INTASC Standard	Description of Teacher Performance	Chapter Objective	Descr[illegible] Teach[illegible]
Principle 6	Uses knowledge of communication techniques to foster active inquiry, collaboration, and supportive interaction	Ch. 4 (Obj. 1–7)	Imple[illegible] studei[illegible]
		Ch. 5 (Obj. 1–5)	Uses effective questioning strategies
		Ch. 6 (Obj. 3–4	Implements strategies for responsive instruction
		Ch. 7 (Obj. 1–4)	Uses technology to promote deep understanding and engagement
		Ch. 8 (Obj. 1–3)	Implements effective classroom management strategies
		Ch. 9 (Obj. 1–7)	Uses cooperative learning strategies
Principle 7	Plans instruction based on knowledge of subject matter, students, the community, and curriculum goals	Ch. 2 (Obj. 1–3)	Identifies key characteristics of effective planning
		Ch. 3 (Obj. 1–4)	Writes and uses instructional objectives
		Ch. 6 (Obj. 4–6)	Differentiates instruction based on student readiness, interest, and learning profile
Principle 8	Understands and uses formal and informal assessment strategies	Ch. 4 (Obj. 6–7)	Implements strategies for ending lessons effectively
		Ch. 5 (Obj. 1–5)	Implements questioning strategies to assess student learning
		Ch. 6 (Obj. 3–4)	Develops understanding of student needs through informal assessment strategies
		Ch. 7 (Obj. 3–4)	Uses technology to assess student learning
		Ch. 9 (Obj. 3–7)	Assesses student mastery through cooperative learning activities
		Ch. 10 (Obj. 1–8)	Implements effective assessment strategies
Principle 9	Reflects on teaching	Ch. 1	Identifies the teacher as a reflective decision maker
		Ch. 10 (Obj. 1–8)	Uses a variety of ways to collect information to form judgments in order to make decisions
Principle 10	Fosters relationships with colleagues, parents, and agencies in the larger community	Ch. 9 (Obj. 6–7)	Gains support for cooperative learning strategies from colleagues administrators, and parents

Classroom Teaching Skills

Classroom Teaching Skills

SEVENTH EDITION

James M. Cooper,
GENERAL EDITOR
University of Virginia

Susan R. Goldman
University of Illinois, Chicago

Ted. S. Hasselbring
University of Kentucky

Mary S. Leighton
Dorchester County (MD) Public Schools

Greta Morine-Dershimer
University of Virginia

James W. Pellegrino
University of Illinois, Chicago

Bob Plants
Vanderbilt University

David Sadker
The American University

Myra Sadker
The American University

Robert D. Sherwood
Peabody College, Vanderbilt University

Robert Shostak
Florida International University

Terry D. TenBrink
Kirksville College of Osteopathic Medicine

Carol Ann Tomlinson
University of Virginia

Wilford A. Weber
University of Houston

Susan M. Williams
University of Texas, Austin

Houghton Mifflin Company
Boston New York

Senior Sponsoring Editor: Sue Pulvermacher-Alt
Senior Development Editor: Lisa Mafrici
Editorial Associate: Sara Hauschildt
Project Editor: Ylang Nguyen
Editorial Assistant: Wendy Thayer
Designer: Henry Rachlin
Production/Design Coordinator: Lisa Jelly Smith
Senior Manufacturing Coordinator: Priscilla Bailey
Marketing Manager: Nicola Poser

Front inside cover credit: Interstate New Teacher Assessment and Support Consortium (1992). *Model Standards for Beginning Teacher Licensing and Development: A Resource for State Dialogue.* Washington, D.C.: Council of Chief State School Officers.

Photo credits: p. 1, © Elizabeth Crews; p. 19, © Elizabeth Crews; p. 53, Elizabeth Crews; p. 77, © Elizabeth Crews; p. 101, © Michael Newman/PhotoEdit; p. 149, © Elizabeth Crews/Stock Boston; p. 181, © Elizabeth Crews/Stock Boston; p. 225, © Elizabeth Crews; p. 273, © Elizabeth Crews; p. 313, © PhotoEdit.

Printed in the United States of America.

Library of Congress Catalog Card Number: 0-618-193-146

International Standard Book Number: 2001133239

3456789–QUD–06 05 04 03

Contents

Preface

Changes in the Field

At one time in the not-too-distant past, teacher education consisted of a few courses on education theory, some courses on methods, and a topping of student teaching. Except for the student teaching, and maybe a little observation experience, the program consisted of campus-based courses.

Teacher education today differs considerably from the preceding description. Programs are much more field-oriented than ever before, requiring prospective teachers to spend more time on-site working with students in schools. The present emphasis on practical experience with students should not be interpreted as a movement away from theory. Rather, educational theory is being integrated with practice. This integration recognizes that theory, to be internalized, must be learned in the context in which it is to be applied. In the past, prospective teachers were expected to translate theory into practice with little help. Usually they were unsuccessful. Today, with the help of newly developed curriculum materials, including case studies, teacher educators help prospective teachers apply the theory in situated contexts and give them feedback on their efforts.

The standards movement has also changed teacher education just as it has changed elementary and secondary education. In 1987, the National Board for Professional Teaching Standards (NBPTS) began developing standards for accomplished performance for experienced teachers in a number of different content areas and age-levels. The Interstate New Teachers Assessment and Support Consortium (INTASC), created in 1987 as a project of the Council of Chief State School Officers (CCSSO), has been developing teaching standards for beginning teachers that are modeled after those developed by the NBPTS. INTASC's primary constituency is state education agencies responsible for teacher licensing and professional development. Its work is guided by one basic premise: An effective teacher must be able to integrate content knowledge with pedagogical understanding to ensure that all students learn and perform at high levels.

Toward this end, INTASC has created model core standards for licensing teachers that reflect those principles which should be present in all teaching, regardless of the subject or grade level taught, and serve as a framework for the systemic reform of teacher preparation and professional development. These core standards are currently being translated into standards for discipline-specific teaching. Many state departments of education are requiring teacher educators to demonstrate that the core INTASC standards are reflected in their teacher education programs, and requiring prospective teachers to provide evidence that they have met those standards. An important attribute of these core standards—and the content-specific standards to be developed in the next phase of the work—is that they are performance-based; that is, they describe what teachers should know and be able to do rather than listing courses that teachers should take in order to be awarded a license.

Because of the growing emphasis on standards for teacher education, this edition of *Classroom Teaching Skills* identifies the particular core INTASC standards that are addressed in each chapter and matches them with each chapter's objectives. A correlation table can be found in the inside front cover of this book. We have done this both to show how each chapter in the book addresses particular teaching standards and to facilitate each teacher education program's documentation of where and how INTASC standards are addressed in the program. The core standards are listed in the appendix on pages 379–384. Readers who would like to understand the rationale for these standards and assumptions underlying them are urged to visit the INTASC web site at <http://www.ccsso.org/intascst.html#draft>.

Purposes of This Text

The seventh edition of *Classroom Teaching Skills* will help beginning teachers meld theory with practice. The book conceptualizes the teacher as a reflective decision maker, one who makes planning, implementing, evaluation, and management decisions as part of the instructional role. To make and carry out these decisions the teacher needs certain teaching skills. The conceptual framework of the teacher as a reflective decision maker is presented in Chapter 1. Each subsequent chapter addresses a particular skill by first discussing the theory behind the skill and then giving the reader practice situations in which knowledge about the skill can be applied and feedback received. Because each chapter presents specific learning objectives as well as mastery tests, the reader receives immediate feedback on this learning.

After students have completed the chapters, the instructor may want to set up experiences that will enable the students to practice the skills with actual learners. Ultimate acquisition of the skill must, of course, take place in actual classroom situations with expertise developing over time.

From the outset our goal was to produce instructional materials that are (1) important, (2) flexible, (3) readable, and (4) scholarly. A word about each of these features follows.

First, the teaching skills contained in this book have been identified by many research studies and best practices literature as being *important* to the success of teachers. Studies of expert teachers demonstrate that these skills are essential to effective teaching. Furthermore, our experience indicates that prospective teachers emphatically want to master practical teaching skills that will enable them to cope successfully with their classroom responsibilities. It is our belief that these instructional materials, dedicated as they are to the mastery of basic teaching skills, will be retained and used by most students as an ongoing self-evaluation tool—to be referred to both during and after their field experiences.

Our second goal, to produce a highly *flexible* text, has been met in two ways. First, the content itself is ubiquitous; the skills reach into virtually every course in the teacher-education curriculum. Second, we designed the book as a self-contained teacher-education learning package that can be used in a variety of capacities in many parts of the curriculum. Some instructors may choose to use particular chapters for one course, while other instructors may use different chapters for another course, thus permitting students to use *Classroom Teaching Skills* for more than one course. How the book is used will depend on the structure and organization of a given teacher-education program. In addition, the book has been often used for professional development courses and workshops with experienced teachers.

Our third goal, *readability*, is achieved by our commitment to communicating clearly and directly with our audience: teachers. Although this is a multi-authored book, all of its chapters are edited to retain the book's ease and utility. While each author's unique writing style is consciously preserved, the level and structure of writing is adjusted for accessibility to readers. Moreover, each chapter presents a consistent five-step, self-teaching format: (1) a statement of objectives, (2) a presentation of written information, (3) practice exercises with answers, (4) a mastery test with an answer key, and (5) observation worksheets.

Our fourth goal, developing materials representative of the best current *scholarship,* has been met by experienced authors, all recognized authorities on the particular skill about which they have written. Further information on each author is presented in the "About the Authors" section following this preface.

Key Features of the Revision

Before revising *Classroom Teaching Skills,* questionnaires were mailed both to professors who had used the book in their classes and nonusers, asking them to evaluate the various chapters and to suggest changes for improvement. These evaluations and comments were mailed to each author, along with my suggestions for revision. The resulting product is a seventh edition that addresses the reviewers' specific concerns and suggestions. Besides general updating, the following are significant changes in the seventh edition.

- **A new chapter on differentiating instruction,** written by Carol Ann Tomlinson, the nation's foremost expert on this topic, replaces the chapter on concept-learning and higher-level thinking. Differentiating instruction has gained tremendous popularity in professional development workshops for teachers, and the opportunity to include this topic seemed particularly timely.
- **A new emphasis is placed on standards.** Each chapter's objectives correlate to the INTASC model standards to assist both instructors and students in providing evidence that their teacher education curriculum is addressing these standards.
- The **use of technology** is emphasized in each chapter, including screening and selecting many web site references relevant to the particular skills. In addition, Chapter 7, "Technology for Teaching and Learning with Understanding," has been thoroughly updated.
- The concept of **teacher reflection** is expanded in Chapter 1, where the relationship of teacher reflection and decision making is explored.
- **Chapter 1 also includes a description of Charlotte Danielson's popular "Framework for Teaching"** and how the chapters of this book address the four domains of her framework.

Acknowledgments

We appreciate the assistance offered in the revision of this text by the following reviewers:

Gail Gregg, Florida International University
Linda Broughton, University of Southern Alabama
Lillie West, Millersville University
Barbara Witteman, Concordia College
Betty Hubschman, Barry University
Sara Sage, Liberty University
Beverly Sanders, Bethune-Cookman College

I would also like to thank the editorial staff at Houghton Mifflin Company for all their support and help in bringing this edition of *Classroom Teaching Skills* to fruition. I am especially thankful to Sara Hauschildt, Editorial Associate, for her careful review of each chapter and her helpful suggestions; Ylang Nguyen, Project Editor, for seeing the book through to completion; Lisa Mafrici, Senior Development Editor, for getting this edition started and putting the authors in such good hands; and Sue Pulvermacher-Alt, Senior Sponsoring Editor for Education, for her overall support of me in this and in other projects with Houghton Mifflin. On behalf of all the authors, I offer my deep thanks and appreciation for all their important contributions to this seventh edition.

James M. Cooper
University of Virginia

Using This Book

The Book's Design

The purpose of *Classroom Teaching Skills* is to help you develop competence in selected teaching skills that are basic to implementing the reflective decision-making model. To acquire these complex teaching skills, you will need to follow the three-stage model represented in Figure 1.4 (see page 17). Accordingly, *Classroom Teaching Skills* incorporates this model of complex skill acquisition in its design.

Each chapter in the book focuses on a particular teaching skill. Within each chapter, a cognitive map of the skill you are to acquire is provided. This cognitive map includes the purpose of the skill, its various elements and their sequencing, and the nature of the final performance.

Each chapter consists of self-contained materials that require practice and provide you with feedback on your efforts. If circumstances permit it, your instructor may also provide you with opportunities to practice these skills in classroom contexts.

To develop smoothness and a high level of competence in teaching skills, far more practice is necessary than can be provided in this book. If you are an elementary school teacher, many of these skills must be practiced within the context of different subject matter areas. Your competence in questioning skills, for example, is greatly a product of your knowledge of the subject about which you are asking questions.

Format of Each Chapter

Each chapter is written with a common format that contains (1) objectives, (2) a rationale, (3) learning materials and activities, (4) mastery tests, and (5) observation worksheets.

1. Objectives. The objectives, stated in terms of learner outcomes, specify the competency or competencies you will be expected to demonstrate. Wherever it is appropriate, the objectives will be arranged in a learning hierarchy, leading you from relatively simple objectives to more complex ones.

2. Rationale. The rationale describes the purpose and importance of the objectives within the chapter. It attempts to explain why you should want to spend your time acquiring the competencies the chapter is designed to produce. The rationale is considered important because, if you are not convinced that the particular skill you are being asked to develop is important to effective teaching, then it is unlikely that you will be willing to spend the time and effort needed to acquire competence in that skill.

3. Learning Materials and Activities. Each objective has an accompanying set of reading materials written specifically for that objective. In addition, some of the authors have provided backup activities for those who want additional work on a particular objective. The nature of the reading materials and activities varies depending on the specific objective for which they were constructed.

4. Mastery Tests. Each chapter contains mastery tests with answer keys to enable you to assess whether or not you have achieved the objectives. These mastery tests assess your learning after you have completed the reading and backup activities related to each objective. This technique allows you to discover immediately after completing each section whether you have met the objective satisfactorily. In addition, at the end of some of the chapters there are final mastery tests that serve as a last check on your achievement.

5. Observation Worksheets. Observation worksheets have been included to help guide you in observing and analyzing the skills taught in this book when you are observing in schools. Watching experienced classroom teachers and analyzing their implementation of these skills will provide you with insights as to how the skills can be used with students in classrooms. You can also compare in what ways the teacher does or does not use the skills in the same ways as advocated in the book.

This format (objectives, rationale, learning activities, mastery tests, and observation worksheets) has been successfully tested in hundreds of teacher education programs. It is an efficient design because all the materials are geared to help students achieve the stated objectives. Extraneous and inconsequential materials are eliminated, allowing students to make best use of their time. If used properly, the format increases the probability that you will be able to acquire a beginning level of competency in these basic teaching skills.

Description of the Skills

Skills were included in this book on the basis of their importance in implementing the reflective decision-making model of teaching. Although other skills may have been included, those that were selected are among the most crucial to the model.

The three basic elements of the reflective decision-making model are to plan, to implement, and to evaluate. Each skill is important in carrying out at least one of these three functions. Some skills are useful for more than one function. The nine skills that make up this book are:

Plan	Planning Instructional objectives
Implement	Involving students in learning Questioning Differentiating instruction Technology skills Classroom management Cooperative learning
Evaluate	Assessment

Planning. Planning is perhaps the most important function a teacher performs—the whole decision-making model is based on this skill. In Chapter 2, Greta Morine-Dershimer emphasizes the key characteristics of productive planning. On the basis of research studies, Morine-Dershimer examines the differences in how novice and expert teachers plan. Expert teachers establish and effectively use routines such as collecting homework, distributing materials, and calling on students. They also have repertoires of alternative routines and procedures to use for different situations. Instead of having only one way of accomplishing an objective, expert teachers plan for and execute different procedures as needed. Morine-Dershimer also examines characteristics of effective lesson and unit plans by comparing teacher planning to dramatic productions, including the use of scripts, scenes, and improvisation.

Instructional Objectives. Writing instructional objectives is a basic planning skill. By specifying instructional objectives, teachers define their purposes in terms that are clear and understandable. In Chapter 3, Terry TenBrink makes the distinction between well-written and poorly written objectives. Opportunities are provided within the chapter to (1) write well-defined instructional objectives, (2) use instructional objectives in planning, and (3) use objectives in implementing instruction. Well-written instructional objectives enable teachers to plan and implement their instructional strategies. The success of teachers' implementation skills greatly depends on the thoughtfulness and clarity of their instructional objectives.

Involving Students in Learning. In Chapter 4, Robert Shostak presents three basic skills for involving students in learning—planned beginnings, planned discussions, and planned endings—that research studies have demonstrated to be important components of engaging students in learning. Planned beginnings refer to teacher-initiated actions or statements that are designed to establish a communicative link between the experiences of students and the objectives of the lesson. Planned discussions encourage students to acquire new knowledge, reflect on ideas different from their own, and to share personal opinions. Planned endings refer to actions or statements designed to bring a lesson to an appropriate conclusion and to consolidate student learning. The effective use of these three skills will help establish and maintain student interest in the lesson, and will ensure that the main part of the lesson has been learned.

Questioning. Probably no teaching behavior has been studied as much as questioning. This is not surprising because most educators agree that questioning strategies and techniques are key tools in the teacher's repertoire of interactive teaching skills. In Chapter 5, Myra and David Sadker chose Bloom's *Taxonomy of Educational Objectives: Cognitive Domain* as their system for classifying questions because it is the most widely used cognitive classification system in education. They provide opportunities to classify and construct questions according to the six levels of Bloom's Taxonomy; to identify the seven habits of effective questioners; to explore the related areas of wait time, probing, scaffolding, and feedback that can enhance questioning skills; and to explore how the growing diversity and multicultural nature of America's students affect questioning strategies. If the skills presented in this chapter are utilized in teaching, the net effect will be students who are more active participants in the learning process.

Differentiating Instruction. A given in classrooms is that students learn what the teacher has planned in different ways, at different times, and at different levels of sophistication. To teach all students in a class effectively, a teacher must take into account the variety of ways in which students differ from one another, and offer instruction that responds to this variety. Differentiated instruction is teaching with student variance in mind. As Carol Ann Tomlinson, the author of Chapter 6 writes, "... differentiated instruction is 'responsive' teaching rather than 'one-size-fits-all' teaching."

In this highly interactive chapter, Tomlinson helps the reader develop a personal rationale for teaching to address learner needs; provides specific ways to differentiate content, activities, and products in response to student readiness, interest, and learning profile; and helps the reader think about practical ways to become a responsive teacher.

Technology for Teaching and Learning with Understanding. The use of computer technology in schools has increased dramatically in recent years and shows few signs of slowing down. While obtaining the latest hardware and software is always a challenge for schools, figuring out how to use the technology effectively is an even greater task. The authors of Chapter 7 (Susan Goldman, Susan Williams, Robert Sherwood, Jim Pellegrino, Robert Plants, and Ted Hasselbring) are pioneers in researching how technology can support and enhance student learning with understanding. All were major researchers in the Cognition and Technology Group at Vanderbilt University. In this chapter, they use their knowledge and experience to articulate the principles of learning with understanding and to explore how teachers can use hardware and software to support student learning.

Classroom Management. No problem concerns beginning teachers more than the problem of classroom management. Most new teachers are worried about not being able to control their students and are aware that lack of control will impede effective instruction. Few areas in teacher education curricula have been neglected as much as classroom management. The major reason for this neglect has been that educators formerly had a poor systematic understanding of classroom dynamics; however, our knowledge in this area has expanded to the point where systematic instruction in classroom management is now possible.

In Chapter 8, Will Weber emphasizes that teachers need to establish and maintain proper learning environments. While the purpose of teaching is to stimulate desired student learning, the purpose of classroom management is to establish the conditions that best promote student learning. Classroom management skills are necessary for effective teaching to occur, but they do not guarantee such behavior. Weber examines several different philosophical positions regarding classroom management, including behavior modification, socioemotional climate, and group processes, and provides numerous opportunities for diagnosing classroom situations according to each of these three viewpoints.

Cooperative Learning. One of the elements in the hidden curriculum of our schools is the emphasis on competition. Children learn how to compete with each other in numerous ways. Recently, the value of cooperation among learners to increase achievement levels has been recognized by educators. In Chapter 9, Mary Leighton examines various research-based cooperative learning strategies to help students significantly improve their academic achievement, as well as develop social skills.

Cooperative learning strategies are organized around systematic methods that usually involve presentations of information, student practice and coaching in learning teams, individual assessment of mastery, and public recognition of team success. The three key characteristics of cooperative learning strategies are group goals, individual accountability, and equal opportunities for success. In this chapter, several of the most widely used cooperative learning strategies are described in some detail.

Assessment. Assessment (evaluation) and knowledge of results are essential if teachers are to improve their teaching effectiveness. The critical nature of assessment is rarely disputed; nevertheless, few teachers receive adequate training in assessment concepts and procedures. Terry TenBrink's chapter on assessment focuses on critical components of the evaluation process. His basic position is that educational assessment is useful only if it helps educators make decisions.

TenBrink perceives assessment as a four-stage process: (1) preparing for evaluation, (2) obtaining needed information, (3) forming judgments, and (4) using judgments in making decisions and preparing reports. Throughout the chapter, examples of problems and decisions that teachers are likely to face are used. Developing test items, checklists, and rating scales for evaluating student knowledge, products, and performance is a major focus of the chapter. This practical emphasis should make assessment concepts and procedures for making better instructional decisions easier to understand and apply.

About the Authors

James M. Cooper is Commonwealth Professor of Education in the Curry School of Education at the University of Virginia, where he also served as Dean from 1984 to 1994. Prior to coming to the University of Virginia, he was on the faculties of the University of Houston (1971–1984) and the University of Massachusetts–Amherst (1968–1971). He received four degrees from Stanford University—two in history and two in education, including his Ph.D. in 1967. He taught junior and senior high school social studies for four years in Palo Alto, California. He has authored, co-authored, and edited numerous publications, including *Those Who Can, Teach* and *Kaleidoscope: Readings in Education*, both in their ninth editions. His books and articles address the areas of teacher education, supervision of teachers, case studies in teacher education, and technology and teacher education. His articles have appeared in such journals as *Phi Delta Kappan, Journal of Teacher Education, Educational Leadership, Elementary School Journal, Elementary English, Journal of Research and Development in Education, Education and Urban Society, Theory Into Practice, Action in Teacher Education,* and *Teaching and Teacher Education.* Cooper's most recent service and leadership contribution to education was serving on the American Association of University Women's Commission on Technology, Gender, and Teacher Education. He also chaired the National Council for Accreditation of Teacher Education Technology and Teacher Education Task Force, which produced the report, *Technology and the New Professional Teacher.* He has been on the Board of Directors for the American Association of Colleges for Teacher Education, the Holmes Group, the Organization of Institutional Affiliates of the American Educational Research Association, and NCATE's Unit Accreditation Board, which he chaired for one year. He is currently the principal investigator for a $2.8 million grant from the U.S. Department of Education for the Preparing Tomorrow's Teachers to Use Technology program. Honors that Cooper has received include a Fulbright-Hays Award for Lecturing in Portugal, recognition as one of the nation's Distinguished Teacher Educators from the Association of Teacher Educators, and being named the Outstanding Professor in the Curry School of Education for 2001. He has been listed in *Who's Who in America* and *Who's Who in American Education* since 1990.

Susan R. Goldman is Distinguished Professor of Cognitive Psychology and Education at the University of Illinois at Chicago and Co-Director of the UIC Center for the Study of Learning, Instruction, and Teacher Development. Dr. Goldman's research and teaching focus on integrating technology with research-based instructional approaches, especially in areas of language, reading, writing, and problem solving. Goldman previously spent twelve years as Professor and Co-Director of the Learning Technology Center at Vanderbilt University.

Susan M. Williams is Assistant Professor of Instructional Technology in the Department of Curriculum and Instruction at the University of Texas at Austin. Her research interests include student learning as it occurs during problem solving and ways that software can support students as they solve complex problems. Her teaching focuses on helping students understand the theoretical assumptions implicit in the design of educational software and ways to integrate technology into classroom teaching.

Robert D. Sherwood is Associate Professor of Education in the Department of Teaching and Learning and a Research Scientist in the Learning Technology Center at Peabody College, Vanderbilt University. His research and development efforts focus on ways to use technology to improve science instruction. He teaches courses in educational technology and science education at Peabody/Vanderbilt.

James W. Pellegrino is Distinguished Professor of Cognitive Psychology and Education at the University of Illinois, Chicago, and Co-Director of the UIC Center for the Study of Learning, Instruction, and Teacher Development. He has been involved in numerous collaborative projects on the uses of technology and media in creating meaningful learning and instructional environments, especially for mathematics and science learning. Pellegrino previously served as Frank W. Mayborn Professor of Cognitive Studies and Dean of Peabody College, Vanderbilt University.

Bob Plants is project manager for Vanderbilt University Learning Technology Center's PT3 Catalyst grant, "Information Technology and Teacher Education: Leveraging the Power of Learning Theory and Technology," and is a recent graduate of the University of Memphis' doctoral program in Instructional Design and Technology. His experiences have focused on the integration of technology in K–12 curriculum and instruction. Plants has been involved in the evaluation of several school reform models including the Schools for Thought program and the New American Schools' Co-NECT program.

Ted S. Hasselbring is the William T. Bryan Professor and Endowed Chair in Special Education Technology at the University of Kentucky. Over the past twenty years Hasselbring has conducted research on the use of technology for enhancing learning in students with mild disabilities and those who are at risk of school failure. He has authored more than a hundred book chapters and articles on learning and technology and serves on the editorial boards of six professional journals. He is also the author of several computer programs, including Scholastic's Read 180. Hasselbring previously spent seventeen years as Professor and Co-Director of the Learning Technology Center at Vanderbilt University.

Mary S. Leighton is the high school supervisor in a small, rural school district on the Eastern Shore of Maryland. She has also served as the principal of a private elementary school in inner-city Washington, D.C., and as the assistant principal of a suburban middle school. Since beginning her career as a teacher in Chicago public schools, she has taught grades preK–12 in urban, suburban, and rural schools and served on teacher education faculties in several institutions. Before undertaking the principalship, Dr. Leighton worked at Johns Hopkins University on the Success for All development and dissemination team and in a private research firm, where she reported regularly on effective programs and practices for students at risk of school failure. As an independent consultant, she helped many secondary and postsecondary faculties adapt cooperative learning strategies to their particular circumstances. She graduated from the University of Chicago and earned a doctorate in curriculum and supervision from the University of Oregon.

Greta G. Morine-Dershimer is an Emeritus Professor of the Curry School of Education, University of Virginia, where she served as Director of Teacher Education (1992–1996) and Senior Researcher in the Commonwealth Center for the Education of Teachers (1988–1994), retiring in May 1998. She is editor of *Teaching and Teacher Education: An International Journal of Research and Studies*, published by Elsevier Science of Oxford. She received her Ed.D. from Teachers College, Columbia University, in 1965 after teaching in elementary and junior high schools for ten years. She has been a teacher educator in New York and California and developed teacher-education materials at the Far West Laboratory for Educational Research and Development in San Francisco. Her research has focused on teacher and pupil information processing, and she has recently investigated changes in the concepts and thinking of prospective teachers during their professional preparation. She served as Vice President of Division K (Teaching and Teacher Education) for the American Educational Research Association (AERA) from 1988 to 1990 and was a member of the Research and Information Committee of the American Association of Colleges for Teacher Education (AACTE) from 1995 to 1998. Her publications include six books, twenty book chapters, and articles in many journals, including *Teachers College Record, Elementary School Journal, Theory into Practice, Social Education, Journal of Teacher Education, Teaching and Teacher Education, Curriculum and Teaching, Educational Theory,* and *American Educational Research Journal.*

The late **Myra Sadker** was a Professor and Dean at American University until 1995. **David Sadker** is currently a Professor at American University. This edition of questioning skills was revised in collaboration with **Phyllis Lerner,** a nationally known trainer of trainers for Teacher Expectations–Student Achievement (TESA) as well as other teacher in-service programs. The Sadkers' writings and research have appeared in a wide array of publications, ranging from *Phi Delta Kappan* and the *Harvard Educational Review* to *Parade, Glamour,* and *USA Weekend* magazines. Their research has been reported in the *New York Times,* the *London Times,* and the *Wall Street Journal.* They have appeared on numerous radio and television programs, including National Public Radio's *All Things Considered, The Today Show, Good Morning, America,* and *Dateline: NBC.* The Sadkers co-authored scores of articles and six books. Their publications include *Failing at Fairness: How Our Schools Cheat Girls* (Touchstone, 1995), a book that reported on their research documenting how teachers interact more frequently and more precisely with male students than with female students. Their introductory textbook, *Teachers, Schools, and Society* (McGraw-Hill, 2003), is now in its sixth edition. The Sadkers' writing and research have been recognized by the Educational Press Association of America, and a variety of universities and professional associations. In 1991, the American Educational Research Association acknowledged the Sadkers for co-authoring the best review of research published that year, and in 1995 they received the Professional Service Award, the same year they were honored with the Eleanor Roosevelt Award from the American Association of University Women. In 2001, David Sadker was given the Gender Equity Architect Award from the American Association of Colleges for Teacher Education, for his "pioneering work in gender equity." Their degrees are from the City College of New York, Boston University, Harvard University, and the University of Massachusetts. Together they provided training in more effective and equitable teaching strategies in over forty-five states and abroad.

Robert Shostak was formerly Coordinator of the English Education program and Administrative Director of the International Institute for Creative Communication at Florida International University. He received his bachelor's degree in humanities from Colgate University, an M.S. in teaching English from the State University of New York at Albany, and a Ph.D. in curriculum and instruction from the University of Connecticut. He taught high school English for six years before focusing his career on higher education and teacher training. Author of textbooks, monographs, and numerous articles, he has devoted his most recent publishing efforts to writing about computers and the teaching of English. Dr. Shostak's most current educational projects are in the field of telecommunications. Presently he is a full-time educational consultant.

Terry D. TenBrink is recently retired from administrative duties at the Kirksville College of Osteopathic Medicine in Kirksville, Missouri. Formerly on the faculty at the University of Missouri at Columbia, Dr. TenBrink received his Ph.D. in educational psychology from Michigan State University in 1969. His graduate studies emphasized learning theory, evaluation, measurement, and research design. His teaching experience spans elementary, junior high school, high school, and college students, and he has been principal of an elementary school. He stays in touch with the classroom through numerous consulting activities in public schools and in adult education and by teaching seminars and workshops to classroom teachers. While at the University of Missouri, Dr. TenBrink taught courses in evaluation, learning, human development, and general educational psychology. He has published numerous journal articles and is engaged in continuing research on the conditions under which learning occurs efficiently. In 1974 his textbook *Evaluation: A Practical Guide for Teachers* was published by McGraw-Hill.

Carol Ann Tomlinson is a faculty member at the University of Virginia's Curry School of Education, where she is Professor of Educational Leadership, Foundations and Policy. Tomlinson's career as an educator includes twenty-one years as a public school teacher, including twelve years as a program administrator of special services for struggling and advanced learners. She was Virginia's Teacher of the Year in 1974. Special interests throughout her career have included curriculum and instruction for struggling learners and advanced learners and effective instruction in heterogeneous settings. Tomlinson is author of over a hundred articles, book chapters, books, and other professional development materials. For ASCD, she has authored *How to Differentiate Instruction in Mixed Ability Classrooms, The Differentiated Classroom: Responding to the Needs of All Learners, Leadership for Differentiating Schools and Classrooms,* the facilitator's guide for the video staff development sets called *Differentiating Instruction,* and *At Work in the Differentiated Classroom,* as well as a professional inquiry kit on differentiation. She works throughout the U.S. and abroad with teachers whose goal is to develop more responsive heterogeneous classrooms.

Wilford A. Weber is Professor of Education and Chair of the Department of Curriculum and Instruction, College of Education, University of Houston. He holds a bachelor's degree in psychology from Muhlenberg College and a doctorate in educational psychology from Temple University. He has taught at Temple University, Villanova University, Syracuse University, and the University of St. Thomas. Dr. Weber has been at the University of Houston since 1971. For six years, he served as a member of the Committee of Examiners for the National Teacher Examinations Core Battery Test of Professional Knowledge. Dr. Weber has directed numerous funded research projects and has authored more than 200 papers, articles, chapters, monographs, and books concerned with teacher education, teacher effectiveness, classroom management, and school discipline. His major publications include "A Review of the Teacher Education Literature on Classroom Management," a chapter—co-authored with Linda A. Roff—in *Classroom Management: Reviews of the Teacher Education and Research Literature* (a monograph published by Educational Testing Service in 1983). During his career, Dr. Weber has conducted scores of seminars and workshops on the subject of classroom management and school discipline. His audiences have included teachers, administrators, and teacher educators throughout Texas and the United States and in Germany, Italy, Malaysia, and Mexico. Dr. Weber stays in touch with the realities of the classroom and the school through consulting and research activities that take him into the schools, by doing substitute teaching, by teaching graduate courses for classroom teachers, and through his involvement in several professional organizations. His interest in classroom management and school discipline stems from his experience as a teacher of court-committed juvenile delinquents.

Classroom Teaching Skills

1

The Teacher As a Reflective Decision Maker

James M. Cooper

What Is a Teacher?

At first glance such a question seems obvious. A teacher is a person charged with the responsibility of helping others to learn and to behave in new and different ways. But who is excluded from this definition? Parents? Band directors? Drill sergeants? Boy Scout leaders? At some time or another we all teach and, in turn, are taught.

We generally reserve the term *teacher*, however, for persons whose primary professional or occupational function is to help others learn and develop in new ways. While education, learning, and teaching can, and do, take place in many different settings, most societies realize that education is too important to be left to chance. Consequently, they establish schools to facilitate learning and to help people live better and happier lives. Schools are created to provide a certain type of educational experience, which can be called the curriculum. Teachers are trained and hired by societies to help fulfill the purposes of the curriculum. Teachers, in the formal educative process of schooling, are social agents hired by society to help facilitate the intellectual, personal, and social development of those members of society who attend schools.

Until modern times, teachers themselves had little formal schooling; often they knew barely more than their students. As late as 1864 an Illinois teacher described the image of the teacher as "someone who can parse and cypher; has little brains and less money; is feeble minded, unable to grapple with real men and women in the stirring employments of life, but on that account admirably fitted to associate with childish intellects."[1] Needless to say, this image of the teacher has changed considerably for the better. Today teachers are better educated, earn more money, and are more highly respected members of society than their nineteenth-century counterparts. Society requires its teachers to obtain a college education and specific training as teachers. This increase in the educational level of teachers is recognition that, if teachers are to facilitate the intellectual, personal, and social development of their students, then they must be much better educated than ever before.

Effective Teaching

Possession of a college degree does not in any way ensure that teachers will be effective. But what is an effective teacher? What is a good teacher? Are they the same?

Good teaching is difficult to agree on because the term *good* is so value laden. What appears to be good teaching to one person may be considered poor teaching by another because each one values different outcomes or methods. One teacher may run the classroom in an organized, highly structured manner, emphasizing the intellectual content of the academic disciplines. Another may run the class in a less structured environment, allowing the students much more freedom to choose subject matter and activities that interest them personally. One observer, because of personal values, may identify the first teacher as a "good" teacher, while criticizing the second teacher for running "too loose a ship." Another observer may come to the opposite conclusion with respect to which teacher is better—again, because of a different set of values.

While it remains difficult to agree on what "good" teaching is, "effective" teaching can be demonstrated. *The* **effective teacher** *is one who is able to bring about intended learning outcomes.* The nature of the learning is still most important, but two different teachers, as in the example above, may strive for and achieve different outcomes and each be judged effective. The two critical dimensions of effective teaching are *intent* and *achievement*.

Without intent, student achievement becomes random and accidental; however, intent is not enough by itself. If students do not achieve their intended learning goals (even if the failure is due to variables beyond the control of their teacher), the teacher cannot truly have been effective.

While effective teachers are defined as teachers who can demonstrate the ability to bring about intended learning outcomes, what enables them to achieve desired results with students? Have you ever stopped to think about what, if anything, makes teachers different from other well-educated adults? What should effective, professional teachers know, believe, or be able to do that distinguishes them from other people? Think about these questions seriously because they are central questions, the answers to which should be at the heart of your teacher education program.

Some people will state that the crucial dimension is the teacher's personality. Teachers, they will say, should be friendly, cheerful, sympathetic, morally virtuous, enthusiastic, and humorous. In a massive study, David Ryans concluded that effective teachers are fair, democratic, responsive, understanding, kindly, stimulating, original, alert, attractive, responsible, steady, poised, and confident. Ineffective teachers were described as partial, autocratic, aloof, restricted, harsh, dull, stereotyped, apathetic, unimpressive, evasive, erratic, excitable, and uncertain.[2] But as two educational researchers once remarked, "... what conceivable human interaction is not the better if the people involved are friendly, cheerful, sympathetic, and virtuous rather than the opposite?"[3] These characteristics, then, while desirable in teachers, are not uniquely desirable to that group alone.

It might be difficult to reach a consensus on exactly what knowledge and skills are unique to the teaching profession, but most educators would agree that special skills and knowledge are necessary and do exist. Certainly teachers must be familiar with children and their developmental stages. They must know something about events outside the classroom and school. They must possess enough command of the subject they are going to teach to be able to differentiate what is important and central from what is incidental and peripheral. They must have a philosophy of education to help guide them in their role as teachers. They must know how human beings learn and how to create environments that facilitate learning.

General Areas of Teacher Competence

B. O. Smith has suggested that a well-trained teacher should be prepared in four areas of teacher competence to be effective in bringing about intended learning outcomes.[4]

1. Command of theoretical knowledge about learning and human behavior
2. Display of attitudes that foster learning and genuine human relationships
3. Command of knowledge in the subject matter to be taught
4. Repertoire of teaching skills that facilitate student learning

A fifth area of teacher competence, personal practical knowledge, will also be considered in addition to the four areas identified by Smith.

1. Command of Theoretical Knowledge About Learning and Human Behavior. For years education has been criticized for its "folkways" practices. Educational recipes and standardized procedures were formally and informally passed on to new teachers to help them survive in classrooms. While this practice still exists, many scientific concepts from psychology, anthropology, sociology, linguistics, cognitive sciences, and related disciplines are now available to help teachers interpret the complex reality of their classrooms. Those teachers who lack the theoretical background and understanding provided by such scientifically derived concepts can only interpret the events of their classrooms according to popularly held beliefs or common sense. Although common sense often serves us well, there is ample evidence that teachers who habitually rely on it will too often misinterpret the events in their classrooms.

Beginning teachers frequently face the difficult situation of receiving different, contradictory messages from their professors and from the teachers with whom they work. While their professors are apt to focus on theoretical knowledge, the experienced teacher may often advise them, "Forget the fancy theoretical stuff and listen to me. I'll tell you what works in real life." This folkways approach to education may be in conflict with what the new teacher has learned and create a dilemma about how to handle a situation.

The problem confronting new teachers is not that the theories put before them are unworkable, but that they simply haven't internalized those theories to the point where they can be used to interpret and solve practical problems. They have not been provided with sufficient opportunities to apply the knowledge, to translate it from theory into practice, and thereby to master it.

An example of a theoretical concept that is derived from psychology and that has enormous implications for teachers is the concept of reinforcement. From their educational psychology courses, most teachers know that a behavior that is reinforced will be strengthened and is likely to be repeated. Nevertheless, these same teachers often respond to a disruptive pupil by calling his or her actions to the attention of the class. If the pupil is misbehaving because of a need to be recognized, the teacher, by publicly acknowledging the misbehavior, may be reinforcing it. When the pupil continues to act up periodically, the teacher doesn't understand why. Although the teacher may have intellectually grasped the meaning of reinforcement, this understanding is not synonymous with internalizing or mastering the concept. Mastery requires practical application to concrete situations.

Because **theoretical knowledge** can be used to interpret situations and solve problems, many classroom events that might otherwise go unnoticed or remain inexplicable can be recognized and resolved by applying theories and concepts of human behavior. This is not an easy task. It requires understanding, insight, practice, and feedback from colleagues and professors. Proficiency will not be achieved as a result of formal training alone; it is a lifelong process involving both formal training and an unending program of on-the-job self-improvement.

2. Display of Attitudes That Foster Learning and Genuine Human Relationships. The second area of competence identified as essential for effective teaching has to do with attitudes. An **attitude** is a predisposition to act in a positive or negative way toward persons, ideas, or events. Virtually all educators are convinced that teacher attitudes are an important dimension in the teaching process. Attitudes have a direct effect on our behavior; they determine how we view ourselves and interact with others.

The major categories of attitudes that affect teaching behavior are: (a) teachers' attitudes toward themselves, (b) teachers' attitudes toward children, (c) teachers' attitudes toward peers and parents, and (d) teachers' attitudes toward the subject matter.

(a) *Teachers' Attitudes Toward Themselves.* There is evidence from psychology that persons who deny or cannot cope with their own emotions are likely to be incapable of respecting and coping with the feelings of others. If teachers are to understand and sympathize with their students' feelings, they must recognize and understand their own feelings. Many colleges are responding to this need by including counseling sessions, reflective thinking, and awareness experiences as part of their teacher education programs. These experiences emphasize introspection, self-evaluation, and feedback from other participants. The goal is to help prospective teachers learn more about themselves, their attitudes, and how others perceive them.

(b) *Teachers' Attitudes Toward Children.* Most teachers occasionally harbor attitudes or feelings toward students that are detrimental to their teaching effectiveness. Strong likes and dislikes of particular pupils, biases toward or against particular ethnic groups, low learning expectations for poverty-level children, and biases in favor of or against certain kinds of student behavior—all can reduce teaching effectiveness. Self-awareness of such attitudes toward individual pupils or classes of children is necessary if teachers are to cope with their own feelings and beliefs. If teachers possess empathy for their students and value them as unique individuals, they will be more effective and will derive more satisfaction from their teaching.

Considerable research on teacher expectations indicates that when teachers hold low expectations for students and, consciously or unconsciously, communicate these low expectations to the students, a self-fulfilling prophecy may occur.[5] That is, the students may conform to the teacher's low expectations, thus confirming the teacher's original expectations. Conversely, when teachers hold high expectations for students and communicate these high expectations, students will often act in ways to live up to the teacher's expectations. A teacher's attitude toward and expectation of students are powerful influences on whether or not students learn.

(c) *Teachers' Attitudes Toward Peers and Parents.* Teachers do not exist in isolated classrooms. They interact with fellow teachers and administrators and often have sensitive dealings with parents. Sometimes they can be effective in dealing with children, but because of negative attitudes toward the adults they encounter, their professional life is unsuccessful. For example, some teachers may resent persons in authority positions, resisting their suggestions for improvement. Other teachers may yield too easily to suggestions from persons in authority, only to later feel guilty about complying instead of sticking up for their own convictions. Or some teachers may feel the need to compete with other teachers for administrative or student approval. Many of the comments already made regarding teachers' attitudes toward themselves and children also apply to their attitudes toward peers and parents.

(d) *Teachers' Attitudes Toward Subject Matter.* The message, in one word, is ENTHUSIASM! Just as students are perceptive in discovering the teacher's attitude toward them, they are also sensitive to the teacher's attitude toward the subject matter. Teachers who are not enthusiastic about what they teach can hardly hope to instill enthusiastic responses in their pupils. After all, if you don't care about the subject matter, how can you ever hope to motivate your students into learning about it?

3. Command of Knowledge in the Subject Matter to Be Taught. Command of the subject matter to be taught is an obvious necessity for any teacher. But taking courses in biology or history or mathematics is not sufficient. A teacher's subject-matter preparation really has two aspects: (1) a study of the subject matter itself and (2) a judicious selection of the material that can be transmitted successfully to the student.

College courses taken in disciplines such as mathematics or English help teachers acquire an understanding of the disciplines, their basic concepts, and their modes of inquiry; but college courses are not directed toward what should be taught to elementary or secondary school students. What should be taught is obviously much less extensive and advanced than the content of the college courses and requires that teachers know the school curriculum as well.

Knowledge of the school curriculum is related to **pedagogical content knowledge,** that is, knowledge that bridges content knowledge and pedagogy. Pedagogical content knowledge represents the "blending of content and pedagogy into an understanding of how particular topics, problems, or issues are organized, represented, and adapted to the diverse interests and abilities of learners and presented for instruction."[6] Teachers who possess pedagogical content knowledge can translate the content knowledge they possess into forms that have great teaching power and that meet the needs and abilities of students. Such teachers understand the central topics in each subject, those aspects that are most difficult for students to learn, and what student preconceptions are likely to get in the way of learning. These teachers draw on powerful examples, illustrations, analogies, demonstrations, and explanations to represent and transform the subject so that students can understand it. For example, using the analogy of water flowing through a pipe to explain how electricity flows through a circuit might be useful initially. However, a teacher with pedagogical content knowledge would also understand the limitations of such an analogy and how it might later interfere with student understanding of other properties of electricity.

Teachers must, therefore, rethink much of the content of a particular discipline as it relates to the lives of their pupils. To be effective communicators, teachers need an understanding of both children and subject matter and, beyond that, special training in linking the two.

4. Repertoire of Teaching Skills That Facilitate Student Learning. The fourth area of competence required of effective teachers is possession of a repertoire of **teaching skills.** Such a repertoire is necessary if teachers are to be effective with students who have varied backgrounds and learning aptitudes. Teacher education programs must, therefore, include a training component focusing on the acquisition of specific teaching skills, such as the effective use of technology to foster student learning. No program can afford to concentrate so exclusively on the acquisition of knowledge that it ignores or slights the "practice" dimension of teaching. Whereas the knowledge components involved in teacher preparation focus on the contexts or situations that confront teachers, the skills component focuses directly on the trainees—on the observation, analysis, and modification of their teaching behavior.

5. Personal Practical Knowledge. **Personal practical knowledge** is the set of understandings teachers have of the practical circumstances in which they work.[7] These understandings include teachers' beliefs, insights, and habits that enable them to do their jobs in schools. This personal practical knowledge tends to be time bound and situation specific, personally compelling, and oriented toward action. For years, researchers denigrated teachers' personal practical knowledge because they placed greater value on scientifically derived knowledge than on practical and personal knowledge. In more recent years, however, researchers have accorded much more importance to teachers' personal practical knowledge. Teachers use their personal practical knowledge to solve dilemmas, resolve tensions, and simplify the complexities of their work.

Because teachers' personal practical knowledge is so closely tied to them as individuals, research on this type of knowledge has not added up to a codified body of teaching knowledge.[8] However, case studies of teachers have provided rich pictures of how teachers use their knowledge to make sense of complex, ill-structured classrooms. These case studies provide evidence that teachers' personal practical knowledge provides an important dimension to a teacher's competence.

A Framework for Professional Practice

We have briefly examined five general areas of competence in which teachers must develop proficiency to be effective. While this examination is useful for obtaining an overview of the basic components of a well-designed teacher education program, it does not provide any guidelines on what a teacher does when teaching. To better understand the responsibilities of teachers, a framework for professional practice will be examined.

Danielson's Framework for Teaching

Charlotte Danielson has developed a framework for teaching that identifies aspects of a teacher's responsibilities that empirical studies have demonstrated as promoting improved student learning.[9] Because teaching is an extremely complex activity, this framework is useful in laying out the various areas of competence in which professional teachers need to develop expertise. Danielson divides the complex activity of teaching into twenty-two components clustered into four domains of teaching responsibility: (1) *planning and preparation,* (2) *the classroom environment,* (3) *instruction,* and (4) *professional responsibilities.* (These domains and their components are shown in Figure 1.1.*) A brief review of each of these domains will provide a road map of the skills and competencies new teachers need to develop. The chapters in this book specifically address many of these competencies.

Domain 1: Planning and Preparation. The components in Domain 1 outline how a teacher organizes the content of what students are expected to learn—in other words, how the teacher designs instruction. These include *demonstrating knowledge of content and pedagogy, demonstrating knowledge of the students, selecting instructional goals, demonstrating knowledge of resources, designing coherent instruction*, and *assessing student learning.* The chapters in this book that address these components are Chapter 2: Instructional Planning; Chapter 3: Instructional Objectives; and Chapter 10: Assessment.

Domain 2: The Classroom Environment. The components in Domain 2 consist of the interactions that occur in a classroom that are noninstructional. These consist of *creating an environment of respect and rapport among the students and with the teacher, establishing a culture for learning, managing classroom procedures, managing student behavior,* and *organizing the physical space.* The chapter that addresses these components is Chapter 8: Classroom Management.

Domain 3: Instruction. The components in Domain 3 are what constitute the core of teaching—the engagement of students in learning content. These include *communicating clearly and accurately, using questioning and discussion techniques, engaging students in learning, providing feedback to students,* and *demonstrating flexibility and responsiveness.* The chapters that address these components are Chapter 4: Involving Students in Learning; Chapter 5: Questioning Skills; Chapter 6: Differentiating Instruction; Chapter 7: Technology for Teaching and Learning with Understanding; and Chapter 9: Cooperative Learning.

---

*From Charlotte Danielson, "Enhancing Professional Practice: A Framework for Teaching," Association for Supervision and Curriculum Development, © 1996, pp. 3–4. Reprinted by permission of the author.

Components of Professional Practice

Domain 1: Planning and Preparation

- Component 1a: *Demonstrating Knowledge of Content and Pedagogy*
  - Knowledge of content
  - Knowledge of prerequisite relationships
  - Knowledge of content-related pedagogy
- Component 1b: *Demonstrating Knowledge of Students*
  - Knowledge of characteristics of age group
  - Knowledge of students' varied approaches to learning
  - Knowledge of students' skills and knowledge
  - Knowledge of students' interests and cultural heritage
- Component 1c: *Selecting Instructional Goals*
  - Value
  - Clarity
  - Suitability for diverse students
  - Balance
- Component 1d: *Demonstrating Knowledge of Resources*
  - Resources for teaching
  - Resources for students
- Component 1e: *Designing Coherent Instruction*
  - Learning activities
  - Instructional materials and resources
  - Instructional groups
  - Lesson and unit structure
- Component 1f: *Assessing Student Learning*
  - Congruence with instructional goals
  - Criteria and standards
  - Use for planning

Domain 2: The Classroom Environment

- Component 2a: *Creating an Environment of Respect and Rapport*
  - Teacher interaction with students
  - Student interaction
- Component 2b: *Establishing a Culture for Learning*
  - Importance of the content
  - Student pride in work
  - Expectations for learning and achievement
- Component 2c: *Managing Classroom Procedures*
  - Management of instructional groups
  - Management of transitions
  - Management of materials and supplies
  - Performance of noninstructional duties
  - Supervision of volunteers and paraprofessionals
- Component 2d: *Managing Student Behavior*
  - Expectations
  - Monitoring of student behavior
  - Response of student misbehavior
- Component 2e: *Organizing Physical Space*
  - Safety and arrangement of furniture
  - Accessibility to learning and use of physical resources

Figure 1.1 A framework for teaching

Components of Professional Practice (continued)

Domain 3: Instruction

- Component 3a: *Communicating Clearly and Accurately*
  - Directions and procedures
  - Oral and written language
- Component 3b: *Using Questioning and Discussion Techniques*
  - Quality of questions
  - Discussion techniques
  - Student participation
- Component 3c: *Engaging Students in Learning*
  - Representation of content
  - Activities and assignments
  - Grouping of students
  - Instructional materials and resources
  - Structure and pacing
- Component 3d: *Providing Feedback to Students*
  - Quality: accurate, substantive, constructive, and specific
  - Timeliness
- Component 3e: *Demonstrating Flexibility and Responsiveness*
  - Lesson adjustment
  - Response to students
  - Persistence

Domain 4: Professional Responsibilities

- Component 4a: *Reflecting on Teaching*
  - Accuracy
  - Use in future teaching
- Component 4b: *Maintaining Accurate Records*
  - Student completion of assignments
  - Student progress in learning
  - Noninstructional records
- Component 4c: *Communicating with Families*
  - Information about the instructional program
  - Information about individual students
  - Engagement of families in the instructional program
- Component 4d: *Contributing to the School and District*
  - Relationships with colleagues
  - Service to the school
  - Participation in school and district projects
- Component 4e: *Growing and Developing Professionally*
  - Enhancement of content knowledge and pedagogical skill
  - Service to the profession
- Component 4f: *Showing Professionalism*
  - Service to students
  - Advocacy
  - Decision making

Figure 1.1 A framework for teaching (*cont.*)

Domain 4: Professional Responsibilities. The components in Domain 4 represent the wide range of a teacher's responsibilities outside the classroom. These include *reflecting on teaching, maintaining accurate records, communicating with families, contributing to the school and district, growing and developing professionally,* and *showing professionalism.* Teachers who demonstrate these competencies are highly valued by their colleagues and administrators, as well as being seen as true professionals. Because of its focus on classroom teaching skills, this book does not cover many of the components in this domain. However, this chapter treats *reflecting on teaching*, and some aspects of *maintaining accurate records* are addressed in Chapter 10: Assessment.

The benefits of having a framework for professional practice, as Danielson notes, are several. First, a framework offers the profession of teaching a shared vocabulary as a way to communicate about excellence. For novice teachers, a framework provides a pathway to excellence by laying out the twenty-two important components that constitute professional practice. A framework for teaching provides a structure for discussions among teachers and also serves to sharpen the focus for professional development. A framework also serves to communicate to the larger community the array of competencies needed to be an effective teacher.

The Teacher As a Reflective Decision Maker

There are many different models depicting the teacher's role. Each is based on different assumptions about effective teaching and the nature of teachers' work. The model of the teacher as a **reflective decision maker** was selected as the organizing rubric of this book because of the model's simplicity and its power to capture the essence of what teachers do in the instructional process. Teachers are professionals who are educated and trained to make and implement decisions. Admittedly, this conceptualization is a simplification of what occurs in teaching, but that is why models are useful. They allow us to see the forest without being confused by the trees.

This particular model represents a theory of teaching and makes several basic assumptions. First, the model assumes that teaching is goal directed; that is, some change in the students' thinking or behavior is sought. Second, the model assumes that teachers are active shapers of their own actions. They make plans, implement them, and continually adjust to new information concerning the effects of their actions. Third, the model assumes that teaching is basically a rational and reflective process that can be improved by examining its components in an analytical manner. Analytic decision making is particularly important because teachers often have to make their decisions quickly and under uncertain conditions. Reflecting on the decisions they have made will help teachers over time to develop personal practical knowledge. Fourth, the model assumes that teachers, by their actions, can influence students to change their own thinking or behavior in desired ways. Stated another way, the model assumes that teachers can affect student learning. Let's look at an example of the kind of decisions teachers are called on to make each and every day.

First consider the following situation. You are a middle school social studies teacher. You want to teach your students what a protective tariff is. What decisions must you make before this can be accomplished? First, *you have to decide exactly what you want them to know about protective tariffs.* You probably will want them to know how protective tariffs differ from revenue tariffs, why countries impose protective tariffs, how other countries are likely to respond, and who benefits and who suffers when protective tariffs are imposed.

Second, *you must decide what student behavior you will accept as evidence that the students understand protective tariffs and their ramifications.* Will they have to repeat a definition from memory? Will they have to give examples? Will they have to analyze a hypothetical situation and describe the pros and cons of imposing a protective tariff?

Third, *you will have to plan a strategy for obtaining the desired pupil learning.* Will you have the students do some reading? Will you lecture to them? Will you use a CD-ROM or computer program to help explain the concept? How many examples will you need to show them? What provisions will you make for those students who don't understand? Will you assess what the students already know about tariffs before beginning instruction? Will you differentiate instruction based on students' prior learning or their learning styles? How much time will you allot for this learning activity?

Fourth, *as you teach the lesson, you will have to decide, based on student reactions, which parts of your strategy to adjust.* Are the students responding in the manner you thought? Are there any new classroom developments that will force you to change your tactics or the decisions you had previously made?

Fifth, *you will need to assess the impact and outcomes of your teaching.* Have the students satisfactorily demonstrated that they understand what protective tariffs are? How should they do that? If they have not grasped the concept, what is the deficiency in their understanding? What can you do about it? How effective were the strategies you used to teach the concept?

All these questions require **decisions** about alternative choices. Even the initial decision to teach the concept of protective tariffs required choosing it from other social studies concepts. As this example demonstrates, the teacher is constantly making decisions with regard to student learning and appropriate instructional strategies.

What kinds of decisions? In the example of the protective tariff, you would have to decide how the students would best learn the characteristics of protective tariffs, based on their previous learning experiences. If you had decided to lecture, you would be predicting that, given the particular students and the available material, they would learn best through a lecture method.

Suppose that midway through the lecture you pick up cues from the students that they do not really understand the concept of a protective tariff. It might be that they weren't ready to understand the concept, or it might be that your lecture was ineffective. Now you have to decide whether to continue, try a different strategy, or reintroduce the concept later. The various steps of this decision-making model are depicted in Figure 1.2. Within the instructional role, teachers must make decisions related to the three basic teaching functions shown in Figure 1.2: (1) planning, (2) implementation, and (3) evaluation.

The *planning* function requires that teachers make decisions about their students' needs, the most appropriate goals and objectives to help meet those needs, the content to be taught, the motivation necessary to attain their goals and objectives, and the instructional modes and teaching strategies most suited to the attainment of those goals and objectives. The planning function usually occurs when teachers are alone and have time to reflect and consider long- and short-range plans, the students' progress toward achieving objectives, the availability of materials, the time requirements of particular activities, and other such issues. Some teaching skills that support the planning function include observing pupil behavior, diagnosing pupil needs, setting

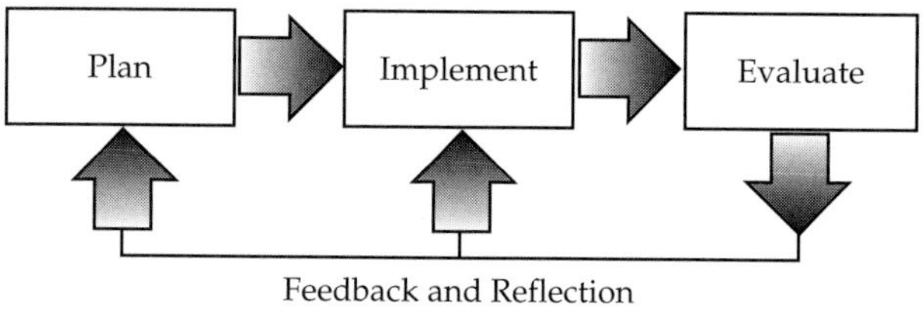

Figure 1.2 Model of the teacher as decision maker

goals and objectives, sequencing goals and objectives, and determining appropriate learning activities related to the objectives.

The *implementation* function requires that teachers implement the decisions that were made in the planning stage, particularly those related to instructional modes, teaching strategies, and learning activities. While much of the planning function is accomplished when teachers are alone, the implementation function occurs when teachers are interacting with students. Research indicates that teachers make an average of one interactive decision every two to six minutes.[10] These decisions frequently must be made rapidly in response to classroom situations. Often, teachers have to make adjustments in their plans based on student questions and how the teachers perceive the lesson to be going. Teaching skills that support the implementation function include presenting and explaining, questioning, listening, introducing, demonstrating, eliciting student responses, and achieving closure.

The *evaluation* function requires decisions about the suitability of chosen objectives as well as the teaching strategies keyed to those objectives and, ultimately, whether or not the students are achieving what the teacher intended. To make the necessary decisions, teachers must determine what kind of information they need and then gather it. Teaching skills that support the evaluation function include specifying the learning objectives to be evaluated; describing the information needed to make such evaluation; obtaining, analyzing, and recording that information; and forming judgments.

The **feedback** and **reflection** dimension of the decision-making model simply means that you examine the results of your teaching, reflect on their meaning, and then decide how adequately you handled each of these three teaching functions. On the basis of this examination, you determine whether you have succeeded in attaining your objectives or whether you need to make new plans or try different implementation strategies. Feedback and your reflection on the feedback, then, is the new information you process into your decision making to adjust your planning, implementation, or evaluation functions—or to continue as before. It is the decision-making system's way of correcting itself.

Reflection

The term ***reflection*** deserves more comment. There are many different conceptions regarding reflection, but the idea of the professional teacher as a reflective practitioner has developed great currency among many teacher educators.[11] The model of the teacher as a reflective practitioner is quite similar to the model of the teacher as a decision maker. Using the skills related to observation, analysis, interpretation, and decision making, reflective practitioners are able to inquire into teaching and to think critically about their work. Reflection typically includes reconstructing the experience, making connections to prior knowledge or skills, testing understanding, and making decisions about how to apply the knowledge or skills in a new situation. Walter Doyle identifies the knowledge base for reflective practitioners as including personal knowledge, craft knowledge of skilled practitioners, and propositional knowledge from classroom research and from the social and behavioral sciences.[12] According to Doyle, theoretical and empirical knowledge, along with teaching skills, are embedded in a conceptual framework that permits the teacher to deliberate about teaching problems and practices. Instead of blindly following rules and prescriptions that are derived from research, reflective practitioners use this theoretical and empirical knowledge, along with knowledge about themselves and craft knowledge derived from skilled teachers, to arrive at decisions that make sense to them given the particularities related to their students and their learning environment.

Reflection on the moral and ethical issues in the decision-making process is strongly urged and supported by many teacher educators. Teachers make moral and ethical decisions every day by the personal examples they set, by the classroom climate they create, and by their interactions with students, parents, and colleagues. These everyday ethics of teaching influence everyone with whom teachers come into contact. When teachers decide how they treat students and others, they make ethical decisions. When they elect to create a classroom climate that fosters safety, trust, and cooperation, they make ethical decisions. When they choose particular examples from history or literature for students to study, they make ethical decisions. In other words, you cannot teach without making ethical decisions.

In addition to the everyday ethics of teaching, teachers are often confronted with ethical dilemmas that demand action but involve competing values. For example, a normally uninterested student has spent hours and hours on a term paper, but its quality is quite poor. He expresses his hope that you will take effort into account when grading the paper. You want to encourage his new engagement in schoolwork, but you also feel the need to be fair to the other students. What do you do? Teaching is filled with many such ethical dilemmas. For further reading on the moral and ethical aspects of teaching, see the Strike and Soltis book listed at the end of the chapter.

Reflection on problems of practice can occur in many ways, including informal debriefing sessions following teaching and written responses to various teaching experiences. Many teachers keep a journal to record their thoughts and reactions to each day's events. The act of writing and describing problems that occurred provides the writer the opportunity to reexamine the day's events and actions taken to address the problems. The journal provides an ongoing record of a new teacher's growth, thinking, and problem-solving ability. Viewing a videotape of one's teaching invariably reveals patterns of behavior that we didn't know existed. Reflecting on the effects of these behavioral patterns on student learning provides motivation either to continue or to change these patterns.

Working with a mentor or colleague allows the teacher to obtain another perspective and to get new ideas regarding classroom problems. Donald Schön argues the benefits of reflecting with another person when he states: "When inquiry into learning remains private, it is also likely to remain tacit. Free of the need to make our ideas explicit to someone else, we are less likely to make them explicit to ourselves."[13] If ideas remain tacit, one is less likely to take steps to address the problems or opportunities.

Factors Influencing Instructional Decisions

Teachers do not make instructional decisions in a vacuum; many factors influence the decision-making process. For example, knowing and understanding your students and their backgrounds is imperative if you are to plan and implement instruction effectively. Your students will represent many kinds of diversity that will affect how they learn. They will differ from one another in terms of racial, ethnic, and cultural backgrounds. These differences influence their perspectives on many issues and often their preferred ways of learning and behaving. Some will speak a primary language other than English, which poses a particular challenge to teachers as they plan and implement their lessons.

Some students will come from poverty backgrounds, which may influence their readiness to learn certain concepts and principles. Many studies have demonstrated the deleterious effects of poverty on student achievement. For example, children from poverty backgrounds are much more likely to suffer from the effects of inadequate health care, shelter, clothing, and nutrition. These negative conditions affect the children's abilities to attend school regularly, concentrate on learning, and do homework. Children from poverty backgrounds pose a particular challenge to schools, partly because schools tend to be more oriented toward serving middle-class children. Many more school dropouts come from poverty backgrounds than from middle-class backgrounds. Making the curriculum and instructional experiences relevant to poor children constitutes a major challenge that schools and teachers must meet.

Students' gender also influences how we think of them and what we often expect of them. Treating boys and girls equitably as individuals rather than as gender stereotypes is a challenge for both male and female teachers. Students also differ in terms of their needs for belonging, safety, and self-esteem. Children from stable, secure homes may have different needs from children who have not had this kind of security. Recognizing diverse needs will help you to better understand students and why they behave the way they do. Students will also come to your classroom with different abilities, achievements, and learning styles. A huge challenge for you as a teacher will be to provide a variety of learning experiences to accommodate your students' diverse backgrounds, needs, learning styles, and abilities.

The teacher's personal practical knowledge also influences decision making. Richard Kindsvatter and colleagues argue that a well-informed belief system is the most credible basis for rational teacher decisions.[14] They assert that teachers should become aware of the assumptions and beliefs that compose their belief systems. Then, as they develop attitudes and habits of practice (e.g., patterns of decision making), these should be examined carefully to ensure conformity to accepted educational principles. As teachers plan instruction, interact in classrooms, and evaluate instructional outcomes, these attitudes and habits of practice, tested against sound educational principles, will become a safeguard against poor education decision making.

The five general areas of teacher competence discussed earlier represent the broad categories of preparation that teachers need to make intelligent, effective decisions. Thus, competence in theoretical knowledge about learning, attitudes that foster learning and positive human relationships, knowledge in the subject matter to be taught, a repertoire of teaching skills, and personal practical knowledge developed over time and with classroom experience provide teachers with the tools necessary to make and implement professional judgments and decisions. Figure 1.3 depicts this relationship.

As you think about Figure 1.3, it should become obvious to you that people may strive toward mastery of the reflective decision-making model without ever achieving it. To achieve mastery would require total command of the four general areas of competence and the ability to apply expertly the knowledge, attitudes, and skills acquired in each instructional decision. Even if decision making cannot be mastered, *through reflection* teachers can become increasingly competent at it and, consequently, become increasingly effective with their students. The use of cases, simulation activities, action research, and reflection are powerful means by which teacher decision making can be developed and fostered within the context of teacher education programs.

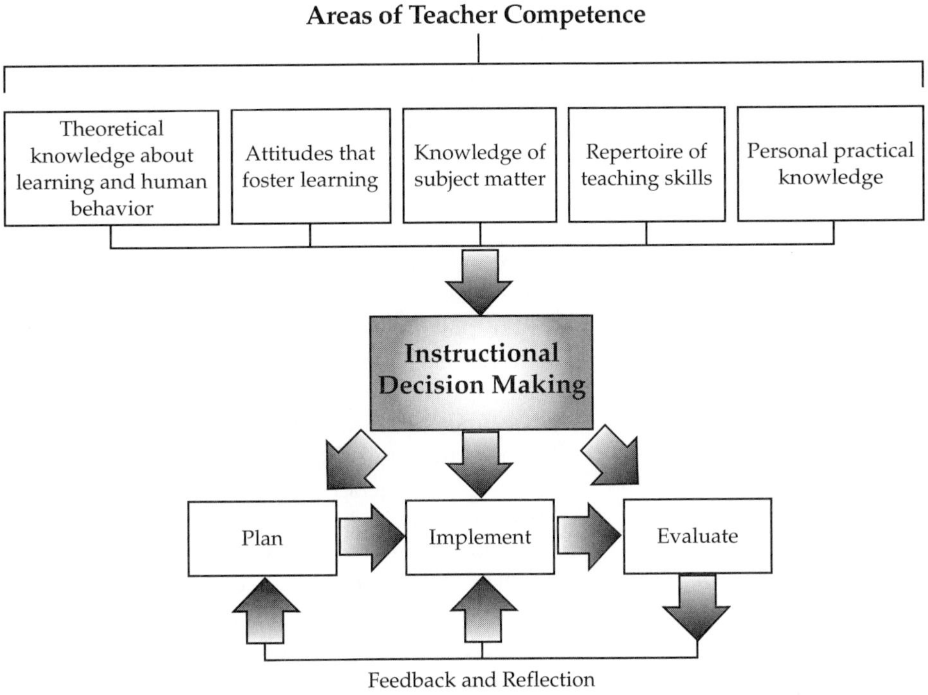

Figure 1.3 Relationship of teacher-competence areas to process of instructional decision making

How Are Teaching Skills Acquired?

Classroom Teaching Skills is designed to equip you with a repertoire of teaching skills crucial to the decision-making process and professional practice. Without such a repertoire of skills, your decision-making alternatives are severely limited. The skills chosen for this book are skills supported by many teacher educators on the basis of their own teaching experience and their diagnosis of the teacher's role as a decision maker, as well as evidence provided by educational research. These skills are complex, not simple, ones. Their acquisition requires both careful study and diligent practice. This book is designed to start you thinking about the skills; understanding their purposes and how they fit into the instructional act; and practicing their application in analytical, simulated, or classroom situations. It will be up to you and your instructors to provide opportunities where you can practice the skills in more complex and realistic situations, eventually practicing them in a classroom context with students.

How does one go about learning complex teaching skills so that they become part of one's teaching style? One researcher has described very well a three-stage process of complex skill acquisition.[15] The first phase is a *cognitive* one. The learner must form a cognitive map of the skill he is to learn. He should know the purpose of the skill and how it will benefit him. Further, this cognitive phase helps the learner to isolate the various skill elements, their sequencing, and the nature of the final performance. In this phase, the learner forms a concept of what is contained in the skill, how its elements fit together, and how his present knowledge and experience can contribute to what he is to learn.

The second phase for complex skill acquisition is *practice.* We have all heard the old saying, "Practice makes perfect." While this statement may not take into account many other requisites, it is certainly true that complex skills cannot be learned without a good deal of practice. The seemingly effortless motion of an Olympic swimmer is not acquired without thousands of miles of swimming practice. Similarly, the skill of driving a car is not learned without a lot of practice. So, too, with complex teaching skills.

The third phase for acquiring a complex skill is *knowledge of results.* Practice will not really make perfect unless the persons trying to acquire the skill receive feedback regarding their performance. This point has been repeatedly demonstrated in psychological experiments in which subjects are given great amounts of practice in a given skill but are deprived of any feedback regarding their performance. Without such feedback, their performance does not improve, while other subjects, whose practice of the same skill includes feedback, do improve on their initial performance.

Since learning complex teaching skills requires (1) cognitive understanding, (2) practice, and (3) knowledge of performance (feedback), any materials aimed at helping teachers develop such skills should incorporate these three conditions into their design. This book has such a design. *Classroom Teaching Skills* is also self-contained; that is, you can acquire conceptual aspects of a particular skill without reliance on outside instructors, materials, or the availability of a group of students to teach. There will be times, however, when you will be asked to work with some of your peers and provide feedback to one another.

You might be asking yourself, "Can teaching skills really be mastered in the absence of pupils to be taught?" Ultimately, no, but there are various intermediate stages that are helpful to go through as you acquire skills. These stages are presented in Figure 1.4.*

Stage 1 involves a conceptual understanding of the skill, its elements, their sequence, and the nature of the final performance. Usually this first stage is accomplished by reading about the skill and its elements and/or by seeing the skill demonstrated and having its various elements explained. It does not normally involve practice.

Stage 2 is accomplished through self-contained training materials directed at each of the major elements composing a model of the skill. Appropriate feedback must also be provided for each of the elements within the model. The training materials should themselves be prepared in accordance with the elements of the model.

Stage 2a requires that the practice exercises contained in the training materials be developed around data obtained from studies of children. In other words, practice situations, drawn from actual data, should be used to make them as realistic as possible and highly transferable to classrooms.

Stage 3 represents classroom situations in which the skill can be practiced with students. This is the context where the teacher tries to "put it all together" and receives feedback on his or her performance. The importance of Stages 2 and 2a becomes apparent when one thinks of moving directly from Stage 1 to Stage 3. Reading about the skill and then immediately practicing it in a classroom is analogous to reading a manual on how to operate an automobile and then taking it out into heavy traffic to practice. Obviously, no responsible driver educator would use this procedure. Instead, the learners would be

*From Bryce B. Hudgins, "Self-Contained Training Materials for Teacher Education: A Derivation from Research on the Learning of Complex Skills," Report 5 National Center for the Development of Training Materials in Teacher Education (Bloomington: School of Education, Indiana University, 1974), p. 23. Reprinted by permission.

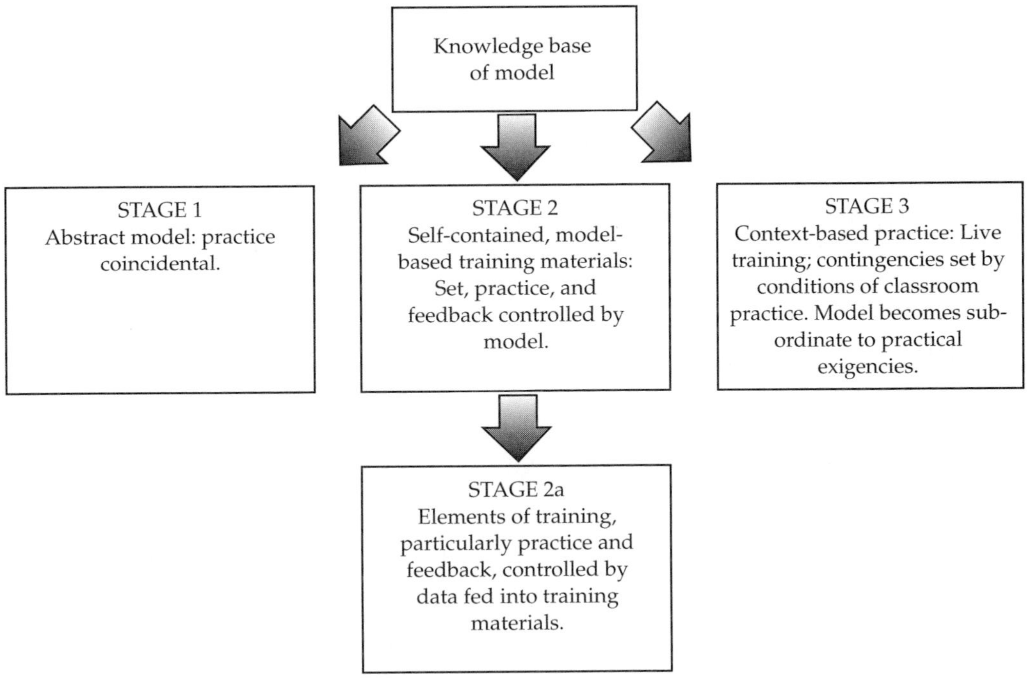

Figure 1.4 Self-contained training materials in a teacher-training sequence. Figure shows (1) the dependence of training materials on an adequate knowledge base for the model and (2) the position of the materials as the reality dimension of training is varied

required to practice various elements in simulated or controlled situations before allowing them to take a car out alone.

Because teacher education has too often lacked the training materials needed to develop basic teaching skills, beginning teachers have sometimes been asked to move directly from Stage 1 to Stage 3. Occasionally, the teacher has succeeded in spite of these circumstances, but in many instances, the results have been disastrous. Although ultimately you must exercise these skills with students in real teaching situations, your probability of success will be greatly increased if you first develop a thorough understanding of the skill and its elements, have controlled practice situations that are reality based, and receive feedback to adjust your performance in necessary ways.

NOTES

1. Myron Brenton, *What's Happened to Teacher?* (New York: Coward-McCann, 1970), p. 71.
2. David Ryans, *Characteristics of Teachers* (Washington, D.C.: American Council on Education, 1960).
3. J. W. Getzels and P. W. Jackson, "The Teacher's Personality and Characteristics," in *Handbook of Research on Teaching*, ed. N. L. Gage (Chicago: Rand McNally, 1963), p. 574.
4. B. O. Smith, *Teachers for the Real World* (Washington, D.C.: American Association of Colleges for Teacher Education, 1969), p. 122.
5. Thomas L. Good and Jere E. Brophy, *Looking in Classrooms*, 8th ed. (New York: Longman, 2000), pp. 75–80.
6. Lee S. Shulman, "Knowledge and Teaching: Foundations of the New Reform," *Harvard Educational Review* 57 (February 1987): 8.
7. Kathy Carter and Walter Doyle, "Personal Narrative and Life History in Learning to Teach," in *Handbook of Research on Teacher Education,* 2nd ed., ed. John Sikula (New York: Macmillan, 1996), pp. 124–125.
8. Kathy Carter, "Teachers' Knowledge and Learning to Teach," in *Handbook of Research on Teacher Education,* ed. W. Robert Houston (New York: Macmillan, 1990), pp. 299–302.
9. Charlotte Danielson, *Enhancing Professional Practice: A Framework for Teaching.* (Alexandria, Va.: Associ-

ation for Supervision and Curriculum Development, 1996).
10. Christopher Clark and Penelope Peterson, "Teacher Stimulated Recall of Interactive Decisions" (Paper presented at the annual meeting of the American Educational Research Association, San Francisco, 1986); Richard Shavelson, "Review of Research on Teachers' Pedagogical Judgments, Plans, and Decisions." *Elementary School Journal,* 83, no. 4 (1983): 392–413.
11. Linda Valli, ed., *Reflective Teacher Education: Cases and Critiques* (Albany, N.Y.: State University of New York Press, 1992).
12. Walter Doyle, "Themes in Teacher Education Research," in *Handbook of Research on Teacher Education,* ed. W. R. Houston (New York: Macmillan, 1990), p. 6.
13. Donald Schön, *Educating the Reflective Practitioner* (San Francisco: Jossey-Bass, 1987), p. 300.
14. Richard Kindsvatter, William Wilen, and Margaret Ishler, *Dynamics of Effective Teaching* (White Plains, N.Y.: Longman, 1996), pp. 2–3.
15. Bryce B. Hudgins, "Self-Contained Training Materials for Teacher Education: A Derivation from Research on the Learning of Complex Skills," Report 5, National Center for the Development of Training Materials in Teacher Education (Bloomington: School of Education, Indiana University, 1974).

ADDITIONAL RESOURCES

Readings

Arends, Richard I. *Learning to Teach,* 5th ed. New York: McGraw-Hill, 2001.

Danielson, Charlotte. *Enhancing Professional Practice: A Framework for Teaching.* Alexandria, Va.: Association for Supervision and Curriculum Development, 1996.

Fenstermacher, Gary D., and Jonas F. Soltis. *Approaches to Teaching,* 3rd ed., New York: Teachers College Press, 1998.

Good, Thomas L., and Jere E. Brophy. *Looking in Classrooms,* 8th ed. New York: Longman, 2000.

Shavelson, Richard J. "What Is the Basic Teaching Skill?" *Journal of Teacher Education* 24 (Summer 1973): 144–149.

Strike, Kenneth A., and Jonas F. Soltis. *The Ethics of Teaching,* 3rd ed. New York: Teachers College Press, 1998.

Web Sites

Teacher's Edition Online: http://www.teachnet.com
A versatile site for teachers that includes lesson plans, educational news, opportunities to share ideas and problems, and a "Top 100" list of Web sites for educators.

Teacher Information Network: http://www.teacher.com/
Contains Web connections to educational organizations, resources, teacher sites, the USDOE, and state DOEs.

Teacher Education: The Next Step: http://www.teachers.ash.org.au/teachereduc/
An Australian site for student teachers that deals with methodologies, theories, and learning concepts. Bloom's taxonomy, behavior management, multiple intelligences, Piaget, multiculturalism, special needs, lesson ideas, classroom resources, discussions, Web polls, and much more.

Mid-Continent Research for Education and Learning: http://www.mcrel.org/
A regional educational laboratory funded by the U.S. Department of Education, the site contains resources on content standards, school improvement, assessment, curriculum, technology, and much more.

Education Week: http://www.edweek.org
An educational newspaper published forty-three times a year. Contains an archive of articles on educational reform, policy, and schools.

2

Instructional Planning

Greta Morine-Dershimer

OBJECTIVE 1 **Given two concept maps depicting a prospective teacher's "before and after" perspectives of teacher planning, to compare these concept maps and determine what the teacher learned about instructional planning**

OBJECTIVE 2 **Given information from studies of the instructional planning of experienced teachers, to identify key characteristics of productive planning**

OBJECTIVE 3 **Given a description of teacher planning analogous to a dramatic production, to generate additional analogies that highlight important aspects of teacher planning**

To Plan Is Human . . .

All people engage in planning on a regular basis. We think in advance about things we want to do and make preparations that enable us to do them. All planning has a future orientation, and all planning involves some intention for action to fulfill some purpose. According to one theory of planning, there are two important reasons why human beings plan in advance for many of our purposeful actions.[1] First, because humans are, to some extent, rational creatures, we tend to deliberate about what we do. But deliberation takes time, and at the moment when we must act, we rarely have time to deliberate at length about exactly how we want to act. So we deliberate in advance, deciding how we intend to act at some future point, and we call this deliberation *planning.* Second, because we live in groups and must relate to other people, we need to coordinate our own activities with those of others. Also, because we all play more than one role, we frequently need to coordinate these roles, engaging in a series of activities, which we must complete within a short space of time, and determining the best sequence in which to carry them out. We manage such coordination by constructing plans for future action.

Clearly, you have already had experience in making plans. But how effective are your plans? To what extent are they fully realized? If you are at all typical, many of your plans undergo some change before you put them into action. Because plans involve anticipation of future events, we can never specify fully what we will do at the point when we begin to act on our plan. Usually we begin with partial plans, filling in more and more details as we get closer and closer to the time for action. This is an efficient way to proceed, for we can rarely predict future events with great accuracy.

Since you have probably been planning important events in your life for several years, you bring a useful experience to one of the most important tasks of teaching. In many ways, instructional planning requires the same skills as the everyday planning you already do.[2] But the planning that a teacher must do is more complex, and this added complexity necessitates some special skills and knowledge.

One of the ten principles developed by the Interstate New Teachers Assessment and Support Consortium (INTASC) as model standards[3] for licensing beginning teachers delineates the knowledge, dispositions, and performances considered essential for effective instructional planning. The relevant principle and supportive details are presented in Figure 2.1.* This chapter introduces ideas related to the special skills and knowledge that are important in planning for instruction. This book as a whole provides information about the complex variety of skills and knowledge that must be brought to bear in order for instructional plans to be carried out effectively.

INTASC Core Standard on Planning

Principle #7: The teacher plans instruction based upon knowledge of subject matter, students, the community, and curriculum goals.

Knowledge

The teacher understands learning theory, subject matter, curriculum development, and student development and knows how to use this knowledge in planning instruction to meet curriculum goals.

The teacher knows how to take contextual considerations (instructional materials, individual student interests, needs, and aptitudes, and community resources) into account in planning instruction that creates an effective bridge between curriculum goals and students' experiences.

The teacher knows when and how to adjust plans based on student responses and other contingencies.

Dispositions

The teacher values both long-term and short-term planning.

The teacher believes that plans must always be open to adjustment and revision based on student needs and changing circumstances.

The teacher values planning as a collegial activity.

Performances

As an individual and a member of a team, **the teacher selects and creates** learning experiences that are appropriate for curriculum goals, relevant to learners, and based upon principles of effective instruction (e.g. that activate students' prior knowledge, anticipate preconceptions, encourage exploration and problem-solving, and build new skills on those previously acquired).

The teacher plans for learning opportunities that recognize and address variation in learning styles and performance modes.

The teacher creates lessons and activities that operate at multiple levels to meet the developmental and individual needs of diverse learners and help each progress.

The teacher creates short-range and long-term plans that are linked to student needs and performance, and adapts the plans to ensure and capitalize on student progress and motivation.

The teacher responds to unanticipated sources of input, evaluates plans in relation to short- and long-range goals, and systematically adjusts plans to meet student needs and enhance learning.

Figure 2.1

*From Interstate New Teacher Assessment and Support Consortium (1992). *Model Standards for Beginning Teacher Licensing and Development: A Resource for State Dialogue.* Washington, D.C.: Council of Chief State School Officers.

OBJECTIVE 1

Given two concept maps depicting a prospective teacher's "before and after" perspectives of teacher planning, to compare maps and determine what the teacher learned about instructional planning

Where Do We Start?

A good place to start thinking about any relatively new topic is with your own ideas. What do you think is involved in teacher planning? One useful way to clarify and explicate your own ideas is to construct a concept map.[4] A **concept map** is a way of organizing your ideas about a particular topic so that the relationships you see among the various subtopics can be displayed visually.

You may already be familiar with concept mapping or know it by another name, such as *webbing* or *semantic mapping*. If not, this is a good technique for you to learn; it can be useful in organizing your ideas for a writing task, or in reviewing a topic you have been studying, or in organizing information for a unit of instruction you are planning to teach.[5] Software is available to assist teachers and their students in designing and developing a variety of types of visual maps for a variety of types of purposes.[6] These maps are useful tools for helping learners construct, organize, and communicate their knowledge.

LEARNING ACTIVITY 1

To construct a concept map of your ideas about teacher planning, follow these simple procedures. First, make a list of all the words and phrases you associate with the topic of teacher planning. Second, group the items in your list together in some way that makes sense to you, and label your groups to indicate what characteristic the items in the group have in common. Third, combine your initial groups to form larger, more inclusive groups. Finally, draw a concept map, or graphic display, that shows how your groups and subgroups relate to each other and to the major topic of teacher planning.

Before you read any further in this chapter, you might want to construct a concept map of your ideas about teacher planning. Then you will have an opportunity to compare your ideas about teacher planning to the ideas of another prospective teacher. Later, as you read further in this chapter and in this book, you can see how the information presented relates to the ideas about instructional planning that you already have.

Concept Mapping: Before and After

One of the most interesting things about people is that their ideas can change. One of the most interesting things about concept maps is that they can help us trace how our ideas change as a result of education and experience. In this section, you will examine before and after concept maps of a secondary prospective teacher to see what changes occurred in his thinking about teacher planning as a result of planning and teaching a series of lessons.

The student whose ideas are presented was enrolled in a teacher preparation program at Syracuse University. He constructed his initial concept map at the beginning of a course on strategies of teaching. During the course, he engaged in **peer teaching** in addition to reading and discussing information about various important aspects of planning and teaching. Each student in the course planned a series of three or four lessons on a given topic, using different instructional procedures in each lesson.[7] They taught these lessons to small groups of their peers.

At the end of the class, each student constructed a new concept map to show how his or her concepts of teacher planning had changed. Pre and post (before and after) maps for one of these students are presented in this section. If you and your classmates chose to construct concept maps, you should find it interesting to compare your own "before map" with the one presented here, as well as with those of fellow students in your own teacher preparation program. In addition, you will be asked to compare the pre and post maps presented here to determine what kinds of changes you can observe in the thinking of this prospective teacher. These changes occurred as a result of coursework and practice in planning and carrying out plans for instruction.

YOUR TURN

Considering a Real Case

Ted was a secondary education major working on a master's degree in social studies education. He had done his undergraduate work in business administration. His pre and post maps of teacher planning are presented in Figures 2.2 and 2.3. Between constructing these two maps, he taught four lessons to a group of his peers on the general topic of the free-enterprise system. At the end of his peer-teaching experience, he began student teaching, teaching social studies to eighth- and ninth-graders in a suburban middle school.

Consider Ted's pre and post maps. What changes do you see? What new ideas have emerged? Do these new ideas appear to be important things to consider? How might Ted's teaching experience have contributed to the changes you observe? After studying these maps, how do you think your own concept map might change, given some practice in planning and teaching lessons in a peer-teaching or classroom setting?

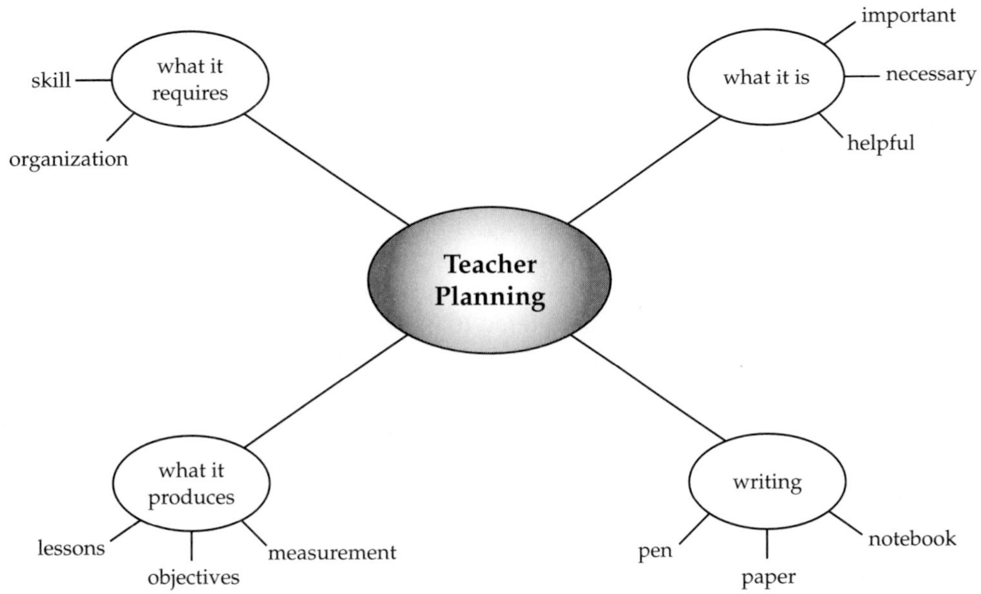

Figure 2.2 Ted's pre map of teacher planning

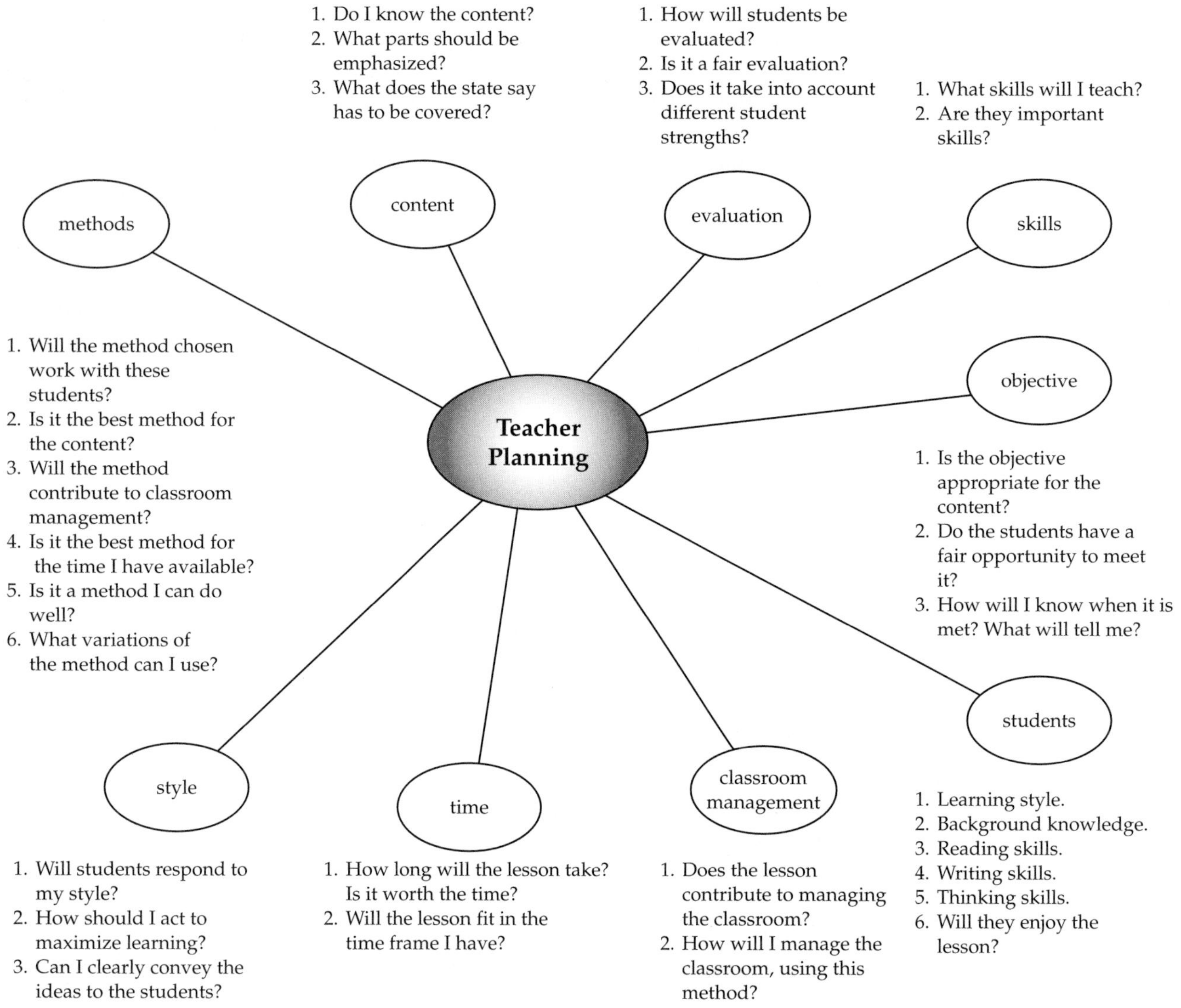

1. Do I know the content?
2. What parts should be emphasized?
3. What does the state say has to be covered?
1. How will students be evaluated?
2. Is it a fair evaluation?
3. Does it take into account different student strengths?
1. What skills will I teach?
2. Are they important skills?
methods
content
evaluation
skills
1. Will the method chosen work with these students?
2. Is it the best method for the content?
3. Will the method contribute to classroom management?
4. Is it the best method for the time I have available?
5. Is it a method I can do well?
6. What variations of the method can I use?
objective
Teacher Planning
1. Is the objective appropriate for the content?
2. Do the students have a fair opportunity to meet it?
3. How will I know when it is met? What will tell me?
students
style
time
classroom management
1. Learning style.
2. Background knowledge.
3. Reading skills.
4. Writing skills.
5. Thinking skills.
6. Will they enjoy the lesson?
1. Will students respond to my style?
2. How should I act to maximize learning?
3. Can I clearly convey the ideas to the students?
1. How long will the lesson take? Is it worth the time?
2. Will the lesson fit in the time frame I have?
1. Does the lesson contribute to managing the classroom?
2. How will I manage the classroom, using this method?

Figure 2.3 Ted's post map of teacher planning

In His Own Words. Ted compared his own maps and noted similarities and differences. Here are some of his comments.

> *Ted:* Two months ago I didn't know what teacher planning was. This showed in my pre concept map with its skeletal nature. My post map focuses on what goes into teacher planning. I thought of all these things and how they are related to each other and affect each other—that any change in one component affects another. These components of teacher planning do not stand independently. Two months ago I thought they did. The peer teaching and the preparation that went into it helped open my eyes to all that is important. I was no longer watching teacher planning, but doing it. If I failed to plan for any of these components, my lesson turned out not to be as good.

Patterns of Change. Ted's experience is not unique. It illustrates patterns of changes in thinking about teacher planning that have been identified in studies of prospective teachers like yourself. As students engage in planning and teaching lessons, they increase their awareness of the many elements to be considered in conducting a successful lesson, identify the relationships among these various elements, and reorganize their ideas to give priority to different aspects of teaching.

The pre and post concept maps presented here are evidence of **professional development.** A *professional* is a person who possesses some specialized knowledge and skills, can weigh alternatives, and can select from among a number of potentially productive actions one that is particularly appropriate in a given situation. The post concept map of Ted, a soon-to-be-professional teacher, shows that he has begun to develop specialized knowledge, specialized skills, an awareness of alternatives, and a sense of the situational characteristics to be considered in determining which alternative to choose. For example, the questions raised on Ted's post map ("Is the objective appropriate for the content?," "Will the method chosen work with these students?," "Is it the best method for the content?," "Will the method contribute to classroom management?," "Is it the best method for the time I have available?," "Will students respond to my style?") show that he has developed an awareness of alternatives as well as a sense of some situational characteristics to be considered in choosing from among instructional alternatives.

Prospective teachers at the University of Virginia's Curry School of Education have also developed pre and post concept maps of teacher planning, in conjunction with classes on alternative instructional strategies and associated field experiences. The most common changes in professional thinking that they exhibited involved increased attention to students' background knowledge and characteristics, instructional materials, and evaluation processes. All of these are critical aspects of planning for instruction.[8]

These examples provide evidence that these prospective teachers are beginning to think and act like professionals. You should be able to observe similar changes in your own knowledge, skills, and awareness of alternatives as you progress through this book. Several of the terms and topics in the concept maps Ted developed are introduced and discussed in detail in later chapters: objectives (Chapter 3), classroom management (Chapter 8), and evaluation/assessment (Chapter 10). Other important considerations for planning, not mentioned as clearly by Ted, are also discussed in later chapters: questioning (Chapter 5), differentiating instruction (Chapter 6), and cooperative learning (Chapter 9). Involving students in learning (Chapter 4) and technology skills (Chapter 7) are important in carrying out your instructional plans successfully.

When you have finished the reading and activities in this book, you might construct a final concept map of teacher planning. If you compare your own pre and post maps, you will have solid evidence of your own professional development.

OBJECTIVE 2

Given information from studies of the instructional planning of experienced teachers, to identify key characteristics of productive planning

Myths and Realities

Many people believe that planning is one of the most important skills a teacher can have and that teachers who plan better must also teach better. Some people think that planning is something teachers do in the quiet of their classrooms—before pupils arrive for the day or after they leave for the night. Others may suspect that many teachers never really plan at all, except to write down the page numbers of the textbook to be covered each day. The truth, of course, is that neither of these views is completely accurate.

The myths about teacher planning are legion. Unfortunately, they are influential in determining what prospective teachers learn about the process of planning. Which of the following statements are myths, and which are probably accurate descriptions of the reality of teacher planning?

- Everybody's doing it.
- A little goes a long way.
- A plan a day keeps disaster away.
- Plans are made to be broken.
- One size fits all.
- Time is of the essence.
- Don't look back!
- You can do it yourself.
- Try it—you'll like it.

Thirty years ago, it would have been difficult to determine which of these statements were myths and which were realities. Little was known about how teachers went about planning in their classrooms. Since then, however, a number of researchers have observed and interviewed teachers as they were engaged in instructional planning. While there is still much to be learned, a useful base of knowledge has been established. Several of the myths discussed here were debunked by a flurry of studies conducted in the late 1970s and early 1980s. These studies have been capably summarized in some excellent reviews.[9] Only more recent studies are specifically cited in the commentary below.

Everybody's Doing It—In a Variety of Ways

Teachers do plan, and they plan in a variety of ways. There are four basic types of planning in which teachers regularly engage: yearly, unit, weekly, and daily planning. All are important for effective instruction.

While all teachers plan, they do not all plan in exactly the same way. Some may jot down a few notes in a lesson plan book. Others may write outlines detailing lessons or units they intend to teach. Many teachers write more detailed daily plans for their substitutes than they do for themselves, wanting to ensure that established routines are understood and maintained. Teachers who have fully embraced the computer age may keep a file of lesson or unit plans stored on disks, updating or revising these each year to fit new circumstances.

Studies have shown that few experienced teachers plan precisely according to the procedures recommended by curriculum experts for many years. Rather than beginning by stating instructional objectives, and then selecting and organizing instructional activities to meet those objectives, many elementary teachers begin by considering the context in which teaching will occur (for example, the instructional materials and time available), then think about activities that will interest and involve their pupils, and finally note the purposes that these activities will serve. Secondary teachers focus almost exclusively on content and preparation of an interesting presentation. This does not mean that teachers have no real goals, but it does suggest that a basic consideration for most teachers is maintaining the interest and involvement of their pupils. Since research has shown that pupil attention and on-task behavior are associated with achievement, pupil involvement is important for teachers to keep in mind when planning for instruction.

Recent research has focused on variation in the ways teachers plan to respond to students' individual differences. Teachers in many classrooms today work with children who vary in cultural background, who have many languages other than English as their first language, and who may either have learning disabilities or be gifted and talented. As classroom diversity has increased, regular classroom teachers have had to learn to adapt their instruction to meet students' special needs and abilities. Studies indicate that elementary teachers do more planning than secondary teachers to meet the needs of students with learning disabilities and also collaborate more with special education teachers in developing appropriate adaptations for these students.[10] Planning with colleagues who have special expertise can improve any teacher's ability to adapt instructional plans to serve diverse pupil populations. Some useful guides are available to help teachers as well.[11]

A Little Goes a Long Way—Especially at the Beginning

The tricky thing about teacher planning is that one kind of plan is *nested* within another. This means that plans made at the beginning of the year have important effects on the weekly and daily plans that will be made throughout the year. Before the students ever enter the room, most teachers have planned the physical arrangement of the classroom: where and how students will be seated, where materials will be kept, what areas will be set up as centers for particular types of activities, and how bulletin board or wall space will be utilized. Decisions about daily and weekly scheduling of subjects are usually completed by the end of the first week of school. Within the first few weeks, student abilities are assessed and plans are made for instructional grouping. Classroom rules or management procedures are also established during these early weeks. Not all of these plans are made by individual teachers in isolation. A grade-level or subject-area team may work together to schedule classes or group pupils. General time schedules and rules for student behavior may be determined by school administrators. Wherever these plans originate, however, they will set the framework within which later plans will develop.

Many teachers identify unit planning as their most important type of planning. Weekly and daily plans are nested within unit plans. Since teachers tend to focus on activities in their planning, unit plans serve to organize a flow of activities related to a general topic for an extended period of time (two weeks to a month, typically).

A Plan a Day Keeps Disaster Away—For Novice Teachers

Experienced teachers report that unit, weekly, and daily planning are the most important types of planning that they do during the year. Few of them write out complete lesson plans on a regular basis, though they will make lesson plans when they are dealing with new content or curriculum materials. They do recommend, however, that student teachers and beginning teachers write lesson plans. This suggests that lesson plans are particularly useful tools in less familiar teaching situations, such as working with new students, new subject matter, or new procedures. For novice teachers, all these aspects of teaching are new and unfamiliar, and lesson plans can be helpful.

In their daily as well as yearly planning, experienced teachers rely heavily on curriculum guides and textbook materials to determine the content and pace of their lessons. Plans for lessons may consist of selecting and adapting activities suggested in the textbook's teacher's guide so that these are particularly interesting or suitable for the instructional needs of their particular pupils. These teachers have established instructional routines over the years, and they fit these suggested activities into their routines; therefore, extensive planning of procedures does not seem as necessary. Novice teachers are in the process of developing routines, experimenting to see what procedures will work for them. More detailed planning of lessons is an essential activity at this stage of their professional development.

Plans Are Not Made to Be Broken— Just Bent

Lesson plans serve several important functions, and teachers say that one of the most important of these is using the plan as a guide for their interactions with students. A written plan can ensure that directions are structured in exactly the right way when an activity is begun. A plan can operate like a secretary's "tickler file," reminding the teacher about what to do next if the rapid-fire interaction of the lesson causes a sudden lapse of memory. A plan can also provide a framework for later evaluation of a lesson, assisting the teacher in identifying productive learning activities.

Because a lesson plan can be such a useful guide, teachers rarely change their plans drastically in the middle of a lesson. They do make adjustments in their plans as they are teaching, and effective teachers seem to be particularly capable at noting how certain pupils are reacting and fine-tuning their procedures accordingly. Some teachers seem to have a "steering group" of pupils who are in the low-average range of achievement, and they adjust the pace of their lessons depending on how well these students are doing. Thus, lesson plans are not made to be broken, but rather to be flexible enough to bend a little when adjustments are needed.

One Size Fits All— But Not Very Well

Most lesson plans are designed to guide instruction for a whole class of students. Thus, the typical plan aims to motivate and involve the "average" student. But of course it is a rare student who fully exemplifies the profile of the average student, just as there are few people whose measurements exactly duplicate those used to design clothing for the average or medium-sized figure. Even a small group of students is made up of individuals who can exhibit a bewildering array of differences in characteristics that influence instruction, including academic performance, prior knowledge or experience, language acquisition, social skills, cultural background, physical development, intellectual ability, and home and family resources. No general lesson plan will be a perfect fit for every student in the class or group. In fact, it is the rare lesson plan that is a *perfect* fit for *any* individual student.

Most teachers make adaptations to accommodate to individual students as they implement their plans, but sometimes these adaptations are not carefully thought through. Some typical accommodations may have negative consequences for student learning. For example, studies show that many teachers call on boys to participate more frequently than girls, presumably because they anticipate more off-task behavior from boys. Teachers also tend to wait longer for high achievers to answer a question but provide less time for lower achievers to respond before redirecting the question or answering it themselves, presumably expecting that only the higher achievers will figure out the answer for themselves if given time to think. White teachers have been observed to make negative judgments about the narrative style of black children (topic-associating style, moving from topic to topic rather than focusing on a single theme) and thus to interrupt their stories frequently to ask questions, while permitting white children, using a topic-centered style, to develop their stories without interruption. These types of adaptations lead to unequal opportunities to learn and unfortunately often provide extra advantages to students who already enjoy a preferred classroom status.

Teacher beliefs can affect the ways teachers plan for diverse pupil populations. Elementary teachers with strong beliefs in the importance of student work habits reportedly plan lessons that are more responsive to student performance, and thus their students learn more.[12] Teachers who believe that all children can learn, and that all children have talents and ideas to contribute to classroom lessons, generally plan lessons that engage students more actively, thus enabling their students to become more self-directed learners.[13]

Classroom diversity compels teachers to make adaptations in their lesson plans to accommodate the instructional needs of individual students and thus promote the learning of all students. Such adaptations are more likely to be effective if they are consciously considered in advance. For example, specific activities designed to encourage student expression of personal feelings, experiences, and opinions *related to the subject matter* of the lesson can accommodate individual differences, celebrate diversity, and contribute to effective pupil achievement. Lesson plans that regularly include such activities enable teachers to tailor their lessons to achieve a better fit for all students.

Time Is of the Essence

Time truly is a crucial factor in teacher planning. Studies of teacher effectiveness have emphasized the importance of providing efficient classroom management. Techniques include establishing routines for rapid homework checks, providing for smooth transitions from one activity to another, and arranging for efficient distribution and collection of materials. These types of procedures save time, allowing teacher and students to concentrate on the content to be learned.

Time is important in another way as well. It takes time for beginning teachers to learn how to plan instruction effectively. There are several reasons for this. During the first year of teaching, it is difficult for teachers to gain a year-long view of the content they are teaching. In most cases, the curriculum, the textbooks and other instructional materials, and the district or state instructional goals and evaluation systems are all unfamiliar to the first-year teacher, yet all these factors must be taken into account in planning daily lessons as well as longer-term instructional units. Some beginning teachers have difficulty planning for classroom discipline and evaluation, possibly because they have had little or no opportunity to organize systems for these elements of instruction during their student teaching. Planning for instruction can be a very time-consuming activity for first-year teachers. By the second year of teaching, however, teachers have a better sense of what to anticipate over the course of the year and have developed a more coherent philosophy of teaching to guide their planning. As time goes on and teachers gain experience with the curriculum and get to know their students' characteristics and abilities, planning tasks become more manageable.[14]

Do Look Back—It Helps in Planning Ahead

Experienced teachers report that soon after a lesson has been taught, they do rethink it and consider how it might be improved or varied another time. This helps them in planning future lessons. Looking back can be especially helpful in long-term planning, such as unit or yearly planning. Teachers who keep records of their plans from prior years can start by considering what activities or procedures worked well and what revisions might be made in sequencing or selection of topics and activities. This is more efficient than starting from scratch every year, and it is an effective aid to teachers who want to improve by learning systematically from their own experience.

Looking back can be useful in another way. Prospective teachers need to reflect on their own early school experiences, because their beliefs about teaching and learning have been deeply affected by their long experience as students. These beliefs have an impact on what and how teachers plan for instruction, and they make it difficult for some to use more innovative and student-centered instructional methods. Only by examining their past experiences and resultant beliefs critically can teachers be free to make informed choices about the instructional activities that will best serve their students.[15]

You Can Do It Yourself—With a Little Help from Your Friends

Teachers rarely rely solely on their own knowledge and inspiration to design classroom instruction. For many years resources such as textbooks, teacher's manuals, and state or district curriculum guides have been available to assist them with instructional planning. Furthermore, in many schools teachers have worked with colleagues to plan lessons or instructional units, sharing ideas and materials. A recent emphasis in public school curricula has been interdisciplinary teaching. When language and methods of inquiry from more than one discipline or subject area are combined to explore a central theme or problem, students may see the topic as more relevant to real life.[16] Some state standards for new teachers require that they collaborate with their colleagues and help students make connections across subject areas.[17] Interdisciplinary instruction can be enhanced when teachers work together to plan lessons and units. This is particularly true at the secondary level, where teachers tend to see themselves as specialists in a single subject area. One prospective English teacher, after planning and teaching an interdisciplinary unit with a prospective science teacher, commented as follows:

> The fact that I was lacking in the science subject area had a positive benefit because I became dependent on [my partner] to help me understand the subject. I found this collaboration rewarding because I wasn't afraid to ask questions. Since teachers too often feel like they have to be infallible experts, being in the position of a "learner" reminded me how important it is to be constantly learning as a teacher.[18]

More recently, teachers have been able to draw readily on the professional knowledge of distant colleagues to enrich their instructional planning. Now, through the resources of the Internet, many opportunities exist for teachers and their students to share ideas electronically with other teachers and students in far-flung places. Because web sites are in constant flux, a published list of useful sites would soon be outdated. The George Lucas Educational Foundation has published an extensive list of electronic resources for educators[19] and has promised to update its web site (http://www.glef.org) regularly to provide current resources. The variety of resources available at the time of publication of this text included instructional projects, documents, visual media, and discussion networks, as well as links to resources on specific topics and subject areas. Searches using terms such as "teacher planning" or "lesson plans" will turn up many other resources. The *New York Times* web site, listed in the Additional Resources at the end of this chapter, is particularly useful. Tomorrow's teachers need to know how to access Internet resources for use in instructional planning. They also need to know how to evaluate them to determine what will or will not be useful. The sections that follow provide some helpful criteria for purposes of such evaluation.

Try It—You May Like It AND You Can Learn from the Process

Teachers report that, besides serving as a guide for interactions with students and as an organizational tool (assisting them to organize time, activities, and materials for a lesson), a lesson plan can provide them with a sense of security. Security is a valuable commodity for a beginning teacher. A well-constructed lesson plan or unit plan can provide a strong foundation for a novice teacher, who may be more than a little shaky about those first few days and weeks with a new group of students.

One study of experienced teachers indicates that planning activities contribute to teachers' development of expertise. Three of the six activities rated by teachers as highly relevant for improving teaching effectiveness were planning activities—preparing materials, mental planning, and written planning. (The other three all related to evaluation of student learning. Planning and evaluation go hand in hand.) Teachers noted that preparing materials and mental planning were more enjoyable activities than written planning, but all three were seen as important tasks. As one teacher commented about mental planning, "If you are always thinking about what you are going to do, then you are constantly getting new insights into what you want to do or how you are going to do it."[20]

To summarize, while we still have things to learn about teacher planning, we do know that teachers think ahead; that they consider planning to be an essential activity; and that designing lessons and units is, for many teachers, one of the most interesting parts of teaching, providing them with an opportunity to use their imagination and ingenuity. We know that a great deal of variety exists in the ways different teachers approach planning. We also know the following:

- Plans are nested, so that plans made to organize the classroom at the beginning of the year have a strong influence on later plans.
- Lesson plans of experienced teachers rely heavily on textbooks and curriculum guides, and they make use of established routines for basic instructional and managerial activities in the classroom.
- Lesson plans of effective teachers are flexible enough to allow for fine-tuning of procedures, adjusting to pupil responses to tasks.
- Teachers' beliefs about teaching and learning strongly influence the options they consider in planning for instruction.
- Effective teachers adapt instructional plans to suit the needs of diverse learners.
- Teachers' planning can be greatly enhanced by collaboration with colleagues as well as by the variety of instructional resources that are available on the Internet.

Novices and Experts

Some interesting research on teaching has built on studies in cognitive psychology that compare the thinking of novices and experts in a given field. Studies of experts and novices in a variety of fields indicate that experts recall meaningful information better than novices and use different criteria to judge the relevance or utility of the information that they perceive and remember.[21]

Some studies of teacher planning suggest that expert teachers are similar to experts in other fields in their patterns of thinking. One study compared the responses of novice and expert mathematics and science teachers on a simulated task in which they had to prepare to take on a new class five weeks after school had started. One of the major differences between experts and novices had to do with how they planned to begin. Experts concentrated on learning what students already knew by planning to have them work review problems and answer questions about their understanding of the subject matter covered so far. Novices planned to ask students where they were in the textbook and then to present a review of important concepts. In other words, experts planned to gather information from students, and novices planned to give information to students. Expert teachers planned to "begin again" by explaining their expectations and classroom routines to students. Novices were more apt to ask students how the former teacher ran the classroom, with the implication that they would follow the same practices.

Expert and novice teachers differed in their judgments of the importance of different types of information. The most important information for experts was what students knew of the subject. The most important information for novices was what management system students were accustomed to following. Expert teachers planned to institute their own routines. Novices planned to adapt to someone else's routines. The expert teachers understood the nested nature of planning. They knew that the classroom management structures they adopted during the first few days of class would shape the plans they would be able to make for the rest of the year.

The Function of Routines

To some people, **routine** connotes dull, dreary, repetitive, unthinking behavior. Thus, the idea that establishing routines is important for instructional planning may be distasteful. But consider the relationship between routines and plans in your everyday life. What are your established routines as a student? Do you have a seat where you habitually sit in each of your classes? Do you have a time of the day or week when you usually read assignments? Do you have a place in the library or computer lab or in your room where you typically work when you have a paper to write? Do you have some materials that you regularly carry with you when you go to class? If you don't have some established routines for any of these activities, you are a rare person.

Everyday routines such as these are important in relation to planning our daily activities because they free our minds to think about other things. If you had to consider a number of alternatives and choose from among them every time you performed any action, you would soon be worn out from the constant decision making. Setting some patterns for your behavior enables you to concentrate on making the really important decisions. Having some established routines also makes it possible for others to predict your behavior to a certain degree. A friend who knows where you will probably sit in class can take the seat next to you, even if you haven't yet arrived.

Having established routines enables teachers to operate more efficiently for similar reasons. In planning lessons, a teacher who has a routine for collecting homework or distributing materials can concentrate on more important decisions about what information to present or what questions to ask students. In conducting lessons, a teacher who has routines for calling on students to participate can more readily concentrate on listening to what the student has to say, rather than worrying about whom to call on next. Lesson routines also help to make teacher behavior predictable to students, and when students know what to expect, they are better able to concentrate on content and are apt to learn more.

Routines can operate at several different levels of teacher planning. For example, at the level of planning for a unit of instruction, routines related to evaluation may include giving a pretest to identify what students already know, scheduling weekly quizzes to assess how well students are mastering concepts presented, and preparing a unit test to determine how much new knowledge students have gained. If students learn that these evaluations are a regular part of the teacher's units of instruction, they will prepare for weekly quizzes by learning material as they go along, rather than waiting and cramming for a final test.

At the level of planning for a daily lesson, routines related to a sequence of activities may include checking homework, presenting new information, conducting group practice with the new information through questioning and discussion, providing for individual supervised practice using new information in assigned seatwork, and providing for independent practice by assigning new homework. This is a pattern of lesson activities followed by many expert teachers of mathematics,[22] and it is a pattern found useful in improving student achievement in many studies of effective teaching.[23] When this sequence of activities is an established pattern for most lessons, the teacher can focus planning decisions on how best to explain and illustrate (with examples) the new information to be presented.

At the level of planning for specific activities within a lesson, management routines become important. When calling on students to participate, a teacher may regularly call only on volunteers when new information is first discussed, believing that volunteers are more apt to be able to answer questions accurately and thus move the lesson along at a lively pace. In the review portion of the lesson, however, the same teacher may use a routine of going up and down rows of students, calling on each in turn, as a way of checking whether all students clearly understand the material previously discussed. A teacher who has such established routines does not need to spend much time planning these specific details of a lesson. Students who become familiar with such routines pay more attention in initial presentations of information, knowing they can expect to be called on in a later review.

The Importance of Repertoire

Routines are an important part of teacher planning for instruction, but expert teachers do not rely on routines alone. Can you imagine an expert chess player who had only one routine way to make an opening move, or to respond to an opponent's opening move, in a chess match? A chess master has a repertoire of alternate ways to open a game and, for each opening move of an opponent, a repertoire of alternate responses. Because different actions are appropriate in different situations, expert teachers also have repertoires that they call on when necessary.

A **repertoire** is a set of alternate routines or procedures, all of which may serve some common, general purpose and each of which may be particularly appropriate in a different situation. For example, a teacher may have a repertoire of procedures for classroom organization that includes whole-class instruction, cooperative group work, individualized seatwork, and peer tutoring. Each of these classroom organizations can be effective in promoting student learning, but cooperative group work can be particularly effective for developing student independence, while supervised, individualized seatwork may be particularly effective for maximizing individual achievement gains. With a repertoire of procedures that are appropriate for different situations, a teacher does not need to spend hours of planning time to devise possible alternate actions. The repertoire provides a range of alternatives to be considered, and knowledge of the specific situation (e.g., type of students to be taught, content to be learned, time available) enables the expert teacher to choose an alternative that fits the situation.

Much of the early research on effective teaching produced generic principles of instruction that tended to emphasize planning for teacher-directed whole-class lessons—beginning with review of prior knowledge, moving on to presentation of new knowledge, and ending with individual practice supervised by the teacher to consolidate the new knowledge. Much of the more recent work on subject-specific instruction has tended to emphasize planning for varied instructional processes, including inquiry or problem-solving strategies, small-group discussion, and "authentic" activities that enable students to use primary source materials and artifacts or that encourage them to apply learning to their lives outside of school.[24] This kind of planning requires teachers of all subject areas to develop a repertoire of alternative instructional procedures.

One useful way to think about instructional repertoire is illustrated by the grid in Figure 2.4. The vertical line denotes possible variation in the instructional process, moving from teacher-directed processes, in which the teacher selects, organizes, and presents information, to student-constructed processes, in which students share in generating, analyzing, and synthesizing information. The horizontal line denotes possible variation in the type of learning goals intended, moving from learning "accepted" knowledge (i.e., understanding and using knowledge produced by experts in the various academic disciplines) to "inventing" new ways of perceiving (i.e., developing and communicating divergent thoughts). Different instructional strategies can be located in different quadrants on this grid.

A teacher who wants to meet the needs of a diverse group of learners will need to develop a varied instructional repertoire, using strategies from each of the four quadrants over time. For example, in planning an integrated "unit" of instruction on the television media, a teacher could plan a sequence of lessons, starting in Quadrant A and moving on to each of the other three quadrants, not necessarily in strict clockwise sequence. Sample lessons could include the following types of activities.

Activity 1 (Quadrant A). The teacher asks students to name the television programs that are watched most frequently in their homes, listing them on the board as they are named. When a good list has been developed, students work in pairs to determine groups of programs that have some feature or features in common. Pairs report their groups and category systems back to the class, and the teacher leads a discussion on the various types of program features students have noted. The lesson concludes with the class developing clusters of program groupings that are similar in some way (grouping the groups), thus forming their own hierarchical category system for describing types of television programs. (This activity is based on a strategy called Concept Formation.[25])

For homework, using the category system they have developed, each student interviews one family member and one neighbor to learn what category of television programs these individuals watch most frequently. The following day, the class compiles the data from their interviews and constructs a bar graph to show the viewing preferences of their families and friends. They plan

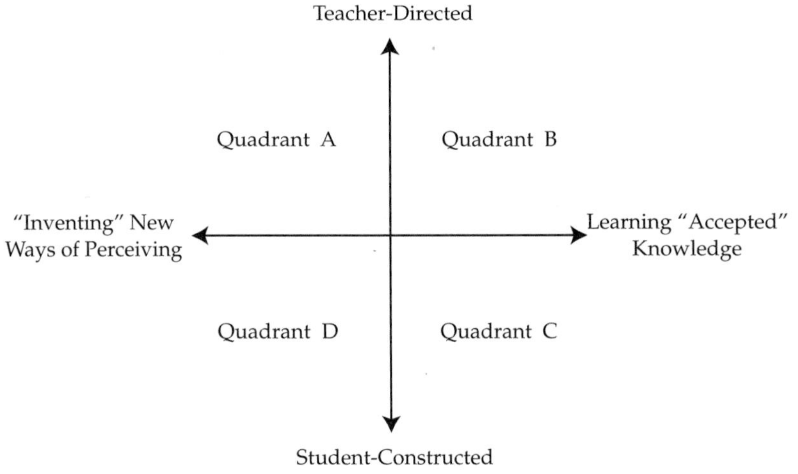

Figure 2.4 Repertoire grid

to "publish" their category system and bar graph on the World Wide Web through Academy One,[26] and they invite other classes to collect, compile, and publish similar data.

Activity 2 (Quadrant C). Based on the class's survey data, the teacher notes that television documentaries are popular fare. She suggests that the class prepare a video documentary on an interesting historical event of local interest. The class decides together on a set of subtopics to be addressed, and students select the subtopic they will investigate. Students organize themselves into groups, with each group assigned to gather information about a particular subtopic. Groups work together over several days to access resources from a variety of locations (school library, community library, local historical museum, Internet) and prepare summary reports. When reports are ready, students share the information gathered in a new group formation. Each "sharing" group has one or two members from each of the original investigative groups, and students report to each other on their findings, so all students learn something about each subtopic. (This activity is based on a cooperative learning strategy called Jigsaw.[27])

Activity 3 (Quadrant B). The teacher introduces students to the technique of writing scripts, drawing on prior work they have done on writing essays, writing dialogue, and reading plays. She provides examples of sample segments of television scripts for documentaries, pointing out the need for attention to camera angle and background scenery, as well as to sequence of speakers and content of commentary. Students view a brief segment of a video documentary and then practice writing a script that provides necessary information for that segment. (This activity is based on a Direct Instruction strategy.[28])

Activity 4 (Quadrant D). Students work together in their original investigative groups to write television scripts providing information about their particular subtopics. Within these groups, students decide what message or perspective they want to convey to their audience and plan their script accordingly. When preliminary plans are set, the groups share their plans with their classmates, and receive reactions and suggestions. Together the class decides on the overall message for the documentary and the sequence of subtopical segments that will best convey that message.

The groups finish writing their individual segments for the documentary. Each group assigns roles to students within the group (actors, commentator, camera person, etc.) and then videotapes a segment of the documentary. When all segments have been taped, the class views them in the planned sequence and makes recommendations about any needed revisions. The completed video is shown to other classes in the school and presented to parents in a special evening meeting. (This activity is based on a Group Investigation strategy.[29])

In planning an instructional unit of this nature, teachers must draw on a repertoire of instructional strategies and play a variety of roles, from director to facilitator of student learning. Students also must draw on and practice a repertoire of academic, social, and technical skills as they engage in learning related to a variety of content areas, including language arts, mathematics, and social studies/history. Planning an integrated unit such as this requires the teacher to have a repertoire of information about all the basic elements of instructional planning (goals, curriculum content, learners and learning, instructional resources, instructional strategies, classroom management techniques, and evaluation/assessment procedures) and to view all these elements in terms of the local school and community context.

The Requirement for Practice

The reason that experts and novices see things differently in any field is that experts have a great deal of experience. With extensive experience in any activity, we learn what types of situations commonly arise, as well as which of our reactions to those situations work to our advantage and which do not. Experts recognize a new situation as being similar to a type of situation they have faced before and quickly call on a repertoire of routines that they have used in the past. Novices face a new situation without much prior experience to draw on. They cannot quickly identify a situation as belonging to a familiar category of situations. Even if they could, they would not have an extensive repertoire of developed routines available to use in response to the situation. Novices can become experts with time, however; all experts began as novices. To become an expert requires a great deal of practice and thought.

Novice teachers are different from novices in other fields in one respect: they are already quite experienced in classroom settings. Most novice teachers are expert students. They have had years of practice at recognizing certain types of classroom situations from the student's perspective. They know which of their fellow students have ideas to contribute to class discussions, and they respond by listening carefully to those students. They quickly recognize the student who rambles on at length and says nothing, and they will tune that student out even on the first day of class. On meeting a new teacher, expert students rapidly determine whether assignments must be in on time; if this is a requirement, they adjust their schedules to ensure that the work gets completed. As expert students, most novice teachers have a ready repertoire of classroom behaviors. To become expert teachers, they must develop a new perspective and a new repertoire of behaviors. And that requires additional practice.

Planning and Practice

Planning is an unusual kind of activity because it can never really be practiced unless a plan is carried out. We learn from practice only if we can get some feedback about the effectiveness of our actions. Can you imagine learning to bowl if there were a curtain across the end of the lane that made it impossible to see where your ball went or how many pins you knocked down? Hours of practice without any information about the results of your actions would be useless. Practice in making instructional plans that you never try out in any real or simulated setting would be useless in helping you to develop skill or expertise in planning. Unless you carry out a plan, you can never tell how effective it is. Plans must be tested in action.

One study of novice teachers found that they spent a great deal of time planning lessons during their student teaching assignments and that they mentally rehearsed their lessons before presenting them by practicing what they would say and trying to anticipate what pupils might say.[30] Where possible, these student teachers also gained extra practice by using the same lesson plan to teach more than one group or class of pupils. By teaching the same lesson again within a short period of time, they were able to make revisions and improve their plans, thereby improving their lessons. The students in this study thought that both forms of practice helped to develop their skills in planning.

Ted, the novice teacher whose concept maps you studied earlier in this chapter, received practice in planning through peer-teaching lessons. He also would mentally rehearse his planned lessons frequently before presenting them to his peers. At the end of the lessons, his peers provided feedback about the procedures that worked well and indicated where they had been confused about procedures or content. Ted then reviewed his lesson plans to consider how he might improve the lesson if he were to present it again. In a sense, peer teaching is only a simulated setting for instruction, but it provides an opportunity for novice teachers to practice planning skills, try out a variety of routine procedures, and develop a repertoire of routines for instruction.

Throughout this book, you will be presented with ideas about effective instructional procedures for presenting information, differentiating instruction, questioning pupils, reacting to pupil responses, managing classroom tasks, using cooperative learning, and evaluating pupil learning. These ideas can make it possible for you to learn useful routines and develop teaching repertoires, but routines and repertoires require practice. As you work through the activities in this book, be prepared to take advantage of every opportunity you have to practice thinking and acting like a teacher. You will not become an expert overnight, but you will get a head start.

YOUR TURN

Choosing Key Characteristics

List six important characteristics of teacher planning that you will want to keep in mind as you begin the transformation from expert student to novice teacher. You may want to review this section as you construct your list. There are more than six characteristics mentioned, so choose the ones that seem most important to you.

OBJECTIVE 3

Given a description of teacher planning analogous to a dramatic production, to generate additional analogies that highlight important aspects of teacher planning

The Play's the Thing

Analogies can be useful in helping us understand new ideas and processes. Researchers engaged in studying the planning and teaching of expert teachers use descriptive terms such as *scripts, scenes,* and *improvisation* to describe teacher thinking. These terms suggest that teacher planning may be thought of as being analogous to a dramatic production. This section builds on that analogy to explore important aspects of teacher planning, including lesson plans, **unit plans,** and classroom organization.

Scripts

The script is a basic feature of a dramatic production. The script provides the dialogue, which carries the message that the play is supposed to convey to the audience. It also frequently indicates specific actions that will convey nonverbal messages to the audience. Actors and actresses follow the script as they perform a play. Before performances, they memorize their lines and rehearse their parts together, so that the play runs smoothly. A script has a fairly standard form, which usually includes some description of the stage arrangements and the props, as well as a careful delineation of who will say what. The scripts of successful writers are performed over and over again, year after year, for many audiences. Frequently, the first draft of a script, even one by a highly successful writer, must be revised during trial runs of the play in out-of-the-way places. This process of polishing a script after seeing the reactions of audiences is an accepted part of the tradition of the theater.

Teachers' lesson plans and unit plans are similar to scripts in many ways. A script is typically organized as a series of acts. Most plays have three acts, and if a change of setting is required, an act may include more than one scene. A lesson plan is analogous to the script for one act of a play. It outlines the procedures to be carried out in a single time segment, and it may include a shift from one type of activity to another, similar to a change of scene within one act of a play. A unit plan is analogous to the full play in that it covers a larger topic and outlines a series of lessons to be carried out in relation to that topic. Like the acts of a play, the lessons in a unit plan are carefully sequenced to build to a climax. Lessons early in the unit may foreshadow information to be developed more fully at a later point. Units vary in length more than does the typical play, for they are acted out over a period of days or weeks rather than a few hours. Each of these types of plans is written with the intention of conveying an important message to an "audience." The teacher follows the plans while "performing" the lesson or the unit of instruction. Before performance of the plan, the teacher mentally rehearses the procedures to help ensure that the lesson or unit will run smoothly. When a lesson or unit is completed, the teacher frequently makes notes about possible revisions for the next time that lesson or unit is taught.

Of course, there are important differences between teachers' plans and dramatic scripts. A script that is rewritten after a trial run will be performed in its revised form almost immediately. A lesson plan or unit plan that is revised after teaching may not be taught again for a full year. Actors and actresses rarely write their own scripts, but teachers typically write their own plans. A script provides the dialogue for all the roles in a play, and everyone can be counted on to play their role as scripted. Teachers can plan specific activities for students to carry out as part of a lesson or unit plan, but there is no guarantee that students will play their roles exactly as the teacher planned. In mental rehearsals of their plans, teachers may envision student responses to their questions, but students rarely "speak their lines" in a classroom dialogue precisely the way that teachers envision. Students in lessons are part of the "act" at some points and part of the "audience" at others.

Like scripts, lesson and unit plans have a typical format. Most plans for lessons or units of instruction include five parts. A statement of the *goal or purpose of instruction* (what students are expected to learn or what message the teacher intends to convey) is an important part of a lesson or unit plan. Expert teachers have a clear goal in mind for any lesson, although they do not always write the goal out explicitly. Similarly, the author of a script hopes to engender a particular mood in audiences. Different types of plays engender different moods. Comedies generate laughter, satires produce awareness of social issues, and dramas encourage reflection on personal experience. The successful author selects a dramatic form that will produce the desired audience mood. Like plays, lessons can take a variety of forms. Because the goal or purpose of instruction influences the form a lesson or unit may take, novice teachers are advised to begin a lesson or unit with a clear goal statement.

Academic standards are now an important part of education policy in most states, and teachers and schools are being evaluated on their ability to demonstrate that a majority of students meet the state content of learning standards in basic subject areas. Many states and school districts have curriculum guides that are keyed to content standards. In order to keep such standards clearly in mind, it can be useful for a teacher to include a reference to an appropriate content standard as part of the goal statement of any lesson plan. [See the website of the Mid-continent Research for Education and Learning (McREL) Laboratory for a compilation of content standards for K–12 curriculum (www.mcrel.org/standards-benchmarks).]

A clear statement of the *central content to be addressed* in the lesson or unit is the second important piece of a lesson or unit plan. Content descriptions may identify concepts or generalizations to be developed, procedures to be implemented, controversial issues to be explored, or a set of facts to be memorized. The expert teacher is thoroughly familiar with the curriculum content and can describe it explicitly. Similarly, the author of a script must have a clear idea of the message or theme of the play. Although the theme may not be stated explicitly anywhere in the script, it dictates the dialogue and development of the action. Because the content drives the interaction (questions, answers, explanations) of a lesson, and because novice teachers may not be fully conversant with the curriculum being taught, they need to pay particular attention to careful articulation of the content to be learned.

A statement or list of the *instructional materials* to be used in a lesson or unit is the third important part of a lesson or unit plan. A statement about needed materials is similar to a notation about props to be used in a script. It alerts the teacher to the preparations to be made before instruction begins, just as information about props alerts the stage manager to the materials that must be available to the actors. A stage manager cannot wait until the night of the performance to begin gathering the props for the play, and a teacher who is an effective manager does not wait until the last minute to gather or prepare materials for a lesson.

The fourth part of a lesson plan includes a *set of procedures* to be followed in the lesson. These procedures involve a series of activities, generally including some details about specific directions to be given or questions to be asked, in relation to each activity. The fourth part of a unit plan usually includes a series of topics to be dealt with across several lessons in the unit of instruction. Within each topic, specific plans for activities to be used may be included. This part of the lesson or unit plan is similar to the main body of a script. The set of activities or the series of topics are like the separate acts in a play script. The specific plans for directions, questions, or activities are like the specific written dialogue that is provided within each act of the script. The set of procedures in a lesson plan and the series of topics in a unit plan both require skill in devising appropriate sequences of activities. Similarly, sequencing is important in the acts of a play, as some problem is set, developed, and carried to a conclusion.

The fifth part of a typical lesson or unit plan involves a statement about *evaluation procedures.* A teacher may evaluate what students have learned from a lesson or unit in a variety of ways, including tests, written homework, and observation of student responses to oral questions. While many useful means of evaluation exist, teachers need to plan their evaluation procedures in advance. Lesson and unit plans differ from scripts in this respect. Scripts are evaluated by the audiences and critics who attend the plays. The importance of evaluation in the theater is evident in the opening night tradition, in which the whole company stays up all night to read the critics' reviews in the morning papers to learn whether or not the play is a success. Teachers' lesson and unit plans are rarely required to pass such public scrutiny, but systematic evaluation of student learning by the teacher is a critical aspect of effective teaching. If learning is not taking place, the "script" for the next lesson will need to be revised.

The five basic parts of a lesson or unit plan denote essential aspects of instruction that a teacher needs to consider in preparing for a lesson. Of course, it is possible to develop a lesson or unit plan that does not include all of these basic components, but such incomplete plans will have much less potential for successful student learning. A script that has no indication of which character is to speak which lines, or one that provides no stage directions, will be difficult to follow, and we should not be surprised if such an incomplete script results in an unsuccessful production. Similarly, a lesson or unit plan that is lacking one or more of the five basic parts will be an insufficient guide to the teacher during the "performance" of the lesson or unit.

The teacher who simply writes down the page numbers in the textbook that are to be covered in the next lesson has not really planned a lesson. Such a teacher has indicated the materials to be used in the lesson but has evidently not determined the procedures to be used for involving students in interacting with these materials. The teacher who writes an outline of steps to be followed in a lesson, without any indication of the particular skills or concepts that students are expected to learn as a result of engaging in the activities, has also developed an incomplete plan or script. A set of procedures that are not tied to any particular goal statement or content description provides the teacher with little or no guidance in making the frequent immediate decisions that confront every teacher during a lesson.

Figures 2.5 and 2.6 present examples of lesson plans that include the five basic parts described above. Both of the lessons were designed to teach the general skill of writing "expanded sentences" (sentences that provide more descriptive information to the reader). The first lesson plan was written for use with elementary school children and the second for secondary school students. Either of these lessons could be part of a unit plan designed to develop skill and interest in expository writing.

Alternative instructional strategies are most readily recognized by examining the Procedures section of a teacher's lesson plan. The sequence of activities in the lesson will vary as a teacher moves from one quadrant to another in the repertoire grid discussed earlier and shown in Figure 2.4. To illustrate, for a lesson such as the one described for Quadrant A in the illustrative unit on the television media, the Procedures section in the lesson plan would include the following sequence of phases, or major activities:

- Students identify and list data related to the topic and content area selected by the teacher.
- Students group data items that have common features and label the groups to identify relevant features.
- With teacher guidance, students group the groups or categories they have developed to form a hierarchical category system.

By contrast, for a lesson such as the one described for Quadrant B in that unit, the Procedures section of the lesson plan would include a very different sequence of phases, or major activities:

- The teacher orients students to the lesson topic, states the lesson objective, and reviews relevant prior learning.
- The teacher explains and demonstrates scriptwriting, the new skill to be learned.
- The teacher provides guidance as students practice using the new skill of scriptwriting.
- Students continue to practice the skill independently.

Lesson Plan A (Elementary)

Objective:

Most of the children will be able to add words to a simple two-word sentence, which will change the meaning of the original sentence in at least two ways.

Related Standard:

Uses the stylistic and rhetorical aspects of writing.

Related Benchmark:

Uses a variety of sentence structures in writing (e.g., expands basic sentence patterns).

Content (Concept/Generalization/Procedure):

A simple sentence can be expanded by adding adjectives, adverbs, and modifying phrases at the beginning or end of the sentence. Sentence expansion extends the meaning of a simple sentence.

Materials:

1. Wooden chart for sentence strips
2. Sample strips of two-word sentences with companion expanded sentences
3. Two-word sentence suggestions for the children in the group

Procedures:

1. *Introduction.* Place a simple two-word sentence on the chart with the expanded sentence under it. Children will be asked to find *similarities* and *differences.*

   Sample:
   Birds fly.
   The graceful birds fly swiftly in the sky.
   (Have another sample ready if children seem to need it.)

2. *Lesson for Children.* Each child will be provided a two-word sentence to expand. (Option for children—to originate their own if sample doesn't "appeal.") Since these will be prepared in advance, reading levels and interests of the children will be considered.

David C.	Airplanes fly.
Mike D.	Firefighters work.
Larry G.	Planets rotate.
Judith H.	Flowers bloom.
Billy M.	Astronauts prepare.

3. *Summary.* Have children read their sentences aloud. Lead children to discuss which sentences "tell more" and to think about opportunities they have to use expanded sentences.

Evaluation:

Collect written work. How complex are the sentences that the children have written? Have they added single words or phrases? Are they placed at the beginning, end, or middle of the sentence? What forms of expansion need further practice?

Figure 2.5

Lesson Plan B (Secondary)

Objective:

Given a set of simple sentences and a group of logical connectives, students will expand a sentence in at least four different ways while maintaining logical sense.

Related Standard:

Uses the stylistic and rhetorical aspects of writing.

Related Benchmark:

Uses a variety of sentence structures and lengths (e.g., complex sentences, parallel or repetitive sentence structure).

Content (Concept/Generalization/Procedure):

A simple sentence can be expanded by adding a logical connective followed by a clause at the beginning or end of the sentence. Sentence expansion extends or modifies the meaning of the simple sentence.

Materials:

1. Overhead projector
2. Chalkboard

Procedures:

1. Have each student write a simple sentence on his or her paper by completing the sentence frame, The ___________________.
2. Have several students read their sentences aloud. Record these sentences on the chalkboard.
3. On the overhead projector write "The helicopter landed *because*. . . ." Have students suggest ways to end the sentence. Write these on the transparency.
4. Ask pupils to expand their own simple sentences by adding *because* and an appropriate clause. Have several examples read aloud.
5. Proceed in the same manner for *but, therefore, whenever, since, then,* and *so.*
6. On the overhead projector write "*Although* the helicopter landed, . . ." Have students suggest ways to end the sentence. Write a few on the transparency.
7. Ask students which of the logical connectives already discussed could be used at the beginning of their sentence. Have them write one or two, and have some read aloud.

Evaluation:

Ask each pupil to take any three of the sentences written on the board at the beginning of the lesson and to expand each sentence in four different ways, using the logical connectives listed on the transparency.

Figure 2.6

The specific format for a lesson plan can vary widely, and elements within specific segments of a lesson plan, such as descriptions of Procedures, can also vary widely, but effective lesson plans include the five basic features we have discussed here. Some school districts favor a particular format for lesson plans and ask all teachers to use the same format. Some education professors may require their students to use a particular format for lesson or unit plans. You may be introduced to new formats and terms for the various parts of a lesson or unit plan as you face new situations in your teacher preparation program and in your later teaching. Whatever the format or terms, look for the five basic parts of a plan and be sure to consider these critical aspects of instruction as you develop your own "scripts" for the lessons you teach.

Scenes

While scripts are an important feature of play production, there are other things to be considered as well. Scenery is an important part of any dramatic production. The scenery provides the backdrop against which the play will be performed. The design of the set determines where and how the actors can move around the stage. A change of scene can trigger a change of mood in the audience. There is a great deal of symbolic meaning in the scenery of a dramatic production—some of the message of any play is conveyed to the audience by the way the scene is set.

Similarly, when teachers plan lessons, they communicate a message in the way they set the scene for the lesson, as well as in what they say or ask students to do during the lesson. The teacher's stage is the physical classroom, and the teacher sets the scene by arranging the physical space of the classroom. In addition, the teacher sets the stage for lessons by determining the social organization of the classroom. In a well-designed classroom "scene," the physical and social organizations will complement each other.

It should be noted that, although the two lesson plans in Figures 2.5 and 2.6 have similar "scripts" (both include the same five basic parts of a lesson plan), the teachers who planned these lessons envisioned different classroom "scenes." In Lesson Plan A (Figure 2.5), the teacher envisions a scene (social organization) in which children will be working individually at their seats for part of the lesson, then discussing examples of expanded sentences together in a large group for another. There are several "scene changes" required for this lesson. First, students will meet in a large group to discuss sample sentences; then they will work individually at their desks. Next, they will share the sentences they have written, again in a large-group discussion. In planning for these scene changes, the teacher needs to be sure that the physical arrangement of desks in the classroom will facilitate discussion as well as independent seatwork. If children are seated in rows of single desks, they may be able to work alone without being distracted by their neighbors. But this type of seating arrangement is not conducive to a group discussion. Most children will see only the backs of other students' heads. In this type of classroom scene (physical arrangement), students talk to the teacher, not to one another. To use these two types of activities as routines in the classroom, the teacher needs to set the scene so that discussion and independent work are both facilitated. Arranging desks in a large semicircle could be one alternative.

In Lesson Plan B (Figure 2.6), the teacher envisions a scene (physical arrangement) in which the overhead projector and screen are the focus of attention. The major activity throughout the lesson involves large-group discussion, and the teacher needs to set the scene so that students can see one another as well as the screen at the front of the room. For this activity, a large semicircle of desks might not be appropriate because students at each end of the semicircle might have difficulty seeing the screen.

When planning for lessons, teachers must think in advance about how the physical arrangement of the classroom will help or hinder students as they carry out the instructional activity of the lesson. If the type of activity changes frequently within lessons, or from one lesson to another, the classroom arrangement must be flexible enough to support a variety of activities and social organizations (small-group work, individual work, or large-group discussion). When planning units of instruction, teachers must envision a series of scenes that can encompass these various types of organization. Teachers are the stage managers and set designers as well as the scriptwriters and the actors.

Improvisation

While lesson and unit plans may function like scripts to cue the teacher about what to do next, no plan for instruction is detailed enough to tell a teacher exactly what to say, as a script for a play does. The teacher's guide for a textbook often provides a set of suggested questions to ask as teachers lead discussions based on readings in the text. But even if a teacher used the teacher's guide as a "script," and asked all the questions provided for a given lesson, some improvisation would still be necessary. Students never answer all questions correctly, and a teacher must react to partial or incorrect answers by asking follow-up questions or by providing additional information. Furthermore, students ask questions of their own, and neither these questions nor the answers to them are included in a teacher's guide to the textbook.

An actor or actress in a scripted play is not expected to improvise lines, except perhaps in an emergency, such as when someone misses a cue and dead silence ensues. But there is a place in the theater for improvisation. In fact, some particularly gifted actors and actresses specialize in improvisation. In improvisational theater, the audience is frequently invited to suggest characters and a situation. The actors then take on the suggested roles and, without any prior rehearsal, act out the situation. The dictionary gives the synonym *unprepared* for the term *improvised,* but it would be a mistake to believe that actors who engage in improvisational performances are unprepared. They have studied a variety of characters and situations through careful observation of people in everyday encounters and extensive reading of plays and other literature. They can call on this rich background of information when they are challenged to react on the spot to requests from the audience. Prior to performing before an audience, they will have practiced improvising skits in response to a variety of possible situations.

Teachers are called on to improvise on a regular basis, just like improvisational actors, but their improvisations may not be as extensive. They may engage in only a brief extemporaneous dialogue with an individual student, rather than carrying out a whole skit. Expert teachers, like actors, are never unprepared for these extemporaneous performances. They also have studied a variety of "characters" (students) and situations through careful observation over time in their own classrooms. They also have a rich background of information about the subject they are teaching. They can call on this background of experience and knowledge when they are challenged to react on the spot to questions or suggestions from students.

In one sense, a teacher can never plan ahead for the improvisational demands of the classroom. Even experienced teachers cannot predict everything that will happen in a lesson. An effective teacher needs to be flexible enough to respond to the ideas and queries of students. In another sense, it is possible for a teacher to be prepared to deal effectively with situations that are not predictable and thus require improvisation. This is one way in which routines and repertoires become invaluable. One way to improvise is to call on a familiar routine and use it in a new setting.

Novice teachers do not come into the classroom armed with a set of routines and repertoires. They must develop their routines and repertoires by careful observation and practice, just as expert teachers and improvisational actors have done before them. Early field experiences that include systematic observation in classroom settings and opportunities for practice in working with small groups can be useful to novice teachers who want to become experts. The prospective teachers can observe the routines employed by experienced teachers and can practice using them. They should also discuss these routines with the teachers from whom they are borrowing them, so that they understand the purposes the routines serve and the situations in which they are most appropriately used. Eventually, they can adapt these borrowed routines and invent their own; in this way they will develop their own repertoire of routines.

Alternative Analogies

The analogy of teacher planning as a dramatic production is a useful one because it highlights some important features of teacher planning: the need to consider the "mood" and "message" (goal and content) that the lesson is intended to convey, the need to have the "props" (materials) prepared in advance, the need to have a "script" (sequence of planned procedures) to follow, and the importance of evaluation by "critics" (the thoughtful teacher). The analogy also emphasizes the importance of setting the "scene" (social organization and physical arrangement) for a successful lesson and indicates that an effective teacher must be skillful at improvising (responding to unpredictable events), drawing on a well-developed repertoire of routines. Like any analogy, this one does not fit completely. No teacher repeats the same script or lesson plan day after day to a series of new audiences, for example.

While the analogy of a dramatic production is a useful one for exploring the concept of instructional planning, it is not the only analogy for teacher planning. Each new analogy tends to highlight different features of a concept, so it can be helpful when clarifying a new concept to consider a variety of possible analogies.

YOUR TURN

Explaining Additional Analogies

One additional analogy for teacher planning is that of a road map. Can you think of some important characteristics of a road map that are also characteristic of teacher planning? Try listing three or four common characteristics now, and then discuss your ideas with your fellow students.

How does the analogy of a road map fail to fit the characteristics of teacher planning? List two ways in which a road map is different from a teacher plan.

What new aspects of teacher planning are highlighted by this new analogy? Describe one important characteristic of teacher planning that stands out particularly in relation to the analogy of a road map.

What other analogies can you think of for the concept of teacher planning? Stretch your imagination and invent an analogy of your own. Can you think of a machine or some natural phenomenon that has some characteristics in common with a teacher's plan? Explore your analogy by listing similarities, differences, and highlighted features of teacher planning in relation to the new analogy. Share your analogy with your fellow students.

Only the Beginning

Since all plans are only intentions to act, a plan is only the beginning. And in the beginning, most plans are vague sketches of possible actions. These partial plans are gradually filled out with more and more definite decisions as the time for action approaches. But the phrase *only the beginning* is a deceptive one. Shakespeare wrote that "All's well that ends well," but it is equally true that things are more apt to end well if they begin well. Because a plan is the beginning, planning is one of the most critical skills that a teacher can have.

Instructional planning requires more than information about what is included in a lesson or unit plan. To plan effectively and efficiently, a teacher needs a clear understanding of the subject to be taught, as well as information about alternate goals and objectives, available instructional materials and resources, productive use of classroom questions, ways to provide for students' individual differences, procedures for classroom management, and techniques for evaluation of student learning. To carry out instructional plans, a teacher must have skills in lesson presentation and in interpersonal communication. Just as a plan is only the beginning, so is this chapter only the beginning. To develop real skill in instructional planning, you will need to absorb and apply the information in all the chapters of this book. You will also need to practice making plans for instruction, carrying them out in peer teaching or with small groups in classroom settings, and revising them on the basis of what you learn from the resulting action.

A concept map of teacher planning can serve as a record of your thoughts at this early stage of your development as a professional teacher. It can mark a point in your thinking that is "only a beginning." If you made such a map earlier, save it. When you have completed the activities in this book and have had an opportunity to practice instructional planning by putting your plans into action, construct another concept map of teacher planning. You will see that you are learning to think like a teacher. You already have a sound beginning.

Observation Worksheet

Focus on Teacher Planning

Teacher planning is not easy to observe, since it is mainly a mental activity. Here are three tasks you can carry out in a classroom to gather information about teacher planning.

Directions: Do not use actual names of schools, teachers, administrators, or students when using this worksheet.

Observer's Name: ______________________________

Date: ______________________________

Grade Level: ______________________________

Subject: ______________________________

Class Size: ______________________________

Background Information: Give a brief general description of the school's social, economic, and ethnic makeup.

____

____

Task 1. The Plan Book and the Actual Lesson

What to Record: Before observing a classroom lesson, ask to see what the teacher has written in his/her lesson plan book as a guide for the lesson. As you observe the lesson, make a record of three things that the teacher does that were *not noted* in the written comments in the plan book. After the lesson is over, interview the teacher briefly about these three procedures and record the answers.

Questions to Ask the Teacher:

1. When did you decide that you were going to do this in this lesson? ______________________________

____

____

2. Is this a procedure that you use often with these students? ______________________________

____

____

____

3. What is your main reason for using this procedure? ______________________________

____

____

____

4. Have you ever written this procedure down as part of a lesson plan? Why or why not?

______

______

______

Task 2. The Plan Book and the Substitute's Lesson Plan(s)

What to Record: Most schools require teachers to keep lesson plans for a substitute teacher on file, to be used in case of the teacher's absence. Ask to see a plan the teacher has prepared for a substitute teacher (either a plan for a single lesson, or a plan for a day's activity). Compare this plan to the plans written in the teacher's plan book. Ask the teacher to tell you the reasons for the differences you note.

Reflections on Your Observation:

1. If you were a substitute in this classroom, which set of plans would you prefer to have, and why?

______

______

______

2. What would you want to know that is not included in either set of plans? ______

______

______

______

Task 3. Teacher Planning and Student Planning

What to Record: Learning to plan and organize your own activities is an important part of becoming an independent learner. The degree to which students are encouraged to engage in the planning and organizing of instructional tasks may vary a great deal based on students' stage of development. As you observe in a classroom setting, try to identify two or three instances in which students are given opportunities to plan or structure some aspect of an activity or assignment.

Questions to Ask the Teacher:

1. Ask the teacher about how and when students are given practice in planning or structuring an individual or group activity.

______

______

______

Mastery Test

A. Prospective teachers at the University of Virginia's Curry School of Education, at the end of an early field experience in which they planned and taught several lessons to full classes, were asked to state a maxim exemplifying an important principle they had learned as a result of their classroom experience. (A maxim is a terse or pithy statement of a rule to guide one's behavior, such as "An apple a day keeps the doctor away" or, for new teachers, "Don't smile before Christmas.")

A number of the maxims they developed are listed below. Some, but not all, provide some useful guidelines related to instructional planning. Organize these maxims into groups or categories, based on similarities you note in the ideas they emphasize. You should develop at least four different groups, but you may form as many more than four as you like, and you may have as many items in a group as you like. Label or name each group to denote what important characteristic(s) are shared by items you place in the group. Write a brief statement for each group to explain how/whether that set of maxims is related to some important aspect of instructional planning.

Maxims

A little fun never hurt anyone.

Assume the students' mindset.

Be wise—Don't be afraid to improvise.

Clock watchers end well.

Don't be afraid to look outside yourself.

Don't do anything for students that they can do for themselves.

Don't stand still or you'll be a pill.

Don't underestimate your students.

Engage a student and the student will learn.

If you fail to plan, you plan to fail.

Kind but firm will help them learn.

Learning can be a team effort.

Look for written proof of students' knowledge.

Make sure students stay on task.

Never let them see you sweat.

Not knowing your students is preparing for trouble.

Organization is the key to elation.

Overplan—Things can blow big!

Pace the race.

Plan for the unexpected.

Prepare or beware.

Put limits on chaos, not creativity.

Students can teach, and teachers can learn.

The best discipline strategy is an engaging lesson.

The more you expect, the more they give.

Think before you speak.

Those who know don't always show.

Try to be wrong once a week.

Wear a poker face.

You can't win 'em all, but you can keep on trying.

B. Pick two lesson plans from one or two web sites of your choice—one plan that contains all the essential elements of a good plan and one that is lacking in two or more essential elements. Print out a copy of each plan.
   1. Identify each of the essential elements in the complete plan and note two additional positive features of the plan, explaining why you consider these to be valuable features.
   2. Fill in the missing elements of the incomplete plan in a way that is consistent with the elements already present and that improves the overall quality of the plan.

NOTES

1. Michael E. Bratman, *Intention, Plans, and Practical Reason* (Cambridge, Mass.: Harvard University Press, 1987).
2. Margaret E. Herbert and Jean P. Dionne, "Planning Perspectives by Academic, Business, Lay, and Teacher Experts" (Paper presented at Annual Meeting of the American Educational Research Association, New York, 1996).
3. INTASC, "Model Standards for Beginning Teacher Licensing and Development: A Resource for State Dialogue" (http://www.ccsso.org/intascst.html, 1992).
4. Joseph D. Novak and D. Bob Gowin, *Learning How to Learn* (Cambridge, England: Cambridge University Press, 1984).
5. Charles R. Williams, "Semantic Map Planning: A Framework for Effective, Reflective Teaching, Teacher Development, and Teacher Research" (M.A. thesis, School for International Training, Brattleboro, Vt., 1994).
6. David Hyerle, *Visual Tools for Constructing Knowledge* (Alexandria, Va.: Association for Supervision and Curriculum Development, 1996).
7. Bruce R. Joyce and Marsha Weil, *Models of Teaching* (Needham Heights, Mass.: Allyn & Bacon, 1992). See also Paul D. Eggen and Donald P. Kauchak, *Strategies for Teachers: Teaching Content and Thinking Skills* (Needham Heights, Mass.: Allyn & Bacon, 1996).
8. Greta Morine-Dershimer, "Tracing Conceptual Change in Preservice Teachers," *Teaching and Teacher Education* 9, no. 1 (1993):15–26.
9. Hilda Borko and Jerry Niles, "Descriptions of Teacher Planning: Ideas for Teachers and Researchers," in *Educator's Handbook: A Research Perspective,* ed. Virginia Richardson-Koehler (New York: Longman, 1987).
10. Jeanne S. Schumm et al., "General Education Teacher Planning: What Can Students with Learning Disabilities Expect?", *Exceptional Children* 61, no. 4 (1995): 335–352.
11. Carol Ann Tomlinson, *How to Differentiate Instruction in Mixed-Ability Classrooms* (Alexandria, Va.: Association for Supervision and Curriculum Development, 1995).
12. Lynn S. Fuchs et al., "The Relation Between Teacher Beliefs About the Importance of Good Student Work Habits, Teacher Planning, and Student Achievement," *Elementary School Journal* 94, no. 3 (1994):331–345.
13. Gloria Ladson-Billings, *The Dreamkeepers: Successful Teachers of African American Children* (San Francisco: Jossey-Bass, 1994).
14. Deborah Sardo-Brown, "A Longitudinal Study of Novice Secondary Teachers' Planning: Year Two," *Teaching and Teacher Education* 12, no. 5 (1996):519–530.
15. Greta Morine-Dershimer and Stephanie Corrigan, "Teacher Beliefs," in *Psychology and Educational Practice,* ed. Herbert J. Walberg and Geneva Haertle (Berkeley: McCutchan, 1997).
16. Andy Hargreaves and Shawn Moore, "Curriculum Integration and Classroom Relevance: A Study of Teachers' Practices," *Journal of Curriculum and Supervision* 15, no. 2 (2000):89–112.
17. Education Professional Standards Board, *New Teacher Standards for Preparation and Certification* (Frankfort, Ky.: Education Professional Standards Boards, 1994).
18. Elizabeth Spalding, "Of Organelles and Octagons: What Do Preservice Secondary Students Learn from Interdisciplinary Teaching?" *Teaching and Teacher Education* 18, no. 6 (2002): in press.
19. George Lucas Foundation, *Learn and Live* (Nicasio, Calif.: George Lucas Foundation, 1997).
20. Thomas G. Dunn and Constance Shriner, "Deliberate Practice in Teaching: What Teachers Do for Self-Improvement," *Teaching and Teacher Education* 15, no. 6 (1999):641.
21. Kathy Carter, Donna Sabers, Katherine Cushing, Stefinee Pinnegar, and David Berliner, "Processing and Using Information About Students: A Study of Expert, Novice, and Postulant Teachers," *Teaching and Teacher Education* 3, no. 2 (1987):147–157.
22. Gaea Leinhardt, "Math Lessons: A Contrast of Novice and Expert Competence" (Paper presented at the Psychology of Mathematics Education Conference, East Lansing, Mich., 1986).
23. Jere Brophy, ed., *Subject-Specific Instructional Methods and Activities* (*Advances in Research on Teaching,* vol. 8) (Amsterdam: JAI Press, 2001).
24. Ibid.
25. Joyce and Weil, *op. cit.*
26. George Lucas Foundation, *op. cit.*
27. Robert E. Slavin, *Cooperative Learning: Theory, Research, and Practice* (Englewood Cliffs, N.J.: Prentice-Hall, 1990).
28. Eggen and Kauchak, *op. cit.*
29. Joyce and Weil, *op. cit.*
30. Hilda Borko and Carol Livingston, "Expert and Novice Teachers' Mathematics Instruction: Planning, Teaching, and Post-Lesson Reflections" (Paper presented at the Annual Meeting of the American Educational Research Association, New Orleans, 1988).

ADDITIONAL RESOURCES

Readings

The book *Psychology and Educational Practice*, edited by Herbert Walberg and Geneva Haertle (Berkeley, Calif.: McCutchan, 1997) includes several chapters with information pertinent to the planning decisions that teachers make. The following chapters are particularly useful:

Blumenfeld, P. C., and R. W. Marx. "Motivation and Cognition," pp. 79–106.

Brown, A. "The Advancement of Learning," pp. 52–78.

Fraser, B. "Classroom Environments," pp. 323–341.

Kaplan, A., and M. Maehr. "School Cultures," pp. 342–355.

Wilson, S. "Teaching in the Content Areas," pp. 233–250.

Web Site

New York Times: www.nytimes.com/learning/teachers/index.html
Has daily lesson plans for grades 6–8 and 9–12, as well as daily news "snapshot" activities that can be developed into lesson plans for grades 3–5. These are based on current events and use interdisciplinary resources and activities. This site can be a valuable resource for exemplary lessons and activities. A particularly useful feature of the daily lesson plan is the information provided to identify academic content standards that can be addressed by each lesson. Users can access the related academic standards for many individual states as well.

3

Instructional Objectives

Terry D. TenBrink

OBJECTIVE 1 **To recognize well-defined instructional objectives**

OBJECTIVE 2 **To write well-defined instructional objectives**

OBJECTIVE 3 **To use instructional objectives in instructional planning**

OBJECTIVE 4 **To use objectives in implementing instruction**

Think for a moment about what teachers do. Sit back and try to remember the *one* teacher whom you felt had the most influence on you. Write down the characteristics of that teacher as well as you can remember them. Chances are that among the characteristics of your favorite teacher was the fact that the teacher knew you as an individual and knew what he or she wanted for you. This favorite teacher probably had a significant influence on your life, playing a part in the development of your attitudes, the formation of your habits, and the acquisition of information that was new and exciting to you. This teacher may have guided you subtly or may have directly "pushed" you toward these goals. The teacher may have used a great many visual aids or none at all, or may have given multiple-choice tests, essay tests, or no tests at all. What effective teachers have in common is *not* their techniques, their teaching styles, or the kinds of tests they use. It is *what* they accomplish, not how they accomplish it, that makes the difference.

If teachers are going to make a significant difference in the lives of their students, they must know what they want their students to accomplish. Having formulated such goals, teachers can share them with their students so that the students will *also* know where they are going and what is expected of them.

There is considerable evidence to support the contention that when teachers have clearly defined instructional objectives and have shared them with their students, a number of things happen:[1]

1. Better instruction occurs.
2. More efficient learning results.
3. Better evaluation occurs.
4. The students become better self-evaluators.

Teachers need to define **instructional objectives,** however, so that they will be clear, valid statements of what they want their students to know or be able to do. Then they must learn to use those objectives in ways that will improve their teaching and their testing. The rest of this chapter is designed to help you do just that.

Before we discuss the criteria for useful objectives and help you learn to write good objectives, you should know that there are numerous sources of instructional objectives. These sources may provide you with objectives you can use exactly as they are, or you may wish to modify them slightly before using them.

Textbooks and teacher's manuals frequently include well-written instructional objectives; check them to make certain they meet the criteria for useful instructional objectives. Another important source for objectives is the school-provided curriculum syllabus for the course you teach. These syllabi are most commonly supplied by the school system for middle school, junior high, and high school subjects.

A more recent and rapidly growing source for instructional objectives is the Internet. There are several very good World Wide Web sites that provide curricular materials, including objectives and teaching strategies. At the end of the chapter is an annotated list of some of these web sites. Check them out and use the various search engines to search for other sites because new sites are being added regularly.

As you begin the process of defining and/or identifying objectives for your classroom, it would be wise to develop objectives that consider the state and national educational standards that form the basis for much of today's educational reform movement (see Additional Resources at the end of this chapter for references). Note that there is currently an ongoing discussion on how local needs can be met while at the same time adhering to state and national standards.[2,3] This discussion will become especially relevant to you when you find yourself in your classroom trying to meet the needs of your individual students as you prepare them to function in a truly global society.

OBJECTIVE 1

To recognize well-defined instructional objectives

LEARNING ACTIVITY 1

Instructional objectives that are useful in the classroom must meet certain criteria. We have outlined these criteria* below. Look them over carefully, and then we will discuss each of them in turn.

A Useful Instructional Objective Must Be:

1. Student-oriented
2. Descriptive of an appropriate learning *outcome*
3. Clear and understandable
4. Observable

1. Good Instructional Objectives Are Student-Oriented. An instructional objective that is student-oriented places the emphasis on what the *student* is expected to do, not on what the teacher will do. Look at the following examples; notice that they all describe student behavior, not teacher behavior.

Examples of Student-Oriented Objectives

1. Students should be able to solve long-division problems using at least two different methods.
2. Students should be able to list the five punctuation rules discussed in the textbook.
3. Students should be able to write down their observations of a simple experiment, stating what was done and what happened.

*List taken from *Evaluation: A Practical Guide for Teachers,* by T. D. TenBrink. Copyright © 1974 by McGraw-Hill Book Company. Used with permission.

4. When given the description of a form of government, students should be able to classify that form of government and list its probable strengths and weaknesses.

Sometimes teachers use instructional goals that emphasize what they themselves are expected to do rather than what they expect of their students. Such teacher-oriented objectives only have value if they direct the teacher to do something that ultimately leads to student learning. A teacher attempting to help students attain the goal of solving long-division problems may work out some of the problems on the chalkboard, explaining each of the steps involved. A teacher-oriented objective associated with this goal might read: "To explain the steps in long division on the blackboard." Notice that this might be a helpful teacher activity, but it is only *one* of many possible activities that could help students reach the goal of solving long division.

YOUR TURN

Recognize Student-Oriented Objectives

The following exercise will give you practice in distinguishing between student-oriented and teacher-oriented objectives. Place an *S* before each student-oriented and a *T* before each teacher-oriented objective.

______ 1. To read at least 250 words per minute with no less than 80 percent comprehension

______ 2. To show students proper eye movements for scanning material

______ 3. To outline my lecture on the board before class begins

______ 4. When given the description of a complex machine, to identify the simple machines contained within it

______ 5. To help the students appreciate classical music

______ 6. To lecture on the basic steps in the scientific method

______ 7. To carry out an investigation using the scientific method

______ 8. To maintain discipline in my class

______ 9. To write a unified paragraph on a single topic

______ 10. To evaluate a poem on the basis of the criteria for good poetry as discussed in class

Now check your answers against the Answer Key. If you missed more than three, you may wish to reread this section before going on.

2. Good Instructional Objectives Describe Appropriate Learning Outcomes. The first thing to keep in mind here is that we are interested in what the students will learn to do. In other words, it is the learning *outcome* that is important, not the learning activities that lead to that outcome. To say that students will practice long-division problems using two different methods is not to specify a learning outcome. It specifies an activity designed to help the students reach some outcome. As such, it is a student-oriented activity, *not* an outcome.

Second, keep in mind that useful objectives are appropriate. To begin with, they must occur in an appropriate place in the instructional sequence (sequentially appropriate). They must also be developmentally appropriate; that is, they should be appropriate for the developmental level of the students.

For an objective to be sequentially appropriate, all prerequisite objectives must already have been attained. Always make certain the prerequisite skills have been attained before starting to work on a new objective.

Model Standards for Beginning Teacher Licensing and Development have been developed by the Interstate New Teacher Assessment and Support Consortium (INTASC). I would encourage you to read these standards carefully, since they represent the most current thinking about the competencies needed by beginning teachers (see the reference to the web site www.ccsso.org, listed in Additional Resources at the end of this chapter). One of the knowledge standards reads as follows: "The teacher is aware of expected development progressions and ranges of individual variation within each domain (physical, social, emotional, moral and cognitive), can identify levels of readiness in learning, and understands how development in any one domain may affect performance in others."

Elementary school teachers, especially, must be aware of the developmental stages of their students. No author or researcher has more clearly defined the stages of intellectual development than Jean Piaget.[4] Do take the time to study Piaget's work carefully. It would be a good idea to take a child development course and learn about other child development theories as well (e.g., Vygotsky's language development,[5] Erikson's social development,[6] and Kohlberg's moral development[7]).

Note, too, that not all instructional objectives are cognitive in nature. There is widespread agreement among educators that instructional objectives fall into three categories or domains: cognitive, affective, and psychomotor. *Cognitive objectives* refer to outcomes that focus on what the mind is able to accomplish (e.g., memorizing knowledge, forming concepts, solving problems, analyzing and/or synthesizing information). *Affective objectives* refer to outcomes that focus on emotional reactions to people, places, things, ideas, and so forth. Many of the affective objectives that are part of an educational curriculum have to do with the attitudes that students exhibit. Although these kinds of objectives are difficult to measure, they are obviously important to the full development of our students as we prepare them to become contributing citizens. The alternative assessment strategies discussed in Chapter 10 are especially useful when trying to measure affective objectives. *Psychomotor objectives* refer to outcomes that focus on physical movement and the control of muscles and muscle groups. Many school subjects require students to master psychomotor objectives. For example, penmanship requires eye–hand coordination, as do drawing, painting, and sculpture. All sports require muscle control, and playing any musical instrument requires a great deal of fine- and gross-motor coordination.

3. Good Instructional Objectives Are Clear and Understandable. The first prerequisite for a clear and understandable objective is explicitness. It should contain a clearly stated verb that describes a definite action or behavior and, in most cases, should refer to an object of that action. Examine the examples that follow. In each case, the verb and its object have been italicized. As you read these examples, try to see if there is more than one possible meaning for any of them. If they are well stated and explicit, only one meaning should be possible.

Examples of Clearly Stated Objectives

1. The student should be able to *label* the *parts of the heart* correctly on a diagram of the heart similar to the one on page 27 of the text.
2. When given words from the list in the back of the spelling book, the student should be able to *identify words that are incorrectly spelled* and make any necessary corrections.

3. The student should be able to use a yardstick to *measure* the *length, width, and height* of any piece of furniture in the room. The measurements should be accurate to within half an inch.
4. The student should be able to *identify* correctly the *ingredients in a mixture of chemicals* prepared in advance by the teacher.
5. When given a *contemporary poem,* the student should be able to *evaluate* it according to the criteria discussed in class.
6. The student should be able to *list* the *major parts of a friendly letter,* briefly *describing* the *function of each part.*
7. Given several occasions to listen to different types of music, the student will *select* at least *three different types of music* that he or she likes.
8. The student should be able to *list* at least *five benefits* of working on a project with students from a variety of cultures.

Notice that in each of the preceding examples, not only are there a clearly defined verb and accompanying object, but there is only one possible meaning for each of the statements. It is also important to note that most people observing someone engaged in the behaviors described above, or observing the products of those behaviors, would agree in their judgments about whether the behavior had occurred as stated. In other words, the preceding objectives are not only explicitly stated but are also observable. This characteristic (observability) will be described in the next section.

A Word of Caution

Let me digress from the present discussion to caution you against something that occurs frequently when teachers are first learning to write instructional objectives. It is easy to confuse the notion that an objective must be explicit with the idea that it must be highly specific. Objectives should be explicit, that is, unambiguous and understandable. However, being explicit does not mean they have to be highly specific, written down to the minutest of details and the lowest level of a given behavior. Below is an example* of an instructional objective that has been written in general terms and then rewritten several times, each time becoming a bit more specific.[8]

1. Students should be able to read with understanding.
2. When given a story to read, the student should be able to answer questions about the content of the story.
3. When given a short story, the student should be able to identify the passages that describe the traits of the main characters.
4. Students should be able to identify the passages that describe the personality traits of the main characters in *Catcher in the Rye.*
5. Students should be able to identify at least five passages from *Catcher in the Rye* that illustrate Holden's confidence in himself.
6. Students should be able to recognize five passages cited in Handout 3 that illustrate Holden's lack of confidence in himself.[9]

Notice that the most useful instructional objectives in the above examples are those that fall somewhere in the middle of the continuum from very general to very specific. When instructional objectives become too specific, they lose much of their value as a guide to study and become

*Examples taken from *Evaluation: A Practical Guide for Teachers,* by T. D. TenBrink. Copyright © 1974 by McGraw-Hill Book Company. Used with permission.

little more than test questions to be answered. Instructional objectives that are too specific might very well encourage poor study habits. Students may tend to learn just enough to meet the specific objectives, but not enough to meet the more general end-of-the-course objectives. The value of getting students to identify the passages from *Catcher in the Rye* illustrating descriptions of personality traits is that this ability will transfer to other short stories as well. Transferability makes the objective more valuable than one asking the student to recognize those passages from *Catcher in the Rye* that had previously been discussed and identified (such as objective 6).

YOUR TURN

Clear and Unambiguous Objectives

For each of the following objectives, determine whether it has a single meaning (mark it with a *1*) or two or more meanings (mark it with a *2*). The first three items have been done for you. The first is ambiguous. In fact, it could be interpreted to mean the same thing as items 2 and 3. The problem with item 1, of course, is the fact that the verb is not explicit. Using a more explicit verb (as in item 2 or 3) clears up the ambiguity.

__2__ 1. To know the presidents of the United States

__1__ 2. To list in writing the presidents of the United States

__1__ 3. To recognize and call by name each president of the United States on seeing his picture

______ 4. To see the connection between well-written sentences and well-written stories

______ 5. To identify the vanishing points in a three-point perspective drawing

______ 6. To establish eye contact with at least five different persons during a three-minute persuasive speech

______ 7. To develop a roll of 35-mm, black-and-white film

______ 8. To run a ten-minute mile

______ 9. To appreciate music

______ 10. To mold a lump of clay into the shape of an animal that can be recognized and correctly named by the rest of the class

______ 11. Not to show favoritism to any given child in the preschool

______ 12. To understand the workings of an atomic energy plant

______ 13. To plan a miniature garden according to the criteria for such a garden as described in the article "Apartment Gardening"

______ 14. To enlarge your concept of realism

4. Good Instructional Objectives Are Observable. The evaluation of learning outcomes hinges on the observability of those outcomes. The key to an observable objective is an observable verb. Consequently, when selecting instructional objectives for use in your teaching, *watch the verbs!* As discussed earlier, an effective objective contains an explicit verb and (usually) a well-defined object of the verb. Both these requirements help make an objective clear and unambiguous. Now we add another requirement: the verb must describe an observable action or an action that results in an observable product.

The verbs in the following box are vague and unobservable. Avoid them.

Vague, unobservable verbs that should be avoided*

to know	to enjoy
to understand	to familiarize
to comprehend	to value
to grasp	to realize
to believe	to like
to appreciate	to cope with
to think	to love

The kind of verb you hope to find in instructional objectives is exemplified in the following box. When you write objectives, use these kinds of verbs.

Verbs describing observable actions or actions that yield observable products†

to identify	to analyze
to speak	to predict
to list	to locate
to select	to explain
to choose	to isolate
to compute	to divide
to add	to separate
to draw	to infer

There are many processes and skills that cannot be directly observed but produce observable products. It is not possible for us to observe the thinking process of a student as he strives to solve an algebraic equation. However, we can examine the solution he arrives at and decide whether or not it is correct. We may be able to look at each of the steps he takes to arrive at that solution if he writes them down for us (displaying his thinking as a product). On the other hand, a well-written prose paragraph, a poem, and an oil painting can all be observed and analyzed. These end products and others like them can serve as "observables," which may help to indicate whether or not an expected learning outcome has occurred.

When selecting or writing instructional objectives, it is helpful to distinguish between those that specify observable behaviors and those that specify end products of behaviors.

The use of strong, active verbs, such as those in the second box, will yield objectives that are either observable or whose end products are observable. If the object of any of these verbs does not describe an observable end product, however, the resulting objective would be vague and nonobservable. For example, examine the following objective: "To explain diversity."

*Taken from *Evaluation: A Practical Guide for Teachers,* by T. D. TenBrink. Copyright © 1974 by McGraw-Hill Book Company. Used with permission.

†For a more complete list of these kinds of verbs, see Appendix 3 in N. E. Gronlund's *Stating Behavioral Objectives* (London: Collier-Macmillan Ltd., 1970).

What is supposed to be explained? The *value* of diversity within a society? The *reasons* why diversity in an organization is often feared? The various *strategies* that organizations can take to help individuals adapt positively in a diverse workforce? All of these, and more, are possible explanations. The problem is not in the verb, but in the object of the verb. Make certain that both the verb and its object are clearly defined, pointing to observable actions or observable end products.

Observation Worksheet
Analysis of Objectives

This activity is designed to give you the opportunity to examine instructional objectives, identifying their strengths and weaknesses according to the criteria set forth in this chapter.

Directions: Do not use actual names of schools, teachers, administrators, or students when using this worksheet.

Observer's Name: ______________________________

Date: ______________________________

Grade Level: ______________________________

Subject: ______________________________

Class Size: ______________________________

Source of Objectives: ______________________________

Background Information: Give a brief general description of the school's social, economic, and ethnic makeup.

____

____

What to Record: Ask the teacher you are observing for copies of the objectives he/she is using to guide his/her teaching for that day or week. These objectives may be a part of the teacher's lesson plans, the course syllabus, or in the teacher's manual.

Reflections on Your Observation: Summarize your findings, indicating the major strengths and weaknesses of the objectives you reviewed. For each objective, determine if it meets the following criteria:

1. Well defined? ______________________________
2. Student oriented? ______________________________
3. Sequentially appropriate? ______________________________
4. Developmentally appropriate? ______________________________
5. Describes a learning outcome? ______________________________
6. Clear, unambiguous? ______________________________
7. Observable? ______________________________

Mastery Test

OBJECTIVE 1 **To recognize well-defined instructional objectives**

For each of the following pairs, check the objective that best meets the requirements for useful objectives.

1. _______ (a) To be able to develop a roll of black-and-white film
   _______ (b) To understand how a developing agent works
2. _______ (a) To select useful objectives
   _______ (b) To know what makes an objective useful
3. _______ (a) To select from a list of definitions the one that best defines the terms provided on Handout 10
   _______ (b) To know the meaning of the terms on Handout 10
4. _______ (a) To solve math problems requiring an understanding of the place holder
   _______ (b) To understand problem-solving techniques
5. _______ (a) To recognize the pictures of people in the news
   _______ (b) To match the names of people in the news with their pictures
6. _______ (a) To select the good poems from good and bad examples
   _______ (b) To evaluate a set of poems
7. _______ (a) To remember the life cycle of the butterfly
   _______ (b) To label, from memory, a diagram of the life cycle of a butterfly
8. _______ (a) To hear clearly short and long vowel sounds
   _______ (b) To distinguish between short and long vowel sounds
9. _______ (a) To know the phonetic rules and their application in reading
   _______ (b) To sound out nonsense words
10. _______ (a) To punctuate a prose paragraph correctly
    _______ (b) To list the punctuation rules

For each of the following objectives, determine the primary fault.

11. To grasp the meaning of conservation
    (a) affectively oriented
    (b) teacher-oriented
    (c) vague and unobservable
12. To demonstrate to the students the need for cleanliness
    (a) teacher-oriented
    (b) unobservable
    (c) student-oriented
13. To paint
    (a) poorly defined product
    (b) vague
    (c) teacher-oriented
14. To do workbook pages 18–20
    (a) vague
    (b) poorly defined product
    (c) a learning activity
15. To listen to the guest speaker talk about diversity
    (a) teacher-oriented
    (b) a learning activity
    (c) vague

OBJECTIVE 2

To write well-defined instructional objectives

LEARNING ACTIVITY 2

There are three simple steps for writing effective instructional objectives. Although these steps should normally follow the given order, you may occasionally wish to go back and rework a step before moving on. This constant monitoring of your own work, always checking against the criteria for well-defined objectives, will help you produce a clear list of objectives for your own use.

Three Steps for Writing Instructional Objectives*

1. Specify the general goals.
2. Break down the general goals into more specific, observable objectives.
3. Check objectives for clarity and appropriateness.

Although these three steps can be applied to course planning as well as lesson planning, it is important to remember that you will not be able to write a set of objectives for an entire course in a short time. You will find it useful, therefore, to work on small units of instruction, one at a time. Eventually, you will have a set of objectives that will cover the full course you are teaching; however, your unit objectives and daily objectives should fit into the overall plan for your course. Consequently, the first step should be nearly complete before you begin working on the objectives for specific units of instruction or for daily lesson plans.

Step 1. Specify the General Goals

In this first step, you will determine in general terms what you want your students to accomplish. At this point, don't worry too much about the wording; just get your general goal(s) written down. These goals can then be rewritten to make them more specific as well as more observable. Often a single goal will lead to several objectives, each one helping the students to attain that goal.

Look at the general end-of-course goals found in Exhibit A. These represent some of the possible goals for a high school psychology course. Most of these goals will each yield several specific, observable objectives.

Exhibit A General Goals for High School Psychology Course

I. Terminal Goals
   A. Students should understand what it means when we say that psychology is a science.
   B. Students should know the major facts about the way in which humans develop.
   C. Students should know, in general, how humans interact with their environment, including their interactions with other humans.
   D. Students will be aware of the various theories of personality, motivation, learning and mental health, and social psychology.

---

*Taken from *Evaluation: A Practical Guide for Teachers,* by T. D. TenBrink. Copyright © 1974 by McGraw-Hill Book Company. Used with permission.

E. Students should be aware of the most recent writings on diversity in our society.
F. Students should be able to apply major findings of psychology to the solutions of specific problems of human behavior and interaction.
G. Students should be more aware of their own typical behavior and the reasons for that behavior.

YOUR TURN

Specifying General Goals—Parts 1 and 2

Now try writing some general end-of-course goals for the psychology course. Do not duplicate those found in Exhibit A. You should be able to write at least five more general goals for this course. Examples of such additional goals are found in the Answer Key for Part 1. Compare what you have written with those examples.

Once the end-of-course goals have been determined, intermediate goals can be written for each unit of instruction. Again, do not worry about whether or not they are observable now. First get them down in a general way, and then they can be rewritten.

Exhibit B presents some possible goals for Unit I: Psychology as a Science. Three cognitive and three affective goals have been written. Read them carefully and then try writing some yourself. *Remember:* Unit-level goals should reflect the broader, end-of-course goals. Compare your work with the further examples of Unit I goals presented in the Answer Key for Part 2.

Exhibit B

II. The General Intermediate Goals for Unit I: Psychology as a Science
- A. Cognitive Goals
  1. Students should know the major dates in the history of psychology.
  2. Students should know the major avocations that have made psychology an important applied science.
  3. Students should know the steps taken from the development of a theory, to the research and testing of that theory, to the final application of the research findings to practical situations.
- B. Affective Goals
  1. Students should appreciate the value of the science of psychology to a civilized country.
  2. Students should show appreciation for the usefulness of various psychological theories.
  3. Students should be sensitive to the needs and opinions of people from diverse backgrounds.

Step 2. Break Down the General Goals into More Specific, Observable Objectives

In this step, each general goal is broken down into its two major parts: the subject-matter content and the expected student response to that content. Take a look at the following general cognitive goal from a high school psychology course.

> Students should know the major founders of psychological theory and the important points in their theories.

First of all, notice that the subject-matter content is divided into (1) the major founders of psychological theories and (2) the important points in each of these theories. When we finalize our list of objectives, these two areas should be kept separate, each serving as the basis for at least one objective. It is usually best to deal with only one area of the subject matter in a given objective.

Now we will take these descriptions of subject-matter content and answer the following questions about each.

1. Is the subject-matter content clearly defined and specific enough?
2. Precisely what response(s) do I want the students to make to that subject-matter content?

In the above goal, the subject-matter content (that is, the founders of psychological theory and points important to each theory) is fairly well defined. This goal could be made more specific, however, by listing the major founders of the theories. The most important concepts for each theory might also be listed. Of course, the real problem with the above goal lies in the use of the vague, unobservable verb "to know." What observable student response could be accepted as evidence that a student "knows"? Would "to list in writing" be acceptable?

The following three objectives were derived from the above general goal. The subject-matter content of that goal was clarified, and the expected student response to that content was more precisely specified.

1. Students should be able to list in writing all the founders of psychological theories discussed in the textbook.
2. Students should be able to match each important concept to the theory with which it is associated. (This goal is limited to the theories found in Unit I in the text.)
3. When given the name of an early psychological theorist, students should be able to identify the concept(s) that are central to the theory.

Try breaking down an **affective goal:**

Students should become interested in finding out more about the specific aspects of human behavior that have been studied by psychologists.

Sometimes teachers fail to plan for the teaching of affective goals because these goals seem difficult to define in observable terms. It is relatively easy, however, if you clearly define the subject-matter content and then specify the *behavior(s)* that are likely to accompany the desired attitude toward that content. The following objective was derived from the above goal in just that way.

In an open discussion about the value of psychology, students should ask questions that would help them discover what aspects of human behavior psychologists have studied.

In this objective, the content is "questions that would help them discover what aspects of human behavior psychologists have studied." The behavior expected is "to ask." Notice, however, that something else has been added: "In an open discussion about the value of psychology." This phrase suggests a condition or type of situation under which we expect the desired student behavior to occur.

Although not necessary to the formation of an effective objective, a statement describing the *condition* under which we expect the student to respond is often helpful. Here is another such objective, derived from the above goal (the condition is italicized):

When given the task of formulating questions to be sent to famous living psychologists, the student will include questions such as: "What aspects of human behavior have psychologists studied?"

Besides a statement specifying the condition under which the student response is expected to occur, there is one other useful (though not necessary) addition that can be made to most objectives. There are times when it may be useful to specify the *level of performance* expected of the students.[10] For example, we might derive the following objective from the above goal:

When books and pamphlets describing the aspects of human behavior studied by psychologists are placed in the class library, the students will sign out *two or more* of these resources.

This objective has the criterion for success built in: two or more resources signed out.

Not only is it possible to set a standard (level of performance expected) for each student, but this can also be done for the class as a whole. By determining the level of performance for each student, each student's performance on that objective can be evaluated. By determining how well the class as a whole should learn, you assess your performance as a teacher. Suppose, for example, the above objective is written so it reads:

When books and pamphlets describing the aspects of human behavior studied by psychologists are placed in the class library, *at least 75 percent of the students* will sign out two or more of these resources.

If fewer than 75 percent of the students reach the expected level of performance, the goal has not been reached (even though some of your students may have signed out two or more resources).

A review: Breaking down general goals into specific, observable objectives

1. Break the goal into two parts: (1) subject-matter content and (2) student response to that content.
2. Clarify the subject-matter content and, where necessary, make it more specific.
3. Determine the expected student response(s) to each statement of subject-matter content.
4. As needed, identify the conditions under which the student response is expected to occur and/or any useful criteria for judging the level of performance expected.

YOUR TURN

Breaking Down a General Goal into Specific, Observable Objectives

Write observable objectives for the following goal. Make certain you:

1. Identify the subject-matter content and decide whether or not it is clearly enough defined. If not, describe what is needed to clarify it.
2. For each aspect of subject-matter content identified above, describe at least one *observable* response the students might be expected to make to it.
3. If appropriate, specify the conditions under which the student response is expected to occur, and specify an acceptable level of performance.

Goal: The students should understand the major concepts, terms, and principles used in psychological research.

Step 3. Check Objectives for Clarity and Appropriateness

To some extent, this last step may be unnecessary. If you do a good job in the first two steps, your objectives should be ready to use. A final check on your work, however, may save you the embarrassment of trying to explain to your students what it was that you "really meant to say."

A way to check for the clarity of your objectives is to have a friend (preferably one teaching the subject matter under consideration) review them. If your friend can tell you in his or her own words what each objective means, you can usually tell whether or not the objective is understandable. If it isn't, that objective probably needs clarification.

Not only must an objective be clearly stated in observable terms, but it must also be appropriate for your students. Use the following checklist to help you determine whether or not an objective is appropriate.

Criteria for Appropriate Objectives

_______ 1. Developmentally appropriate

_______ 2. Attainable by the students within a reasonable time limit

_______ 3. In proper sequence with other objectives (not to be accomplished prior to a prerequisite objective)

_______ 4. In harmony with the overall goals of the course (and curriculum)

_______ 5. In harmony with the goals and values of the institution

If your objectives are clearly stated in observable terms and meet the above criteria, they should be useful to both you and your students. Now take the Mastery Test below for this objective.

Mastery Test

OBJECTIVE 2 **To write well-defined instructional objectives**

1. List the three steps involved in writing instructional objectives.
2. General, end-of-course goals do not need to be written in observable terms. (True or False)
3. Write at least two observable objectives for each of the following three goals:
   (a) Students should understand how people learn.
   (b) Students should know what motivates people to act.
   (c) Students should understand the value of diversity in the classroom.
4. What are the two parts needed to complete a well-written instructional objective?
5. What are the two useful (although not always needed) parts of a well-written objective?

OBJECTIVE 3

To use instructional objectives in instructional planning

LEARNING ACTIVITY 3.1

Despite the fact that there has been considerable controversy over the usefulness of instructional objectives, it is quite clear that they serve an important function in instructional planning.[11] Well-defined instructional objectives can help you:

1. Focus your planning
2. Plan effective instructional events
3. Plan valid evaluation procedures

1. Instructional Objectives Can Help You Focus Your Planning. Teachers often complain that they do not have enough time to cover the material. The process of writing instructional objectives forces you to decide, out of all the material to be covered, what you really want your students to know or be able to do. This helps to focus your planning in two ways. First, it helps you eliminate topics that are of lesser importance and highlight the more important subject matter. Second, it helps you plan for a balance of different levels of learning. By examining your final list of instructional objectives for a course (or unit within a course), you can determine whether your plans include a balance of memorization, conceptualization, problem solving, and so forth. Use taxonomies of learning such as those proposed by Bloom[12] or Gagné[13] to help determine whether you have planned for sufficient higher-order learning outcomes and whether you have included appropriate affective and psychomotor objectives. Finally, a note of caution is in order here: once you have brought your plans into focus, check your final list of objectives to make certain they will help your students meet state and national standards.

2. Instructional Objectives Can Help You Plan Effective Instructional Events. In any given **instructional event,** the most important thing is what is happening in the minds of the students. Everything the teacher does should be designed to get the students to do the thinking that will produce the expected learning outcome. If an instructional objective calls for the students to memorize information, the learner activities should be designed to get them to repeat that information, to form appropriate associations, and so forth. If an instructional objective calls for the students to form a new concept, the learner activities should be designed to get students to focus on the criterial attributes of the concepts to be learned, and to compare and contrast positive and negative instances. In each of these cases, the teacher activities should be designed to help the students do the thinking (memorizing, conceptualizing) required to attain the instructional objective.

It is important that you understand the concept of an instructional event. An instructional event is any activity or set of activities in which students are engaged (with or without the teacher) for the purpose of learning (for example, attaining an instructional objective). Listening to a teacher's explanation, watching a film, doing an assignment in history, and completing a workbook page are all examples of instructional events.

Each instructional event should be designed to optimize the learning conditions and provide appropriate activities for both the learner and the teacher. Different kinds of learning require different learning conditions.[14] Note that teachers can use carefully developed questions to help learners reach different levels of learning in Bloom's *Taxonomy.* Sadker and Sadker, in their discussion of questioning skills (see Chapter 5), point out the fact that questions can be categorized according to the level of thinking required as defined by Bloom's *Taxonomy.* Objectives can also be classified according to Bloom's *Taxonomy;* and the various lists of words suggested in Chapter 5 by Sadker and Sadker as tools to determine the level of Bloom's *Taxonomy* for questions can also be applied to objectives.

Once you have determined the level of learning required by an objective using any number of available educational taxonomies, you can then plan the kinds of activities that will be most effective in helping students to attain those objectives at those levels.

The first step in planning appropriate learner and teacher activities is to determine, for each instructional objective, the kind of learning involved. If your instructional objectives are well defined, this should be relatively easy. The secret is in the verbs. The verbs should signal the kind of learning. For example, verbs such as *list, recall,* and *describe* suggest memory learning. Verbs such as *distinguish, differentiate,* and *contrast* suggest discrimination learning. *Identify, categorize,* and *recognize* suggest concept learning. *Solve, diagnose, resolve,* and *determine* suggest problem solving. *Like, enjoy, desire,* and *prefer* suggest affective learning. *Manipulate, perform, do,* and *physically control* suggest skill learning.

Once you have determined the kind of learning called for by an objective, your next step is to determine the kind of activities that the students have to do to accomplish that kind of learning. There are a number of books that can help you in this task,[15] and some of the other chapters in this book will also help (see, for example, Chapters 2, 4–6, and 8). You might also wish to read some of the learning research literature to find the latest information on how humans achieve particular kinds of learning outcomes. (*The Psychological Abstracts* are a particularly useful source.)

Now you are finally ready to determine the teacher activities. The key principle to remember is that everything the teacher does should be designed to help the learners do what they need to do to learn. Therefore, you should not only be providing the students with the information they need, but you should also be helping them process that information in appropriate ways. This is why it is so important for teachers to ask the right kinds of questions at the right time (see Chapter 5).

3. Instructional Objectives Can Help You Plan Valid Evaluation Procedures. Validity and reliability are the two most important considerations when evaluating learning (see Chapter 10). Instructional objectives define the expected learning outcomes and, therefore, are the key to developing valid tests. A test is valid if it measures what it is supposed to. Consequently, whenever teachers want to know how well their students have learned the subject material, they should measure how well those students have attained the outcomes specified in the instructional objectives. Chapter 10 tells you how to use instructional objectives to develop tests and authentic assessment tools that are both valid and reliable. For now, remember that if a test is to be a valid measure of classroom achievement, it must measure as directly as possible each of the instructional objectives taught in that classroom.

LEARNING ACTIVITY 3.2

The education community has accepted the usefulness of instructional objectives in the planning process. An analysis of available instructional plans will help you appreciate more fully the value of instructional objectives in the planning process. Gather together completed copies of several different instructional plans (course syllabi, completed lesson plans, teacher's manuals, etc.). Examine these to determine whether objectives are included and, if they are, try to decide how (if at all) the objectives influenced the student activities and/or the teacher activities. Finally, look at the objectives and try to come up with alternate student activities and/or alternate teacher activities that would also be effective in helping the students reach the objectives.

Mastery Test

OBJECTIVE 3 **To use instructional objectives in instructional planning**

1. List three ways in which instructional objectives can help in instructional planning.
2. Which activities should be determined first?
   (a) Teacher activities
   (b) Learner activities
   (c) It doesn't matter which is determined first.
3. Which part of an instructional objective is most helpful when trying to determine the kind of learning required by that objective?
   (a) The verb
   (b) The description of the subject matter
   (c) The criteria for performance
   (d) The conditions of performance
4. Why is it important to determine the kind of learning required to accomplish an objective?
5. Which criterion for an effective assessment strategy is most reinforced by the use of instructional objectives in evaluation planning?
   (a) Usefulness
   (b) Reliability
   (c) Validity

OBJECTIVE 4

To use objectives in implementing instruction

LEARNING ACTIVITY 4.1

Well-defined instructional objectives can be a big help to you and your students during the teaching process. First, when used correctly, they can help you clarify the expectations for your students, and clarity has been shown to be a critical element in successful teaching.[16] Second, they can serve as a useful guide to the students as they listen, do assignments, and study for tests.[17] Finally, well-defined instructional objectives can help you stay on track as you teach and help you deal more effectively with sidetracks. To improve your teaching, you can use instructional objectives:

1. As handouts prior to instruction
2. To prepare students for instruction
3. As a guide throughout instruction

1. Using Objectives as Handouts Prior to Instruction. There is some evidence in the literature suggesting that students perform better on tests when they have been provided with handouts of well-defined instructional objectives.[18] There are a number of things you can do to make these handouts as effective as possible. Objectives that are clearly articulated, meeting the criteria specified earlier in this chapter, will contribute most to student achievement.[19] According to Melton,[20] however, objectives should also be of interest to the students, at the correct level of difficulty, and relevant to the content to be mastered.

It has been my experience that if too many objectives are given to students all at once (for example, all the objectives for a six-week period), they are not used effectively and do little to improve achievement. Try handing out a separate set of objectives for each unit of instruction for each subject. Then review those objectives daily as you work with your students. Finally, keep in mind that we must always consider the great diversity that exists in our classrooms. Adjust your teaching strategies to accommodate that diversity[21] and, where necessary, adapt to the individual needs of your students. See Chapter 6 for ways to differentiate instruction.

2. Using Objectives to Prepare Students for Instruction. Madeline Hunter has been a strong advocate of producing an appropriate learning set in students by telling them what they should be able to expect from any given instructional event.[22] This concept is occasionally criticized by those who advocate a discovery or inquiry approach to learning. The concern is that, if students know the outcome from the beginning, the discovery process will not work effectively. It is my contention, however, that one can adequately prepare students for learning without giving away the answers, and well-written instructional objectives can help you do that. Recall that a well-written objective should not be too specific (though it must be explicit and unambiguous). Therefore, students should be told that they will be expected to be able to solve certain types of problems or that they should be able to discover things such as relationships or causes and effects. They should not be told, however, which specific finding or answer they are expected to discover. The focus should be on the learning outcome—the skill they are expected to acquire during the discovery process—not on the specific outcome of their discovery activities.

Because each instructional activity may require something different of the learner, teachers should prepare students at the beginning of each new instructional event. There are at least four kinds of information that will help prepare students for any given instructional event:

a. Learning outcome
b. Learner activities
c. Teacher activities
d. Assessment activities

a. Learning Outcome

A well-written objective is the best statement of learning outcome and is, therefore, especially useful in preparing students for an instructional event. Telling students what they will be expected to know or be able to do on completion of the instructional event will help prepare them for the activities involved.

b. Learner Activities

For many students, knowing just the expected learning outcome may not be enough information to help them get the most out of an instructional event. Some students, for example, when told to study Chapter 19 (an instructional event) so that they will be able to describe the major causes of the Civil War (a learning outcome), may not know how to study for such an outcome. Consequently, when preparing students for an instructional event, it is helpful to tell them what they need to do to get the most out of the activities involved and to accomplish successfully the expected outcome. When instructional objectives are well defined, it is much easier to determine the kind of learning activities that would be most appropriate.[23]

c. Teacher Activities

In most instructional activities, the teacher has a definite role. The teacher activities may involve providing explanations, giving feedback, observing student performance, and so forth; however, they should always involve guiding the learner through the learner activities to the accomplishment of the learning outcome (instructional objective). It is helpful for students to know from the beginning of an instructional event exactly what the role of the teacher will be and exactly how much guidance can be expected.

d. Assessment Activities

How will the students know if they have accomplished an expected learning outcome? How will the teacher judge a student's performance relative to that learning outcome? Providing students with the answers to these two questions helps prepare them for an instructional event and increases the efficiency of their learning. Well-defined objectives are stated in measurable, observable terms, and the type of evaluation is easily determined. Such is not the case when objectives are poorly written.

3. Using Objectives As a Guide Throughout Instruction. Objectives are not only helpful in preparing students to learn, but they can also serve to keep students and teacher alike focused throughout the instructional process. By keeping instructional objectives constantly in students' minds throughout the instructional process, teachers can significantly reduce the problems of getting off track or focusing on the wrong topics during instruction. This strategy is especially effective in a constructivist approach to instruction, where the learning/discovering process is paramount. Better learning occurs when the goals to be accomplished are kept in mind throughout the discovery process. If you make it obvious that you are using instructional objectives to guide what you do as teacher, if the things you ask your students to do are designed to help them accomplish the instructional objectives, and if your tests do indeed evaluate the instructional objectives, then both you and your students will stay better focused. This is not to say that sidetracks are always bad or that it is not worth learning if an objective has not been written to cover it. But your instructional objectives should serve as a primary guide for what you teach, what your students learn, and what you assess.

LEARNING ACTIVITY 4.2

Here is a simple exercise that can help you understand the value of using objectives as a regular part of the instructional process. You and your classmates should divide into small groups, five to six per group. Each group will develop a handout of four or five objectives for a given unit of instruction (specify the grade level as well as the subject). Using the above guidelines, prepare a brief presentation (it may not take more than a few seconds to present) designed to prepare the students to learn. One member of your group should use the handout and present an overview of the unit, preparing the students for that unit. Each of the other members of your group should make a presentation, preparing the students to begin learning a given objective from those on the handout. Make certain that you tell the students the learning outcome and describe for them the learner activities, teacher activities, and evaluation activities.

Mastery Test

OBJECTIVE 4 **To use objectives in implementing instruction**

1. List three ways in which you can use instructional objectives to improve your teaching.
2. Which of the following schedules for handing out objectives to students is most likely to be effective?
   (a) All course objectives provided on a handout as an overview at the beginning of the course.
   (b) Unit objectives provided on a handout as an overview at the beginning of each unit.
   (c) Each objective provided as a handout at the beginning of the class when that objective will be taught.
3. List four things that should be told to students to prepare them for an instructional event.
4. Instructional objectives should guide:
   (a) Teaching
   (b) Evaluating
   (c) Learning
   (d) All of the above

NOTES

1. W. J. Popham, "Instructional Objectives 1960–1970," *Performance and Instruction* 26, no. 2 (1987):11–14. Also see Additional Resources at the end of this chapter.
2. T. Gibbs and A. Howley, "'World-Class Standards' and Local Pedagogies. Can We Do Both?" *ERIC Digest* (December 2000). (Full text available at *http://www.ael.org/eric/digests/edorc008.htm*)
3. T. Chrochunis et al., "Equity and High Standards: Can We Have It Both Ways?" *LAB Education Notes* 2 no. 1 (2000). (Providence, R.I.: Northeast and Islands Regional Educational Laboratory at Brown University)
4. Jean Piaget, *Science of Education and the Psychology of the Child* (New York: Orion, 1970); Jean Piaget and Bärbel Inhelder, *The Growth of Logical Thinking from Childhood to Adolescence*, trans. A. Parsons and S. Seagrin (New York: Basic Books, 1958).
5. Lev Vgotsky, *Thought and Language* (Cambridge, Mass.: MIT Press, 1962).

6. Erik Erikson, *Identity: Youth and Crisis* (New York: Norton, 1968).
7. Lawrence Kohlberg, "The Cognitive-Developmental Approach to Moral Education," *Phi Delta Kappan* 56 (1975):567–677.
8. For additional examples, see Chapter 4 in T. D. TenBrink, *Evaluation: A Practical Guide for Teachers* (New York: McGraw-Hill, 1974).
9. This list was adapted from T. D. TenBrink, *Evaluation: A Practical Guide for Teachers* (New York: McGraw-Hill, 1974), p. 102.
10. Some authors use the term *performance* to refer to student outcome, *condition* to refer to conditions under which the performance is expected to occur, and *criteria* to refer to the level of performance expected.
11. S. J. Frudden and S. B. Stow, "Eight Elements of Effective Preinstructional Planning," *Education* 106, no. 2 (1985):218–222.
12. Lorin W. Anderson and David R. Krathwohl, eds., *Taxonomy for Learning, Teaching, and Assessing: A Revision of Bloom's Taxonomy of Educational Objectives* (New York: Longman, 2000).
13. R. M. Gagné, "Learning Outcomes and Their Effects: Useful Categories of Human Performance," *American Psychologist* 39, no. 4 (1984):377–385.
14. R. M. Gagné, *Conditions of Learning and Theory of Instruction,* 4th ed. (San Diego: Harcourt Brace Jovanovich, 1992).
15. See Additional Resources for recent books on educational psychology and teaching/learning strategies.
16. C. V. Hines, D. R. Cruickshank, and J. J. Kennedy, "Teacher Clarity and Its Relationship to Student Achievement and Satisfaction," *American Educational Research Journal* 22, no. 1 (1985):87–99.
17. J. Hartley and I. Davies, "Preinstructional Strategies: The Role of Pretests, Behavioral Objectives, Overviews and Advance Organizers," *Review of Educational Research* 46 (1976):239–265.
18. P. C. Duchastel and P. F. Merrill, "The Effects of Behavioral Objectives on Learning: A Review of Empirical Studies," *Review of Educational Research* 45 (1973): 53–69.
19. G. T. Dalis, "Effects of Precise Objectives upon Student Achievement in Health Education," *Journal of Experimental Education* 39 (1970):20–23.
20. R. F. Melton, "Resolution of Conflicting Claims Concerning the Effects of Behavioral Objectives on Student Learning," *Review of Educational Research* 48 (1978): 291–302.
21. T. J. Lasley II and T. J. Matczynski, *Strategies for Teaching in a Diverse Society: Instructional Models.* (Belmont, Calif.: Wadsworth, 1997).
22. Madeline Hunter, "Teacher Competency: Problem, Theory, and Practice," *Theory into Practice* 15, no. 2 (1976):162–171.
23. R. M. Gagné, "What Should a Performance Improvements Professional Know and Do?" *Performance and Instruction* 24, no. 27 (1985):6–7.

ADDITIONAL RESOURCES

Readings

Carver, Sharon, and David Klahr, eds., *Cognition and Instruction: 25 Years of Progress.* Mahwah, N.J.: Earlbaum, 2001.

Gagné, R. M., et al. *Principles of Instructional Design,* 5th ed. San Diego: Harcourt Brace Jovanovich, 1997.

Gallagher, Suzanne. *Educational Psychology: Disrupting the Dominant Discourse.* New York: P. Lang, 2001.

Gronlund, Norman E. *How to Write Instructional Objectives,* 6th ed. Upper Saddle River, N. J.: Prentice-Hall, 1999.

Krathwohl, David R., Benjamin S. Bloom, and Bertram B. Masia. *Taxonomy of Educational Objectives: Vol. 2. Affective Domain.* Reading, Mass.: Addison-Wesley, 1999.

Mager, Robert F. *Preparing Instructional Objectives: A Critical Tool in the Development of Effective Instruction,* 3rd ed. Atlanta, Ga.: Center for Effective Performance, 1997.

Marzano, Robert J., Debra Pickering, and Jane E. Pollock. *Classroom Instruction That Works: Research-Based Strategies for Increasing Student Achievement.* Alexandria, Va.: Association for Supervision and Curriculum Development, 2001.

Web Sites

Access Eric: http://www.eric.ed.gov

ACCESS ERIC, the promotional and outreach arm of the U.S. Department of Education's Educational Resources Information Center (ERIC) system, keeps you informed of the wealth of information offered by the ERIC components and other education-related organizations. This site is a beginning point for access to all of the ERIC web sites and can help you in your search for the latest information on all aspects of education, including sources of information on appropriate instructional objectives for various subjects at various grade levels.

www.ericae.net/digests/tm9505.htm
The digest at this site discusses several aspects of **assigning grades.** It is a thorough and well-written discussion of the whole process of assigning grades that are fair and equitable.

The Council of Chief State School Officers: http://www.ccsso.org
This is the web site for the Council of Chief State School Officers and includes the INTASC standards, as well as information on council projects, federal legislative positions, policy statements, and news releases of interest to educators.

Yahoo's Directory of K–12 Lesson Plans: http://dir.yahoo.com/Education/K_12/Teaching/Lesson_Plans/
This web site consists of a variety of lesson plans and resources that are already developed for a variety of subjects. It also talks about different types of media and learning activities that are helpful in teaching the subject material. Under this site, click on the appropriate icon or highlighted word to bring you into the different subject areas. In addition, the "AskERIC Lesson Plans" search (http://ericir.syr.edu/Virtual/Lessons/) will provide a listing of new lesson plans submitted to this web site for different months during the year. Each month contains many different specific lesson plans, with the subject and appropriate grade levels listed.

Teacher's Net, Lesson Bank: http://www.teachers.net/lessons/posts/posts.html
This web site contains around 200 prepared lesson plans that have been submitted by teachers around the world. The specific topic is listed, along with the grade level and subject area (e.g., *Mini Page Term Paper,* Elementary, Reading/Writing). It also provides you with the capability to submit lesson plans you have developed, search for specific lessons, and request lesson plans from certain topics.

Chemistry Resources: http://198.110.10.57/Chem/Chem1Docs/Index.html
This web site specifically looks at chemistry resources and lesson plans for demonstrations, laboratory investigations, teaching tips, and other topic areas. (A specific site for life science resources is located at http://198.110.10.57//Chem/Bio1Docs/Index.html, and a specific site for math problems is located at http://falcon.cc.ukans.edu/~danherm/prob.html)

http://www.mcrel.org/standards-benchmarks/index.asp
This web site has an accumulation of the different subject areas in categories and lists topical areas under each subject. These sites provide national standards for benchmarking in these areas.

AskEric's Lesson Plans: http://ericir.syr.edu/VirtualLessons/
"Contains more than 1,100 unique lesson plans that have been written and submitted to AskERIC teachers from all over the United States."

New York Times Education Resources: http://www.nytimes.com/learning/
"Free news and education resources for teachers, their students and parents. Includes lesson plans, vocabulary and geography builders and more."

Funbrain.com: http://www.funbrain.com
This site enables teachers to integrate games and thousands of assessment quizzes into their daily lesson plans.

JDL Technologies: Resources for Students and Educations: http://www.k-12world.com
Lots of great resources for students and teachers. This site provides numerous links to educational sites and resources.

4

Involving Students in Learning

Robert Shostak

OBJECTIVE 1 **To define a planned beginning (set), explain its purposes, and give examples of when it is used to involve students in learning**

OBJECTIVE 2 **To create original planned beginnings (sets) for involving students in learning**

OBJECTIVE 3 **To define planned discussion, explain its purposes, and give examples of when it is used to involve students in learning**

OBJECTIVE 4 **To identify student behaviors that reflect their ability to engage in effective classroom discussion**

OBJECTIVE 5 **To create original planned discussions for use in a given learning situation**

OBJECTIVE 6 **To define a planned ending (closure), explain its purposes, and give examples of how it is used to involve students in learning**

OBJECTIVE 7 **To create original planned endings (closure) for use in a given learning situation**

Teaching and learning are two sides of the same coin. It is extremely difficult to talk about one without including the other. However, if you were to examine the nature of professional writing and research dealing with teaching and learning, you would discover an interesting phenomenon. Educators shift their emphasis from teaching to learning in a regular, almost predictable fashion. In the early 1990s the focus was on teaching and measuring effective teaching performance. Now the emphasis has shifted, and professional educators have turned their attention to the task of involving students in learning.

Researchers are now describing the classroom as a "complex social environment" in which "the characteristics of the students . . . ha[ve] implications for the way in which instruction is delivered and the effects that teachers have on student learning."[1] These researchers view learning as a social process heavily influenced by the sociolinguistic, ethnic, and cultural characteristics of the students. **Constructivist theorists** are emphasizing that students are not sponges—passive recipients of knowledge—and that effective learning occurs when students are interacting with one another and the teacher to make their own meaning and construct their own knowledge.[2]

And now the Council of Chief State School Officers, in its project to develop core standards for beginning teachers, has brought much of the current research and theory together to describe the following performance requisite:

> The teacher stimulates student reflection on prior knowledge and links new ideas to already familiar ideas, making connections to students' experiences, providing opportunities for active engagement, manipulation, and testing of ideas and materials, and encouraging students to assume responsibility for shaping their learning tasks.[3]

This standard of teacher performance helps form the basis for the three most important skills a teacher must acquire to successfully involve students in learning: (1) beginning a lesson, or creating a *set;* (2) generating productive discussions; and (3) ending a lesson, or making effective *closure.*

Remember that regardless of the grade level you teach, the necessity of exposing students to new facts, ideas, and complicated relationships requires the teacher to involve students in the learning process.

OBJECTIVE 1

To define a planned beginning (set), explain its purposes, and give examples of when it is used to involve students in learning

LEARNING ACTIVITY 1.1

The Planned Beginning

A planned beginning, or **set,** is a combination of actions and statements designed to relate the experiences of the students to the instructional objectives of the lesson.[4] Planned beginnings are used to involve students more effectively in learning. Involving students in learning requires accomplishing the following critical tasks: *gaining students' attention, establishing expectations for what is to be learned, motivating students to become involved, and using students' prior knowledge to make meaningful connections to new material.*

A story is told about a traveler who came upon an old man beating his donkey in an effort to make the animal rise. The animal sat placidly in the middle of the road refusing to get up, and the old man continued to whip the animal until a stranger stepped up and stopped his hand. "Why don't you tell the donkey to rise?" asked the stranger. "I will," replied the old man, "but first I have to get his attention."

The first purpose of a planned beginning is *to focus student attention on the lesson.* Effective teachers know that one of their primary tasks is to involve the student in the learning process. The Kelwynn Group, an educational consulting firm that developed a list of twenty criteria for effective teaching performance based on the work of Madeline Hunter, Jane Stallings, Barak Rosenshine, and others, echoes the same notion.[5]

As its second purpose, a planned beginning attempts *to establish expectations for what is to be learned.* This is done by creating a framework for the ideas, principles, or information that is to follow. Gage and Berliner, in discussing the importance of lecture introductions, speak of **advance organizers**—"telling students in advance about the way in which a lecture is organized is likely to improve their comprehension and ability to recall and apply what they hear."[6] Effective teachers frequently share their goals and objectives with students as a means of helping them establish a framework for their learning and involving them in the lesson.

The third purpose of a planned beginning is *to motivate students to become involved in the lesson.* A great deal of research has been carried on over the years on student motivation and the need to increase students' interest in learning. Maria Montessori observed how deep involvement in play activities can keep a young child motivated and interested in a single game over an extended period of time. The point here is that active involvement at the beginning of a lesson can increase curiosity and stimulate student interest in the lesson.[7] A good example is the teacher who wishes to teach the concept of categorizing and brings a collection of baseball cards, CDs, or even a basket of leaves to class. Then the students, divided into groups, are asked to categorize their collections and explain how and why they did what they did.

The fourth and last purpose of the planned beginning is *to relate students' prior knowledge to the new material to be learned.* An idea or principle that is abstractly stated can be difficult for many students to comprehend. Moreover, many students who do understand an idea or principle have difficulty applying their knowledge to new situations. The clever use of examples and analogies can do much to help students relate their prior knowledge to new material to be learned.

LEARNING ACTIVITY 1.2

Now that the planned beginning has been defined and its purposes explained, you are ready to focus on when it is used in the course of a lesson. To better understand the use of planned beginnings, think of a classroom lesson as a game. Bellack, in his research on the language used by teachers to engage students in learning, talks about "structuring moves [that] set the context for the entire classroom game."[8] Furthermore, he views the lesson as containing several "subgames," each of which is identified primarily by the type of activity taking place during a given period of play.

For example, you may plan to use several different activities such as reading, writing, and discussion, each dealing with different subject matter. Each new activity can be seen as a subgame within the context of a larger game, the entire day's lessons. Each activity must be designed so that students are involved (play) actively in the lesson (game). Specific examples are illustrated in the sample lessons in the section discussing Objective 2.

The kinds of classroom activities (subgames) for which it is necessary to employ a planned beginning are innumerable. For help in learning when to use a planned beginning in your own lessons, carefully study the following list.

Examples of When to Use the Planned Beginning

To start a long unit of work in which the class might be studying plants, rockets, or local government

To introduce a new concept or principle

To initiate a discussion

To begin a skill-building activity such as reading comprehension or visual discrimination

To introduce a film, TV program, or video

To demonstrate a particular function of a computer

To prepare for a field trip

To present a guest speaker

To introduce a homework assignment

To begin a laboratory exercise

To redirect a presentation when you see that students do not understand the content

Mastery Test

OBJECTIVE 1 **To define a planned beginning (set), explain its purposes, and give examples of when it is used to involve students in learning**

These questions are designed to determine your knowledge and comprehension level. Successful completion of these questions meets the objective of the learning activity.

1. Define the planned beginning, and explain three specific purposes it serves to involve students in learning.
2. Describe briefly three different situations in which you would use a planned beginning in your lessons.

OBJECTIVE 2

To create original planned beginnings (sets) for involving students in learning

LEARNING ACTIVITY 2.1

Now that you know what a planned beginning is and the general purposes for which it is used, you are ready to begin practicing how to create your own planned beginnings. Before you actually begin doing this, you should take time to familiarize yourself with some examples of how experienced teachers might use planned beginnings in their lessons.

Uses of Planned Beginnings

Below is a list of specific planned beginnings used by experienced teachers. Study them carefully. Then read each of the sample lessons that follow and the accompanying analysis. You should then be ready to create your own planned beginnings for a given teaching situation.

1. To focus students' attention on the lesson by employing an activity, event, object, or person that relates directly to students' interests or previous experiences
2. To establish expectations for learning by providing a structure or framework that enables the student to visualize the objectives, content, or activities of the lesson
3. To motivate students to become involved in the lesson by employing student-centered activities or student-developed examples
4. To provide a smooth transition from known or already covered material to new or unknown material by capitalizing on students' present knowledge, past experiences, familiar examples, or analogies

Sample Lesson 1

The teacher has planned to get into the topic of percent and is aware of student interest in the local baseball team. The teacher decides to introduce the unit with a brief discussion of the previous day's game. Talk is directed to batting averages, and the teacher demonstrates how they are calculated. Students are encouraged to work out one or two of the averages for favorite players.

Analysis. This planned beginning is most appropriately used for introducing a unit on percent or the concept of percent itself. Referring to the list of uses for planned beginnings mentioned above, note:

1. It uses an event, yesterday's baseball game, that is familiar and of interest to students to gain their attention.
2. It provides a ready frame of reference (batting averages) for the new concept to be learned, percent.
3. It motivates students to become involved by engaging in an activity the students enjoy—talking about a favorite sport.
4. It relates prior knowledge and experiences (previously learned math concepts and the term *batting average*) to the new concept of percent.

Sample Lesson 2

The students working in a science unit have already demonstrated in the first part of their lesson some basic understanding of mixtures. The teacher has planned to conduct an experiment to demonstrate visually the concept of mixtures. She brings to class several bottles of different kinds of popular salad dressings. The students are directed to experiment with the various bottles and to observe differences in their appearance before and after they are vigorously mixed.

Analysis. This planned beginning is most appropriately used to begin a laboratory exercise. Referring to the list of uses for planned beginnings mentioned above, note:

1. It uses popular salad dressings as a device to gain students' attention.
2. It establishes expectations for what is to be learned by focusing on what students are to look for while "experimenting" with the salad dressings.
3. It motivates students to become involved by engaging them in a meaningful activity.
4. It uses the students' prior knowledge of mixtures to help them discover new knowledge related to the topic they are studying.

Sample Lesson 3

The students have been learning how to type messages in their new computer e-mail program. The teacher announces that they are now ready to select a pen pal and begin to learn how to send their messages.

Analysis. This planned beginning is most appropriately used to introduce a new skill in a series of related skills. Referring to the list of uses for planned beginnings mentioned above, note:

1. It focuses students' attention on the lesson by involving them in an activity they enjoy and have been anticipating—the selection of a pen pal.
2. It establishes a framework for learning by relating what they have already accomplished to the next skill to be mastered in using e-mail.
3. It motivates students to become involved by allowing them to use what they have learned in an activity they enjoy.
4. It uses students' knowledge of language skills and the computer to create new opportunities to build meaningful relationships with others.

LEARNING ACTIVITY 2.2

Up until this point in the chapter, you have been engaged solely in paper-and-pencil-type activities. Now it is time to observe in real classrooms where students are actually involved in learning. Before scheduling your first observation, review the material on field-based observation in Chapter 1. When you are ready to observe, make a copy of the Observation Worksheet that follows to gather your data. You will be able to compare the results of your observations with others in a subsequent class activity.

Mastery Test

OBJECTIVE 2 **To create original planned beginnings (sets) for involving students in learning**

Following these directions are five hypothetical teaching situations. Read each one carefully and create a planned beginning of your own that you feel would work effectively in that particular situation. You may refer to the list of uses for planned beginnings on page 81 and the sample lessons that follow to help you complete this task.

Situation 1. The class has been working on a unit comparing different cultures. During the first part of the period, the students saw a short videotape that provided an overview of important cultural differences. The teacher wishes to use the remainder of the period for a new activity that will involve students more directly in the lesson.

Situation 2. You are introducing the study of pollution and the environment to your class. It is important that you get off on the right foot.

Situation 3. You are introducing the use of search engines on the World Wide Web.

Situation 4. Your class has been studying the letters of the alphabet. You wish to use part of the day to take up this subject again and to determine how far your students have come in being able to place the letters in order.

Situation 5. Your class has been working on different techniques to put life into their writing. In this lesson, you wish to present the idea of using descriptive words to paint verbal pictures.

Observation Worksheet

Beginning a Lesson

This observation activity gives you the opportunity to compare what you've learned about beginning a lesson to what you actually see in classrooms.

Directions: Do not use actual names of schools, teachers, administrators, or students when using this worksheet.

Observer's Name: ______________________________

Date: ______________________________

Grade Level: ______________________________

Subject: ______________________________

Class Size: ______________________________

Background Information: Give a brief general description of the school's social, economic, and ethnic makeup.

____

____

What to Record: While observing teachers in action, pay attention to those times in the instructional process when the teacher introduces a new lesson. Use the following format to record what the teacher says to get students ready for that lesson.

1. How are the students made aware that the lesson is beginning? ______________________________

____

____

2. How are the students motivated to become involved in the lesson? ______________________________

____

____

3. What frame of reference is provided to help students organize their learning? ______________________________

____

____

4. How does the teacher make use of students' prior knowledge as it relates to the new material to be learned? ______________________________

____

Reflections on Your Observation: Compare what you've seen the teacher do in beginning a lesson with the steps advocated by this chapter's author. In what ways are they similar and different? In your judgment, was the lesson beginning effective? Why or why not?

____

____

____

OBJECTIVE 3

To define planned discussion, explain its purposes, and give examples of when it is used to involve students in learning

LEARNING ACTIVITY 3.1

Planned Discussion

Many of the changes in what has been happening in the classroom in recent years have been the result of sociolinguistic research investigating the instructional function of classroom talk. The idea that students are passive recipients of knowledge and that teachers are the transmitters of that knowledge is giving way to the notion that students learn better when they are involved in the process of creating knowledge for themselves.[9]

The educators who are bringing about these changes follow the precepts of what is known as constructivist learning theory. The research base for this theory stems from recent studies of the brain and how learning occurs. Although there is not widespread agreement on a definition of the constructivist theory of learning, many theorists can agree on some basic assumptions about how humans learn, or "construct knowledge."

Basic to constructivist theory is the notion that the individual student, not the teacher, is the focus in every *learning situation* and that classroom social interaction is critical in the learning process. Specifically, learning occurs when students interact directly with whatever materials or events encompass the learning experience and when they create their own ideas and understandings from this interaction. This means that constructivism focuses on learning, not telling. Students are encouraged to take chances, given opportunities to experiment on their own, and accept responsibility for their own learning. Moreover, great emphasis is placed on creating a classroom environment that encourages students to interact with one another.

The constructivist views the teacher, for the most part, as a facilitator. The teacher provides learning situations in which students have an opportunity to conceptualize for themselves and create their own understandings. The teacher also encourages cooperative learning and emphasizes the need for students to engage in meaningful dialogue. That is why dialogue, or classroom discussion, is being viewed as one of the more important learning situations teachers can use to help students create knowledge for themselves.[10]

Furthermore, the Council of Chief State School Officers describes the following performance requisite for beginning teachers in its INTASC Core Standards:

> The teacher knows how to ask questions and stimulate discussion in different ways for particular purposes, for example, probing for learner understanding, helping students articulate their ideas and thinking processes, promoting risk-taking and problem-solving, facilitating factual recall, encouraging **convergent** and **divergent thinking,** stimulating curiosity, helping students to question. [11]

A planned discussion is one that permits open interaction between student and student as well as between teacher and student. Although the teacher initiates the activity, he or she does not assume a leadership role but rather participates as a member of the group. And everyone adheres to the guidelines for acceptable discussion behavior. Discussion serves several important purposes as a vehicle for involving students in learning:

1. Students acquire new knowledge.
2. They learn to express clearly their own ideas or views.
3. They learn to evaluate their own thinking and the thinking of others.
4. They learn to reflect on ideas different from their own.
5. They learn to share personal opinions.

LEARNING ACTIVITY 3.2

Now that planned discussion has been defined and you understand its purposes for involving students in learning, you need to know when to use discussion most effectively in a lesson. For help in completing this task, carefully study the following list.

Examples of When to Use Discussion

To compare different solutions to the same problem

To determine what can be learned from a completed laboratory experiment, an extended research project, or a meaningful field trip

To compare a novel, play, or biography to its filmed version

To examine different political ideologies

To evaluate new or proposed changes in social policy

To explore the similarities and differences across cultures

Mastery Test

OBJECTIVE 3 **To define planned discussion, explain its purposes, and give examples of when it is used to involve students in learning**

The following questions are designed to determine your knowledge and comprehension level. Successful completion of these questions meets the objective of the learning activity.

1. Define in your own words the term *planned discussion.*
2. State three specific purposes for using planned discussion in a lesson.
3. Describe briefly three different situations in which you would use a planned discussion in your lessons.

OBJECTIVE 4

To identify student behaviors that reflect their ability to engage in effective classroom discussion

LEARNING ACTIVITY 4

Preparing Students for a Discussion

Although learning how to plan for a successful discussion is extremely important, it is just as important to know how to prepare students to participate effectively in discussion. Most experts in group dynamics agree that one of the keys to preparing for successful classroom discussion is the ability of the teacher to create an atmosphere of trust among students and between teacher and students. Students must be made to feel that the classroom is a safe place to express their ideas and feelings without running the risk of being embarrassed or ridiculed.

Many teachers make the mistake of thinking that students are born with the ability to communicate effectively in an open discussion. This is just not true. Students must learn the basic skills required to participate effectively in a discussion. Before you implement your plan for conducting a discussion, be certain to include time for familiarizing your students with the skills needed to participate effectively in an open group discussion. The list that follows contains a set of basic skills that most experts in human communication would agree are necessary for participants to be successful in a large-group classroom discussion. Study the list carefully before initiating your first classroom discussion.

1. Listen respectfully even if you disagree with what is being said.
2. Learn to avoid interrupting others when they are speaking.
3. Learn to keep an open mind to different points of view.
4. Learn to take responsibility for getting a task done.
5. Learn to cooperate for the purpose of seeking solutions to the problem at hand.
6. Learn to listen critically.
7. Learn to stay focused on the issue and avoid irrelevant comments, questions, or stories.
8. Learn how to come to a common understanding to which all can agree.

Mastery Test

OBJECTIVE 4 **To identify student behaviors that reflect their ability to engage in effective classroom discussion**

Now that you know the purposes for using planned discussion, know when to use them in a lesson, and are aware of the importance of preparing students to engage in effective discussion, you are ready to test your observational skills in a real classroom situation. Your task is to identify student behaviors that reflect their ability to engage in effective classroom discussion. Before scheduling this observation, review the material on field-based observation in Chapter 1. When you are ready to observe, make a copy of the Observation Worksheet that follows to gather your data. You will be able to compare the results of your observations with others in a subsequent class activity.

Observation Worksheet
Planned Discussion

This observation activity gives you the opportunity to identify student behaviors that reflect their ability to engage in effective classroom discussion.

Directions: Do not use actual names of schools, teachers, administrators, or students when using this worksheet.

Observer's Name: ______________________________

Date: ______________________________

Grade Level: ______________________________

Subject: ______________________________

Class Size: ______________________________

Background Information: Give a brief general description of the school's social, economic, and ethnic makeup.

____

____

____

What to Record: You will be observing student behaviors reflecting their ability to engage in effective discussion. Use the following format to record what the students do during discussion.

1. How do students demonstrate their respect for others? ______________________________

____

____

2. In what ways are students maintaining an open mind? ______________________________

____

____

3. In what ways are students demonstrating their willingness to accept responsibility for getting the task done? ______________________________

____

____

4. What evidence is there that students are trying to reach a consensus? ______________________________

____

____

5. How do students demonstrate their ability to stay focused on the issues?

____

____

6. What evidence is there that students are thinking about the issues being discussed? ______________________________

____

____

7. How do students demonstrate their ability to work cooperatively?

____

____

____

Reflections on Your Observation:

1. Summarize your general impressions about the students' ability to engage in effective discussion.

____

____

____

2. If you had been leading the discussion, what changes would you have made? Why?

____

____

____

OBJECTIVE 5

To create original planned discussions for use in a given learning situation

LEARNING ACTIVITY 5.1

Planning a Discussion

Although good discussion can evolve spontaneously, there is no guarantee this will happen on a regular basis. Ensuring meaningful discussion requires the same care you give to planning an entire lesson. This does not mean that the outcome of a discussion is something one should predict or predetermine. On the contrary, an effective plan for discussion must provide only the organizing framework to ensure meaningful and productive dialogue. This can best be accomplished by applying what you have learned in the preceding two chapters about lesson planning and writing instructional objectives. Before you begin doing this, you should take time to familiarize yourself with the kind of organizing framework an experienced teacher might use for planning a successful discussion:

1. Have a goal (objective) in mind to serve as a guideline for what students are expected to learn.
2. Develop a clear statement of the content to be covered, that is, concepts to be developed or issues to be explored.
3. Prepare the materials to be used, that is, readings, CDs or web sites to be explored, list of discussion questions.
4. Formulate a set of procedures or guidelines for participation.
5. Create a means to evaluate discussion results through written homework, classroom activity, test, or observation of student response to oral questions.

LEARNING ACTIVITY 5.2

Before undertaking this task, be sure you have had the opportunity to see an experienced teacher carry on a discussion in a real classroom and to compare the data on your Observation Worksheet with the information gathered by other students in your class. Remember that planning a discussion is like planning a lesson. Assuming you have the knowledge of the subject matter to be discussed and have led your students to understand how they must interact in a discussion, you now need to prepare a framework that will help to elicit meaningful and productive deliberation. First, return to Learning Activity 5.1 and study the organizing framework provided there. Then examine the model outline that follows. When you have finished this task, you should be ready to create your own planned discussions for a given teaching situation.

Planned Discussion—A Model

Goal	To develop a heightened awareness of the rhythm in oral and written language and increase the facility in both oral and written communication.
Content	Investigate the use of rhythm as it is used in oral and written communication and discover how it helps convey and enhance meaning.
Materials	Limericks [prepare a set of limericks appropriate for the grade level you teach] Prose selections [prepare a set of prose selections containing specific rhythmic devices—for example, alliteration—that are appropriate for the grade level you teach] Nursery rhymes [select several nursery rhymes with which you feel most of your students might be familiar] Prepare a set of questions to help guide students during the discussion. Create a limerick completion sheet that requires students to fill in alternate lines of a limerick that you provide.

Procedures	1. A third of the students in the class are given a copy of a limerick; a second third are given a copy of the selected prose examples; and the last third are given a copy of the nursery rhyme. They are asked to take home their selections and practice reading them aloud. 2. On the day you plan to conduct your discussion, begin by distributing the discussion question sheet you prepared in advance. Then have one student from each group read that group's selection aloud. Commence the discussion using the prepared questions as a guide. At the appropriate time, have the second group read its selection and continue the discussion using the question sheet as a guide. Repeat this procedure with the next selection. Try to close by having students summarize the conclusions reached during the discussion.
Evaluation	Distribute to each student a copy of the prepared limerick completion sheet and instruct them to complete this activity according to the directions on the sheet. Finally, read orally and in a new discussion compare and contrast the results.

Mastery Test

OBJECTIVE 5 **To create original planned discussions for use in a given learning situation**

Following these directions are five hypothetical teaching situations. Read each one carefully and select one for which you will develop your own planned discussion. You may refer to the preceding model for help in generating ideas for your plan.

Situation 1. Your class has been working on different techniques used by fiction writers for developing character. Select some appropriate fictional material for your grade level and plan to conduct a discussion of some specific selections that clearly illustrate the technique you are studying.

Situation 2. Part of your computer literacy curriculum includes material on some of the problems we face as we rely more and more on computers to accomplish everyday tasks such as shopping, banking, bill paying, and ordinary socializing. Develop a plan that will involve your students in a discussion of the problems, both real and potential, that will arise as computers increasingly become a part of our everyday lives.

Situation 3. Select a topic from current events that is appropriate for your grade level or subject area and develop a planned discussion dealing with the issue or issues pertinent to that topic.

Situation 4. Your students have been studying the Pilgrims and in particular the Thanksgiving feast. As part of their study you have introduced materials on feasts of thanksgiving held by people of other cultures. Plan a discussion in which your students can compare and contrast the thanksgiving celebration as it occurs across cultures.

Situation 5. Safety has been a major topic of study in your class, and you have visited the neighborhood fire department, where your students were able to view an excellent film on preventing fire in the home. Plan a discussion around the important ideas learned on the students' recent field trip.

OBJECTIVE 6

To define a planned ending (closure), explain its purposes, and give examples of how it is used to involve students in learning

LEARNING ACTIVITY 6.1

Planned Endings

Anyone familiar with weekly television shows will find it very easy to understand the concept of planned endings (closure) when it is used to involve students in learning. Television scriptwriters use planned endings when, each week, they faithfully bring their shows to a satisfying close—that is, the audience has the comfortable feeling that all the loose ends have been tied up, the conflict has been resolved, and things are as they should be with the main characters. But the planned ending, when used by the successful teacher, is much more sophisticated than the technique used by the TV scriptwriter.

If a teacher wishes to create for students the same sense of satisfaction or completion achieved by the TV writer, then that teacher must learn how to use planned endings, or closure, skillfully. **Closure** is a term used to refer to those actions or statements by teachers that are designed to help students bring things together in their own minds, to make sense out of what has been going on during the course of the lesson. Research in the psychology of learning indicates that learning increases when teachers make a conscious effort to help students organize the information presented to them and perceive relationships based on that information.

Another way to look at the planned ending is to compare it to the paper-and-pencil process of lesson planning. An effective lesson plan will usually indicate where the students will be going, how they will get there, and how they will know when they have arrived. In their discussion of the results of research on cognitive learning strategies, Rosenshine and Meister suggest that summarizing serves "a comprehension-fostering function" that leads to "deeper processing."[12] And making certain that students know *when they have arrived* is the result of the skillful teacher's use of the planned ending. Constructivist learning theorists such as Gagnon and Collay emphasize as one of the six building blocks of their learning model the need for "reflections." "Reflections" come at the close of the lesson, permitting students to review what they have just experienced and connect it to what they already know in order to create new knowledge.[13]

And again, the Council of Chief State School Officers in its INTASC Core Standards for beginning teachers has brought much of the current research and theory together to describe the following performance requisite:

> The teacher appropriately uses a variety of formal and informal assessment techniques (e.g., observation, portfolios of student work, teacher-made tests, performance tasks, projects, student self-assessment, peer assessment, and standardized tests) to enhance her or his knowledge of learners, evaluate students' progress and performances, and modify teaching and learning strategies. [14]

The planned ending, then, has as its first purpose *to draw attention to the end of a lesson segment.* Unfortunately, many teachers have neglected the development of this important skill. Your own experience will tell you that many teachers will close the lesson something like this:

Teacher A: Okay. There's the bell! Get going—you'll be late for your next class!
Teacher B: Enough of this! Let's close our books and line up for recess.
Teacher C: The bell? All right, we'll stop here and pick up at the same point tomorrow.
Teacher D: Any questions? No? Good. Let's move on to the next chapter.

The students are certainly aware that something has concluded in each case, but that is about all. These rather unsophisticated attempts at closing a lesson completely ignore the fact that effective learning is a direct result of careful planning. And one of the most important parts of your lesson plan is making provision for feedback and review, or what we are calling planned endings.

Planned endings alert students to the fact that they have reached an important point in the lesson and that the time has come to wrap it up. This activity must be planned just as carefully as its counterpart, the planned beginning, and timing is critical. The teacher must be aware of the clock and must begin to initiate closure proceedings well before the lesson is due to end.

Consequently, a second major purpose of the planned ending is *to help consolidate student learning.* Simply calling attention to the lesson's conclusion is not enough. A great deal of information may have been involved and a number of activities may have taken place, and it is the teacher's responsibility to tie it all together into a meaningful whole. The learner, just like the television viewer, should not be left with a feeling of incompleteness and frustration. Like the TV detective who explains to the audience how the various pieces of the puzzle finally came together to form a complete picture, the skillful teacher needs to provide students with an opportunity to create new knowledge by consolidating what they already know with what they have just experienced.

Finally, the planned ending has as its third purpose *to reinforce the major points to be learned.* Having signaled the end of the lesson and made an effort to organize what has occurred, the teacher should briefly refocus on the key ideas or processes presented in the lesson. The ultimate objective here is to help students retain the important information learned in the lesson and thus increase the probability that they will be able to recall and use the information at a later time. Gagné and Briggs, in discussing information storage and retrieval, have this to say: "When information or knowledge is to be recalled . . . *the network of relationships* in which the newly learned material has been embedded provides a number of different possibilities as cues for its retrieval."[15] The planned ending does this by calling attention to the end of the lesson, tying key points together into a coherent whole, and, finally, ensuring their later use by anchoring them in the student's larger conceptual network.

LEARNING ACTIVITY 6.2

Now that the planned ending has been defined and its purposes explained, you are ready to focus specifically on when the teacher uses it in the course of the lesson. You should be able to understand more easily when the planned ending is used if you completed the learning activity on planned beginnings. In that section, a lesson was compared to a game containing several "subgames." In the classroom such "subgames" might involve a lesson introducing some new concept or skill or an activity with some combination of reading, writing, viewing, or discussing. Each of these activities can be viewed as a "subgame" within the context of the larger game—the entire class period in a particular subject or a full day of nondepartmentalized instruction.

The role of the teacher is to plan a lesson (subgame) so that it begins and ends in such a way as to involve the students in learning. This is the function of both planned beginnings and planned endings. For help in learning when to use a planned ending in a lesson, carefully study the following list of situations.

Examples of When to Use a Planned Ending

To end a long unit of work that the class might be studying, such as animals, or the family, or a country

To consolidate learning of a new concept or principle

To close a discussion

To end a skill-building activity, such as locating words in the dictionary or practicing basic functions in arithmetic

To follow up a film, TV program, or video

To end a planned activity on the computer

To consolidate learning experiences on a field trip

To reinforce the presentation of a guest speaker

To follow up a homework assignment reviewed in class

To end a laboratory exercise

To organize thinking around a new concept or principle (e.g., all languages are not written, or different cultures reflect different values)

Mastery Test

OBJECTIVE 6 **To define a planned ending (closure), explain its purposes, and give examples of how it is used to involve students in learning**

1. Define the term *planned ending (closure)* in your own words, and explain three specific purposes it serves in involving students in learning.
2. Try responding to the following statements by placing the letter *T* next to those that are true and the letter *F* next to those that are false.

______ (a) A planned ending is a natural complement to planned beginnings.

______ (b) A planned ending is less important than planned beginnings because students can tell by the clock when the class period ends.

______ (c) A planned ending helps students know when they have achieved lesson objectives.

______ (d) One of the purposes of a planned ending is to draw attention to the end of a presentation.

______ (e) A planned ending provides an opportunity for students to review what they are supposed to have learned.

______ (f) A planned ending is a natural phenomenon and does not require planning.

______ (g) One of the purposes of the planned ending is to help organize student learning.

______ (h) Timing is critical in using a planned ending.

______ (i) A planned ending helps to get your lesson off on the right foot.

______ (j) One of the purposes of a planned ending is to consolidate or reinforce the major points to be learned in a presentation.

3. Describe briefly three different situations in which you could use a planned ending to involve students in learning.

OBJECTIVE 7

To create original planned endings (closure) for use in a given learning situation

LEARNING ACTIVITY 7.1

Now that you know what a planned ending is, the general purposes for which it is used, and when it is used to involve students in learning, you are ready to begin practicing how to create your own planned endings. Before you actually begin doing this, you should take time to familiarize yourself with some examples of how experienced teachers might use planned endings in their lessons.

Uses of Planned Endings

A list of specific uses of the planned ending employed by experienced teachers follows. Study them carefully. Then read each of the sample lessons and the accompanying analysis. You should then be ready to create your own planned ending for a given teaching situation.

1. Attempts to draw students' attention to a closing point in the lesson
2. Reviews major points of teacher-centered presentation
3. Reviews sequence used in learning material during the presentation
4. Provides a summary of important student-oriented discussion
5. Relates lesson to original organizing principle or concept

6. Attempts to lead students to extend or develop new knowledge from previously learned concepts
7. Allows students to practice what they have learned

Sample Lesson 1

The lesson is in geography, and the teacher has planned to introduce two basic concepts: (1) humans as the active shapers of their environment and (2) environment as a limiting context within which humans must live. The teacher has reached the critical point in the lesson when it is time to call students' attention to the fact that the presentation of the first concept is ready for closure.

> *Planned Ending:* "Before moving to the next important idea, the restrictions that environment places on humans, let's review the main points I've already covered on how humans can play a critical role in shaping the environment." The teacher then proceeds to review the major points of the presentation, using either a prepared outline or one developed on the chalkboard during the lesson.

Analysis. This type of planned ending is appropriate to use when you wish to help students organize their thinking around a new concept before moving on to a new idea. Referring to the list of uses for planned endings, note:

1. The teacher draws attention to the end of the lesson with a verbal cue—"Before moving to the next important idea . . ."
2. The teacher reviews important points made in the lesson.
3. The teacher helps organize student thinking around the first concept presented by using an outline on the chalkboard.

Sample Lesson 2

The lesson is in language arts, social studies, science, or some other subject, and the teacher is conducting a discussion around some specific issue that is important in the lesson plan for that particular day. The time has come to bring the discussion to a close.

> *Planned Ending:* The teacher calls on a specific student and says, "Jessica, would you please summarize what has been said thus far and point out what you felt were the major points covered?"

Analysis. This type of planned ending is appropriate to use when you wish to bring a classroom discussion to a close. Referring to the list of uses for planned endings, note:

1. The teacher draws attention to the fact that the time has come for a temporary end to discussion by requesting a student summary.
2. The teacher summarizes what students have been discussing.
3. The teacher helps students to organize or rearrange their own ideas by specifically asking students to list major points made in the discussion.

Sample Lesson 3

The lesson is on search techniques using the World Wide Web. The class has been given the homework assignment of recording the steps they used to gather specific information from the web on vitamins. After reading student responses to the assignment and sharing some of them, the teacher believes that the students have successfully learned the first steps in an effective computer search technique. She is ready to go on to new material and wishes to close.

> *Planned Ending:* "You did very well with your computer searches and turned up some interesting information. Now let's use these new

techniques to help you find answers to the questions you asked about nutrition to which our textbook had no answers."

Analysis. This type of planned ending is appropriate to use when following up on a homework assignment being reviewed in class before moving on to the application of newly learned techniques. Referring to the list of uses for planned endings, note:

1. The teacher draws attention to the close of the assignment with a comment of approval: "You did very well with your computer searches and turned up some interesting information."
2. The teacher reviews material covered in the assignment by having students extend their knowledge of what they have already learned to a new problem.

Sample Lesson 4

The lesson is in mathematics, and the teacher is presenting a general reading skills approach to problem solving: (1) preview, (2) identify details or relationships, (3) restate problem in one's own words, and (4) list computational steps to be taken. The time has come to see how well the students have understood the use of the new procedure.

> *Planned Ending:* "Before you try to use this new approach to problem solving by yourselves, let's list the steps on the chalkboard and try to apply them to the first problem in your textbooks on page 27. When you finish, I will ask some of you to share with the class your experience using this new technique."

Analysis. This type of planned ending is effective when you are ending a skill-building activity and wish to help students consolidate what they have learned. Referring to the list of uses for planned endings, note:

1. The teacher draws attention to the close of the presentation with a verbal signal, "Before you try to use this approach . . . let's list the steps . . ."
2. The teacher reviews the sequence used in learning new reading skills during the lesson.
3. The teacher permits students to practice immediately what they have learned.

LEARNING ACTIVITY 7.2

Once again you have reached the point in this chapter when it is time to observe in real classrooms where students are actually involved in learning. When you are ready to observe, make a copy of the Observation Worksheet that follows to gather your data. You will be able to compare the results of your observations with others in a subsequent class activity.

Observation Worksheet

Ending a Lesson

This observation activity gives you the opportunity to compare what you've learned about ending a lesson to what you actually see in classrooms.

Directions: Do not use actual names of schools, teachers, administrators, or students when using this worksheet.

Observer's Name: ______________________________

Date: ______________________________

Grade Level: ______________________________

Subject: ______________________________

Class Size: ______________________________

Background Information: Give a brief general description of the school's social, economic, and ethnic makeup.

____

____

What to Record: While observing teachers in action, pay attention to those times in the instructional process when the teacher is ending a lesson. Use the following format to record what the teacher says and does to bring the lesson to a close.

1. How are students made aware that the lesson is ending? ______________________________

____

____

2. In what ways are students helped to organize or consolidate what they have learned?

____

____

____

3. In what ways is student learning reinforced? ______________________________

____

____

Reflections on Your Observation:

1. In your judgment, was the lesson ending effective? Why or why not?

____

____

2. Think of at least one other way that the lesson could have been ended and describe that ending.

____

____

Mastery Test

OBJECTIVE 7 **To create original planned endings (closure) for use in a given learning situation**

Following these directions are five hypothetical learning situations. Read each one carefully and plan a closure of your own that you feel would work effectively in that particular situation. You may refer to the list of uses for closure on page 95–96 for help in generating ideas for your own closures.

Situation 1. You have just completed a presentation on the steps one takes in preparing a green salad.

Situation 2. You have just completed a demonstration of how to save a file to a disk.

Situation 3. You have reached a point in a class discussion at which it would be appropriate to close.

Situation 4. You had begun a lesson on the use of theme in literature by comparing it to the threads running through a colorful tapestry. Now it is time for closure.

Situation 5. You have presented an important concept in science to the class and have asked the students how the idea might be used in other situations.

NOTES

1. Thomas J. Shuell, "Teaching and Learning in a Classroom Context," in *Handbook of Educational Psychology,* ed. D. C. Berliner and R. C. Calfee (New York: Macmillan, 1996), p. 745.
2. Catherine Fosnot, *Constructivism: Theory, perspectives, and practice* (New York: Teachers College Press, 1996).
3. Interstate New Teacher Assessment and Support Consortium (INTASC), *Model Standards for Beginning Teacher Licensing and Development: A Resource for State Dialogue,* Draft. (Washington, D.C.: the Council of Chief State School Officers, 1992), p. 10.
4. Set induction as a lesson presentation skill was developed for use in teacher training by J. C. Fortune and V. B. Rosenshine for the School of Education, Stanford University, Stanford, Calif.
5. "Criteria for Effective Teaching Performance," *Effective School Report* (February 1991):6–7.
6. N. L. Gage and David C. Berliner, *Educational Psychology,* 6th ed. (Boston: Houghton Mifflin, 1998), p. 405.
7. Maria Montessori, *The Montessori Method* (New York: Schocken Books, 1964), p. 170.
8. Arno A. Bellack et al., *The Language of the Classroom* (New York: Teachers College Press, 1966), p. 134.
9. George W. Gagnon, Jr., and Michelle Collay, "Constructivist Learning Design." Paper available at www.prainbow.com/cld/cldp.html
10. C. T. Adger, M. Kalyanpur, D. B. Peterson, and T. L. Bridger, *Engaging Students: Thinking, Talking, Cooperating* (Thousand Oaks, Calif.: Corwin Press, 1995), p. 1.
11. INTASC, *op. cit.,* p. 15.
12. Barak Rosenshine and Carla Meister, "Reciprocal Teaching: A Review of Nineteen Experimental Studies" (Paper presented at the Annual Meeting of the American Educational Research Association, Chicago, April 1991).
13. Gagnon and Collay, *op. cit.*
14. INTASC, *op. cit.,* p. 17.
15. Robert M. Gagné, Leslie J. Briggs, and Walter W. Wager, *Principles of Instructional Design,* 4th ed. (Fort Worth: Harcourt Brace Jovanich College, 1992), p. 123.

ADDITIONAL RESOURCES

Readings

Clyde, J. A. and M. W. F. Condon. *Get Real: Bringing Kids' Learning Lives into the Classroom.* York, Maine: Stenhouse, 2000.

Finkel, Donald L. *Teaching with Your Mouth Shut.* Portsmouth, N.H.: Heinemann, Boynton/Cook, 2000.

Graves, Donald H. *Bringing Life into Learning: Create a Lasting Literacy.* Portsmouth, N.H.: Heinemann, 1999.

Kaufman, Douglas. *Conferences and Conversations: Listening to the Literate Classroom.* Portsmouth, N.H.: Heinemann, 2000.

Larson, C. L. and C. J. Ovando. *The Color of Bureaucracy: The Politics of Equality in Multicultural School Communities.* Belmont, Calif.: Wadsworth, 2001.

Web Sites

Blue Web'n: www.kn.pacbell.com/wired/bluewebn
Excellent searchable database of over 1,000 sites targeting only those educational sites most useful to online learners.

Digital Education Network: www.actden.com
Teachers, parents, and students can access tutorials and courses for classroom or home use. Interactive lessons provide students the opportunity to engage in the online learning experience.

The Future of Children: www.futureofchildren.org
This site provides teachers and parents with timely information related to children's total well-being through several publications and online resources.

5

Questioning Skills

Myra Sadker
David Sadker

OBJECTIVE 1 **To explain the seven characteristics of effective classroom questions**

OBJECTIVE 2 **To classify questions according to Bloom's *Taxonomy of Educational Objectives: Cognitive Domain***

OBJECTIVE 3 **To construct classroom questions on all six levels of Bloom's *Taxonomy of Educational Objectives: Cognitive Domain***

OBJECTIVE 4 **To write examples of questioning strategies that enhance the quality of student participation**

OBJECTIVE 5 **To describe how the growing diversity and multicultural nature of America's students impact questioning strategies**

The student teacher was composed. She quickly dispensed with the administrative details of classroom organization—attendance records and homework assignments. The classroom chatter about the Saturday night dance and the upcoming football game subsided as the tenth-grade students settled into their seats. The students liked this teacher, for she had the knack of mixing businesslike attention to academic content with a genuine interest in her students. As the principal of Madison High walked by her room, he paused to watch the students settle into a discussion about *Hamlet.* Classroom operation appeared to be running smoothly, and he made a mental note to offer Ms. Ames a contract when her eight weeks of student teaching were over. Had he stayed a little longer to hear the discussion, and had he been somewhat sophisticated in the quality of verbal interaction, he would not have been so satisfied.

Ms. Ames: I would like to discuss your reading assignment with you. As the scene begins, two clowns are on stage. What are they doing? Cheryl?
Cheryl: They are digging a grave.
Ms. Ames: Right. Who is about to be buried? Jim?
Jim: Ophelia.
Ms. Ames: Yes. One of the gravediggers uncovers the skull of Yorick. What occupation did Yorick once have? Donna?
Donna: He was the king's jester.
Ms. Ames: Good. A scuffle occurs by Ophelia's graveside. Who is fighting? Bill?
Bill: Laertes and Hamlet.
Ms. Ames: That's right. In what act and scene does Ophelia's burial occur? Tom?
Tom: Act V, Scene 1.

Throughout the fifty-minute English class, Ms. Ames asked a series of factual questions, received a series of one- and two-word replies—and Shakespeare's play was transformed into a bad caricature of a television quiz show.

It is extremely important that teachers avoid ineffective questioning patterns such as the one just described because the questioning process has always been crucial to classroom instruction. The crucial role that questions play in the educational process has been stated by a number of educators.

> To question well is to teach well. In the skillful use of the question more than anything else lies the fine art of teaching; for in it we have the guide to clear and vivid ideas, and the quick spur to imagination, the stimulus to thought, the incentive to action.[1]
>
> What's in a question, you ask? Everything. It is the way of evoking stimulating response or stultifying inquiry. It is, in essence, the very core of teaching.[2]
>
> The art of questioning is . . . the art of guiding learning.[3]

It was John Dewey who pointed out that thinking itself is questioning. Unfortunately, research indicates that most student teachers, as well as experienced teachers, do not use effective questioning techniques. Think back to your own days in elementary and secondary school. You probably read your text and your class notes, studied (or, more accurately, memorized), and then waited in class for the teacher to call on you with a quick question, usually requiring only a brief reply. It did not seem to matter much whether the subject was language arts or social studies or science; questions revealed whether or not you remembered the material. But questions need not be used only in this way, and the appropriate use of questions can create an effective and powerful learning environment. Consider the following description of Mark Van Doren's use of questions:

> Mark would come into the room, and, without any fuss, would start talking about whatever was to be talked about. Most of the time he asked questions. His questions were very good, and if you tried to answer them intelligently, you found yourself saying excellent things that you did not know you knew, and that you had not, in fact, known before. He had "educed" them from you by his questions. His classes were literally "education"—they brought things out of you, they made your mind produce its own explicit ideas. . . . What he did have was the gift of communicating to [students] something of his own vital interest in things, something of his manner of approach; but the results were sometimes quite unexpected—and by that I mean good in a way that he had not anticipated, casting lights that he had not himself foreseen.[4]

It is all too easy to describe Van Doren as a gifted teacher and to dismiss his technique of questioning as an art to which most teachers can never aspire. It is our strong belief that the teacher's effective use of questions is far too important to dismiss in this way. Unfortunately, research concerning the use of questions in the classroom suggests that most teachers do *not* use effective questioning techniques. If one were to review the research on questioning, the results would reveal both the importance of questioning in school and the need for teachers to improve their questioning technique.

OBJECTIVE 1

To explain the seven characteristics of effective classroom questions

LEARNING ACTIVITY 1

What Do We Know About Questioning?

If you are going to teach, you are not only going to ask questions, you are going to ask quite a lot of questions. Researchers have determined that during a career in the classroom, a typical teacher will ask about *one and a half million* questions. (They are still working on how many of those questions will be answered correctly.) Other educators estimate that teachers average between *30 and 120 questions an hour!* And this extraordinary reliance on questioning has not changed over time. Back in 1912, in one of the first major classroom studies, it was determined that about 80 percent of classroom discussions consisted of asking, answering, or reacting to questions. In fact, only lecturing is a more common teacher strategy. And once teachers develop their questioning pattern, this is likely to become a habit—with all its strengths and faults—for their entire career.[5]

Although teachers ask a large number of questions, they generally show little tolerance in waiting for student replies. Typically, only *one second* passes between the end of a question and the next verbal interaction! After the answer is given, only nine-tenths of a second passes before the teacher reacts to the answer. The tremendous number of questions asked and the brief amount of time provided before an answer is expected reinforce the finding that most questions do not require any substantive thought. Classroom questions simply call for the rapid recall of information.[6]

But asking a lot of questions is not the same as asking good questions. The great majority of questions that teachers ask are lower-order, memory questions. How many are lower order? While estimates vary, studies suggest that between 70 and 95 percent of all teacher questions are the kind of questions that do not require deep thinking. One of the problems is that without more higher-order, thought-provoking questions, learning becomes little more than memorization. Although the research on higher-order classroom questions is at times contradictory, there is a growing consensus that higher-order questions increase the level of student thinking and lead to an increase in student achievement.[7]

Studies also reveal that the quality and quantity of student answers increase when teachers provide students with time to think. If teachers can increase the one second of silence that usually follows a question to three seconds or more, student answers will reflect more thought and more students will actively participate in the classroom.[8]

Although learning is designed to help students receive answers for their questions, become independent citizens, and understand their world, little provision is made in schools for student questions.[9]

The significant number of research findings related to classroom questions indicates that questions play a crucial role in the classroom and that teachers need to improve their questioning strategies.[10] The activities in this chapter are designed to do just that, to increase your mastery of questioning skills.

The Seven Habits of Highly Effective Questioners

In his best-selling book *Seven Habits of Highly Effective People,*[11] Stephen Covey offers practical suggestions for personal improvement. Borrowing from the Covey approach, this chapter will translate the research findings in the previous section into seven strategies, habits if you prefer, that will improve your use of classroom questions:

1. Asking fewer questions
2. Differentiating questions
3. Questioning for depth
4. Questioning for breadth
5. Using wait time
6. Selecting students
7. Giving useful feedback

(Unlike Covey, we make no claim that this will enhance your personal life. Then again, it might).

1. Asking Fewer Questions

While it may seem contrary to the purposes of this chapter, it is possible to have too much of a good thing. Most teachers today ask too many questions. In fact, the typical teacher asks *hundreds of questions a day.* One way to improve teaching effectiveness becomes painfully obvious: ask fewer questions. While that may not sound particularly challenging, changing any habit, whether personal or professional, can be quite difficult. And teachers offer an impressive range of reasons to explain their seemingly endless string of questions. All of the following reasons have been given to explain the role of questions in the classroom. Any wonder why the classroom is heavy with questions?

- By asking questions, teachers reinforce their image as the authority figure, the person in charge, the "expert" who knows the right answers.
- Since lecturing can be seen as dogmatic, old-fashioned, and teacher-centered, perhaps questions are viewed as the opposite. If a lecturing teacher is autocratic, then it follows, as the night the day, that questioning teachers are democratic.
- The more questions teachers ask, the harder students work, and the more students learn.
- Questions help teachers stay on schedule so all critical topics are "covered."
- Questions keep the students "on their toes" and on-task, reducing or eliminating discipline problems.
- The students' role in class, their "job," is to study a subject and to answer questions. The teachers' role, their "job," is to ask questions.
- Questioning is the *only* tool some teachers have for getting students involved.

- When teachers were themselves young, their teachers asked lots of questions, and so they are simply "modeling" the teaching style they experienced as children.

2. *Differentiating Questions*

The sheer number of different, even contradictory, explanations for using questions might help to explain why the typical classroom is the scene of a questioning deluge, but this need not be the case. To reduce this torrent of questions, teachers need to **differentiate questions.** Although students in the same class may be the same chronological age, they differ in readiness, learning styles, interests, and personal backgrounds. As a teacher formulates questions, it is useful to consider individual student differences and craft quality questions based on each student's need. Teachers might ask themselves: How does this question build on this student's knowledge? Am I asking a question that is far too difficult—or far too simple—for this student's capabilities? Am I using an effective questioning technique for this particular student's learning style? What interests does this student have, and how can my questions build on those interests? Can my questions tie into this student's background and experiences?

Teachers who know both their students and their content area can effectively differentiate their questions and engage their students. For example, if you are an English teacher and you know a student is interested in women's rights, you might fashion a question that builds on this interest: "Would the plot in *Lord of the Flies* be different if girls rather than boys were stranded on the island?" Questions based on a student's interest can transform subjects from academic tasks to personal, exciting quests. Some teachers can take this one step further, formulating questions that connect not only with student interests but also with their personal experiences. These are called **authentic questions.**[12] Authentic questions respond to the unspoken student query: "What's this have to do with me? How does this issue relate to my life and experiences?" Authentic questions that would tie students into *Lord of the Flies* might include: "What island experiences have you had?" "Have you ever felt lost and frightened like the kids on the island?" "How do your peer conflicts compare with those in *Lord of the Flies*?" "How might your presence on the island affect this story?"

But matching questions to students' background is only part of the challenge; teachers also want their questions to push students slightly beyond where they are. One purpose of questions should be to help students grow and develop new skills and insights. Effective questions cause students to wrestle with new ideas, to call on what they have learned in the past in order to connect to what they have not yet learned. Too many of today's questions are mundane and routine, little more than drill and practice. Too few classroom questions actually challenge students. Challenging questions cause students to stretch, to risk, to grow . . . and sometimes to fail. Obviously, both teachers and classmates need to be part of a supportive community, one that respects the individual and encourages risk taking and experimentation. And the challenging questions that a teacher formulates must be within the student's grasp and not so challenging as to frustrate the student (and the teacher).[13]

3. *Questioning for Depth*

"When did Columbus come to America?" is the kind of teacher question familiar to most of us. Nothing particularly wrong with it, as far as it goes—but it doesn't go particularly far. It requires simple recall. However, questions should go beyond simple recall and *deepen a student's understanding* of a topic. A related but more demanding question could be, "How might the United States be different if Columbus had arrived a century earlier—or a century later?" Here are some additional examples of more powerful higher-order questions, questions that give meaning and substance to our learning:

Create a fictional conversation that might have occurred if Abraham Lincoln met Malcolm X.

Analyze Margaret Sanger's impact on the women's rights movement.

Contrast Picasso with Mondrian.

While the questions described above promote a deeper understanding of content, **delving** or **probing questions** focus less on the subject and more on individual students. In order *really* to understand how much a student knows, or doesn't know, we may need to go beyond the student's first response and dig deeper. We call these follow-up questions *delving* and *probing*. Examples of probing or delving questions include:

What are your reasons for selecting that answer?

What characteristics of this candidate did you find most appealing?

Could you give us an example of that?

Probing puts the teacher on the frontier of a student's knowledge. On one side of the frontier is what a student knows, manifested by a correct answer. On the other side is what the student does not know or does not really understand, manifested by the wrong answer or no answer at all. In educational literature, this gap between what a student *does* know and what a student is *capable* of learning, but does not yet know, is called the "zone of proximal development."[14] Effective probing is one teaching tool to move students through this zone. By providing students with new insights, probing questions can bridge the gap between what students know and what they have yet to learn. However, one or two probing questions may not always be enough: sometimes the probe uncovers serious gaps in the student's knowledge that need more teaching and development than just several more probing questions. Teachers need to be skilled in helping children to bridge both small and large gaps in their learning.

When students are unable to answer a question, teachers can also use questions to help them, to *cue* them to the right answer. In a sense, cuing is the opposite of probing and delving. In probing, for example, questions are used to explore the thinking behind the student's original answer. In cuing, we are using questions to help a student get to the right answer. By offering more information, or hints, cuing questions put the student on the road to success. Here is an example:

We are looking for the name Europeans gave to New York City before the British took control. If you remember which European nation settled New York before the English, that will help you to recall that name.

Sometimes a simple cue is not enough, and a more intricate strategy is called for, a strategy educators call **scaffolding.** "Scaffolding" conjures up the image of a building under construction. A new building is barely visible at the beginning of the construction cycle, hidden behind supporting beams and platforms, a temporary support called the scaffold. But the scaffold is critical, because it gives workers the ability to slowly construct the new building from the bottom up, assisting but not obstructing others. They surround the new structure, adding to it slowly to ensure that it is solid. As the edifice takes shape, the scaffolding is reduced, and as the building nears completion, the scaffolding is finally removed. So much for buildings, but what about students?

Educators have borrowed this scaffolding imagery to describe the teacher's role in "building" a student's competencies. Educational scaffolding is substantial at the beginning of "the construction," as the teacher carefully diagnoses a student's competencies and determines where new knowledge will need to be built. Once the scaffold is planned, the teacher begins to build the student's knowledge through carefully crafted questions, well-phrased explanations, and thoughtfully designed student activities. Most of the skills described in this chapter will help teachers scaffold. As the student internalizes information, the teacher's scaffolding can be reduced. Once the student becomes fully competent, the scaffolding is removed.[15]

4. Questioning for Breadth

All questions and answers fall into one of two categories: no, we are not talking about "right and wrong" but rather *convergent* and *divergent.* A convergent question, also called a *closed* question, generates a single answer that is clearly right or wrong—for instance, "Who wrote this poem?" Many convergent questions are lower order and require little more than memory. But not all. A convergent question could also require higher-order thinking. For example, a complex math or science equation may have one single answer, but getting to that convergent answer could be quite challenging.

As you might have suspected by now, unlike convergent questions, divergent questions always have more than one correct answer and are usually higher order. Divergent questions are also called *open* questions—for instance, "What does this poem mean to you?" or "How would your life be different without the invention of the computer?" Teachers use divergent questions when they want to generate different ideas, infuse breadth into the classroom, and provide students with a creative springboard.

Howard Gardner's work on **multiple intelligences** has dramatically increased our ability to question for breadth.[16] Gardner believes that a serious problem with today's schools is their limited focus on only two types of intelligence, linguistic and mathematical-logical:

1. *Linguistic:* speaking, poetic, and journalistic abilities; sensitivity to the meanings and the rhythm of words and to the function of language
2. *Mathematical-logical:* scientific and mathematical abilities, skills related to mathematical manipulations, and discerning and solving logical challenges

According to Gardner and others, much of school life, including standardized tests such as the SATs, emphasizes these two types of intelligence almost exclusively while ignoring others. What are the other areas of intelligence? Here are some suggested by Gardner:

3. *Bodily-kinesthetic:* physical skills related to controlling one's body movements and to handling objects skillfully, such as athletic and dancing abilities
4. *Musical:* vocal, compositional, and instrumental abilities and the ability to produce and appreciate rhythm, pitch, and timbre; appreciation of music
5. *Spatial:* abilities to perceive the physical world accurately, such as those of a sculptor, navigator, or architect
6. *Interpersonal:* the ability to analyze and respond to the moods, temperaments, desires, and needs of others, such as that shown by a salesperson, teacher, or psychologist
7. *Intrapersonal:* knowledge of one's own needs, strengths, and weaknesses and the ability to use this information to guide behavior; useful within and beyond most careers
8. *Naturalist:* ability to live wisely and respect the world's resources; associated with careers in conservation and related fields

Gardner does not view these as a definitive inventory of intelligences, for he believes that many more intelligences will be recognized in the years ahead. But his vision is instructive and useful today because his work suggests that *all* these areas of intelligence should be represented in classroom questions. Can you think of other areas of intelligence that Gardner has not yet identified?

With some planning and practice, we can move beyond questions that are limited to the traditional linguistic or logical-mathematical areas to questions such as:

Can you express what you are feeling through movement?

Can you create a physical model of your plan?

What are your personal strengths in this area?

How can you influence your classmates on that issue?

5. Using Wait Time

In the typical classroom, the teacher waits less than a second after asking a question before calling on a student to respond. For those students who need more than a fraction of a second to formulate their answer, class participation becomes a real challenge. Not only do fewer students participate, but the quality of their responses is lowered. Less than a second is not a great deal of time to consider what to say, much less how to say it. Teachers are also victims of this brief **wait time.** With little time to think about which student to call on, teachers tend to call on the "fastest hand in the class."

There is a second wait time, less well known but just as important, that occurs directly after a student response. This is sometimes referred to as wait time 2, and, like wait time 1, it is also less than a second in length. The brevity of wait time 2 can typically be seen in the frequent teacher interruptions of student answers, often with little more than a quick "uh-huh," "okay," or "I see." Students have little time to complete or extend their answers or their thoughts. As a result of their quick retorts and the pressure to keep moving, teachers also short-circuit themselves. After hearing the student's answer, teachers have little time to consider the student's response or to formulate their own reaction. As a result, teachers frequently react to student answers with a bland, imprecise, and ineffective comment. While less has been written about this incredibly brief second wait time, it also short-circuits effective teaching and learning.

6. Selecting Students

As you probably recall from your own elementary or secondary school days, it is not unusual for a few students to monopolize classroom interaction, while the rest of the class looks on. The fast pace of classroom exchanges leads many teachers to call on the first hand that is raised. Even a fraction of a second is too long for some students to wait. Very active and animated students can sometimes eliminate even the teacher from the decision-making role by simply shouting out the answer.

But even when the teacher maintains control and selects which students to call on, there is a tendency to call on students who want to be called on. As Ted Sizer wrote in *Horace's Compromise,* this is a very comfortable situation for all concerned. Students who want to talk get to talk. Students who want to stay silent, stay silent. The teacher's lesson moves along at a good pace, and the main points are all covered. Everybody is having their needs met; everybody is happy. So what's the problem? There are several problems, including the fact that the purpose of school is not to eliminate all anxieties and make everyone happy (although that *sounds* awfully good!). The purpose of schools, and teachers, and questions is to educate. When the teacher selects only students who quickly volunteer, many students are left out. Reticent students often find themselves on the sidelines, unable and unwilling to participate. Females also

Tricks and traps: Ways *not* to use questions

Unfortunately, not all questions are wondrous, and teachers have been known to use questions inappropriately. Here are some examples of *ineffective* and *inappropriate* uses of questions. We will explain enough about these misapplications to tell you what to avoid. But we will stop there. (After all, we don't want to invest too much time in teaching you "malquestioning" strategies.)

- *To "control" misbehavior:* Some teachers use questions to prevent or stop misbehavior, a sort of "I see you; here's a question; can't answer it?—well, stop misbehaving and *listen!*" Rather than reducing student distractions, this "question as punishment" approach actually serves to reward misbehaving students with extra instructional attention. The problem is compounded because students who are acting appropriately are being ignored. Questions should be used to teach everyone in the class—not used to manage a few. (We might add that teachers who use effective questioning strategies that keep all students on-task *reduce* the likelihood that management problems will emerge.)
- *To help "needy" students:* Some teachers see questions as an opportunity to "help" weaker students. When asked easy questions or given really obvious "hints," a weak student miraculously comes up with the right answer. This is a patronizing strategy, and in most instances this charade is obvious to both children and adults. Patronizing weak students is a poor reason for asking questions.
- *To "put down" a student:* The converse of the above occurs when teachers use questions as a tool of humiliation, a way to put down a difficult student with a really tough question, a zinger few could answer. Or if the student somehow manages to answer the question, the teacher might respond with a sarcastic comment. Questions should not be used as weapons.
- *To "manipulate" answers:* Teachers have been known to take great liberties in restating student answers in order to move the lesson along a predetermined path. As a result, it is the teacher's idea rather than the student's that is heard. Such dramatic paraphrasing devalues students and should not be used as a tool for manipulating class discussions.
- *To offer the infamous "yes, but" teacher response:* Some teachers, caught between the desire to accept a student's answer and the urge to correct or disagree with that answer, fall into the trap of revealing their conflict with a "yes, but" reaction. Such teacher comments tend to discredit student contributions.
- *To promote student "involvement":* An easy way to get a number of students responding to a topic in class is to shower the students with questions. While *Jeopardy* may be a popular show on television, "Classroom Jeopardy" is often overused. The teacher who regularly asks a torrent of nonstop questions in an attempt to involve a large number of students is far from creating an ideal learning environment.

receive less of an opportunity to get into the dialogue and are more likely to be interrupted when they do participate. Children of color become second-class citizens, receiving fewer opportunities to hear their voices or ideas in a public setting. Students who need a little more time to think—because they are by nature thoughtful, or because English is a new language, or because their cultural background encourages a slower response—also become spectators to rapid classroom exchanges. When teachers allow their classroom dialogue to be dominated by a few animated students, they are abandoning one of their key educational responsibilities: the responsibility to include *all* their students in active learning.

7. Giving Useful Feedback

While educators label questions as either *higher* or *lower order,* they do not apply such labels to the reactions teachers give to student answers. If we were to label these reactions, most teacher reactions would be rated as lower order. Teacher reactions are generally imprecise and offered without the careful thought that might help student learning. Imprecise teacher feedback means that students rarely are offered a powerful reward when they have given a superb answer. When they do poorly, they are often not told what they did wrong or how best to improve their performance. Teacher feedback generally lacks specificity, with "fine" and "okay" capturing the tone of the typical feedback.

Unfortunately, figuring out the reasons for the poor quality of these reactions is not surprising: simply look at what has already been described about questions. Since most questions involve only simple memory, terrific teacher reactions are hardly merited. When hundreds of questions flood the airwaves, teachers have a difficult time focusing on their reactions—or focusing at all. The incredibly short wait time afforded by teachers short-circuits their ability to thoughtfully consider what students have said, much less what their reactions should be. All these factors contribute to an environment that neither requires nor encourages quality teacher reactions. The result is a less than enriching educational experience for students.

Practicing these seven "habits" will be helpful in creating classrooms marked by meaningful learning and by the active participation of all students. The following Your Turn gives you the opportunity to review these seven characteristics of effective questioning.

YOUR TURN

Characteristics of Effective Questions

For items 1–5, mark *T* for true and *F* for false statements.

______ 1. Typically, teachers wait three to five seconds after asking a question before calling on a student.

______ 2. Most classroom questions can be categorized as *lower order,* requiring little thought to answer.

______ 3. It is not unusual for teachers to ask several questions a minute and hundreds of questions every day.

______ 4. Teachers wait less than a second after a student answers a question before they offer their feedback.

______ 5. Teacher feedback to student answers could accurately be described as precise, honest, and helpful.

6. Briefly describe at least three purposes for asking questions in class, as well as one inappropriate reason for using a questioning strategy in the classroom.

Mastery Test

OBJECTIVE 1 **To explain the seven characteristics of effective classroom questions**

The principal of your school has just developed a new approach to staff development. She has decided that new teachers, like yourself, should be responsible for some aspects of professional development. She sees it as a way to keep her faculty up-to-date with current thinking at the university, as well as offering leadership opportunities to junior faculty members. You really liked the idea—until she asked *you* to participate. You have been asked to prepare a ten-minute presentation on the effective uses of classroom questions. Luckily, you have just read the first part of this chapter, so you feel extremely qualified. Outline the main points of your talk. Be sure to include all seven habits of effective questioners, and, whenever possible, offer an example or illustration to help explain your point.

OBJECTIVE 2

To classify questions according to Bloom's *Taxonomy of Educational Objectives: Cognitive Domain*

LEARNING ACTIVITY 2

As the research in the introductory section reveals, questioning plays an important role in the classroom. Ever since Socrates, teaching and questioning have been viewed as integrally related activities. To be an effective teacher, one must be an effective questioner. The first step in effective questioning is to recognize that questions have distinct characteristics, serve various functions, and create different levels of thinking. Some questions require only factual recall; others cause students to go beyond memory and to use other thought processes in forming an answer. Both kinds of questions are useful, but the heavy reliance teachers place on the factual type of question does not provide the most effective learning environment. Learning the different kinds of questions and the different functions they serve is a crucial step in being able to use all types of questions effectively.

There are many terms and classifications for describing the different kinds of questions. Most of these classification systems are useful because they provide a conceptual framework, a way of looking at questions. We have selected only one system, however, to simplify the process and eliminate repetitive terms. Bloom's ***Taxonomy***[17] is probably the best-known system for classifying educational objectives as well as classroom questions. There are six levels of Bloom's *Taxonomy*, and questions at each level require the person responding to use a different kind of thought process. Teachers should be able to formulate questions on each of these six levels to encourage their students to engage in a variety of cognitive processes. Before teachers are able to formulate questions on each of these levels, they must first understand the definitions of the six categories and be able to recognize questions written on each. The six levels are:

1. Knowledge
2. Comprehension

3. Application
4. Analysis
5. Synthesis
6. Evaluation

The following definitions, examples, and exercises are designed to help you recognize and classify questions on the six cognitive levels of Bloom's *Taxonomy.* (By the way, *taxonomy* is another word for *classification.*)

Level 1. Knowledge

The first level of the *Taxonomy,* knowledge, requires the student to recognize or recall information. The student is not asked to manipulate information, but merely to remember it just as it was learned. To answer a question on the knowledge level, the student must simply remember facts, observations, and definitions that have been learned previously.

Examples of Knowledge Questions

What is the capital of Maine?

What color did the solution become when we added the second chemical?

Who is the secretary of state?

Who wrote *Hamlet?*

It has become fashionable to scoff at questions that ask the student to rely only on memory. For example, a common complaint about some college exams is that they ask students to "spit back" the information they have memorized from their text and class notes. Memorization of material, however, is important for several reasons. The knowledge, or memory, category is critical to all other levels of thinking. We cannot ask students to think at higher levels if they lack fundamental information. Some memorization of information is also required to perform a variety of tasks in our society, ranging from being an effective citizen to being a good parent. Our society expects that many things be memorized. Further, use of **knowledge questions** promotes classroom participation and high success experiences for students. Students from lower socioeconomic backgrounds achieve more in classrooms characterized by a high frequency of knowledge questions. Studies show that effective teachers provide both low-ability and high-ability students with high success opportunities and that, in these successful classrooms, students are responding correctly at least 70 to 80 percent of the time.[18] The use of knowledge questions plays a key role in establishing this high success rate.

Although important, the knowledge category does have severe drawbacks, the main one being that teachers tend to overuse it. Most questions that teachers ask both in class discussions and on tests would be classified in the knowledge category. Another drawback to questions on this level is that much of what is memorized is rapidly forgotten. And a third drawback to memory questions is that they assess only a superficial and shallow understanding of an area. Parroting someone else's thoughts does not, in itself, demonstrate any real understanding. Some words frequently found in knowledge questions are listed in the following box.

Words often found in knowledge questions

define	who	list	name
recall	what	identify	reproduce
recognize	where	recite	
remember	when	review	

YOUR TURN

Knowledge

The following questions will test your understanding of knowledge-level questions and your ability to classify questions at the knowledge level of Bloom's *Taxonomy* correctly. Your answers will also provide you with a useful study guide when preparing for the Mastery Test.
In items 1–5, mark a *T* for true and an *F* for false statements.

_____ 1. The first level of Bloom's *Taxonomy* requires higher-order thinking.

_____ 2. Most classroom and test questions that teachers ask are memory questions.

_____ 3. A drawback to knowledge, or memory, questions is that they are unimportant.

_____ 4. Knowledge, or memory, questions are important because they are necessary steps on the way to more complex, higher-order questions.

_____ 5. All the questions asked so far in this activity (items 1–4) are on the first level of the *Taxonomy*—knowledge and memory.

Mark a *K* in the space in front of those questions that are at the knowledge level and a "–" for those that are not.

_____ 6. Who discovered a cure for yellow fever?

_____ 7. Can you analyze the causes of the Gulf War?

_____ 8. Where does the United States get most of its tin from?

_____ 9. What does this music mean to you?

_____ 10. Define *antediluvian.* (The class has previously been given the definition of this word.)

_____ 11. Can you think of a title for this painting?

_____ 12. What do you think might happen to teachers if a recession were to continue over several years?

Check your answers with the answers and comments included in the Answer Key. If you answered all correctly—terrific! One wrong is pretty good also. Two wrong suggests that you should check each answer and perhaps reread the section. If you got three or more wrong, reread the section, underlining key points as you read, before you proceed to the next level.

Level 2. Comprehension

Questions on the second level, comprehension, require the student to demonstrate sufficient understanding to organize and arrange material mentally. The student must select those facts that are pertinent to answering the question. To answer a comprehension-level question, the student must go beyond recall of information. The student must demonstrate a personal grasp of the material by being able to rephrase it, give a description in his or her own words, and use it in making comparisons.

For example, suppose a teacher asks, "What is the famous quote of Hamlet's that we memorized yesterday, the quotation in which he puzzles over the meaning and worth of existence?" By asking students to recall information, in this case a quotation, the teacher is asking a question on the knowledge level.

If the teacher had asked instead, "What do you think Hamlet means when he asks, 'To be or not to be: that is the question'?," the teacher's question would have been on the comprehension level. With the second question, the student is required to rephrase information in his or her own words.

Frequently, **comprehension questions** ask students to interpret and translate material that is presented in charts, graphs, tables, and cartoons. For example, the following are comprehension questions.

Examples of Comprehension Questions

What is the main idea that this chart presents?

Describe in your own words what Herblock is saying in this cartoon.

This use of the comprehension question requires the student to translate ideas from one medium to another.

It is important to remember that *the information necessary to answer comprehension questions should have been provided to the student.* For example, if a student has previously read or listened to material that discusses the causes of the Revolutionary War and then is asked to explain these causes in his or her own words, the student is being asked a comprehension question. If the student has *not* been given material explaining the causes of the Revolutionary War and is asked to explain why the war started, he or she is *not* being asked a comprehension question, but, rather, a question on a different level of the *Taxonomy.*

Words often found in comprehension questions	
describe	rephrase
compare	put in your own words
contrast	explain the main idea

YOUR TURN

Comprehension

In items 1–4, mark a *T* for true and an *F* for false statements.

______ 1. A comprehension question may require the student to use new information not previously provided.

______ 2. Comprehension questions may require students to rephrase information.

______ 3. It is possible to remember a definition without being able to put the definition in your own words.

______ 4. A comprehension question asks students to recall information exactly as they have learned it.

Some of the following questions are at the knowledge level and others are at the comprehension level. Write a *C* next to those questions on the comprehension level and a *K* next to those questions on the knowledge level.

______ 5. When did the Berlin Wall come down?

______ 6. Use a Venn diagram to compare whales and sharks.

______ 7. What is the meaning of this cartoon?

______ 8. Who is the author of *The Color Purple?*

______ 9. Describe what we saw on our visit to the planetarium.

______ 10. Explain in your own words what the speaker suggests are the main reasons for the "Internet explosion."

Check your answers with those in the Answer Key. If you missed two or more, you should reread the description of comprehension questions and take notes. As you perhaps have already discovered, taking notes in your own words will ensure that you are comprehending the comprehension level.

Level 3. Application

It is not enough for students to be able to memorize information, or even to rephrase and interpret what they have memorized. Students must also be able to apply information. A question that asks a student to apply previously learned information to reach an answer to a problem is at the application level of the *Taxonomy.*

Application questions require students to apply a rule or process to a problem and thereby to determine the single right answer to that problem. In mathematics, application questions are quite common. For example,

$$\text{If } x = 2 \text{ and } y = 5$$
$$\text{then } x^2 + 2y = ?$$

But application questions are important in other subjects as well. For example, in social studies, a teacher can provide the definitions of *latitude* and *longitude,* and ask the student to repeat these definitions (knowledge). The teacher can then ask the student to compare the definitions of *latitude* and *longitude* (comprehension). At the application level, the teacher would ask the student to locate a point on a map by applying the definitions of *latitude* and *longitude.*

To ask a question at the application level in language arts, the following procedure might be used. After providing students with the definition of a *haiku* (a type of poem), a teacher would hand out a sheet with several different types of poems, then ask the students to select the poem that is a haiku, that is, the one that fits the definition of a haiku poem. To do this, the students must apply the definition to the various poems and select the poem that fits the definition.

In all the examples given, the student must apply knowledge to determine the single correct answer. Here are some other examples of questions at the application level.

Examples of Application Questions

In each of the following cases, which of Newton's laws is being demonstrated?

According to our definition of *socialism,* which of the following nations would be considered socialist today?

Write an example of the sexual harassment policy we have just discussed.

If Brian works three hours to wash the car and it takes Alicia only two, how many hours would it take them to wash the car together?

What is the rule that is appropriate in Case Study 2?

Words often found in application questions

apply	write an example	show	demonstrate
classify	solve	translate	diagram/map
use	how many	make	record/chart
choose	which	illustrate	
employ	what is	teach	

YOUR TURN

Application

Indicate the level of the *Taxonomy* that each of the following questions represents. Use a *K* for those at the knowledge level, *C* for those at the comprehension level, and *Ap* for those at the application level.

_____ 1. What does *freedom of speech* mean to you?

_____ 2. Using the Internet, locate this university's web page.

_____ 3. Who is the author of *The Joy Luck Club*?

_____ 4. If these figures are correct, will the company make a profit or suffer a loss?

_____ 5. Categorize the plants according to the classification system we reviewed.

_____ 6. Having read about runners and swimmers, clarify the similarities shared by these athletes.

Check your answers with those provided in the Answer Key. If you missed two or more, reread this section and answer the additional questions. If you would like extra practice, the additional questions will provide you with that opportunity. When you feel ready, go on to the next level of the *Taxonomy.* At this point, you're halfway through with this learning activity.

Additional Questions

_____ 7. Solve this problem by using the procedure we enumerated in our discussion of conflict resolution.

_____ 8. Rephrase the definition of *CPR.*

_____ 9. Restate the three safety steps we have learned that should be followed on a mountain hike.

_____ 10. According to our definition of a mammal, which of the five animals in the photo would be considered a mammal?

Check your answers in the Answer Key. If you still need help, you may want to check with your instructor, with some other students who are getting the exercises correct, or the Additional Resources at the end of the chapter. If you understand the application level, move on to the analysis level.

Level 4. Analysis

Analysis questions are a higher order of questions that require students to think critically and in depth. Analysis questions ask students to identify reasons, uncover evidence, and reach conclusions.

Following are examples of three kinds of analysis questions.

1. To identify the motives, reasons, and/or causes for a specific occurrence

   What factors influenced the writings of Anne Frank?
   Why did the congresswoman decide not to run for the presidency?
   How do your personal finances respond to economic upswings and downturns?

   In all these questions, students are asked to discover the causes or reasons for certain events through analysis.

2. To consider and analyze available information to reach a conclusion, inference, or generalization based on this information

After reading this story, how would you characterize the author's background, attitude, and point of view?
Look at this new invention. What do you think the purpose of this invention is?
After studying about major developments in South Africa and China, what can you now conclude about the various causes of revolutionary change?

This type of analysis question calls on the learner to reach a conclusion, inference, or generalization based on evidence.

3. To analyze a conclusion, inference, or generalization to find evidence to support or refute it

Which of the speaker's points support affirmative action?
How did the role-play promote cultural understanding?
What evidence can you cite to validate that smoking cigarettes is more harmful than drinking alcohol?

These questions require students to analyze information to support a particular conclusion, inference, or generalization.

If you tried to answer any of these questions, you probably realized that several answers are possible. Because it takes time to think and analyze, these questions cannot be answered quickly or without careful thought. The fact that several answers are possible and that sufficient time is needed to answer them is an indication that analysis questions are higher-order ones. A student cannot answer an analysis question by repeating information or by reorganizing material to put it into his or her own words or by applying a rule. Analysis questions not only help students learn what happened but also help them search for the reasons behind what happened.

Words frequently found in analysis questions		
identify motives or causes	why	categorize/dissect
draw conclusions	compare/contrast	deduce
determine evidence	order/sequence	investigate
support	summarize	justify
analyze		

YOUR TURN

Analysis

_____ 1. Analysis questions call for higher-order thinking. (true or false)

_____ 2. Which of the following processes is *not* required by analysis questions? (a) identifying evidence to support a statement, (b) making a statement based on evidence, (c) explaining motives or causes, (d) making evaluations

_____ 3. "Why" questions are often on the analysis level. (true or false)

_____ 4. Analysis questions require students only to rephrase information, to state it in their own words. (true or false)

_____ 5. Analysis questions require students to use or locate evidence in formulating their answers. (true or false)

Identify the levels of the following questions (*K* = knowledge, *C* = comprehension, *Ap* = application, *An* = analysis).

______ 6. Why didn't Hamlet act when he first learned of the treachery? (The reasons have not been discussed in the text or class.)

______ 7. What was Hamlet's position or title in Denmark?

______ 8. In your own words, how did we characterize Hamlet in yesterday's discussion?

______ 9. What evidence can you now propose to support the statement that Hamlet was a coward?

______ 10. According to our definition of *moral dilemma,* when did Hamlet confront a moral dilemma?

Check your answers with the Answer Key. Two or more wrong answers suggest you should review this section. Consider working out loud with a peer to help you analyze your thinking. If you made fewer than two errors, go directly to the fifth level of the *Taxonomy,* synthesis.

Level 5. Synthesis

Synthesis questions are higher-order questions that ask students to perform original and creative thinking. These kinds of questions require students to produce original communications, to make predictions, or to solve problems. Although application questions also require students to solve problems, synthesis questions differ because they do not require a single correct answer but, instead, allow a variety of creative answers. Here are some examples of the different kinds of synthesis questions.

1. To produce original communications

   Construct a collage of pictures that represents your values and feelings.
   What would be a descriptive and exciting name for this video game?
   Write an e-mail to a local newspaper editor on a social issue of concern to you.

2. To make predictions

   What would the United States be like if the South had won the Civil War?
   How would your life be different if school were not mandatory?
   After studying about forestry on the West Coast, what do you suspect is happening in the South American rain forests?

3. To solve problems

   How would you measure the height of a building without being able to go into it?
   How can we successfully raise money to fund our homeless shelter project?
   Design a musical instrument (with materials found in our lab) that effectively demonstrates three principles of physics.

Teachers can use synthesis questions to help develop the creative abilities of students. Unfortunately, as in the case of analysis questions, teachers too often avoid synthesis questions in favor of lower-order questions, particularly knowledge questions. Synthesis questions rely on a thorough understanding of material. Students should not make wild guesses to answer synthesis questions. For example, one synthesis question that we suggested, "What would the United States be like if the South had won the Civil War?," requires the student to have a firm grasp of information before being able to offer a sound prediction. To review, synthesis questions require predictions, original communications, or problem solving in which a number of answers are possible.

Words often found in synthesis questions		
predict	construct	create
produce	how can we improve . . . ?	imagine
write	what would happen if . . . ?	hypothesize
design	can you devise . . . ?	combine
develop	how can we solve . . . ?	estimate
synthesize		invent

YOUR TURN

Synthesis

In items 1–10, identify the level of the question by using the code provided (*K* = knowledge, *C* = comprehension, *Ap* = application, *An* = analysis, and *S* = synthesis).

______ 1. What is the state capital?

______ 2. Where is it located?

______ 3. Point it out on the map.

______ 4. If you could decide on a location for a new state capital, what location would you choose?

______ 5. Why?

______ 6. What would happen if we had two state capitals?

______ 7. Draw a simple blueprint of your ideal state capital.

______ 8. Quote what your textbook says about the primary function of a state capital.

______ 9. Describe this primary function.

______ 10. Given the categories of different kinds of state capitals, how would you classify the capital of Maine?

______ 11. Synthesis questions require students to do all the following *except*
(a) Make predictions
(b) Solve problems
(c) Rely primarily on memory
(d) Construct original communication

______ 12. Synthesis questions require original and creative thought from students. (true or false)

The Answer Key will provide you with feedback on your progress in this section. If you missed more than two, review the box of words often found in synthesis questions to correct your errors. If you made two or fewer errors, go directly to the final level of the *Taxonomy,* evaluation.

Level 6. Evaluation

The last level of the *Taxonomy* is evaluation. Evaluation, like synthesis and analysis, is a higher-order mental process. **Evaluation questions** do not necessarily have a single correct answer. They require the student to judge the merit of an idea, a solution to a problem, or an aesthetic work. They may also ask the student to offer an opinion on an issue. Following are some examples of different kinds of evaluation questions.

Examples of Evaluation Questions

Decide why young children should or should not be allowed to read any book they want.

How do you assess your performance at school?

Give three reasons that support why this picture is your best.

Taking the role of cultural critic for your local public radio station, offer reviews of three current movies.

Defend your choice as to whether or not busing is an appropriate remedy for desegregating schools.

Which U.S. senator is the most effective and why?

To express your opinion on an issue or to make a judgment on the merit of an idea, solution, or aesthetic work, you must use some criteria. You must use either objective standards or a personal set of values to make an evaluation. For example, if you answer the last question in the list of examples using a personal set of values, you might decide that the senator whose voting record is most congruent with your own political philosophy is the most effective senator. If you are strongly against defense spending or strongly in favor of civil rights legislation, these personal values would be reflected in your evaluation of the most effective senator.

Another way of evaluating senators would be through the use of objective criteria. Such criteria might include attendance records, campaign-financing practices, influence on other senators, number of sponsored bills that became law, and so forth. By comparing each senator to these criteria, a judgment can be made in relation to "the most effective senator."

Of course, many individuals use a combination of objective criteria and personal values when making an evaluation. The important thing to remember about evaluation questions is that they are not casual, careless, or offhand judgments: some standard must be used and different answers are possible.

Words often used in evaluation questions

judge	give your opinion	verify
argue	which is the better picture, solution, etc.	rate
decide		select
evaluate	do you agree	recommend
assess	would it be better	conclude

Observation Worksheet

Focus on Higher Order Questions

Given the rapid pace of classroom dialogue, capturing the level of a teacher's question can be quite challenging. Here is an approach that will help you analyze the teacher's use (or nonuse) of higher-order questions.

Directions: Do not use actual names of schools, teachers, administrators, or students when using this worksheet.

Observer's Name: ______________________________

Date: ______________________________

Grade Level: ______________________________

Subject: ______________________________

Class Size: ______________________________

Background Information: Give a brief general description of the school's social, economic, and ethnic makeup.

____

____

What to Record: Write down each question asked in class for later analysis. After the observation, assess each question in terms of Bloom's *Taxonomy* to determine which of the six cognitive levels most appropriately describes the cognitive demand of each question. Some questions may be related to class procedures or other nonacademic areas, so you may want to create a seventh category called "Other" for these noninstructional questions.

Reflections on Your Observation:

1. How are the teacher's questions distributed across Bloom's *Taxonomy?* ______________________________

____

____

2. Are some levels underutilized or not used at all? Are some categories overused?

____

____

____

3. Although no one has defined an "ideal" distribution, as a result of this observation, what are some factors that you think are important in using the different levels of the *Taxonomy?*

____

____

____

YOUR TURN

Evaluation

Using all levels of the *Taxonomy,* classify the following questions (*K* = knowledge, *C* = comprehension, *Ap* = application, *An* = analysis, *S* = synthesis, and *E* = evaluation).

______ 1. Who was the founder of the school of abstract art?

______ 2. Describe the first attempts of the pioneers of abstract art.

______ 3. Paint your own abstract piece.

______ 4. What is your opinion of abstract art?

______ 5. Which native crafts are most like these abstract oils?

______ 6. Why have women been a central image of abstract art?

______ 7. Which artist do you prefer, Miro or Picasso?

At this point, we have reviewed all levels of the *Taxonomy,* and you should know whether or not you are ready for the Mastery Test. In the Mastery Test, you will be asked to identify the levels of a number of questions; all six levels of the *Taxonomy* will be represented.

Mastery Test

OBJECTIVE 2 **To classify questions according to Bloom's *Taxonomy of Educational Objectives: Cognitive Domain***

Read the paragraph below and then classify the following questions according to their appropriate level on Bloom's *Taxonomy* (*K* = knowledge, *C* = comprehension, *Ap* = application, *An* = analysis, *S* = synthesis, and *E* = evaluation).

To pass the Mastery Test, you should classify eleven of the thirteen questions accurately. Good luck!

> School reading texts were also studied. It was found that the major reading series used in almost all public and private schools across the country teach that being a girl means being inferior. In these texts, boys are portrayed as being able to do so many things: they play with bats and balls, they work with chemistry sets, they do magic tricks that amaze their sisters, and they show initiative and independence as they go on trips by themselves and get part-time jobs. Girls do things too: they help with the housework, bake cookies and sit and watch their brothers—that is, assuming they are present. In 144 texts studied, there were 881 stories in which the main characters are boys and only 344 in which a girl is the central figure.
>
> —Nancy Frazier and Myra Sadker, *Sexism in School and Society* (New York: Harper & Row, 1973), pp. 103–104.

_____ 1. In your own words, compare the portrayal of males and females in school texts.

_____ 2. Assess how racist texts might be similar and different from the sexist materials described above.

_____ 3. What do boys do in the school reading texts that were studied?

_____ 4. What is the main idea of this paragraph?

_____ 5. Considering the category descriptions of sexist and nonsexist books that we have studied, how would you classify *Miracles on Maple Hill*?

_____ 6. What would your ideal nonsexist book be like?

_____ 7. What is your opinion on the issue of sexism in books?

_____ 8. If all books became gender neutral, gender balanced, or gender affirming during the next five years, what do you predict would be the effects on children?

_____ 9. Why do you think that girls and boys have been historically portrayed in such a stereotyped manner in school texts?

_____ 10. How many texts were analyzed for sexism?

_____ 11. Do you think that sexist books should be banned from children's libraries?

_____ 12. Why do you think educators are concerned with the passive way in which girls are portrayed in textbooks?

_____ 13. Cite examples of sexist patterns in *this* text.

OBJECTIVE 3

To construct classroom questions on all six levels of Bloom's *Taxonomy of Educational Objectives: Cognitive Domain*

LEARNING ACTIVITY 3

The first, and perhaps the most difficult, step in learning to ask effective classroom questions is that of gaining a thorough understanding of Bloom's *Taxonomy.* Now that you have demonstrated your ability to classify questions, you are ready to focus on constructing them. Effective classroom questions make provision for student thinking on all levels of the *Taxonomy.* Although during a short period of time only one or two levels of the *Taxonomy* may be reflected in a teacher's questions, over the course of an entire semester, students should have ample opportunity to answer questions phrased at all levels. The sample questions and the information in this Learning Activity provide you with useful information for constructing questions. The following review should provide you with a reference as you construct questions on the various levels of the *Taxonomy.*

Suggestions for Constructing Questions

In the next few pages, we will review the nature of the cognitive processes and verb prompts that are frequently associated with specific levels of the *Taxonomy.* As you go over this review, remember that it is important to analyze each question you write because inclusion of key words is not an unconditional guarantee of the taxonomic level of a particular question. After a brief review, you will get a chance to practice constructing questions that pertain to a specific reading selection.

Before proceeding to the exercises in this Learning Activity, you may find it helpful to remember to phrase your questions carefully. You have probably been a student in more than one class where the teacher's questions were so cumbersome or wordy that you lost the meaning of the question. In fact, some studies indicate that almost half of teacher questions are ambiguous and poorly phrased. You should be explicit enough to ensure understanding of your questions, but, at the same time, you should avoid using too many words. When a question is too wordy, students become confused and unable to respond; frequently, the result is that the question has to be rephrased.

Now you are ready to construct questions at each of the six levels of Bloom's *Taxonomy.* Read the paragraph in the Your Turn that follows. Then construct at least twelve questions relating to it. When you are done, you should have two questions on each of the six levels of the *Taxonomy.* As you construct your questions, keep the following in mind. What facts are in the paragraph that you might want students to recognize or recall (knowledge level)? What are the main points in the reading selection that you would want students to comprehend and be able to rephrase in their own words (comprehension level)? What information is there in the paragraph that students could apply to solving problems, classifying, or giving examples (application level)? What questions can you ask about the reading selection that require students to consider reasons and motives, examine the validity of a conclusion, or seek evidence to support a conclusion (analysis level)? Using this paragraph as a

Levels of the *Taxonomy:* Word Prompts

Knowledge	Comprehension	Application	Analysis	Synthesis	Evaluation
define recall recognize remember who what where when list reproduce recite name describe identify review	describe compare contrast rephrase put in your own words explain the main idea	apply classify use choose employ write an example solve how many which what is show translate make illustrate teach record/chart diagram/map demonstrate	support analyze why summarize compare/contrast order/sequence deduce investigate categorize classify draw conclusions identify motives or causes determine evidence justify	predict produce write design develop synthesize construct improve what if devise solve create imagine hypothesize combine estimate invent	judge argue decide evaluate assess give your opinion which is better do you agree would it be better verify rate select recommend conclude

springboard, how can you stimulate original student thought—creative problem solving, the making of predictions, and the production of original communication—in writing, music, dance, art, and so forth (synthesis level)? Finally, what issues can you raise from the material in this paragraph that will cause students to judge the merit of an idea, the solution to a problem, or an aesthetic work (evaluation level)?

After you have finished writing your questions, compare them with the sample questions in the Answer Key. Obviously, a wide variety of questions could be written pertaining to this particular selection. The sample questions are simply meant to give you a basis for comparison and to indicate the kinds of questions that can be asked on each of the six levels of the *Taxonomy.*

Compare your questions with the information and examples in the previous Learning Activities. Discuss the questions you develop with your instructor and with other members of your class. If eleven or twelve of your questions accurately reflect the appropriate level of the *Taxonomy,* you are doing well. If you miss two or three, you will probably want to review previous sections and study the sample questions carefully, particularly those on the levels where you did not construct the questions accurately. If you missed more than three, a careful rereading and additional practice in constructing questions may be necessary before you take the Mastery Test.

YOUR TURN

Constructing Questions on the Six Levels of Bloom's *Taxonomy*

In Des Moines, Iowa, two high school students and a junior high student, in defiance of a ban by school authorities, wore black armbands to class as a protest against the Vietnam War. As a result, they were suspended from school. But the U.S. Supreme Court later ruled the suspensions were illegal, holding that the first amendment to the Constitution protects the rights of public school children to express their political and social views during school hours.

This case illustrates a significant new trend in American life. Young people, particularly those under twenty-one, are demanding that they be granted rights long denied them as a matter of course. And, with increasing frequency, they are winning those rights.

—Michael Dorman, *Under 21* (New York: Delacorte, 1970), pp. 3, 5.

Write two questions at each level of the *Taxonomy* based on the above material: (1) knowledge level, (2) comprehension level, (3) application level, (4) analysis level, (5) synthesis level, and (6) evaluation level.

Mastery Test

OBJECTIVE 3 **To construct classroom questions on all six levels of Bloom's *Taxonomy of Educational Objectives: Cognitive Domain***

Read the following paragraphs and then construct twelve questions based on this reading selection. Two of your questions must be at the knowledge level, two at the comprehension level, two at the application level, two at the analysis level, two at the synthesis level, and two at the evaluation level. To pass this Mastery Test successfully, nine of the twelve questions should accurately reflect the level of the *Taxonomy* at which they are constructed.

> Death may be an unwelcome, terrifying enemy, a skeleton with an evil grin who clutches an ugly scythe in his bony hand. Or death may be a long awaited friend who waits quietly, invisibly, beside the bed of a dying patient to ease his pain, his loneliness, his weariness, his hopelessness.
>
> Man alone among the things that live knows that death will come. Mice and trees and microbes do not. And man, knowing that he has to die, fears death, the great unknown, as a child fears the dark. "We fear to be we know not what, we know not where," said John Dryden. But what man dreads more is the dying, the relentless process in which he passes into extinction alone and helpless and despairing. So he puts death and dying out of his mind, denying that they exist, refusing to discuss them openly, trying desperately to control them. He coins phrases like "never say die," and somehow, when he says something is "good for life," he means forever. Unable to bear the thought of ceasing to be, he comforts himself with thoughts of a pleasant afterlife in which he is rewarded for his trials on earth, or he builds monuments to himself to perpetuate at least his memory, if not his body.
>
> —John Langone, *Death Is a Noun* (Boston: Little, Brown, 1972), pp. 3–4.

Now that you have read the paragraphs, construct twelve questions, two at each level of the *Taxonomy.* When you write the application-level questions, you may find it helpful to consider that the following information has previously been given to the class: (1) definitions of various literary images, including metaphor, simile, and personification; (2) a list of terms and definitions that characterize various psychological states; and (3) several novels that portray death as a central or minor theme.

1. Two knowledge questions
2. Two comprehension questions
3. Two application questions
4. Two analysis questions
5. Two synthesis questions
6. Two evaluation questions

OBJECTIVE 4

To write examples of questioning strategies that enhance the quality of student participation

LEARNING ACTIVITY 4

While most of this chapter has focused on how to ask higher-order questions, this section explores several related areas that will enhance your questioning skills. Two of these areas are post-question follow-up skills: wait time and feedback. The last topic explores techniques for moving the responsibility of asking questions back to the students, where it actually all began.

Wait Time

If we were to stop and listen outside a classroom door, we might hear classroom interaction similar to this.

Teacher: Who wrote the poem "Stopping by Woods on a Snowy Evening"? Tomás?
Tomás: Robert Frost.
Teacher: Good. What action takes place in the poem? Sally?
Sally: A man stops his sleigh to watch the woods get filled with snow.
Teacher: Yes. Emma, what thoughts go through the man's mind?
Emma: He thinks how beautiful the woods are—*(pauses for a second)*
Teacher: What else does he think about? Joe?
Joe: He thinks how he would like to stay and watch. *(pauses for a second)*
Teacher: Yes—and what else? Rita? *(waits for half a second)* Come on, Rita, you can get the answer to this. *(waits for half a second)* Well, why does he feel he can't stay there indefinitely and watch the woods and the snow?
Rita: He knows he's too busy. He's got too many things to do to stay there for so long.
Teacher: Good. In the poem's last line, the man says that he has miles to go before he sleeps. What might sleep be a symbol for? Sarah?
Sarah: Well, I think it might be—*(pauses for a second)*
Teacher: Think, Sarah. *(waits for half a second)* All right then—Mike? *(waits again for half a second)* John? *(waits for half a second)* What's the matter with everyone today? Didn't you do the reading?

There are a number of comments we could make about this slice of classroom interaction. We could note the teacher's development from primarily lower-order questions to those of a somewhat higher order. We could comment on the inability of the students to answer her later questions and on the teacher's increasing frustration. But perhaps the most devastating thing we could say about this interaction segment is that it lasts for less than a single minute.

In less than one minute of dialogue, this teacher manages to construct and ask six questions—some of them, at least, requiring a fairly high cognitive level of response. As discussed earlier, a rapid questioning rate is not at all atypical of many classrooms across the country. The mean number of questions a teacher asks averages between two and three per minute, and it is not unusual to find as many as seven to ten questions asked by a teacher during a single minute of classroom instruction.

The effect of this rapid "bombing rate" is that students have little time to think. In fact, research shows that the mean amount of time a teacher waits after asking a question (wait time 1) is approximately *one second!* If the students are not able to think quickly enough to come up with a response at this pace, the teacher repeats the question, rephrases it, asks a different question, or calls on another student. If a student manages to get a response in, the teacher reacts or asks another question within an average time of nine-tenths of a second (wait time 2). It is little wonder that high rates of teacher questioning tend to be associated with low rates of student questions and student declarations. In classrooms where questions are asked at this bombing rate, students have little time or desire to think or to express themselves in an atmosphere so charged with a sense of verbal evaluation and testing.

When teachers break out of the bombing-rate pattern and learn to increase wait time 1 (after asking a question) and wait time 2 (after a student responds) from one second to three or five seconds, many significant changes occur in their classrooms. For example:[19]

1. Students give longer answers.
2. Students volunteer more appropriate answers, and failures to respond are less frequent.
3. Student comments on the analysis and synthesis levels increase. They make more evidence-inference responses and more speculative responses.
4. Students ask more questions.
5. Students exhibit more confidence in their comments, and those students whom teachers rate as relatively slow learners offer more questions and more responses.
6. Student achievement is higher.

Simply by increasing their ability to wait longer after asking a question, especially a higher-level question, teachers can effect some striking changes in the quantity and quality of student response and achievement. It is not as easy as you might think to learn to wait three to five seconds after asking a question. If a teacher does not get an immediate response to a question, the natural reaction seems to be one of panic—an assumption that the question is not an effective one and that the student does not know the answer. Indeed, teachers who have experimented with trying to increase their wait time find that they become frustrated at about the second or third week of practice. They go through a period of indecision about how long exactly they should wait after asking a question. If they receive encouragement during this difficult time, however, most teachers are able to increase wait time from one second to three or five seconds. Some teachers have found the following suggestions helpful as they try to increase their wait time.

1. Avoid repeating portions of student response to a question (teacher echo).
2. Avoid the command "think" without giving the students clues to aid their thinking or sufficient time in which to get their thoughts together.
3. Avoid dependence on comments such as "uh-huh" and "okay."
4. Avoid the "yes, but" reaction to a student response. This construction signals teacher rejection of the student's idea.

Currently, too many classrooms are characterized by a rapid rate of interaction, as teachers fire one question after another at students without giving them sufficient time to think, formulate their answers, and respond. If teachers can master the skill of increasing wait time from one second to three or five seconds, particularly after questions at a higher cognitive level, they will probably find some positive changes in both classroom discussion and student achievement.

Teacher Feedback

Not too long ago, noted educator John Goodlad and his research team conducted an in-depth observation study of more than a thousand classrooms. And what were their impressions? Goodlad observed:

> [T]here is a paucity of praise and correction of students' performance as well as of teacher guidance, in how to do better next time. Teachers tend not to respond in overtly positive or negative ways to the work students do. And our impression is that classes generally tend not to be strongly positive or strongly negative places to be. Enthusiasm and joy and anger are kept under control.[20]

Goodlad concluded that the emotional tone of schools is neither punitive nor joyful. Rather, he says, the school environment can best be characterized as "flat." Part of the reason for this bland quality may lie in the way teachers deal with student answers to questions. Trained observers visited more than a hundred classrooms along the East Coast and analyzed teacher reactions to student answers and comments. They found the following:

- Teachers don't often praise students. Approximately 10 percent of teacher reactions praise students. In approximately 25 percent of the classrooms observed, teachers never praised students.
- Teacher criticism is even more rare. (In this study, criticism was defined as an explicit statement that a student's behavior or work was wrong.) Approximately two-thirds of the one hundred classrooms observed contained no criticism. In the approximately thirty-five classrooms where teachers did criticize students, such criticism constituted only 5 percent of teacher interaction.
- Teacher remediation of student answers was quite frequent. It occurred in all classrooms and constituted approximately 30 percent of all teacher reactions. (Teacher remediation was defined as teacher comments or questions that would help students reach a more accurate or higher-level response.)
- But neither praise, criticism, nor remediation is the most frequent teacher response. Teachers most often simply *accept* student answers. Acceptance means that they say "uh-huh," or "okay," or nothing at all. Acceptance occurred in all of the classrooms, and it constituted more than 50 percent of teacher reactions. There was more acceptance than praise, remediation, and criticism combined.[21]

Some teachers seem committed to using "bland" feedback, although they don't call it that. They advise new teachers to "avoid saying an answer is wrong or even inadequate" for fear of wounding a student's ego. "Find something good in all answers, and keep students happy and involved" is their advice. The following true incident illustrates the kind of problem that ensues when this advice is followed:

> A teacher in an eastern city asked students one of the most popular of all classroom questions: "When did Columbus arrive in America?"
>
> "1942" was the quick retort offered by a fifth-grade boy in the front row.
>
> "Close" replied the teacher.

Although Columbus did not arrive in the Americas in 1942, or even close to 1942, the teacher later explained that although the answer was not correct, all the digits were; just the order of the digits needed work. Rather than risk hurting the "student's ego," the teacher found something correct and accepted the answer. Teachers often avoid saying that a student is wrong, and many even find it difficult to say that an answer is wrong. The fact that thirty-five other students might be more confused as a result of this imprecise teacher reaction probably did not occur to the teacher. The teacher's good intentions led to a poor educational judgment. And, unfortunately, this is all too common.

The way the classroom question cycle most often goes is:

- Teacher asks a question.
- Student gives an answer.
- Teacher says, "Okay."

The "okay" classroom is probably a bland, flat place in which to learn. Further, the okay classroom may not be okay in terms of encouraging student achievement. Research on teaching effectiveness indicates that students need specific feedback to understand what is expected of them, correct errors, and get help in improving their performance. If a student answers or questions, and the teacher reacts by saying "uh-huh" or "okay," the student is not getting the specific feedback he or she needs. Also, these flat "acceptance" reactions to student comments are not likely to encourage high-quality student thought and discussion.

Teachers give feedback in two ways: verbal and nonverbal. While either can be effective, sometimes messages are more powerful when they are not spoken. Nonverbal feedback refers to physical messages sent through eye contact, facial expressions, and body position. Does the teacher smile, frown, or remain impassive as a student comments in class? Is the teacher looking at or away from the student? Where is the teacher standing? Does the teacher appear relaxed or tense? All these physical messages indicate to the student whether the teacher is interested or bored, involved or passive, pleased or displeased with a student's comment.

Several studies comparing the relative effect of nonverbal and verbal feedback on students have been undertaken. One study had teachers send out conflicting messages to determine which message students accepted as the more powerful. In one group, the teacher displayed positive nonverbal rewards (smiled, maintained eye contact, indicated positive attitude to student answers with facial and body cues) but, at the same time, sent out negative verbal messages. In the second case, the process was reversed, and negative nonverbal disapproval was coupled with positive verbal praise (frowns, poor eye contact, and the like, coupled with "good," "nice job," etc.).

Although no evidence was accumulated as to whether the teacher was perceived as having multiple personalities, the results of the study were nonetheless interesting. In both cases, the nonverbal message was perceived as the stronger message by the majority of students. Whether the nonverbal message was positive or negative, most students responded to the nonverbal rather than to the verbal comments. This study provides fascinating support for the notion of "silent language," or "body language," and it emphasizes the importance of teachers' attending to what they do not say as well as to what they do say when they reinforce student participation.

For many years educators have assumed that rewards, verbal and nonverbal, were a positive tool in promoting student learning, and certainly this is frequently the case. But reward is not always an effective teaching skill. In some cases reward is ineffectual, and, on occasion, it is detrimental to learning.[22]

When a teacher relies totally on one or two favorite types of feedback and uses these repeatedly, the eventual result may become ineffectual. The teacher, for example, who continually says "good" after each student response is not reinforcing but simply verbalizing a comment that has lost its power to reward. Overusing a word or phrase is a pattern that many teachers, both new and experienced, fall into. Continual repetition of a word such as *good* seems only to ease teacher anxiety and to provide the teacher with a second or two to conceptualize his or her next comment or question.

In other cases feedback can detract from educational objectives and student learning when given too quickly and too frequently. When students are engaged in problem-solving activities, continual teacher comments can be an interruption to their thought processes—and may even terminate the problem solving altogether. Teachers who react to each student comment refocus the discussion on themselves, inhibiting the possibility of student-to-student interactions.

Finally, it should be pointed out that different individuals respond to different kinds of feedback. Teachers should learn to recognize that while some students find intensive eye contact rewarding, others find it uncomfortable; some students respond favorably to a teacher's referring to their contributions by name, but others find it embarrassing. Although it is unrealistic to expect that a teacher will be able to learn the various rewards to which each individual student responds, it is possible for teachers to try, in general, to be sensitive to the effects of different rewards on students.

Researchers who have studied teacher feedback conclude that effective feedback has the following characteristics:[23]

1. Effective feedback is *contingent* on the student's answer or behavior. When someone is doing something right, praise that behavior then and there. When a student is making an error, correct it as soon as possible. Feedback that is directly related to the student's performance in both time and focus is far more effective than late, nonexistent, unfocused, or general teacher reactions.
2. Effective feedback is *specific,* communicating what precisely is praiseworthy ("Using a chronological framework made your essay clear and logically organized!") or what needs to be corrected ("Check your rules for writing footnotes; you are making several mistakes with the punctuation."). Specificity of feedback provides the student with precise direction for building on strengths or correcting errors.
3. Effective feedback is *honest* and *sincere.* Teachers who provide a constant stream of syrupy rewards are quickly dismissed by students. Effective questions and thoughtful answers merit honest feedback.

Student-Initiated Questions

Think back to conversations you may have had with two-, three-, or four-year-olds. Do you remember how it felt to be the center of a storm of questions, the target of a constant stream of *whats* and *hows?* With the patience of Job, you answered each question, only to be confronted by a predictable follow-up: "Why?" Before they enter school, young children are filled with questions, from "Why is the sky blue?" to "Where do babies come from?" (When given these two options, most adults make a beeline to answer the "sky" question.) In fact, children initiate more than half the questions asked in their conversations with adults.[24] Children ask questions to learn about their world, and their quest for knowledge seems insatiable—insatiable, that is, until they arrive at school. Once in school, children's natural tendency to learn by questioning mysteriously evaporates. On that first day of school, the adult becomes questioner, while the child becomes the answerer. One insightful story that captures this role transformation describes a conversation between a parent and a child.

> The parent asks his son how he liked his first day of school. "Fine," says the child, "except for the grownup who kept interrupting."

By the upper grades, students are asking fewer than 15 percent of classroom questions.[25] And even these questions are not typically about what is being taught; they are more likely to be concerned with management and organization, such as "Is this going to be on the test?" "Where do we line up?" or that ever-popular, "Can I go to the bathroom?" Real questions about learning are very rare. Why this dramatic decline when children pass through the classroom door? If you would like to take a minute and try your hand at solving this problem, this is the ideal time to do just that. What is happening at school to dampen student questions?

Did your detective work uncover time pressure as one of the critical school factors? Teachers report that they feel pressured to "cover" the curriculum and feel that the school day is simply too short to be given over to students. In addition to the persistent pressure to "cover" material, there is also a new pressure added to today's schools: the pressure to "raise student test scores." Local, state, and even national tests put schools and educators under a very intense public spotlight. Encouraging **student-initiated questions,** questions unlikely to be included on these standardized tests, is certainly not the path to higher scores.

But we need not focus only on time and testing pressures, because the very organization of school inhibits student questions. Picture today's classroom (a room fundamentally unchanged in decades): the teacher's desk and chalkboard dominating a room populated by smaller desks—furniture that seems to be saying, "the teacher is the authority figure and the students are the followers; look to the teacher for direction." And unlike one child asking a parent a question, in school we have twenty or thirty students vying for the teacher's attention. This can lead to the "control" issue. Classrooms engulfed by student voices, even voices created by the excitement of questions, are classrooms some educators view as threatening, a sign that the teacher has "lost control."

Teachers can change this situation and encourage student questions through both *direct* and *indirect* techniques.[26] In fact, if your teaching reflects the skills in this chapter (you remember—"The Seven Habits of Highly Effective Questioners"), you are already using an indirect technique, one called *modeling.* Your thoughtful use of wait time, asking of both higher- and lower-order questions, and use of probing and delving questions, for example, will serve to model the kind of questioning skills that you want your students to develop. These indirect techniques create classrooms characterized by good questioning, and students, as if by osmosis, begin to model good questioning skills.

While the indirect approach is useful, more direct efforts are usually needed to develop good student questions.[27] While we do not have the space in this chapter to detail all of these direct approaches, we can offer some suggestions that will get you started in creating classrooms that encourage student inquiry.[28]

1. *Create a classroom climate that encourages student questions.* Some teachers have found that fun questioning activities and games can be very effective in promoting student questions. The game of "Twenty Questions" is one example. In this game, a student secretly selects a person, place, or thing, and the rest of the class has to guess what it is. The class is allowed to ask twenty questions that can only be answered with a "yes" or "no." Another fun activity is to provide students with answers to topics being studied and ask them to formulate the appropriate question. Many students find this role reversal enjoyable. Even fun activities can build a climate that supports questioning and fundamental skills used to ask questions.
2. *Overtly reinforce student questioning.* Teachers can promote student questions through encouragement and praise. "What a wonderful question. Let me think about that for a moment." "Your questions are getting better and better." Questioning can be risky business, and a reward for the effort can make the risk worth taking.
3. *Support the questioner.* While "smart" questions broadcast the questioner's insight and intellect, a bad question announces a student's ignorance to all

within earshot. Stupid questions can draw a groaning "duh" or other humiliating put-downs from peers. But from the teacher's side of the desk, a "stupid" question can provide a valuable insight: the student who has the courage (even the ineptitude) to ask a "stupid" question shows that more teaching may be needed for others as well. But if students feel intimidated about the risk of asking a "stupid" question, fewer student questions of all kinds will be asked.

4. *Establish helpful guidelines.* Establishing guidelines about questioning can create a supportive class norm. Sample guidelines might include: share the floor with others, stay on the point, treat each other with respect, accept and listen to all questions, think about your question before you ask it, and everyone must write down at least one question per topic studied. You can include key questioning words as hints to help students formulate their questions at all levels of the taxonomy. You and your students may want to add to or modify this list together, and then display it prominently in class.
5. *Cue your students.* Teachers can get the ball rolling by focusing students on questioning opportunities. Direct teacher cues might include:

   As you read this chapter, write down questions that you might want to ask the characters.
   Write down questions to ask tomorrow's guest speaker.
   After you answer the questions at the end of the chapter, add one of your own.

6. *Have students write study guide and exam questions.* Some teachers ask students to write and submit their own questions as a study guide to help them prepare for an exam. Other teachers go one step further and ask students to create the questions that actually will be used on their exams. (This can be a real motivator for some students!)
7. *Encourage student-to-student questions.* After one student gives a report, offers an explanation, or even answers a teacher's question, other students are encouraged to direct a question to the speaker. Courteous cross-questioning promotes open dialogue and more in-depth understanding of issues being studied.
8. *Use authentic questions.* The use of authentic questions, questions that tie into student interest and genuine curiosity, can generate not only student enthusiasm but also student questions. Teachers can ask students to list subject-related questions that interest them, and then the teacher and students can work together on finding the answers. Authentic student questions can serve as a springboard to a meaningful classroom curriculum.
9. *Teach questioning directly.* Elements of good questioning can be taught directly. For instance, different ways of phrasing questions can be discussed and practiced in class. In fact, the seven habits of highly effective questioners described in this chapter can be taught to your students. Asking effective questions is not intended to be a teacher monopoly; it is an important learning skill as well.

The purpose of this section has been to remind you that you have an invaluable partner in your teaching responsibilities: students. While this book focuses on refining your teaching skills, classrooms are not just about you. As you develop your own questioning skills on the road to being an effective teacher, remember the importance of student-initiated questions on the road to more successful learning.[29]

YOUR TURN

Questioning Strategies

Here we will use the *Taxonomy* to strengthen your knowledge of effective questions. Using *analysis,* briefly write about the strategies that enhance student participation (wait time, effective feedback, and student-initiated questions). The correct answers are found in the previous sections. As a reminder, the italicized words ask you to analyze. (But you knew that already, right?)

1. Based on your reading, *identify motives* teachers might have for extending their wait time.
2. *Provide one reason* that supports using criticism before remediation.
3. *Why* might your understanding of multiple intelligences promote student-initiated questions?
4. *Summarize* at least one example of wait time that you observed this week (inside or outside a classroom).
5. What can you *conclude* about acceptance when it is used as the primary feedback by teachers?

In items 6–12, identify the level of the question by using the code provided (*K* = knowledge, *C* = comprehension, *Ap* = application, *An* = analysis, and *S* = synthesis). After you have identified the level, actually *do* the *synthesis*-level questions as directed. (Hint: there are three!)

______ 6. Share your responses to questions 1–5 with a peer and discuss and improve them until you both agree that your work is correct.

______ 7. Create a short poem or rap that embodies something you have learned about questioning skills.

______ 8. What do you notice about this section and the previous section of Your Turn?

______ 9. Explain the main idea of the synthesis level.

______ 10. Choose, from the above tasks, the portions that will be relevant for your use.

______ 11. Why might the pattern shift (beyond knowledge and comprehension) in these Your Turn exercises be motivating for you?

______ 12. Write down a question that you have about this chapter. Working in a group of two or three, propose a possible answer to this question.

For items 1–5, review your comments carefully and check the Answer Key for suggestions. If further analysis and note taking aren't working for you, check with another student or with your teacher. For items 6–12, check your answers in the Answer Key. Hopefully, you are able to evaluate your own work and remediate any weaknesses!

Observation Worksheet
Wait Time and Teacher Reactions

Effective questioning in the classroom depends on a number of factors, including the length of the teacher's wait time and the specificity of the teacher's reactions. In this activity, you will have several opportunities to investigate these critical variables.

Directions: Do not use actual names of schools, teachers, administrators, or students when using this worksheet.

Observer's Name: ______________________________

Date: ______________________________

Grade Level: ______________________________

Subject: ______________________________

Class Size: ______________________________

Background Information: Give a brief general description of the school's social, economic, and ethnic makeup.

Wait Time

What to Record: Determining a teacher's wait time requires little more than some patience, a watch that can measure seconds (or the ability to count seconds), and an ear that can hear silence. Remember, the wait time is silent time, without rephrasing of questions or any other verbal interruption. After the teacher has asked a question, simply write down the number "1" if the student receives a wait time of a second or less. If longer, write down the number that represents how many seconds long each wait time lasts.

Teacher Reactions

What to Record: Teacher reactions fall into one of four categories: praise, acceptance, remediation, or criticism. In this activity, you will determine how the teacher distributes these reactions. Write down each reaction the teacher gives to each student response or comment. You may be able to listen to the reactions and immediately record which category applies. If you need more time to classify the teacher's reactions, you could write down the reactions verbatim and classify them after the observation when you have more time. If the teacher follows a student response with a probing question, record that as well.

Reflections on Your Observation:

1. How long is this teacher's typical wait time? ______________________________

____

2. How many times did the teacher wait longer than three seconds? ______________________________

____

3. Do you believe that a longer wait time would be useful in this class? ______________________________

____

4. What percentage of teacher reactions went to each of the four categories? ______________________

5. What conclusions can you draw from that distribution? ______________________

6. Considering your observation data, were student-initiated questions encouraged? How? ______________________

Mastery Test

OBJECTIVE 4 **To write examples of questioning strategies that enhance the quality of student participation**

Create one scenario (much like the examples in this chapter) that incorporates effective questioning. You should include the following in your vignette:

(a) *wait time* during a teacher–student interaction (*WT*)
(b) feedback (*specific praise*) for a correct answer (*SP*)
(c) feedback (*remediation*) of an incorrect response (*R*)
(d) *student-initiated questioning* as created by the teacher (*SIQ*)

Indicate (with parentheses) the dialogue portions that model the four strategies and label them *WT, SP, R,* and *SIQ.*

OBJECTIVE 5

To describe how the growing diversity and multicultural nature of America's students impact questioning strategies

LEARNING ACTIVITY 5

While diversity and multicultural issues are currently "hot" topics in America's schools, our national history is replete with examples of simplistic and unflattering stereotypes of Americans based on race, ethnicity, religion, and class. It is not surprising that the typical teacher wants nothing to do with such inaccurate and frequently demeaning stereotypes. It is not surprising to hear a teacher proclaim: "I don't see color; I only see children." Such a statement suggests that the teacher is working hard to treat all students fairly. Unfortunately, pretending that group differences do not exist does not necessarily lead to either fair or effective teaching. In fact, denying group differences can make teaching in general, and questioning strategies in particular, more difficult.

Many Asian Americans excel in math, many African Americans become athletes, and Jewish Americans are known for their educational drive. Are these **stereotypes?** Or is this reality? According to educator Carlos Cortés, this is reality, and recognizing the validity of such **generalizations** is an important step in becoming a more effective teacher.[30] So what is the difference between potentially helpful generalizations and potentially destructive stereotypes? Cortés draws three fundamental distinctions between the two.

1. *Flexibility:* Generalizations are open to change, especially as new information develops or new theories emerge. On the other hand, stereotypes are inflexible, rigid, and impervious to new information.
2. *Intragroup heterogeneity:* Generalizations recognize that within a group, there are amazing differences and diversity; not all members of a group are the same. Stereotypes make the assumption that all group members are homogeneous. When an individual does not easily "fit" the group definition, a stereotypic perception would conclude that the individual is atypical, an anomaly, the exception that proves the rule.
3. *Clues:* Since we know that groups have different characteristics, when we learn that an individual belongs to a particular group, we then have a clue about that individual. Generalizations give teachers a start, an insight about group members. Stereotypes replace clues with assumptions. Because an individual belongs to a group, a stereotype assumes that certain characteristics must apply to that individual. While generalizations are subtle, stereotypes are blatant.

While each of us is a unique individual, our group memberships create certain similarities as well. Understanding the power of group membership helps teachers to understand students better and therefore to design more effective teaching strategies. How to focus eye contact when talking to a Native American, how best to approach the parents of a Mexican American, or how most effectively to use wait time with students who have limited English proficiency are all group strategies that provide teachers with a helpful direction.

Although generalizations can be beneficial, it is important to remember to use them cautiously. Boundaries can be murky, and crossing from a generalization to a stereotype is always a danger. As Carlos Cortés warns, careless generalizations can lead to damaging stereotyping and unintended bias.

When you begin teaching, nearly one-third of schoolchildren in the United States will be students of color. In fact, in many of our communities today, "minority" students are already the majority.[31] Teachers, on the other hand, are overwhelmingly white.[32] Educators need to learn about our diversity in order to question (and teach!) effectively. Let's look at some classroom scenarios that demonstrate questioning behaviors that we've discussed in this chapter. Only this time, let's look at these behaviors as they are played out in multicultural classrooms.

Room .25

The teacher tends to call on students who quickly and actively raise their hands. It feels good. The pace is hot. The material is being covered, and there are always some good answers.

But . . . Many fast hand-raisers are males of the dominant culture who see themselves as achievers. They want to be called on and are comfortable in the spotlight. Many are animated learners and may even shout out answers without waiting for the teacher's okay. A few Asian-American students avoid answering questions by keeping their hands down and eyes lowered. For them, shyness is prized, while talking, especially about oneself, may not be acceptable.[33] Other students less sure of their ability, simply choose not to raise their hand and "hide" as the teacher seeks out a "volunteer." While the class moves forward, it is with the momentum of only one-fourth of the group.

Room 911

This teacher asks a question, barely waits for a student response, then quickly calls on someone else. He wouldn't want to embarrass students by pressuring them to answer. And besides, if the answer isn't on the tip of their tongue, it will probably take too long to dig it out.

But . . . A closer look reveals that the teacher is giving some students more time to formulate answers. Teachers tend to wait for students they perceive as worth waiting for. A few bright youngsters benefit and receive more "airtime" to develop and share their thoughts. They are verbal and seem to "hit" the points the teacher values. Ability level can dictate participation level—unless the teacher is proactive. Several other students, however, with limited or nonstandard English, could use more time to respond, but the teacher usually feels the need to move on.[34] A small group of Hispanic females, culturally conditioned to the spectator role, are hesitant to display their academic ability in this mixed-gender setting.[35] They sit silently during the rapid verbal exchanges.

Room 411

Another teacher tends to ask many knowledge-based, factual questions. She relishes these questions because the students' correct answers build self-esteem. Unlike so many other teachers, she gets plenty of participation and is pleased with how well her students are doing.

But . . . Some students thrive on factual questions, which are compatible with their learning style and their need to achieve. A number of African-American students feel successful when the questions are concrete and factual. They feel the teacher is really teaching what they need to learn.[36] However, there are other African Americans who want more challenging questions, drawn from real life, and would appreciate a chance to be more expressive and thoughtful.[37] They are not being engaged by the teacher's questions. In fact, a number of students find the class boring. Several of them have generated their own questions—questions they never get to ask![38]

Room 007

This teacher takes pride in delving, probing, and scaffolding to help students deepen their understanding of the topic. High expectations are held for everybody. In this class, no one gets off the hook with a quick answer or an "I don't know." When someone answers incorrectly, the teacher firmly refocuses the student.

But . . . A few students, who are of a different race from the teacher, feel intimidated by the display of the teacher's power. The two American Indian students in the class say a great deal with very few words, but they appear uncomfortable when probed to expand an answer. Most students are comfortable with this classroom culture and are thrilled with the chance to expand their answers. They feel the teacher's guidance is supportive.[39] At one point, the teacher's critical feedback unintentionally left one Hispanic student feeling humiliated.[40]

Room OK

The teacher in this room tells students that their answers are "okay" so often that some students actually count her "okays" during the lesson (and have nicknamed her Annie

Okay). A few high achievers get specific feedback for correct answers, and praise for them is quite positive. Most of the time, things are "okay."

But . . . This teacher's feedback reflects biased expectations and is probably a predictor of her students' achievement. This is even more evident among culturally diverse pupils. Most of the time, she merely accepts their answers. When she was surprised at the brilliance of an African-American student, her praise was particularly enthusiastic, some would say patronizing. She didn't remediate an Asian-American youngster who was working quietly, as she was grateful for the good behavior and didn't focus on the work.[41]

These scenarios show how questioning might be experienced differently by students from various ethnic or racial groups. Many teacher decisions, often instantaneous and unconscious, can have a negative impact on some students. None of these teachers intended to be biased, and some were even practicing the "Seven Habits of Highly Effective Questioners." Yet, while they were practicing them, they were *not* being responsive to cultural and individual differences. As a result, some students benefited from their skills, while others did not.

Researchers who have observed classroom interaction closely have discovered gender differences as well. Analyze the following discussion, which took place in a seventh-grade class. See if you can detect any gender biases.

Room 5050

Teacher: How many of you have decided, maybe you're not 100 percent sure but you have considered, what you want to be when you grow up? *(The teacher looks around; about half the students shoot their hands up.)* Justin? *(Teacher walks to the area where Justin and a few other males are seated.)*

Justin: I want to be a lawyer.

Teacher: Okay, how come? What interests you about the law?

Justin: Well, my dad's a lawyer and he works hard; he likes it a lot and is really successful. Plus, I watch TV and the lawyers really have amazing stuff going on.

Teacher: Give me an example, Justin.

Justin: Well, last week they flew my dad out to California to review some medical papers for a lawsuit they're doing on diet pills.

Teacher: Sounds intriguing, Justin, and it's good to hear you're following your dad's case. What about the TV lawyers?

Justin: Most of them are like working with criminals and the court system. It's super exciting because it's really life-and-death trials.

Teacher: Great. So, you're really up for an exciting, life-and-death work life. That's going to require plenty of academic skills. What school skills do you think Justin will need? Anyone? James?

James: Lots of reading and writing work. And probably that speech class we take next semester.

Teacher: Exactly! Would you add research to that, Marcia, like our library Internet searches last week?

Marcia: Yeah. He'd have to use the Internet to find out case histories.

Teacher: Okay. *(Teacher moves to the front of the room near the chalkboard.)* Class, the list I have put on the overhead includes some "Hot Careers" for the next twenty-five years. It's not too soon for you to realize how important your course choices are as you determine your working future. And the more you learn about different careers and build your interests and skills, the better your choices will be. *(Overhead projector light flashes on revealing "Hot Careers.")*

Hot Careers

Biotech—Patent attorney

Geriatric—Rehabilitation therapist

Psychopharmacologist

Health lawyer

Webmaster—On-line content developer

Malcolm: What's a psychophar . . . molist?

Teacher: Psy-cho-pharm-a-col-o-gist. What do you think, Malcolm? What word parts do you see in there?

Malcolm: Well, the guy who works at a drug store—pharmacist or something.

Teacher: Great start, Malcolm. The first part—psycho—you've heard that before.

Malcolm: People who work with crazy people?

Teacher: Who can help Malcolm? Isaac?

Isaac: —It's, hmm—like a, hmm, a psychologist?

Teacher: And what's that? Someone knows—yes, Hillary?

Hillary: Someone who studies people?

Teacher: No. James?

James: Someone who studies people's minds.

Teacher: Close enough. So, put it all together. What's a psychopharmacologist? Write down in your notebook, everybody, what you think it is. Great, check with your neighbor. If you both agree and really think you got it right, put a hand up. All right. Jamal?

Jamal: *(who paired with Lissa)* Someone who checks out people and how they feel, mentally and stuff, but works at a drug store.

Teacher: Hey, that's one way to go and maybe not a bad idea. But, it's not quite right. Someone else? Arturo?

Arturo: Someone who gives out drugs but just for people who are feeling bad mentally.

Teacher: Absolutely! It's two jobs in one. Someone who specializes in pharmaceuticals and drugs. *And* someone who knows how the mind works. So, this single career puts the two jobs together into a new specialization. We get someone who has high expertise in understanding chemistry, drugs, the human brain, and feelings. And *that's* what I wanted you to sort out about these other hot careers. They're all double jobs. Who can figure another one out? Jennifer? You have your hand up.

Jennifer: Well, another thing is that two of the jobs have lawyer in them and four have something like in health or medicine.

Teacher: Okay. If the hot careers involve two jobs put together, I want you all to think of what you might like to be when you grow up. Settle down, Jorge, you're going to like this part. The challenge is to take two things you like to do and put them together to make a whole new and interesting profession.

If you read this scenario carefully, you might have noticed that the teacher directs more questions to boys than to girls. Also, boys receive more of the questions that call for higher-order thinking and more creative responses. Several studies indicate that boys, particularly high-achieving boys, are likely to receive most of the teacher's active attention.[42] They receive more praise on the quality of their academic work,[43] and they are asked more complex and abstract questions.[44] Other research has shown that teachers in mathematics classrooms give significantly more wait time to boys than to girls. The researchers conclude that "this difference could possibly have a negative effect on girls' achievement in mathematics."[45]

When teachers realize that they are distributing their attention and their questions in an unfair manner, they can change their teaching behavior. It is important to check yourself for equity in interaction and questioning so that you actively involve all your students in classroom discussions.[46]

If some students are denied their fair share of the teacher's questions, then the talents of even the most effective teachers do them little good. If teachers are not responsive to the cultural, racial, gender, and ethnic differences in their classes, then a growing number of America's children will be shortchanged. The Your Turn and Mastery Test that follow will start you down the path not only of more effective teaching but also of more inclusive teaching.

YOUR TURN

Responding to Diversity

Take a walk back through the school hallway and revisit Rooms .25, 911, 411, and the other classes described in these scenarios. In each room, the teacher missed at least one, and often more than one, opportunity to include all the students in the instruction. Briefly rewrite these scenarios, correcting the teacher's omission and describing how the instructional changes in your scenarios create a more responsive and effective learning environment for all students.

Observation Worksheet

Equality of Distribution of Teacher's Questions

In this activity, you will discover how teachers distribute their questions in class. Obtain a seating chart indicating the location of each student, either by asking the teacher or creating one yourself. Write down the position of each student in the class, and record student names as soon as you learn them. It may also be useful to write down student gender, race, or ethnic information, since you may want to analyze the role these factors might play in class participation. You may want to practice collecting data with a seating chart by first coding information for a small group of students before collecting observational data on a whole class.

Directions: Do not use actual names of schools, teachers, administrators, or students when using this worksheet.

Observer's Name: ______________________

Date: ______________________

Grade Level: ______________________

Subject: ______________________

Class Size: ______________________

Background Information: Give a brief general description of the school's social, economic, and ethnic makeup.

____

____

Measure Response Opportunities

What to Record: Every time a student participates, either because the teacher called on the student or because the student called out, make a mark next to that student's name on your seating chart. You may want to record "SI" for *s*tudent-*i*nitiated responses and "TI" for *t*eacher-*i*nitiated opportunities, such as calling on a student to answer a question. You will want to capture every time the teacher asks a student a question, even if the student is unable to answer. Every question the teacher asks a student, including several in a row to the same student, should get a separate mark. This will capture information about which students the teacher stays with over an extended time. If a teacher has everyone respond together to a question (a choral response), the best way to record this is to simply create a category at the bottom of the page entitled "group response" and make a mark next to that category.

Reflections on Your Observation:

1. Which students were most involved in interaction? Did they create their own opportunities by calling out or vigorously waving their hands, or did the teacher tend to call on the same students repeatedly?

____

____

____

2. Do these highly participatory students fit into any special group? (For example, did they sit in a specific location or did they belong to a particular racial, ethnic, or gender group?)

____

____

____

3. Were any students left out entirely? Can you suggest any reasons to explain why these students did not participate?

____

____

____

4. Can you offer any suggestions for getting them involved? ______________

____

____

5. What other conclusions can you draw from your observation data? ______________

____

____

____

Mastery Test

OBJECTIVE 5 **To describe how the growing diversity and multicultural nature of America's students impact questioning strategies**

Review the scenario you developed for Mastery Test, Objective 4. You were asked to incorporate *effective* questioning strategies that included: wait time, feedback (specific praise, remediation), and student-initiated questioning. Set your classroom in a *real* school, one that reflects the diversity of an urban center, rural community, or suburban neighborhood. As you picture the students, imagine how issues of race, ethnicity, gender, and class might impact the learning. Begin by briefly describing your classroom "culture." Develop a statement for each effective strategy (wait time, specific praise, remediation, and student-initiated questioning) that demonstrates your knowledge, high expectations, and sensitivity to groups and individuals while avoiding stereotypes!

> *Sample:* Wait time—Many of the youngsters are refugee immigrants from Southeast Asia and are the first in their family to speak English or even attend high school. Wait time will give them the chance to shift between two languages, carefully consider content, and rehearse "in their heads" before they respond aloud. Providing five seconds of teacher silence will allow them to process information and produce answers. A side benefit will be that other students will learn to be better listeners!

NOTES

1. Charles DeGarmo, *Interest and Education* (New York: Macmillan, 1902), p. 179.
2. John Dewey, *How We Think,* rev. ed. (Boston: D. C. Heath, 1933), p. 266.
3. Joseph Green, "Editor's Note," *Clearing House* 40 (1966): 397.
4. Thomas Merton, *The Seven Storey Mountain* (Garden City, N.Y.: Doubleday, 1948), p. 139.
5. Romiett Stevens, "The Question as a Measure of Classroom Practice," *Teachers College Contributions to Education,* no. 48 (New York: Teachers College Press, 1912); Trevor Kerry, "Classroom Questions in England," *Questioning Exchange* 1, no. 1 (1987):33; Arthur C. Graesser and Natalie K. Person, "Question Asking During Tutoring," *American Educational Research Journal* 31 (1994):104–137; William S. Carlsen, "Questioning in Classrooms: A Sociolinguistic Perspective," *Review of Educational Research* 61 (1991): 157–178; Meredith D. Gall, "Synthesis of Research on Teacher's Questioning," *Educational Leadership* 42 (1984):40–47.
6. Mary Budd Rowe, "Wait-Time and Rewards as Instructional Variables: Their Influence on Language, Logic and Fate Control" (Paper presented at the Annual Meeting of the National Association for Research in Science Teaching, Chicago, April 1972); Kenneth Tobin, "Effects of Teacher Wait Time on Discourse Characteristics in Mathematics and Language Arts Classes," *American Educational Research Journal* 23 (1986):191–200.
7. L. M. Barden, "Effective Questions and the Ever-Elusive Higher-Order Question," *American Biology Teacher* 57, no. 7 (1995):423–426; Meredith D. Gall and T. Rhody, "Review of Research on Questioning Techniques," in *Questions, Questioning Techniques, and Effective Teaching,* ed. William W. Wilen (Washington, D.C.: National Education Association, 1987), pp. 23–48; G. Brown and R. Edmondson, "Asking Questions," in *Classroom Teaching Skills,* ed. E. Wragg (New York: Nichols, 1984), pp. 97–119; William W. Wilen and Ambrose A. Clegg, "Effective Questions and Questioning: A Research Review," *Theory and Research in Social Education* 14 (1986):153–161.
8. Mary Budd Rowe, "Science, Silence, and Sanctions," *Science and Children* 34 (September 1996):35–37.
9. Angelo V. Ciardiello, "Training Students to Ask Reflective Questions," *The Clearing House* 66 (May/June 1993): 312–314; Robert J. Sternberg, "Answering Questions and Questioning Answers," *Phi Delta Kappan* 70, no. 2 (October 1994):136–138; S. J. Doenu, "Soliciting," in *The International Encyclopedia of Teaching and Teacher Education,* ed. M. J. Dunkin (Oxford and New York: Pergamon Press, 1987), pp. 407–413.
10. J. T. Dillon, "Research on Questioning and Discussion," *Educational Leadership* 42, no. 3 (1984):50–56.

11. Stephen R. Covey, *The Seven Habits of Highly Effective People.* (New York: Simon & Schuster, 1990).
12. Norah Morgan and Juliana Saxton, *Teaching, Questioning and Learning* (London and New York: Routledge, 1991), p. 76; Beverly A. Busching and Betty Ann Slexinger, "Authentic Questions: What Do They Look Like? Where Do They Lead?" *Language Arts* 72 (September 1995):341–351.
13. Carol Ann Tomlinson, "Reconcilable Differences? Standards-Based Teaching and Differentiation," *Educational Leadership* 58, no. 1 (September 2000):6–11.
14. P. Smagoinsky, "The Social Construction of Data: Methodological Problems of Investigation Learning in the Zone of Proximal Development," *Review of Educational Research* 65, no. 3 (1995):191–212.
15. J. V. Wertsch, *Vygotsky and the Social Formation of the Mind* (Cambridge, Mass.: Harvard University Press, 1985).
16. Howard Gardner, "Probing More Deeply into the Theory of Multiple Intelligences," *The National Association of Secondary Principals Bulletin* 80, no. 583 (November 1996):1–7; Howard Gardner, "Reflections on Multiple Intelligences: Myths and Messages," *Phi Delta Kappan* 77, no. 3 (November 1995):200–209.
17. Benjamin Bloom, ed., *Taxonomy of Educational Objectives, Handbook I: Cognitive Domain* (New York: McKay, 1956).
18. Jere Brophy and Carolyn Evertson, *Learning from Teaching: A Developmental Perspective* (Boston: Allyn and Bacon, 1976).
19. The findings in this section are based on the work of Mary Budd Rowe. See also Kenneth Tobin, "The Role of Wait Time in Higher Cognitive Level Learning," *Review of Educational Research* 57, no. 1 (1987):69–95.
20. John Goodlad, *A Place Called School* (New York: McGraw-Hill, 1984), p. 124.
21. Myra Sadker, Joyce Bauchner, David Sadker, and Leslie Hergert, *Promoting Effectiveness in Classroom Instruction: Final Report* (Contract No. 400-80-0033) (Washington, D.C.: U.S. Department of Education, 1984); see also K. Watson and B. Young, "Discourse for Learning in the Classroom," *Language Arts* 63, no. 2 (1986):126–141.
22. Jere Brophy, "Teacher Praise: A Functional Analysis," (Occasional Paper No. 2) (East Lansing: Michigan State University, Institute for Research on Teaching, 1979).
23. *Ibid.*
24. A. E. Edwards and D. G. P. Westgate, *Investigating Classroom Talk,* Social Research and Educational Studies Series: 4 (London and Philadelphia: Falmer, 1987), p. 170.
25. D. Bridges, "A Philosophical Analysis of Discussion" in *Questioning and Discussion: A Multidisciplinary Study,* ed. J. Dillon (Norwood, N.J.: Ablex, 1988), p. 26.
26. Morgan and Saxton, *op. cit.,* pp. 105–111; Francis P. Hunkins, *Teaching Through Effective Questioning* (Boston: Christopher-Gordon, 1989).
27. Ciardiello, *op. cit.*
28. Morgan and Saxton, *op. cit.,* pp. 113–125.
29. See also Margaret A. Cintorino, "Discovering Their Voices, Valuing Their Words," *English Journal* 83, no. 6 (October 1994):33–40; Ciardiello, *op. cit.;* Sternberg, *op. cit.;* Debby Deal and Donna Sterling, "Kids Ask the Best Questions," *Educational Leadership* 54, no. 6 (March 1997):61–63; M. Beth Casey and Edwin C. Tucker, "Problem-Centered Classrooms: Creating Lifelong Learners," *Phi Delta Kappan* 76, no. 2 (October 1994): 139–143.
30. Carlos E. Cortés, *The Children Are Watching: How the Media Teach About Diversity* (New York: Teachers College Press, 2000), pp. 149–150.
31. Marie Carbo, "Educating Everybody's Children" in *Educating Everybody's Children: Diverse Teaching Strategies for Diverse Learners,* ed. Robert W. Cole (Alexandria, Va.: Association for Supervision and Curriculum Development, 1995), p. 1.
32. National Education Association, *NEA Study of the Status of Public School Teachers.* (Washington, D.C.: Author, 1987); Rick A. Breault, "Preparing Preservice Teachers for Culturally Diverse Classrooms," *The Educational Forum* 59 (Spring 1995):262–275.
33. J. C. McCroskey and V. P. Richmond, *Quiet Children and the Classroom Teacher,* 2d ed. (Annandale, Va.: Speech Communication Association, 1991).
34. Ron Scollon and Suzanne B. K. Scollon, *Narrative, Literacy, and Face in Interethnic Communication: An Athabaskan Case,* Working Papers in Sociolinguistics, no. 59, 1995.
35. Lisa Delpit, *Other People's Children: Cultural Conflict in the Classroom* (New York: New Press, 1995).
36. *Ibid.;* Sylvia Brice Heath, *Ways with Words* (New York: Cambridge University Press, 1983), p. 280.
37. Delpit, *op cit.;* J. J. Irvine, *Black Students and School Failure: Policies, Practices and Prescriptions* (Westport, Conn.: Greenwood, 1990); Asa G. Hillard, "Teachers and Cultural Styles in a Pluralistic Society," *NEA Today* 7, no. 6 (1989):65–69; Jeanne Oakes, *Keeping Track: How Schools Structure Inequality* (New Haven, Conn.: Yale University Press, 1985); J. J. Irvine, "Making Teacher Education Culturally Responsive," in *Diversity in Teacher Education,* ed. M. E. Dilworth (San Francisco: Jossey-Bass, 1992), pp. 72–92.
38. Jim Chesebro, Roy Berko, Carol Hopson, Pamela Cooper, and Helene Hodges, "Strategies for Increasing Achievement in Oral Communication," in Cole, *op. cit.,* p. 156.
39. Delpit, *op. cit.*
40. Chesebro et. al., *op. cit.,* p. 152.
41. James Banks, *Multiethnic Education* (Boston: Allyn and Bacon, 1987); Donna M. Gollnick and P. C. Chinn, *Multicultural Education in a Pluralistic Society,* 3d ed. (New York: Macmillan, 1990); Christine Sleeter and Carl Grant, *Making Choices for Multicultural Education* (Columbus, Ohio: Merrill, 1988).
42. Jere Brophy and Thomas Good, *Teacher–Student Relationships: Causes and Consequences* (New York: Holt, Rinehart & Winston, 1974).
43. Carol Dweck, William Davidson, Sharon Nelson, and Bradley Enna, "Sex Differences in Learned Helplessness: II. The Contingencies of Evaluative Feedback in the Classroom, and III. An Experimental Analysis," *Developmental Psychology* 14, no. 3 (1978):268–276.

44. Sadker, Bauchner, Sadker, and Hergert, *op. cit.*
45. Delores Gore and Daniel Roumagoux, "Wait Time as a Variable in Sex Related Differences During Fourth-Grade Mathematics Instruction," *Journal of Educational Research in Education* 17 (1991):269–334.
46. For a comprehensive review of the impact of gender in schools, see Myra Sadker and David Sadker, *Failing at Fairness: How Our Schools Cheat Girls* (New York: Touchstone, 1995); Myra Sadker, David Sadker, and Susan Klein, "The Issue of Gender in Elementary and Secondary Schools," *Review of Research in Education* 17 (1991):269–334.

ADDITIONAL RESOURCES

Readings

Brandt, Ronald. *Powerful Teaching.* Alexandria, Va.: Association for Supervision and Curriculum Development, 1998.

Cole, Robert W., ed. *Educating Everybody's Children: Diverse Teaching Strategies for Diverse Learners.* Alexandria, Va.: Association for Supervision and Curriculum Development, 1995.

Delpit, Lisa. *Other People's Children: Cultural Conflict in the Classroom.* New York: New Press, 1995.

Dillon, J. T. *The Practice of Questioning.* New York: Routledge, 1990.

Dillon, J. T. *Questioning and Teaching: A Manual of Practice.* New York: Teachers College Press, 1989.

Gollnick, Donna, and P. C. Chinn. *Multicultural Education in a Pluralistic Society,* 5th ed. New York: Prentice-Hall, 1997.

Hogan, Kathleen, and Michael Pressley. *Scaffolding Student Learning: Instructional Approaches and Issues.* Cambridge, Mass.: Brookline Books, 1997.

Hunkins, Francis P. *Teaching Thinking Through Effective Questioning.* Boston: Christopher-Gordon, 1989.

Hyman, Ronald T. *Strategic Questioning.* Englewood Cliffs, N.J.: Prentice-Hall, 1979.

Sadker, Myra, and David Sadker. *Failing at Fairness: How Our Schools Cheat Girls.* New York: Touchstone, 1995.

Wilen, William. *Questioning Skills for Teachers.* Washington, D.C.: National Education Association, 1991.

Web Sites*

Effective Questioning Techniques: http://www.oir.uiuc/edu/did/booklets/question/question.html
This on-line booklet is a helpful reference for instructors who wish to improve their questioning skills or review and assess their current questioning techniques. Strategies are offered to help teachers ask good questions and create environments in which students are encouraged to ask questions.

How Better Questioning Leads to Improved Learning: QUILT: http://www.ael.org/rel/quilt/questng.htm
QUILT—Questioning and Understanding to Improve Learning and Thinking—helps make the classroom learning environment more active, student-centered, constructivist, inquiry-based, and metacognitive. Students may also link to an annotated bibliography.

Teaching Tips for TAs: Effective Questioning Enhances Student Learning: http://www.jd.ucsb.edu/ICTA/tips/quest.html
A helpful site for teachers of all grade levels. Teachers learn how to implement Bloom's *Taxonomy,* wait time, and probing questions to develop critical thinking in their students.

Beginning Teachers: http://www.nea.org/bt/1-students/1-1-nres.html
The National Education Association offers new (and longtime) teachers a breadth of resources, including the article "Hints on Effective Questioning Techniques."

A Questioning Toolkit: http://www.fno.org/nov97/toolkit.html
The *Educational Technology Journal* integrates philosophy and pragmatism to assist teachers in developing effective questioning techniques.

---

*Web site information provided by Karen Zittleman and Sarah Irvine Belson.

Collaboration to Advance Teaching Technology and Science: http://www.geo.arizona.edu/catts/resources/educators.html
As a gateway to on-line resources, this site gives a wealth of information on effective questioning techniques, reform efforts in math and science education, learning styles, personality types, motivations, cooperative learning, and assessment.

Teacher Talk: What Is Your Classroom Management Profile?: http://education.indiana.edu/cas/tt/v1i2/what.html
Is your management style authoritative, laissez-faire, or indifferent? This brief quiz will help you assess your classroom approach.

6

Differentiating Instruction for Academic Diversity

Carol Ann Tomlinson

OBJECTIVE 1	**To develop an informed, personal definition of *differentiated instruction***
OBJECTIVE 2	**To construct an informed, personal rationale for teaching to address learner needs**
OBJECTIVE 3	**To depict ways in which learner, learning environment, and curriculum are integral to differentiated or academically responsive instruction**
OBJECTIVE 4	**To apply specific ways to differentiate content, activities, and products in response to student readiness, interest, and learning profile**
OBJECTIVE 5	**To analyze and understand general principles of effective differentiation**
OBJECTIVE 6	**To propose personal first steps in becoming a responsive teacher**

OBJECTIVE 1

To develop an informed, personal definition of *differentiated instruction*

Nearly 100 years ago, third-grader Betsy moved from a small town to the country and found herself—in mid-year—in a one-room schoolhouse. On Betsy's first day in her new school, the teacher asked her to read aloud to the class during a group reading session. She read at length, with ease and with feeling. The teacher told her to work later in the day with the Level 7 readers. Nine-year-old Betsy was bewildered, pleased, and worried. She was puzzled because, she thought, her teacher must surely recognize that she was too small to be a seventh-grader. Shouldn't all third-graders read third-grade books? Betsy was happy because she had always wanted to read books with interesting words and ideas, and this might be her chance. She was afraid, too, however, and the fear ultimately sent her to the teacher to explain why it would not work for her to be a part of Level 7 reading. She confessed to the teacher that she would be a dismal failure with Level 7 math. Math, she explained, was her hardest subject.

Now it was the teacher's turn to look puzzled. "I've not said anything about your math," the teacher reflected. "I haven't yet checked to see what you need in math."

By the end of the first day, Betsy (also called Elizabeth Ann) had assignments for working in all her subjects—and she was confused. This wasn't like her old classroom, where everyone did the same thing at the same time.

> Elizabeth Ann fell back on the bench with her mouth open. She felt really dizzy. What crazy things the teacher said! She felt as though she was being pulled limb from limb.

"What's the matter?" asked the teacher seeing her bewildered face.

"Why—why," said Elizabeth Ann, "I don't know what I am at all. If I'm second-grade arithmetic and seventh-grade reading, and third-grade spelling, what grade *am* I?"

The teacher laughed. "*You* aren't any grade at all, no matter where you are in school. You're just yourself, aren't you? What difference does it make what grade you're in? And what's the use of your reading little baby things too easy for you just because you don't know your multiplication table?"[1]

Almost a century ago, Betsy's teacher understood a reality that is, if anything, more evident today than at any time in our country's past: students in a single classroom vary in important ways. The teacher also understood a correlate truth that it's easy to lose sight of in a busy classroom: a good teacher studies and actively addresses student differences as an integral part of planning and instruction.

What Is "Differentiated Instruction"?

The term **differentiated instruction** is relatively new on the educational scene. Its practice, however, is likely as old as teachers and classrooms. A given of teaching is that as long as there's more than one student in the room, the students won't all learn what the teacher has planned in the same ways, to the same degree of sophistication, or on the same timetable. In fact, even if there *were* only one student in the room, that student would exhibit noteworthy learning differences at varied developmental stages of life, across subjects, within different parts of the same subject, and even at different times of the day.

On a simple level, differentiated instruction is teaching with student variance in mind. It means starting where the kids are rather than adopting a standardized approach to teaching that seems to presume that all learners of a given age or grade are essentially alike. Thus differentiated instruction is "responsive" teaching rather than "one-size-fits-all" teaching.

A fuller definition of *differentiated instruction* is that a teacher proactively plans varied approaches to what students need to learn, how they will learn it, and/or how they can express what they have learned in order to increase the likelihood that each student will learn as much as he or she can as efficiently as possible.

The rest of this chapter "unpacks" this latter definition by examining key underpinnings of differentiation, important components of differentiation, and some practical ways to accomplish differentiation. The overarching aim of the chapter is to help prospective teachers reflect on ways in which their early professional practice can begin with the needs of learners at its center.

LEARNING ACTIVITY 1

This chapter has suggested several definitions of *differentiated instruction.* Differentiation is the following:

- Starting where the kids are rather than adopting a standardized approach to teaching that seems to presume that all learners of a given age or grade are essentially alike
- Responsive teaching
- Proactively planning varied approaches to what students need to learn, how they will learn it, and/or how they can express what they have learned in order to increase the likelihood that each student will learn as much as he or she can as efficiently as possible

Here are a few more definitions. Differentiation is also the following:

- Making a match between learner and material to be taught[2]
- Rising to the challenge of educating every child in the classroom[3]
- Teaching that connects with the learner[4]
- Personalizing the prescribed curriculum by offering a range of learning options and support systems, and using a range of teaching and learning strategies[5]
- Proactively planning, student-centered instruction that is rooted in assessment and blends whole-class, individual, and small-group instruction to provide multiple approaches to content, process, and product with the goal of maximizing the capacity of each learner[6]

YOUR TURN

Developing a Definition of Differentiation

1. Think about a time when a learning experience (in school or out of school) was a poor fit for you. Write or sketch your impressions of what that felt like to you. Include both cognitive (learning) and affective (feeling) descriptors.
2. Now, write a note or memo to the adult in charge of that setting explaining what he or she might have done to make the situation more appropriate for your needs. If you'd rather, make a list of dos and don'ts you'd like that adult to have understood and practiced.
3. Based on the definitions here and your own reflections, develop your own preliminary definition of *differentiated instruction.*
4. Come back to your definition at the end of the chapter and your class discussion on the chapter and revise the definition to reflect new insights you have developed.

OBJECTIVE 2

To construct an informed, personal rationale for teaching to address learner needs

Why Differentiate Instruction

Differentiating instruction certainly calls on teachers to develop more complex professional skills than does the more typical practice of teaching as though all students in the classroom were essentially alike. It makes sense, then, to ask the question: Is it really worth the time and effort to differentiate instruction?

There are many compelling reasons to craft classrooms that vigorously attend to student differences. A rationale for differentiated instruction comes from theory, research, and educational common sense. Consider the following.

- Today's classrooms are becoming more academically diverse in most regions of the United States (and elsewhere, for that matter). Many, if not most, classrooms contain students representing both genders and multiple cultures, frequently include students who do not speak English as a first language, and generally contain students with a range of exceptionalities and markedly different experiential backgrounds. These students almost certainly work at differing readiness levels, have varying interests, and learn in a variety of ways.[7]
- Psychologists tell us that a student learns only when a task is a little too hard for that student. When a student can do work with little effort, and virtually independently, that student is not learning, but rather rehearsing the known. When a student finds a task beyond his or her reach, frustration, not learning, is the result. Only when a task is a bit beyond the student's comfort level, and the student finds a support system to bridge the gap, does learning occur. This optimum degree of difficulty for learning is referred to as a student's zone of proximal development.[8] Considering today's diverse classrooms, it is unlikely that a teacher will be consistently able to develop one-size-fits-all learning experiences that are in the zones of proximal development of all students in a particular class.
- Brain research suggests that when tasks are *too hard* for a learner, the brain "downshifts" to the limbic area of the brain that does not "think," but rather is designed to protect an individual from harm. Also, when tasks are *too easy* for learners, those learners do not show thoughtful brain activity, but rather display patterns that look more like the early stages of sleep. Only when tasks are moderately challenging for an individual does the brain "think" in a way that prompts learning.[9] Once again, teachers will find it difficult to consistently find single tasks that are moderately challenging for all learners in a class that includes a range of readiness and experiential levels.
- It is likely that male and female learning patterns and preferences vary. The variance probably has biological, cultural, and environmental origins. There is also, of course, great variety among both male and female populations in regard to learning. Nonetheless, it is likely counterproductive to assume that gender is an irrelevant factor in what individuals learn and how they learn.[10]
- Culture has an important bearing on how individuals learn. While it is clearly not the case that all members of a given culture learn in similar ways, it is the case that learning environments and procedures that are comfortable for many members of one cultural group may not be so to many members of other cultural groups. Students whose classrooms are a cultural misfit often do poorly in school.[11] In classrooms where varied cultural groups are represented, a single approach to teaching and learning is unlikely to serve all students well. In fact, because students in any cultural group also vary, even classrooms that are more culturally homogeneous would benefit from multiple approaches to teaching and learning.
- Student motivation and task persistence increase when students can work with topics that are of personal interest. Modifying instruction to draw on student interests is likely to result in greater student engagement, higher levels of intrinsic motivation, higher student productivity, greater student autonomy, increased achievement, and an improved sense of

self-competence.[12] Encouraging students to link required learning to that which is personally interesting to them seems an important modification for teachers in most classrooms.

- The opportunity to learn in ways that make learning more efficient is also likely to make learning more effective. Attention to a student's preferred mode of learning or thinking promotes improved achievement.[13]

LEARNING ACTIVITY 2

Beyond information provided by theory and research, most of us can draw on both personal experience and classroom observation to understand the positive impact of instruction that fits the individual and the negative impact of instruction that is a poor fit for the individual. Consider the likely outcomes for students in the following paired statements.

A	B
Juan cannot read the text in his history class and cannot understand the teacher's lectures. No provisions are made for him to get access to the information, and he doesn't know where to begin.	Juan has a textbook in his class in which the teacher has highlighted key passages so he can focus his efforts on translating essential segments. In addition, there is always the opportunity to read with a partner or to use tape-recorded text. The teacher consistently uses small-group discussions to encourage students to summarize and make sense of notes they have taken in class.
Latisha is quite a good reader. Although a first-grader, she reads at a fourth-grade level. Her teacher makes certain every student works with the same reading materials and exercises.	Latisha's teacher is aware that she is an advanced reader. Sometimes everyone in the class reads together, but most of the time students work with a variety of peers to read books of common interest at common reading levels or to share books with classmates. The teacher also works with the students in small groups to be sure she is closely addressing their needs to continue to grow as confident readers.
David has a learning disability. He understands ideas well but has a great deal of difficulty reading quickly and writing efficiently. Nearly all assessments in David's class are written. Most tests and papers have strict time limits.	David and his teacher work together to establish timetables for his written assignments. This flexibility enables him to write with less tension and to proofread his work. The teacher also generally provides more than one way to express ideas, so that David and other students can use diagrams, sketches, oral presentations, hands-on demonstrations, and so on to show their knowledge and skill.

It does not take a great deal of thought to understand the wear and tear on Juan, Latisha, and David in the "A" scenarios. It also seems evident that student attitude and work are likely to improve in the "B" scenarios. While it's important to have theory and research to inform our classroom practice, an observant teacher receives clear clues every day that students benefit from classrooms that address their individual needs.

We know a great many things about learners and learning that suggest the importance of attending to students' differences in the classroom. We also know, however, that few classrooms are vigorously attentive to learner variance. This is the case whether students have learning disabilities, are advanced, represent varied cultures, or are second-language learners.[14]

YOUR TURN

Developing a Rationale for Differentiation

1. Divide a sheet of paper into two columns. In the left-hand column, list all the reasons that you think cause teachers to differentiate instruction when they do so. In the right-hand column, list all the reasons that you think cause teachers not to differentiate instruction when they do not do so.
2. Examine your two lists. What patterns do you see? What do you make of the patterns? If possible, compare your lists and patterns with those of colleagues to see whether the lists and patterns are similar in any way. Write a brief paragraph about your conclusions and thoughts resulting from this exercise. If you'd prefer, you might simply list thoughts that stem from analysis of the lists or draw an editorial-type cartoon that depicts one or more of your insights.
3. Write or tape-record a letter to yourself that provides the rationale you'd like to use in deciding whether or not to teach in ways that are responsive to learner variance in your classes. Do this with the thought that you'll read the letter or listen to the tape when you complete your teaching internship and then again when you complete your first year of teaching. You may want to add to or revise the letter or tape when you conclude your work with this chapter (and other related parts of the book).

OBJECTIVE 3

To depict ways in which learner, learning environment, and curriculum are integral to differentiated or academically responsive instruction

The Classroom Origins of Differentiated Instruction

The idea of differentiated or responsive teaching is not an isolated one. Neither is it a strategy to be used on occasion when there is extra time. Differentiation is actually a way of thinking about teaching and learning that, over time, pervades everything a teacher does. The reason for the pervasiveness is that differentiation stems from increasing awareness of a key classroom element—

students. That awareness then impacts all other classroom elements and a teacher's decision about those elements.

LEARNING ACTIVITY 3

A helpful way of thinking about the origins and impacts of differentiation is to examine the approach in regard to four classroom elements: *who* we teach, *where* we teach, *what* we teach, and *how* we teach. A brief look at the classroom as a system in which those four elements are tightly interdependent helps us understand more about what differentiation is, where it comes from, why teachers elect to teach in a differentiated way, and even a little about how differentiation might look.

Who We Teach

Howard Gardner suggests that one of the greatest mistakes we make in teaching is to assume that all learners in a given classroom are essentially the same. Once we allow ourselves to believe, for example, that all our kindergartners are basically alike or that our Spanish I learners are a homogeneous group, or that our seventh-grade social studies students are pretty much the same, we give ourselves permission to teach them the same things, to use a single method, and to allot the same amount of time for each student's learning.[15]

Consider Gardner's caution as it applies to a teacher's brief description of learners in a real classroom of twenty-five students in a very recent year. This group, the teacher noted, was fairly typical of her students in past years as well. The teacher's name is Judy Rex.[16]

- Several students appeared to work on grade level in some areas but a bit above or below grade level in other areas.
- Three students had identified learning disabilities.
- Three students were second-language learners.
- Four students were identified as gifted, one of whom consistently worked as much as five years above grade level.
- Three students were taking medication for attention and hyperactivity disorders.
- Two students had diagnosed emotional difficulties.
- Three students were working with speech and/or occupational therapists.
- Several students in the class displayed problems and needs similar to those of students who had been identified as having special needs, but they had not been formally identified as needing special assistance.

Even this listing of learning variance omits important information. The students also varied in level of security at home, economic status, degree of parental support, experiences that affect school performance, culture, gender, talents and interests, preferences for how to learn, personality, social skills, and so on.

Mrs. Rex comes to her classroom each fall not only expecting significant academic diversity in her students but also holding several other important beliefs about the students she will teach. She believes the following:

- Each student is a person of worth—deserving of dignity as they are, worthy of respect by both teacher and peers, and worthy of the teacher's investment of time and attention.

- Each student is an individual—like all other humans in important ways and unlike others in important ways, bringing positives that need to be developed and negatives that need to be modified in order to help the student develop effectively.
- Each student in the room is building a life—with an evolving relationship to others and to learning, with the student's potential largely hidden from view.
- Each student is someone the teacher must come to know and understand in order to show respect, recognize individuality, develop strengths, address weaknesses, and discover potential. While she will never know any child fully, she believes she must continually attempt to learn more about each student and to use what she learns to help students grow and develop as learners and as people.

Because of Mrs. Rex's beliefs about the students she teaches, she simply cannot disregard the obvious differences among her learners. Both their commonalities and differences become central to her instructional thinking and planning. Her mindset about teaching is significantly shaped by her beliefs about the students she teaches.

Where We Teach

Both because of her beliefs about who she teaches and because of what she knows about the impact of environment on learning, Mrs. Rex has also developed some key beliefs about where she wants to teach and where her students can best learn:

- The classroom must be a place that feels safe to students—a place where their strengths are acknowledged and affirmed, where their weaknesses are dealt with honestly but supportively, where errors are seen as an important and acceptable part of the learning process, and where the teacher teaches for success.
- The classroom must provide ongoing opportunities for each student to be known by and know the other students—a place where every student is acknowledged in positive ways, a place where each student feels a connection or affiliation.
- The classroom must accord dignity and respect through basic expectations for each learner—attending class regularly, meeting deadlines, demonstrating growth as a learner, displaying a commitment to learning evidenced through hard work, and being a valuable colleague for peers.
- The classroom must be a place where an ethic of hard work—propelled by purpose, joy, and pride—is engendered; where there is continual support for individual growth; where growth is acknowledged and celebrated; and where clear classroom routines support efficiency, clarity about expectations, and success.
- Both to make time for the teacher to work with individuals and small groups and to develop learner independence and a sense of ownership in learning, the classroom must support shared teaching and learning—a place where everyone has something academically important to contribute to others, where everyone has something personally important to contribute to others, where the teacher is a learner, and where students are teachers.

These beliefs about the kind of classroom she wants to help develop stem in part from Mrs. Rex's beliefs about students. The kind of classroom she develops will also contribute to or inhibit her capacity to act upon her beliefs about students. Likewise, her beliefs about where she should teach and where her students should learn both stem from and impact her beliefs about what she should teach—in other words, the nature of curriculum.

What We Teach

Elsewhere in this book, authors write about key elements of curriculum. What a teacher believes about curriculum greatly affects both who the teacher teaches and where the teacher teaches. A teacher who is fascinated by his or her discipline and sees its power to make people's lives richer approaches curriculum with a curricular compass different from that of the teacher who simply sees curriculum as something to be covered.

Mrs. Rex has also developed beliefs about curriculum, or what she will teach. Again, it both stems from and shapes her beliefs about her students and the learning environment she will share with them:

- Curriculum should be clear and focused—the teacher must recognize and help students master what is essential for learners to know, understand, and be able to do as a result of a learning sequence.
- Curriculum should spotlight high-quality knowledge, ideas, and skills—knowledge, ideas, and skills that lead to competence in the discipline; help students make meaning of the discipline; are valued by experts in the discipline; support retention, retrieval, and transfer of knowledge; lead students toward expertise in the discipline; and necessitate thought, reflection, application, and production on the part of students.
- Curriculum should be invitational—important, illuminating, intriguing, purposeful, and challenging to the individual.
- Curriculum should play a role in developing a hunger for learning. It is a catalyst for developing self-awareness as a learner and for developing habits and attitudes that cause a learner to effectively pursue understanding and skill.

How We Teach

Differentiated instruction really has to do with *how* we teach. However, *how* we teach is not an entity separate from *who* we teach, *where* we teach, or *what* we teach. Rather, *how* we teach is a response to the other three elements.

Mrs. Rex teaches in a differentiated way. She would say she really has no other good options. If she believes every student is worthy of respect, time, and investment, she will accept the responsibility of getting to know them. The more she knows and understands them, the more invested she is in making the learning environment a good fit for each learner. The more she knows and understands them, the more determined she is to share with each of them the power of knowledge to help them develop their capacities and build more rewarding and productive lives. It becomes her mission to help each student she genuinely cares about come to love the subject matter she finds so powerful. At that point, *how* she teaches is a given. She will not develop a highly responsive or differentiated classroom in a short period of time. In fact, she will spend her career working toward the goal of responsive teaching, but that journey will be propelled by her growing sense of the four elements and their interrelationship:

- To maximize individual growth and success, instruction must be crafted to maximize the opportunity for the growth and success of each learner in mastering essential knowledge, understanding, and skill.
- To maximize individual growth and success, instruction must be a good fit for the readiness levels, interests, and modes of learning of individual learners.

- To maximize individual growth and success, instruction must employ varied modes of presentation and varied approaches to learning—to match both curricular goals and student needs.
- To maximize individual growth and success, instruction will involve a range of student groupings—to allow for a match between learner and what is to be learned, to allow students to work in a variety of contexts to enhance opportunities for success, to "audition" students in different settings in order to understand which approaches to learning work best for different learners, and to allow the teacher to teach in ways more targeted to the needs of individuals and small groups of learners.
- To maximize individual growth and success, instruction will build student–teacher partnerships—for determining approaches that work best, for goal-setting, for monitoring growth, and for building scaffolding for success.

The next section examines concrete strategies a teacher might use to "differentiate instruction." It's important to remember, however, that differentiated teaching is most powerful when it is an outgrowth of beliefs about teaching and learning, not when it is simply a collection of techniques applied to a classroom in which students are often taught as though they were indistinguishable from one another, or in a setting that is impersonal or intimidating, or using a curriculum that feels stale and remote to learners.

YOUR TURN

Examining Classroom Connections in Responsive Teaching

It is likely that classrooms in which you teach *will* be academically diverse. You probably can't escape academic diversity in your teaching career. What you *can* control is your response to it. Even as you begin your career as a teacher, what you believe about your work as a professional will begin to shape how you practice that profession.

1. Draw a flowchart or some other graphic representation that shows the interrelationship among who we teach, where we teach, what we teach, and how we teach in the thinking and practice of Mrs. Rex. Annotate your graphic to make sure the connections you make are clear to colleagues who look at your work.
2. Draw a similar flowchart that reflects the thinking and practice of a teacher in a one-size-fits-all classroom. Annotate this graphic with your thoughts, too. Beneath the graphic, write a statement of comparison and contrast for the two representations.
3. Develop a list of three or four of the most important beliefs you now hold about who you will teach, where you will teach, what you will teach, and how you will teach. Beside each of the beliefs, write how you think that belief will shape your teaching.
4. It's easy to think of grading as a process that is highly prescribed—that exists apart from a teacher's beliefs about teaching. In fact, it is often the case that because we see grading as fixed, grading shapes our beliefs about teaching rather than our beliefs about teaching shaping the way we grade. What impact would you suppose Mrs. Rex's beliefs have on her grading? How would you grade to reflect the beliefs you listed in item 3?

OBJECTIVE 4

To apply specific ways to differentiate content, activities, and products in response to student readiness, interest, and learning profile

LEARNING ACTIVITY 4

Some Approaches to Responsive Teaching

There is no formula for differentiation—no single way to respond to student variance. While that is uncomfortable in some ways, it's also positive. Teachers vary just as their students do, and it's important for teachers to be able to develop processes and procedures for addressing their learners' needs in ways that simultaneously address the personality and developing expertise of the teacher.

It is nonetheless helpful, however, for a teacher to have a way of organizing his or her thinking about and planning for academically responsive teaching. For that reason, it's useful to think in terms of differentiation in response to three student traits (readiness, interest, and learning profile) in regard to three elements of curriculum (content, process, and product) and in terms of two instructional roles (teacher role and student role).

This section presents just a few examples of how a teacher might differentiate *content* (what the student should learn or how the student gets access to the information and ideas), *process* (activities, or how the student comes to make sense of and "own" the content), and/or *product* (how the student shows what he or she has come to know, understand, and be able to do) in response to student *readiness* (proximity to a learning goal), *interest* (affinity for a topic or task), and/or *learning profile* (preferred way to learn), depending on whether the focus of instruction at a given moment is *teacher as presenter* or *student as worker*.[17]

Differentiation in Response to Learner Readiness

Readiness has to do with a student's current understandings and skills relative to a particular learning goal. A task presented at a readiness level appropriate for a student will be just a little too difficult for the student to complete independently. Often, the learning goal for a task will not change in response to student readiness, but the "degree of difficulty," or degree of complexity at which the student is asked to work with the goal, should match the student's current preparedness for the work. Recall that when tasks are too difficult or too simple for a learner's readiness level, achievement is likely to be impaired. Thus the goal of readiness differentiation is to make sure a learner (1) has enough background to understand the assigned material or task, (2) has to work to link what he or she already knows to something unfamiliar introduced in the material or task, (3) has a support system in the classroom to help bridge the known and the new, and (4) generally finds that success follows effort.

The following table lists strategies teachers can use to make the classroom fit better for a range of learners. The list is by no means complete, but it illustrates ways in which teachers teach important content with the needs of learners forming a central part of their instructional thinking and planning.

Some Approaches to Differentiating Instruction for Student Readiness

Adjusting for Readiness: When the Teacher Presents

Strategy	Example
Provide organizers to help students follow the presentation sequence and focus on main ideas.	To support students who have difficulty following a lecture or other oral presentation, Mr. Jameson gives students blank graphics with spaces to record main ideas and illustrations. He also completes the graphic on the overhead as he talks.
Use concrete illustrations of complex or abstract ideas.	To support students who have difficulty with abstract information, Ms. Higgins nearly always uses objects she's brought from home to demonstrate how principles of physics work.
List key vocabulary for student reference.	To support second-language learners and other students with reading or writing difficulties, Ms. Ahmad posts a chart of important words about a topic and discusses what students know or guess about the words before she begins a discussion on that topic. She then has her students adjust their thoughts about the words as they gain new information.
Use small-group instruction as a regular means of teaching.	Ms. Abel frequently conducts mini-workshops on skills or ideas she knows will be difficult for some of her students. She individually asks some students to attend and also invites anyone who'd like help with the topic to come to the session as well. She also regularly plans reteaching sessions for students who struggle with fundamental ideas and skills and small-group sessions to extend the thinking of students whose thinking and skills are advanced.
Stop often for student reflection and questions.	Mr. Garcia stops about every seven to ten minutes when he is explaining and demonstrating at the board or overhead. Sometimes he asks students to summarize key points or apply a skill with a partner. Sometimes he asks students individually to write a summary statement or question about what they are understanding. He walks around the room to hear or read student ideas and then concludes with questions from the class before moving ahead.
Ask questions of escalating difficulty.	To make certain everyone in the class is challenged by discussions, Ms. Rentz plans question sequences that begin by asking for fundamental information and concepts and continues by increasing the complexity of questions until everyone in the class has been both affirmed and stretched by her questioning.

Adjusting for Readiness: When the Student Is Worker

Strategy	Example
Provide materials at varied readability levels.	Ms. Glenn uses text materials, supplementary print materials, and Internet resources at a wide range of reading levels on the same topics to ensure that each student has resources that are appropriately challenging for that learner.
Bridge the language gap for second language learners.	Ms. Hendrix finds resource materials in the native languages of students whenever she can. She also ensures that in group work, there are students who can speak both English and the language of students who are just learning English. She encourages new English learners to write first in their own language and then translate into English so their ideas are not muted by language difficulties. In addition, she meets with these students as often as possible to coach them in their new language.
Assess often and use findings to adjust plans.	Mr. Peterson thinks of everything his students do as an assessment tool. He preassesses prior to each unit. He makes quick notes during discussions, as he spot-checks homework, as he sits with individuals and small groups, and as he grades tasks in order to be more aware of students' proficiency levels. He often uses "exit cards" on which students respond briefly to questions about a day's lesson. All these are helpful to him in knowing how to adjust instruction tomorrow or in a few days.

(*continued*)

Some Approaches to Differentiating Instruction for Student Readiness (cont.)

Adjusting for Readiness: When the Student Is Worker

Strategy	Example
Provide highlighted texts.	Mr. Lupinski keeps several texts on a shelf behind his desk. In each of them, he has highlighted the most essential passages. Students with learning disabilities, who are new to English, and who have other reading problems often begin by using the highlighted books to focus their energies on important ideas. Reading seems much more manageable with the highlighted texts.
Use tape recordings of text and supplementary materials.	Ms. Ishmael nearly always has a listening station in the classroom where students can hear important materials read aloud. She records some of the materials herself but often uses student and parent volunteers to make the recordings.
Provide reading partners or reading buddies.	Ms. Feinstein uses several read-aloud strategies, including reading buddies, with similar readers paired together; interest-based read-alouds of students' own choosing; and choral reading pairs in which a more able reader reads a brief passage that is then repeated by the partner, who has more difficulty with reading. She finds that paired readings not only support her struggling readers but can also be designed to challenge and support very advanced readers.
Allow students to express what they have learned in multiple ways.	Mr. Arnold often gives students the option of writing prose to explain ideas or generating annotated diagrams or other graphics that are explanatory. He also often gives students both a hands-on product and a test on a topic. He invites students with serious reading or language problems to tell him test responses or to tape-record them so that language problems don't mask understanding of content.
Provide tasks and products at different "degrees of difficulty" or different levels of complexity.	Ms. Avila routinely uses tiered tasks and tiered products to ensure that all of her students are working with the same essential ideas and skills, but at challenge levels that are appropriate for them individually.
Use rubrics with clear indicators of quality at varied levels of sophistication.	Mr. Fierro uses rubrics that reflect key elements of skill and understanding, and specific descriptors of student work at varied levels of competency. He works with students to set goals for next steps in growth on the rubrics, not assuming that excellence will look the same for all students at a given time.
Vary the pacing of student work.	Ms. Askins knows that her students will need different amounts of time to work on a task. Some students may need additional time for practice, others additional time for in-depth exploration of a topic. She uses "anchor activities" that give her students directions for what to do if they finish a task early.
Provide homework options.	Mr. Bandy often has students diagnose their strengths and weaknesses at a given point in a unit, then provides homework options so that students can select work most likely to help them improve.
Vary test questions.	Although Mr. Conklyn's tests cover the same core knowledge, understanding, and skill, he will often vary some questions on tests. His goal is to have at least some questions targeted to a student's current level of understanding and skill.
Coach for success.	Ms. Bellin actively moves among her students whenever they are working on a task. She monitors their progress, assesses their understanding, and coaches them individually to help them reach and extend both group and personal goals for achievement.

Much of the time, a teacher can help virtually all students explore the same important concepts, understandings, and skills by varying the complexity of student tasks, adjusting pacing, and providing different support systems. Sometimes, however, it is necessary to change what students are studying. This is particularly true when students are working on a relatively linear sequence of skills, as is often the case in spelling, math computation, and some foreign-language acquisition. In many of these instances, a student simply cannot move to a new step of proficiency until he or she has mastered the previous step. Once a student has mastered a step, there is no growth as long as the student continues to work at the same level of mastery. In such instances, teachers do well to consider opportunities for students to work on the skills they need in order to progress rather than force-fitting everyone into a lesson that misses the target for most learners. For example, it makes little sense for every sixth-grader always to have the same list of spelling words when some of the students are spelling at a first-grade level and others like college students. Similarly, a student who has not developed number sense will not likely succeed with addition and subtraction. Likewise, a student who is already adding and subtracting gains nothing from a continuing study of what a number is and how it is represented.

Teaching in response to students' varying readiness levels begins when a teacher asks the question: Is what I'm teaching today and how I'm teaching today likely to stretch each student a bit beyond his or her comfort level? When the answer is "no" for some students in the class, a teacher who intends to make the day work for each student in the classroom begins to ask: What adjustments can I make to ensure that each learner is challenged in a way that enhances his or her opportunity to work hard and succeed as a result of the work? Remember that "working hard" and "success" are highly individual concepts.

Differentiation in Response to Learner Interest

Interest has to do with a student's proclivity for a topic. When a student finds a topic interesting, motivation and engagement increase and achievement is likely to follow. Teachers can learn to incorporate students' interests into most facets of the curriculum. Teachers also have a great opportunity to help students develop *new* interests because of curriculum and instruction that are dynamic and relevant to students. The goal of differentiation based on learner interest is to help a student connect his or her particular talents, experiences, and preferences to required content. Given the interrelatedness of all knowledge, capturing student interest and relating it to what students "have to learn" is really not so difficult.

As is the case with differentiation in response to student readiness, there is no formula for how to modify instruction to tap into student interest. The next table suggests a few approaches to differentiation based on learner interest.

A teacher who differentiates instruction based on learner interest asks the questions: How can the content I teach become a catalyst for developing personal interests and talents, and how can personal talents and interests become a catalyst for developing students' passion about the content I teach? These teachers understand that learning is a two-way swinging door in which what students care about and what they need to learn can provide a common passageway to achievement and personal development.

Differentiation in Response to Learner Profile

Learning profile relates to preferences for how to learn. The goal of learning profile differentiation is to tap into a learner's best ways of learning, while perhaps also helping learners expand the number of avenues to learning that work for them. Learning profile is influenced by at least four factors: learning style, intelligence preference, gender, and culture.

Learning style refers to the environmental conditions in which a person is mostly likely to concentrate on, internalize, and retain information and skills, and it often relates to categories such as environment, physical needs, and interactions with others.[18] Used in that way, learning style might include such factors as level of noise, degree of movement, kind of seating, preference for a mode of presentation, preference for working alone or with a partner, and so on.

Some Approaches to Differentiating Instruction for Student Interests

Adjusting for Interest: When the Teacher Presents

Strategy	Example
Link required subject matter and interests of students.	Mr. Brewster frequently uses examples from music, sports, literature, current events, and other areas of interest to his students to illustrate concepts and skills from the content he teaches.
Find out what is appealing to students about their areas of interest, and show them those elements in what you teach about.	Ms. D'Angelo looks for *why* her students like what they like. They may, for example, be drawn to humor, action, reflection, human stories, making or creating things, and so on. She then teaches in a way that brings out those elements in her presentations. She helps students come to understand why they like what they do and that those things are a part of what she teaches.
Show students how what you teach connects with and furthers your own interests.	Ms. Aiken often uses one of her interests as a metaphor for what she is teaching. For example, she recently talked about how themes in history are like themes in music. She explained to students that thinking about her content in relation to something else she liked made both things more interesting for her. Then she challenges students to reflect on how elements of her subject are related to their own interests.
Show students how the content you teach shapes people's lives.	Ms. Lightfoot makes it a point to share with her students stories about people who have shaped the discipline she teaches and about people whose lives are now centered in that discipline in one way or another. She is careful to use illustrations from various cultures, occupations, and walks of life. She finds that many of her students develop new interests in a subject when they see it as attached to life in some way.
Teach with joy in mind.	Mr. Washington always reminds himself as he plans presentations that students respond to joy, mystery, purpose, and enthusiasm. He finds that his young learners often develop ownership in ideas and skills he presents with those characteristics at the heart of his teaching.

Adjusting for Interest: When the Student Is Worker

Strategy	Example
Use interest surveys.	Early in the year, Ms. Todd gives her students general-interest surveys she has developed. As the year goes on, she seeks other ways to elicit student interests, for example, discussions, bulletin boards where students post questions of interest, and journal writing about interests. She also asks students to give her ideas about how she can draw on their interests in class.
Use interest centers and interest groups.	Mr. Leland keeps a space in the room where he and the students contribute materials related to the topic they are studying. He encourages the students to use the area to learn more about ideas and people of special interest to them as they study. He also uses interest-based discussion groups from time to time so students can discuss topics of interest in the content with peers who share the same interests. He also likes to use the cooperative strategy called Group Investigation, which teaches students skills of investigation and presentation as they learn about a student-selected aspect of the content.
Allow students to specialize in subtopics of a larger topic.	Mr. Francisco often asks his students to select one aspect of the unit they will study in which they would like to specialize. He provides time and structures for students to explore these preference areas as a way to strengthen their affinity for the subject and expand their knowledge about it.
Design tasks and products that invite students to link concepts and skills in your content to areas of interest.	Ms. Kiernan routinely asks students to show how key concepts and skills they are learning in language arts are related to student interests. For example, students have examined how the "rules" of writing vary in novels, journalism, music, science, and so on. They have also recently examined how the concept of interdependence is evidenced in athletics, the arts, science, families, governments, and literature, their primary content area.

Some Approaches to Differentiating Instruction for Student Interests (cont.)

Adjusting for Interest: When the Student Is Worker

Strategy	Example
Provide choices.	Mr. Lin finds his students' interest enhanced almost any time he gives them choices about their work—where to sit, with whom to work, resources to use, timelines for accomplishing tasks, criteria for success, topics for investigation, and so on.
Encourage students to select modes of expressing learning.	Ms. Larsen carefully outlines for students which basic information, ideas, and skills their work must demonstrate, but she provides options for how students present their work. Among the options may be such things as monologues, editorial cartoons, video clips, museum exhibits, essays, and panel discussions.
Provide opportunities for guided independent investigations of interest areas.	Ms. Wannamaker includes independent study as a part of each year's curriculum. The lengths of the studies vary with student readiness and breadth of interest. She meets with students to work on aspects of independent learning such as posing good questions, using resources effectively, analyzing data, drawing conclusions, setting goals and timelines, and so on. Her goal is to help each student stretch in capacity to learn independently. The choice of topic is largely set by student interest.
Help students develop mentorships in interest areas.	Ms. Elkins uses mentorships with a variety of students to help them develop or extend interests. Mentors may be professionals or older students with developed interests in areas of interest shared by her students. She finds mentors can be particularly helpful in showing students how to apply ideas and skills in authentic ways and how to assess the quality of their work in authentic ways.

Intelligence preference refers to thinking style. Robert Sternberg suggests that individuals are likely to have a preference for learning analytically (in a sort of typical school-oriented fashion with an emphasis on logical arrangement of ideas, summary and repetition of information, and dealing with ideas in a text–lecture–test format), practically (in a way that encourages seeing how people use ideas and skills in the "real world" and learning ideas and skills in a real world context), or creatively (in ways that tap into problem solving and imagination).[19] Howard Gardner suggests that individuals have proclivities for one of eight intelligences that he calls verbal-linguistic, logical-mathematical, bodily-kinesthetic, musical, spatial, interpersonal, intrapersonal, and naturalist. These intelligences are described briefly in Chapter 5 on page 108.[20] Gardner and Sternberg suggest that both heredity and environment affect our intelligence preferences. Both propose that attending to an individual's intelligence preferences in the learning process enhances learning.

Culture and *gender* also affect our preferences for learning. While culture and gender help shape both environmental and intelligence preferences, they can also affect how we relate to others (e.g., whether we prefer to work alone or in groups; whether we focus more on groups or individuals; whether we are more responsive to messages from self, peers, adults, or a combination), how we process information (e.g., whether we learn better from whole to part or from part to whole, in a linear or nonlinear way, through collaboration or competition, orally, visually, or spatially; whether we are people-oriented or task-oriented; whether we learn best inductively or deductively; whether we relate best to facts or meanings; whether we are creative or conforming), and how we see ourselves in the world (e.g., whether we see ourselves as capable or incapable, whether we are present-oriented or future-oriented, whether we see ourselves as rule makers or rule followers, whether we see ourselves as vulnerable or powerful, whether we are self-directed or other-directed). While it is always a mistake to assume homogeneity within any culture or gender, it is the case that *patterns* of learning preference exist within a culture or gender. In general, schools serve best those whose culture is dominant in schools. There are exceptions to that trend, too, however.

The goal of a teacher who differentiates instruction in response to student learning preferences should *not* categorize students by gender, culture, intelligence preference, and so on and draw conclusions about the student based on those categories. The teacher should not prescribe how a student will learn or limit how that student might learn. Rather the teacher's goal is to create a classroom that is flexible enough—offers enough options—for students to investigate how they learn best and make informed choices about what approaches to learning will serve them well.

We know a great deal about learning profile—so much, in fact, that it can be daunting to consider the options. It is likely that no teacher could address all the possible learning profile factors and options. A more realistic goal is to begin by selecting a few learning profile options that seem both important and obtainable, talking with students about them, and establishing a classroom in which students have enough choices about learning to find an approach that seems comfortable. The following table presents a few ways of thinking about learning profile differentiation. The goal of the figure, as with the two previous ones, is to be not exhaustive but illustrative.

Understanding the variety of learning profile options takes study and time. It is particularly important in today's culturally diverse classrooms that teachers invest time in understanding the traditions, values, and perspectives of all the students they serve. It's much easier for a teacher to assume everyone sees the world (including school) as he or she does. But this is an inaccurate assumption that contributes to considerable discomfort, disenfranchisement, discouragement, and lowered achievement in large numbers of students.

No teacher can know every student thoroughly. Every teacher can, however, learn far more about more students by setting out to do so than by assuming it is impossible to know them. In the beginning, just give students learning profile choices and have them share what they learn about themselves with you. It's also a wonderful habit to develop early in teaching to ask students often to share with you their ideas about how to make the class a better fit for all of them.

Some Approaches to Differentiating Instruction for Student Learning Profile

Adjusting for Learning Profile: When the Teacher Presents

Strategy	Example
Highlight past and contemporary contributions to the discipline by people from varied cultures and both genders.	Ms. Phillips talks about contributors to the field she teaches as a routine part of each unit. She includes contributors from many cultures and both genders. She also carefully relates instances of people at work in the discipline throughout the local area.
Present multiple perspectives on topics and issues.	Ms. Losario raises complex issues and multifaceted problems that call on students to use their knowledge and think deeply. She encourages students to look for varied viewpoints on the issues and lets them know they are thinking effectively when they do so.

Some Approaches to Differentiating Instruction for Student Learning Profile (cont.)

Adjusting for Learner Profile: When the Teacher Presents

Strategy	Example
Present in oral, visual, and tactile modes.	Mr. Barsel always uses an overhead projector as he talks with the class. He consistently uses pictures of what he is talking about and often constructs models in front of the class. Often he provides manipulatives for students so they can work along with him.
Design presentations to move through a cycle of intelligence or other learning preferences.	Ms. Tepper often plans for analytical, practical, and creative illustrations and questions in her presentations. This approach ensures that each student identifies with at least one segment of the presentation and also helps students expand their learning options.
Use wait time and other approaches to reflection and student participation.	Ms. Akimba regularly uses strategies like Think–Pair–Share to ensure participation by students, including those who are less assertive in speaking before the class, those who like to reflect before they speak, those who enjoy speaking more often, and those who are reticent. She also honors the need for reflection by alerting students early in the week or marking period to tasks that will come later.
Use whole-to-part and part-to-whole approaches.	Mr. Lloyd is always certain to explain the purpose of the lesson as well as its details—to be sure students are clear on both the "what" and the "why" of what they are learning. He also routinely uses concept maps of the unit and year to help students see how parts of the curriculum connect.
Use concrete examples of abstract ideas.	Mr. Peterson shows students how the ideas he teaches look when they are used in people's daily lives, jobs, and hobbies. He also guides students in using objects (the familiar) that can serve as metaphors for what they are studying (the unfamiliar).

Adjusting for Learner Profile: When the Student Is Worker

Strategy	Example
Develop tasks and assessments that ask students to examine multiple perspectives with empathy for various vantage points.	Mr. Malonowski uses "Think Tanks" in his class during many units. Small groups of students work together throughout the unit to develop one of several possible positions on issues. As the unit concludes, the Think Tank groups present and defend their perspectives. They also assess the effectiveness of all Think Tank presentations using a rubric developed by the students and teacher. One criterion for success is helping peers understand perspectives other than their own on an issue.
Honor student needs to work alone or with peers.	Ms. Lukin often encourages students to work alone, with one peer, or with a small group in completing activities and products. She also works with students to gain the skills they will need to succeed in whichever setting they select.
Offer multiple modes of investigation to students.	Mr. French often gives students the choice of a practical, analytical, or creative task as they work to develop new understandings and skills.
Offer multiple modes of expressing learning.	When possible, Mr. Largent develops product assignments with several modes of presenting student understanding. In a given unit, students can write a how-to piece, develop a PowerPoint presentation, or present a video or live demonstration. In each case, the same essential knowledge, understanding, and skill are requirements for whichever mode a student selects.
Offer options for competition or collaboration.	Ms. McAlister sometimes uses competitions as a mode of review for tests, sometimes uses collaborative study groups, and often gives students a choice of which way to prepare for tests.
Develop a classroom with flexible spaces.	Often Ms. Ellis's students have the option of working at a table, in a stand-alone desk, or on the floor.

(continued)

Some Approaches to Differentiating Instruction for Student Learning Profile (cont.)

Adjusting for Learner Profile: When the Student Is Worker

Strategy	Example
Develop a classroom that attends to varied needs for sound and visual stimulation.	Mr. Renfrow has some sections in his classroom that do not have things posted on walls and bulletin boards to make it easier for students who are distracted by "busy" space to work. He also uses "quiet zones," headsets, and earplugs to help students who need to screen out noise. He and his students work together to balance the needs of students whose visual and auditory needs differ.
Balance structure and openness.	Ms. Carver has learned to present task and product directions in a more structured way for some of her students and a more open-ended way for others. However, she also works with highly structured students to become more flexible and highly creative students to attend to structured requirements.
Accommodate students who need to move.	In Ms. Smith's classroom, students who need to get up and move around are free to do so as long as they don't disrupt other students. She has found that these learners are far more successful and she is far less frustrated than when she tried to keep them seated and still all the time. Sometimes she even invents jobs for them to do so that they will need to move around and use some of their energy.
Help students learn to be aware of their own learning preferences.	Ms. Gwaltney asks her students to record their experiences in varied learning modes. She guides them in analyzing what they learn about themselves and in making decisions about ways they elect to learn.

YOUR TURN

Plannning to Differentiate Instruction Based on Learner Need

It is great practice to look at a variety of lessons through the lens of differentiation in response to students' readiness levels, interests, and learning profile. The more you think about the available options to make the classroom a better fit for more learners, the more likely you are to develop practices that allow you to do so.

1. Look at a chapter in a textbook for students of the age you might teach or in a college text you have used. Create a pre-assessment you think would be appropriate to determine student readiness to master the knowledge, understandings, and skills in the chapter. Have a colleague review the chapter and your pre-assessment to see whether there is a good match between the learning goals of the chapter and your pre-assessment.
2. Select a lesson that you have taught, that you have been taught recently, or that you have observed. Record what you think the learning goals for the lesson were. Then develop an activity for the lesson that you believe clearly addresses the learning goals. Next, develop at least two more versions of the activity—one that is more appropriately challenging for a very advanced learner and one that is more appropriately challenging for a student who has great difficulty with reading, writing, and abstract thinking. Remember that (1) the learning goals for the versions should remain the same, (2) the activities don't need to be totally different from each other, and (3) the versions need to be more and less complex, not to provide more work or less work.
3. Think about a teacher you've had who was successful in either extending an interest you already had or developing a new interest in you.

Write a letter to that teacher explaining what the teacher did to foster your interest and what that has meant to you over time.

4. Interview someone who may have a different view about school based on gender, culture, economic status, or particular life experiences. Find ways in which that person experienced school differently than you did. Note insights the conversation gives you as a teacher. If possible, share what you found out with several other peers who completed the same task.

5. Add at least one additional strategy for differentiation and an example of it to all three tables in this chapter.

OBJECTIVE 5

To analyze and understand general principles of effective differentiation

LEARNING ACTIVITY 5

Key Principles of Differentiated Instruction

There is no formula or template for developing a differentiated or academically responsive classroom. Precisely how a teacher develops processes and procedures that ensure attention to varying needs of learners will vary with the personality of the teacher, age of students, stage of professional development of the teacher, subject being taught, length of time available for teaching a given subject, and so on.

There are, however, some general principles that guide effective differentiation. They stem from knowledge about learners and learning, and from the common sense of experience in a classroom. Below are ten key principles of effective differentiation. The list is not complete, but it illustrates some important hallmarks of most effectively differentiated classrooms:

- *The core of the differentiation is proactive rather than reactive.* The teacher comes to class with several routes to learning already planned rather than with a one-size-fits-all lesson that he or she will adjust on the spot when it becomes apparent the lesson is not working well for one or more students. On-the-spot adjustment can be very important in any classroom. However, it is unlikely that impromptu modifications to lesson plans can consistently be robust enough to address the needs of learners who are far behind in understanding, far ahead in understanding, don't speak English fluently, and so on.
- *The teacher is clear about what constitutes essential knowledge, understanding, and skill for any segment of the curriculum.* This is not only necessary to achieve sound learning in any classroom but also takes on additional importance in a differentiated classroom. It is these content essentials that must serve as the focus of instruction for students who have learning problems, should generally serve as the focus for additional challenge for advanced learners,

and will give all learners a common opportunity for sharing and discussion even though their routes to the content essentials will sometimes differ.

- *The teacher provides "respectful tasks"*[21] *for all learners.* When student tasks vary, the teacher works to ensure that each one is equally interesting, equally inviting, and equally powerful. The goal is for each student to find his or her work as appealing as that of any other student. This principle also reinforces the belief that virtually all students should work at a high level of thought with the essential knowledge, understanding, and skill that is key to the particular activity or product.
- *The teacher continually assesses student understanding and adjusts instructional plans based on what the assessment reveals.* A teacher in an effectively differentiated classroom doesn't give more tests or assignments than do teachers in most other classrooms. Rather, the teacher in a responsive classroom sees everything the student does as a source of information about how learning is progressing. Thus discussions, homework, activities, small-group conversations, and student products all become indicators of student growth. The teacher looks for clues in all these indicators, reflects on what he or she sees, and modifies instructional plans based on those reflections.
- *The teacher works hard to establish a sense of community.* In these classrooms, students come to understand and value the contribution of each member of the community. Students feel safe and accepted as they are, but they also feel a sense of persistent encouragement to grow and support in doing so.
- *Flexibility is a hallmark.* The teacher seems always to be asking: What's another way to do this? How else can we help students learn effectively and efficiently? Teachers work to use time, materials, and space in flexible ways. Flexible grouping is also a central goal in effective differentiation. That is, the teacher plans for individual, whole-class, and small-group work in each learning cycle. In addition, the teacher ensures that each student regularly works in a variety of student groupings—sometimes based on readiness, sometimes based on interest, and sometimes based on learning profile. Sometimes the groupings are more homogeneous in nature (e.g., students at similar readiness levels or with similar interests) and sometimes they are more heterogeneous (e.g., mixed readiness groups or groups in which students bring a variety of talents to accomplish a common goal). Sometimes the teacher assigns students to groups, sometimes students decide on groupings, and sometimes groups are assigned randomly. A goal of flexible grouping is to balance a student's opportunity to experience work targeted to his or her particular needs with the opportunity to work in varied contexts and with a variety of peers.
- *There are clear operational routines.* Students know how to move around the room efficiently and quietly. They know how to get and return materials appropriately. They know what to do when they are assigned to a particular task or area of the room. They know how to get help when the teacher is busy. They know how to turn in work. It's safe to say that in classrooms where multiple tasks occur simultaneously and smoothly, the teacher has taught the routines for success every bit as carefully as he or she has taught math or art.
- *The teacher and students share responsibility for the classroom, for teaching, and for learning.* A teacher's role is both enhanced and streamlined when the teacher comes to understand that students are teachers, too—and that teachers are learners. Teachers in student-centered classrooms ask the question: What tasks and roles am I now assuming that my students could learn to do for

the class? The teacher not only enlists student help in those roles but also consistently asks student advice on how to make virtually all aspects of the class more effective. Further, a teacher in an effectively differentiated classroom works with the students to envision and bring into being a classroom in which individual differences are honored. Both philosophy and practice are shared among all members of the class.

- *The teacher "teaches up."* It's likely that we underestimate the potential of nearly all students. If the goal of a differentiated classroom is to maximize the capacity of each learner, then the teacher must continually encourage each student to "stretch." Thus it is generally the case in a differentiated classroom that the teacher is looking for ways to push each student a bit beyond his or her comfort level and trying to avoid student opportunities to "coast." This can be a particular challenge for the teacher in regard to advanced learners, who are not accustomed to stretching because school often assumes students are successful when they reach a norm. No student is well served in school, however, unless that student finds his or her capacity extended by school.
- *There is a focus on growth.* This means at least two things. First, each student is accountable for progressing or growing in important knowledge, understanding, and skill, and the teacher is accountable for guiding and supporting that growth. A student's point of entry into a subject is out of the control of the teacher and student. Both, however, can accept responsibility for growth from that point on. Second, this focus necessitates that growth (or lack of growth) be acknowledged as part of grading.

YOUR TURN

Examining the Principles of Effective Differentiation

1. Divide a sheet of paper into two columns. Label the left-hand column "Proactive Differentiation" and the right-hand column "Reactive Differentiation." Now, examine the three tables in this chapter. List all the examples of proactive or preplanned differentiation from all three figures in the left-hand column and all the examples of reactive, or on-the-spot, differentiation in the right-hand column. Also include your own examples generated for Learning Activity 4. Finally, list as many reasons as you can that proactive differentiation is likely to be more effective than reactive differentiation in academically diverse classrooms.
2. Earlier in the chapter, it is asserted that effective differentiation grows from a teacher's philosophy about whom we teach, where we teach, what we teach, and how we teach. Write a brief statement about how each of the ten key principles of differentiation in this section is related to beliefs about these four elements of a teacher's philosophy. If you'd prefer, create and annotate a graphic that shows the connections.

OBJECTIVE 6

To propose personal first steps in becoming a responsive teacher

Starting the Journey Toward Responsive Teaching

Beginning teachers, like the students they teach, vary in important ways. Some are younger, some older. Some have many experiences leading groups of people, some have few such experiences. For these and many other reasons, the professional development of new teachers does not follow a single timetable or a single path.

Nonetheless, it is generally the case that beginning teachers are developing the "gross-motor skills" of teaching. Differentiation is a "fine-motor skill" of teaching.[22] Creating a classroom that attends to the multiple needs of learners might then seem out of reach to someone at the beginning of a teaching career. It is the case, however, that refined skills of teaching, like refined skills in any human endeavor, are developed over time. A beginning teacher generally cannot fully differentiate instruction in the first year or two of teaching. However, there are first steps in the process of learning to be a responsive teacher—and some of these are within the reach of teachers new to the profession. Excellence in teaching is progressive—earned year by year when teachers set their own sights on the kind of continual growth we ask of students.

LEARNING ACTIVITY 6

Here are a few possible early steps toward developing an academically responsive classroom. They reflect the early stages of practices that can become more refined in each successive year as a teacher moves along a continuum of professional knowledge, understanding, and skills from novice toward expert educator.

- *Reflect on students.* Be a student of your students. Study them. Take notes on what you see whenever you can. Try to understand how their attitudes, behaviors, and achievements change as circumstances in the classroom change. Particularly try to understand the link among classroom structures, classroom behavior, and classroom success. When you can, share your thinking about the classroom with your students and ask them to help you make the classroom better. This early focus on students ultimately develops the root system of responsive teaching.
- *Work for increasing clarity about the curriculum.* Continue to ask yourself: What really matters in this lesson or unit? How can I present this in a way that helps students genuinely understand what it means and why it matters? How can I share the important knowledge, understanding, and skill with

my young learners in a way that makes learning inviting for them? Clarity about the essentials, meaning, and power of the curriculum will ultimately enable you to be both focused and flexible with the curriculum and to find multiple routes to inviting students to learn.

- *Develop and practice management routines.* In the beginning, management routines may be as simple as taking attendance without wasting time or returning papers without losing the attention of students. Take time in your planning to envision how you'd like a procedure to look, then plan step by step to make it work that way. After you've tried your plans, take time to reflect on what worked and what you can do to make it work even better next time. Not only does each success increase your capacity to handle more complex classroom routines, but it also clarifies your role as leader for both your students and you.
- *Think of assessment as more than grading.* Remind yourself often that what goes in the grade book is of less value to you and your students than what you can learn about student understanding from examining work, giving students feedback on it, and using what the student work shows you as you plan instruction. Become a hunter-and-gatherer of information about students from any source at your disposal.
- *Keep an eye on the goal of student-centered teaching.* Our best understanding of learning tells us clearly that it must happen *in* students, not *to* them.[23] Continue to ask yourself what you can do to put the focus on students as workers rather than teacher as worker. Perhaps you can provide a few minutes in each lesson for students to answer a key question in pairs or use learning logs in which students reflect their understanding of subject matter and raise questions about what they are studying. Whatever you can do to put students on center stage as active learners takes you down the road toward differentiation.
- *Work for flexibility.* Early on, establishing yourself as a classroom leader is critical. Even at that stage of growth, however, there are things you can do to aim for flexibility. You may be able to give students two choices of how to do a task, ask students to give you a suggestion on an index card for the best due date for a project in a week you specify, assign individual students responsibility for one or two classroom chores, provide students two options for work to do when they finish an assigned task, or examine two ways you might present tomorrow's lesson rather than only one. Once again, working toward flexibility is more likely to make you a flexible teacher than is developing early habits of "one-way" teaching.
- *Use resource staff as partners in your classroom.* Teachers of English as a second language, resource specialists in gifted education or special education, reading specialists, psychologists, counselors, media specialists, and others on a faculty have a rich store of understanding and skill they can share with you. Cultivate the habit of asking these people how they might address a particular classroom situation. Better still, ask them to come into your classroom and observe or co-teach with you. Most teaching would probably be stronger if it were a team sport. This is particularly true given the range of needs and challenges in most contemporary classrooms.
- *Find and work with like-minded colleagues.* Many teachers spend their careers developing the skills of responsive teaching. Many do not. Find teachers who are willing to expend the mental and physical effort it takes to reach out to their learners on a daily basis. Cultivate these professional friendships. Work together. Share successes and failures. Celebrate your growth together.

- *Reflect on your beliefs about who, where, what,* and *how you teach, and examine the match between your beliefs and your practice.* Early on, your practices may be a bit of a mismatch for what you believe, but if you cultivate the habit of checking for match, you'll continue working toward the classroom that exists in your mind's eye.

In many sports, athletes are encouraged to see themselves as they execute a particular move. This sort of mental rehearsal is part of training for success. A similar practice in teaching may be helpful in a similar way. In day-by-day planning, it can be quite useful to "see" how you'd like it to look when you return papers, ask students to get into groups, or wrap up a class. On a longer-term basis, this sort of reflection can provide a kind of internal compass for thinking about decision making. At this point in your development as a teacher, you can only speculate on how you would like things to be in your classroom. Even now, however, you have many experiences, values, and considerable knowledge to direct your mental rehearsal.

YOUR TURN

Thinking About Your Own Response to Academic Diversity

1. Return to your notes from item 3 in the Your Turn for Learning Activity 3, where you listed key beliefs you now have about whom you teach, where you teach, what you teach, and how you teach. For each of those beliefs, list two or three concrete actions or steps you might take in your classroom as you begin teaching full time so that you also begin the process of developing a classroom where your practices and beliefs are a match.

2. Below are brief scenarios that give the perspective of three students on their experiences in school. Read the scenarios, then create advice from each of the students to their teachers based on what you read and infer from your reading. Express the advice in a list, letter, written dialogue, or oral presentation—in the student's voice.
   - My name is Tia. The class seems awfully long to me. I finish my work quickly because I pretty much know the answers before class even begins. I have some other things I'd like to work on when I get through with assignments, but that seems to make my teacher unhappy, so I sit and wait a lot. I have a lot of questions I'd like to ask about what we study, but I don't want to talk so much that my friends in class don't have a chance to talk. Besides, when I do ask the questions, I sometimes get the feeling that people are rolling their eyes. I don't know if it's because my questions seem wrong or because people don't understand them. Sometimes I wish there were time for the teacher to talk with me during class, but she always seems to need to work with kids who are having lots of trouble with what we are learning. I pretty much get A's in class, and I guess that should be satisfying, but somehow, it doesn't feel right.
   - My name is Carlos. I wish I could understand what the teacher is asking us to do. I try. I really do. Sometimes I get tired of trying and I kind of drift off for a few minutes, but mostly, I really try to listen. I have a hard time writing down all the stuff the teacher says. He goes fast, and I don't always know how to spell all the words. Sometimes he tells stories that make us laugh, but they are still hard to write down. When I try to study for tests, it's like my head gets full really fast, and when I try to cram more in my head, everything gets all mixed up. I don't get why other people can follow the directions so much better than I can in class. But it's mostly been that way for me in school. I guess I'm just no good at school.
   - My name is Sam. If I have to sit still for one more minute, I think I'll just explode. The teacher gets really crabby when I move around or tap on the desk, but I just can't stay as still as she wants me to. When I try to stay still all the time, it seems like that's all I can think about, and so I miss what she's telling

us, and then that makes me get behind some more and that makes me feel worse and that makes me need to move even more. The teacher gets mad when I move around. She tells me to stay still, and I get embarrassed or mad or something and it makes me have to move more. I like it in PE when we get to do things and talk to people. I wish we could have PE twice every day. I wish I knew why we had to learn all this stuff anyhow. It seems like a lot of lists of things that people have to sit still to learn. Maybe why I don't do well in school is because I can't sit still to learn.

3. In what ways would your first steps toward responsive teaching from item 1 be helpful to each of these three students? What else would you like to be able to do to teach them even more effectively if they were part of your class in your fifth year of teaching?

Mastery Test

Use the first-person descriptions of Tia, Carlos, and Sam in item 2 in the Your Turn for Learning Activity 6 as a basis for your work in this mastery activity.

First, reflect on the perspectives of the students in the three scenarios and make a list of specific learning needs for each of the three students.

Second, develop a lesson (or use one you have already developed) for a "typical" student in a class you might teach. Be sure that you state the goals of the lesson clearly. Then explain how you would differentiate the lesson to ensure that each of the three students finds it appropriately challenging. (In other words, differentiate the lesson based on the students' readiness needs.) Note also what you might do to make the lesson interesting for each of the three learners as well as to make the way in which students work a good fit for each of the three. (In other words, make some suggestions for differentiation based on student interest and learning profile also.) Be sure to address portions of the lesson in which you are presenting directions, examples, or information and parts of the lesson in which the student is working. For each modification you make, explain whether you are addressing readiness, interest, and/or learning profile, and why you believe your adaptation is likely to be helpful to the student.

Third, write a brief statement of ways in which your own beliefs about the nature of students, learning environments, curriculum, and instruction are reflected in your plans for differentiation.

Observation Worksheet
Thinking About Responsible Instruction

The goal of this observation is to help you reflect on the "fit" of a classroom for particular learners in that classroom and to examine ways a teacher can differentiate instruction to improve the fit for more students. Before you begin the observation, ask the teacher to point out to you one or two students who have a hard time with the content of the class, one or two who have behavior problems, and one or two who are particularly advanced. Take a few minutes as class begins to locate these students and observe them briefly. Then select three of them whom you will watch for the remainder of the observation.

Directions: Do not use actual names of schools, teachers, administrators, or students when using this worksheet.

Observer's Name: ______________________________

Date: ______________________________

Grade Level: ______________________________

Subject: ______________________________

Class Size: ______________________________

Background Information: Give a brief general description of the school's social, economic, and ethnic makeup.

____

____

What to Record: First, write a very brief description of each student as a learner. Then, in the boxes that follow, take notes on the three students as the class proceeds. Do you have any evidence that they are participating actively in the class? That they are understanding the content, are confused, or are bored? What sorts of behavior do they exhibit? Why do you think they are behaving as they do? What is working well for them? Or poorly? Does the class seem interesting to them? In the fourth box, take notes on anything the teacher does to make the class successful for the three students you've selected. Has he or she tried to make the environment seem safe and inviting to the students? Are there materials or activities particularly appropriate for these learners? Do the students have choices about how to work? Are questions targeted to address particular learner needs? Are there opportunities to meet with the teacher to clarify or extend learning? Jot down whatever you think affects the learning of your three target students and reflects teacher attempts to actively address varied learner needs.

Student #1 Name ____________________ Description ____________________

____

Student #2 Name ____________________ Description ____________________

____

Student #3 Name ____________________ Description ____________________

____

Student #1	Student #2

Student #3	Teacher

Reflections on Your Observation:

1. To what degree did you feel the content and activities of the class matched the readiness level of the students you observed? On what do you base your conclusions?

2. What ideas do you have about how a teacher might effectively address the readiness needs of the students you observed?

3. In what ways did the teacher work to make the content and activities link to student interests?

4. What ideas do you have about other ways in which a teacher might tap into student interests at some point during the unit that you observed briefly?

5. In what ways did the teacher work to address varied student preferences for *how* to learn?

6. What other ways can you think of to give students a range of ways to learn in this class, both when the teacher is presenting and when the student is the worker?

7. In what ways do you think the learning environment in the classroom encourages and supports learning for the students you observed?

8. What other ways can you think of to make the learning environment even more encouraging and supportive of the learning success of the students you observed?

NOTES

1. Dorothy Canfield Fisher, *Understood Betsy* (New York: Henry Holt and Company, 1917, 1999), pp. 89–84.
2. Tim O'Brien and Dennis Guiney. *Differentiation in Teaching and Learning: Principles and Practice*. (London: Continuum, 2001).
3. Ochan Kusuma-Powell and William Powell, eds. *Count Me In!* (Washington, D.C.: Overseas School Advisory Council, 2000).
4. O'Brien & Guiney, *op. cit.*
5. Kusuma-Powell and Powell, *op. cit.*
6. Carol Ann Tomlinson, *How to Differentiate Instruction in Mixed Ability Classrooms*, 2nd Ed. (Alexandria, Va.: Association for Supervision and Curriculum Development, 2001).
7. Y. Lou, P. Abrami, J. Spence, C. Poulsen, B. Chambers, and S. d'Apollonia, "Within-Class Grouping: A Meta-Analysis." *Review of Educational Research* 66 (1996) 423–458.
8. Lev Vygotsky, *Mind in Society* (Cambridge, Mass.: Harvard University Press, 1978).
9. Pierce Howard, *An Owner's Manual for the Brain* (Austin, Tex.: Leornian Press, 1994); Eric Jensen, *Teaching with the Brain in Mind* (Alexandria, Va: Association for Supervision and Curriculum Development, 1998).
10. Michael Gurian, *Boys and Girls Learn Differently: A Guide for Teachers and Parents* (San Francisco: Jossey-Bass, 2001).
11. Lisa Delpit, *Other People's Children: Cultural Conflict in the Classroom* (New York: The New Press, 1995; Shirley Brice Heath, *Ways with Words: Language, Life and Work in Communities and Classrooms*. (Cambridge, England: Cambridge University Press, 1983); Thomas Lasley, and Thomas Matczynski, *Strategies for Teaching in a Diverse Society: Instructional Models* (Belmont, Calif.: Wadsworth, 1997).
12. Teresa Amabile, *The Social Psychology of Creativity* (New York: Springer-Verlag, 1983); Teresa Amabile, *Creativity in Context* (Boulder, Colo.: Westview, 1996); Mihaly Csikszentmihalyi, Kevin Rathunde, and Samuel Whalen. *Talented Teenagers: The Roots of Success and Failure* (New York: Cambridge University Press, 1993); Paul Torrance, "Insights About Creativity: Questioned, Rejected, Ridiculed, Ignored." *Educational Psychology Review* 7 (1995):313–322.
13. Robert Sternberg, "What Does it Mean to Be Smart?" *Educational Leadership* 55 (1997):20–24; M. Sullivan, "A Meta-Analysis of Experimental Research Studies Based on the Dunn and Dunn Learning Styles Model and its Relationship to Academic Achievement and Performance." Unpublished doctoral dissertation, St. John's University, Jamaica, N.Y., 1993.
14. F. Archambault, K. Westberg, S. Brown, B. Hallmark, C. Emmons, and W. Zhang, *Regular Classroom Practices with Gifted Students: Results of a National Survey of Classroom Teachers* (Research Monograph 93102) (Storrs: University of Connecticut, National Research Center on the Gifted and Talented, 1993); T. Fletcher, C. Bos, and L. Johnson, "Accommodating English Language Learners with Language and Learning Disabilities in Bilingual Education Classrooms." *Learning Disabilities Research & Practice* 14 (1999):80–91; L. Fuchs and D. Fuchs. "General Educators' Instructional Adaptation for Students with Learning Disabilities." *Learning Disability Quarterly* 21 (1998):23–33.
15. J. Siegel and M. Shaughnessy, "Educating for Understanding: A Conversation with Howard Gardner." *Phi Delta Kappan* 75, no. 7 (1994):563–566.
16. L. J. Kiernan. *A Visit to a Differentiated Classroom* (Alexandria, Va.: Association for Supervision and Curriculum Development, 2001), videocassette.
17. *Ibid.*; Carol Ann Tomlinson, *The Differentiated Classroom: Responding to the Needs of All Learners.* (Alexandria, Va.: Association for Supervision and Curriculum Development, 1999).
18. Rita Dunn, *How to Implement and Supervise a Learning Styles Program* (Alexandria, Va.: Association for Supervision and Curriculum Development, 1996).
19. Robert Sternberg, *The Triarchic Mind: A New Theory of Intelligence* (New York: Viking, 1988); Robert Sternberg, "What Does It Mean to Be Smart?" *Educational Leadership* 54, no. 6 (1997):20–24.
20. Howard Gardner, *Multiple Intelligences: The Theory in Practice* (New York: Basic Books, 1993); Howard Gardner, "Reflections on Multiple Intelligences: Myths and Messages," *Phi Delta Kappan*, 78, no. 5 (1997):200–207.
21. Tomlinson, *op. cit., The Differentiated Classroom.*
22. C. Tomlinson, C. Callahan, E. Tomchin, N. Eiss, M. Imbeau, and M. Landrum, "Becoming Architects of Communities of Learning: Addressing Academic Diversity in Contemporary Classrooms." *Exceptional Children* 63 (1997):269–282.
23. National Research Council, *How People Learn: Brain, Mind, Experience, and School* (Washington, D.C.: National Academy Press, 1999).

ADDITIONAL RESOURCES

Readings

Azwell, T., and E. Schmar. *Report Card on Report Cards: Alternatives to Consider*. Portsmouth, N.H.: Heinemann, 1995.

Delpit, Lisa. *Other People's Children: Cultural Conflict in the Classroom*. New York: The New Press, 1995.

Strachota, Bob. *On Their Side: Helping Children Take Charge of Their Learning*. Greenfield, Mass.: Northeast Foundation for Children, 1996.

Tomlinson, Carol Ann. *The Differentiated Classroom: Responding to the Needs of All Learners*. Alexandria, Va.: Association for Supervision and Curriculum Development, 1999.

Tomlinson, Carol Ann. *How to Differentiate Instruction in Mixed Ability Classrooms*, 2nd ed. Alexandria, Va.: Association for Supervision and Curriculum Development, 2001.

Winebrenner, Susan. *Teaching Gifted Kids in the Regular Classroom: Strategies Every Teacher Can Use to Meet the Needs of the Gifted and Talented*. Minneapolis: Free Spirit Publishing, 1992.

Winebrenner, Susan. *Teaching Kids with Learning Difficulties in the Regular Classroom*. Minneapolis: Free Spirit Publishing, 1996.

Web Sites

The Council for Exceptional Children: http://www.cec.sped.org
The National Association for Gifted Children: http://www.nagc.org
There are web sites that deal with particular categories of exceptional learner and can provide information, materials, and links to related sites. These sites are examples.

Inspiration Software: http://www.inspiration.com/home.cfm
There are web sites that provide software helpful to teachers and students with particular learning styles or needs. This site is an example.

HottLinx, University of Virginia: http://curry.edschool.virginia.edu/hottlinx/
Eastern Suffolk BOCES (New York): www.sricboces.org/Goals2000/
Montgomery County (Maryland) Public Schools: http://www.mcps.k12.md.us/departments/eii/diffexemplaryex.html
Ball State University: http://www.bsu.edu/teachers/services/ctr/javits/Instruction/instruction.htm
The Internet TESL (Teachers of English as a Second Language) Journal: http://www.iteslj.org
There are web sites that provide examples of differentiated lessons or ideas helpful in differentiation. These sites are examples.

LD/ADD Pride Online: http://www.ldpride.net/learningstyles.MI.htm
Chaminade College Preparatory School: http://www.chaminade.org/inspire/learnstl.htm
State University of New York at Oswego: http://www.oswego.edu/~shindler/lstyle.htm
There are web sites designed to help teachers and/or students understand and use their preferred learning styles or intelligences. These sites are examples.

Association for Supervision and Curriculum Development: http://www.ascd.org/frametutorials.html
Montgomery County (Maryland) Public Schools: http://mcps.k12.md.us/departments/eii/eiimanagepracticespage.html
Rockwood (Missouri) School District: http://www.rockwood.k12.mo.us/staffdev/diff/index.htm
There are web sites that provide information about differentiated instruction or tutorials on differentiated instruction. These sites are examples.

7

Technology for Teaching and Learning with Understanding

Susan R. Goldman,
Susan M. Williams,
Robert D. Sherwood,
James W. Pellegrino,
Robert Plants, and
Ted S. Hasselbring

OBJECTIVE 1 **To examine assumptions about learning and technology**

OBJECTIVE 2 **To examine the principles of learning with understanding and how technology can support them**

OBJECTIVE 3 **To understand principled uses of technology to support learning with understanding**

OBJECTIVE 4 **To understand how to make hardware and software work for you and your students**

Perspectives on Technology in Schools

Technological literacy has fast become one of the "basic skills" of teaching. The sheer increase in availability of electronic resources in schools and classrooms makes it important for teachers to be prepared to integrate technology with instruction. In 1999, 84 percent of public school teachers surveyed by the National Council for Educational Statistics reported that they had a computer in their classroom and 95 percent had computers available elsewhere in the school. At the same time, school connectivity to the Internet was 95 percent and classroom connectivity had risen to 63 percent.[1] As the number of resources have grown, the focus now is turning to how they are being used.

Survey data indicate that while many teachers, especially those under 35, are comfortable using computers for personal productivity, at least two-thirds feel unprepared to integrate technology into instruction. Only half of the teachers with computers available use them for instruction, and when they do use a computer, it is poorly integrated with other classroom activities. Word processing and basic skills practice are the most frequent uses of computers. At the same time, use of software applications that engage analytical thinking through simulations and multimedia production is relatively infrequent.[2] At the same time, there are a number of exemplary schools, teachers, and students who demonstrate the catalyzing impact that technology can have on rethinking instructional goals, practices, and student work.[3]

The contrasts between traditional and innovative technology use underscore the observation that classroom teachers can use technology to support a variety of instructional models that differ in their goals and approaches to learning and teaching.[4] Some of the debates over whether classrooms need computers and whether technology "works" hinge on differences in philosophies of schooling, theories of learning, and visions of the role(s) of technology. Initial uses of electronic technology some thirty years ago mirrored the then-dominant models of instruction: teacher-directed instruction in which students memorized facts and procedures.[5] As the limitations of this kind of learning became evident, many began exploring ways for technology to support models of instruction that emphasized learning with understanding and more active involvement on the part of the student. Teachers who are proficient with technology report that it makes classrooms more student-centered, allows them to meet students' needs more fully, and lets them demand more of their students. They report that computers impact students' inquiry-based analytical skills, problem solving, and critical thinking.[6] The latter reflects uses of technology to go beyond fact-based, memorization-oriented curricula to curricula in which learning with understanding is a major goal.

In brief, technology can make it quicker or easier to teach the same things in the same ways, or it can make it possible to adopt new and better ways of teaching. Decisions about when to use technology, what technology to use, and for what purposes cannot be made in isolation from theories of learning. The overarching objective of this chapter is to examine instructional technology from the perspective of principles that support learning with understanding. The focus is on how technology can support the creation and implementation of environments that focus on learning with understanding.

OBJECTIVE 1

To examine assumptions about learning and technology

LEARNING ACTIVITY 1

Debates about technology's role in education are part of the public discourse and appear in the popular press with some frequency. The following article is a typical example. As you read it, consider the issues about technology and learning that it raises.

> *Rethinking Computers: More Than a Toy?*[7]
>
> Blasphemies are beginning to be heard from outside the church of technology. Criticism of computers in the classroom is surfacing nationwide, according to a N.Y. TIMES editorial written by Ethan Bronner (11/30). Most of what passes for education on computers "is akin to glorified video games offered in the vague but firm belief that access to endless information, regardless of quality, must be good," pens Bronner.
>
> Bronner describes an "intellectual backlash" against technology in the schools, particularly in the lower grades. "At the moment, the most mindless use of computers is at the elementary school level," said Judah Schwartz, professor of education at Harvard U.
>
> Interestingly, some of the criticism has leaked from the lips of computer gurus themselves, writes Bronner. Many computer experts "point out that since it doesn't take 12 years of school to master computers, they can become a distraction from other learning that takes longer," writes Bronner.
>
> David Gelernter, professor of computer science at Yale U: "Computers themselves are fine. But we are in the middle of an education catastrophe. Children are not being taught to read, write, know arithmetic and history. In those circumstances, to bring a glitzy toy into the classroom seems to me to be a disaster."
>
> Other computer masters, however, predict a new age of education—one in which students are liberated from authoritarian teachers and rote learning, reports Bronner. This group includes Don Tapscott, author of

Growing Up Digital and Idit Harel, founder of MaMaMedia, "a creative new educational Web Site for children," writes Bronner. According to Tapscott, the "Net Generation" is "beginning to process information and learn differently than the boomers before them. New media tools offer great promise for a new model of learning—one based on discovery and participation."

Tapscott predicts that computers will support a shift from teaching to "the creation of learning partnerships and learning cultures. The schools can become a place to learn rather than a place to teach."

Astronomer and computer expert Clifford Stoll disagrees. "Maybe I'm the weird one, but I never thought learning was supposed to be fun. It requires discipline, responsibility, and attention in class." He added: "Learning is work. Turning scholarship and class work into a game is to denigrate the most important thing we can do in life. Someone has to react against all this bogus stuff."

Bronner admits that computer literacy for children "may not be all bogus." He cites research that found college and high school students who learned algebra with computers "have done markedly better than those without them in a series of tests." Although studies have not yet found that reading and arithmetic achievement have increased due to computer use, the technology has improved other skills including communication, presentation and initiative-taking, reports Bronner. Some experts also point out that writing and editing skills are completed with "more ease" on computers.

Yet, many still view the technology as the classroom toy of the 1990s. "The idea that children are in educational trouble because they don't have access to enough glitz and what they really need is a bigger database is staggeringly ludicrous," said Gelernter. "They need practice in the basics."

YOUR TURN

Conduct a search for brief articles that have appeared in major newspapers, in magazines, or on the World Wide Web in the last six months debating the role of technology in children's education. Select one for comparison with the preceding 1997 article. Based on these two articles and your current understanding of learning and technology, what questions do these articles raise for you? What assumptions are the different "speakers" in the articles making about learning? What does and should go on in classrooms? What are appropriate roles for technology? Have the current concerns that are expressed in the popular press changed significantly from 1997? After you have generated your individual list, share ideas across the class.

OBJECTIVE 2

To examine the principles of learning with understanding and how technology can support them

LEARNING ACTIVITY 2

What Is Learning with Understanding and Why Do We Need It?

Learning with understanding is more than memorizing information. It involves understanding the significance of information so that it can be used as a tool to solve problems in the future. Consider the following statements: "The Indians of the Northwest lived in slant-roof houses made of cedar planks. . . . Some California Indians lived in simple earth-covered or brush shelters. . . . The Plains Indians lived mainly in teepees. . . ." It is simple enough for students to memorize these facts, but to use this knowledge as a tool, they need to understand that the Indians used the raw materials that were available to them; that slant-roof houses were useful for shedding rain in the wet Northwest climate; and that teepees were portable, an essential feature for Indians who moved frequently to follow the buffalo herds that were their primary food source. With this additional information, a student might be able to figure out new problems, such as predicting what kind of house an Alaskan Indian might build. When students learn with understanding, they are developing their abilities to think, solve problems, and become independent learners.

Teachers are often dismayed when even their best students fail to develop the deep understanding that can help them solve problems. In the words of a fifth-grade teacher:

> My students can memorize facts, but they can't tell you why these facts are significant . . . they haven't had to take in facts and try to assimilate or synthesize and spit it back out into some form that has meaning. They are not used to having to attach meaning to what they are doing.

Likewise, employers are often dissatisfied with the graduates of our schools. Rapid change in workplace technology demands that all workers must be adaptable, continuing to learn and do new jobs in new ways throughout their lives. According to a 1999 U.S. Department of Commerce report, by 2006 almost 50 percent of the workforce will be employed in technology production industries or in industries that use information technology products and services.[8] However, the United States is currently experiencing an extreme shortage of workers specializing in the information technology industry. During 2000, 1.6 million technology jobs were created in the United States, but about half remained unfilled.[9] U.S. schools have just not kept pace with society's expectations and needs for the rapidly changing world of the twenty-first century. Immediate changes in our schools are needed if America is to compete in global markets.

The idea of preparing people for a rapidly changing world is a daunting challenge. Rapid change requires lifelong learning, and this means that people who enter the workforce must be prepared to learn on their own. The skills required for effective work following high school graduation are now essentially equivalent to those that were required for college-bound students in the 1980s. It is not sufficient merely to memorize a body of knowledge. Given today's information explosion, it is not even possible to do so! People need to be able to reason with and about that knowledge. They need to make decisions about what they know and what they need to learn.[10]

Accordingly, many educators argue that the kinds of learning necessary for the twenty-first century are quite different from those required in the twentieth century. *All* students need to learn with understanding and become independent learners, not just a select few. There is remarkable consensus regarding the conditions that promote these kinds of learning competencies. In standards for student achievement authored by professional associations, state boards of education, and federal task forces, the process of learning is described as a dynamic one in which learners actively construct knowledge through experiences of sustained inquiry and reflection. Inquiry includes the ability to ask questions about interesting and important natural phenomena, formulate hypotheses to answer these questions, collect evidence, and argue the answers to peers. Such inquiry facilitates the development of a rich body of subject-matter knowledge and the ability to gain new understandings in contexts beyond the classroom.

Learning with understanding goes well beyond learning that emphasizes memorization of facts and fluent execution of procedures. Many of the exciting uses of technology make it easier to create rich, inquiry-based projects in which children learn with understanding. This is not to deny the importance of mastering the basics, but knowledge of the basics and a memorized body of knowledge are not adequate goals for twenty-first century educational systems.

Instructional Design Principles for Learning with Understanding and Technology's Role in Supporting Them

Research on cognitive and social issues in learning suggests four design principles for instruction that are important if one is to achieve learning with understanding.

1. Instruction is organized around the solution of meaningful problems.
2. Instruction provides scaffolds for achieving meaningful learning.
3. Instruction provides opportunities for practice with feedback, revision, and reflection.
4. The social arrangements of instruction promote collaboration, distributed expertise, and independent learning.

We describe each principle in turn and briefly describe how technology can help realize that principle. In Learning Activity 3, we provide a more detailed look at technology-based support for these design principles.

Principle 1: Instruction Is Organized Around the Solution of Meaningful Problems

When students acquire new information in the process of solving meaningful problems, they are more likely to see its potential usefulness than when we ask them to memorize isolated facts. Meaningful problems also help students overcome the "inert knowledge" problem, defined as knowledge previously learned but not remembered in situations where it would be potentially useful.[11] Seeing the relevance of information to everyday problems helps students understand when and how the information may be useful.

When students see the usefulness of information, they are motivated to learn. Research on the relationship between interest and learning indicates that personal interest in a topic or **domain** positively affects academic learning in that domain.[12] New approaches to motivation emphasize authentic tasks that students perceive as real work for real audiences. This emphasis contrasts with an earlier emphasis on elaborate extrinsic reinforcement for correct responding.

Problem solving is at the core of inquiry- or project-based learning. Students work on problems that are interesting and personally meaningful. Several contemporary educational reform efforts use dilemmas, puzzles, and paradoxes to "hook" students or to stimulate their interest in the topic of study.[13]

Principle 1: Technology's Role

One major challenge for inquiry-based learning environments is to develop problems that are rich and complex enough to engage students in the kinds of sustained inquiry that will allow them to deeply understand important new concepts. Bringing complex problems into the classroom is an important function of technology. Unlike problems that occur in the real world, problems that are created with graphics, video, and animation can be explored again and again. These multimedia formats capture children's interest and provide information in the form of sound and moving images that is not available in text-based problems and stories. Multimedia formats are more easily understood and allow the learner to concentrate on high-level processes such as identifying problem-solving goals or making important inferences.[14]

Although technology-based problem environments come in many forms, an important characteristic is that they are under the learner's control. Students can review stories on an interactive videodisc many times and freeze specific frames or pictures in order to study them. Problems presented on the World Wide Web or in hypermedia allow students to search easily for the parts that interest them most. Simulations or exploratory environments called **microworlds** allow students to carry out actions, immediately observe the results, and attempt to discover the rules that govern the system's behavior. No matter what form of technology is involved, the student is primarily responsible for deciding how to investigate the problem, and the technology creates an environment in which flexible exploration is possible.

Principle 2: Instruction Provides Scaffolds for Achieving Meaningful Learning

Although students benefit greatly from the opportunity and responsibility of exploring complex problems on their own, the mere presence of these opportunities does not lead to learning with understanding. Because of the complexity of the problems and the inexperience of the students, **scaffolds** must be provided to help students carry out the parts of the task that they cannot yet manage on their own.

Cognitive scaffolding assumes that individuals learn through interactions with others who are more knowledgeable, just as children learn through adult–child interactions. Adults model good thinking, provide hints, and prompt children who cannot "get it" on their own. Children eventually adopt the patterns of thinking reflected by the adults.[15] Cognitive scaffolding can be realized in a number of ways, including modeling and coaching by experts, and providing guides and reminders about the procedures and steps that are important for the task.[16]

Principle 2: Technology's Role

Teachers can also use technologies to scaffold the solution of complex problems and projects by providing resources such as visualization tools, reference materials, and hints. Multimedia databases on CD-ROMs, videodiscs, or the World Wide Web provide important resources for students who are doing research. Technology-based reference materials provide several advantages over those in book format. Most importantly, they allow the presentation of information in audio or video format. In many cases, students can see an actual event and create their own analysis rather than reading someone else's description. Electronic references are easy to search and provide information quickly, while students are in the midst of problem solving. For example, definitions of words and their pronunciations are readily available while a student is reading or writing a story. A student who is stuck while setting up a math problem can effortlessly access hints and examples. Students will highly value and easily remember the knowledge acquired in these **just-in-time learning** situations because they understand why it is useful to them.

Technology can help learners visualize processes and relationships that are normally invisible or difficult to understand. For example, students might use spreadsheets to create a graph that demonstrates a trend or shows whether one result is out of line with the rest. These graphs are useful in initial interpretations of numerical data and also valuable for reporting it to others. Charts, maps, and other graphic representations can be created by students or automatically generated by simulation programs to depict the changes brought about by student actions.

Principle 3: Instruction Provides Opportunities for Practice with Feedback, Revision, and Reflection

Feedback, revision, and reflection are aspects of **metacognition** that are critical to developing the ability to regulate one's own learning. In 1933, John Dewey noted the importance of reflecting on one's ideas, weighing our ideas against data and our predictions against obtained outcomes.[17] In the context of teaching, Donald Schön emphasizes the importance of reflection in creating new mental models.[18]

Content-area experts exhibit strong self-monitoring skills that enable them to regulate their learning goals and activities. Self-regulated learners take feedback from their performance and adjust their learning in response to it. Self-monitoring depends on deep understanding in the domain because it requires an awareness of one's own thinking, sufficient knowledge to evaluate that thinking and provide feedback to oneself, and knowledge of how to make necessary revisions. In other words, learners cannot effectively monitor what they know and make use of the feedback effectively (in revision) unless they have a deep understanding in the domain. The idea that monitoring is highly dependent on knowledge creates a catch-22 for novices. How can they regulate their own learning without the necessary knowledge to do so? Thus, the development of expertise requires scaffolds for monitoring and self-regulation skills so that deep understanding and reflective learning can develop hand in hand.

Analyses of expert performance indicate that the development of expertise takes lots of practice over a long period of time.[19] Cycles of feedback, reflection, and opportunities for revision allow students to practice using the skills and concepts they are trying to master. Cognitive theories of skill acquisition place importance on practice because it leads to fluency and a reduction in the amount of processing resources needed to execute the skill.[20] Practice with feedback produces better learning than practice alone. About fifty years ago, the noted psychologist of learning Edward L. Thorndike provided a simple but elegant illustration of the importance for learning of practice with feedback. He spent hundreds of hours trying to draw a line that was exactly 4 inches long. He did not improve—until he took off his blindfold. Only when he could see how close each attempt had come to the goal was Thorndike able to improve. Unless learners get feedback on their practice efforts, they will not know how to adjust their performance in order to improve it. Recent surveys of multiple research studies in which formative feedback was provided to students about the correctness of their answers during the learning process have shown substantial positive effects on students' overall levels of achievement for many areas of the curriculum.[21]

Principle 3: Technology's Role

An early and major use of technology involved providing opportunities for extended practice of basic skills. It is important to distinguish between two stages of basic skill development, *acquisition* and *fluency*. Acquisition refers to the initial learning of a skill, and fluency refers to being able to access this skill in a quick and effortless manner (such as math facts). If students do not develop basic skills to fluent levels, then the learning process is incomplete and they will not be able to function well in the real world.

Although there is no question that the nature of a drill-and-practice application makes it ideal for providing endless practice in almost any curricular area, when a student is in the acquisition phase of learning the use of drill-and-practice is inappropriate. As the name implies, computer-based drill-and-practice is designed to reinforce *previously learned information* rather than to provide direct instruction in new skills. If technology is to be used during the acquisition phase of a new skill or concept, the tutorial is more appropriate than drill-and-practice. A technology-based tutorial differs from a drill-and-practice application in that a tutorial attempts to play the role of a teacher and to provide direct instruction on a new skill or concept. The tutorial presents the student with new or previously unlearned material in an individualized manner, providing frequent corrective feedback and reinforcement.

It is important to remember that tutorials and drill-and-practice software came into existence at a time when teacher-led lecture and recitation were widely accepted and that these applications frequently mirror this instructional approach. For some, the mere mention of this type of software evokes a negative response. However, when students encounter difficulties in the process of solving meaningful problems, the opportunity for individualized instruction and practice can be very valuable. This is especially true when the curriculum provides students a chance to apply what they have learned by revising their solutions to the problem that caused them difficulty.

Software that provides for extended practice with feedback has been easier to develop for low-level subskills, such as word recognition or the recall of math facts, than for higher-order thinking skills. However, software programs that provide this kind of feedback do exist for specific areas of the curriculum.[22] Using technology in this way can encourage the kind of self-assessment skills that are frequently seen in expert performance.

Principle 4: The Social Arrangements of Instruction Promote Collaboration, Distributed Expertise, and Independent Learning

The view of cognition as socially shared rather than individually owned is an important shift in the orientation of cognitive theories of learning. It reflects the idea that thinking is a product of several heads in interaction with one another.[23] In the theoretical context of cognition-as-socially-shared, researchers have proposed having learners work in small groups on complex problems as a way to deal with complexity. Working together facilitates problem solving and capitalizes on distributed expertise.[24] Collaborative environments are also excellent venues for making thinking visible, generating and receiving feedback, and revising.[25]

Principle 4: Technology's Role

A number of technologies support collaboration by providing venues for discussion and communication among learners. Through the use of computer networks, many schools today are connecting their computers to other computers, often thousands of miles away. If computers are networked within a room, building, or larger geographic area, students can send and receive information from other teachers or students not in their physical location. Teachers and students are freed from the constraints of location and time. For example, students can log on to a network at any time that is convenient to send or receive information from any location that is part of their network. Also, given the heavy dependence on text in most networked systems, students have a reason to use text to read, write, and construct thoughts and ideas for others to read and respond to. In addition, a massive amount of information is available through the Internet.

A vast array of communications services is rapidly becoming available to schools. For example, two-way video and two-way audio systems now allow students and teachers at remote sites to see and hear each other. In this way, face-to-face interactions can take place over great distances in real time. Communal databases and discussion groups make thinking visible and provide students with opportunities to give and receive feedback, often with more reflection because the comments are written rather than spoken.

To summarize, in this section you have been introduced to principles of learning for the design of environments that support learning with understanding. We have briefly described ways in which technologies can help realize these principles in the classroom. Learning Activity 3 will elaborate with specific examples of technology-based programs that attempt to realize inquiry-based learning.

Mastery Test

OBJECTIVE 2 **To examine the principles of learning with understanding and how technology can support them**

In the following activity you are asked to analyze, compare, and contrast the teaching and learning reflected in each example using the principles and technologies discussed in this section.

Analyze each pair of cases. For each case, think about what the teacher is doing to promote learning with understanding. How is the teacher using technology, and how does it fit into the curriculum? Compare your analyses with those of other members of your class. Develop a joint list.

Contrasting Cases—Pair 1

A. For much of this semester, Ms. Gale's fourth-grade students have been studying punctuation and parts of speech. She has embedded these skills in many different writing tasks. For example, writing thank-you letters after a field trip and addressing the envelopes gave students an opportunity to learn about capitalization of proper nouns and punctuation of dates and addresses. Ms. Gale decides to give a test on these skills before moving on to new topics, partly to help her prepare report cards. She uses a computer program that allows her to create questions that specifically target the skills she has taught and to display the results of the test for each student in several different formats. The students go to the computer one by one to take the test. After each question that they miss, the program gives them the correct answer and an explanation. It also gives them a final score.

B. Mr. Webster believes that his fourth-grade students should spend as much time as possible writing. He gives them many opportunities to create original stories and research reports. Students often use computers to create drafts of these projects, which he then edits and returns to them for revision. Every week throughout the year, the students use a computer program to take a test on the basics of writing mechanics and language usage. The program focuses on the skills required for fourth-graders by the local school district. It gives students feedback on specific questions and also prints out a graph for each student that shows this week's score on each skill as compared with scores in the previous weeks. The students are always excited to see the line on the graph move upward. The results of the program tell Mr. Webster, the students, and their parents exactly what they need to focus on in next week's writing project.

Contrasting Cases—Pair 2

A. Ms. Hardcastle's sixth-grade students are busy designing a playground as part of a mathematics unit on geometry. A video called *Blueprint for Success* gives specifications for this project, describing a specific playground site and the type of equipment that is needed. Each student is creating a scale drawing of a slide. They know from the video that very steep slides can be dangerous, so they take care to measure the angle of the sliding surface in their drawing. Ms. Hardcastle notices that some of the students are having difficulty using their protractors to measure the angles. She suggests that they spend some time using a computer program that helps them understand how to use a protractor and provides opportunities for practice and feedback.

B. Mr. Jones is a sixth-grade teacher who typically begins his math lessons with a demonstration of a new skill followed by opportunities for students to practice. This week, students are learning about angles. Mr. Jones asks students to watch as he uses an overhead projector to demonstrate measuring angles with a protractor. As he works, he carefully explains what he is doing. After the demonstration, he asks several students to construct and measure angles while the class watches. Then the entire class goes to the computer lab, where the lab teacher shows them how to use a program designed for practicing measurement skills, including the use of a protractor. The program checks students' work as they solve problems by trial and error. They can also get specific hints or watch as the computer solves a similar problem.

Contrasting Cases—Pair 3

A. The dissection of frogs in Ms. Coble's middle school biology class is a complex, time-consuming project, but she feels it is important for students to have the actual experience of locating and identifying each of the organs. So that they will not make mistakes and ruin expensive specimens, Ms. Coble always demonstrates in advance many of the things that the students will be doing. Not all of her thirty students will be able to see if she uses a real frog, so she plans to use a computer program that simulates the dissection of a frog and to project the image on a screen in front of the class. The simulation will allow her to show the location and appearance of the important organs and also to demonstrate the function of the organs and how they are related to each other.

B. It's very noisy in Mr. Klein's science class. Small groups of students are gathered around the computers, talking and frequently pointing to animations on the monitors. The students are using a computer-based simulation to discover the laws of force and motion. Each group develops alternative hypotheses and makes predictions. The software enables them to alter parameters (e.g., vary the amount of gravity or step slowly through an experiment to see how velocity changes over time). Students also plan and carry out experiments in the real world by rolling balls down a ramp and measuring the distance. After conducting these investigations, the students work together to organize their data and determine whether the results match their predictions, which of their hypotheses have been disproved, and whether they need to conduct further experiments.

OBJECTIVE 3

To understand principled uses of technology to support learning with understanding

LEARNING ACTIVITY 3

Creating and implementing instructional environments that support learning with understanding involve several challenges. In the preceding section we discussed design principles for learning with understanding and briefly identified ways in which technology can help realize these principles in classrooms. In this section, we elaborate on the ways in which various technologies can be helpful in **inquiry-based learning.** We discuss four functions and needs for technology in classrooms where the instructional goals include learning with understanding.

1. Bringing interesting and complex problems into the classroom
2. Providing resources and scaffolds that support learning and problem solving
3. Providing opportunities for feedback, reflection, and revision
4. Supporting communication and community building

Maximal effectiveness of instruction is achieved when a program supports all four of these functions, either by itself or in conjunction with other technology or classroom-based activities. In providing examples of existing and available technologies for each function, we highlight the aspect of a program that matches that function. In a number of cases, we describe particular programs as examples of several functions. However, our descriptions are not exhaustive, either of the capabilities of individual programs or of all existing programs. They reflect those with which we are most familiar or which are particularly good exemplars. New and exciting programs appear all the time. We hope to provide you with a useful framework for analyzing new programs and technologies as they emerge.

Bringing Interesting and Complex Problems into the Classroom

One important use of technology is to encourage problem finding and problem solving by bringing interesting and complex real-world problems into the classroom and illustrating them realistically. Students attempt to solve such problems as "How can we save this wounded eagle?" or "How can we design a playground that fits the constraints of this neighborhood?" or "How can we determine if this river is polluted?" The complexity of real-world problems like these can create difficulties for learners who have limited experience, knowledge, and reading skills. Many students may have trouble understanding complex problem situations when they are presented as text. The use of interactive video and dynamic graphics helps make this complexity manageable. By providing a dynamic representation of events that includes visual and spatial information, video allows students to form more accurate mental models of the problem situation that can support their comprehension.[26] Video environments can also include numerous scenes designed to scaffold students' learning.

Interactive video also allows students to scan the video rapidly forward and backward when they need to locate important information in the problem. Although it is possible to use videotape in this way, even more opportunities are available when students use videodiscs and CD-ROMs that can be controlled by bar-code readers or computers. Using the random-access capabilities of this technology, teachers can instantly access important scenes to use as illustrations for class discussion, and students can show data from the video as evidence to support their solutions to problems. The interactive nature of technological environments is very important for helping students manage complexity and achieve in-depth understanding of content. Interactivity makes it easy for students to return to specific parts in order to explore them more fully. Noninteractive environments such as linear videotape are much less effective for creating contexts that students can collaboratively reexamine and explore.

Complex problems help students appreciate the value of working collaboratively, because it is unlikely that any one student can solve the problems alone.[27] The organization of instruction around the collaborative solution of realistic problems is quite different from classroom organizations in which individual students spend most of their time learning the facts from a lecture or text and answering questions at the end of the chapter.

Programs That Bring Problems into the Classroom

Resources that bring projects and problems into the classroom can be found in a variety of media and forms. Many are accessible on the web as well as being available in "package" forms, that is, videodiscs, CD-ROMs, and print materials. Increasingly, programs that involve problem- and project-based activities are also including ways to support problem solving, provide feedback, and afford opportunities for communication and community building. This is especially true for programs that are primarily web based. In this section we describe several programs to illustrate the range of content areas and formats that are available. We first describe programs that are available via specific CD-ROM and print-based materials, and then we discuss Internet-based programs.

CD-ROM and Print-Based Programs

The Jasper Woodbury Problem Solving Series, consisting of twelve interactive video environments, presents authentic challenges that require students to understand and use important concepts in mathematics.[28] For example, in *Rescue at Boone's Meadow,* Larry is teaching Emily to fly an ultralight airplane. During the lessons, he helps Emily learn about the basic principles of flight and the specific details of the ultralight she is flying, such as its speed, fuel consumption, fuel capacity, and how much weight it can carry. Not long after Emily's first solo flight, her friend Jasper goes fishing in a remote area called Boone's Meadow. Hearing a gunshot, he discovers a wounded bald eagle and radios Emily for help in getting the eagle to a veterinarian. Emily consults a map to determine the closest roads to Boone's Meadow, then calls Larry to find out about the weather and to see if his ultralight is available. Students are challenged to use all the information in the video to determine the fastest way to rescue the eagle.

After viewing the video, students review the story and discuss the setting, characters, and any unfamiliar concepts and vocabulary introduced. After they have a clear understanding of the problem situation, small groups of students work together to break the problem into subgoals, scan the video for information, and set up the calculations necessary to solve each part of the problem. Once they have a solution, they compare it with those that other groups generate and try to choose the optimum plan. Like most real-world problems, *Jasper* problems have multiple correct solutions. Determining the optimum solution involves weighing factors such as safety and reliability as well as making the necessary calculations.

The *Jasper* series focuses on providing opportunities for problem solving and problem finding. It is not intended to replace the entire mathematics curriculum. Frequently, while attempting to solve these complex problems, students discover that they do not have the necessary basic skills. Teachers use these occasions as opportunities to conduct lessons in which they review the necessary concepts and procedures.

The *Little Planet Literacy Series* introduces kindergarten, first-, and second-grade students to problems in the form of literacy challenges that encourage them to research and write books in order to solve the challenges.[29] The challenges are presented as animated anchor stories that contain information relevant to literacy, science, and mathematics. In *Ribbit and the Magic Hats,* the characters on the little planet are visited by a stranger named Wongo who convinces the animals that they need to buy his "magic" hats if they want to use their imaginations and tell good stories. All the animals are taken in by his pitch, except for Ribbit. Ribbit doubts Wongo, becoming a lonely dissenter (see Figure 7.1). As the story progresses, Ribbit learns to use components of the scientific method to test whether the hats really are magic. With these tests, all the animals soon discover that they've been duped. They get their money back from Wongo, but they learn that he plans to take his hats to other parts of the planet. This leaves the animals with a challenge: How can they prevent other animals from being tricked by Wongo? The answer, of course, is to write a book, and the animals in the story enlist the aid of children in the classroom. The activities in the program integrate video, software, and print. The purpose of the technology is to provide support for rich discussions, to motivate read-

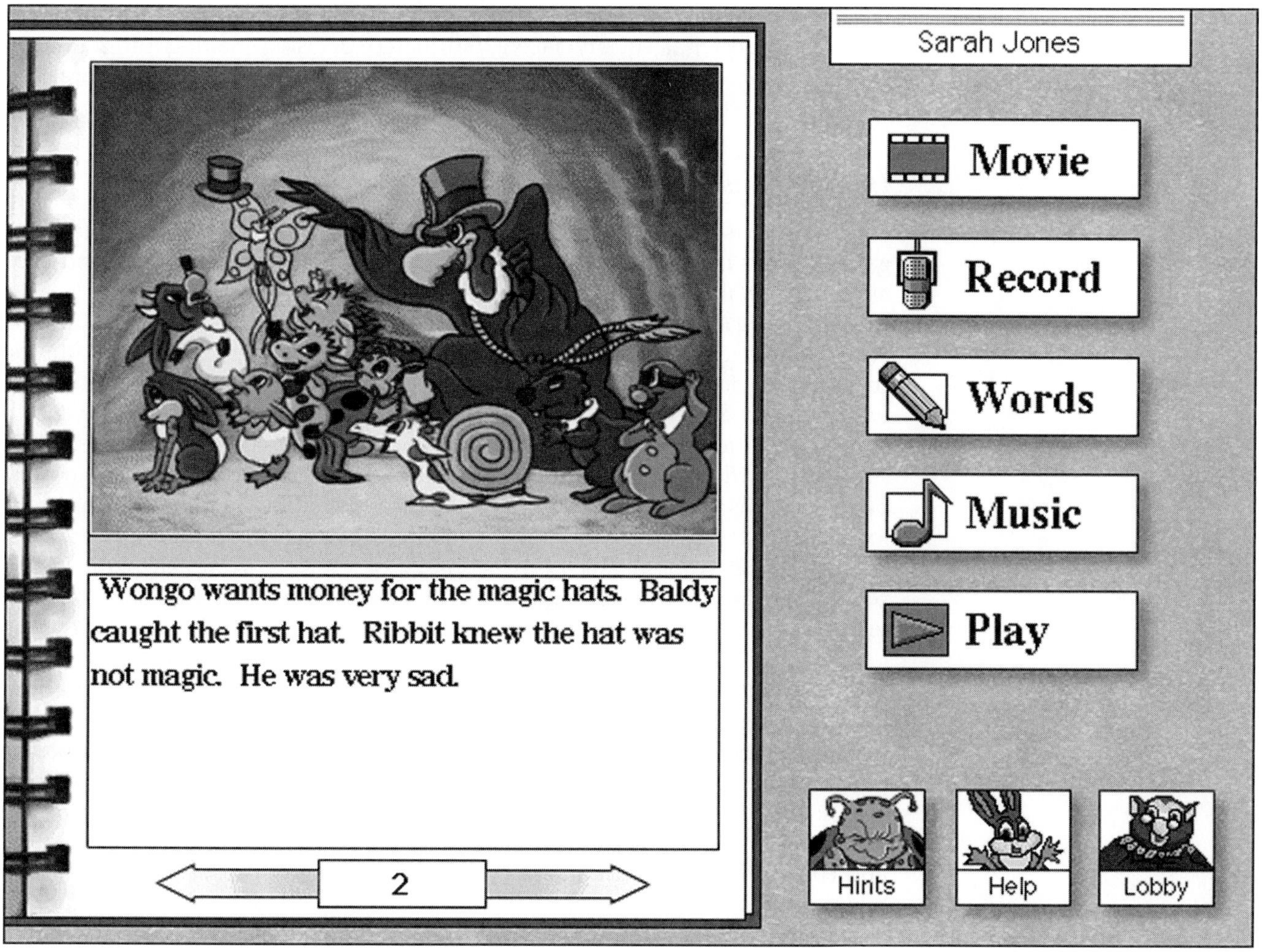

Figure 7.1
Screen shot copyright © by Little Planet Publishing. Reprinted by permission.

ing and writing, and to enable children to share their readings and written work with authentic audiences.

Simulations and microworlds are other forms of programs that bring problems into classrooms. A computer simulation of a complex system can create an ideal educational environment by modeling or re-creating a real-life event that cannot be carried out easily in a traditional teaching environment. Simulations allow the student to experience vicariously such real-life events as traveling in space, homesteading in the 1800s, conducting a science experiment, or living as prey or predator in a food chain. Classroom teachers can use simulations to introduce a sense of realism into what are often abstract subjects that frustrate the learner. Further, simulations provide for active participation rather than the passive role often taken by many learners. Rather than merely describing systems to students, simulations bring naturally occurring processes under students' control.[30]

Many simulations develop decision-making skills, an important aspect of thinking and problem solving. For example, a series called *Decisions, Decisions,* produced by Tom Snyder Productions, engages students in collaboration and role-playing in various content areas. In one program, students participate as members of ancient Greek society in simulations of important economic and political issues that society faced. Simulated decision-making programs on contemporary issues such as AIDS, prejudice, and substance abuse are also available.

Internet-Based Programs

The Internet is home to a growing number of learning environments that engage learners in problem solving by getting them involved in asking and then answering challenges related to their interests.

The *Web-based Inquiry Science Environment* (*WISE*) brings problems into the classroom in the form of current scientific controversies. Students examine real-world evidence and analyze it with respect to the controversies. Students work collaboratively, with most of the work done on computers. They use a web browser to take notes and to discuss and organize their arguments. *WISE* projects use data visualization and modeling to support students' inquiry processes. They are designed to help students develop "lifelong learning skills including critiquing, comparison, and design" of scientific solutions.[31]

The *WISE* web site includes a library of projects, complete with lesson plans, learning goals, and connections to national standards. Tools are provided that allow teachers to customize the projects to suit the developmental level of their classes. Teachers can also use and grade the on-line assessments provided with the projects. *WISE* projects engage students in thinking about their existing beliefs and evaluating evidence for consistency, bias, and accuracy. For example, in *How Far Does Light Go?* students decide between two hypotheses by examining the scientific properties of light. Other kinds of projects involve the use of scientific information to solve complex design problems. In *House in the Desert* students use knowledge of thermodynamics, insulation, and conduction to design an energy-efficient house in the face of the extreme temperatures typical of desert habitats. Other projects involve earthquakes and water quality.

Another inquiry-based problem environment, *BGuILE,* focuses specifically on biology content. The problems are the same ones that scientists are working on, and one goal is that students will come to understand the nature of science and scientific investigation. "Students working with BGuILE learn to plan and perform an investigation, construct, evaluate, and improve upon their own explanations, critique other's explanations, and understand science as a process of building and refining explanations."[32] Sample curriculum units treat topics such as microevolution (*The Galapagos Finches*) and the importance of careful observation and behavioral analysis (*The Animal Landlord*).[33]

The GLOBE Program (*Global Learning and Observations to Benefit the Environment*) involves students in gathering data about the local environment and creating a global database open to the *GLOBE* community. At their local sites, students use instruments and observations to carry out investigations that have been designed by scientists. The students submit their data to the *GLOBE* student data server so that all participating students and scientists can use it in analyses. Currently more than 800 schools in more than thirty-four countries are participating, allowing for data collection around the globe. Several earth science areas (e.g., atmosphere, hydrology, land cover/biology, and soils) are under investigation. Each investigation is introduced by a letter and an interview with the scientist who conducted the investigation. The letters describe the purpose and place of the investigation in the global and scientific world.

The Annenberg/Center for Public Broadcasting's (CPB) Internet-based project *Journey North* focuses on the study of global and interdependent ecological systems. It engages students in a global study of wildlife migration and seasonal change. Students track migrations of various species and interact with teachers and *Journey North* scientists in "Ask the Expert" interviews. Students also respond to specific "challenge" questions.

Other programs conduct "electronic field trips" and allow students to visit places they would not otherwise be able to visit. For example, the *JASON* project uses advanced interactive telecommunications to enable teachers and students all over the world to take part in global explorations. Each year, the project selects different environments—for example, Belize or Baja California—for students to study. Curricula and on-line programs are developed by *JASON* scientists. Students work with these materials to prepare to participate in the culminating event—a "virtual" electronic field trip—through a live, interactive broadcast from the expedition site. The advantage of electronic field trips over watching a video is that they occur in real time and are more authentic. Through two-way audio connections, students can actually ask the scientist questions about what they are seeing and get an immediate response. Although these types of programs have been largely experimental, advances in communication technology are making them more affordable and accessible to larger numbers of schools.

Sources of open-ended problems are not only becoming more ubiquitous but are also relying more on the web to provide the resources needed to solve them. For example, the Center for Problem Based Learning and the Illinois Problem Based Learning Network sponsor the *Summer Sleuths* program, targeted specifically at seventh- eighth- and ninth-grade students. For each challenge, the site provides materials that help structure the problem solving and suggests informational resources.[34] Another site, *ThinkQuest,* poses challenges and junior challenges that are designed to stimulate the formation of on-line communities. The communities do research and construct web pages to address the challenges. Winning pages are posted to the web site. For example, according to the "About This Site" information, *World War II: The Homefront* is a web site designed by Jacob Crouch, Ben Gould, and Scott Hays for *ThinkQuest.* The designers say, "We felt the need to bring educational material on this topic to the Internet, a dynamic way of teaching people anywhere on the planet. We hope that you enjoy this site and learn something from it as well. Also, be sure to check out our Acknowledgments page for information on the sources used on this site." *ThinkQuest* challenges extend to all subject-matter content areas, and communities are free to generate and suggest challenges.[35]

Providing Resources and Scaffolds That Support Learning and Problem Solving

Resources and scaffolds for problem solving range from time-honored lectures and directed teaching for key concepts to technologically sophisticated simulations that allow students to discover the relationships among variables. They can also include technologies that allow students to practice particular skills needed to solve authentic problems, such as rate calculations. The particular form of support, resource, or scaffold depends on the sophistication of the students as well as the teachers' knowledge in the problem domain. Resources and scaffolds can frequently support a number of different problems that are brought into the classroom.

Information Databases

Most types of resources and scaffolds are becoming "technologized," with many forms of print-based materials now available in electronic form. For example, CD-ROM resources include the entire set of *National Geographic* magazines. Encyclopedia resources such as *Encarta* and *Grolier's* provide youngsters with access to vast stores of information. These resources take advantage of **hypermedia,** the ability to jump in a nonlinear fashion to related information, whether that information is text, graphics, video, or sound. Hypermedia provides a way to weave together written language, static and dynamic images, and sound under computer control. Multimedia encyclopedias exploit the use of hypermedia. In many of the electronic encyclopedias currently on the market, students can actually create a physical link between topics. The link remains and is noted the next time they access the topics.

The use of hypermedia has some potential disadvantages. It is easy for students to become distracted or lost in the hypermedia environment, which is filled with interesting information. Although it is wonderful to have access to vast amounts of information through clicking and browsing, the usefulness of this information comes from developing a conceptual framework within which to make sense of it. Students must develop meaningful links between discrete bits of information and larger information domains. Teachers must take an active role in helping students to construct a conceptual understanding of how this information is related.

In addition to technologies that might be on-site, Internet sites available over the World Wide Web provide vast information resources, including print, video, CD-ROM, and other web sites. The Annenberg/CPB web site even provides a video preview room that allows you to view recently broadcast PBS programs that can be ordered. In fact, the information available on the World Wide Web (WWW) is so vast that the function of many sites is simply to organize and classify resources. For example, the *Perseus Project* is a digital library of resources for studying the ancient world. Materials include "ancient texts and translations, philological tools, maps, extensively illustrated art catalogs, and secondary essays on topics like vase painting." The site currently has a large collection of materials on Greece. They are preparing material on Rome.[36]

A more general web site for social studies information contains lesson plans, lessons, journals, magazines, and special program announcements on topics in social studies, as well as web site addresses (URLs) for museums, magazines, and journals. In addition, there are a number of professional organizations and commercial web sites that organize resources for teachers to use in preparing curriculum units and projects for students, and many of the sites are explicitly for students. For example, the National Council for the Social Studies (www.ncss.org) provides resources grouped thematically (e.g., culture; time, continuity, and change; and power, authority, and governance). The National Council for Teachers of English (www.ncte.org) site has a "Teaching Ideas" section in which members can share activities and ideas that have worked for them. Channel 13 in New York City sponsors a site (www.thirteen.org) that organizes and reviews resources in science, mathematics, and social studies. Other sites provide tools that foster discipline-based analysis. For example, the National Archives and Records Administration provides written document analysis tools that guide students through the process of evaluating everything from written documents to cartoons, maps, and motion pictures (www.nara.gov/education/teaching/analysis/analysis.html).

Programs That Supply Their Own Resources

Many of the programs that bring problems into the classroom also provide resources for problem solving. For example, two design characteristics of the *Jasper Adventures* are **embedded data** and **embedded teaching.** One scene in *The Big Splash,* a business-planning adventure, demonstrates the calculation of a cumulative distribution and illustrates principles of sampling and extrapolation to the population. The *Jasper Adventures* also include opportunities for practice and extended learning of particular skills. Related problems provide opportunities for practicing the skills needed to solve the overall problem. They utilize the same principles needed to solve the main problem but "tweak" them by changing the values of the variables involved. A related problem on the sampling concept asks students to consider a new sample with a different distribution of responses and to extrapolate to a different-sized population. Through multiple examples in which the underlying principle remains the same, students gain practice and proficiency using the principle to solve different problems. Equally important, this practice is motivated by the meaningful situation in which it was originally embedded.

In the *Little Planet Literacy Series,* children prepare to write a book based on the video adventures by discussing and sequencing pictures of important events from the animated story. Storyboard tools allow the children to move the pictures into any order they wish and to receive audio or visual help as needed (see Figure 7.2). After they sequence the pictures, children use a multimedia storybook maker to retell the story in their own words. The software also allows children to write a summary of the story, receive spelling help

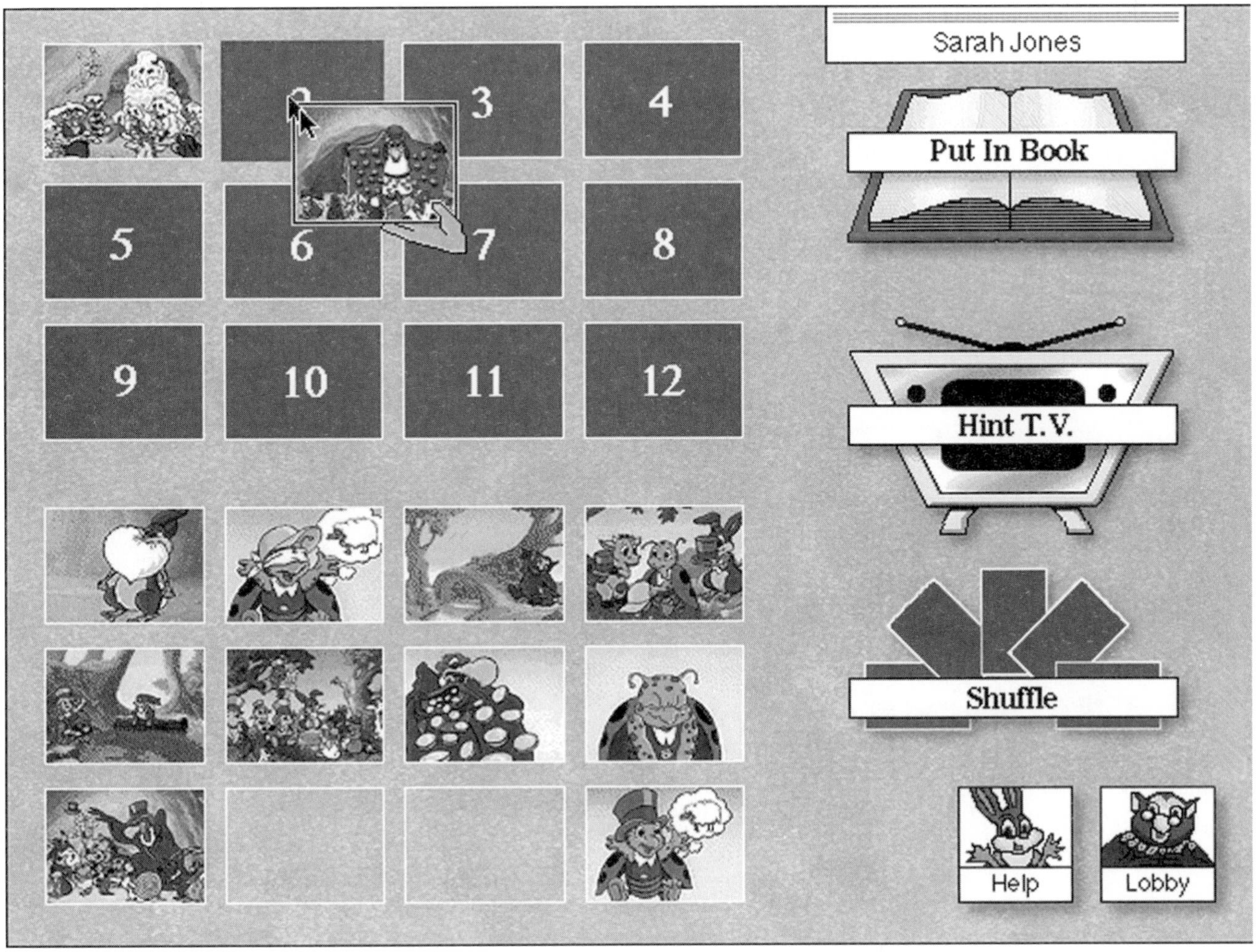

Figure 7.2
Screen shot copyright © by Little Planet Publishing. Reprinted by permission.

when needed, make a recording of their voices reading the story, and add music to their stories. These activities encourage in-depth understanding of the affective as well as the narrative elements of stories. Eventually, the students print their stories in a traditional book format to take home and share with their families. Again, an essential motivational tool is the anchor story, which is about something of importance to the children.

To help teachers include phonics instruction as part of the program, the *Little Planet* software includes Read-Along books. These books feature characters from the Little Planet and are composed exclusively of short, decodable words. As children practice reading the text, they can click on words or sentences to hear them read aloud. Printed versions of the Read-Along books include bar codes. Children use the bar-code reader and a videodisc player to hear printed text read aloud.

The *Web-based Inquiry Science Environment* (*WISE*) provides a series of resources and tools that support students in developing skills of scientific investigation and argumentation. *WISE* uses a variety of web resources in combination with pop-up windows for taking notes and seeking help. The *WISE* environment breaks the project down into inquiry steps (e.g., reading, examining data, taking notes, reflecting). Students navigate through the content (evidence) by selecting appropriate buttons. Help in the form of hints is also available (see Figure 7.3). Some of the hints ask questions to foster deeper thinking about the issues presented in the evidence. Note taking is similarly designed to foster reflective thinking in that students are asked to provide written responses to evidence they have encountered. The *WISE* environment also features tools for visualizing data, drawing flowcharts and causal maps, sorting evidence, and holding on-line discussions. The evidence-sorting function of the Sensemaker tool is particularly important because it helps students think about the information as they sort it. For example, students can group different pieces of evidence according to the hypothesis they think it supports. This process encourages them to think about the credibility and relevance of each piece of evidence for the problem on which they are working. Along with online and class discussions, Sensemaker is designed to make thinking visible so that students can reflect on it—sometimes orally, sometimes in writing.[37]

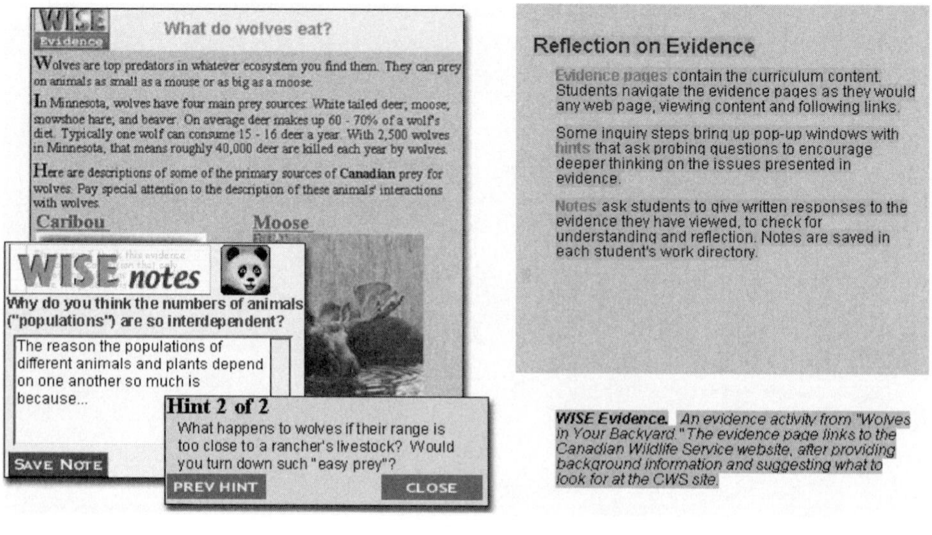

Figure 7.3 Examples of hints provided in the WISE environment.

Reprinted by permission of The WISE Project. http://wise.berkeley.edu

The *BGuILE* project has constructed software that is unique to each of its units but suited to the nature of the biological investigations. The software fosters different ways of visualizing, representing, and analyzing the different forms of data relevant to each challenge problem.

The *GLOBE* program investigations include a variety of learning activities that are designed to be completed along with collecting the data in the field. These activities are a means by which students can learn more about the domain, the instruments, and procedures. For example, one of the learning activities for the atmosphere unit focuses on careful observation, description, and identification of clouds. Students first generate their own sketches and descriptions and then compare them to official weather bureau ones. More advanced activities examine the correlation between wind and clouds by having students chart the wind direction and speed for each observable cloud type and explain the connection between the hydrologic cycle and atmospheric conditions.

Especially in science and mathematics, software that supports visualization of the relationships among variables has been found to be extremely useful. *GLOBE* provides visualization tools that allow students to see how their data fit into that collected all over the world. Students select the variable they want, and the data are displayed on a map.

Co-Vis provides another web-based visualization tool. It uses real-time data on weather and global climate. The Weather Visualizer provides a graphical interface that uses real-time weather data. Students select variables they want to see displayed on a customized weather map, and the images are then generated on demand. It is also possible to get satellite images using this visualization software. *Co-Vis* also provides *WorldWatcher,* a visualization environment that supports looking at global climate and climate change as well as human and physical geography data. These data allow students to look at causes and implications of climate change. The *Co-Vis* web page also provides some resources that explain the phenomena under consideration, such as the greenhouse effect or global seasonal variation. These are text resources such as one might find in a textbook.

Students select the variables reflected in the *GLOBE* and *Co-Vis* visualizations, but the software designers specify the relationships. However, simulations can provide visualizations based on both student-selected variables and student-specified relationships among the variables. For example, *Model-It* software provides system contexts (e.g., ecosystems, human nutrition systems) in which students qualitatively "model" the system by selecting variables and defining the relationships among them (see Figure 7.4). Students can run these models to see the results, which are displayed graphically. Because they have access to and control over the underlying relationships, students can explain the results in terms of these relationships. Note that "canned" simulations such as *SimCity, SimEarth,* or *SimLife* do not provide students access to the relationships that underlie the system's operation. Scientists and teachers have developed system domains for *Model-It* that include ecosystems, nutrition, and photosynthesis. Additional *Model-It* software tools support data gathering and reporting.[38]

Access to Experts

Teachers often face the dilemma of not "holding all the answers" to authentic problems posed to students. In such cases, technology can provide a useful resource to the teacher as well as the students. Distance learning increasingly provides access to lectures on a wide range of subjects and at multiple levels of sophistication. Currently, distance learning programs are most often relevant to high school and college coursework. The ability to interact quickly and

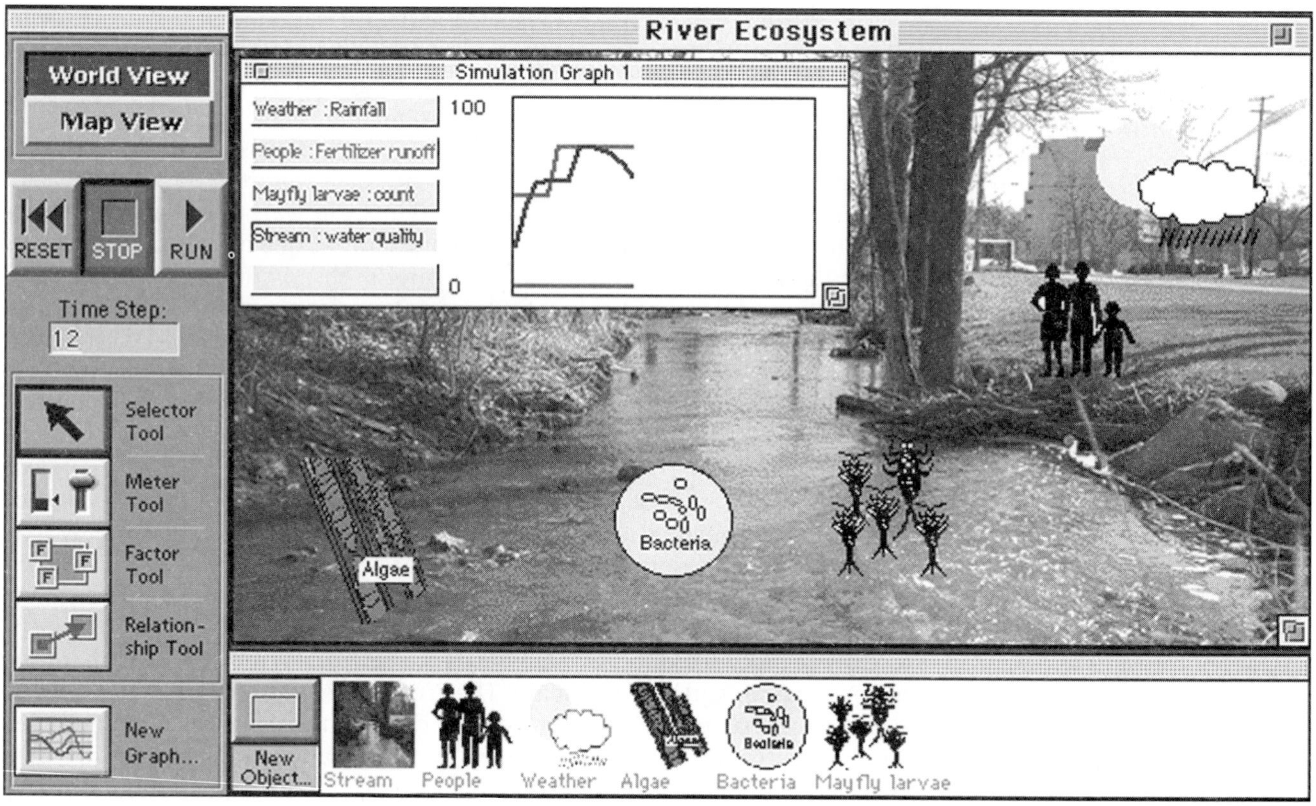

Figure 7.4
Used by permission of Joseph Krajcik, Center for Highly Interactive Computing in Education.

directly with experts in a variety of fields is enhanced via e-mail and the WWW. For example, many of the museum and general reference databases provide ways to contact individuals about specific questions and issues that arise in the context of projects that students and teachers are working on. General search engines (e.g., Ask Jeeves and Google) are also frequently effective at finding information relevant to specific questions.

Providing Opportunities for Feedback, Reflection, and Revision

Students need opportunities to receive feedback and reflect on the implications of that feedback for revising their work. These self-assessment skills are critical for setting appropriate learning goals and becoming independent and lifelong learners. A variety of technology tools can assist in providing feedback and opportunities for reflection and revision. We provide several examples of technology-based support for these processes.

Technology tools vary greatly in the amount of flexibility that they allow students during learning and problem solving. They can range from open-ended exploratory systems in which students have complete control to coached practice systems that assign problems and provide highly directive feedback.[39]

BioLogica is at the more open-ended part of the continuum. It is an innovative computer-based program designed to help students learn key concepts of genetics and develop scientific reasoning skills. The centerpiece is the open-ended software tool that permits students to manipulate models of genetic information at multiple levels, including cells, family trees, and whole populations. Using *BioLogica,* students can create and vary the biological traits of an imaginary species of dragons—for example, by altering a gene that codes for the dragon's color and exploring how this alteration affects generations of offspring and the survivability of a population. *BioLogica* embeds formative assessment into the computerized activities: the system poses sequences of challenges to students as they work, monitors their actions, intervenes with hints or feedback, asks questions intended to elicit student understanding, provides tools the students can use to meet the challenge, and directs them to summon the teacher for discussion. The *BioLogica* scripts are based on numerous hours of observation and questioning of children as they worked. The system can also create personal portfolios of a student's notes and images, and record the ongoing interactions of multiple students in a massive log that can be used for formative or summative assessment.[40]

The previously discussed *Web-based Inquiry in Science Education* (*WISE*) environment combines features of the more opened-ended systems with those of more directive approaches. *WISE* provides feedback through scaffolds and hints that structure reflection and revision on the evidence gathered as well as on the process of gathering evidence and addressing the target controversy.

At the highly directive end of the continuum is the *PUMP Algebra Tutor,* a sophisticated intelligent tutoring program designed to help students learn algebra as they solve problems and receive individualized feedback. The program monitors each action that a student takes to solve a problem and compares it with a set of operations that are based on the performance of successful students as well as the mistakes that students frequently make. When help is needed, the tutor knows where the student is in the problem-solving process and can provide immediate feedback that is tailored to the student's particular approach to the problem. Because every step of the performance is monitored, the student cannot get too far off track. The *PUMP* tutor also monitors learning from problem to problem. A statistical procedure identifies a student's strengths and weaknesses, selects problems, and creates an optimal pace through the curriculum. Similar tutors have been developed for other areas of the curriculum, such as geometry.[41]

Although students with more expertise may become impatient with this highly directive approach, the tutor's immediate feedback is useful in the early stages of learning and for relatively simple tasks. It is not as effective for tasks in which the goal is to understand mechanisms that underlie the behavior of complex systems—a central goal of learning about science. To achieve this kind of understanding, it is important for students to be able to explore competing alternatives and to construct their own models of a system.

Simulation software is a type of technology that models systems. Simulations provide both resources for exploring the principles that govern a particular domain and opportunities for feedback, reflection, and revision. The simulation results are immediately available for interpretation and for guidance in additional problem-solving attempts. Recent research validates the effectiveness of computer-based simulations in instruction and the strategies that students use as they explore them.[42] Almost all studies indicate that students are able to learn the targeted material while using the simulations. Students solve more problems and produce better-quality solutions after instruction that includes simulations. Moreover, students have more confidence in their solutions.[43] For example, researchers developed an interactive *Jasper Adventureplayer* software program that allows students to suggest solutions to a *Jasper* adventure and then see simulations of the effects of their solutions. Studies show this has positive effects on the quality of the student-generated solutions because students make use of the feedback to modify and amplify their solutions.[44]

Simulation environments are also called *microworlds* because they portray simple versions of real-world phenomena. Within these microworlds, students can carry out actions and immediately observe the results. The combination of immediate feedback and a controlled environment provides excellent opportunities to scaffold reflection and revision of student thinking. By reflecting on the outcomes of successive experiences within the simulation, students are able to construct and refine their own qualitative model of how it operates. The reflection feature of the instructional environment has been shown to be extremely important.

Another example of the power of simulations for learning is in the area of physics. Most children and many adults have misconceptions about what happens when a force acts on a moving object, but sixth-grade students using the *ThinkerTools* simulations developed a more expert understanding of Newton's law than traditionally taught high school physics students.[45] Traditional approaches to physics instruction frequently introduce students to physical laws via equations to be memorized and used to solve problems. Students often fail to make connections between these equations and the principles that they represent. For additional information on *ThinkerTools,* please see the boxed information below.

One potential difficulty with the use of simulations is that it is often difficult for teachers and students to keep track of the variables they have manipulated,

ThinkerTools: A simulation environment for Newtonian physics

ThinkerTools guides students to discover the principles of Newtonian physics by doing experiments in a series of four increasingly complex microworld simulation environments. In the first simulation, students can move a dot left or right by applying a force either in the same direction that the dot is moving or in the opposite direction. By changing the amount or the direction of the force, students gradually come to understand that force causes an object to change speed, stop, or reverse direction. Student understanding is facilitated in several ways. First, the problems that are presented in the first simulation are similar to activities that most children understand, for example, kicking a ball. Second, the first microworld is an oversimplification of the real world because gravity and friction, and the complexity that they introduce, are not included. Third, the simulation environment employs multiple graphic representations for speed and force that are easy to understand and similar to the behavior of objects in the real world. Each subsequent microworld increases the complexity of the problems that can be represented. For example, gravity is not part of the system until the fourth microworld. The simulations are effective because they are easy to interpret: outcomes are represented as a series of cause-and-effect events. Use of *ThinkerTools* in the context of an instructional cycle that includes reflection on the results of experiments, hypothesis revision, and additional experimentation has been shown to significantly enhance students' understanding of the cause-and-effect relationships.[46]

the results of these manipulations, and their impact on the problem-solving process. Technologies that "track" the course of problem solving provide a window into the problem-solving process. One of the most sophisticated examples of technology that tracks the course of problem solving is the *IMMEX Project* (*Interactive Multimedia Exercises*). *IMMEX* presents realistic, complex problems and uses neural network technology to make sense of the actions students take during problem solving. *IMMEX* consists of a variety of software tools for authoring problem-solving tasks and collecting performance data. An example is the *IMMEX* problem set called *True Roots,* where learners play the part of forensic scientists trying to identify the real parents of a baby who may have been switched with another in a maternity ward. Students can access data from various experts, such as police and hospital staff, and can conduct laboratory tests such as blood typing and DNA analysis.[47]

The moves that students make in solving a problem in the *IMMEX* system are tracked; they can be presented graphically as well as compared with patterns previously exhibited by both skilled and less skilled problem solvers. Feedback can be generated at multiple levels of detail for both teacher and student. For the teacher, data are available on how individual students and whole classes are doing on particular problems as well as over time on multiple problems. At a deeper level of analysis, teachers and students can obtain visual maps of their search for a given problem. These maps are rich in information, and teachers and students can use them in multiple ways to review and discuss the problem-solving process. By comparing earlier maps with later ones, teachers and students can also judge refinements in problem-solving processes and strategies.[48]

Students also need experiences in which they learn to be more self-reflective about what they understand and what they do not. Some of the hints provided in the *WISE* environment are intended to foster that process. In the physics area, *DIAGNOSER* is a computerized assessment tool that allows students to test their own understanding of critical concepts. Students work through various parts of the curriculum and receive feedback on their understanding of key math and science concepts. On the basis of students' responses to the carefully constructed questions, the program can pinpoint areas of possible misunderstanding, give feedback on students' reasoning strategies, and prescribe relevant instruction. The program also keeps track of student responses, information that teachers can use for monitoring overall class performance. The assessment questions are in a multiple-choice format, with each possible answer corresponding to a correct, partially correct, or incorrect state of understanding. The choices are based on research identifying specific difficulties that students have with concepts in various areas of the physics or math curriculum. Studies have shown that use of the *DIAGNOSER* software system significantly enhances student learning in high school physics. It helps students appreciate what they still don't understand and to develop more appropriate ways to think about the content.[49]

Curriculum Based Measurement (*CBM*) is an assessment system in mathematics and reading that provides students and teachers with feedback on whether students are making progress in their learning for the year.[50] *CBM* assessments sample from the range of competencies expected by the end of the school year at a particular grade level. Students complete short assessments several times a month, which are scored by the computer. Each score becomes a data point on an individual child's graph. By looking at the shape of the graph over time, students and teachers can quickly see whether the student's performance is improving. A more detailed analysis of the student's correct and incorrect responses assists the teacher in determining the curriculum areas to concentrate on with particular students. Teachers have found the results of

CBM assessments to be powerful ways of providing parents with information about their children's learning and development.

Little Planet "Knock Knock" software is a game environment that provides a means of systematically presenting and assessing skills in a context in which students must use their knowledge to accomplish a goal. It encourages writing as well as listening and provides a way for students to learn to externalize and represent their thoughts. Students learn the passwords of Little Planet animals so they can admit them to the Little Planet Clubhouse. Passwords can be anything from letter–sound correspondences to mathematical equations to definitions of scientific concepts. For example, if one animal's password is the letter sound for *b* and another's is the letter sound for *p*, the children will first have to write down the correct password for each animal in a form that they can read. They then use their written "code sheet" to help them identify the character who slips a "note" under the door with the written password (e.g., *b*). There are endless possibilities for the skills that can be assessed in this fashion. New games are easy to create and the *Little Planet* web site contains additional games that can be downloaded.

In addition to technology-based simulations and microworlds that provide opportunities to explore specific domains of knowledge and problem solving, there are more general and domain-independent technology tools and environments that support the inquiry processes of exploration, feedback, reflection, and revision.

In many areas of the curriculum, extended written responses are often an excellent means of determining how well students have understood important concepts embedded in a text and can express their interrelationships. In classroom instruction and assessment contexts, the process of providing feedback on such written products can be problematic because it is so time- and labor-intensive. Technology tools have been developed to aid in this process by automatically scoring a variety of extended written products, such as essays. One example is the *Summary Street* program, experimental software for language arts, that helps middle school students improve their reading comprehension and writing skills by asking them to write summaries of materials they have read. Using a text analysis program based on Latent Semantic Analysis, the computer compares the summary with the original text and analyzes it for certain information and features. The program also gives students feedback on how to improve their summaries before showing them to their teachers. Research with this system has shown substantial improvements in students' summary generation skills, and these generalize to other classes.[51]

An example of a domain-independent technology-based environment is *Knowledge Forum* [formerly *Computer-Supported Intentional Learning Environments* (*CSILE*)], a communal computer database.[52] It allows for asynchronous communication among individuals located within the same classroom, school, or Internet-linked community. Because the database can be accessed at any time, communication is asynchronous. Students communicate electronically with their peers by posting notes and commenting on one another's notes. Teachers often pose questions to which students enter answers. Everyone has access to everyone else's thinking, as reflected in the notes and comments made in the database. This database affords possibilities for feedback on ideas, as well as providing opportunities for teachers to formatively assess what students are thinking; that is, to "get a read on" students' ideas on a particular topic. (It can also be a resource when a student asks for help in understanding something or when experts log on and respond.)[53]

Engaging in conversations in *Knowledge Forum* makes it possible for students to get much more feedback on their ideas than would be possible if they had to rely solely on the teacher. Peers can generate questions and provide feedback, and often this is sufficient to get students to revise their thinking. On other occasions, teachers or outside experts can "seed" the discussion to stimulate students' thinking. In the example below, RB, a sixth-grade teacher, began a critical dialogue in the database by asking students to compare which of two protagonists from different books had been in a worse predicament in trying to survive: (1) Miyax, in *Julie of the Wolves*,[54] is trained in wilderness survival skills by her father but runs away from home when he fails to return from a hunting trip and is presumed dead. (2) Brian, a self-proclaimed "city boy" in *Hatchet*,[55] is stranded in the Canadian woods after a plane crash. After students had generated their initial responses, RB inserted the following note to foster deeper discussion on the issue.

[Comment]: To Everyone: We have a definite "split" in our opinion on whose situation is the worst. Read everyone's theory and see if you can bring someone of a different opinion around to agreement with you by asking specific questions or clarifying, perhaps, a misconception. [RB]

This prompt stimulated students to make comments and provide feedback to their peers, as in the following notes:

[Comment]: To Brandon: Didn't Miyax have grass and stuff that she could eat? [WD]
[Comment]: CF, what do you mean that the girl is going to die in the cold? [DP]
[Comment]: DP, I am saying that she is in more danger than Brian. [CF]
[I Need To Understand]: Jennifer: Don't you think that Brian's condition is worse than Miyax's because he had no food or anything and Miyax does?

As mentioned earlier, outside experts can also visit classrooms electronically and provide feedback to students. This helps students continually deepen their understanding of particular domains.

Supporting Communication and Community Building

One of the major advantages of technology is that it enables teachers and students to communicate their ideas more effectively through the use of multiple media and frequently to communicate with a wide audience beyond their classroom walls.

Students as Multimedia Developers

Recently, educators have begun to see the usefulness of having students create authentic products that are seen by other students, parents, and community members. The products are multimedia presentations about important and timely issues, such as drugs and alcohol, AIDS, driving safety, pollution, and recycling. Student production teams do the research necessary to create products that can teach and inform others. In creating the products, the students learn about the topic in a meaningful way as well as learn communication skills and gain the confidence to present and argue their point of view.

The multimedia products produced by students incorporate text, sound, pictures, graphics, and video. Students collect visual images from sources in the public domain. They combine these images with text and narration that they supply, as well as with music that they either select or create. Since the development of the student products involves a wide range of talents (e.g., in music, drawing, and writing), the process allows students to use talents that often are not emphasized in school. The fact that students are creating products to show to others appears to be highly motivating. Researchers who have conducted similar types of authentic projects report that the motivation of at-risk students improves markedly in situations such as these.[56]

Other key outcomes of students as multimedia developers are noteworthy. Classmates are extremely interested in one another's presentations. Teachers often report surprise at the level of attention and detail exhibited in many students' work. When completed, student products can be displayed in their school. In addition, the products can be transferred to videotape so that the students can take them home for their parents to see. Once the products are on videotape, students at different schools have opportunities to share them with one another.

When working with students who are producing multimedia products, teachers need to monitor the development process so that it is beneficial to the student. The following guidelines should be kept in mind:

1. Students should select their own topics so that they are motivated to complete the project.
2. Students should complete all research and plan the presentation before creating the product on the computer.
3. The teacher or student should select a multimedia presentation tool that is simple to learn and gives only a limited number of options—otherwise students get consumed with the technology and forget the content of their presentation. New products for students to use to create multimedia presentations appear frequently. Students frequently learn to use products marketed for adults quite quickly (e.g., Microsoft's PowerPoint and Hyperstudio). There are also a number of products that are specifically targeted to building web pages, such as the WebPage Builder (available through Tom Snyder productions: www.tomsnyder.com).
4. The teacher can use the projects as great opportunities for teaching grammar, writing, and spelling, for example, within a context that is meaningful and motivating for the student.

Students will not produce masterpieces the first time. (No one does.) They will need to rewrite their texts and edit and polish their supporting media (pictures, graphics, and video). These types of improvements require effective teaching, student reflective thought, and practice followed by feedback. Over time, the students will produce some very interesting and professional products—and learn while they are doing it.

Connecting and Community

Technology also makes it possible for students and teachers to connect with other students, teachers, homes, and communities regardless of physical distances. We have already discussed the value of having peers and "outsiders" participate in classroom instruction as providers of resources and feedback. Another advantage to widening the dialogues in which students participate is the sense of community that develops, both within the classroom and outside the classroom walls. When the dialogues are about learning, a vital learning community develops. All members of the learning community are valued for what they uniquely bring to the conversation. Especially in asynchronous systems, individuals often feel more able to contribute because they have more time to reflect on what they wish to say and how they wish to say it.[57]

Internet-based collaborative projects also provide a means of developing community that extends beyond the walls of the classroom. Projects like *Global Schoolhouse* establish learning clusters of four to six schools that work as collaborative teams. Clusters study topics such as groundwater pollution, solid waste management, alternative energy sources, space exploration, natural disasters, and weather. Sites contribute data relevant to their topic and exchange the information in a database available over the WWW to all the schools in the cluster. The *Global Schoolhouse* format allowed students to share data and pool their resources and findings across several sites as they developed evidence and solutions for various environmental problems. The project is now in its second phase as Global SchoolNet Foundation, continuing to serve as an information exchange and publication forum for K–12 sites that choose to participate in the project.

Most web-based programs provide on-line dialogue possibilities for students engaged in working on common projects. *WISE* features on-line asynchronous and synchronous "chat" capabilities; *Co-Vis* uses an asynchronous communal database called the Collaboratory Notebook; *ThinkQuest* provides chat rooms and mail lists. On-line discussion can provide interesting and rich environments for building learning communities though dialogic interaction about content. As such, on-line discussions provide opportunities for feedback, reflection, and revision.

On-line discussion forums and chat rooms are being used increasingly as venues for teacher communities at both preservice and inservice career stages. Professional organizations such as teachers' unions, nonprofit and for-profit companies, and the various sites that provide resources for teaching typically all have a discussion forum feature for exchange of information among those who use the site. The synchronous conferencing system *TAPPED IN* (http://www.tappedin.org/) hosts a series of teacher-hosted discussions among small, focused interest groups. *TAPPED IN* staff provide a monthly list of scheduled on-line events through e-mail messages to members of the *TAPPED IN* community. *TAPPED IN* allows users to leave messages and other artifacts in various conference center locations for subsequent reference. Thus, while the system is designed for simultaneous participation by multiple teachers, information can be accessed at later points in time.[58]

Productivity tools for teachers

Many of the productivity software tools that are a mainstay of the business community are also very useful for teachers, both for their general productivity as professionals and for instruction. Usually these productivity tools include word-processing, spreadsheet, database, and presentation software. For general productivity, word processors are used for correspondence, reports, and so on; spreadsheets for budget management; databases for class roles and student information; and presentation software for lecture outlines and notes. However, all these software applications can also be used in more instructional roles. A few examples are presented here, but many creative teachers have found ways to use these kinds of software in classrooms. Also, many software publishers have web sites with tips for use of their productivity software, (e.g., www.microsoft.com/education).

Word processors allow teachers to prepare quizzes and tests but also can be used in class for group-writing assignments. Students can collect comments and notes for later use in oral presentations or in handouts that are shared with the whole class. Word processors can also be used in a similar manner as presentation software to create overhead transparencies or blank charts for data collection.

Spreadsheets can often be used to present mathematical relationships, trends in data, and simple statistical analyses, as well as to carry out complex calculations that students might find to be a hurdle to conceptual understanding. For example, in science and mathematics the concept of "doubling time" is a very useful idea that can be applied to many situations, such as why bacterial infections can quickly become very serious and how natural resources such as fossil fuels can be used up faster than expected. A very simple spreadsheet that compares percentage increases, such as 2 percent with 7 percent, can illustrate the concept of doubling time very dramatically. With a 2 percent increase, if it is based on yearly increases, it takes about thirty-five years for an amount of money or number of insects to double, while with a 7 percent increase, the doubling time is reduced to about ten years. Spreadsheet programs are usually paired with graphing subprograms that allow a visual representation to be constructed by the computer based on the spreadsheet. In this manner the students can see the sharp difference in slope between the two percentages for the example just mentioned.

Database programs, especially the relatively simple versions, can be used by students to collect and sort information for a variety of situations. Samples collected in science class can be classified by various aspects; for example, insects might be classified by number of wings or antennae and then similar insects could easily be found by searching the database. In social studies, data might be collected from old cemeteries to see whether there was a pattern to the dates of death: Did an epidemic occur sometime in the past? Sometimes external databases, such as census data from the nineteenth century, are also available for student use and can provide interesting local and national information.

Presentation software is usually thought of as being used for preparing linear presentations (i.e., one screen followed by the next), that might be enhanced by color, graphics, audio, and video. However, most presentation programs can also be used in a nonlinear format. The objects on the screen (text, graphics, icons, etc.) can be considered to be "action buttons" and clicking on them can take the user to different screens, not necessarily the next one. This is sometimes useful for developing discussion questions, with students choosing an action and then receiving additional information or feedback on their choice. While not usually as flexible as some of the multimedia programs mentioned in other parts of this chapter, presentation software does allow teachers and students to create nonlinear multimedia-enhanced programs with software that is often included with computer systems or can be purchased at a relatively low cost.

Mastery Test

OBJECTIVE 3 **To understand principled uses of technology to support learning with understanding**

Using the web or product catalogues, identify two technology-based programs. Analyze and discuss them from the standpoint of how each satisfies, or could satisfy, the four functions important to meeting the instructional goal of learning with understanding. Your examples might come from different content areas or reflect different types of technologies.

OBJECTIVE 4

To understand how to make hardware and software work for you and your students

LEARNING ACTIVITY 4

The previous two Learning Activities of this chapter have outlined some powerful ways that learning and learning with technology can take place. How do these ideas fit into "normal" classrooms, where a variety of issues can interact to make implementing some of the ideas difficult for teachers? In order to answer this question, we will identify these implementation issues and consider how they may make an impact on teachers' decisions about how to use technology.

District-Level Issues

As technology becomes more prevalent in the nation's schools, many school systems have designed and implemented technology plans for districts. Visiting any moderately large system's web site, you will usually find an entry about technology's projected role in the district. The system's overall commitment to technology is often apparent in the mission statement of the district. If technology aspects are not considered in such a statement, the administration and school board may see technology as an expensive "frill," making it difficult for classroom teachers to become involved with technology. By reading a technology plan, teachers can often find out what resources they will have to work with in their school. If the district has made a commitment to replacing hardware according to a reasonable timetable and has plans to connect all classrooms to the Internet, it gives teachers an idea of what resources might be available in the future. Several organizations have presented ideas about what might be appropriate to consider as a district-level plan is developed. For example, the International Society for Technology in Education (ISTE; www.iste.org), the Milken Family Foundation (www.mff.org/edtech), and the CEO Forum (www.ceoforum.org) all provide documents that can be helpful for both districts and schools.

YOUR TURN

Visit the web site of a school system in your area to see what they have done in regard to plans for technology. [If you can't easily find a site, visit the Williamson County (Tennessee) home page (www.wcs.edu)]. Why are overall district and/or school technology plans important to individual teachers?

School-Level Issues

As with districts, many individual schools are developing technology plans as part of overall mission statements and/or site-based management initiatives. Teachers may be able to influence mission statements at a school level more readily than at the district level. What things should a classroom teacher consider if asked to work on a technology planning committee?

1. What goals does the school have for technology? Will it use technology to develop the understanding that has been suggested previously in this chapter or will it use technology to practice basic skills? While neither of these two goals is ever completely independent of the other, a school that decides to spend its technology dollars on an "integrated learning system" (one that emphasizes students' coming to a computer laboratory for a set period of time each week for skills development) is making a statement that is different from one that plans for four to six computers in every classroom with Internet access and software oriented to problem solving.
2. Who will assist teachers with technology at the school level? Not only are initial training issues important in a school-level technology plan, but continuing support for classroom teachers is also essential. Many schools use the "mentor" model whereby a small number of teachers, perhaps one from each grade level, receive more extensive computer training and serve as mentors to other faculty. One drawback of this model is that an individual teacher cannot get assistance or advice on a particular problem during the school day, since most mentor teachers will be involved with their classes and unavailable for questions until after school. Districts usually have a technology support person or team that can be contacted either on the Internet or by phone, but, again, this person may not be available for immediate questions—such as "Why doesn't my printer work anymore?"—that can be frustrating for both teachers and students. As computer systems become more user-friendly and as more classroom teachers become more experienced with technology either in their preservice or in-service programs, some of these basic support issues may be resolved. Nevertheless, support for classroom teachers is an issue that schools must address at the building level in order for technology to be used effectively.

YOUR TURN

Visit a local school web site to see if you can find a technology plan or goals for that school.

Classroom Issues

Issues related to technology use on the classroom level generally fall into three major areas: the instructional philosophy of the teacher, which is the most critical, as well as the more technical issues of hardware and software selection and support. We discuss each of these in the following sections.

Instructional Philosophy

Overall instructional goals for a district and a school often provide classroom teachers with useful direction in developing their own instructional goals. In many schools, teams of teachers develop grade-level goals and objectives. In many states, there have been efforts to produce "standards" or "guidelines" for using technology in school. A check of your state department of education web site will usually quickly allow you to see what the guidelines are for your state. Some preliminary national standards have been proposed by ISTE and can be found at their web site (www.iste.org).

However, in the long run, individual teachers are still the primary decision makers as to what happens on a daily basis in their classrooms. While the first two objectives of this chapter outline some interesting and challenging methods compared to more traditional ideas of teaching and learning, it is up to the classroom teacher to implement these ideas. The issues you have read about in this chapter will have an impact on what direction technology use will take in classrooms. Your basic instructional philosophy is the most important aspect of implementation. If teachers believe strongly that a challenge-based problem-solving method is important to implement in their classroom, even if it means less instructional time on traditional "teaching is telling" methods, they will be willing to take some instructional risks and try some alternative ways of instruction. You as teachers need to take time to think about, discuss, and clarify what your instructional philosophy is and how you can use technology to assist in implementing it.

Hardware

Technology changes so rapidly that it is especially difficult for schools with limited resources to prevent the equipment that they purchase from rapidly becoming obsolete. While a district- or school-level plan for replacing or upgrading computers on a three- to four-year cycle helps overcome some of these problems, individual teachers may need to make decisions about hardware if special funding becomes available. Nothing can stop the continuous rapid change in hardware, but some planning when purchasing microcomputers may help extend the useful life of machines. Issues for you or technology planners in your school to consider include the following:

1. What is the upgradeability of the computer system? Purchasing a system that allows for a new microprocessor to be installed instead of a whole new system can result in substantial savings. Increases in speed of 50 to 75 percent are common when a faster, more powerful processor is installed. Additionally, computer memory (RAM) should be expandable to at least twice what originally comes with the machine. Many of the software packages mentioned earlier in this chapter make use of video and animation, which often require additional RAM for good functioning.
2. Can additional peripheral devices be added or upgraded easily? While almost all systems now come with some type of video card for the computer monitor, a sound card for audio, a hard disk subsystem for storage, and a CD-ROM player, all these components may need to be upgraded to faster speeds or larger storage capacities. Knowing that these can be replaced without purchase of a new system is a plus when comparing systems.

3. How will the computer be connected to a local area network (LAN) and/or the Internet? Many schools have "wired" their buildings to provide for network connections—some for local networks only, but most for connection to the Internet. Generally a network interface card must be used in the computer for a connection to be made to the network. A system that already comes with a card that is compatible with the school network saves an additional installation step. Wireless networks are also beginning to find a home in schools. While generally not as fast as wired networks when groups as large as full classes are all using the Internet, they do offer the advantage of not requiring as much cabling inside the classroom.

Special education technology—What is it?

The use of assistive technology by individuals with disabilities is not a new development. For centuries, individuals have used a variety of assistive devices to help them overcome environmental demands, such as a horn held to the ear to enhance hearing or a wooden peg on an amputated leg to allow walking. Historically, it was up to individuals to find appropriate devices to help them ameliorate their disability. Today, however, with support from federal legislation, schools and businesses are required to help individuals with disabilities find and use appropriate assistive technologies and services. Beginning in July 1998, federal law mandated that assistive technology *must be considered* for all students eligible for special education services. Assistive technology for students with special needs is defined as "any item, piece of equipment, or product system, whether acquired commercially off the shelf, modified, or customized, that is used to increase, maintain, or improve functional capabilities of individuals with disabilities" (Individuals with Disabilities Education Act, PL 101-476). This is a very broad definition and encompasses a wide variety of technologies. Assistive technologies, including devices and services, can be categorized into seven functional areas: (1) existence; (2) communication; (3) body support, protection, and positioning; (4) travel and mobility; (5) environmental interaction; (6) education and transition; and (7) sports, fitness, and recreation.[59] Numerous high-tech devices exist within these seven categories, such as hearing amplifiers for individuals with hearing disabilities, communication devices for individuals with speech impairments, word-prediction software for students with learning disabilities, computer screen readers and Braille printers for people with visual impairments, and even speech-recognition systems and robotic devices to assist people with severe physical disabilities. When employing an assistive technology, it is important to remember that each and every individual faces a unique set of challenges and demands that must be considered.

Software

Over the years, many software "evaluation" forms or methods have been presented by various authors. Many of these are appropriate to use in selecting particular programs. However, instead of using a form or checklist, classroom teachers might want to ask the following questions as they think about software for their classrooms:

1. Will the software "run" on my current or planned hardware?
2. Are the activities that the students engage in with the software developmentally appropriate?
3. What will the students actually be learning if they use the software?
4. What issues of classroom management will I have to consider to use the software?

Technical Considerations: Will It Run?

A careful reading of information about the technical requirements for using a software package, either from the materials on the "side of the box" or in a catalogue, will answer most questions about whether the software will run on a particular machine. The speed of the processor and the amount of RAM needed are almost always listed, as well as which operating system is required. Most current software programs have automated the installation processes and provide on-line help to make the initial use less of a problem than in previous years.

Developmental Level

The development level of the students using a particular software package is an issue that should be of concern to the classroom teacher. For example, a complicated word-processing program will not be useful with very young children who lack the keyboarding or literacy skills to effectively use such a program. For older children, the power to integrate graphics, charts, and so on into documents would be a plus as they prepare reports and presentations based on research and problem-solving activities. More subtle levels of developmental appropriateness may be hard to judge if teachers must rely on advertisements or company literature. Discussions with other teachers, either in their own district or over the Internet, is often a way to discuss issues of software appropriateness. Also, teacher-oriented journals or Internet web sites (see listing at the end of this chapter) may contain reviews of particular software packages. Some publishers are adding "previews" of their software by placing a sample version on the Internet. This is often very useful in getting a better idea of the appropriateness of the software.

The migration of software from being CD-based to web-based is also beginning to occur. Some programs still sell a CD, but updates, hints, and alternative activities may reside on the web and be downloaded as needed. Other publishers are going toward full web implementations, meaning that no physical media are used and schools "subscribe" to web sites that contain the full software. As Internet speeds increase, this is likely to be a method of distribution for more publishers. The disadvantage, however, is that schools have to make "big-ticket" purchases of subscriptions that may or may not be appropriate for all students.

What Is Being Learned

A program that is designed to have students practice skills such as multiplication has a different learning goal from one that creates a problem-solving environment in which the student needs multiplication skills to solve the "adventure." Both share the goal of improving students' ability to do multiplication in other settings, but their implementation is quite different. Teachers need to look at the software not only for what it says it is designed for but also for what they believe the students will actually learn. Does the practice program really meet the goal of improving student ability to do multiplication in *new* situations? Research on application of knowledge to new situations (discussed earlier) suggests that students may need teacher assistance to use what they have "learned" with specific software in other learning contexts. In other words, teachers need to extensively use software that they plan to use with their students. They need to decide if what the package lists as "learning objectives" are likely to occur when students use the software.

Management Issues

Developing a philosophy and goals for a classroom in which problem-based activities are a major component of instruction, but having only one or two computers, is an example of how resource and management issues will have an impact on instructional goals. If students are to spend substantial time researching, revising ideas, and preparing presentations about problem scenarios, it will be very difficult to achieve this with limited technology resources. It is not impossible, however, to implement a problem-based curriculum in classrooms with limited hardware. Some programs are designed to involve students in the decision-making process by presenting problems to the whole class via one computer and a projection device. Tom Snyder Productions (www.tomsnyder.com) produces many of these. *The Jasper Woodbury Problem Solving Series,* initially released on videodisc and now on CD-ROM is another example of software that can be used in this manner. Problems are presented and individuals or groups of students work on developing solutions or alternative ideas that they then discuss in a whole-class environment. Additionally, many teachers have developed rotation systems by which individual students can use software while other classroom activities are going on.

Mastery Test

OBJECTIVE 4 **To understand how to make hardware and software work for you and your students**

Place yourself in the role of a "mentor" technology teacher for your particular grade or subject in a school. You have received some additional training both in your preservice work and in your school system. You need to write a short report to other teachers about what things the group might want to consider in their planning for next year. In the report, address the teaching philosophy the group has been working on for the past two years, mention the school and district technology goals, and then outline two or three ways in which the group might want to implement some of these goals in each classroom. Assume that each of the classrooms in your grade or subject area has at least two computers, one of which is connected to the Internet. Also assume that your group shares a projection device that allows the teacher (or students) to project the computer screen to a size large enough that everyone in the class can see it at the same time. Your software budget, mainly provided through parent donations and fundraisers, is not large ($10 per student), but the group can spend it as they see fit.

YOUR TURN

Observation of Technology Use in a School

As part of your field-work component for this course, make a school visit in which you focus on what a school is doing with technology. You will need to visit the school web site before you go to the school, e-mail the principal asking for his or her views on technology, and then visit the school and at least one teacher's classroom. Try not to focus too much on the technology itself (how many computers, etc.) but rather on what is happening with the computers. Write a short narrative of your visit that includes your views on what is happening in the school and some ideas that you would like to implement if you were teaching in that environment. To help you write your narrative, use the observation sheet below on your visit.

Mastery Test

Entire Chapter

Design a technology-enhanced instructional unit. Your design should incorporate the design principles that support learning with understanding. In describing your unit, be sure to include the following:

- The broad theme of the unit in which this lesson will be used
- Specific learning goals and purposes of the lesson
- How and what technology is used
- How learning with understanding is supported by the technology

Observation Worksheet

Technology Use in a Classroom

Directions: Do not use actual names of schools, teachers, administrators, or students when using this worksheet.

Observer's Name: ______________________________

Date: ______________________________

Grade Level: ______________________________

Subject: ______________________________

Class Size: ______________________________

Technology in Place in Classroom: ______________________________

Location and Placement in the Room: ______________________________

Background Information: Give a brief general description of the school's social, economic, and ethnic makeup. Summarize the information that is published (usually on a web site) about the school's goals for use of technology.

Observation: During your observations, notice how many students use technology in the classroom and how it is used. For example, if the teacher is using a large monitor with a computer to explore the Internet on a particular subject, this is a different use than having individual students go to computers in the room for individual drill-and-practice activities. These observations can be recorded in narrative form. Some things you may want to look for include:

- The instructional goals the technology is meeting (e.g., bringing problems in, resources and scaffolds, feedback, communication and community)
- How familiar students seem to be with the technology
- The kinds of software students are using
- Engagement levels of students
- How the teacher interacts with the students at computers
- Use of other materials along with computers
- What the students appear to be learning as they use the software

Teacher Questions: Try to arrange to speak with the teacher for a few minutes about his or her use of technology. Ask questions such as the following:

1. What kinds of things do you use technology for?
2. Do you think technology has been useful for your students?
3. What learning do you believe is taking place when your students use technology?
4. What kinds of technologies would you like to have in your classroom?
5. How good is the support that you get at a school and district level for working with technology?

Student Questions: If the teacher agrees, ask a few questions to one student in the class. Ask questions such as the following:

1. Do you like using technology?
2. What are your favorite things to do?
3. What kinds of technology would you like to have in the class that you do not have now?
4. What kinds of things do you think you are learning from the software?

Reflections on Your Observation: Write a summary paragraph or two about your observation, reflecting on the level of technology use and what might be good things for the teacher you observed to try in his or her class using technology.

NOTES

1. Becky Smerdon, Stephanie Cronen, Lawrence Lanahan, Jennifer Anderson, Nicholas Iannotti, and January Angeles, *Teachers' Tools for the 21st Century: A Report on Teachers' Use of Technology* (NCES 2000-102), Washington, D.C.: U.S. Department of Education, 2000) (http://nces.ed.gov).
2. H. J. Becker, "Teaching, learning, and computing." Irvine, Calif: University of California, Department of Education, June 1999 (http://www.crito.uci.edu/TLC).
3. Some exemplary uses of technology are Hunterdon Central's Online Literary Magazine (www.hcrhs.hunterdon.k12.nj.us/esoup/welcome.html); an Alaskan teacher using the Internet to report on the Iditarod (www.mff.org/newsroom/news.taf?page=177). In addition, the Milken exchange has a series of case studies of classrooms involved in innovative uses of technology (www.edweek.org/sreports/tc98/cs/cs-n.htm).
4. Cognition and Technology Group at Vanderbilt, "Looking at Technology in Context: A Framework for Understanding Technology and Education," in *Handbook of Educational Psychology,* eds. D. C. Berliner and R. C. Calfee (New York: Macmillan, 1996), pp. 807–840.
5. P. Suppes and M. Morningstar, "Computer-Assisted Instruction," *Science* 166 (1968):343–350.
6. M. Hadley and K. Sheingold, "Commonalities and Distinctive Patterns in Teachers' Integration of Computers," *American Journal of Education* 101 (1993):261–315.
7. December 5, 1997, the Daily Report Card, appearing on the World Wide Web (Pape, 1997 http://www.negp.gov). Copyright by the Education Policy Network, Inc. EPN, Inc. hereby authorizes further reproduction and distribution with proper acknowledgment.
8. David, Henry, Patricia Buckley, Gurmukh Gill, Sandra Cooke, Jess Dumagan, Dennis Pastore, and Susan LaPorte, *The Emerging Digital Economy II* (Washington, D.C.: United States Department of Commerce, 1999) http://www.ecommerce.gov/ede/ede2.pdf).
9. D. Feyerick, "U.S. Schools Fall Behind in High-Tech Education." 2000. (www.cnn.com/2000/TECH/computing/09/27/tech.schools).
10. L. Resnick, *Education and Learning to Think* (Washington, D.C.: National Academy Press, 1987).
11. A. N. Whitehead, *The Aims of Education* (New York: Macmillan, 1929).
12. B. L. McCombs, "Motivation and Lifelong Learning," *Educational Psychologist* 26 (1991):117–127; P. A. Alexander, J. M. Kulikowich, and T. L. Jetton, "The Role of Subject-Matter Knowledge and Interest in the Processing of Linear and Nonlinear Texts," *Review of Educational Research* 64 (1994):201–252.
13. A. L. Brown and J. C. Campione, "Guided Discovery in a Community of Learners," in *Classroom Lessons: Integrating Cognitive Theory and Classroom Practice,* ed. K. McGilly (Cambridge, Mass.: MIT Press, 1994), pp. 229–272; Cognition and Technology Group at Vanderbilt, *The Jasper Project: Lessons in Curriculum, Instruction, Assessment, and Professional Development* (Mahwah, N.J.: Erlbaum, 1997); C. E. Hmelo and S. M Williams, eds., *Learning Through Problem Solving,* Special Issue of the *Journal of the Learning Sciences* 7, (no. 3/4 1998); S. Jackson, S. J. Stratford, J. S. Krajcik, and E. Soloway, "Making System Dynamics Modeling Accessible to Pre-College Science Students," *Interactive Learning Environments* 4 (1996):233–257.
14. D. L. M. Sharp, J. D. Bransford, S. R. Goldman, V. J. Risko, C. K. Kinzer, and N. J. Vye, "Dynamic Visual Support for Story Comprehension and Mental Model Building by Young, At-Risk Children," *Educational Technology Research and Development* 43 (1995):25–42.
15. L. S. Vygotsky, *Thought and Language* (Cambridge, Mass.: MIT Press, 1962); S. S. Wood, J. S. Bruner, and G. Ross, "The Role of Tutoring in Problem Solving," *Journal of Child Psychology and Psychiatry* 17 (1976):89–100.
16. A. Collins, J. S. Brown, and S. E. Newman, "Cognitive Apprenticeship: Teaching the Crafts of Reading, Writing and Mathematics," in *Knowing, Learning and Instruction: Essays in Honor of Robert Glaser,* ed. L. B. Resnick (Hillsdale, N.J.: Erlbaum, 1989), pp. 453–494.
17. J. Dewey, *How We Think, a Restatement of the Relation of Reflective Thinking to the Educative Process* (Boston: Heath, 1933).
18. D. A. Schön, *The Reflective Practitioner: How Professionals Think in Action* (New York: Basic Books, 1983); D. A. Schön, "Coaching Reflective Teaching," in *Reflection in Teacher Education,* ed. P. P. Grimmett and G. L. Erickson (New York: Teachers College Press, 1988), pp. 17–29.
19. R. Glaser and M. T. H. Chi, "Introduction: What Is It to Be an Expert?" in *The Nature of Expertise,* ed. M. T. H. Chi, R. Glaser, and M. J. Farr (Hillsdale, N.J.: Erlbaum, 1988), pp. xv–xxiix.
20. W. Schneider, S. T. Dumais, and R. M. Shiffrin, "Automatic and Controlled Processing and Attention," in *Varieties of Attention,* ed. R. Parasuraman and D. R. Davies (Orlando, Fla.: Academic Press, 1984), pp. 1–27.
21. P. Black, and D. William, "Inside the Black Box: Raising Standards Through Classroom Assessment." *Phi Delta Kappan,* 80 no. 2 (1998):139.
22. E. Kintsch, D. Steinhart, G. Stahl, C. Matthews, R. Lamb, and L. R. Group, "Developing Summarization Skills Through the Use of LSA-Backed Feedback." *Interactive Learning Environments,* 8 (2000):87–109. (http://lsa.colorado.edu/content.html#top); K. C. Hurst, A. M. Casillas, and R. H. Stevens, *Exploring the Dynamics of Complex Problem-Solving with Artificial Neural Network-Based Assessment Systems* (CSE Technical Report No. 387). (Los Angeles: University of California at Los Angeles, National Center for Research on Evaluation, Standards, and Student Testing, 1988) (http://www.immex.ucla.edu/).
23. C. Bereiter, "Aspects of an Educational Learning Theory," *Review of Educational Research* 60 (1990):603–624; E. Hutchins, "The Social Organization of Distributed Cognition," in *Perspectives on Socially Shared Cognition,* ed. L. Resnick, J. M. Levine, and S. D. Teasley (Washington, D.C.: American Psychological Association, 1991), pp. 283–307.

24. A. L. Brown, D. Ash, M. Rutherford, K. Nakagawa, A. Gordon, and J. C. Campione, "Distributed Expertise in the Classroom," in *Distributed Cognitions: Psychological and Educational Considerations,* ed. G. Salomon (New York: Cambridge University Press, 1993), pp. 188–228; R. D. Pea, "Practices of Distributed Intelligence and Designs for Education," in Salomon, *op. cit.,* pp. 47–87.
25. Cognition and Technology Group at Vanderbilt, *op. cit., The Jasper Project;* G. Hatano and K. Inagaki, "Sharing Cognition Through Collective Comprehension Activity," in Resnick, et al., *op. cit.,* pp. 331–348.
26. Sharp, et al., *op. cit.*
27. Cognition and Technology Group at Vanderbilt, *op. cit., The Jasper Project.*
28. *Ibid.*
29. *Ibid.*
30. A. Collins and J. S. Brown, "The Computer As a Tool for Learning Through Reflection," in *Learning Issues for Intelligent Tutoring Systems,* ed. H. Mandl and A. Lesgold (New York: Springer-Verlag, 1988), pp. 1–18.
31. M. C. Linn and S. Hsi, *Computers, Teachers, and Peers: Science Learning Partners.* Mahwah, N.J.: Erlbaum, 2000 (http:wise.berkeley.edu).
32. Biology Guided Inquiry Learning Environments, July 31, 2001 (www.letus.org/bguile).
33. B. J. Reiser, I. Tabak, W. A. Sandoval, B. Smith, F. Steinmuller, and T. J. Leone, BGuILE: *Strategic and Conceptual Scaffolds for Scientific Inquiry in Biology Classrooms,* in *Cognition and Instruction: Twenty-five Years of Progress,* ed. S. M. Carver and D. Klahr (Mahwah, N.J.: Erlbaum, 2001) (www.letus.org/bguile).
34. Information on the Center for Problem Based Learning can be found at www.imsa.edu/team/cpbl and on the Illinois Summer Sleuths program at www.imsa.edu/team/cpbl/ipbln/
35. J. Crouch, B. Gould, and S. Hays, "World War II: The Homefront," July 31, 2001. (http://library.thinkquest.org/15511). The ThinkQuest web site is www.thinkquest.org.
36. G. R. Crane, ed., *The Perseus Project* (http://www.perseus.tufts.edu, September, 1997).
37. P. Bell, "Using Argument Representations to Make Thinking Visible for Individuals and Groups," in *Proceedings of the Conference on Computer Support for Collaborative Learning '97,* ed. R. Hall, N. Miyake, and N. Enyedy (Mahwah, N.J.: Erlbaum, 1997), pp. 10–19.
38. S. Jackson, S. J. Stratford, J. S. Krajcik, and E. Soloway, "Making System Dynamics Modeling Accessible to Pre-College Science Students," *Interactive Learning Environments* 4 (1996):233–257.
39. K. R. Koedinger and J. R. Anderson, "Intelligent Tutoring Goes to School in the Big City," in *Proceedings of AI-ED 95, World Conference on Artificial Intelligence in Education* (Charlottesville, Va.: Association for the Advancement of Computers in Education, 1995), pp. 421–428.
40. P. Horwitz, and M. T. Christie, "Hypermodels: Embedding Curriculum and Assessment in Computer-Based Manipulatives." *Journal of Education,* 181, no. 2 (1999): 1–23 (http://biologica.concord.org).
41. J. R. Anderson, C. F. Boyle, and G. Yost, "The Geometry Tutor," *Journal of Mathematical Behavior* 5 (1986):5–19; (see www.carnegielearning.com); L. Schauble, "Belief Revision in Children: The Role of Prior Knowledge and Strategies for Generating Evidence," *Journal of Experimental Child Psychology* 49 (1990):31–57.
42. Anderson et al., *op. cit.;* Schauble, *op cit.*
43. S. P. Lajoie, "Computer Environments as Cognitive Tools for Enhancing Learning," in *Computers as Cognitive Tools,* ed. S. P. Lajoie and S. J. Derry (Hillsdale, N.J.: Erlbaum, 1993), pp. 261–288.
44. T. R. Crews, G. Biswas, S. G. Goldman, and J. D. Bransford, "Macrocontexts Plus Microworlds: An Anchored Instruction Approach to Intelligent Learning Environments," *Journal of AI in Education* 8. no. 2 (1997):142–178.
45. B. Y. White, "ThinkerTools: Causal Models, Conceptual Change, and Science Education," *Cognition and Instruction* 10 (1993):1–100.
46. B. Y. White and J. Frederiksen, "Inquiry, Modeling, and Metacognition: Making Science Accessible to All Students," *Cognition and Instruction* 16, no. 1 (1998):3–118.
47. Hurst, et al., *op cit.*
48. *Ibid.*
49. Information on *DIAGNOSER* and other facet-based projects is available at www.talariainc.com/facet
50. L. S. Fuchs, D. Fuchs, C. L. Hamlett, and P. M. Stecker, "Effects of Curriculum-Based Measurement on Teacher Planning and Student Achievement in Mathematics Operations," *American Educational Research Journal* 28 (1991):617–641.
51. E. Kintsch et al., *op cit.*
52. M. Scardamalia, C. Bereiter, and M. Lamon, "The CSILE Project: Trying to Bring the Classroom into World 3," in McGilly, *op. cit.,* pp. 201–228.
53. S. M. Williams, K. L. Burgess, M. H. Bray, J. D. Bransford, S. R. Goldman, and the Cognition and Technology Group at Vanderbilt, "Technology and Learning in Schools for Thought Classrooms," in C. Dede, ed. *Association for Supervision and Curriculum Development Handbook* (Alexandria, Va.: Association for Supervision and Curriculum Development, 1998), pp. 97–119.
54. J. C. George, *Julie of the Wolves* (New York: Harper Trophy, 1974).
55. G. Paulsen, *Hatchet* (New York: Simon & Shuster, 1987).
56. S. M. Carver, R. Lehrer, T. Connell, and J. Erickson, "Learning by Hypermedia Design: Issues of Assessment and Implementation." *Educational Psychologist* 27 (1992):385–404; A. Collins, J. Hawkins, and S. M. Carver, "A Cognitive Apprenticeship for Disadvantaged Students," in *Teaching Advanced Skills to At-Risk Students,* ed. B. Means, C. Chelemer, and M. S. Knapp (San Francisco: Jossey-Bass, 1991), pp. 216–243.
57. M. Lamon, T. J. Secules, T. Petrosino, R. Hackett, J. D. Bransford, and S. R. Goldman, "Schools for Thought: Overview of the Project and Lessons Learned from One of the Sites," in *Innovations in Learning: New Environments for Education,* ed. L. Schauble and R. Glaser (Mahwah, N.J.: Erlbaum, 1996), pp. 243–288.
58. M. S. Schlager, and P. K. Schank, "TAPPED IN: A New On-Line Teacher Community Concept for the Next

Generation of Internet Technology, in *Proceedings of the Second International Conference on Computer Support for Collaborative Learning,* 1977, ed. R. Hall, N. Miyake, and N. Enyedy (www.tappedin.org/info/papers/cscl97/); M. Schlager, J. Fusco, & P. Schank, (1998). "Cornerstones for an On-Line Community of Education Professionals," in *IEEE Technology and Society* 17, no. 4 (1998) (www.tappedin.org/info/papers/ieee.html/).

59. University of Kentucky Assistive Technology (UKAT) Project, Department of Special Education and Rehabilitation Counseling, "UKAT Toolkit" (Lexington, Ky.: University of Kentucky, 1999).

ADDITIONAL RESOURCES

Readings

Anderson, J. R. "A Spreading Activation Theory of Memory." *Journal of Verbal Learning and Verbal Behavior* 22 (1983):261–296.

Anderson, J. R., and A. T. Corbett. "Tutoring of Cognitive Skill." In *Rules of the Mind,* ed. J. R. Anderson. Hillsdale, N.J.: Erlbaum, 1993, pp. 235–255.

Bruer, J. T. *Schools for Thought.* Cambridge, Mass.: MIT Press, 1993.

Cognition and Technology Group at Vanderbilt. "Designing Learning Environments That Support Thinking: The *Jasper* Series As a Case Study." In Designing Environments for Constructive Learning, ed. T. M. Duffy, J. Lowyck, and D. H. Jonassen. New York: Springer-Verlag, 1993, pp. 9–36.

Cognition and Technology Group at Vanderbilt. "The *Jasper* Experiment: Using Video to Furnish Real-World Problem-Solving Contexts." *Arithmetic Teacher* 40 (1993): 474–478.

Cognition and Technology Group at Vanderbilt. "The *Jasper* Series: Theoretical Foundations and Data on Problem Solving and Transfer." In *The Challenges in Mathematics and Science Education: Psychology's Response,* ed. L. A. Penner, G. M. Batsche, H. M. Knoff, and D. L. Nelson. Washington, D.C.: American Psychological Association, 1993, pp. 113–152.

Cognition and Technology Group at Vanderbilt. "From Visual Word Problems to Learning Communities: Changing Conceptions of Cognitive Research." In *Classroom Lessons: Integrating Cognitive Theory and Classroom Practice,* ed. K. McGilly. Cambridge, Mass.: MIT Press, 1994, pp. 157–200.

Collins, A. "Design Issues for Learning Environments." In *International Perspectives on the Psychological Foundations of Technology-Based Learning Environments,* ed. S. Vosniadou, E. De Corte, R. Glaser, and H. Mandl. Hillsdale, N.J.: Erlbaum, 1996, pp. 347–362.

Collins, A., J. Hawkins, and S. M. Carver. "A Cognitive Apprenticeship for Disadvantaged Students." In *Teaching Advanced Skills to At-Risk Students,* ed. B. Means, C. Chelemer, and M. S. Knapp. San Francisco: Jossey-Bass, 1991, pp. 216–243.

Goldman, S. R. (2001). "Professional Development in a Digital Age: Issues and Challenges for Standards-Based Reform." *Interactive Educational Multimedia* 2 (March 2001): 19–46.

Grabe, M., and C. Grabe. *Integrating Technology for Meaningful Learning.* Boston: Houghton Mifflin, 1998.

Kim, A. J. *Community Building on the Web.* Berkeley: Peachpit Press, 2000.

Lajoie, S. P., and S. J. Derry, eds. *Computers as Cognitive Tools.* Hillsdale, N.J.: Erlbaum, 1993.

Lesgold, A., S. P. Lajoie, M. Bunzo, and G. Eggan. "A Coached Practice Environment for an Electronics Troubleshooting Job." In *Computer Assisted Instruction and Intelligent Tutoring Systems: Establishing Communication and Collaboration,* ed. J. Larkin, R. Chabey, and C. Cheftie. Hillsdale, N.J.: Erlbaum, 1992, pp. 201–238.

Lewis, R. A. *Special Education Technology: Classroom Applications.* Pacific Grove, Calif.: Brooks/Cole, 1993.

McCombs, B. L. "Alternative Perspectives for Motivation." In *Developing Engaged Readers in School and Home Communities,* ed. L. Baker, P. Afflerbach, and D. Reinking. Mahwah, N.J.: Erlbaum, 1996, pp. 67–87.

Resnick, L. B., and D. P. Resnick. "Assessing the Thinking Curriculum: New Tools for Educational Reform." In *New Approaches to Testing: Rethinking Aptitude, Achievement and Assessment,* ed. B. R. Gifford and M. O'Connor. New York: National Committee on Testing and Public Policy, 1991, pp. 37–76.

Salomon, G., ed. *Distributed Cognitions: Psychological and Educational Considerations.* New York: Cambridge University Press, 1993.

Salomon, G. "On the Nature of Pedagogic Computer Tools: The Case of the Writing Partner." In *Computers as Cognitive Tools,* ed. S. P. Lajoie and S. J. Derry. Hillsdale, N.J.: Erlbaum, 1993, pp. 179–196.

Schauble, L., R. Glaser, K. Raghavan, and M. Reiner. "Causal Models and Experimentation Strategies in Scientific Reasoning." *Journal of the Learning Sciences* 1 (1991): 201–238.

Schwartz, J. L., M. Yerushalmy, and B. Wilson, eds. *The Geometric Supposer: What Is It a Case of?* Hillsdale, N.J.: Erlbaum, 1993.

Secules, T., C. D. Cottom, M. H. Bray, L. D. Miller, and the Cognition and Technology Group at Vanderbilt. "Schools for Thought: Creating Learning Communities." *Educational Leadership* 54, no. 6 (1997):56–60.

Shute, V., and R. Glaser. "A Large-Scale Evaluation of an Intelligent Discovery World Smithtown." *Interactive Learning Environments* 1 (1990):51–77.

Vye, N.J., S.R. Goldman, J.F. Voss, C. Hmelo, S. Williams, and the Cognition and Technology Group at Vanderbilt. "Complex Mathematical Problem Solving by Individuals and Dyads." *Cognition and Instruction* 15, no. 4 (1997): 435–484.

Vye, N. J., D. L. Schwartz, J. D. Bransford, B. J. Barron, L. Zech, and the Cognition and Technology Group at Vanderbilt. "SMART Environments That Support Monitoring,

Reflection, and Revision." In *Metacognition in Educational Theory and Practice,* ed. D. Hacker, J. Dunlosky, and A. Graesser. Mahwah, N.J.: Erlbaum, 1998, pp. 305–346.

White, B. Y., and J. R. Frederiksen. "Causal Model Progressions as a Foundation for Intelligent Learning Environments." *Artificial Intelligence* 42 (1990): 99–157.

Yackel, E., P. Cobb, and T. Wood. "Small Group Interactions as a Source of Learning Opportunities in Second-Grade Mathematics." *Journal for Research in Mathematics Education* 22, no. 5 (1991):390–408.

Web Sites: Sample Projects

Adventures of Jasper Woodbury: peabody.vanderbilt.edu/projects/funded/jasper/Jasperhome.html

Biology Guided Inquiry Learning Environments (BGuILE): www.letus.org/bguile

Co-Vis Project, Learning Through Collaborative Visualization: www.covis.nwu.edu/

Global Schoolhouse Project: www.gsn.org

The Jason Project: www.jasonproject.org

Knowledge Forum: www.learn.motion.com/lim/kf/KF0.html

Little Planet Literacy Project: littleplanettimes.com/

Perseus Project: www.perseus.tufts.edu

PUMP Algebra Tutor: www.carnegielearning.com

SimCalc: tango.mth.umassd.edu

The Globe Program (Global Learning and Observations to Benefit the Environment) www.globe.gov

Thinkquest: www.thinkquest.org

Thinkertools: thinkertools.berkeley.edu:7019

Web-based Inquiry Science Environment (WISE): www.wise.berkeley.edu

The Math Forum: mathforum.org/

Web Sites: General Learning Resources, Museums, and Libraries

Annenberg/CPB Project: www.learner.org/about/aboutus.html

CNNfyi: www.Cnnfyi.com

Educational Resources Information Center (ERIC): www.eric.ed.gov
Funded by the U.S. Department of Education, this organization supports clearinghouses of information (lesson plans, student resources, etc.) related to a variety of subject areas.

Federal Resources for Educational Excellence: www.ed.gov/free
This site is a portal to a panoply of resources for educators and students in all content domains including educational technology.

International Educational Resource Network: www.iearn.org

National Geographic: www.NationalGeographic.com
Home page for the on-line version of the magazine.

NOVA Online: www.pbs.org/wgbh/nova
On-line resources produced by the Public Broadcasting System for the NOVA documentary TV series.

Public Broadcasting System: www.pbs.org
Home page of the Public Broadcasting System.

Teacher Prep STAR Chart: www.ceoforum.org/tp-questions.cfm
The CEO Forum's Interactive Teacher Preparation School Technology and Readiness (STaR) Chart is a self-assessment tool designed to enable schools, colleges, and departments of education to assess their level of readiness in preparing tomorrow's teachers to use technology.

700 Great Sites: www.ala.org/parentspage/greatsites/amazing.html
These are sites recommended for children from preschool through age 14, their parents, and other caregivers, compiled by the Children and Technology Committee of the Association for Library Service to Children, a division of the American Library Association.

Web Sites: Sample of Libraries and Museums

The Library of Congress: www.loc.gov
The library preserves a collection of nearly 121 million items, more than two-thirds of which are in media other than books. These include the largest map, film, and television collections in the world. The library serves all Americans through its popular web site and in its twenty-two reading rooms on Capitol Hill.

The Louvre Museum: www.louvre.fr/louvrea.htm
Home page of the museum located in Paris, France.

Online Evaluation Resource Library: oerl.sri.com/instruments/instruments/htm
OERL is composed of plans, instruments, and reports that have been used to conduct evaluations of projects funded by the Directorate for Education and Human Resources (EHR) of the National Science Foundation (NSF).

The Smithsonian Museum: www.museumspot.com/features/smithsonian.htm
The Smithsonian Institution has evolved into the world's largest museum complex, with sixteen museums, the National Zoo, and various research centers. Virtual Smithsonian offers an interactive tour through the museum complex, complete with video highlights.

The Smithsonian Center for Education and Museum Studies: educate.si.edu
The Smithsonian Center for Education and Museum Studies interprets the collective knowledge of the Smithsonian and serves as a gateway to its educational resources.

Web Sites: Sample of Professional Resources and Organizations

Examples of web sites maintained by professional organizations and/or foundations that provide instructional resources.

Association for the Advancement of Computers in Education (AACE): www.aace.org/pubs/
The AACE publishes several journals on a variety of educational technology themes.

Benton Foundation: www.benton.org
The foundation works at the intersection of telecommunications policy and practice, with a repertoire of tools including research and publishing, convening and networking, technical assistance, and grantmaking.

The Children's Partnership: www.childrenspartnership.org
This site provides information for leaders and the public about the needs of children. This organization undertakes research and policy analysis, as well as publishing reports and multimedia materials. The partnership focuses particular attention on identifying new trends and emerging issues that will affect large numbers of America's children and on providing early analysis and strategies for action.

International Society for Technology Education (ISTE): www.iste.org/
ISTE also publishes educational technology journals.

Milken Family Foundation: www.mff.org/edtech/
Education Technology presents cutting-edge research on the effective integration of technology into America's schools, and it also helps educators and policy makers to assess their progress in implementing technology through interactive on-line tools such as the State Education Technology Financial Model.

National Center on Education and the Economy (NCEE): www.ncee.org
The hallmark of the national center's work is standards-based reform.

National Council for the Social Studies: www.socialstudies.org/resources
This site provides access to a vast range of resources for social studies teaching and investigation.

National Council of Teachers of English: www.ncte.org
The NCTE web site provides a large number of different types of resources for professional growth, teaching, and learning.

Web Sites: Sample of Commercial Web Sites

Bigchalk: www.bigchalk.com

Blackboard: www.blackboard.com

Encarta: encarta.msn.com/Default.asp

Grolier's: auth.grolier.com/cgi-bin/authV2

Houghton-Mifflin's Eduplace: www.eduplace.com

MaMaMedia: www.mamamedia.com

Plato: www.plato.com

Riverdeep: www.riverdeep.net

Sunburst Software: www.sunburst.com/

Tom Snyder Productions: www.tomsnyder.com

8

Classroom Management

Wilford A. Weber

OBJECTIVE 1 **To describe the four stages of the analytic-pluralistic classroom management process**

OBJECTIVE 2 **To describe the nature and dynamics of the authoritarian, intimidation, permissive, cookbook, instructional, behavior-modification, socioemotional-climate, and group-process approaches to classroom management**

OBJECTIVE 3 **To analyze a given classroom situation and to describe and justify the managerial strategy or strategies most likely to be effective in facilitating and maintaining those classroom conditions deemed desirable**

No other aspect of teaching is so often cited as a major concern by prospective, beginning, and experienced teachers as classroom management. No other aspect of teaching is more frequently discussed in the professional literature—or the faculty lounge. The reason is quite simple. Classroom management is a complex set of behaviors the teacher uses to establish and maintain classroom conditions that will enable students to achieve their instructional objectives efficiently—that will enable them to learn. Thus, effective classroom management is the major prerequisite to effective instruction. Classroom management may be considered the most fundamental—and the most difficult—task the teacher performs.

Teachers' competence in classroom management is largely a function of their understanding of the dynamics of effective classroom management. Therefore, the purpose of this chapter is to enable you to cope more effectively with classroom management problems by helping you to understand more fully the management dimension of teaching. Because no one best approach to classroom management has been found, eight different approaches are examined: the authoritarian, intimidation, permissive, cookbook, instructional, behavior-modification, socioemotional-climate, and group-process approaches. Your own teaching should be more effective if you understand the managerial process and the range of managerial strategies that characterize each of those eight approaches and if you are able to select and apply those specific managerial strategies most likely to be effective in a given situation.

A search of the literature on teaching reveals a number of rather different definitions of the term **classroom management.** They differ because each represents a particular philosophical position and operational approach regarding classroom management. Each approach has its advocates and its practitioners; however, no one of these managerial approaches has been proved best. Therefore, you are discouraged from adopting any one position and from relying on only one managerial approach. Rather, you are encouraged to consider accepting a pluralistic definition of the term *classroom management.* Such a definition broadens the range of approaches from which to select managerial strategies having the potential to create and sustain conditions that facilitate effective and efficient instruction. Only teachers who adopt a pluralistic operational definition—who draw from each of the eight approaches—are able to select from a full range that managerial strategy most likely to be effective, given an accurate analysis of a particular situation. A pluralistic approach does not tie teachers to only one set of managerial strategies as they attempt to establish and maintain those conditions in which teachers can instruct and students can learn. Teachers are free to consider all strategies that appear workable.

A definition sufficiently broad to reflect a pluralistic approach might state: classroom management is that set of activities by which the teacher establishes and maintains those classroom conditions that facilitate effective and efficient instruction.

OBJECTIVE 1

To describe the four stages of the analytic-pluralistic classroom management process

LEARNING ACTIVITY 1

The previous section argued for a definition of classroom management that views it as a process—a set of activities—by which the teacher establishes and maintains those conditions that facilitate effective and efficient instruction. The purpose of this section is to expand on that position by providing a description of classroom management as a four-stage, analytic-pluralistic process in which the teacher (1) specifies desirable classroom conditions, (2) analyzes existing classroom conditions, (3) selects and utilizes managerial strategies, and (4) assesses managerial effectiveness.

Specifying Desirable Classroom Conditions

The classroom management process is purposive; that is, the teacher uses various managerial strategies to achieve a well-defined, clearly identified purpose—the establishment and maintenance of those particular classroom conditions the teacher feels will facilitate effective and efficient instruction with students. Consequently, the first step in an effective classroom management process is the specification of those conditions the teacher deems desirable—the specification of "ideal" conditions. Teachers should develop a clear, thoughtful conceptualization of those conditions they believe will enable them to instruct effectively. In so doing, teachers should recognize that the conditions identified as desirable will, to a large extent, reflect their personal philosophy. That is, the conditions teachers deem desirable will reflect their personal view of teaching rather than any set of universally accepted and empirically validated truths. Additionally, teachers should recognize the need to continually assess the utility of their conceptualization and to modify it as circumstances dictate.

Teachers who take care to specify the classroom conditions they believe are desirable have two major advantages over teachers who do not: (1) they will be far less likely to view classroom management as a process in which they simply react to problems as they occur, and (2) they will have a set of objectives—managerial objectives—toward which their efforts are directed and by which their accomplishments are evaluated. Teachers who have a clear understanding of their managerial objectives are far more likely to be effective than teachers who do not.

Analyzing Existing Classroom Conditions

Having specified desirable classroom conditions, the teacher is in a position to analyze existing classroom conditions—to compare the "real" with the "ideal." Such an analysis allows the teacher to identify (1) discrepancies between existing conditions and desired conditions and decide which require immediate attention, which require eventual attention, and which require monitoring; (2) potential problems—discrepancies that are likely to arise if the teacher fails to take preventive measures; and (3) those existing conditions the teacher wishes to maintain, encourage, and sustain because they are desirable. Thus, the second stage of the process is based on the assumption that the effective teacher is one who is skilled at analyzing classroom interaction and particularly sensitive to what is happening in the classroom; that is, the teacher has an accurate understanding of what the students are doing—and not doing—and what they are likely to do. He or she is sensitively aware of "what's going on."

Selecting and Utilizing Managerial Strategies

When analysis of existing conditions suggests the need for intervention, the teacher should carefully select and apply the managerial strategy or strategies having the greatest potential to achieve the goal—be it to solve a problem, prevent a problem, or maintain a desirable condition. The effective teacher understands the full range of managerial strategies implied by each of a variety of approaches to classroom management, and selects and applies the strategy or strategies most appropriate to a particular situation. The teacher is most likely to be effective if the strategy selected is "situation specific" and "student specific." That is, the teacher makes a thoughtful, informed, reasoned decision based on an insightful understanding of the circumstances and the anticipated reaction of the student or students. For example, a teacher seeking to reinforce appropriate student behavior might publicly praise a student known to find public praise rewarding but avoid this strategy for a student known to find public praise punishing.

This selection process may be thought of as a "computer search," in which the teacher considers the strategies "stored" in his or her "computer bank" and selects that strategy or those strategies holding the greatest promise in promoting the conditions deemed desirable.

Assessing Managerial Effectiveness

The fourth stage of the managerial process involves the teacher's self-assessment of managerial effectiveness. From time to time, teachers should evaluate the extent to which their efforts are establishing and maintaining desirable conditions—the extent to which they are narrowing the gap between the "real" and the "ideal." This evaluation process focuses on two sets of behaviors: teacher behaviors and student behaviors. In the first case, teachers evaluate the extent to which they are using those managerial behaviors they intend to be using. Teachers assess whether the managerial strategies being used are most likely to bring about those conditions deemed desirable. In the second case, the more important of the two, the teacher evaluates the extent to which the students are behaving in desirable ways. Here, the major emphasis is on the extent to which students are behaving appropriately—the extent to which they are doing what they are supposed to be doing. Teacher and student behavioral data may be collected from three sources: the teacher, the student, and an independent observer.

Mastery Test

Objective 1 **To describe the four stages of the analytic-pluralistic classroom management process**

Briefly describe each of the four stages of the analytic-pluralistic classroom management process. When you have done so, compare your responses to those in the Answer Key at the end of the book.

OBJECTIVE 2

To describe the nature and dynamics of the authoritarian, intimidation, permissive, cookbook, instructional, behavior-modification, socioemotional-climate, and group-process approaches to classroom management

Earlier, the third stage of the analytic-pluralistic managerial process was described as a "computer search," in which teachers select and apply the managerial strategy or strategies that appear to have the greatest potential to be effective in a particular situation, given their analysis of that situation. It was emphasized that teachers are most likely to be effective if the strategy they select is "situation specific" and "student specific." Teachers must base their selection on an insightful understanding of both the situation and the student. In effect, teachers must predict how that particular student will react to their intervention. That prediction should be based on what the teacher knows about that student, not on gender or ethnic stereotypes. For example, the teacher should publicly praise Mark because he *knows* that Mark feels rewarded by public praise and should avoid publicly praising Phil because he *knows* that Phil feels punished by public praise.

Earlier, it was also noted that this stage requires the teacher to understand the full range of managerial strategies implied by each of a variety of approaches to classroom management. The purpose of this section of the chapter is to increase your understanding of the authoritarian, intimidation, permissive, cookbook, instructional, behavior-modification, socioemotional-climate, and group-process approaches. It is not unreasonable to expect that a teacher might utilize strategies from a number of these approaches during a typical school day; however, primary attention will be given to the behavior-modification, socioemotional-climate, and group-process approaches because both the literature and research seem to point to their effectiveness. Somewhat less attention is given to the other five approaches. Limitations of space preclude an in-depth examination of any of the approaches. Consequently, you are encouraged to read the books and check out the web sites listed in the Additional Resources at the end of this chapter.

LEARNING ACTIVITY 2.1

The Authoritarian Classroom Management Approach

The authoritarian approach to classroom management views the managerial process as one in which student behavior is controlled by the teacher. The approach places the teacher in the role of establishing and maintaining order in the classroom through the use of controlling strategies; the major goal of the teacher is to control student behavior. The teacher assumes responsibility for controlling the conduct of the student because the teacher "knows best." The teacher is "in charge." This is most often done by creating and enforcing classroom rules and regulations.

One should not view authoritarian strategies as intimidating. The teacher who draws from the authoritarian approach does not force compliance, demean the student, or use harsh forms of punishment. The authoritarian teacher acts in the best interests of the student. This position is perhaps best explained by Canter and Canter, advocates of an approach they have called "assertive discipline."[1] Canter and Canter argue that the teacher has the right to establish clear expectations, limits, and consequences; insist on acceptable behavior from the students; and follow through with an appropriate consequence when necessary. Canter and Canter take great pains to emphasize that assertive discipline is a humane approach. They argue that all students need limits and that teachers have the right to set and enforce such limits.

Although it is an oversimplification, it is suggested here that the authoritarian approach offers five strategies that the teacher might wish to include in his or her repertoire of managerial strategies: (1) establishing and enforcing rules; (2) issuing commands, directives, and orders; (3) utilizing mild desists; (4) utilizing proximity control; and (5) utilizing isolation and exclusion.

Establishing and Enforcing Rules

The process of *establishing rules* is one in which the teacher sets limits by telling the students what is expected of them and why. Thus, it is a process that clearly and specifically defines the teacher's expectations concerning classroom behavior. Rules are statements—usually written—that describe and make public appropriate and inappropriate student behaviors. Rules are formalized guidelines that describe acceptable and unacceptable student behaviors; their purpose is to guide and limit student conduct. It is argued that well-defined rules are necessary if students are going to work within known boundaries. Rules that specify what is and is not acceptable are necessary if students are to know where they stand; students have a right to know "the rules of the game." In addition, they have a right to know the consequences of breaking the rules. Advocates of the authoritarian approach insist that the teacher should establish and enforce rules that are realistic, reasonable, well defined, limited in number, and clearly understood—and do so beginning on the first day of the school year. They stress that no group can work together successfully without established standards of behavior—rules that are public and enforced.

Many recommendations have been made about the establishment of classroom rules. Space limitations allow only two major issues to be highlighted here. The first issue has to do with the extent to which students are involved in making the rules. The second issue, somewhat related to the first, has to do with the number of rules that should be established. There are various positions concerning student involvement in rule establishment. The polar positions are (1) students should have a central role in making rules because they are more likely to follow rules they have had a hand in developing—the role of the teacher is to guide the students' efforts to develop good rules; and (2) the teacher should make the rules because the teacher, not the students, has the responsibility to determine which student behaviors are acceptable and which are not—the role of the students is to follow the rules, not to make them.

A position somewhere between these extremes seems to be most attractive; that is, the teacher should first specify a limited number of nonnegotiable rules and then work with students to add additional rules deemed necessary. This viewpoint also incorporates what appears to be the most appealing position about the number-of-rules issue: teachers should work to keep the number of rules to a minimum. The argument is that fewer rules, consistently enforced, are more likely to be effective than are many rules because having a great number of classroom rules makes enforcement impossible. When rules go unenforced, the teacher's ability to manage the classroom is greatly diminished. Thus, the teacher should establish a reasonable number of enforceable rules.

Issuing Commands, Directives, and Orders

The use of *commands, directives, and orders* is the second authoritarian managerial strategy discussed here. A command is a statement the teacher uses to tell students that they are supposed to do something the teacher wants them to do. Clearly, there are times when it is necessary and appropriate for the teacher to tell students that they are supposed to do something the teacher wants them to do. The kindly kindergarten teacher who asks her students to move to the story center is issuing a command; the friendly French teacher who asks his students to open their texts to page 47 is issuing a command; and the businesslike calculus teacher who asks one of her students to distribute the midterm examinations is issuing a command. Even in the most democratically run classrooms, teachers issue commands. Advocates of this authoritarian strategy argue that the use of clearly stated, easily understood commands, directives, and orders is a perfectly acceptable way for the teacher to control student behavior so long as the teacher does not use force to compel the student to obey. They recommend that commands should describe what the student is expected to do in specific terms. One is hard-pressed to disagree with this viewpoint.

Utilizing Mild Desists

A variety of recommendations have been made about the enforcement of classroom rules. Most typically, these recommendations have ranged from mild to harsh forms of punishment. Many who support the authoritarian viewpoint recognize that severe types of punishment have been shown to be ineffective in the classroom setting. They do point, however, to the effectiveness of a mild form of punishment—mild **desist behaviors.** The terms *mild desist, gentle desist, soft reprimand,* and *corrective* are used as labels for that managerial strategy in which the teacher reproves students for behaving in an unacceptable way—for violating a rule. The teacher—in a kindly manner intended to promote more acceptable behavior, not in a hostile manner intended to condemn the unacceptable behavior—informs students that they are behaving inappropriately, should stop behaving inappropriately, and should return to behaving appropriately. The literature suggests that the use of mild desists is an effective strategy for helping the student who is exhibiting minor forms of misconduct—who is off-task—to get back on-task with a minimum of fuss. Those who support the use of this strategy are quick to remind others that mild desist behaviors are intended to be helpful, not hostile. They are verbal or nonverbal teacher behaviors intended to inform, not to indict.

Utilizing Proximity Control

A teacher may be described as utilizing *proximity control* when he or she moves closer to a student who is misbehaving or who seems to be on the verge of misbehaving. This sort of action is based on the assumption that the physical presence of the teacher will be sufficient to cause the student to refrain from misbehaving. Proximity control is intended to defuse a disruptive or potentially disruptive situation; it is not intended to be punitive or intimidating. Its primary function is to let the student know—by the teacher's presence—that the teacher is aware of the student's behavior. Much like the mild desist, its intent is to inform, not to indict.

Utilizing Isolation and Exclusion

Isolation, exclusion, in-school suspension, in-school detention, suspension, and other forms of exile are strategies that teachers and school administrators are encouraged to consider as a response to serious student misbehavior. Authors representing a wide range of philosophies support the use of various types of exile. All attest to the effectiveness of these strategies, and most view them as nonpunitive. On the other hand, Wallen and Wallen describe isolation as the "ultimate punishment," the most severe allowable form of punishment.[2] The growing use of isolation suggests that various forms of exile—particularly in-school suspension—are viewed as effective in dealing with more serious forms of student misbehavior.

Summary

Given the arguments presented here, teachers who build a repertoire of classroom management strategies would do well to consider the inclusion of at least five authoritarian managerial strategies: the establishment and enforcement of classroom rules; the use of commands, directives, and orders; the use of mild desists; the use of proximity control; and the use of isolation and exclusion.

LEARNING ACTIVITY 2.2

The Intimidation Classroom Management Approach

The intimidation classroom management approach—like the authoritarian approach—views classroom management as the process of controlling student behavior. Unlike the authoritarian approach, which stresses the use of humane teacher behavior, the intimidation approach emphasizes the use of intimidating teacher behaviors—harsh forms of punishment such as sarcasm, ridicule, coercion, threats, force, and disapproval, for example. The role of the teacher is viewed as one of forcing students to behave according to the teacher's dictates.

The student behaves in a manner acceptable to the teacher out of a fear of doing otherwise.

Although intimidation strategies are widely used, few authors who have written in the area of classroom management acknowledge that they believe the intimidation approach to be workable. On the contrary, it is often criticized in the literature. Its most articulate critics may be Johnson and Bany, who point to the ineffectiveness of "punitive and threatening practices" and "dominative and pressuring practices," strategies at the core of the intimidation approach.[3] They assert—and it is agreed here—that objective evaluation of intimidation managerial strategies leads to the conclusion that they are, for the most part, ineffective. Their use usually results in only temporary solutions followed by even greater problems, the most serious of which are student hostility and the destruction of teacher–student interpersonal relationships. At the very best, intimidation strategies deal only with a problem's symptoms, not with the problem itself.

Utilizing Harsh Desists

The literature suggests that teachers who wish to build a repertoire of effective classroom management strategies will find "slim pickings" in the intimidation approach. The one intimidation strategy that might be viewed as useful in certain situations is the *harsh desist.* A harsh desist or reprimand is a loud, verbal command issued in a situation in which the intent of the teacher is to immediately stop a serious student misbehavior. For example, the teacher who comes upon two students fighting in the hallway may yell "Stop!" in the hope that the students—hearing the voice of a teacher—would be afraid to continue to misbehave and break the rules in the presence of a teacher who could bring serious sanctions to bear. Obviously, this type of intimidating behavior would be best used only to *stop* the fight—to stop the misconduct at once. When the fighting has stopped, the continued use of intimidating teacher behaviors would not be as productive as other strategies. The viewpoint here is that the teacher who relies heavily on intimidation managerial strategies—who attempts to control student behavior through the use of intimidating teacher behaviors—is likely to be ineffective.

LEARNING ACTIVITY 2.3

The Permissive Classroom Management Approach

The permissive classroom management approach stresses the need to *maximize student freedom.* The major theme is that the teacher should allow students to do what they want whenever and wherever they want. The role of the teacher is to promote the freedom of students and thereby foster their natural development. In essence, the teacher is expected to interfere as little as possible. The teacher is to encourage students to express themselves freely so that they might reach their fullest potential. Frankly, the permissive approach has few advocates. It represents a point of view that most consider impossible to put into operation in the public school context. It fails to recognize that the school and the classroom are social systems and, as such, make certain demands on those who are major actors in them. Students—and teachers—are expected to exhibit socially acceptable behavior, for to do otherwise is to risk violating the rights of others.

On the other hand, many who contend that the permissive approach in its "pure" form is not productive in school and classroom environments suggest that the teacher should give students an opportunity to "do their own thing" when it makes sense to do so. Students, they argue, must have the opportunity to be "psychologically free"; to take "safe risks"; to negotiate those aspects of the school experience that are negotiable; and to develop self-directedness, self-discipline, and self-responsibility. If the teacher does not encourage a measure of freedom when it is appropriate, those things are not likely to happen. Clearly, the teacher must find ways to provide students with as much freedom as they can handle in a responsible manner. Those who would consider drawing on managerial strategies that are representative of the permissive approach would do well to consider the validity of such arguments.

LEARNING ACTIVITY 2.4

The Cookbook Classroom Management Approach

The fourth approach discussed here is the cookbook, or "bag-of-tricks," approach. This approach to classroom management—an ill-fitting combination of old wives' tales, folklore, and common sense—takes the form of recommendations touted as remedies for all managerial ills. Descriptions of the cookbook approach usually consist of lists of things a teacher should or should not do when confronted with various types of classroom management problems. These lists of dos and don'ts are commonly found in articles with titles like "Thirty Ways to Improve Student Behavior." Because these lists often have the appearance of being quick and easy recipes, this approach is known as the cookbook approach. The following are typical of the kinds of statements one might find on such a list:

Always reprimand a pupil in private.

Never raise your voice when admonishing a student.

Always be firm and fair when dealing with students.

Never play favorites when rewarding students.

Always be sure that a student is guilty before punishing him or her.

Always be sure that all students know all your rules and regulations.

Always be consistent in enforcing your rules.

Because the cookbook approach is not derived from a well-conceptualized base, it lacks consistency. Even though many suggestions put forward by advocates of the cookbook approach make a great deal of sense, there is no set of principles that permits the teacher to generalize to other problems. The cookbook approach tends to cause a teacher to be *reactive* in dealing with classroom management. In other words, the teacher who uses a cookbook approach usually is reacting to specific problems and using short-range solutions. It is more effective to be *proactive,* to anticipate problems, and to use long-range solutions. The cookbook approach does not foster this type of managerial behavior, which attempts to deal with (1) possible problems before they surface in the classroom and (2) causes rather than symptoms.

Another difficulty caused by acceptance of the cookbook approach is that when the specific prescription fails to achieve its intended goal, the teacher cannot posit alternatives because the cookbook approach deals in absolutes. If "such and such" happens, the teacher does "so and so." On the other hand, advocates of a pluralistic approach assert that if "such and such" happens, the teacher can do "this or this." And if one of those fails to work, it is simply a matter of reanalyzing the situation and selecting from a variety of other attractive alternatives. Teachers who operate from a cookbook framework put themselves at a disadvantage and are unlikely to be effective classroom managers.

A final word of caution: the cookbook approach should not be confused with either an eclectic approach or a pluralistic approach. The cookbook approach consists of ill-fitting bits and pieces of advice concerning the managerial behaviors the teacher is to use in particular situations. An eclectic approach is one in which the best aspects of a variety of managerial approaches are combined to create a well-conceptualized and philosophically, theoretically, and psychologically sound whole from which the teacher selects that particular managerial behavior appropriate to a situation. As noted previously, a pluralistic approach is one in which the teacher selects from a wide variety of managerial approaches that managerial strategy or combination of strategies having the greatest potential, given an analysis of the situation. It is argued here that the wise teacher places value on those managerial approaches and strategies that are conceptually sound. The wise teacher does not blindly follow a recipe.

LEARNING ACTIVITY 2.5

The Instructional Classroom Management Approach

The instructional approach to classroom management is based on the contention that carefully designed and implemented instruction will prevent most managerial problems and solve those it does not prevent. This approach argues that effective management is the result of high-quality instructional planning. Thus, the role of the teacher is to carefully plan "good lessons"—learning tasks that are tailored to the needs and abilities of each student—provide each student with a reasonable opportunity to be successful, gain and hold the interest of each student, and motivate each student. The "war cry" of those who advocate the instructional managerial approach is: "make your lessons interesting."

Advocates of the instructional approach to classroom management tend to view instructional teacher behaviors as having the potential to achieve two central managerial goals: (1) preventing managerial problems and (2) solving managerial problems. It is argued here that well-planned and well-executed instructional activities make a major contribution to the first of these goals—the prevention of managerial problems—and little contribution to the second goal—the solving of managerial problems. There is considerable evidence to indicate that well-designed, well-implemented instructional activities are a primary factor in preventing managerial problems. In addition, there is overwhelming support for the contention that poorly designed, poorly implemented instructional activities are a major contributor to managerial problems. There is little evidence, however, to support the notion that instructional activities are effective in solving managerial problems once they have occurred. At best, it seems that instructional managerial behaviors are useful in dealing with only minor sorts of student misbehavior.

An examination of the arguments made by advocates of the instructional approach suggests that the teacher should consider the following instructional managerial strategies: (1) providing interesting, relevant, and appropriate curriculum and instruction; (2) employing effective movement management; (3) establishing classroom routines; (4) giving clear directions; (5) utilizing interest boosting; (6) providing hurdle help; (7) planning for environmental changes; (8) planning and modifying the classroom environment; and (9) restructuring the situation.

Providing Interesting, Relevant, and Appropriate Curriculum and Instruction

Davis states that "a well-planned curriculum implemented by a well-prepared teacher who presents a study topic so that it holds the interest of the students has traditionally been considered a deterrent to disruptive classroom behavior."[4] Kounin has reported research findings that are particularly relevant about this topic.[5] He found that the key to effective classroom management is the teacher's ability to prepare and conduct lessons that prevent inattention, boredom, and misbehavior. He found that successful teachers teach well-prepared, well-paced lessons that proceed smoothly with a minimum of confusion or loss of focus, waste little time moving students from one activity to another, and provide seatwork activities geared to the abilities and interests of students. Successful teachers, he found, are prepared and therefore able to exhibit what he called "smoothness" and "momentum." Such teachers employ effective movement management.

Employing Effective Movement Management

Effective **movement management** is evidenced by a teacher who is able to move students smoothly from one activity to the next (smoothness) and to maintain momentum within an activity (momentum). The ability to regulate the flow and pace of classroom activities is viewed by many as crucial to preventing student off-task behavior.

Kounin also found that unsuccessful teachers are inadequately prepared and therefore unable to exhibit smoothness and momentum; they exhibit "jerkiness" and "slowdowns." They do not move students smoothly from one activity to the next, nor do they maintain momentum within an activity. Instead, they display behaviors Kounin saw as contributing to jerkiness (*thrusts, dangles, truncations,* and *flip-flops*) and slowdowns (*overdwelling* and *fragmentation*). A *thrust* is an instance in which the teacher suddenly bursts into an activity with a statement or direction for which the group is not ready. A *dangle* is an instance in which the teacher leaves one activity dangling in midair to start another activity, and then returns to the first activity. A *truncation* is an instance in which the teacher simply leaves one activity dangling in midair and starts another activity. A *flip-flop* is an instance in which the teacher terminates one activity, starts a second, and then returns to the first. *Overdwelling* is an instance in which the teacher spends too much time giving explanations and/or directions. *Fragmentation* is an instance in which the teacher breaks down an activity into several unnecessary steps when it could have been appropriately handled as a whole.

Kounin's contention is that these teacher behaviors hinder smoothness and momentum, and contribute to jerkiness and slowdowns, resulting in student inattention, boredom, and misbehavior. It is his position that unsuccessful teachers display ineffective behaviors primarily because they have not given adequate attention to planning and preparing the instructional activities they would have their students undertake. Since space does not permit a thorough description of Kounin's work, you are encouraged to refer to his 1970 book if you feel that his findings are of particular interest; that book has become something of a classic in the classroom management literature.

Establishing Classroom Routines

The process of *establishing classroom routines* is one in which the teacher—beginning with his or her first encounter with the classroom group—helps students understand what it is they are to do with regard to typical daily activities. Clear explanations of the teacher's expectations regarding classroom routines are viewed as a critical first step in effectively managing the classroom and developing a productive classroom group. It is a process that minimizes the potential for problems.

Giving Clear Directions

A number of authors emphasize the importance of giving *clear, concise directions.* Long and Frye argue that clear, simple instructions are fundamental to promoting desired behaviors.[6] Others argue that directions should be clear, precise, concise, to the point, and carefully sequenced. The effective classroom manager gives clearly understood directions. The teacher who says to students, "Please open your books to the problems you worked for homework," is much more likely to create problems than the teacher who says, "Please open your math book to page 47 so we can take a look at the six problems you did for last evening's homework." Obviously, students are far more likely to do what the teacher would like them to do if the teacher is clear in communicating what they are to do. Giving clear directions contributes to managerial effectiveness because it helps avoid problems that can result from poor directions.

Utilizing Interest Boosting

Interest boosting is a process in which the teacher makes a special effort to show genuine interest in a student's work when the student first begins to show signs of boredom or restlessness. The teacher might look at the student's work, compliment his or her effort, and make suggestions for further improvements. In this way the teacher helps the student stay on-task and prevents misbehavior.

Providing Hurdle Help

Hurdle help is assistance given by the teacher to help the student cope with a frustrating problem just when the student really needs it to avoid exploding or giving up. The intent is to provide assistance before a situation gets out of hand. Hurdle help is a particularly useful way to prevent disruptive behavior.

Planning for Environmental Changes

The classroom management literature suggests that, to minimize managerial problems, the teacher should anticipate certain environmental changes and prepare the classroom group to deal with them. For example, students should be prepared for the possibility of a substitute teacher in the teacher's absence. Advance planning helps students know how to behave before potentially disruptive situations arise. Thus, managerial problems are prevented.

Planning and Modifying the Classroom Environment

A number of authors have pointed to the importance of a classroom environment that is cheerful and orderly, that is organized to maximize productivity and minimize misbehavior, and that is well designed with regard to the physical placement of students. These authors stress the need to plan and modify the classroom environment to prevent or eliminate certain types of unacceptable behaviors. The best set of suggestions regarding classroom arrangement may be those found in the works of Evertson, Emmer, and Worsham.[7] Their "five keys to good room arrangement," stated briefly, are: (1) use a room arrangement consistent with your instructional goals and activities; (2) keep high-traffic areas free of congestion; (3) be sure students are easily seen by the teacher; (4) keep frequently used teaching materials and student supplies readily accessible; and (5) be certain students can easily see instructional presentations and displays. Any teacher can benefit from further examination of what Evertson, Emmer, and Worsham have written on this topic.

Restructuring the Situation

Situation restructuring is a managerial strategy in which the teacher, through the use of a simple cue—a sentence or two at most—initiates a new activity or causes an old activity to be performed in a different manner. Changing the nature of the activity, changing the focus of attention, or finding new ways of doing the same old thing appear to be effective in preventing managerial problems, particularly those that result from boredom.

Summary

In summary, the teacher should remember the following about instructional managerial strategies: (1) well-planned and well-conducted instructional activities are a key factor in preventing managerial problems, but not in solving them; (2) the teacher should design instructional activities that take into account the abilities and interests of each student; (3) the teacher should move students smoothly from one activity to the next and should maintain momentum within an activity; (4) the teacher should establish classroom routines and give clear directions; (5) the teacher should use interest boosting and hurdle help; and (6) the teacher should plan the classroom environment, plan for environmental changes, and restructure the situation when necessary. The use of these instructional managerial strategies will prevent many managerial problems.

LEARNING ACTIVITY 2.6

The Behavior-Modification Classroom Management Approach

The behavior-modification approach is based on principles from behavioral psychology. The major principle underlying this approach is that behavior is learned. This applies to both appropriate and inappropriate behavior. Advocates of the behavior-modification approach contend that a student misbehaves for one of two reasons: (1) the student has learned to behave inappropriately or (2) the student has not learned to behave appropriately.

The behavior-modification approach is built on two major assumptions: (1) there are four basic processes that account for learning and (2) learning is influenced largely, if not entirely, by events in the environment. Thus, the major task of the teacher is to master and apply the four basic principles of learning that behaviorists have identified as influencing human behavior. They are positive reinforcement, punishment, extinction, and negative reinforcement.

Utilizing Positive Reinforcement, Punishment, Extinction, and Negative Reinforcement

Terrence Piper[8] provides an easily understood explanation of the four basic processes. He suggests that when a student behaves, that behavior is followed by a consequence. He argues that there are only four basic categories of consequences: (1) when a reward is introduced, (2) when a punishment is introduced, (3) when a reward is removed, or (4) when a punishment is removed. The introduction of a reward is called **positive reinforcement,** and the introduction of a punishment is simply called **punishment.** The removal of a reward is called either **extinction** or **time out,** depending on the situation. The removal of a punishment is called **negative reinforcement.**

Behaviorists assume that the frequency of a particular behavior is contingent (depends) on the nature of the consequence that follows the behavior. Positive reinforcement, the introduction of a reward after a behavior, causes the reinforced behavior to increase in frequency. Rewarded behavior is thus strengthened, and it is repeated in the future.

Example

Brad prepares a neatly written paper, which he submits to the teacher (student behavior). The teacher praises Brad's work and comments that neatly written papers are more easily read than those that are sloppy (positive reinforcement). In subsequent papers, Brad takes great care to write neatly (the frequency of the reinforced behavior is increased).

Punishment is the introduction of an undesirable or aversive stimulus (punishment) after a behavior and causes the punished behavior to decrease in frequency. Punished behavior tends to be discontinued.

Example

Jim prepares a rather sloppily written paper, which he submits to the teacher (student behavior). The teacher rebukes Jim for failing to be neat, informs him that sloppily written papers are difficult to read, and tells him to rewrite and resubmit the paper (punishment). In subsequent papers, Jim writes less sloppily (the frequency of the punished behavior is decreased).

Extinction is the withholding of an anticipated reward (the withholding of positive reinforcement) in an instance in which that behavior was previously rewarded. Extinction results in the decreased frequency of the previously rewarded behavior.

Example

Susie, whose neat work has always been praised by the teacher, prepares a neatly written paper, which she submits to the teacher (student behavior previously reinforced by the teacher). The teacher accepts and subsequently returns the paper without comment (withholding of positive reinforcement). Susie becomes less neat in subsequent papers (the frequency of the previously reinforced behavior decreases).

Time out is the removal of the student from the reward; it reduces the frequency of reinforcement and causes the behavior to become less frequent.

Example

The students in Ms. Clark's English class have come to expect that she will give them an opportunity to play a word game if their work is satisfactory. This is an activity they all enjoy. Ms. Clark notes that all their papers were neatly done except Jim's paper. She tells Jim that he will not be allowed to participate in the class game and must, instead, sit apart from the group (removal of the student from the reward). Subsequently, Jim writes less sloppily (the frequency of the behavior decreases).

Negative reinforcement is the removal of an undesirable or aversive stimulus (punishment) after a behavior, and it causes the frequency of the behavior to be increased. The removal of the punishment serves to strengthen the behavior and increase its tendency to be repeated.

Example

Jim is the one student in the class who consistently presents the teacher with sloppy papers. Despite the teacher's constant nagging, Jim's work becomes no neater. For no apparent reason, Jim submits a rather neat paper. Ms. Clark accepts it without comment—and without the usual nagging (the removal of punishment). Subsequently, Jim's work becomes neater (the frequency of the behavior is increased).

Utilizing Positive Reinforcement

In summary, the teacher can encourage appropriate student behavior by using positive reinforcement (the introduction of a reward) and negative reinforcement (the removal of a punishment). The teacher can discourage inappropriate student behavior by using punishment (the introduction of an undesirable stimulus), extinction (the withholding of an anticipated reward), and time out (the removal of the student from the reward). It must be remembered that these consequences exert influence on student behavior in accordance with established behavioral principles. If the teacher rewards misbehavior, it is likely to be continued; if the teacher punishes appropriate behavior, it is likely to be discontinued.

According to Buckley and Walker,[9] timing and frequency of reinforcement and punishment are among the most important principles in behavior modification. Student behavior that the teacher wishes to encourage should be reinforced immediately after it occurs; student behavior that the teacher wishes to discourage should be punished immediately after it occurs. Behavior that is not reinforced at once tends to be weakened; behavior that is not punished at once tends to be strengthened. Thus, the teacher's timing of rewards and punishment is important. "The sooner the better" should be the motto of those teachers who want to maximize their management effectiveness.

Of equal importance is the frequency with which a behavior is reinforced. Continuous reinforcement, reinforcement that follows each instance of the behavior, results in learning that behavior more rapidly. Thus, a teacher who wishes to strengthen a particular student behavior should reward it each time it occurs. While continuous reinforcement is particularly effective in the early stages of acquiring a specific behavior, once the behavior has been established, it is more effective to reinforce it intermittently.

There are two approaches to intermittent reinforcement: an interval schedule and a ratio schedule. An **interval schedule** is one in which the teacher reinforces the student after a specified period of time. For example, a teacher using an interval schedule might reinforce a student every hour. A **ratio schedule** is one in which the teacher reinforces the student after the behavior has occurred a certain number of times. For example, a teacher using a ratio schedule might reinforce the student after every fourth occurrence of the behavior. For the most part, an interval schedule is best for maintaining a consistent behavior over time, while a ratio schedule is best for producing more frequent occurrence of a behavior.

Positive reinforcement has been defined as the introduction of a reward; extinction and time out have been defined as the removal of a reward. Punishment has been defined as the introduction of a punishment; negative reinforcement has been defined as the removal of a punishment. In other words, behavioral consequences have been discussed as either the introduction or the removal of rewards, or the introduction or removal of punishment. Therefore, let's take a closer look at the notions of reward and punishment.

By definition, a reward or reinforcer is any stimulus that increases the frequency of the behavior that preceded it; and, by definition, a punishment (or aversive stimulus) is anything that decreases the frequency of the behavior that preceded it. Different authors classify reinforcers differently. The behavior-modification literature is replete with labels. There is general agreement, however, that reinforcers may be classified into two major categories: (1) **primary reinforcers,** which are not learned and which are necessary to sustain life (food, water, and warmth are examples); and (2) **conditioned reinforcers,** which are learned (praise, affection, and money are examples). Conditioned reinforcers are of several distinct types, including *social reinforcers*—rewarding behavior by other individuals within a social context (praise or applause), *token reinforcers*—intrinsically nonrewarding objects that may be exchanged at a later time for tangible reinforcers (money or a system of checkmarks that can be traded in for free time or school supplies), and *activity reinforcers*—rewarding activities offered the student (outdoor play, free reading time, or being allowed to choose the next song).

Space limitations preclude a complete description of how various types of unconditioned and conditioned reinforcers can be used by the teacher to manage student behavior effectively. Many of the books and web sites listed in the Additional Resources at the end of the chapter do that quite well. It is important to emphasize one point here: a reward is defined in terms of its ability to increase the frequency of the rewarded behavior. Thus, reward (and punishment) can be understood only in terms of an individual student. One student's reward may be another student's punishment. A response that the teacher intended to be rewarding may be punishing, and a response intended to be punishing may be rewarding. The latter is often the case. A common example occurs when a student misbehaves to get attention. The teacher's subsequent scolding rewards rather than punishes the attention-hungry student and, consequently, the student continues to misbehave in order to get attention.

The above example suggests that the teacher must take great care in selecting a reinforcer that is appropriate to a particular student. While this is true, the selection process need not be difficult. Because reinforcers are idiosyncratic to the individual student, the student is in the best position to designate them. Thus, the best reinforcer is one selected by the student. Givener and Graubard[10] suggest three methods to identify individually oriented reinforcers: (1) obtain clues concerning potential reinforcers by observing what the student likes to do; (2) obtain additional clues by observing what follows specific student behaviors; that is, try to determine what teacher and peer behaviors seem to reinforce the student's behavior; and (3) obtain additional clues by simply asking students what they would like to do with free time, what they would like to have, and what they would like to work for.

Teachers who think it is important to reward appropriate student behavior do so in many ways. These range from "pats on the back" to "happy notes" informing a student's parents that the student has improved his or her conduct. Most teachers recognize that praise and encouragement are powerful social reinforcers. Additionally, behavior modification offers the teacher a number of managerial strategies that involve the use of reinforcement. Although much has been written about each of these strategies and their effectiveness, space allows only a brief description here. While the position taken here is that positive reinforcement—properly used—is a very powerful managerial strategy, it should be recognized that there are those who argue that the use of positive reinforcement—when combined with the use of punishment—is counterproductive in that it produces students who are compliant, not self-disciplined.

Utilizing Modeling

Modeling is a process in which the student, by observing another person's behavior, acquires new behaviors without being exposed to the consequences of the behavior. Modeling, as a managerial strategy, may be viewed as a process in which the teacher's own behavior demonstrates the values and behaviors he or she wants students to acquire and display.

Utilizing Shaping

Shaping is a procedure in which the teacher requires the student to perform a series of behaviors that approximate the desired behavior. Each time the student performs the required approximation or one a bit closer to the desired behavior, the teacher reinforces the student until the student is consistently able to perform the desired behavior. Thus, shaping is a behavior-modification strategy used to encourage the development of new behaviors.

Utilizing Token Economy Systems

A *token economy system* usually consists of three elements intended to change the behavior of students: (1) a set of carefully written instructions that describe the student behaviors the teacher will reinforce, (2) a well-developed system for awarding tokens to students who exhibit the behaviors that have been specified as appropriate, and (3) a set of procedures that allows students to exchange tokens they have earned for "prizes" or opportunities to engage in special activities. The implementation and operation of a token economy requires a great investment of time and energy on the part of the teacher. Consequently, its most typical—and efficient—use is in situations where a large percentage of the students in a class are misbehaving and the teacher seeks to rapidly change the behavior of those students. A well-managed token economy can be an effective means for modifying the behavior of groups of students.

Utilizing Contingency Contracting

A *contingency contract* or behavioral contract, an agreement negotiated between the teacher and a misbehaving student, specifies the behaviors the student has agreed to exhibit and indicates what the consequences—the payoff—will be if the student exhibits those behaviors. A contract is a written agreement between the teacher and a student detailing what the student is expected to do and what reward will be given for doing those things. As in all contracts, both parties obligate themselves. The student is committed to behave in certain ways deemed appropriate, and the teacher is committed to reward the student for doing so. Contracting tends to be a somewhat time-consuming process. Therefore, it is usually reserved for those instances in which a student is exhibiting serious misbehaviors on a rather routine basis. Contracting can be an effective tool in such instances.

Utilizing Group Contingencies

Group contingencies consist of using a procedure in which the consequences—reinforcement or punishment—that each student receives depend not only on his or her own behavior but also on the behavior of the group. Usually, it involves an instance in which the rewards for each individual member of the class are dependent on the behavior of one or more or all of the other students in the class.

Reinforcing Incompatible Alternatives

Reinforcing an incompatible alternative involves a situation in which the teacher rewards a behavior that cannot coexist with the disruptive behavior the teacher wishes to eliminate.

Utilizing Behavioral Counseling

Behavioral counseling is a process involving a private conference between the teacher and the student—a conference intended to help the misbehaving student see that a certain behavior is inappropriate and to plan for change. It is argued that such conferences help the student to understand the relationship between his or her actions and the resulting consequences, and to consider alternative actions likely to result in desired consequences.

Utilizing Self-Monitoring

Self-monitoring (self-management, self-recording) is a strategy in which the student records some aspect of his or her behavior in order to modify that behavior. Self-monitoring systematically increases the student's awareness of a behavior the student wishes to decrease or eliminate. Self-monitoring promotes self-awareness through self-observation.

Utilizing Cues, Prompts, and Signals

A *cue* is a verbal or nonverbal prompt or signal—a reminder—given by the teacher when the student needs to be reminded either to behave in a certain way or to refrain from behaving in a certain way. Thus, a cue can be used to encourage or discourage a given behavior. Unlike a reinforcer, a cue precedes a response; it "triggers" a behavior.

Administering Punishment

Having briefly discussed the use of rewards, let us now turn to the thorniest of dilemmas faced by advocates of the behavior-modification approach—the use of punishment to eliminate inappropriate behavior. This is a subject of great controversy, controversy that is far from resolution. While it appears that every author has a somewhat different opinion, three major viewpoints seem most prominent: (1) the appropriate use of punishment is highly effective in eliminating student misbehavior; (2) the judicious use of punishment in limited types of situations can have desirable immediate, short-term effects on student misbehavior, but the risk of negative side effects requires its use to be carefully monitored; and (3) the use of punishment should be avoided completely because student misbehavior can be dealt with just as effectively with other techniques that do not have the potential negative side effects of punishment.

Few authors present a viewpoint other than their own; however, Sulzer and Mayer[11] do help the reader examine the advantages and disadvantages of using punishment. They identify the following advantages: (1) punishment does stop the punished student behavior immediately, and it reduces the occurrence of that behavior for a long period of time; (2) punishment is informative to students because it helps them discriminate rapidly between acceptable and unacceptable behaviors; and (3) punishment is instructive to other students because it may reduce the probability that other class members will imitate the punished behaviors. Disadvantages include: (1) punishment may be misinterpreted (sometimes a specific, punished behavior is generalized to other behaviors; for example, the student who is punished for talking out of turn may stop responding, even when appropriate to do so); (2) punishment may cause the punished student to withdraw altogether; (3) punishment may cause the punished student to become aggressive; (4) punishment may produce negative peer reactions; for example, students may exhibit undesirable behaviors (ridicule or sympathy) toward the punished student; and (5) punishment may cause the punished student to become negative about him- or herself or about the situation; for example, punishment may diminish feelings of self-worth or produce a negative attitude toward school.

In weighing the advantages and disadvantages of using punishment, Sulzer and Mayer conclude that alternative procedures for reducing student behaviors should always be considered. They contend that once a punishment procedure is selected, it should be employed with the utmost caution and its effects should be carefully monitored. They also suggest that the teacher anticipate and be prepared to handle any negative consequences that might arise. Finally, they recommend that teachers find desirable behaviors to reinforce at the same time they are withholding reinforcement or punishing undesirable behavior.

Other behaviorists also point to research that suggests punishment is largely ineffective in the classroom setting and argue against its use. As noted earlier, advocates of the authoritarian approach view mild forms of punishment (mild desists) as effective, whereas advocates of the intimidation approach view harsher forms of punishment as effective. Advocates of the socioemotional-climate approach argue for the effectiveness of another form of punishment—the application of logical consequences. Many behaviorists argue that the effective teacher is one who is able to modify inappropriate student behavior through the use of strategies other than punishment; they advocate the use of extinction and time out. Several other strategies are also advocated; these include overcorrection, response cost, negative practice, satiation, and fading.

Utilizing Overcorrection

Overcorrection is a mild form of punishment in which the teacher requires a disruptive student to restore the environment to a better condition than existed before the disruptiveness occurred. The student is required to go beyond simple restitution and to make things better than they were before the misbehavior.

Utilizing Response Cost

Response cost is a procedure in which a specified reward is removed following an inappropriate behavior. The teacher arranges the rules of the classroom so that a particular cost—a fine—is levied for certain misbehaviors. Inappropriate behavior costs the student an already earned reward.

Utilizing Negative Practice

Negative practice is a process in which the student who exhibits an undesirable behavior is required by the teacher to repeatedly perform that behavior until it becomes punishing—to repeat that behavior to the point at which the behavior itself becomes aversive. Those who advocate the use of negative practice encourage teachers to use this procedure only to eliminate undesirable behaviors that can be repeated without causing additional harm or disruption.

Utilizing Satiation

Satiation—saturation—is the process of presenting a reinforcing stimulus so frequently that it is no longer desirable and becomes aversive. An "oversupply" of a particular reinforcer is presented so that the effectiveness of the reinforcer is diminished. In the typical situation, a teacher might insist that a misbehaving student continue to perform that misbehavior until he or she tires of doing it.

Utilizing Fading

Fading is a process in which the teacher gradually eliminates the cues and prompts for a given kind of behavior. Supporting stimuli—cues and prompts—originally provided are gradually omitted until the student can perform the desired behavior without assistance.

Summary

Clearly, this section on the behavior-modification approach cannot begin to describe in detail the many managerial strategies that constitute this approach. Should you feel the need for more information on this subject, books by Axelrod[12] and Clarizio[13] provide in-depth descriptions of behavior-modification strategies. Given the discussion in this section, the following seems to be an accurate summary of the lessons to be gained from the behavior-modification approach: (1) rewarding appropriate student behavior and withholding the rewarding of inappropriate behavior are effective in achieving better classroom behavior; (2) punishing inappropriate student behavior may eliminate that behavior but may have serious negative side effects; and (3) rewarding appropriate behavior is probably the key to effective classroom management.

LEARNING ACTIVITY 2.7

The Socioemotional-Climate Classroom Management Approach

The socioemotional-climate approach to classroom management has its roots in counseling and clinical psychology and, consequently, places great importance on interpersonal relationships. It builds on the assumption that effective classroom management—and effective instruction—is largely a function of positive teacher–student relationships. Advocates of the socioemotional-climate approach emphasize that the teacher is the major determiner of interpersonal relationships and classroom climate. Consequently, the central managerial task of the teacher is to build positive interpersonal relationships and to promote a positive socioemotional climate.

Communicating Realness, Acceptance, and Empathic Understanding

Many of the ideas that characterize the socioemotional-climate approach may be traced to the work of Carl Rogers.[14] His major premise is that the facilitation of significant learning is largely a function of certain attitudinal qualities that exist in the interpersonal relationship between the teacher (the facilitator) and the student (the learner). Rogers has identified several attitudes that he believes are essential if the teacher is to have maximum effect in facilitating learning: realness, genuineness, and congruence; acceptance, prizing, caring, and trust; and empathic understanding.

Realness is viewed by Rogers as the most important attitude the teachers can display in facilitating learning. Realness is an expression of the teacher being him- or herself; that is, the teacher is aware of his or her feelings, accepts and acts on them, and is able to communicate them when appropriate. The teacher's behavior is congruent with his or her feelings. In other words, the teacher is genuine. Rogers suggests that realness allows the teacher to be perceived by students as a real person, a person with whom they can relate. Thus, the establishment of positive interpersonal relationships and of a positive socioemotional climate is enhanced by the teacher's ability to display realness. Sincere expressions of enthusiasm or boredom are typical examples of realness.

Acceptance is the second attitude that Rogers views as important to teachers who are successful in facilitating learning. Acceptance indicates that the teacher views the student as a person of worth. It is nonpossessive caring for the learner. It is an expression of basic trust—a belief that the student is trustworthy. Accepting behaviors are those that make the student feel trusted and respected, those that enhance the student's self-worth. Through acceptance, the teacher displays confidence and trust in the ability and potential of the student. Consequently, the teacher who cares, prizes, and trusts the student has a far greater chance of creating a socioemotional climate that promotes learning than does the teacher who fails to do so.

Empathic understanding is an expression of the teacher's ability to understand the student from the student's point of view. It is a sensitive awareness of the student's feelings, and it is nonevaluative and nonjudgmental. Expressions of empathy are all too rare in the classroom. When they occur, the student feels that the teacher understands what he or she is thinking and feeling. Rogers argues that clearly communicated, sensitively accurate empathic understanding greatly increases the probability that positive interpersonal relationships, a positive socioemotional climate, and significant learning will occur.

In summary, Rogers suggests that there are certain conditions that facilitate learning and that most prominent among these is the attitudinal quality of the interpersonal relationship between the teacher and the student. He has identified three attitudes that are crucial to the rapport-building process: realness, acceptance, and empathy.

Utilizing Effective Communication

Haim Ginott[15] has presented views similar to those of Rogers. His writing, which also stresses the importance of congruence, acceptance, and empathy, gives numerous examples of how these attitudes may be manifested by the teacher. In addition, Ginott has emphasized the importance of *effective communication* in promoting positive teacher–student relationships. How the teacher communicates is viewed as being of decisive importance.

Ginott has written that the cardinal principle of communication is that the teacher talk to the situation, not to the personality and character of the student. When confronted with undesirable student behavior, the teacher is advised to describe what he or she sees and feels as well as what needs to be done. The teacher accepts the student, but not the student's behavior; the teacher "separates the sin from the sinner." This notion has been called unconditional positive regard. (As you can see, it is identical to Rogers's notion of acceptance.) The teacher views the student as a person of worth, regardless of how the student behaves. In addition, Ginott has provided a list of recommendations describing ways in which the teacher might communicate effectively. Although a lengthy explanation of each is not possible here, a summary of these recommendations is:

1. Address the students' specific situations. Do not judge their character and personality because this can be demeaning.

2. Describe the situation, express feelings about the situation, and clarify expectations concerning the situation.
3. Express authentic and genuine feelings that promote student understanding.
4. Diminish hostility by inviting cooperation and providing students with opportunities to experience independence.
5. Decrease defiance by avoiding commands and demands that provoke defensive responses.
6. Recognize, accept, and respect students' ideas and feelings in ways that increase their feelings of self-worth.
7. Avoid diagnosis and prognosis, which result in labeling the student, because this may be disabling.
8. Describe process and do not judge products or persons. Provide guidance, not criticism.
9. Avoid questions and comments that are likely to incite resentment and invite resistance.
10. Avoid the use of sarcasm because this may diminish the student's self-esteem.
11. Resist the temptation to provide students with hastily offered solutions; take the time to give them the guidance needed to solve their own problem. Encourage autonomy.
12. Attempt to be brief; avoid preaching and nagging, which are not motivating.
13. Monitor and be aware of the impact one's words are having on students.
14. Use appreciative praise because it is productive; avoid judgmental praise because it is destructive.
15. Listen to students and encourage them to express their ideas and feelings.

This list cannot do justice to Ginott's views. The reader who desires a fuller explanation of these recommendations and who wishes to examine examples that support Ginott's suggestions is encouraged to refer to his last book, *Teacher and Child*.

Many of those who share Ginott's views about effective communication stress the importance of active listening and humor. **Active listening** is a process in which the teacher listens carefully to the student and then feeds back the message in an attempt to show that he or she understands what the student is trying to say. Advocates of this strategy argue that active listening creates a situation in which the student is more likely to feel understood and valued; some view it as a way to operationalize the concept of acceptance. *Humor* is a strategy that can be used to ease tension in an anxiety-producing situation or to make a student aware of a lapse in behavior. Humor should be genial, kindly, and gentle; it should not be sarcastic or ridiculing, because this endangers teacher–student relationships and student feelings of self-worth.

Utilizing Reality Therapy

A third viewpoint that might be classified as a socioemotional approach is that of William Glasser.[16] Although an advocate of teacher realness, acceptance, and empathy, Glasser does not give these primary emphasis. Rather, he stresses the importance of teacher involvement and the use of a managerial strategy called *reality therapy*.

Glasser asserts that the single basic need that people have is the need for identity—feelings of distinctiveness and worthiness. He argues that to achieve a "success" identity in the school context, one must develop social responsibility and feelings of self-worth. Social responsibility and self-worth are the result of the student's developing a positive relationship with others—both peers and adults. Thus, it is involvement that is crucial to the development of a success identity. Glasser argues that student misbehavior is the result of the student's failure to develop a success identity. He proposes an eight-step, one-to-one counseling process the teacher might use to help the student change problematic behavior. This process has been called *reality therapy* and is in many ways similar to behavior contracting, a behavior-modification strategy discussed in the previous Learning Activity. Glasser suggests that the teacher should do the following:

1. Become personally involved with the student; accept the student, but not the student's misbehavior; indicate a willingness to help the student solve the behavior problem.
2. Elicit a description of the student's present behavior; deal with the problem, do not evaluate or judge the student.
3. Assist the student in making a value judgment about the problem behavior; focus on what the student is doing to contribute to the problem and to his or her failure.
4. Help the student plan a better course of action; if necessary, suggest alternatives; help the student reach his or her own decision based on his or her own evaluation, thereby fostering self-responsibility.
5. Guide the student in making a commitment to the course of action he or she has selected.
6. Reinforce the student as he or she follows the plan and keeps the commitment; be sure to let the student know that you are aware that progress is being made.
7. Accept no excuses if the student fails to follow through on the commitment; help the student understand that he or she is responsible for his or her own behavior; alert the student of the need for a better plan; acceptance of an excuse communicates a lack of caring.
8. Allow the student to suffer the natural and realistic consequences of misbehavior, but do not punish the student; help the student try again to develop a better plan and expect the student to make a commitment to it.

Glasser views the above process—reality therapy—as effective for the teacher who wishes to help the misbehaving student develop more productive behavior. In addition, Glasser proposes a similar process for helping a whole class deal with group behavior problems—the social problem-solving classroom meeting. As a managerial strategy, the classroom meeting is perhaps best thought of as a group-process managerial strategy. Therefore, it is described in Learning Activity 2.8, the next section of this chapter.

Developing a Democratic Classroom and Employing Logical Consequences

A fourth viewpoint that might be seen as a socioemotional-climate approach is that of Rudolf Dreikurs.[17] While it is true that works by Dreikurs and his colleagues contain many ideas that have important implications for effective classroom management, there are two that stand out from the others: (1) an emphasis on the democratic classroom in which the students and the teacher share responsibility for both process and progress, and (2) a recognition of the impact that natural and logical consequences have on the behavior—and misbehavior—of students.

A dominant theme in this approach is the assumption that student conduct and achievement are facilitated in a *democratic classroom.* The autocratic classroom is one in which the teacher uses force, pressure, competition, punishment, and the threat of punishment to control student behavior. The laissez-faire classroom is one in which the teacher provides little, if any, leadership and is overly permissive. Both the autocratic classroom and the laissez-faire classroom lead to student frustration, hostility, and/or withdrawal; both result in a devastating lack of productivity. True productivity can occur only in a democratic classroom—one in which the teacher shares responsibility with students. It is in a democratic atmosphere that students expect to be treated and are treated as responsible, worthwhile individuals capable of intelligent decision making and problem solving. And it is the democratic classroom that fosters mutual trust between the teacher and the students, and among students.

The teacher who attempts to establish a democratic classroom atmosphere must not abdicate leadership responsibilities. The effective teacher, while not an autocrat, is also not an anarchist. The democratic teacher guides, the autocratic teacher dominates, and the laissez-faire teacher abdicates. The democratic teacher teaches responsibility by sharing responsibility.

The key to a democratic classroom organization is regular and frank group discussions. Here the teacher—acting the role of leader—guides the group in group discussions that focus on problems of concern. Three products of that process have been identified: (1) the teacher and the students have an opportunity to express themselves in a way that is sure to be heard, (2) the teacher and the students have an opportunity to get to know and understand one another better, and (3) the teacher and the students are provided with an opportunity to help one another. Dreikurs notes that an essential by-product of such group discussions is the opportunity the teacher has to influence those student values that may differ from those considered more productive.

Although there is an emphasis on the importance of the teacher's developing a democratic socioemotional classroom climate, you will see in the next Learning Activity that these views on the value of shared leadership and group discussions are similar to those of the advocates of the group-process approach.

Dreikurs's second major emphasis concerns the impact of consequences on student behavior. In the classroom setting, natural consequences are those that are solely the result of the student's own behavior. *Logical consequences* are those that are more or less arranged by the teacher but are a logical outcome of the student's behavior. The natural consequence of the student's grasping a hot test tube is a burned hand. The logical consequence of breaking the test tube is that the student will have to pay the cost of replacing it. To be considered a logical consequence, however, the consequence must be viewed by the student as logical. If it is viewed as punishment, the positive effect is lost. Although most behaviorists do not make a distinction between logical consequences and punishments, most advocates of the socioemotional-climate approach do. Dreikurs and Grey suggest five criteria they view as useful in distinguishing logical consequences from punishment:

1. Logical consequences express the reality of the social order, not of the person; punishment expresses the power of a personal authority; a logical consequence results from a violation of an accepted social rule.
2. Logical consequences are logically related to the misbehavior; punishment rarely is logically related; the student sees the relationship between the misbehavior and its consequences.
3. Logical consequences involve no element of moral judgment; punishment inevitably does; the student's misbehavior is viewed as a mistake, not a sin.

4. Logical consequences are concerned only with what will happen next; punishment is concerned with the past; the focus is on the future.
5. Logical consequences are applied in a friendly manner; punishment involves either open or concealed anger; the teacher should try to disengage him- or herself from the consequences.

In summary, logical consequences express the reality of the social order, are intrinsically related to the misbehavior, involve no element of moral judgment, and are concerned only with what will happen next. On the other hand, punishment expresses the power of personal authority, is not logically related to the misbehavior, involves moral judgment, and deals with the past. Like Glasser, Dreikurs stresses the importance of the positive effect that the application of logical consequences has on the behavior of students. Both argue that it is crucial for teachers to help students understand the logical relationship between their behavior and the consequences of that behavior. Both also argue that it is important that the teacher be able to use logical consequences appropriately—and avoid punishment—in helping students change their behaviors to ones that are more desirable.

Recognizing Student Dignity

A fifth and final viewpoint that might be viewed as a socioemotional-climate approach is that of Curwin and Medler,[18] who advocate many of the strategies recommended by others who have written from this viewpoint. They emphasize the importance of effective teacher–student communication and stress the use of active listening, I-messages, and logical consequences, for example. However, they argue that effective classroom management is built on the notion of student dignity and that, consequently, all teacher–student interactions must preserve the dignity of the student. Their arguments are very convincing.

Summary

Teachers who would be effective classroom managers should include the following socioemotional-climate strategies in their behavioral repertoire: communicating realness, acceptance, and empathic understanding; utilizing effective communication; exhibiting unconditional positive regard and active listening; utilizing humor; utilizing reality therapy; developing a democratic classroom; employing logical consequences; and recognizing the dignity of students. All are strategies that facilitate the establishment and maintenance of positive teacher–student interpersonal relationships and a positive socioemotional climate.

LEARNING ACTIVITY **2.8**

The Group-Process Classroom Management Approach

The *group-process approach*—also known as the *sociopsychological approach*—is based on principles from social psychology and group dynamics. The major premise underlying the group-process approach is based on the following assumptions: (1) schooling takes place within a group context—the classroom group; (2) the central task of the teacher is to establish and maintain an effective, productive classroom group; (3) the classroom group is a social system containing properties common to all social systems, and the effective, productive classroom group is characterized by certain conditions that are compatible with those properties; and (4) the classroom management task of the teacher is to establish and maintain such conditions. While there is some disagreement concerning the conditions that characterize the effective, productive classroom group, we will examine the conditions described in three excellent sources: the work of Schmuck and Schmuck, Johnson and Bany, and Kounin.

Developing Effective Classroom Groups

First let us focus on six properties identified by Schmuck and Schmuck[19] regarding classroom management: expectations, leadership, attraction, norms, communication, and cohesiveness.

Clarifying Expectations

Expectations are those perceptions that the teacher and students hold regarding their relationships to one another. They are individual predictions of how self and others will behave. Therefore, expectations about how members of the group will behave greatly influence how the teacher and the students behave in relation to one another. The effective classroom group is one in which expectations are accurate, realistic, and clearly understood. The behavior of the teacher communicates to students what behavior the teacher expects of them, and the students, in turn, tend to conform to those expectations. Thus, if students feel the teacher expects them to misbehave, it is likely that they will misbehave; if students feel the teacher expects them to behave appropriately, it is more likely that they will behave appropriately.

Sharing Leadership

Leadership is best thought of as those behaviors that help the group move toward the accomplishment of its objectives. Thus, leadership behaviors consist of actions by group members; included are actions that aid in setting group norms, move the group toward its goals, improve the quality of interaction between group members, and build group cohesiveness. By virtue of their role, teachers have the greatest potential for leadership. In an effective classroom group, however, leadership functions are performed by both the students and the teacher. An effective classroom group is one in which the leadership functions are well distributed and all group members can feel power and self-worth in accomplishing academic tasks and in working together. When students share classroom leadership with the teacher, they are far more likely to be self-regulating and responsible for their own behavior. Thus, the effective teacher is one who creates a climate in which students perform leadership functions. The teacher improves the quality of group interaction and productivity by training students to perform goal-directed leadership functions and by dispersing leadership throughout the group.

Fostering Attraction

Attraction refers to the friendship patterns in the classroom group. Attraction can be described as the level of friendship that exists among members of the classroom group. The level of attraction is dependent on the degree to which positive interpersonal relationships have been developed. It is clear that a positive relationship exists between level of attraction and student academic performance. Thus, the effective classroom manager is one who fosters positive interpersonal relationships among group members. For example, the teacher attempts to promote the acceptance of rejected students and new class members.

Promoting Productive Group Norms

Norms are shared expectations of how group members should think, feel, and behave. Norms greatly influence interpersonal relationships because they provide guidelines that help members understand what is expected of them and what they should expect from others. Productive group norms are essential to group effectiveness. Therefore, one important task of the teacher is to help the group establish, accept, and maintain productive group norms. Such norms provide a frame of reference that guides the behavior of members. The group, not the teacher, regulates behavior by exerting pressure on members to adhere to the group's norms. It is crucial that the teacher assist the group in the development of productive norms. This is a difficult task. Advocates of the group-process approach argue that productive norms can be developed—and unproductive norms changed—through the concerted, collaborative efforts of the teacher and the students using group discussion methods.

Encouraging Open Communication

Communication—both verbal and nonverbal—is dialogue between group members. It involves the uniquely human capability to understand one another's ideas and feelings. Thus, communication is the vehicle through which the meaningful interaction of members takes place and through which group processes in the classroom occur. Effective communication means the receiver correctly interprets the message that the sender intends to communicate. Therefore, a twofold task of the teacher is to open the channels of communication so that all students express their thoughts and feelings freely and, frequently, to accept student thoughts and feelings. In addition, the teacher should help students develop certain communication skills—paraphrasing, perception checking, and feedback, for example.

Fostering Cohesiveness

Cohesiveness is the collective feeling that the class members have about the classroom group—the sum of the individual members' feelings about the group. Unlike attraction, cohesiveness emphasizes the individual's relation to the group as a whole instead of to individuals within the group. Schmuck and Schmuck note that groups are cohesive for a variety of reasons: (1) the members like one another, (2) there is high interest in a task, and (3) the group offers prestige to its members. Thus, a classroom group is cohesive when most of its members, including the teacher, are highly attracted to the group as a whole.

Cohesiveness occurs to the extent individual needs are satisfied by group membership. Schmuck and Schmuck assert that cohesiveness is a result of the dynamics of interpersonal expectations, leadership style, attraction patterns, and the flow of communication. The teacher can create cohesive classroom groups by open discussions of expectations, dispersion of leadership, the development of several friendship clusters, and the frequent use of two-way communication. Cohesiveness is essential to group productivity. Cohesive groups possess clearly established group norms—strong norms, not necessarily norms that are productive. Thus, the effective classroom manager is one who creates a cohesive group that possesses goal-directed norms.

To summarize the position taken by Schmuck and Schmuck, it can be said that they give importance to the teacher's ability to create and manage an effectively functioning, goal-directed classroom group. The implications of their position, as they suggest, are the following:

1. The teacher should work with students to clarify the interpersonal expectations held by individuals in the group, recognize the expectations he or she holds for each individual student and for the group, modify these expectations on the basis of new information, foster expectations that emphasize student strengths rather than weaknesses, and make a deliberate effort to accept and support each student.
2. The teacher should exert goal-directed influences by exhibiting appropriate leadership behaviors, helping students develop leadership skills, and dispersing leadership by sharing leadership functions with students and by encouraging and supporting the leadership activities of students.
3. The teacher should display empathy toward students and help them develop an empathic understanding of one another, accept all students and encourage them to accept one another, provide opportunities for students to work collaboratively, and facilitate the development of student friendships and teacher-student rapport.
4. The teacher should help students resolve conflicts among institutional rules, group norms, and/or individual attitudes; use various problem-solving techniques and group discussion methods to help students develop productive, goal-directed norms; and encourage students to be responsible for their own behavior.
5. The teacher should exhibit effective communication skills and help students develop effective communication skills; foster open channels of communication that encourage students to express their ideas and feelings freely and constructively; promote student interaction, which allows students to work with and get to know one another; and provide opportunities for students to discuss openly the group's processes.
6. The teacher should foster cohesiveness by establishing and maintaining a classroom group that is characterized by clearly understood expectations; shared, goal-directed leadership; high levels of empathy, acceptance, and friendship; and open channels of communication.

Facilitating and Maintaining Effective Group Processes

Although the views held by Johnson and Bany[20] are, in many ways, similar to those of Schmuck and Schmuck, they represent a contribution that warrants an examination here. Johnson and Bany describe two major types of classroom management activities—facilitation and maintenance. *Facilitation* refers to those management behaviors that improve conditions within the classroom; *maintenance* refers to those management behaviors that restore or maintain effective conditions. The teacher who manages the classroom effectively exhibits both facilitation and maintenance management behaviors.

Johnson and Bany have identified four kinds of facilitation behavior: (1) achieving unity and cooperation, (2) establishing standards and coordinating work procedures, (3) utilizing group problem-solving discussions to improve conditions, and (4) changing established patterns of group behavior. They have identified three kinds of maintenance behavior: (1) maintaining and restoring morale, (2) handling conflict, and (3) minimizing management problems. Although we cannot give a full description of these managerial behaviors—Johnson and Bany used more than 400 pages doing that—a brief explanation of each behavior is presented here.

Achieving Unity and Cooperation

Achieving classroom group unity and cooperation (cohesiveness) is a worthy and necessary goal if the teacher is to help the group be maximally effective.

Because cohesiveness is largely dependent on group members's liking one another and liking the group, the task of the teacher is to make group membership attractive and satisfying. Johnson and Bany assert that cohesiveness is dependent on the amount and frequency of student interaction and communication, the kind of structure that exists within the group, and the extent to which motives and goals are shared. It follows, then, that the teacher should encourage student interaction and communication by providing opportunities for students to work with one another and to discuss their ideas and feelings, accept and support all students while creating a structure within which each student develops a strong sense of belonging, and help students develop and recognize shared goals.

Establishing Standards and Coordinating Work Procedures

Establishing standards and coordinating work procedures are among the most important—and the most difficult—of the teacher's responsibilities. Standards of conduct specify appropriate behaviors in given situations; work procedures are those standards that apply to interactive instructional processes. For example, a behavioral standard might involve the behavior prescribed for students as they stand in the cafeteria line or as they leave the classroom during a fire drill. A work procedure might refer to the behavior expected of students when they are finished with seatwork assignments or when they wish to ask the teacher a question. Clearly, effective instruction is dependent on the extent to which the teacher is able to establish appropriate standards and to facilitate student adherence to those standards. Johnson and Bany emphasize the importance of group decision methods as a means of establishing behavioral standards and gaining adherence to those standards. Standards that are accepted by the group become group norms. In a cohesive group, there is a great deal of pressure on members to conform to those norms. Thus, the effective classroom group is one in which desirable standards and work procedures are accepted group norms.

Utilizing Group Problem-Solving Discussions

Utilizing group problem-solving discussions to improve classroom conditions is a strategy highly recommended by advocates of the group-process approach. The problem-solving process is viewed somewhat differently by different authors but, for the most part, may be thought of as including: (1) identifying the problem, (2) analyzing the problem, (3) evaluating alternative solutions, (4) selecting and implementing a solution, and (5) obtaining feedback and evaluating the solution. The basic premise underlying this strategy is that students, given the opportunity, skills, and necessary guidance, can and will make responsible decisions regarding their classroom behavior. This premise suggests that the teacher should provide students with the opportunity to engage in group problem-solving discussions, foster the development of student problem-solving skills, and guide students in the problem-solving process.

Changing Established Patterns of Group Behavior

Changing established patterns of group behavior involves the use of planned-change techniques similar to those of group problem solving. The difference is that the purpose of the problem-solving process is to find a solution to a problem, while the purpose of the planned-change process is to gain acceptance of an already determined solution. Thus, the planned-change process is one of improving conditions by substituting appropriate goals for inappropriate goals. The group goals exert a strong influence on the behavior of group members, and when group goals are in conflict with those of instruction, students behave inappropriately. Therefore, it is necessary for the teacher to help the group replace inappropriate goals and behaviors with more appropriate ones, goals that satisfy group needs and are consistent with those of the school.

Johnson and Bany argue that group planning is the best process to use for changing inappropriate goals and behaviors to more appropriate ones. Their viewpoint is based on the assumption that such changes are much more likely to be accomplished and accepted if members of the group have participated in the decision to change. This suggests that the role of the teacher is to help students understand the goal to be achieved; to involve students in discussions that result in an examination of various plans for achieving the goals, selecting a plan, and identifying tasks that need to be performed; to implement the plan and perform the necessary tasks; and to assess the plan's effectiveness. During the planned-change process, the teacher encourages group acceptance of externally established goals. Students are engaged in decisions regarding the strategies to be used in achieving those goals.

Simply put, the facilitation management behaviors of the teacher consist of: (1) encouraging the development of group cohesiveness; (2) promoting the acceptance of productive standards of conduct; (3) facilitating the resolution of problems through the use of group problem-solving processes; and (4) fostering appropriate group goals, norms, and behaviors. The intent of these facilitative management behaviors is the improvement of those classroom conditions that promote effective instruction. Maintenance management behaviors are intended to restore and maintain those classroom conditions. Descriptions of the three types identified by Johnson and Bany follow.

Maintaining and Restoring Morale

The ability to *maintain and restore morale* is important because the level of classroom group morale greatly influences group productivity. A group with high morale is far more likely to be productive than a group with low morale. Facilitation behaviors build morale; however, the effective teacher recognizes that many factors can cause morale to fluctuate. Thus, the teacher should understand the factors that influence morale and exhibit those behaviors that preserve high morale. Johnson and Bany note that morale is affected by the level of cohesiveness, the amount of interaction and communication, the extent to which members have shared goals, the extent to which the group's goal-directed efforts are hindered, and environmental conditions that cause anxiety and stress or otherwise affect the group adversely.

Thus, the task of the teacher may be viewed as twofold: (1) the teacher should act to rebuild morale—fostering cohesiveness, encouraging increased interaction and communication, and promoting shared goals; (2) the teacher should act to reduce anxiety and relieve stress—fostering cooperation rather than competition, exhibiting shared leadership, eliminating extremely frustrating and threatening situations, neutralizing disruptive influences, and clarifying stress situations through discussion. Crucial to the teacher's effectiveness is the extent to which the teacher is accepted and trusted by the students. The teacher who is perceived by students as being part of the problem or whose behavior creates new problems cannot hope to be successful in restoring morale. The use of punishment is an all too common example of the latter.

Handling Conflict

Handling conflict in the classroom group is among the most difficult tasks a teacher faces. Hostile, aggressive student behaviors are emotion laden, disruptive, and irritating, especially when directed toward the teacher. But conflict and hostility must be viewed as a normal result of the interactive processes that occur in the classroom. It is not realistic to expect otherwise. Indeed, in the initial phases of a group's development, it is not unusual and can be constructive.

There are many causes of conflict. Primary among them is frustration. When the group is hindered or blocked in achieving its goal, the result is frustration. Feelings of frustration manifest themselves as hostility and aggression or as withdrawal and apathy. The effective teacher should be able to recognize and deal with such problems quickly. Johnson and Bany suggest a process for resolving a conflict: (1) set guidelines for discussion, (2) clarify what happened, (3) explore differences in points of view, (4) identify the cause or causes of the conflict, (5) develop agreements regarding the cause or causes of the conflict and resolution of the conflict, (6) specify a plan of action, and (7) make a positive appraisal of group efforts. To prevent conflict, the teacher is encouraged to reduce frustrations as much as possible by allowing the group to set and reach reasonable goals.

Minimizing Management Problems

If they are to *minimize problems,* teachers must understand their classroom group and must be able to anticipate the influence various environmental factors will have on that group. In minimizing management problems, the effective teacher utilizes two major strategies: (1) facilitation and maintenance behaviors to establish and maintain an effectively functioning, goal-directed classroom group; and (2) continuous diagnosis and analysis of the health of the classroom group as well as action on the basis of that diagnosis. For example, symptoms of disunity call for teacher behaviors intended to promote group cohesiveness. Symptoms of inappropriate norms call for teacher behaviors intended to change those norms to more appropriate ones. In addition, certain types of problems—the new student and the substitute teacher, for example—can and should be anticipated. The teacher should help the class prepare for such possibilities.

Effective classroom management, according to Johnson and Bany, involves the ability of the teacher to establish the conditions that enable the classroom group to be productive—and the ability to maintain those conditions. The latter involves the ability to maintain a high level of morale, resolve conflict, and minimize management problems. Implicit is the need to build effective communication, establish positive interpersonal relationships, and satisfy both individual and group needs. The overriding emphasis is on the ability of the teacher to use group methods of management. These behaviors determine the effectiveness of the group and the success of instruction.

So far in this section, we have presented two somewhat different viewpoints regarding the group-process approach to classroom management—the views of Schmuck and Schmuck and the ideas of Johnson and Bany. A brief examination of several additional ideas from the research of Kounin[21] and the work of Glasser[22] completes the overview presented in this section.

Utilizing Withitness, Overlapping, and Group-Focus Behaviors

As noted in Learning Activity 2.5, Kounin has conducted extensive research on the management dimension of teaching. Several concepts coming from his research were described as instructional managerial strategies. Here, three additional strategies—strategies relevant to the group-process approach—are described:

1. **Withitness behaviors** are those behaviors by which teachers communicate to students that they know what is going on, that they are aware of what students are doing—or not doing. Kounin concluded that withitness is sig-

nificantly related to managerial success; that is, teachers who demonstrate withitness are more likely to have fewer and less serious student misbehaviors.

2. **Overlapping behaviors** are those behaviors by which teachers indicate that they are attending to more than one issue when there is more than one issue to deal with at a particular time. Kounin suggests that overlapping—when combined with withitness—is related to managerial success. Teachers who are able to pay attention to more than one issue at a time are more likely to be effective than teachers who are unable to do so.
3. **Group-focus behaviors** are those behaviors teachers use to maintain a focus on the group—rather than on an individual student—during individual recitations. Kounin identified two aspects of group-focus behaviors: *group alerting,* which refers to the extent to which the teacher involves nonreciting students (maintains their attention and "keeps them on their toes"), and *accountability,* which refers to the extent to which the teacher holds students accountable and responsible for their task performances during recitations. Kounin found that group alerting and accountability are related to student behavior. He suggests that teachers who maintain a group focus are more successful in promoting student goal-directed behavior and in preventing student misbehavior than are teachers who do not.

In summarizing his studies, Kounin suggests there are certain teaching behaviors—withitness, overlapping, and group-focus behaviors—that are related to managerial success. He also notes that these techniques of classroom management apply to the classroom group, not merely to individual students. Thus, Kounin may be described as a staunch advocate of group management—a most interesting dimension of the group-process approach to classroom management.

Utilizing Classroom Meetings

Many behavior problems are best addressed through the use of the class as a problem-solving group under the guidance of the teacher. If each student can be helped to realize that he or she is a member of a working, problem-solving group, and that he or she has both individual and group responsibilities, it is likely that discussions of group problems will lead to the resolution of those problems. Without such help, students tend to evade problems, depend on others to solve their problems, or withdraw. The social–problem-solving *classroom meeting* is intended to provide the assistance students need in this regard. It is a viewpoint shared by most advocates of the group-process approach and best described by Glasser. He suggests three guidelines to enhance the potential effectiveness of social–problem-solving classroom meetings:

1. Any group problem may be discussed; a problem may be introduced by a student or the teacher.
2. The discussion should be directed toward solving the problem; the atmosphere should be nonjudgmental and nonpunitive; the solution should not include punishment or fault finding.
3. The meeting should be conducted with the teacher and students seated in a tight circle; meetings should be held often; meetings should not exceed thirty to forty-five minutes, depending on the age of the students.

The reader who wishes to be more fully informed about these views should refer to Glasser's classic work, *Schools Without Failure.* Also, the reader might find additional value in reading his more recent works, including *Control Theory in the Classroom* and *The Quality School: Managing Students Without Coercion.*[23]

In summary, it appears that the teacher who wishes to develop a behavioral repertoire that draws on the group-process approach should consider the advantages of the following strategies: fostering reasonable, clearly understood expectations; sharing leadership; fostering open communication; establishing and maintaining group morale and attraction; fostering group unity, cooperation, and cohesiveness; promoting productive group standards and norms; resolving conflicts through discussion; exhibiting withitness, overlapping, and group-focus behaviors; and employing problem-solving classroom meetings. This section provides an overview of the group-process approach. Space limitations preclude a more detailed treatment of the subject. It is recommended that the reader who wishes to explore this topic in more detail refer to the work of Schmuck and Schmuck, Johnson and Bany, Kounin, and Glasser. An excellent source of practical suggestions related to classroom group development is Stanford's *Developing Effective Classroom Groups*.[24]

Mastery Test

OBJECTIVE 2 **To describe the nature and dynamics of the authoritarian, intimidation, permissive, cookbook, instructional, behavior-modification, socioemotional-climate, and group-process approaches to classroom management**

Learning Activities 2.1 through 2.8 presented brief descriptions of eight different approaches to classroom management. The following exercise provides you with an opportunity to assess your understanding of the basic principles of each of those approaches. Each of the following fifty statements takes a particular position with regard to the teacher and effective classroom management. Your task is to identify correctly the approach each statement represents. In the space provided in front of each statement, please place the code letters of that approach you feel the statement represents. Please use the following code:

AU—authoritarian approach
BM—behavior-modification approach
CB—cookbook approach
GP—group-process approach
IN—instructional approach
IT—intimidation approach
PM—permissive approach
SE—socioemotional-climate approach

When you have responded to all fifty statements, compare your responses to those presented in the Answer Key at the end of the book.

______ 1. The teacher should recognize that a central role of the teacher is to maintain order and discipline in the classroom by controlling student behavior.

______ 2. The teacher should recognize that classroom climate greatly influences learning and that the teacher greatly influences the nature of that climate.

_____ 3. The teacher should reward acceptable student behavior and avoid rewarding unacceptable student behavior.

_____ 4. The teacher should recognize that an individualized curriculum can eliminate most classroom management problems.

_____ 5. The teacher should address the student's situation, not the student's character or personality, when dealing with a problem.

_____ 6. The teacher should not impose limits on students because this will keep them from reaching their full potential.

_____ 7. The teacher should understand that the use of logical consequences minimizes the potential for the negative side effects that can accompany other forms of punishment.

_____ 8. The teacher should understand that effective management begins with his or her ability to control each student through the use of force as necessary.

_____ 9. The teacher should always be fair and firm in dealing with students because consistency is important.

_____ 10. The teacher should help students understand, accept, and follow established rules and regulations.

_____ 11. The teacher should view a well-managed token system as an effective means of promoting appropriate student behavior.

_____ 12. The teacher should be tolerant of all forms of student behavior.

_____ 13. The teacher should allow students to suffer the natural and logical consequences of their behavior, unless those consequences involve physical danger.

_____ 14. The teacher should behave in ways that let the students know the teacher is aware of what is going on.

_____ 15. The teacher should recognize that a central role of the teacher is the establishment and maintenance of positive teacher–student relationships.

_____ 16. The teacher should understand that the use of punishment and the threat of punishment can be effective management tools when used appropriately.

_____ 17. The teacher should recognize that rewards are unique to the individual student.

_____ 18. The teacher should understand that appropriate classroom activities usually ensure appropriate student behavior because they decrease the potential for frustration and boredom.

_____ 19. The teacher should recognize that the appropriate use of mild desist behaviors can be both effective and efficient in controlling student behavior.

_____ 20. The teacher should treat students with respect and be committed to helping them develop self-responsibility and feelings of self-worth.

_____ 21. The teacher should never punish a student unless there is adequate evidence to establish guilt beyond a reasonable doubt.

_____ 22. The teacher should help students develop a high level of cohesiveness and productive norms.

_____ 23. The teacher should operate on the assumption that both appropriate and inappropriate student behaviors are learned.

_____ 24. The teacher should understand that disruptive students often misbehave because they have been given inappropriate learning tasks.

_____ 25. The teacher should recognize that the manner in which the teacher communicates with students is decisively important.

_____ 26. The teacher should use sarcasm carefully and only after positive interpersonal relationships have been established.

_____ 27. The teacher should always conduct him- or herself in a businesslike and dignified manner when interacting with students.

______ 28. The teacher should observe and/or question students to obtain clues concerning potential rewards.

______ 29. The teacher should understand that the use of classroom meetings and group problem-solving sessions can be an effective means for solving certain managerial problems.

______ 30. The teacher should "separate the sin from the sinner" when dealing with a student who has behaved inappropriately.

______ 31. The teacher should recognize that most classroom management problems can be avoided or solved by effective instructional practices.

______ 32. The teacher should understand that it is important to help students develop communication, leadership, and group problem-solving skills.

______ 33. The teacher should understand that effective classroom management is nothing more than the application of common sense.

______ 34. The teacher should recognize that the proper use of sarcasm and ridicule can be effective in controlling student behavior.

______ 35. The teacher should recognize that a central role of the teacher is to use a variety of instructional strategies to prevent and solve discipline problems.

______ 36. The teacher should understand that it is important to establish and enforce reasonable expectations and rules.

______ 37. The teacher should be fair but firm from the beginning because it is easier to relax control than it is to impose it once it has been lost.

______ 38. The teacher should foster group cohesiveness by helping students perceive membership as attractive and satisfying.

______ 39. The teacher should create discipline with lessons the students will find interesting and motivating.

______ 40. The teacher should view teacher realness, acceptance, and empathy as keys to effective classroom management.

______ 41. The teacher should understand that it is important to establish a physical and psychological environment in which students are completely free to say and do anything they want to.

______ 42. The teacher should understand that well-planned lessons are an effective means of achieving order in the classroom.

______ 43. The teacher should reinforce appropriate student behaviors in ways that recognize that rewards are unique to the individual student.

______ 44. The teacher should understand that effective management is mostly a function of his or her ability to punish student misconduct when it occurs.

______ 45. The teacher should recognize that he or she must often assume responsibility for controlling the behavior of the student.

______ 46. The teacher should recognize that a central role of the teacher is to use tried-and-true techniques to prevent and solve discipline problems.

______ 47. The teacher should recognize that rewarded behavior is likely to be continued and that unrewarded behavior is likely to be discontinued.

______ 48. The teacher should plan and use appropriate instructional activities to ensure appropriate student behavior.

______ 49. The teacher should understand that effective classroom management is the result of the teacher's establishing and maintaining control.

______ 50. The teacher should understand that effective classroom management is intended to help the classroom group become responsible for solving many of its own problems.

OBJECTIVE 3

To analyze a given classroom situation and to describe and justify the managerial strategy or strategies most likely to be effective in facilitating and maintaining those classroom conditions deemed desirable

LEARNING ACTIVITY 3.1

It was previously emphasized that the nature of the problem and its context should dictate the strategy that a teacher uses in attempting to solve the problem. In addition, a strong case has been made for the viewpoint that the teacher might appropriately employ any one of a number of strategies in attempting to solve a particular classroom management problem. Indeed, the effective teacher is one who is able to recognize several equally workable alternatives when confronted with the need to employ a managerial strategy. The following exercise is designed to give you an opportunity to practice that skill.

YOUR TURN

Recognizing Alternative Strategies

For each case study, please (1) describe the type of problem, (2) describe two different strategies a teacher might use in solving the problem, and (3) briefly explain and defend the choices you have made. Because of the wide range of possible responses, this learning activity does not have an Answer Key. After responding to all six case studies, you should analyze your answers. You might consider the extent to which your responses to a particular problem: (1) are really different approaches to the problem; (2) follow logically from the type of problem indicated; (3) deal with the problem's cause, not just the symptoms; (4) would influence a majority of the class in a positive and productive way; (5) would have long-range benefit; and (6) most important, would promote those classroom conditions you deem desirable. If you are pleased with the results of your analysis, you can feel reasonably comfortable with your ability to consider alternative solutions to classroom management problems. If you are not pleased with your responses and feel that additional effort is required, you may find it helpful to review the information contained in Learning Activities 2.1 through 2.8.

1. Although you have no direct evidence that supports the assertion, Eddie has a reputation as a bully. He is large for his age and towers over most of his sixth-grade classmates. Having attended to a chore that required you to leave your room for a few minutes, you return to find Eddie holding Harry, a much smaller boy, by the shirt. Eddie's clenched right hand is cocked as if he is about to deliver a sharp blow.
   a. Problem:
   b. Solution 1
      (1) Description:
      (2) Justification:

c. Solution 2
(1) Description:
(2) Justification:

2. Having finished lunch, you hurry to the gym to set up the equipment necessary for your 1:00 P.M. physical education class. As you enter the gym, you find Phil and Allan, both seniors, smoking. Although school regulations forbid smoking and call for an automatic three-day suspension, some of your colleagues fail to enforce the regulation because they feel the punishment is too severe.
   a. Problem:
   b. Solution 1
      (1) Description:
      (2) Justification:
   c. Solution 2
      (1) Description:
      (2) Justification:

3. While your third-grade class is working quietly at their seats, Cindy approaches your desk and in a near-whisper says, "During recess someone took the pen I got for Christmas out of my desk. I think Ray took it because he's now using one just like it. I don't think he had it before. If I don't get it back, my mom is going to be awful mad."
   a. Problem:
   b. Solution 1
      (1) Description:
      (2) Justification:
   c. Solution 2
      (1) Description:
      (2) Justification:

4. Your eighth-grade American history class is a delight to teach. They are bright and motivated. Although you have taught them for only three months, they have become your "all-time favorites." As you introduce the day's lesson, you notice immediately that they are angry and sullen. Recognizing that this is such unusual behavior for this group and that it is likely to inhibit your effectiveness that day, you decide to find out the reason for their feelings. Brenda, one of the class leaders, speaks out: "It's that Mr. Underhill. He gave us an exam that was totally unfair. It covered two chapters he hadn't even assigned and now he says he did. None of us did well on the exam; a 62 was the highest score. And he won't let us take a makeup. That's not fair." The rest of the class nods in agreement.
   a. Problem:
   b. Solution 1
      (1) Description:
      (2) Justification:
   c. Solution 2
      (1) Description:
      (2) Justification:

5. At recess, you accompany your fifth-grade class to the playground. You are watching a group of students skipping rope when you are attracted by noise coming from a group of boys in a cluster. As you approach them, you find eight or ten boys in a tight circle around another boy, Leslie McClendon. The boys in the circle are chanting, "Leslie is a girl's name, Leslie is a girl's name."

a. Problem:
b. Solution 1
(1) Description:
(2) Justification:
c. Solution 2
(1) Description:
(2) Justification:

6. A month into the school year, you assign small-group projects to your tenth-grade biology students. You allow students to form their own groups of four or five. Although the class of thirty-four students consists of eighteen boys and sixteen girls (twenty white students and fourteen black students), you are surprised and disappointed to see that the groups the students form are composed of white boys, black boys, white girls, or black girls only. Not one of the eight groups is either sexually or racially integrated.
a. Problem:
b. Solution 1
(1) Description:
(2) Justification:
c. Solution 2
(1) Description:
(2) Justification:

LEARNING ACTIVITY 3.2

Thus far in this chapter, emphasis has been given to the notion that the effective classroom manager accurately identifies the nature of the problem and selects the managerial strategy that has the greatest potential for solving the problem. Accurate identification of the problem and selection of an appropriate strategy are crucial factors. Of equal importance is the matter of *timing*. *When* the teacher acts is often as important as *what* the teacher does. Even if the teacher decides not to act, that decision must be made quickly.

There are four such decisions to be made about the timing of an intervention. The teacher must (1) anticipate certain types of problems and act to prevent them from happening; (2) react immediately in instances requiring immediate action; (3) solve problems that do not require immediate action but must be dealt with promptly; and (4) monitor the effectiveness of attempts to solve identified problems. The following exercise gives you an opportunity to practice the ability to react under the pressure of time—the ability to make effective decisions quickly.

YOUR TURN

Making Quick Decisions

Eight problems are briefly described. Your task is to describe what you would do in each case and to justify the course of action you select. In this exercise, your response should also be timed so that you experience the pressure of having to make a decision within a limited amount of time. For each case, you will have two minutes to describe what you would do if faced with the problem described. The following procedures are recommended for this exercise.

Do *not* read the case studies yourself; have a partner read them to you instead. You and your partner can take turns reading the problems. For example, your partner reads problem 1 to you, then you write a timed (two minute) response. Together, you and your partner should discuss your response. Next you would read problem 2 to your partner, who then writes a response which you two should discuss. You can continue using this pattern until you have responded to all the problems. In addition you can make up other scenarios depicting common classroom management problems to read to each other. You should write your solution—and only the solution, *not* the justification—to the first problem during the two-minute interval that follows each reading of a problem. At the end of the first interval, you should move on to the second problem, and so on. After you have finished writing responses to the problems, go back and write justifications for them.

Your justifications ought to describe the reasoning behind your decisions. Additionally, you may find it helpful to describe the assumptions you made about the nature of the problem, other alternatives you considered, and the condition you would be attempting to establish or reestablish. Having finished writing a justification for each response, carefully and thoroughly examine your responses and your justifications with a peer or group of peers. Or put your answers aside for a day or two. Then you might review your responses to determine how good you still feel about your answers. Obviously, this exercise has no right or wrong answers. For this reason, no Answer Key is provided. The best answers are clearly those that make sense to you as you subject them to an objective analysis and recognize the assumptions you have made about the problem and the managerial outcomes you would hope to achieve.

1. Jim is one of the brighter students in your third-grade class, but he constantly misbehaves. He does nothing really serious, just a continuous series of minor incidents—talking out, laughing loudly, slamming his desktop, throwing wads of paper, and teasing fellow classmates, for example. Although these are not major misbehaviors, they are annoying and disruptive. In addition, the other students think these things are funny. They laugh and treat Jim's behavior as a joke. What do you do?

2. You are not sure of the problem, but the symptoms are obvious. Your seventh-period algebra class is not working well. Assignments are generally late. The students are constantly complaining about your assignments, the fairness of tests, and everything in general. During class discussions, no one participates. No one volunteers to answer questions you believe many can answer. Little accidents such as pencils breaking, books falling on the floor, and an overturned wastebasket seem frequent. What do you do?

3. Tom has been a member of your Spanish II class for nearly three weeks now, having transferred to Wilson High School after the Christmas break. Although he seems to be a nice young man, it is obvious that he has not been accepted by his classmates. Small-group projects designed to involve Tom have not helped. Tom remains outside an otherwise cohesive group. The other students seem to ignore him, and he seems to ignore them; however, you have not seen any signs of hostility on anyone's part. What do you do?

4. Your fourth-period social studies class has always been a bit more of a problem than your other tenth-grade students. After six months, however, they now work quite well, with one bothersome exception. Despite your telling them on numerous occasions that they are to wait until you dismiss them when the bell rings for them to go to fifth-period lunch, they invariably get out of their seats and rush to the door, pushing and shoving into the hallway. As luck would have it, today Mr. Blake, the principal, was almost run over by your stampeding students. What do you do?

5. Your eighth-grade history students are working quietly in groups of three or four. As you move around the room checking on the progress the groups are making on their projects, you hear constrained giggling from a far corner of the room. You look up in time to see Bill holding a penknife in his hand. Catching sight of you, Bill slips the knife into his desk. As you near Bill's desk, you notice that an obscene word has been carved in large letters on Bill's desktop. The carving is fresh; indeed, there are still wood chips on the desk. What do you do?

6. The flu kept you out of school for several days. Handling students after they have had a few days with a substitute teacher is generally something of a problem, and you do not really expect the first day back to go too smoothly. That expectation is reinforced by a note left for you by the substitute teacher. It reads: "I had nothing but trouble with all of your classes, but the first-period business math class is perhaps the worst group I've ever met. There isn't a polite person in that entire class. I don't know how you stand it. They gave me nothing but trouble. They are the most discourteous group I've ever met." The first period bell rings, and members of the business math class take their seats. What do you do?

7. When Linda's mother brought Linda to your kindergarten class on the first day of school, she warned you that Linda was "a very sensitive child." After only two weeks of school, you have some idea of the reason she felt the need to warn you. Linda displays a rare gift for temper tantrums. If she can't be first in line—temper tantrum. If she is not allowed to do what she wants—temper trantrum. And Linda's temper tantrums are complete with kicking, crying, screaming, and rolling on the floor. You have tried to ignore her outbursts, but now you find that the other children are making fun of Linda. Typical comments include: "There she goes again!" "What a baby she is!" "Grow up, crybaby!" What do you do?

8. Your ninth-grade social studies class is the best you have ever had. They are both bright and well behaved. Class discussions are a delight; test scores are always high. On numerous occasions, you have praised the class for their accomplishments. The recent assignment of Barbara to the class, however, has created a problem. Barbara has had a miserable home life. She is the illegitimate daughter of a woman with a bad reputation in the community. Barbara herself has been in trouble with the law. Indeed, she has just been released from a school for delinquent girls, having served six months for shoplifting—a third such conviction. The principal has assigned her to your class because she is bright and because he feels that she will be better behaved with "good students." Barbara has been in your class for only a few days when you begin to receive complaints that "things are missing." Pencils, pens, compacts, combs, lipsticks, and other things have begun to disappear. What do you do?

Observation Worksheet
Managerial Objectives and/or Strategies

This observation focuses on observing managerial strategies the teacher uses in the classroom and/or student behaviors that are indicators of good managerial behavior on the teacher's part.

Directions: Do not use actual names of schools, teachers, administrators, or students when using this worksheet.

Observer's Name: ______________________________

Date: ______________________________

Grade Level: ______________________________

Subject: ______________________________

Class Size: ______________________________

Background Information: Give a brief general description of the school's social, economic, and ethnic makeup.

____

____

What to Record: From the two boxed inserts located on pages 267–269, you will construct an observational checklist that lists the behaviors—the teacher behaviors and/or student behaviors—on which you will focus your attention. Your checklist may include: (1) *teacher behaviors*—those managerial strategies you expect the teacher to exhibit during your observation (positive reinforcement would be an example); (2) *student behaviors*—those student behaviors that are indicators of the managerial objectives that you value and that you expect the students to exhibit during your observation (on-task behavior would be an example); or (3) *both* teacher behaviors and student behaviors. Include no more than ten or twelve behaviors on your checklist.

Reflections on Your Observation:

1. What, if any, managerial strategies did you observe the teacher use to prevent managerial problems? In your view, was the use of these strategies effective in preventing managerial problems?

____

____

____

2. What, if any, managerial strategies did you observe the teacher use to solve a managerial problem or problems? In your view, was the use of these strategies effective in dealing with the managerial problem or problems?

____

____

____

3. What, if any, managerial strategies did you observe the teacher use to strengthen a desirable student behavior or behaviors? In your view, was the use of these strategies effective in strengthening the student behavior or behaviors?

____

____

____

4. What, if any, student behaviors did you observe that indicated that the teacher was being successful or unsuccessful in achieving his or her managerial objectives?

____

____

____

Managerial strategies

The following is a listing from which you may select those managerial strategies you wish to include on your Observation Worksheet:

1. Establishing and enforcing rules
2. Issuing commands, directives, and orders
3. Utilizing mild desists
4. Utilizing proximity control
5. Utilizing isolation and exclusion
6. Utilizing harsh desists
7. Providing interesting, relevant, and appropriate curriculum and instruction
8. Employing effective movement management—smoothness and momentum
9. Establishing classroom routines
10. Giving clear directions
11. Utilizing interest boosting
12. Providing hurdle help
13. Planning for environmental changes
14. Planning and modifying the classroom environment
15. Restructuring the situation
16. Utilizing positive reinforcement
17. Utilizing negative reinforcement
18. Utilizing extinction and/or time out
19. Utilizing modeling
20. Utilizing shaping
21. Utilizing token economy systems
22. Utilizing contingency contracting
23. Utilizing group contingencies
24. Reinforcing incompatible alternatives
25. Utilizing behavioral counseling
26. Utilizing self-monitoring
27. Utilizing cues, prompts, and signals
28. Administering punishment
29. Utilizing overcorrection
30. Utilizing response cost
31. Utilizing negative practice
32. Utilizing satiation
33. Utilizing fading
34. Fostering positive interpersonal relationships
35. Communicating realness
36. Communicating acceptance
37. Communicating empathic understanding

38. Utilizing effective communication
39. Exhibiting active listening
40. Utilizing humor
41. Utilizing reality therapy
42. Employing logical consequences
43. Developing a democratic classroom
44. Exhibiting withitness behaviors
45. Exhibiting overlapping behaviors
46. Maintaining group focus
47. Clarifying expectations
48. Sharing leadership
49. Promoting productive group norms
50. Fostering open communication
51. Fostering attraction
52. Establishing and maintaining group morale
53. Developing cooperation
54. Fostering group cohesiveness
55. Employing classroom meetings
56. Involving students in decision making
57. Resolving conflicts through discussion and negotiation
58. Employing role playing

Student behaviors

The following is a listing from which you may select those student behaviors you wish to include on your Observation Worksheet:

1. Students exhibit on-task behavior.
2. Students understand the teacher's expectations and act accordingly.
3. Students exhibit productive work and study behaviors.
4. Students understand and adhere to school and classroom rules.
5. Students evidence feelings of self-worth.
6. Students feel free to express themselves to the teacher and to one another.
7. Students follow clearly established routines and procedures.
8. Students show respect for self, other persons, and property.
9. Students communicate openly and honestly.
10. Students manifest positive interpersonal relationships.
11. Students feel accountable for their own behavior.
12. Students exhibit group cohesiveness.
13. Students understand and accept the consequences of their actions.
14. Students feel that they are treated fairly.
15. Students exhibit cooperation and a sharing attitude.
16. Students display productive group norms.
17. Students quickly return to task after interruptions
18. Students follow directions.
19. Students are prepared for the task at hand.
20. Students function at a noise level appropriate to the activity.
21. Students participate actively in learning tasks.
22. Students display positive feelings about classroom processes.
23. Students manifest the ability to adjust to changing situations.
24. Students exhibit self-discipline and self-control.
25. Students feel comfortable and safe.
26. Students display initiative and creativity.

27. Students serve as resources to one another.
28. Students move from one task to another in an orderly manner.
29. Students accept and respect authority.
30. Students support and encourage one another.
31. Students are responsible for individual supplies and materials.
32. Students pay attention to the teacher and to one another.
33. Students like being members of the classroom group.
34. Students feel that the teacher understands them.
35. Students believe that they have opportunities to be successful.

NOTES

1. Lee Canter and Marlene Canter, *Assertive Discipline* (Los Angeles: Canter & Associates, 1979).
2. Carl J. Wallen and LaDonna L. Wallen, *Effective Classroom Management* (Boston: Allyn & Bacon, 1978), p. 214.
3. Lois V. Johnson and Mary A. Bany, *Classroom Management: Theory and Skill Training* (New York: Macmillan, 1970), pp. 45–49.
4. Jean E. Davis, *Coping with Disruptive Behavior* (Washington, D.C.: National Education Association, 1974), p. 21.
5. Jacob S. Kounin, *Discipline and Group Management in Classrooms* (New York: Holt, Rinehart & Winston, 1970).
6. James D. Long and Virginia H. Frye, *Making It Till Friday: A Guide to Successful Classroom Management* (Princeton, N.J.: Princeton Book Company, 1977), pp. 35–36.
7. Edmund T. Emmer, Carolyn M. Evertson, and Murray E. Worsham, *Classroom Management for Secondary Teachers* (Boston: Allyn & Bacon, 2000); Carolyn M. Evertson, Edmund T. Emmer, and Murray E. Worsham, *Classroom Management for Elementary Teachers* (Boston: Allyn & Bacon, 2000).
8. Terrence Piper, *Classroom Management and Behavioral Objectives: Applications of Behavioral Modification* (Belmont, Calif.: Lear Siegler/Fearon, 1974), pp. 10–18.
9. Nancy K. Buckley and Hill M. Walker, *Modifying Classroom Behavior: A Manual of Procedures for Classroom Teachers* (Champaign, Ill.: Research Press Company, 1970), p. 30.
10. Abraham Givener and Paul S. Graubard, *A Handbook of Behavior Modification for the Classroom* (New York: Holt, Rinehart & Winston, 1974), p. 8.
11. Beth Sulzer and G. Roy Mayer, *Behavior Modification Procedures for School Personnel* (Hinsdale, Ill.: Dryden, 1972), pp. 174–184.
12. Saul Axelrod, *Behavior Modification for the Classroom Teacher* (New York: McGraw-Hill, 1983).
13. Harvey F. Clarizio, *Toward Positive Classroom Discipline* (New York: Wiley, 1980).
14. Carl R. Rogers, *Freedom to Learn* (Columbus, Ohio: Merrill, 1969).
15. Haim G. Ginott, *Between Parent and Child* (New York: Macmillan, 1965); Ginott, *Between Parent and Teenager* (New York: Macmillan, 1969); Ginott, *Teacher and Child* (New York: Macmillan, 1972).
16. William Glasser, *Schools Without Failure* (New York: Harper & Row, 1969).
17. Rudolf Dreikurs and Loren Grey, *A New Approach to Discipline: Logical Consequences* (New York: Hawthorn, 1968); Rudolf Dreikurs and Pearl Cassel, *Discipline Without Tears* (New York: Hawthorn, 1972); Rudolf Dreikurs, Bernice Bronia Grunwald, and Floyd C. Pepper, *Maintaining Sanity in the Classroom: Classroom Management Techniques* (New York: Harper & Row, 1982).
18. Richard Curwin and Allen Medler, *Discipline with Dignity* (Alexandria, Va: Association for Supervision and Curriculum Development, 1988).
19. Richard A. Schmuck and Patricia A. Schmuck, *Group Processes in the Classroom* (Dubuque, Iowa: Brown, 1979).
20. Johnson and Bany, *op. cit.*
21. Kounin, *op. cit.*
22. Glasser, *op. cit.*
23. Glasser, *op. cit.*; William Glasser, *Control Theory in the Classroom* (New York: Harper & Row, 1986); William Glasser, *The Quality School: Managing Students Without Coercion* (New York: HarperPerennial, 1998).
24. Gene Stanford, *Developing Effective Classroom Groups* (New York: A & W Visual Library, 1980).

ADDITIONAL RESOURCES

Readings

Arends, Richard I. *Classroom Instruction and Management.* New York: McGraw-Hill, 1997.

Axelrod, Saul. *Behavior Modification for the Classroom Teacher.* New York: McGraw-Hill, 1983.

Breeden, Terri, and Emalie Egan. *Positive Classroom Management.* Nashville: Incentive Publications, 1997.

Cangelosi, James S. *Classroom Management Strategies.* New York: Wiley, 2000.

Canter, Lee, and Marlene Canter. *Assertive Discipline.* Santa Monica, Calif.: Canter & Associates, 1992.

Charles, C. M. *Building Classroom Discipline.* Boston: Allyn & Bacon, 2002.

Clarizio, Harvey F. *Toward Positive Classroom Discipline.* New York: Wiley, 1980.

Curwin, Richard, and Allen Medler. *Discipline with Dignity.* Alexandria, Va.: Association for Supervision and Curriculum Development, 1988.

DiGiulio, Robert. *Positive Classroom Management.* Thousand Oaks, Calif.: Corwin, 2000.

Dreikurs, Rudolf, and Pearl Cassel. *Discipline Without Tears.* New York: Hawthorn, 1972.

Dreikurs, Rudolf, Bernice Bronia Grunwald, and Floyd C. Pepper. *Maintaining Sanity in the Classroom: Classroom Management Techniques.* New York: Harper & Row, 1982.

Dreikurs, Rudolf, and Loren Grey. *A New Approach to Discipline: Logical Consequences.* New York: Dutton, 1990.

Edwards, Clifford H. *Classroom Discipline and Management.* New York: Wiley, 1999.

Emmer, Edmund T., Carolyn M. Evertson, and Murray E. Worsham. *Classroom Management for Secondary Teachers.* Boston: Allyn & Bacon, 2000.

Evertson, Carolyn M., Edmund T. Emmer, and Murray E. Worsham. *Classroom Management for Elementary Teachers.* Boston: Allyn & Bacon, 2000.

Fields, Marjorie V., and Cindy Boesser. *Constructive Guidance and Discipline: Preschool and Primary Education.* Upper Saddle River, N.J.: Merill Prentice Hall, 2002.

Ginott, Haim G. *Teacher and Child: A Book for Parents and Teachers.* New York: Macmillan, 1972.

Glasser, William. *Schools Without Failure.* New York: Harper & Row, 1969.

Glasser, William. *Control Theory in the Classroom.* New York: Harper & Row, 1986.

Glasser, William. *The Quality School: Managing Students Without Coercion.* New York: HarperPerennial, 1998.

Jones, Fredric H. *Tools for Teaching.* Santa Cruz, Calif.: Fredric H. Jones & Associates, 2000.

Jones, Vernon F., and Louise S. Jones. *Comprehensive Classroom Management.* Boston: Allyn & Bacon, 1998.

Kerr, Mary Margaret, and C. Michael Nelson. *Strategies for Addressing Behavior Problems in the Classroom.* Upper Saddle River, N.J.: Merrill Prentice Hall, 2002.

Nelsen, Jane, Linda Escobar, Kate Ortolano, Roslyn Duffy, and Deborah Owen-Sohocki. *Positive Discipline: A Teacher's A–Z Guide.* Roseville, Calif: Prima Publishing, 2001.

Nelsen, Jane, Lynn Lott, and H. Stephen Glenn. *Positive Discipline in the Classroom.* Roseville, Calif: Prima Publishing, 2000.

Rinne, Carl H. *Excellent Classroom Management.* Belmont, Calif.: Wadsworth, 1997.

Schmuck, Richard, and Patricia A. Schmuck. *Group Processes in the Classroom,* 8th ed. Boston: McGraw-Hill, 2001.

Stanford, Gene. *Developing Effective Classroom Groups.* New York: A & W Visual Library, 1980.

Tauber, Robert T. *Classroom Management: Theory and Practice.* Orlando, Fla.: Harcourt Brace, 1995.

Weinstein, Carol Simon. *Secondary Classroom Management: Lessons from Research and Practice.* New York: McGraw-Hill, 1996.

Weinstein, Carol Simon, and Andrew J. Mignano, Jr. *Elementary Classroom Management: Lessons from Research and Practice.* New York: McGraw-Hill, 1997.

Wolfgang, Charles H. *Solving Discipline Problem: Methods and Models for Today's Teachers.* Boston: Allyn & Bacon, 1999.

Wong, Harry K., and Rosemary T. Wong. *The First Days of School.* Mountain View, Calif.: Harry K. Wong Publications, 1998.

Web Sites

Adprima (Toward the Best): http://www.adprima.com/managing.htm
Adprima, a web site developed and maintained by Robert Kizlik, describes "some of the things that good classroom teachers do to maintain an atmosphere that enhances learning." Recommendations range from suggestions regarding classroom arrangement to guidelines for effective praise.

Education World®: http://www.db.education-world.com/perl/browse?cat_id=1846
Education World® presents a range of information concerning classroom management; this includes a "database" of nearly 100 "teacher resources" concerned with classroom management in addition to articles and classroom management links at http://www.education-world.com/preservice/learning/management/shtml

Expage: http://www.expage.com/ClassroomManagement
Expage presents a list of links to web sites dealing with various aspects of classroom management; titles include "Classroom Management Concepts," "Classroom Management Ideas," and "Strategies for Classroom Management," for example.

The Innovative Classroom: http://www.innovativeclassroom.com/Class_Management/
The Innovative Classroom presents suggestions concerning various aspects of classroom management including "Organization Tips," a section that deals with "the organization of materials and supplies, tips dealing with behavior issues, and suggestions for implementing class routines."

Innovative Teaching Concepts: http://www.twoteach.com/ClassroomManagement.htm
This site offers recommendations regarding "the positive approach to classroom discipline." It also provides ideas concerning character education as well as sample lessons and posters.

Learning Network: http://www.teachervision.com/lesson-plans/lesson-5776.html
This section of the Learning Network web site presents "advice from experienced teachers and specialists" regarding various aspects of "behavior management." Topics range from "Bully-Proof Your Classroom" to "Setting Limits."

Northwest Regional Educational Laboratory: http://www.nwrel.org/scpd/sirs/5/cu9.html
A project of the Northwest Regional Educational Laboratory, the School Improvement Series presents "research you can use." In "Schoolwide and Classroom Disciplines," one in the series, Kathleen Cotton provides a relatively comprehensive review of research in the field of classroom management.

ProTeacher™: http://www.proteacher.com/030000.shtml
ProTeacher™, edited by Sarah Wood, presents "classroom management ideas for elementary school teachers in grades K–6 including tips for new teachers." Topics range from "Classroom Arrangement" to "Classroom Routines."

The Teacher's Guide: http://www.theteachersguide.com/ClassroomManagement.htm
This section of The Teacher's Guide web site provides links to articles providing suggestions regarding various aspects of classroom management from a variety of perspectives.

Teachers Helping Teachers: http://www.pacificnet.net/~mandel/index.html
Teachers Helping Teachers is a web site maintained by Scott Mandel. It provides "basic teaching tips to inexperienced teachers," "new ideas in teaching methodologies for all teachers," and "a forum for experienced teachers to share their expertise and tips with colleagues." The section at http:www.pacificnet.net/~mandel/SpecialEducation.html provides "tips" about special education, many of which have application in "regular" classrooms.

Teachnet: http://www.teachnet.com/index.html
The "Classroom Management" section of the Teachnet website, http://www.teachnet.com/how-to/manage/, presents a wide range of suggestions about "behavior and discipline" representing various viewpoints.

9

Cooperative Learning

Mary S. Leighton

OBJECTIVE 1 **To review the functions of teachers, students, and content in effective lessons**

OBJECTIVE 2 **To describe the attributes of cooperative learning that contribute to student achievement in social and academic arenas and to discriminate academically productive cooperative learning strategies from less formal group activities that may not improve achievement**

OBJECTIVE 3 **To integrate simple cooperative learning structures into more complex or extended lessons**

OBJECTIVE 4 **To implement complex cooperative learning strategies, including Student Teams Achievement Divisions (STAD) and Jigsaw**

OBJECTIVE 5 **To describe some of the process skills students use in cooperative learning and explore some ways of teaching those skills**

OBJECTIVE 6 **To examine how the physical, organizational, and instructional environments support effective use of cooperative learning strategies**

OBJECTIVE 7 **To explore some of the schoolwide dimensions of classroom use of cooperative learning**

The sixth-grade reading and language arts class is working on vocabulary. On Monday, the class members created a list of new and interesting words drawn from the novel they are studying. The teacher, Ms. Harriman, helped the class trim the original list to twenty words and then find sentences in the novel that show what each word means. On Tuesday, she suggested that as a journal-writing exercise they try using the words in sentences about their own lives. Today students are working in learning teams to prepare for a quiz on the spelling and meaning of the words.

As usual, each team has its own lesson packet, which Ms. Harriman uses to distribute and collect materials. The packet for this lesson includes an alphabetized word list with a text sentence for each word; a guide with definitions and some examples of common usage of the words; and four cards, numbered 1 to 4. The Cougars—Isaac, Kate, José, and May—are old hands at team practice. May, assigned the role of materials manager for the week, fetches the team packet from the materials shelf and brings it to the team table. Each member draws a numbered card and glances at the chalkboard, where Ms. Harriman has written starting roles for each number. Isaac has drawn number 1, designated for this practice session as the starting questioner. He reaches for the word list, while Kate—as number 3, the starting checker—takes the answer key. Isaac reads the opening question to May, number 2, the first answerer: "'[Muna] got no closer to those exalted figures than their horses' feed troughs.' What does 'exalted' mean?"[1] May responds promptly, "High class, important, rich." Kate checks May's explanation against the study guide and decides that the definition is acceptable. José looks puzzled, though. Isaac pops up from his chair and mimes kingly stature, pulling Kate into the act to curtsey deeply. José nods, smiling, and the session continues. May spells the word correctly, and the action moves on: May becomes the questioner; Kate, the answerer; and José—as number 4, a listener during round one—becomes the checker. Isaac becomes the listener.

Today's practice session starting roles
1 Questioner
2 Answerer
3 Checker
4 Listener

Because this is José's first year in an English-language reading group, he asks for and gets extra help from his teammates, who have become adept at illustrating word meanings with lots of examples from their daily routines. Occasionally, they recruit the help of Raphael on the Pumas, because as a Spanish speaker like José he can offer examples in Spanish, too. Kate, whose extensive recreational reading makes her a star in this class, is another good resource for José, a peer with whom she previously had limited acquaintance. The Cougars finish their work early and use the extra time to try a practice test. Each is eager to make this week's individual quiz score higher than usual and contribute to the team's improvement points.

Ms. Harriman has been circulating around the room monitoring work, and she stops near the Cougars to check their progress. She has had a private coaching session with Isaac, who is very assertive, to teach him how to exercise his irrepressible initiative (a mixed blessing, in her view!) in drawing out May, who is shy. Ms. Harriman sees that Isaac is making progress in this skill and that everyone is participating appropriately in the practice activity.

The class expects a quiz tomorrow. Each group member's score will be compared to his or her **base score,** calculated by averaging their usual quiz scores in vocabulary. The team earns points when the comparison shows individual progress. All the teams that reach the Super Team standard of growth will be able to display their teams' pennants on the library bulletin board next week. Those that meet the slightly lower Great Team standard will display pennants on the classroom bulletin board. Since Ms. Harriman has been using this strategy, Isaac's quiz scores have risen from 70s to 80s and his interest in reading has visibly increased. José's scores have improved dramatically, and by the end of the semester Ms. Harriman expects to see him reading on grade level in English, as he already does in Spanish. May smiles and participates more often in class discussions now, and her grades have risen to a solid B. Kate, always an A student but sometimes careless in her work, now often makes perfect scores on quizzes. For Kate's 100s and José's dramatic improvement, the team earns a lot of team points and is frequently included among the celebrated Super Teams of the week. Equally important—at least from Kate and José's point of view—they are much more often recruited for playground games and lunchtime socializing than they used to be. Team points do not change students' individual grades, which reflect individual accomplishments, but they lead to public recognition and token rewards, which the children enjoy.

The Cougars are active participants in a learning activity that promotes development on multiple levels and takes advantage of students' diverse resources to meet their diverse needs. In the long run, this activity can help them become valued and productive members of their community. Success in all dimensions of life increasingly depends on the ability to solve problems using the right combination of knowledge, skill, and creativity. Every day, modern life poses new challenges arising out of new social arrangements, technology, political and economic systems, and uses of space (on earth, around it, beyond its orbit). Long after the Cougars leave sixth grade, they will remember how to find answers by using available expertise, to view differences in talent as opportunities to compare and enrich thinking, and to engage in forms of peer leadership and negotiation that sustain collective progress. The care that Ms. Harriman takes to structure the academic tasks leads to sustained, cooperative engagement to meet worthwhile cognitive challenges. The quality and quantity of student work make a significant and measurable contribution to their learning. The way they interact as they work also enhances their social relations.

Cooperative learning strategies, properly structured, have proven to be efficient and effective in promoting mastery of knowledge and skills among students of all abilities and ages. To improve learning in the novel study, the Cougars' teacher is using a form of Student Team Learning,[2] one of several complex configurations of cooperative learning elements that work effectively. In reviews of hundreds of studies conducted in the first ninety years of the twentieth century, Johnson and Johnson found consistent evidence of the effectiveness of cooperative learning strategies.[3] Improved achievement was found in a broad array of subjects, from math and physical education to second-language learning. Such studies often focus on elementary and secondary teaching. However, experimental studies in accounting education[4] and geology education,[5] among other subjects, showed positive results with postsecondary students as well. These studies extend the earlier work of Cooper and his colleagues at California State University, who have documented the success of cooperative learning strategies across the college curriculum.[6] In short, properly structured cooperative learning activities are a reliable way to improve academic achievement.

Furthermore, cooperative learning strategies can enhance creativity by harnessing the power of many kinds of human intelligence and providing task structures that facilitate shared work and responsibility. Considerable evidence suggests that schools where teachers and students are frequently engaged in cooperative activities provide the social and cultural foundations necessary to cultivate general civility and support peaceful and productive conflict resolution. One summary of a major research review reported the regular finding that cooperative learning led to measurable improvement in group cohesion, positive relationships, ability to provide peer support, and appreciation of diversity.[7] In addition, the review noted evidence of the positive impact of cooperative learning on self-esteem, social skills, and stress management. These indicators of good social and psychological health serve as a nurturing context for collective openness and innovation, which in turn stimulate and sustain creativity. When it engages diverse students in productive activity focused on achieving a shared goal, cooperative learning produces positive intergroup relations. Indeed, some of the most intensive research and development work on cooperative learning has been done in situations where social change increased the pressure for groups to learn to live and work together.

In this chapter, we will explore forms of cooperative learning that teachers all over the world have found useful and identify the key elements that define them. For the sake of clarity, the term *cooperative learning* will be used here exclusively to refer to lesson activities of a particular type, elaborated in the next section of the chapter. The term *group work* will be used for other lesson activities that may involve two or more students but that do not possess the defining traits of cooperative learning.

OBJECTIVE 1

To review the functions of teachers, students, and content in effective lessons

LEARNING ACTIVITY 1

The General Context of Cooperative Learning

Teachers, students, and content all play vital roles in good lessons; the fundamental nature and importance of those roles is the same in effective cooperative learning as in other lesson formats. Teachers control the lesson elements that students do not have the knowledge or skill to control. Students work hard to construct and transform lesson content for their own use. Lesson content is substantively adequate and worthy of students' time and effort.

Teachers present the content. That is, they stage an encounter from which students can learn the new material, the structure of relevant knowledge, and the processes of knowing. They may, for example, demonstrate, explain, provide media events (a movie, an interactive computer activity), tell a story, or take the class on a trip. Whatever the format, they ensure a representation of content and process that is just beyond but within reach of the learners' current knowledge. For example, to introduce primary students to the concepts of municipal governance, a teacher might first explore the roles, relationships, and responsibilities of members of families and the school community. Only then would a teacher launch the class into a study of civic authority. Metaphors from family and school life might serve as organizers and illuminators of the general structure; observed discrepancies could illustrate the nature of differences and extensions with respect to familiar social systems.

If students have appropriate print materials, Internet resources, hypertext, opportunities to interview, videotapes, or other sources of data that they can review independently, the teacher may shift from presenter to coach. As coach, the teacher guides students through the lesson content as they become familiar with details of the new information. Teachers must know the general terrain of the curriculum and the present level of student understanding in order to determine what lesson content represents a reasonable, stimulating stretch for students and what presentation mode offers them the richest, most supportive opportunity to learn.

There is a widespread and worrisome misconception that in cooperative learning students are each other's primary teachers. A related concern is that the resulting absence of real expertise limits learning—how can a student learn from someone just as uninformed? Such conditions may occur in some forms of group work, but not in cooperative learning. In effective cooperative learning, the teacher uses presentation strategies that ensure accurate, complete information is available to all students. Lesson activities stimulate students' mediation of each other's learning through sharing insights and examples, collaborating over solutions, and coaching each other's practice of skills. The teacher may rely on good media or well-developed learning centers for content presentation, rather than the traditional lecture and demonstration. However, the teacher's expertise is at work in selecting and organizing the presentation of content. Students' learning is not limited by reliance on peers who may not initially know any more than they about the lesson content; rather, learning is enriched by peers' active involvement in explaining, showing, and motivating as part of their own work.

In the ordinary process of learning, human beings use different combinations of perception, action, and conversation. They watch, attempt to imitate, and discuss what they are doing. Babies offer good examples of this phenomenon: For months and months they watch others closely. Increasingly they attempt to imitate what they see, discovering through practice how to move purposefully, speak intelligibly, and reach their self-selected goals. By age two or three they begin to be able to learn from speech, their own and others'. Alone in a room, they may chatter away, talking themselves through their play, in part because they rely on talking aloud to know what they are thinking and doing. Increased age brings increased ability to "hear" one's own thinking without speaking aloud, but new learning continues to rely on expression to reveal both mastery and misconceptions. Teachers have often used recitation formats to assess students' learning for just this reason.

Expression during the process of learning, in the company of other students, performs the important function of revealing both to the learners and to their audience the nature and extent of their mastery. Whether adults or children, novices frequently think they know something until they try to explain it. As they hear their own words, even before the other listeners can comment, the speakers can assess their own knowledge. If the speakers do not pick up their own inaccuracies, the other listeners generally do. Learners need to express their knowledge as it is developing, both to confirm and to correct its adequacy. Good cooperative learning strategies engage students in sharing how they think, examining it themselves, gaining insight from the critiques of their peers, and enlarging their conceptual understanding by hearing how others understand the same content.

As in other lessons, those using cooperative learning strategies to engage students depend ultimately on the adequacy of the content itself—both the knowledge and the processes of developing it—to promote growth. If the initial presentation of new content is muddled or shallow, if the practice exercise offers too fragmented a view of substance, if meaningful interaction with content is sacrificed for rote learning, then the lesson is doomed no matter how deftly the cooperative learning incentive system is implemented. Reflecting back on Ms. Harriman's class, for example, the quality of the lesson was ensured by the focus on real literature, the use of words in context to enhance vocabulary and spelling, and an activity that productively engaged all students in acquiring mastery. Had students spent the same amount of time in a similar lesson structure based on an ill-conceived, trivial novel, a spelling lesson unconnected with either the novel or their lives, and a practice activity with no controls for quality or extent of participation, real and enduring learning would surely be missing.

The concepts and activities explained in this chapter show how to motivate students to work hard together so that each one makes the most of his or her ability. To lead to measurable gains in achieving mastery of targeted skills and content, however, cooperative learning must operate in a context in which teachers provide accessible and engaging opportunities to learn and the content is substantively compelling.

Mastery Test

OBJECTIVE 1 **To review the functions of teachers, students, and content in effective lessons**

Read the statements below and determine whether they are true or false, based on the information in Learning Activity 1.

_____ 1. Use of cooperative learning usually improves achievement in reading, but not in math.

_____ 2. The achievement outcomes for cooperative learning have been documented in elementary, secondary, and postsecondary classrooms.

_____ 3. Cooperative learning takes advantage of students' diverse talents and resources.

_____ 4. Although cooperative learning may produce achievement effects, it does not significantly change social skills or group cohesion.

_____ 5. In cooperative learning lessons, students are each other's primary teachers.

_____ 6. Teachers seldom use multimedia in cooperative learning, because it is a text-based strategy.

_____ 7. Most students learn from observing their own performance, as well as from observing others or hearing others' feedback.

_____ 8. The quality of lesson content is not as important in cooperative learning as the structure of the task.

OBJECTIVE 2

To describe the attributes of cooperative learning that contribute to student achievement in social and academic arenas and to discriminate academically productive cooperative learning strategies from less formal group activities that may not improve achievement

LEARNING ACTIVITY 2

Essential Features of Cooperative Learning

Cooperative learning is an instructional task design that engages students actively in achieving a lesson objective through their own efforts and the efforts of the members of their small learning team. What distinguishes cooperative learning from other activities that involve working in small groups is a combination of features that weave through an academic task. Different schools of thought propose different ways to name and number these features, but they converge on the basic idea that the structure of the learning task engages students in productive and mutually supportive ways to achieve mastery of the lesson objective. In a good cooperative learning lesson, completing the assignment successfully is easier and more engaging to do as a team and more difficult to do any other way.

Four features have been regularly shown to be central to the success of any cooperative learning lesson. First and foremost is *positive interdependence,* a spirit of "all for one and one for all."[8] Having *goal interdependence* means that if any member is to succeed, all must succeed. With *reward interdependence* the prize or recognition is available to all members of the team when they all achieve a certain standard. For example, each will earn 5 bonus points if all earn a passing score on the test. *Resource interdependence* means that each group member has a share of the materials needed to complete the group task, which requires the shares held by all. *Role interdependence* is what characterized the Cougars' practice session: each student's role interlocked with the others' roles.

Playing jump rope is a good example of positive interdependence: two people must coordinate hand and arm motions while the third jumps in a pattern. The game goes smoothly only when all three do their jobs properly.

Furthermore, the nature of the reward should make it equally available to high-and low-ability students who work hard and make progress.[9] Interdependence is intrinsically unrewarding if the group is denied access to rewards because the members have unequal resources for a given task. Recognizing achievement of a standard of growth—rather than absolute achievement—is one way to support interdependence within a team.

Some models of cooperative learning have highly elaborated roles, while others are fairly simple. All the models that produce improved achievement have built in positive interdependence.

The second key feature is *accountability at the group and the individual level.* That is, the group cannot succeed unless each member demonstrates success or significant progress. The task structure rewards the group for cooperation and at the same time rewards individuals for achieving lesson objectives. In the opening scenario, for example, the Cougars gain recognition as a team for supporting each other's measurable learning, while each member of the team gains recognition for progress and absolute achievement. Whatever form team recognition takes, teams cannot earn it unless they work together and prove their effectiveness by means of individual growth. Slavin has conducted extensive research in this area and consistently come up with the same evidence: grading strategies must be based on individual achievement and team rewards must be based on individual growth if cooperative learning is to work well.[10] Every person who has worked on a team without **individual accountability** has stories to tell about "hitchhikers" who let the hard workers do what needs to be done and coast along on others' efforts. Hitchhikers don't learn; workers learn. If they are to succeed, lesson activities must promote every student's work at learning.

The third essential feature is what the Johnsons call "face-to-face promotive interaction"—*the acts of helping each other learn.*[11] Fine-tuned studies of what exactly goes on in successful cooperative groups have found that explaining what one knows is positively associated with mastery. Now, one might normally assume that the smart students who know more also get to explain more and, of course, eventually show higher achievement on tests. But it is not as simple as that. Among students of equal ability, those who demonstrate mastery by explaining actually reinforce and extend mastery. When students of modest ability in a given academic task explain their answers and thinking to their peers, they learn better. In addition, the opportunity of high-achieving students to explain their knowledge or demonstrate their skills adds materially to their own learning.[12] For this reason, studies of the contribution of cooperative learning strategies to the achievement of academically gifted students usually show benefits to them. The insights gained from translating new knowledge into different terms or modeling new skills for another substantially enhance learning across ability groups.

The fourth essential feature is the *focus on interpersonal and small-group skills* that students use in completing cooperative learning lessons. Working successfully in a team demands particular social skills, which are best learned and practiced in the context of real tasks. Included in this arena is the students' ability to review their own skills critically with a view to improving group effectiveness.

When done properly, cooperative learning not only stimulates cognition but also gives play to the multiple forms of intelligence that students bring to any shared task.[13] In the context of their small learning team, students have a chance to identify and take advantage of each other's strengths and expand their own notions of how to approach a challenge. For instance, think back to the Cougars. José is an English-language learner. His teammates cannot speak Spanish, his first language, but they want him to learn the lesson. Kate's gift for language enables her to provide several alternative English explanations of *exalted.* Isaac, a natural actor, brings the team to giggles demonstrating the meaning of that term. Successful people—adults and children—not only draw

Multiple Intelligences and Cooperative Learning

Gardner[a] has identified at least eight forms of human intelligence that are "rooted in biology" and "valued in one or more cultural settings." He views intelligence as "the ability to solve problems or fashion products that are of consequence in a particular cultural setting or community." Listed below are the types of intelligence, brief descriptions, and a sketch of the contributions each might make to a simple team-learning task, such as the vocabulary and spelling lesson engaging the Cougars. See also Nicholson-Nelson, 1998.[b]

Intelligence	Description	Contribution to Word Study
Linguistic	Uses words and learns languages easily and well	Offers alternative definitions
Logical/mathematical	Thinks scientifically, processes data spontaneously and quickly	Connects ideas logically, shows how the meaning links to other familiar meanings
Spatial	Uses visual cues well to design, navigate, draw, etc.	Draws or creates visual models of meanings
Musical	Uses songs, tunes, sounds, and rhythms	Recalls songs that help fix new words in memory
Bodily/kinesthetic	Controls physical movement with special grace or precision	Acts out meanings
Interpersonal	Perceives the feelings and needs of others accurately and uses that information to approach them	Can see when a struggling teammate is frustrated, offers extra support
Intrapersonal	Knows own feelings and needs well and uses that to make sense of the world	Empathizes, listens, observes
Naturalist	Recognizes the elements and systems of the natural world	Uses images from nature to illustrate meaning

a. H. Gardner, *Multiple Intelligences: The Theory in Practice* (New York: Basic Books, 1993), pp. 15–16.
b. K. Nicholson-Nelson, *Developing Students' Multiple Intelligences* (New York: Scholastic Professional Books, 1998), pp. 10–12.

on their own innate talents; through practice and observing others, they also build up competence in areas where their native gifts may be initially quite modest. The academic task structure and social skill-building emphasis of cooperative learning ensure opportunities for students to use their special gifts and expand their repertoires. Implicitly and often explicitly, cooperative learning promotes metacognition—knowing how one knows, how one learns, and how to enhance others' learning. The challenge of representing knowledge and skill in different ways for the purpose of helping teammates learn takes advantage of students' different learning styles and forms of intelligence.

Three Popular Families of Models

There are three popular families of models of cooperative learning, each with a prominent advocate among many successful others. The models overlap significantly in their research base and to some extent in their practice. But they nevertheless have their own distinctive qualities.

The **Student Team Learning** model promoted by Slavin focuses on task structure, team composition, and reward systems.[14] In most forms of Student Team Learning, task structure ensures that every team member participates. Team composition is carefully determined to create learning groups that are microcosms of the class with respect to diversity. Reward systems for teamwork recognize progress of individual members. Grades for individual achievement are completely determined by individual performance. Student Team Learning models—such as Student Teams Achievement Divisions (STAD), discussed later in this chapter—often have the most detailed scoring systems for team recognition. The skills of teamwork are taught and nurtured as needed to support the academic work, but academic success is the goal of teamwork; social coherence is more an intended side effect. Among the widely used programmatic versions of this model are Team Accelerated Instruction (TAI) in math, Cooperative Integrated Reading and Composition (CIRC), and Success for All.

Johnson and Johnson are more directly concerned with group process and interpersonal skills.[15] While group skills are taught in the context of learning activities, social coherence is viewed as an important goal in itself. Achievement in academic and social arenas is highly valued. Students study, practice, and critique their teamwork skills with a view to improving academic outcomes. Through their models of **Learning Together,** Johnson and Johnson hope to lay the foundations of a society whose members are adept at collaborating and negotiating, who know how to find peaceful and satisfying solutions to social problems. While using the Student Team Learning model has proved to have significant, beneficial effects on social relations, its explicit goal is usually described as academic.[16] Learning Together engages students in both academic and social skill acquisition, and is more often promoted as a community building strategy.

Kagan espouses a kind of molecular model, in which complex lessons may include one or more cooperative elements among other kinds of learning activities.[17] Like the others, Kagan aims for improved efficiency in academic learning and improved social skills. However, his **Structural Approach** views lessons as compositions of interlocking parts, some of which may demand cooperation while others do not. The cooperative structures he uses serve different purposes, which he classifies as team building, class building, mastery, thinking skills, information sharing, and communication skills.

These three schools of thought converge on the principle that an effective cooperative task structure has embedded in it features that elicit and support certain kinds and levels of collaborative effort directed toward achieving a lesson objective. Both carefully controlled studies and the somewhat larger body of less rigorous professional reports consistently indicate that effective strategies include some combination of the key elements. In practice, teachers adapt the characteristics of all three models to fit particular teaching situations.

When Is Group Work Not Cooperative Learning?

Teachers often put students in small groups to move through some part of a lesson or achieve a goal. For example, at the end of a lecture, a teacher might say, "Form a small group with the people sitting next to you and review the main points of my presentation." This is a good way to wake up the listeners and reactivate their engagement, but it involves none of the key features that engage students deeply and extensively enough to improve the rate of learning. In a science or computer lab, a teacher might assign two or three students to the same station to complete a series of tasks. Although they may indeed help each other if they feel like it, there are usually no structures in place to focus and enhance their exchanges, no particular reason to invest in each other's learning. The reason for doubling up may be lack of enough stations to serve each student otherwise.

In a given lesson, any class of students represents a range of interests and abilities. Putting students in small groups with others may encourage them to work or may make it easier for them to coast along. The relatively gifted students may resent the distraction; the students who find the material too challenging may continue to suffer in silence. Nothing about the assignment to a small group under these conditions ensures their engagement. Nothing in such an ad hoc arrangement requires on-task conversation or rewards individual success as a product of group work. No part of the setup instructs students in how to get past interpersonal hurdles or motivates interest in another's achievement. Of course, people are sometimes inspired simply by the opportunity to promote each other's good and to concentrate on the learning at hand, but such opportunities often go unheeded. Group work does little to offset human distractibility; cooperative learning activities use predictable human inclinations to improve conditions for learning.

If a group can earn recognition despite ignoring the needs of a relatively low-performing student or because some gifted members are carrying along the others, the group work is not cooperative learning. If a group's product earns a grade awarded to all students without regard to individual growth or participation, the group work is not cooperative learning. If the reward structure penalizes groups whose members include low achievers by failing to recognize improvement as an important contributor to team success, the group work is not cooperative learning. If a group activity does not involve members in promotion of each other's achievement, it is not cooperative learning. If in the context of group work no instruction is offered on how to work together effectively and how to evaluate effectiveness, the group work is unlikely to generate cooperative learning. Group work may be engaging and lively, but without the key features of cooperative learning, it has not been reliably demonstrated to improve student achievement or promote development of social skills or social cohesion.

The next part of this chapter describes some simple cooperative learning strategies that can be integrated into different kinds of lessons. These strategies embed some of the key features described above, adding effectiveness to group work or whole-class work. They have the merit of being fairly easy to launch and demanding few unfamiliar social skills. While they are not as powerful as complex strategies, they are useful and can be incorporated with little preparation.

Mastery Test

OBJECTIVE 2 **To describe the attributes of cooperative learning that contribute to student achievement in social and academic arenas and to discriminate academically productive cooperative learning strategies from less formal group activities that may not improve achievement**

A. Write short answers to the questions below:

1. List and describe the four essential features of cooperative learning.
2. For each of the three families of models of cooperative learning listed below, name a well-known advocate and describe the approach:
   a. Student Team Learning
   b. Learning Together
   c. Structural Approach

B. Scenarios: Now that you have read something about the factors that generate improved achievement in cooperative learning strategies, see if you can distinguish between strategies that have those critical factors and other group strategies. Indicate your opinion by writing next to each scenario either *CL* (for cooperative learning) or *Other.*

______ 1. During Multicultural Month, Señor Gomez visits each class in the primary grades to read aloud children's stories set in Mexico. The story he reads to the third-graders is about Elida, an eight-year-old girl who lives on a farm in a remote area of the country. When he finishes the story, he has the students sit in their regular, heterogeneous learning teams and write words and phrases describing the life of a rural Mexican child. He reviews their work and tests them individually, rewarding teams that reach preset standards of average individual growth.

______ 2. Ms. Mustard has assigned each of her three reading groups (advanced, on-grade, and remedial) to choose a single book from her list and make a class presentation about it. Each group will receive a collective grade for its report.

______ 3. Mr. Pickle's social studies class has been investigating the contributions of men and women to the development of the first thirteen American colonies. On Friday, he will give a test on where and when the men and women lived and what each contributed. He has assigned students to heterogeneous, four-member teams to review the material they have covered. After grading the tests, Mr. Pickle will post on the "Notable Historians" bulletin board the names of teams (and members) whose average gain scores are 10 or more points.

______ 4. Ms. Juniper taught a lesson on dividing decimal numbers. She assigned students to work on practice problems in heterogeneous, four-member teams. At the end of the lesson, Ms. Juniper administered the test. She rewarded teams on the basis of the team test grade average; Great Teams averaged in the 80s and Super Teams averaged in the 90s.

_____ 5. Mr. Herman has been lecturing and showing films about the structure of DNA, a major component of genes. Before he started the unit, he calculated base scores representing each student's usual achievement in his course. After he finished presenting the material, he assigned students to study together in self-selected learning teams, using a study guide. After administering the unit test in the regular way, he calculated gain scores for each student by comparing the unit test score with the base score. On a special awards bulletin board, he posted the names of the individual students who made exceptional progress.

C. True/False Statements: Indicate whether the following conditions are essential for academic productivity in cooperative learning strategies (*T* = True) or not (*F* = False). If a statement is false, revise it to make it true.

_____ 1. In the first stage of the lesson, students usually conduct independent research on the topic of study.

_____ 2. Productive learning teams are made up of members who have a lot in common, such as gender or membership in a voluntary social group.

_____ 3. Students' participation on learning teams in the classroom usually translates to more cooperative social interactions elsewhere.

_____ 4. Academic progress in cooperative learning activities is measured by having the team take a test together, to build team spirit.

_____ 5. If a student does exceptionally well on a test after working with a learning team, the teacher may recognize the team in public.

_____ 6. Team rewards are usually based on earning high grades on a test; for example, teams earn rewards by scoring an average of 90 percent.

OBJECTIVE 3

To integrate simple cooperative learning structures into more complex or extended lessons

LEARNING ACTIVITY 3

Simple Cooperative Learning Structures

Although most teachers are implementing a variety of new instructional formats made possible by advances in technology and training, many find that well-balanced programs still include on a regular basis occasions when students are all attending to the same instructional event at once—a lecture, demonstration, or film, for example. Several very simple tactics can ensure that students maintain engagement and integrate lesson content with their prior knowledge. Three are described below; Kagan and others have collected and tested ideas for many more that promote active learning, even in lesson formats that are otherwise relatively passive in nature.[18]

Think–Pair–Share (TPS) and Story Buddies

During lessons in which teachers are lecturing or demonstrating, they often ask questions to check comprehension. Addressed to a single person, such a question provides only the respondent with the opportunity to demonstrate learning. Using **Think–Pair–Share (TPS),** teachers offer every student a practice opportunity and get a broader picture of mastery.[19] Here is how it works.

1. *Plan.* Identify places in the lesson where pausing for reflection and exchange of ideas will be helpful to students.
2. *Explain strategy to students.* Before beginning the lesson, explain the Think–Pair–Share strategy: students will have partners with whom they will exchange ideas during the lesson, whenever the teacher signals them to do so.
3. *Form pairs.* Form pairs, using a simple scheme such as having students count off in duplicate—1,1; 2,2; 3,3; 4,4; and so on. If necessary, the last group may be a threesome or the teacher may take a partner.
4. *Pose question; signal "think."* At appropriate points during the lesson, pose a question and call for a short "think-time," perhaps ten seconds or more, depending on the nature of the question. During this think-time, students must remain silent, forming their own answers.
5. *Signal "share."* At a signal, usually just a word—"share"—or the sounding of a timer's bell, have students turn to their partners and exchange answers, spending a minute to explain their thinking and resolve differences, if there are any.
6. *(Optional) Have two pairs share.* After individual silent thinking and partner sharing, have two partnerships compare and discuss responses together before reconvening the whole class for discussion.
7. *Have pairs report.* At the end of share-time, ask a pair (or a pair of pairs) to report. Depending on the lesson and the time available, discuss the item further, invite other pairs to comment, or simply move along to the next lesson segment.

One variation that can enrich storytime is called Story Buddies.[20] Before the teacher begins reading or telling a story, students are assigned a partner or asked to choose someone sitting nearby. As the story unfolds, the teacher pauses briefly at points of special interest and invites buddies to engage in a responsive activity. For example, students might be asked to show their buddies the meaning of a word by assuming a certain facial expression (angry,

Think–Pair–Share (TPS)

1. Plan TPS breaks.
2. Explain strategy to students.
3. Form pairs.
4. Pose question and signal "think."
5. Signal "share."
6. (Optional) Have two pairs share.
7. Have pairs report to class.

3 by 3 by 3

1. Present content.
2. Assign task to trios.
3. Ask for questions.

anxious, delighted), silently to imagine what is coming next and quietly to share their predictions with their buddies, or jointly to create an ordered list of story events.

These activities have little structure and no assurance of accountability, but they attach students' inclination to interact socially to the academic agenda. They also multiply by a large factor the participation rate in comprehension checking. Students are encouraged to internalize the words and images, to follow the action, and to construct meaning.

3 by 3 by 3

"3 by 3 by 3,"* a slightly simpler and more flexible version of Think–Pair–Share, works especially well with older students—including adults—during otherwise conventional large-group lessons, such as lectures. It requires no prior planning or special instruction for students and has been used successfully even in college lecture classes with hundreds in attendance.

1. *Present.* Present a lesson segment—for instance, the first ten or fifteen minutes of a lecture or film—and then pause.
2. *Assign task to trios.* Have students form groups of three with those sitting nearby and *brainstorm* at least three ideas, facts, or issues that have been raised during the previous segment of the lesson. Ask them to *write down questions* they wish the teacher to answer. Give them three minutes to complete this activity.
3. *Ask for questions or continue.* After three minutes, ask for questions or simply continue the lesson, stopping again for a "3 by 3 by 3" whenever necessary or desirable.

As in TPS, the teacher may direct the group's discussion by posing a question. If time does not permit dealing with the questions raised by students in their mini-discussions, the teacher collects written questions at the end of the period and deals with them later. In the normal course of events, many questions raised early in the period are answered either by peers during the three-minute discussions or later in the lecture as the topic unfolds. Students hand in only those questions that remain unanswered at the end of the period.

By means of strategies such as TPS, Story Buddies, and 3 by 3 by 3, teachers enhance students' time on task and encourage the expectation that talking about academic work can be fun. They nurture students' continuous alertness and involvement in situations where whole-group instruction is the method of choice.

Numbered Heads Together

Numbered Heads Together makes drills and quick reviews of facts engaging and productive for the whole class.[21] It may add depth to students' participation in more complex academic work as well. Numbered Heads is easy to use when the class has existing learning teams, but it also adapts readily to situations in which teams are formed on an ad hoc basis for a single lesson. It has six

*"3 by 3 by 3" stands for 3 students, 3 ideas, 3 minutes

Numbered Heads Together

1. Plan.
2. Form teams.
3. Assign numbers.
4. Pose questions.
5. Call for "heads together."
6. Call on numbered respondent.

components: (1) planning; (2) assigning students to teams of four; (3) giving each member of each team a number from 1 to 4; (4) posing a question to the whole class; (5) having students make sure everyone knows the answer; (6) calling on a number to answer and earn points for each team while others wait in silence.

1. *Plan.* Identify appropriate practice material.
2. *Form teams.* Assign students to four-member teams, using five-member teams only as needed. In general, it is best to make teams approximately equal in the range of student ability.
3. *Assign numbers to students.* Give each student on the team a number. In classes where learning teams are already in place, a set of numbered cards may be kept in each team's materials packet; students each draw a number when playing this game. Numbers 4 and 5 on the team may trade off answering when the number 4 is drawn (as described below). After students play this game once or twice, they establish routines for numbering off. In the example at the beginning of this chapter, Isaac, José, Kate, and May use the numbers in their team packet for a variety of tasks.
4. *Pose the question.* When the teams are settled and students numbered, pose a question. This activity is best suited for low-inference, high-convergence questions, such as "How do you find the answer to 25 times 31?" or "What are the main industries of Kansas?" or "What is the shape of a DNA molecule?" or "What is the meaning of the word *exalted*?"
5. *Call for "heads together."* After the question is posed, have the teams put their heads together and talk very quietly to keep other teams from overhearing. Team members must figure out what the answer is and then make sure that each person knows it, whether it is a fact or a process, because they do not know which member's number will be called. The team point will be available only if the person whose number is called can answer accurately on the team's behalf.
6. *Call the number of respondent.* Signal for the teams to stop conferring and call a number at random. Some use a spinner to assure randomness. Have the student on each team with that number raise a hand or stand up. During this stage of the game, enforce absolute silence among teammates in order to maintain conditions that support effective coaching during the assigned "heads together" time. Depending on the circumstances and the nature of the questions, one of two respondent selection tactics can be used at this point. Either call on one of the identified team representatives at random, taking care to give approximately equal numbers of response opportunities to all teams over the course of the lesson or have all of the identified representatives—one from each team—respond simultaneously by writing the answer on a piece of scrap paper or the chalkboard, joining in choral response, or signaling in some predetermined way. The team re-

ceives a point for each correct response made by its randomly selected representative.

Some enterprising student teachers worked out a *Jeopardy*-like variation on Numbered Heads Together, using items from study guides developed for secondary students in various subjects. They created "answer grids" with columns of categories related to unit topics and rows of items of increasing difficulty with increasing point value. They reproduced these grids on either large chart paper or overhead projector transparencies, obscuring the answers with removable covers. In the class sessions scheduled for unit review, they assigned numbers to members of existing learning teams and provided each team with a supply of scrap paper and a marker.

In this version, the order of play goes like this: (1) At the beginning of the game, the teacher gives the answer to the first easy item in the first column and signals for "heads together." (2) After teams confer, the teacher uses a spinner to choose a number. Strict silence is enforced while the team member with that number writes the answer in the form of a question in marker on scrap paper. (If a team member breaks the silence, the team loses the opportunity to answer.) (3) At a signal, all respondents put markers down and reveal to the teacher what they have written. Those who offer the correct question earn the designated number of points for their teams. (4) The teacher allows one of the winners to choose the next category. Winning teams earn one "late homework" pass for each member.

Like more elaborate cooperative learning strategies that are used over a longer period, Numbered Heads Together provides an incentive for students to harness their interest in socializing to an academic agenda, to invest in the learning of their teammates, and to work hard themselves. Furthermore, most students really enjoy playing. However, it does not address some of the underlying problems that erode the motivation of less able students. If one team's Number 2 student happens to be very bright academically and another team's Number 2 has a learning disability, neither the teams nor the individuals experience equal opportunities for success in competition with each other when Number 2 is the respondent and the question is complex or the pace rapid. In addition, the quick pace of the game and necessarily short "heads together" time make it practical for students to give answers rather than explanations to each other. For these reasons, Numbered Heads Together is best used as a small part of an incentive system generally driven by rewards for making progress and achieving "personal bests."

Mastery Test

OBJECTIVE 3 **To integrate simple cooperative learning structures into more complex or extended lessons**

Listed below are ten brief descriptions of lessons that teachers have chosen to offer as whole-class, teacher-centered activities. Most of them would benefit from investing part of the lesson time in simple cooperative structures such as TPS, Story Buddies, Numbered Heads Together, or 3 by 3 by 3. For each lesson, indicate which simple structure could be used effectively or whether the whole-class format should be dropped altogether in favor of a different strategy.

1. The second-grade teacher is reading aloud *The Story of Ping* to her class of twenty-five during their regular half-hour storytime.
2. During a one-hour period, the American history class is watching a forty-five-minute segment of a film series on the Civil War to learn more about how the lives of ordinary soldiers were affected by their participation.
3. The Spanish-language teacher has introduced and explained the new vocabulary in the chapter, and today, after a quick review, he will give students practice in comprehension and use by telling them a story using the words and asking occasionally for responses to questions about content.
4. After spending several days in hands-on experiences with manipulatives, the fifth-grade teacher plans to spend a period demonstrating how to add and subtract fractions.
5. The computer specialist plans to spend one class session in the lab giving students an overview of new software, a practice that experience has taught her works most efficiently. In the next class session, they will try it out for themselves, with her help.
6. The students have worked on a variety of team and whole-class activities in their study of the mid-Atlantic states. In preparation for the district's standardized test for this unit, the teacher wants to spend a period reviewing the basic facts that everyone needs to know.
7. The fourth-grade math class will spend today working all together on computation problems, mixed operations, as a prerequisite for beginning a problem-solving unit tomorrow. The teacher wants to be able to check everyone's understanding and provide additional instruction if it seems necessary.
8. The sixth-grade class is working on essays based on family stories, and in the process of discussing drafts, the teacher has discovered that almost everyone is confused about the placement of quotation marks. He plans to spend twenty minutes of today's class giving the whole class an explanation of quotation marks and using examples paraphrased from their stories for guided practice.
9. Students have asked many questions about the history of settlement in North America, especially about the pre-colonial era, but the syllabus for this course does not allow much time for exploration of the topic. The teacher has decided to devote one class to aspects of the historiography of the pre-Columbian period, responding to students' evident interest in knowing how the stories that make up history texts are put together.

OBJECTIVE 4

To implement complex cooperative learning strategies, including Student Teams Achievement Divisions (STAD) and Jigsaw

Complex Cooperative Learning Structures

LEARNING ACTIVITY 4.1

Student Teams Achievement Divisions (STAD)

Student Teams Achievement Divisions (STAD), one of the Student Team Learning models developed by Slavin, has five basic components: forming heterogeneous learning teams; presenting content; engaging teams in practice or concept development activities; assessing individual student mastery; and calculating team improvement scores and recognizing team accomplishments.[22] Each segment involves some planning.

Student Teams Achievement Divisions (STAD)

1. Form heterogeneous learning teams.
2. Present content.
3. Have teams discuss and practice.
4. Assess individual mastery.
5. Calculate improvement scores and recognize team accomplishments.

Form Heterogeneous Learning Teams

To form learning teams, the teacher first computes the current achievement level of each student in the whole class and ranks students by achievement. A simple way to do this is to average the last three performance scores in the content area in which the team will work. This average is called the base score. For example, to form learning teams for math, one creates a base score by averaging the last three math test scores. It is important to use achievement measures that give a reliable indication of typical end-of-lesson performance. (Teachers are sometimes tempted to use pretest scores, but they are not suited for this purpose because they are intended to reflect entering ability, not final achievement.) The teacher then sorts students into the top 25 percent, the bottom 25 percent, and the middle 50 percent by achievement. Other characteristics that may affect group participation—such as race, gender, handicapping condition, or language-minority status—are then noted for each student.

Using this information, the teacher forms groups of four or five by choosing one or two students from each ability group, attending to the array of other characteristics. For example, in a class of twenty-eight, with seventeen boys and eleven girls, eight minority students, two students with physical handicaps, and one student with a learning disability, every team should have one high, one low, and two average achievers. Every team should have at least one girl, and no team should have more than two. Every team should have at least one minority student, and three teams should include a student with a disability. If the class had thirty students, an additional student of average ability should be added to each of two groups of four. For students in the intermediate grades and above, groups of four are ideal, adding a fifth only when necessary. For younger students, groups of two or three may work a little better; a foursome can be created for some projects by pairing pairs. For adults, groups as large as six may be productive.

Teams composed of members of preexisting social groups may tend to slide off-task or interact over the nonacademic issues that form the basis of their voluntary association. Teams formed for the purpose of academic work and composed of members with different perspectives and abilities are more likely to pursue the academic goals. Evidence suggests that their success in this pursuit creates new, enduring, and positive social ties outside of class.[23]

Three predictable possibilities require teachers to adapt this team formation formula. First, a class conducted in one language may include several students who share a different home language and vary in proficiency in the language of the class. It may be useful to place two of these second-language learners on a team—one with better skills in the class language to provide support for a second with more limited skills in that language.

Second, where relations between two individuals or members of different social groups are actively hostile, discretion is the better part of valor. They should not initially be assigned to the same teams. Ultimately, they will acquire the group-process skills to work together, but it is not wise to force the issue in early days.

Third, occasionally a student will simply refuse to work in a group at all. This initial resistance is not rare, and most reluctant students can be persuaded to try out teamwork by the judicious application of modest incentives. Some students need a few days or even weeks to see how well the system works with their classmates before they will join a team. Very few students hold out for long. Most teachers find that permitting a student to work alone poses no real problems. In that case, the student would *not* be entitled to rewards offered for group work but should receive the report card grade and other recognition that might otherwise be earned by solitary effort. Such students should be offered regular invitations to join teams, and if they do, the scoring formula should reflect concern with fairness to those already on the team.

Learning teams stay together for several weeks (about four to six), long enough to complete a project or a related series of tasks. They are re-formed when work or conditions change. For example, a student who has been functioning as a low achiever may gain sufficient strength to be reclassified as average or even a high achiever. Or the class may finish a unit of study, providing an opportunity for reorganization. Periodic changes in team membership give students ongoing practice in using social skills to create productive work groups and further experience in forging alliances with new, formerly unfamiliar classmates. The balance to be struck is between the benefits of such change and the benefits of remaining on a team long enough to develop insights about teammates that enable teams to make best use of diverse talents.

YOUR TURN

Forming Learning Teams

Use the grades from the class list below to calculate base scores and form a master list of students ranked by achievement. Then form three learning teams balanced according to achievement, gender, and ethnicity.

Name	Quiz 1	Quiz 2	Quiz 3	Gender	Ethnicity
Alvin	70	73	75	M	White
Andy	76	79	70	F	African-American
Carol	62	64	65	F	Other
Danielle	74	85	80	F	White
Eddy	98	94	100	M	Latino
Edgar	79	82	85	M	White
Jack	40	49	50	M	White
Mary	91	100	85	F	African-American
Sarah	100	97	100	F	Latino
Stan	82	73	80	M	Other
Tammy	91	94	85	F	White
Travis	67	64	75	M	African-American

Present Content

Using any format that ensures adequate quantity and quality, the teacher presents the content of the lesson. In a straightforward lesson about a math computation skill, for example, the teacher might explain and demonstrate the skill and lead students through whole-class guided practice. In analyzing the characters of a novel, the teacher might brainstorm with students some of the questions they will use to guide group research. In developing a learning center where groups will explore a topic, the teacher uses materials and tasks that represent the topic effectively. Usually in STAD, the presentation includes three parts: (1) the introduction, including a simple statement of lesson goal, set induction, and a brief review of prerequisite skills; (2) lesson development, which emphasizes meaning and focuses on demonstration, explanation, and informal, ongoing assessment; and (3) guided practice, requiring all students to attempt responses and calling on a random selection of students to sustain attention.[24]

STAD is *not* a self-instruction model but a model in which students help each other learn content that has been presented effectively and clearly. Whether the teacher chooses the role of lecturer, guide, critic, or coach, he or she takes responsibility for the adequacy of lesson content. The teacher provides the resources, materials, and experiences that students need to understand lesson content and begin the process of making it their own.

Have Teams Discuss and Practice

Two factors contribute to the productivity of learning teams. The first factor is the *academic task structure*. The academic tasks and the procedures for completing them are designed to involve each member actively in learning. In many forms of successful cooperative learning, team members engage in group practice, discussion of material, individual practice, and peer coaching. Students attempt practice problems together and, individually, explain their solutions, comment on each other's problem solving, and share insights about the nature of the problem and its relation to familiar issues. The second factor responsible for the productivity of learning teams is *heterogeneity*. Productive teams are microcosms of the larger class. Students with different kinds of intelligence should be represented, if possible, to enrich the discussion of content.

In STAD, teams usually stay together for four to six weeks. They often choose names, sometimes based on sports teams or animals or other positive images.

Assess Individual Student Mastery

Each student must demonstrate mastery of the lesson content in an individual assessment, without assistance from team members during testing. While some engaging practice task structures include filling out worksheets together or creating collective products, the team's goal is for each student to perform well independently. Asking for and giving coaching help to teammates is the norm; asking for and giving answers for a test is a shortcut to individual failure. Teachers' decisions about whether to reteach or move on to the next lesson, how to assign course grades, and how to interpret each student's academic achievement are based on individual test scores, performances, or portfolio items—that is, evidence of individual mastery.

The final test is based on the same material as the study questions or practice items and may take any valid and reliable form. Individual grades reflect whatever system the teacher normally uses—numbers, letters, or other indicators of achievement.

Calculate Team Improvement Scores and Recognize Team Accomplishments

Team points are based on **improvement scores** that are calculated according to a special formula designed to motivate students at all levels and reward teams for attention to the success of all members. A formula often used in STAD is:

Posttest Score (expressed as percentage)	Improvement Points
10 or more below base score	0
Within 10 points (+ or −) of base score	10
11–20 points above base score	20
>20 points above base score or a perfect score	30

Improvement points are calculated for each member of the team and then averaged for the team. Teams whose average improvement scores reach a predetermined level are eligible for rewards.

Good Team: Average team improvement score 5–10
Great Team: Average team improvement score 11–20
Super Team: Average team improvement score higher than 20

In STAD, public recognition goes to all teams that reach a preset standard of individual gain, such as earning an average individual gain score of 10. Terms such as *Super Team, Great Team,* and *Good Team* are used to convey the concept of collective achievement. The recognition is mostly ceremonial, accompanied by appropriate fanfare. Some teachers offer elaborate (photocopied) certificates, sometimes with small additional prizes—for example, Super Teams may be given a "no homework" pass, extra recess, or some other token. For the most part, however, praise and honor serve as the coin of this academic realm. Occasionally, recognition comes from the team's public display of expertise—for example, in a presentation. Outstanding individual progress may be recognized as evidence of effective teamwork as well as of individual effort. If José makes a spectacular showing in the weekly vocabulary test, his team will be honored for its contribution to his learning.

YOUR TURN

Student Team Learning

Imagine that the students in the following teams earned these scores. Use the improvement point formula above to determine which team(s) qualified for Good Team, Great Team, and Super Team awards.

Team A

	Base (%)	*Posttest* (%)
Alice	90	92
Eliz.	80	95
Keith	70	69
Peter	40	49

Team B

	Base (%)	*Posttest* (%)
Auggie	95	85
Ed	85	90
Hattie	65	70
Olivia	50	55

Team C

	Base (%)	*Posttest* (%)
Bernard	90	100
Gertrude	85	94
Jenny	65	76
Ned	55	85

Team D

	Base (%)	Posttest (%)
Collette	95	84
Fred	80	70
Zelda	70	60
Mike	50	59
Debra	40	48

Team E

	Base (%)	Posttest (%)
Laurie	95	90
Kim	70	81
Isaac	60	73
Carl	60	72
Danny	45	52

LEARNING ACTIVITY 4.2

Jigsaw

Jigsaw is designed to promote interdependence. Students participate in **expert groups** and learning teams. In expert groups, students gather information about one aspect of complex content and become experts in this aspect of content. Then they return to their learning teams and share their expertise with their teammates, each of whom has likewise become expert in a different aspect of the content. Teammates coach each other toward mastery of the complex body of information by sharing expertise. All class members are then tested on all aspects of the content. The elements of developing expertise and sharing it with teammates may involve different planning than is otherwise used.

Jigsaw has six elements:

1. *Form learning teams.* Learning teams are formed in the same way for Jigsaw as for STAD. (See above.)
2. *Form expert teams.* One member of each learning team is assigned to each heterogeneous expert group with a focus on a particular area of study within the broader lesson focus. Expert groups may have six to eight members. Because each learning team needs to have an expert in each area of study, normally there will be only four or five expert groups for any lesson.
3. *Develop expertise.* For each expert group, provide a study guide that directs attention to one aspect of the material to be covered. Then direct the group to discover the answers to the questions or problems in its own area. Two variations of Jigsaw have been developed for different work contexts. In Jigsaw I, each expert group receives only the resources that address its particular problem or issue. For example, in an instructional unit about the country of Chile, the expert group assigned to learn about Chile's waterways might be given all of the reference books, web site addresses, and audiovisual materials that focus primarily on that topic. The expert group

Jigsaw

1. Form learning teams.
2. Form expert teams with representatives from each learning team.
3. Develop expertise.
4. Share expertise in learning teams.
5. Assess individual achievement.
6. Calculate improvement scores and recognize teams.

investigating the people of Chile would use different resources to pursue its objective. This variation is most appropriate when the learning materials with the right focus are readily available or the teams have the skills and opportunities to conduct research independently. In Jigsaw II, all expert groups use the same resources but concentrate their learning on finding the information of particular interest to them. For example, the groups might all use the appropriate chapters of their geography texts and other common materials, but each group would gather only data related to its own focus of study. This variation is easier to plan and can involve fewer resources. Furthermore, although the experts are responsible for presenting only the specific information about their topic, their research involves reading through materials that cover the other topics, which provides a sound backdrop for understanding the other experts. Whichever form of Jigsaw is used, the point of the expert team discussion is to pool learning to create the best data set in response to questions posed on the study guide.

4. *Share expertise in learning teams.* Once the expert teams have cultivated their knowledge, they return to learning teams. Using their expert study guides, they present the information developed in expert team discussions. When the experts finish reporting, the learning team turns to discussing the comprehensive study guide, which calls for analysis and evaluation based on the whole data collection activity.
5. *Assess individual achievement.* As in STAD, students take individual tests on the whole unit of study and earn individual grades, which form the basis of individual and team improvement scores.
6. *Calculate team improvement scores and recognize team accomplishments.* Using a system of scoring such as the one for STAD, the teacher determines the level of team improvement and celebrates accordingly.

YOUR TURN

Jigsaw

Several general topics are listed below. For each topic, write at least four subtopics that might be suitable for study by expert groups in a Jigsaw format.

1. Geographical features of a region (specify the region)
2. Analysis of "The Legend of Sleepy Hollow" or some other story
3. Explanation of the elements of a desert community
4. Major ethnic groups in the former Soviet republics

Mastery Test

OBJECTIVE 4 **To implement complex cooperative learning strategies, including Student Teams Achievement Divisions (STAD) and Jigsaw**

A. The following are activities or characteristics of student work groups. Some are typical of groups participating in effective cooperative learning; others are irrelevant or perhaps even inimical to learning. Circle the number in front of those that support cooperative learning.

1. High achievers tell everyone how to fill in the blanks.
2. Team members ask for and get explanations.
3. Everyone in a group belongs to the same social crowd.
4. Group members talk to each other about academic tasks.
5. Group members discuss nonacademic issues of common interest during work time.
6. Minority students are grouped together.
7. Two students with hearing impairments are put in the same group to simplify communication.
8. Team scores are based on the improvement points earned by each member.
9. Average achievers are all put together.
10. Low achievers are put in a remedial-level team.
11. The grade earned on a worksheet or project completed collectively is the grade recorded for each member.
12. Students are tested individually, and individual scores form the basis for team recognition.

B. The following class list includes the average of the last three test scores (given as a percentage) in one subject for each student and information about student characteristics. Form teams whose composition will stimulate positive social interdependence and academic success.

Name	*Average (%)*	*Gender*	*Ethnicity*
Ann	87	F	White
Bud	67	M	White
Charles	86	M	Other
Doris	81	F	Other
Frank	96	M	African-American
George	56	M	White
Hattie	75	F	White
Joy	88	F	White
LaTanya	72	F	African-American
Melissa	45	F	White
Nan	65	F	African-American
Paul	85	M	Latino
Ross	90	M	White
Sam	18	M	White
William	77	M	African-American
Victor	97	M	White

C. List and describe the five elements of STAD. Illustrate briefly how each would be implemented in the subject and grade of interest to you.

D. List and describe the six elements of Jigsaw. Illustrate briefly how each would be implemented in the subject and grade of interest to you.

OBJECTIVE 5

To describe some of the process skills students use in cooperative learning and explore some ways of teaching those skills

LEARNING ACTIVITY 5

Developing Students' Social Skills

Cooperative learning strategies are strengthened by their reliance on the social aspect of learning.[25] Students like to socialize. Acquiring academic competence often involves skills better nurtured in groups, where modeling and feedback occur more frequently than in independent work. In other strategies, students are asked to sacrifice highly desired interaction with peers. In cooperative learning strategies, they are given a structure in which they can and do interact with each other productively. Lessons are organized to use the impulse to chat for developing new interaction patterns and directions and improving learning opportunities for students at all achievement levels through peer coaching. Conversation about content under these circumstances becomes a social event. Participation in the social event is, by virtue of the assigned group task, academic.

Fostering productive teamwork involves teaching prerequisite group-process skills and, in some cases, adopting new classroom management strategies. Many teachers begin by posting guidelines developed jointly with students. Such guidelines might include:

1. Work *quietly* together on team assignments.
2. Ask for and give *explanations,* not answers.
3. Listen carefully to teammates' questions.
4. Ask teammates for help if you need it.
5. Work at the pace that is right for your team.
6. Help each other stay on-task; don't talk about or work on other things.
7. Remember that the team's work is finished only when every member knows the material.
8. Ask the teacher for help only after you have asked everyone on your own team.

In classrooms of diverse students, teachers cannot assume that everyone knows how to follow such rules. In some situations, working "quietly" may mean total silence—which is seldom useful in this group-based learning activity. In others, asking for help from peers may be construed as cheating. Many students will initially feel that the teacher is the only acceptable authority in the class, and they will consequently deluge the teacher with questions about both process and content that peers could answer with equal accuracy and greater speed. Concepts of good manners and respectful behavior vary greatly among different American subgroups, and their importance relative to other social values also varies in interesting ways. Assuming that all students have the prerequisite skills and similar rules about social interactions will be counterproductive and lead to frustration and embarrassment.

Good teamwork

Looks like this:	Sounds like this:
Team members are facing each other; desks or chairs are close to each other.	Team members are using twelve-inch voices
Team members have all material ready.	Team members are asking, "Will you please explain?"
Team members are taking turns.	Team members are saying, "It's your turn now."
Every team member is working hard.	
Team members are listening to each other.	Team members are saying, "Let's see if each of us knows this."

Acquiring social skills necessary for successful group work also contributes to competence in adulthood. For example, recent analyses of the learning demands that adults face at work reveal that the skills recommended for productive participation in cooperative learning activities continue to be useful outside of school.[26] Therefore, during a lesson, time invested in teaching students how to work together may pay great dividends in both the near and the long-term future.

For these reasons, teachers will find it useful to demonstrate how to work in groups and to engage students in rehearsal, practicing to the point of mastery in the same way and with the same patient persistence they would use to teach any new, difficult content. Such practice will contribute to the creation of a classroom culture accessible to all students, not mistakenly assumed to be familiar to students whose experience has not, in fact, prepared them. Once the skills have been demonstrated and practiced, teachers nurture them by circulating among learning teams and shaping behaviors in unobtrusive ways. When they can do so without interrupting ongoing work, teachers can reinforce effective group process by publicly praising good examples. Some post charts on which they list instances of cooperative student behavior observed during a lesson.

Teamwork skills might be sorted into four categories: forming skills, functioning skills, formulating skills, and fermenting skills.[27] Kagan organizes skill categories differently, but his strategies also directly target development of useful group processes.[28]

Forming skills are essentially procedural. They involve, for example, moving quickly and quietly into team workplaces or positions and staying there, speaking softly in "twelve-inch" voices (voices audible from no more than twelve inches away), taking turns, using each other's names, and avoiding put-downs. Once these skills have been mastered, the logistical aspects of teamwork become simple and manageable. (Conversely, as long as students

Teamwork skills

Forming skills make routines flow smoothly.
Functioning skills build group cohesion and participation.
Formulating skills promote solid mastery.
Fermenting skills nurture critical thinking.

are not skilled in this area, teamwork will not go smoothly, and time will be lost in transition.)

To teach turn-taking in conversation, Kagan suggests Talking Chips.[29] In this simple tactic, each member of the group uses one object (a pen, a text) as a marker. When a member takes a turn answering or contributing to the group task, he or she puts the marker in the center of the team table and may not contribute again until all the teammates' markers are in the center. Then they all retrieve their markers and continue. This measure may be intrusive, but it can heighten students' consciousness of the importance of give-and-take in a group activity. Because a response opportunity is a learning opportunity, fair distribution of participation is essential for the success of all students. This process helps promote fairness.

Functioning skills address the routines of working, often on the affective level. Once teams are positioned to work, they use generic functioning skills to move their work forward. Restating directions, paraphrasing each other's contributions, and asking for or offering clarification are all functioning skills that build group cohesion and reinforce the need for full participation. Regular critical assessment of the team's group process in these areas is a key feature of learning together.

A variation of Talking Chips, called Colored Chips, promotes discussion of group process.[30] Each team member is given a set of colored chips or markers, one color per person. As the discussion continues, members put a chip in for each contribution. When the time for discussion ends, teammates count the chips in the center and evaluate whether the discussion involved each fairly. If students decide participation was inequitable, they discuss how to improve it in future discussions. Several other Kagan "chip games" promote improvement in the quality of interpersonal content in task-related discourse. For instance, Affirmation Chips are distributed to all students before a team discussion. Participants deposit one in the center pile each time they make a statement that recognizes how hard a teammate is trying. Gambit Chips remind students how to start statements that have particular purposes. For example, to begin a statement intended to paraphrase a teammate, a student might use the phrase, "Tell me if I have it right . . ."—which is printed on the paraphrase Gambit Chip. The Gambit Chip for practicing feedback might have written on it: "What I like about your idea is . . ." Having the physical object with words written on it can help ensure that every student feels called on to exercise the skill during a particular activity. The need for chips and gambits fades as functioning skills become parts of students' daily repertoires.

Formulating skills help students probe each other's mastery of lesson content. They are often cultivated by assigning roles to students. For example, one student might be the summarizer, another the checker, a third the explainer. Alternatively, skills can be practiced by all participants, after appropriate instruction. The purpose of formulating skills is to ensure that students dig deeply into the content of their lesson and engage in different kinds of mental processing to assist comprehension, application, and retention of learning. Using a strategy such as Kagan's Pairs Check is one way to stimulate growth in formulating skills. In Pairs Check, students on teams divide into pairs to complete a practice exercise. They begin by doing one item each, with the first student working while the second student watches. The first student finishes and explains to his or her partner what has been done. If they agree that the answer is correct, the partner does the next item while the first student watches, listens, and discusses. At this point, they consult with the other pair on their team to see if they agree on the process and the answer. If not, they discuss the differences until they find a solution. Then they continue. During this process, students also practice praising each other's progress.

Fermenting skills challenge students to extend and elaborate their thinking, to analyze and synthesize, and to evaluate. These skills include providing critical or challenging feedback in ways that do not offend the originator of a plan, product, or idea; probing for further information; generalizing to new settings or applications; and synthesizing different elements of information.

The purpose of activities such as these is to ensure that every student has familiarity with and the inclination to use appropriate group-process skills during team learning periods. However, from the first time teachers use cooperative learning strategies, they must balance attention to lesson content with attention to group-process skills. In properly functioning team learning activities, students learn how shared norms of civility can contribute to attaining a worthy end; in school, the worthy end is academic. If cooperative learning activities focus too much on group process, students may benefit in the social skills arena but forfeit the academic gains they have a right to demand from schoolwork. On the other hand, if they do not receive instruction in how to work cooperatively, their squabbling may itself impede access to substantive learning opportunities.

Teaching students how to function effectively in groups is a key factor in cooperative learning, but teachers must also cultivate their own supportive behaviors. In some cases teaching skills useful in cooperative learning are quite different from the behaviors that work well in more directed lesson activities. For example, after students have been dispatched to work on teams, teachers should respect their need for concentration and keep whole-class communications to an absolute minimum. When conferring with individual teams, teachers should speak in voices audible only to the team. When responding to questions, teachers should model coaching and explaining whenever appropriate.

For many teachers, the hardest new skill to practice when students are engaged in team activities is turning individual student questions back to the team instead of answering them immediately. Once the initial presentation of new material in a lesson is complete, answering questions posed by other students is one way that students can improve understanding and retention. Furthermore, once directions have been given, students are usually capable of repeating them for peers. It is amazing how many teachers reinforce student inattention during directions by their willingness to repeat directions over and over, despite having given them quite clearly the first time. When students are required to ask their peers for replays of directions, the peers are quick to note whether the query stems from poor attention and, if so, to comment on the need for improvement.

By creating lesson structures that rely on students to manage independent practice and engage them in meaningful, substantively valuable interactions with each other about lesson content, teachers promote productive effort among students at every ability level. When students work hard and skillfully in the socially appealing task structures of cooperative learning, they improve achievement in basic skills, content, and critical thinking. This positive outcome reinforces a principle underlying most human enterprises: hard work on relevant tasks produces better outcomes.

Mastery Test

OBJECTIVE 5 **To describe some of the process skills students use in cooperative learning and explore some ways of teaching those skills**

A. Students' Social Skills:

1. List and describe four kinds of process skills that can be taught directly in the context of cooperative learning lessons and give an example of how to teach one of each.
2. Explain why interpersonal and process skills must be taught directly.

B. Teacher Types: Each of the imaginary teachers below has a habit that seems helpful when he or she is using teacher-centered instructional methods. Explain how each teacher should adjust his or her behavior to make a cooperative learning lesson format more effective.

1. Ms. Butler, having trained as an opera singer before becoming a teacher, can project her voice so well that she can get the whole class's attention no matter how noisily engaged they are in a project.
2. Mr. O'Hara prides himself on his patience. He willingly answers questions about task directions until every student in the room is able to get to work. Although his directions are always clear from the beginning, he sometimes spends half of the period repeating himself.
3. Ms. Murphy understands that Joey's reticence makes it hard for him to answer a question in front of the class, so she seldom calls on him for answers or comments.
4. Mr. Rogers is famous in his school for having the quietest, most orderly classroom. During language arts, you can hear a pin drop while his students are working on their essays or writing answers to questions about a novel they have just read.

OBJECTIVE 6

To examine how the physical, organizational, and instructional environments support effective use of cooperative learning strategies

LEARNING ACTIVITY 6

Managing Effectively to Support Cooperative Learning

Some typical teaching activities look easy from the outside. For instance, giving a lecture and administering a test appear deceptively simple—the hard parts happen in private, as preparation. Cooperative learning, however, is a complex activity that looks daunting from the start. One learns eventually that developing the perfect lecture or test is also quite a complex undertaking, but one sees at the very beginning that cooperative learning strategies require careful planning. Those who use cooperative learning routinely discover in the long term that their early investment of time pays off—the students soon become active learners, applying their own energy to lessons and moving forward with their own momentum. On the other hand, in teacher-centered strategies, the teacher is often doing the lion's share of the work, pulling the class along; students only have to listen, take notes, and fill in blanks. To be successful in adding cooperative learning strategies to their professional repertoires, teachers must address the physical, organizational, and instructional aspects of environment that affect implementation.

Physical Environment

A classroom's physical arrangements can either support easy use of learning teams or get in the way. The ideal arrangement includes several elements. First, desks, chairs, or tables organize students into groups of four (or five). Students are always sitting in teams, whether or not a given lesson calls for teamwork. In most cases, desks or chairs can be adjusted to face the front when the activity requires it, and individual work can be completed as easily with students seated in clusters as otherwise. Teachers often place movable desks in rows facing front to reduce distractions, but as a practical matter, in the history of education, this tactic has by itself never been able to extinguish all student chatter. Furthermore, seeing students sitting in rows encourages teachers to overuse methods that limit students to an audience role. Seeing the students arranged in teams will spontaneously prompt teachers more often to use strategies like TPS, Numbered Heads Together, or less formal discussion options to promote students' reflection on and application of new ideas, as the content and pace of a lesson permit.

Second, the room should have areas designated for displays and supplies. An awards display site suitable for the grade level of the students should be prominent. If it is a room used by more than one class, there should be enough space for each. Team supplies—team packets, pennants, work-in-progress—and other materials should be easily available. If the room has general use areas, such as a library corner, policies should establish how they may be used during team time.

Third, the arrangements for desks, supplies, and teamwork should minimize the class's impact on others sharing open-space areas or in immediately adjacent rooms. With thoughtfully designed physical arrangements, cooperative learning strategies have been used successfully even in schools where large open spaces serve several classes. The trick is to use area rugs, furniture, floor space, and tightly clustered workgroups to keep noise levels low.

Finally, if the new ways of using furniture, space, or supplies result in different demands on custodial staff, teachers should alert them to the change and find out how to facilitate reasonable maintenance. For instance, diligent custodians might routinely straighten the desks back into rows each night, thinking it their responsibility, if they are not advised of the change. New learning tasks might at first cause undue messiness, which students must learn to manage. Awarding team bonus points for neatness at the end of the day is one useful approach. Teachers often report that more student activity results in more mess—and that sometimes results in active resistance from those who share or clean the space used for teamwork. It is important to keep in mind that cooperative learning pays off generously in student achievement, so solving the problem of more mess should not involve decreasing the use of cooperative learning.

Organizational Environment

Trial and error have shown teachers many ways to gain the support of coworkers as they begin implementing cooperative learning strategies. Starting to learn and apply these methods with a colleague has been a real asset to adoption. Peers can plan together, share resources, critique new ideas, observe each other, and generally provide the moral support to help each other through the first tentative steps.

Teachers report that principals and other supervisors can offer important assistance. Supervisors who have participated in cooperative learning training can, of course, provide insightful feedback on new plans and practices. Those who have little background in this area will need a briefing so they will know what to expect if they drop in to visit. They can be offered a small observation "assignment" for their next planned visit. For example, they can take verbatim data on a team discussion or document the participation of mainstreamed special education or language-minority students in teamwork. Such data are difficult for a teacher to collect, and they are very useful for reflecting on a lesson. Supervisors who have not been alerted to the new practices may mistake the lively buzz of conversation in a properly functioning team activity for off-task chatting. Taking a proactive stance in explaining how the lesson is supposed to work and soliciting supervisors' input can promote their productive participation in implementation.

In a similar fashion, colleagues who are unfamiliar with cooperative learning strategies may be curious about what is happening in a newly cooperative classroom. Definitions of acceptable noise levels may have to be renegotiated. Explanations of the incentive value of team scoring may need to be offered. Some teachers will have the misconception that team points are substitutes for individual achievement; qualms of those who have such misconceptions can often be relieved by giving them the right information. Field experience has already taught every first-year teacher that good practicing teachers do not all agree on what belongs in a complete professional repertoire. Some features of cooperative learning—the hum of teamwork is the most notorious—raise questions that are usually resolved in early conversations with colleagues. Converts are most often won by the evidence of the effectiveness of cooperative learning strategies in achieving academic and social goals with every student.

Teachers often inform parents when they begin using cooperative learning to enlist their support and understanding. Parents of the highest and lowest achievers may have questions. Bright students' parents worry that cooperative learning strategies will make their children the workhorse of the team and that working with a group of less able students will hold their children back. Teachers need to explain how the scoring system requires every child to work hard to earn team points and to review the data that show how much the brightest students gain in real achievement in such settings. Less able students' parents worry that their children will not be able to keep up. While limited ability may indeed result in more modest achievement, the record is clear that in cooperative learning groups less able students gain significantly. Their individual achievement rises because they are working harder. They are unlikely to become the academic stars of the class, but they will learn more than they learned before. Furthermore, they gain in popularity and acceptance because their progress (not their ultimate achievement level) contributes to the team score. Some of the structures of cooperative learning are unfamiliar to parents, and they will appreciate an explanation. Because positive outcomes are evident very soon after implementation begins and so many students eventually earn higher grades based on better performance, parents can become champions of the new strategy. Parent volunteers, appropriately oriented to the principles of cooperative learning, can be of great help in managing materials and supporting productive teamwork during lessons.

Instructional Environment

Whatever complex or simple cooperative learning strategy a teacher is using in a particular lesson, productivity will be increased if students share common expectations about how to proceed. The environment created by general social and behavioral expectations influences instruction. As discussed earlier, teaching prerequisite skills is an important step in successful use of cooperative activities. In addition to teaching such things as how to talk in an "inside" voice that only one's group can hear or how to give an explanation instead of an answer, preparation may include team-building exercises, such as those recommended by Kagan.[31]

To sustain and nurture a productive instructional environment, teachers must help students remain aware of how their civility contributes to their academic progress, creating social and academic achievements that are intrinsically satisfying. A good assignment to launch cooperative learning is choosing a team name. Even high school and adult students enjoy this task. Teams who will work together for several weeks may want to create a team poster or pennant that "flies" at their workplace whenever they are working together. Some teachers use part of the poster for ad hoc rewards such as stickers earned for winning a game of Numbered Heads Together or for demonstrating exemplary skill in group process. Team posters can also serve as displays for weekly team scores. (The actual student grades should not be displayed, but the improvement points, based on gains, could be.)

Teachers have found that two management practices are particularly helpful in implementing cooperative learning strategies. The first is using what this chapter has called **team packets,** which could be large envelopes, boxes, or file folders. The team packet serves many purposes: Teachers can collect and return homework papers by means of the packet, which is handled by the team's materials manager. Packets can hold teams' works-in-progress, practice exercises, score sheet, pennant, number cards for Numbered Heads Together, and any other handouts or supplies that the teacher can place in the packet before class; this makes for easy distribution by team members.

The second is adopting a **zero-noise signal,** which is any signal that can be perceived by the whole class. Teachers use this signal on the very rare occasions when they must interrupt teams' deliberations to make an announcement of general interest, restore more reasonable noise levels, or for some other reason have everyone's attention. The signal may be as simple as raising one hand while catching the eye of the nearest team, each member of which then silently raises a hand until the whole class has noticed and is waiting in silence. Some teachers find that flicking the lights or ringing a small bell works. The most important aspect of this signal is that it must work almost instantly in order to reduce teams' downtime. Rehearsing purposefully with a stopwatch and setting class goals for speedy compliance help most classes learn to respond to the signal effectively. However, teachers should not overuse the signal; working teams ought not be disturbed. Students will not be inclined to take their own teamwork seriously if the teacher is continuously interrupting them.

Mastery Test

OBJECTIVE 6 **To examine how the physical, organizational, and instructional environments support effective use of cooperative learning strategies**

In the interest of refreshing his professional repertoire, Mr. Wilt attended a three-day workshop on cooperative learning strategies at the staff development center. He is now eager to put his new knowledge into practice. He is working with Ms. Deyo, his school's master teacher, to plan for the first lessons and reflect on his practice in the first few months. He has prepared a list of problems that require some action and will discuss them with Ms. Deyo after school today. Read the list below and propose solutions consistent with the recommendations in Learning Activity 6.

1. The individual student tables in his classroom have been arranged in rows since time immemorial.
2. Ms. Jones, the custodian, has been tidying the desks into rows after school since time immemorial.
3. Neither the principal nor the grade-level lead teacher have ever used (or apparently heard of) cooperative learning. The principal often comes in for informal visits.
4. Mr. Zack, across the hall, runs a very orderly and silent classroom and already thinks Mr. Wilt is an easy grader.
5. Alison's mother and father, successful attorneys with a civil law practice, are grooming her for a fast-track Ph.D. program in an Ivy League school. They fret constantly about perceived slights to her considerable intellectual gifts.
6. Mr. Wilt's students are sometimes uneasy about taking leadership roles in academic work; some appear unable to participate productively in group work.

OBJECTIVE 7

To explore some of the schoolwide dimensions of classroom use of cooperative learning

LEARNING ACTIVITY 7

Schoolwide Dimensions of Using Cooperative Learning

As educational research expands its view of the impacts of new programs and practices, new ways of characterizing and measuring progress are being discovered. It may be too early to say with any certainty that, as a result of more widespread use of cooperative learning, dramatic improvements have occurred in addition to those of individual student learning. However, the evidence of improvement is promising in three important dimensions of schooling. First, schoolwide programs that apply cooperative learning strategies across the curriculum have begun to document substantial gains in student achievement.[32] Second, greater use of cooperative learning is being perceived as a sturdy and empowering context for peer mediation and conflict resolution among students.[33] Third, adoption of cooperative learning strategies in the classroom is providing a nurturing and stimulating context for the professional collaboration that underlies successful school reform.[34]

Cooperative Schools

After a continuous stream of research on cooperative learning, adding incrementally over the years to the initial elements of Student Team Learning, the team at the Johns Hopkins University Research Center has developed Success for All (SFA) and Roots and Wings.[35] Both are schoolwide instructional models most often adopted by schools with a high percentage of students at risk of school failure. Success for All focuses on reading, writing, and language arts from kindergarten through grade 6. During an extended reading and language arts block scheduled every day, the whole school devotes itself to this instruction. Children are assigned to small reading groups, homogeneous in reading achievement, with enriched curriculum opportunities from storytelling and decoding to writing workshops and novel studies.

Students use teamwork and partner reading from the very earliest stages of literacy development to make their lessons productive. In addition, carrying out the cooperative theme, the most challenged students receive individual tutoring from a teacher whose goal is to help them succeed in the regular reading program. Students with nonacademic problems are the focus of the work of a family support team, composed of teachers and specialists who provide extra help to families to ensure student success. In Success for All, all teachers embrace the same approach, spend extra time in professional development, and evaluate student growth with a view to continuous improvement. As a result, even the students most at risk gain from one-quarter to one full grade equivalent more than their peers in control groups each year they participate. The results are equally impressive for students in the Spanish/English bilingual and the English as a Second Language groups.

Roots and Wings extends the original SFA program to include math, social studies, and science. As a whole-school model, it was initially funded by the New American Schools project; now it is being disseminated nationally. Strong positive effects have been measured on standardized tests, including those that are performance based and involve complex assessment activities.

These two programs address academic learning with strong and aggressive strategies based on cooperative learning. Their comprehensive and ambitious agenda appears to be generating significantly improved learning for the participating students and changing the way whole faculties approach teaching.

Cooperative Learning as a Context for Violence Prevention

Among the traits regularly characterized as essential to school effectiveness is maintenance of a "safe and orderly environment." Recent reviews indicate that despite a proliferation of violence-prevention programs, the incidence of violence has gone up in schools.[36] This finding seems to arise from two causes. First, most programs define *prevention* narrowly—as squashing the event—and therefore focus on a narrow range of strategies. Second, programs target a broad segment of the population for training, thus having little impact on the fairly small segment whose behavior is most threatening. Johnson and Johnson's alternative prescription is to create a schoolwide cooperative context in which peer mediation and conflict resolution are natural extensions of the usual ways of working together.[37] Then special strategies could be used with the few students whose misbehavior accounts for the most problems.

Building on the skills students learn in cooperative lessons, schools aiming to improve safety should take a six-part approach that extends and enriches the usual violence-prevention curriculum. (1) They should take the role of community service center, doing what they can to help students and their families get the support they need. (2) They should create a cooperative environment that includes widespread use of cooperative learning across the curriculum. (3) They should nurture longer-term relationships between teachers and students. For example, they should extend the time teachers and students spend together by creating schools-within-schools, keeping students with the same teacher for more than one grade, and/or using block schedules that reduce the number of different students teachers see in a day. (4) They should offer an array of extracurricular activities and host community-sponsored clubs and events to reduce the amount of out-of-school time in situations where such time is seldom spent productively or safely. (5) They should establish partnerships with members of the community who can help promote peaceful life choices through such things as mentoring and internships. (6) They should offer mediation and violence-prevention lessons to all students, in a curriculum of increasing complexity.

If a student experiences school as a place where only the "best" person wins—and it's never oneself—and the social valuing that comes with success is routinely awarded to others whose gifts make it easier for them to shine, then the self-respect and discipline required to resist the temptation to violence may be in short supply. Furthermore, the willingness to search for a solution to conflict that all participants can appreciate and the creativity to invent such a solution may not be cultivated in a competitive academic arena. If daily learning routines support the habit of cooperation and the confidence that gives rise to creativity, students are arguably in a better position to view themselves as problem solvers and peacemakers.

Collaborating in School Reform

Finally, cooperation seems to be the key concept in most current approaches to school reform. The movements toward total quality management (TQM) and facilitative leadership rely on developing a collegial approach to reach high levels of proficiency in achieving an organization's mission. Improved training, shared leadership, lowered tolerance for failure, and a commitment to excellence are among the elements that produce powerful collaboration. Continuous improvement is the basis of team rewards—in the classroom and on the faculty. Helping each other adopt and adapt ideas presented in shared professional development activities strengthens the professional culture that is the foundation for faculty growth. Learning together is how the modern school faculty meets the demands of society and the needs of the students. Learning together is not just for kids.

OBSERVATION WORKSHEET
Cooperative Learning

This observation focuses on (1) how the teacher uses cooperative learning strategies to promote student engagement with and mastery of lesson goals and (2) how the organization of the room supports such activities.

Directions: Do not use actual names of schools, teachers, administrators, or students when using this worksheet.

Observer's Name: ____________________

Date: ____________________

Grade Level: ____________________

Subject: ____________________

Class Size: ____________________

Background Information: Give a brief general description of the school's social, economic, and ethnic makeup.

____

____

What to Record: Select a classroom from grades K–12, preferably one in which the teacher frequently uses some form of cooperative learning. Be certain you have discussed your objective with the teacher in advance and have confirmed that the class will be engaged in activities that relate to your assignment.

Orientation to the Lesson

In the preliminary conference with the teacher, find out:

- Which cooperative learning strategies or complex structures are used
- How (if at all) social and procedural skills are taught and reinforced
- How the teacher forms learning teams
- How long learning teams stay together
- What forms of recognition are used (e.g., points, tokens, certificates)
- What the teacher views as the benefits and costs of cooperative learning

Lesson Observation

As you watch the lesson, describe the following:

- The apparent (or stated) lesson objective
- The teacher's role in presenting lesson content
- The academic task—What exactly are students supposed to do? How are they to help each other?
- The things students say to each other about their work (e.g., prompts, corrections)
- The social skills required to perform the work together
- The things the teacher does during team learning time
- How the arrangement of furniture and materials supports or detracts from the lesson format
- How this kind of student activity seems likely to impact on nearby classes

Postlesson Discussion

As soon as possible after the observation, ask the teacher to explain any part of the lesson that did not occur as usual or as planned.

Reflections on Your Observation:

1. To what extent was what you observed consistent with the models for cooperative learning recommended in this chapter?

____

____

____

2. On the day that you visited, did the classroom environment and activities appear to be "normal" or were they modified to accommodate your visit?

____

____

____

3. Identify and discuss any discrepancies between what you observed the teacher doing and the suggestions for strategies and activities advocated in the chapter.

____

____

____

4. If other students had the same assignment, organize in small groups and compare notes with fellow students to evaluate what you observed.

____

____

____

Mastery Test 7

OBJECTIVE 7 **To explore some of the schoolwide dimensions of classroom use of cooperative learning**

Indicate whether the following statements are true (*T*) or false (*F*). Rewrite the false statements to make them true.

_____ 1. Success for All and Roots and Wings are too new to have demonstrated achievement outcomes for participating students.

_____ 2. Having a safe and orderly environment is essential to school effectiveness.

_____ 3. Violence-prevention programs work best if they target their efforts narrowly.

_____ 4. Supporting a wide range of family services is one way to reduce violence in schools.

_____ 5. Extracurricular activities help keep students safe.

_____ 6. Students used to cooperative learning have a harder time than others in conflict resolution.

_____ 7. Cooperative learning in particular and collaboration in general are not just for kids.

NOTES

1. K. Paterson, *The Sign of the Chrysanthemum* (New York: Harper & Row, 1973).
2. R. E. Slavin, *Cooperative Learning: Theory, Research, and Practice* (Englewood Cliffs, N.J.: Prentice-Hall, 1990).
3. D. W. Johnson and R. Johnson, *Cooperation and Competition: Theory and Research* (Edina, Minn.: Interaction Book Company, 1989); D. W. Johnson, R. Johnson, and M. Stanne, "Cooperative Learning Methods: A Meta-Analysis." www.clcrc.com (May 2000).
4. S. Ravenscroft, F. Buckless, G. McCombs, and G. Zuckerman, "Incentives in Student Team Learning: An Experiment in Cooperative Group Learning," *Issues in Accounting Education* 10, no. 1 (Spring 1995):97–110.
5. R. Macdonald and A. Bykerk-Kauffman, eds., "Collaborative and Cooperative Activities as Tools for Teaching and Learning Geology" [theme issue], *Journal of Geology Education* 43, no. 4 (September 1995).
6. J. Cooper, S. Prescott, L. Cook, L. Smith, R. Mueck, and J. Cuseo, *Cooperative Learning and College Instruction: Effective Use of Student Learning Teams* (Carson, Calif.: California State University Foundation on Behalf of the California State University Institute for Teaching and Learning, 1990).
7. D. W. Johnson, R. Johnson, and E. Holubec, *The New Circles of Learning: Cooperation in the Classroom and School* (Alexandria, Va.: Association for Supervision and Curriculum Development, 1994); N. M. Ares, "Students' Appropriation of Power and Roles in a Hierarchical Cooperative Learning System." (Paper presented at the annual meeting of the American Educational Research Association, Seattle, April 2000).
8. *Ibid.*
9. Slavin, *op. cit.*
10. *Ibid.*
11. Johnson, Johnson, and Holubec, *op. cit.*
12. N. Webb, "Small Group Problem-Solving: Peer Interaction and Learning" (Paper delivered at the annual meeting of the American Educational Research Association, New Orleans, April 1988).
13. H. Gardner, *Multiple Intelligences: The Theory in Practice* (New York: Basic Books, 1993); K. Nicholson-Nelson, *Developing Students' Multiple Intelligences* (New York: Scholastic Professional Books, 1998).
14. Slavin, *op. cit.*
15. D. W. Johnson, R. Johnson, and E. Holubec. *Cooperative Learning in the Classroom* (Alexandria, Va.: Association for Supervision and Curriculum Development, 1994).
16. Slavin, *op. cit.*
17. S. Kagan, *Cooperative Learning* (San Clemente, Calif.: Kagan Cooperative Learning, 1994).
18. *Ibid.*
19. F. Lyman, "Think–Pair–Share, Thinktrix, Thinklinks, and Weird Facts: An Interactive System for Cooperative Learning," in *Enhancing Thinking Through Cooperative Learning,* ed. N. Davidson and T. Worsham (New York: Teachers College Press, 1992).
20. L. Baloche and T. Platt, "Sprouting Magic Beans: Exploring Literature Through Creative Questioning and Cooperative Learning," *Language Arts* 70, no. 4 (April 1993):264–271.
21. Kagan, *op. cit.* (Numbered Heads Together is credited by the author to Russ Frank, a teacher in Diamond Bar, Calif.)
22. Slavin, *op. cit.*
23. R. E. Slavin, "Effects of Biracial Learning Teams on Cross-Racial Friendships," *Journal of Educational Psychology* 71 (1979):381–387.
24. Slavin, *op. cit., Cooperative Learning.*
25. L. Corno, "Teaching and Self-Regulated Learning," in *Talks to Teachers,* ed. D. C. Berliner and B. V. Rosenshine (New York: Random House, 1987); J. Trimbur, "Collaborative Learning and Teaching Writing," in *Perspectives on Research on Scholarship in Composition,* ed. B. W. McClelland and T. R. Donovan (New York: Modern Languages Association, 1985).
26. L. Resnick, "Learning in School and Out," *Educational Researcher* 16, no. 9 (December 1987):14–20.
27. Johnson, Johnson, and Holubec, *op. cit. New Circles of Learning.*
28. Kagan, *op. cit.*
29. *Ibid.*
30. *Ibid.*
31. *Ibid.*
32. R. E. Slavin and O. S. Fashola, *Show Me the Evidence: Proven and Promising Programs for America's Schools* (Newbury Park, Calif.: Corwin, 1998).
33. Johnson and Johnson, D. W. Johnson, and R. Johnson, *Reducing School Violence Through Conflict Resolution Training* (Alexandria, Va.: Association for Supervision and Curriculum Development, 1995); *op. cit., Reducing School Violence;* D. W. Johnson and R. Johnson, "Why Violence Prevention Programs Don't Work—And What Does," *Educational Leadership* 52, no. 5 (February 1995):63–68; D. W. Johnson and R. Johnson, "Reducing School Violence Through Conflict Resolution Training," *Bulletin of the NASSP* 80, no. 579 (April 1996):11–18.
34. J. Bonstingl, *Schools of Quality* (Alexandria, Va.: Association for Supervision and Curriculum Development, 1992); *How We Are Changing Schools Collaboratively* (New York: Impact II, The Teachers' Network, 1995). L. Lezotte, *Total Quality Effective School* (Okemos, Mich.: Effective Schools Products, 1992); A. Lieberman, ed., *Building a Professional Culture in Schools* (New York: Teachers College Press, 1988).
35. Slavin and Fashola, *op. cit.*
36. Johnson and Johnson, *op. cit., Reducing School Violence.*
37. Johnson and Johnson, *op. cit., Reducing School Violence.*

ADDITIONAL RESOURCES

Readings

Anderson, R., and K. Humphrey. *61 Cooperative Learning Activities for Computer Classrooms.* Portland, Maine: J. Weston Walch, 1996.

Johnson, D. W., R. Johnson, and E. Holubec. *Cooperative Learning in the Classroom.* Alexandria, Va.: Association for Supervision and Curriculum Development, 1994.

Johnson, D. W., R. Johnson, and E. Holubec. *The New Circles of Learning: Cooperation in the Classroom and School.* Alexandria, Va.: Association for Supervision and Curriculum Development, 1994.

Kagan, S. *Cooperative Learning.* San Clemente, Calif.: Kagan Cooperative Learning, 1994.

Slavin, R. E. *Cooperative Learning: Theory, Research, and Practice.* Englewood Cliffs, N.J.: Prentice-Hall, 1990.

Slavin, R. E., and O. S. Fashola. *Show Me the Evidence: Proven and Promising Programs for America's Schools.* Newbury Park, Calif.: Corwin, 1998.

Web Sites

The Jigsaw Classroom: http://www.jigsaw.org
Developed by Elliot Aronson and the Social Psychology Network, this site contains "how-to" explanations, research summaries, implementation tips, and related links.

The Cooperative Learning Network: http://sheridanc.on.ca/coop_lrn.htm
Sponsored by Sheridan College, this site contains descriptions of cooperative learning in postsecondary schools, on-line discussions, professional development opportunities, and related links.

The Cooperative Learning Center (CLC) at the University of Minnesota: http://www.cooplearn.org
Provided by the CLC, this site contains descriptions of center work; essays and research reports by Johnson and Johnson and others; book and supply catalogues.

Cooperative Learning Site of the California Department of Education (CDE): http://www.cde.ca.gov/iasa/cooplrng2.html
Developed by the CDE, this site focuses on promoting the academic success of diverse learners, especially those from low-income or minority-language backgrounds. It contains descriptions of key elements and applications that stimulate growth in language proficiency.

Cooperative Learning Site in the "Tool Room" of New Horizons for Learning: http://www.newhorizons.org/trm_cooplrn.html
This site contains brief descriptions of the basic features of cooperative learning and links to related sites.

10

Assessment

Terry D. TenBrink

OBJECTIVE 1 **To define *evaluation* and to describe each of the four stages in the assessment process**

OBJECTIVE 2 **To select appropriate information-gathering strategies when seeking to make classroom assessments**

OBJECTIVE 3 **To write effective test items for assessing achievement**

OBJECTIVE 4 **To develop rubrics (including checklists and rating scales) for evaluating student products and performances**

OBJECTIVE 5 **To use portfolios to assess ongoing performance and progress**

OBJECTIVE 6 **To describe how to use information to evaluate; that is, to grade, to judge student progress, and to judge changes in student attitudes**

OBJECTIVE 7 **To describe how to use assessment data to help students learn more effectively**

OBJECTIVE 8 **To select and use standardized instruments**

Educational evaluation is useful only if it helps the educator (administrator, teacher, student) make sound educational judgments and decisions. In this chapter, you will learn about some of the basic principles of evaluation as applied to classroom problems. This chapter can be helpful when you are faced with the task of evaluating your students. I would encourage you, however, to go beyond this introductory level of understanding. Purchase a basic text on classroom evaluation techniques. Practice your test-writing skills whenever possible. Learn from your mistakes as you begin to evaluate your own students, and learn to use evaluation as a necessary and important teacher tool. Use evaluation to help you teach better and to help your students learn better.

OBJECTIVE 1

To define *evaluation* and to describe each of the four stages in the assessment process

LEARNING ACTIVITY 1

In recent years, educators have begun replacing the word **evaluation** with the word **assessment.** Although the two terms basically refer to the same process, the newer term is being used in an attempt to expand our thinking about the role of evaluation. Assessment strategies include far more than formal testing, which has historically been the emphasis in textbooks on measurement and evaluation. Such procedures are finally being recognized as an integral part of the teaching process. Generally, assessment techniques that are authentic provide us with information about behaviors, skills, ideas, attitudes, and so on that are "real world." What we try to measure with authentic assessments are those things that represent skills and so on that are useful in everyday living and important in helping students reach the next level of skill in a given subject. Furthermore, authentic assessment tools seek to obtain information under conditions that are as close as possible to the real-world use of the information or skills being assessed. Assessment tools that are most likely to provide authentic assessment information include rubrics, checklists, rating scales, portfolios, and such like. In this chapter, we will discuss these authentic assessment tools as well as more formal, yet still valuable, tools such as tests and questionnaires. Nevertheless, at the root of all assessment procedures is the act of evaluating.

Stated most simply, to evaluate is to place a value upon—to judge. Forming a judgment is not an independent action. To judge, one must have information. The act of judging depends on this prerequisite act of obtaining information. The act of forming a judgment is itself prerequisite to an action one step further along: decision making. So *evaluation,* the process of forming judgments, depends on information gathering and leads to decision making. Picture it this way:

obtaining information	→	forming judgments	→	making decisions

Or this way:

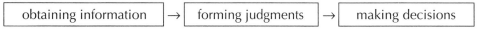

> *Evaluation* is the process of obtaining information and using it to form judgments that, in turn, are used in decision making.

This definition clearly specifies the interrelationships among the various stages in the evaluation process, yet it also clearly indicates the centrality of forming judgments. If you have not formed a judgment, you have not evaluated.

It is important for you to understand the *total* evaluation process. So let's expand this definition. So far, it is obvious that evaluation involves at least three stages: obtaining information, forming judgments, and using those judgments in decision making. By adding a preparation stage and enlarging a bit on the last stage, we come up with the following four stages:

The assessment process

Stage 1: Preparing for assessment
Stage 2: Obtaining needed information
Stage 3: Forming judgments
Stage 4: Using judgments in making decisions and preparing reports

Let's look at a rather typical teaching–learning situation. Notice how this teacher goes through these four stages as she attempts to make her instruction more effective.

Stage 1. Preparing for Assessment. Bonnie, a third-grade teacher, has become concerned about Billy. He seems to be having trouble keeping up in reading. Bonnie wonders how long he will be able to function within the reading group he is in. She wonders whether or not she should move him to a slower group. Perhaps there is something she can do to help—some extra work, for example, or some extra attention. She decides she needs more information before she can accurately judge Billy's level of achievement in reading. After determining the kind of information she needs (for example, information about the kind of errors made when reading orally, Billy's use of various word attack skills, Billy's interests), Bonnie determines when and how to obtain that information.

Stage 2. Obtaining Needed Information. Over a period of several days Bonnie obtains a great deal of information about Billy. She gives him a standardized reading test, listens to him read orally, carefully records the errors he makes, and observes him throughout the day, watching for patterns of behavior that might indicate particular attitudes toward various subjects.

Stage 3. Forming Judgments. After analyzing all the information she has obtained, Bonnie comes to the following conclusions:

Billy is not capable of reading material written at a third-grade level.

Billy reads comfortably only that material written on a second-grade level or lower.

Billy's primary weakness lies in the area of word attack skills.

Billy does not have a comprehension problem. He understands what is read to him.

Billy likes the children in his reading group.

Billy enjoys the stories in the third-grade reader.

Stage 4. Using Judgments in Making Decisions and Preparing Reports. On the basis of her judgments, Bonnie decides that she should keep Billy in his present reading group. She also decides to take the following action:

Prepare a checklist of word attack skills.

Systematically teach Billy those skills on a one-to-one basis.

Continue to have the stories read to Billy so that he will not fall behind on his comprehension skills.

Have Billy check off each word attack skill as he demonstrates competence in using it.

Having made these decisions, Bonnie writes a brief summary of her judgments, noting the actions she anticipates taking. She files this in her own files for future reference. She also calls in Billy's parents and shares her findings with them. She asks them to cooperate, give Billy lots of encouragement and praise, and support him as he struggles to make up the deficiencies she has discovered.

Note the key features of each of the stages:

1. *Stage 1: Preparation.* Determine the kind of information needed and decide how and when to obtain it.
2. *Stage 2: Information gathering.* Obtain a variety of information as accurately as possible.
3. *Stage 3: Forming judgments.* Judgments are made by comparing the information to selected criteria.
4. *Stage 4: Decision making and reporting.* Record significant findings and determine appropriate courses of action.

Mastery Test

OBJECTIVE 1 **To define *evaluation* and to describe each of the four stages in the assessment process**

1. Give a brief definition of *evaluation.*
2. List the four stages in the assessment process. Describe briefly what goes on in each stage. Use examples from the classroom to clarify your descriptions.

OBJECTIVE 2

To select appropriate information-gathering strategies when seeking to make classroom assessments

LEARNING ACTIVITY 2

The first step in preparing to evaluate is determining what you will be evaluating and what kind of information you will need to make your assessments.[1] Once that has been determined, you are ready to choose a strategy for obtaining that information. There are two steps involved: (1) determine the information-gathering technique you want to use and (2) select the type of instrument that should be used.

Step 1. Choose an Appropriate Technique

There are four different techniques classroom teachers use to obtain information about themselves and their students: **inquiry,** observation, analysis, and testing. To inquire is to ask. Whenever you wish to know someone's opinions, feelings, interests, likes and dislikes, and so forth, ask that person. Effective teachers always ask their students how they feel about what is going on. They know the value of information gained through inquiry. **Observations** are made by teachers whenever they look, listen, feel, or use any other senses to find out what is going on in the classroom. Observations of student performances, habit patterns, and interpersonal interactions all provide the teacher with helpful information. Analysis is the process of breaking something down into its component parts. For example, a teacher might analyze a math assignment to discover the kinds of errors students are making, or a vocational education teacher might analyze a coffee table made by a woodworking student to evaluate the project according to the design, overall construction, and finish of the table. Testing is being used whenever there is a common situation to which all students respond (for example, a test question), a common set of instructions governing the students' responses, a set of rules for scoring the responses, and a description (usually numerical) of each student's performance—a score.

The following table compares these four techniques. Study the chart and then do the exercise that follows.

Summary of the Major Characteristics of the Four Information-Gathering Techniques*

	Inquiry	Observation	Analysis	Testing
Kind of information obtainable	Opinions Self-perceptions Subjective judgments Affective (especially attitudes) Social perceptions	Performance or the end products of some performance Affective (especially emotional reactions) Social interaction Psychomotor skills Typical behavior	Learning outcomes during the learning process (intermediate goals) Cognitive and psychomotor skills Some affective outcomes	Attitude and achievement Terminal goals Cognitive outcomes Maximum performance
Objectivity	Least objective Highly subject to bias and error	Subjective, but can be objective if care is taken in the construction and use of the instruments	Objective but not stable over time	Most objective and reliable
Cost	Inexpensive but can be time-consuming	Inexpensive but time-consuming	Fairly inexpensive Preparation time is somewhat lengthy but crucial	Most expensive, but most information gained per unit of time

*Taken from *Evaluation: A Practical Guide for Teachers,* by T. D. TenBrink. Copyright © 1974 by McGraw-Hill Book Co. Used with permission.

OBSERVATION WORKSHEET
Assessment Activities

Talk to a teacher about how he or she decides what to teach, when to teach, and how to teach. Probe for specific answers. Try to identify the various stages in the assessment process as that teacher explains his or her decision making to you. How could you use the terminology of this chapter to explain what the teacher has done?

Directions: Do not use actual names of schools, teachers, administrators, or students when using this worksheet.

Observer's Name: ____________________

Date: ____________________

Grade Level: ____________________

Subject: ____________________

Class Size: ____________________

Background Information: Give a brief general description of the school's social, economic, and ethnic makeup.

____

____

What to Record: Observe the teacher in action. Note how assessment is an integral part of his or her teaching. Use the following format to keep track of the information being gathered, the information-gathering techniques being used, and the judgments being made.

Time	Information Obtained	Assessment & Technique	Judgment(s) Made
9:15–9:45	Students' ability to sound words during reading class	Observation	Most did well. George and Mary had trouble with some words.

Reflections on Your Observation:

1. What variety of assessment techniques did the teacher use?

____

____

____

2. In what ways did the teacher use the results of the assessment? Did he or she adjust instruction or learning activities based on assessment results?

____

____

____

3. If so, in what ways? ______________________________

____

____

4. What questions would you want to ask the teacher regarding his or her use of assessment?

____

____

____

Step 2. Select the Best Instrument to Obtain the Information You Need

Once you have selected an appropriate information-gathering technique, you should choose the type of information-gathering instrument to be used. An information-gathering technique is a *procedure* for obtaining information. An information-gathering instrument is a *tool* we use to help us gather information. We will briefly examine three basic types of instruments: tests, rubrics, and questionnaires.

A **test** is an instrument that presents a common situation to which all students respond, a common set of instructions, and a common set of rules for scoring the students' responses. Tests are used primarily for determining aptitude and achievement. When we want to know how much a student knows, or how well he or she can perform certain skills, a test is an appropriate instrument to use. Most classroom tests are constructed by the teacher and are referred to as *teacher-made tests* or *classroom tests* to distinguish them from *standardized tests.* The instructions on standardized tests have been carefully standardized so that everyone taking the test does so under similar conditions. Most standardized tests are developed and sold by test publishers and have been carefully developed, tried out, revised, standardized, and evaluated for reliability and validity.

A **rubric** is a set of rules for scoring student products or student performance. Rubrics typically take the form of a checklist or a rating scale. They are especially helpful when you are trying to assess learning outcomes and processes that closely match the kind of performances that are useful in daily living and in real-life vocational settings. Such assessment is sometimes called authentic assessment. For example, assessing a student's ability to present a cogent and logical argument for a given political stance is most directly measured by assessing position papers written by the student. A less direct method would be to present students with several statements and ask them to choose the one that best supports a specified position.

A **checklist** is basically a list of criteria (or "things to look for") for evaluating some performance or end product. One uses a checklist by simply checking off those criteria that are met. For example, one could use a checklist to be certain that a student goes through all the routines in an exercise program, or a list of criteria for an effective speech could be checked as an indication of what a student did correctly when making a speech to inform. Whenever it is helpful to know whether an important characteristic is present in a performance (or is found in some end product), a checklist would be an appropriate instrument to use.

If we wish to rate the quality of a performance or end product, a **rating scale** would be the instrument to use. We might judge a speech, for example, by whether or not gestures were used. But if we want to determine the quality of those gestures (whether they were good, fair, poor, etc.), a rating scale should be used. A rating scale provides a scale of values that describe someone or something being evaluated.

Questionnaires are especially useful for getting at opinions, feelings, and interests. They can be used when we are not certain about the type of responses we might get.

The advantages and disadvantages of each type of instrument are highlighted for you in the following table. Again, study the table carefully, and then take Your Turn at selecting an appropriate instrument.

Advantages and Disadvantages of Each Type of Information-Gathering Instrument

Type of Instrument	Advantage	Disadvantage
Standardized tests: used when accurate information is needed.	Usually well developed and reliable. Include norms for comparing the performance of a class or an individual.	Often do not measure exactly what had been taught. Expensive. Limited in what is measured.
Teacher-made tests: used routinely as a way to obtain achievement information.	Usually measure exactly what has been taught. Inexpensive. Can be constructed as need arises.	No norms beyond the class are available. Often unreliable. Require quite a bit of time to construct.
Rubrics: used to assess the quality of student performance.		
Checklists: used to determine the presence or absence of specific characteristics of performance.	Helpful in keeping observations focused on key points or critical behaviors.	Measure only presence or absence of a trait or behavior.
Rating scales: used to judge quality of performance.	Allow observational data to be used in making qualitative as well as quantitative judgments.	Take time and effort to construct. Can be clumsy to use if too complex.
Questionnaires: used to inquire about feelings, opinions, and interests.	Keep inquiry focused and help teacher obtain the same information from each student.	Take time and effort to construct. Difficult to score. No right or wrong answers. Data difficult to summarize.

YOUR TURN

Selecting an Information-Gathering Instrument

Read each of the following classroom situations. First decide what technique is being used (inquiry, observation, analysis, testing), and then write down which instrument you would use and why. Compare your answers with those of your peers and those found in the Answer Key.

1. A second-grade teacher wants to find out if her pupils now understand how to form the vowels in cursive writing.
2. A high school social studies teacher wants to know how his students feel about the outcome of the latest elections.
3. A fourth-grade teacher wants to know how well his class compares to other fourth-grade classes in their achievement of the basics: reading, writing, arithmetic.
4. An eighth-grade teacher just finished teaching her students how to compute the volume of a cube, and she wants to know how well her students learned this skill.
5. A music teacher wants to rank-order her clarinet players so that she can assign them chairs in the band.
6. A shop teacher wants to make sure that all his students follow the safety precautions when operating a radial arm saw.

Mastery Test

OBJECTIVE 2 **To select appropriate information-gathering strategies when seeking to make classroom assessments**

For each of the situations described in the following questions, determine the best technique and/or instrument to be used.

1. A fifth-grade teacher wants to ask all her students how they feel about each of the subjects they are studying.
   a. Testing—classroom test
   b. Observation—questionnaire
   c. Inquiry—rating scale
   d. Inquiry—questionnaire

2. A fifth-grade teacher wants to know if her students are including the new girl from Mexico in their games during recess. Which of the following should she use?
   a. Observation
   b. Inquiry
   c. Testing
   d. Analysis

3. The school superintendent wants an overall picture of the level of achievement for each class in the school system.
   a. Checklist
   b. Classroom test
   c. Standardized test
   d. Rating scale

4. A speech teacher is trying to improve her ability to judge impromptu speeches.
   a. Analysis
   b. Observation
   c. Testing
   d. Inquiry

5. An English teacher examines each student's theme carefully so she can get an idea about each person's particular strengths and weaknesses in writing.
   a. Analysis—checklist
   b. Analysis—test
   c. Inquiry—checklist
   d. Inquiry—test

6. To determine academic aptitude for placement in special programs, one should use which of the following?
   a. Rating scale
   b. Checklist
   c. Classroom test
   d. Standardized test

OBJECTIVE 3

To write effective test items for assessing achievement

LEARNING ACTIVITY 3.1

The first step in test construction is to determine what it is you are trying to test and what kind of item would be best suited to testing that type of information. Most classroom tests are used to measure learning outcomes. The best statements of learning outcomes are instructional objectives. As you may recall from the discussion in Chapter 3, instructional objectives define clearly, in observable terms, the achievement we expect of our students, and the importance of well-chosen verbs in writing instructional objectives was emphasized. The verb should describe precisely the kind of response you expect the student to make to particular subject-matter content. If the verb used in an instructional objective does that, it is a relatively simple matter to determine the type of test item you should use. For example, suppose you are trying to find out if your students have mastered the following objectives:

To list the names of the first ten presidents of the United States

To describe the major contributions of Washington and Lincoln

To explain the changes that occur when a different political party takes control of Congress

The first objective obviously calls for a short-answer question in which the student is asked to list names. The other two objectives would best be tested with an essay question because students would have to describe or explain—not the kind of thing they could do on an objective test such as true/false or multiple choice. What kinds of learning outcomes are best measured with objective-test items (true/false, matching, multiple choice)? These types of items are best suited for measuring learning outcomes for which the student must be able to choose among alternatives. For example:

To choose the word that best describes the author's feelings

To select the sentence that best represents the democratic position

To identify the emotive language in a paragraph

To determine which of several experiments would most likely provide the information needed by a particular researcher

Note that each of these objectives could readily be measured with an objective test; however, it is possible to measure some of them with another type of item. For example, the third objective in the list (to identify emotive language) could be measured with a variety of test items:

1. *True/false:* The statement underlined in the paragraph above uses emotive language.
2. *Multiple choice:* Which of the following sentences (as numbered in the paragraph above) represents emotive language?
   (a) Sentence 2 (c) Sentence 6
   (b) Sentence 3 (d) Sentence 9
3. *Short answer:* Pick out three emotive statements from the paragraph above and write them on your paper.

You can readily see that the first step in selecting the type of item to use is to examine the instructional objectives. There is often still room for choice, however; some objectives can be measured by more than one type of item. Consequently, other things must be taken into account. The following table highlights the advantages and disadvantages of the major types of test items.

Advantages and Disadvantages of Different Types of Test Items

Type	Advantages	Disadvantages
Short answer	Can test many facts in a short time. Fairly easy to score. Excellent format for math. Tests recall.	Difficult to measure complex learning. Often ambiguous.
Essay	Can test complex learning. Can assess thinking process and creativity.	Difficult to score objectively. Uses a great deal of testing time. Subjective.
True/False	Tests the most facts in shortest time. Easy to score. Tests recognition. Objective.	Difficult to measure complex learning. Difficult to write reliable items. Subject to guessing.
Matching	Excellent for testing associations and recognition of facts. Although terse, can test complex learning (especially concepts). Objective.	Difficult to write effective items. Subject to process of elimination.
Multiple choice	Can assess learning at all levels of complexity. Can be highly reliable, objective. Tests fairly large knowledge base in short time. Easy to score.	Difficult to write. Somewhat subject to guessing.

YOUR TURN

Selecting the Type of Item

For each learning outcome, determine the type of test item you would use and briefly state your reason.

1. To explain the value of using strong, active verbs in writing paragraphs.
2. To list the steps to take when processing a film.
3. To select, from among alternatives, the best way to introduce a new topic.
4. To discuss the implications of the new world order.
5. To write down the names of a least five generals from World War II.
6. To choose the most likely cause of a given kind of engine malfunction.
7. To recognize each of the major parts of speech.

Writing Test Items

Writing Essay Questions

The secret to effective item writing is to be as clear and concise as possible. Don't try to trick the students. Test each learning outcome (instructional objective) in as straightforward a manner as possible. When reading a test question, a student should understand exactly what is being asked. If the student knows the material, he or she should be able to answer the question correctly.

The objectivity that comes from an item written in this way is especially difficult to attain when writing and grading essay questions. By following the simple guidelines listed, however, you should be able to produce well-written essay questions.

Guidelines for Writing Essay Questions

1. Make certain that your question really tests the learning outcome of interest.
2. Each essay item should include:
   (a) A clear statement of the problem
   (b) Any restrictions on the answer
3. For each item, construct a model answer. It should include:
   (a) The content of an ideal answer
   (b) Any important organizational features one might expect in an ideal answer

Once you are certain that an essay is the type of item you wish to use, you need to formulate the question so that every student reading it will have the same understanding about what is expected in the answer. Every student need *not* be able to answer the question; however, every student should know what the question is asking. That criterion for a well-written essay question will be easier to meet if you:

1. Use clear, concise language
2. Are precise about any restrictions you want to place on the answer

Examine the following sets of questions. Note that the questions that are easiest to understand are shorter, contain simpler language, involve simple sentence structures, and do not include extraneous verbiage.

Set A

Clear: Describe a wedge, and list three or four of its uses.

Not so clear: Explain what a wedge is and its function with a few examples.

Downright confusing: Produce a descriptive paragraph concerning the wedge and its functional utility.

Set B

Clear: Explain why certain chemicals should always be mixed in a certain order.

Ambiguous: Exploding chemicals can be dangerous, which should not happen. How do you avoid this?

Impossible: Sometimes reactions occur that are potentially volatile when the proper order of mixing certain chemicals is not maintained. Can you explain this?

Using clear, concise language is not enough. An effective essay question must also indicate the level of specificity you expect in the answer. It must let the student know whether opinions are acceptable, whether or not arguments must be substantiated, and, if so, whether or not references are needed. It should provide the student with an indication of just how much freedom he or she has in responding. Take, for example, the following essay item:

Discuss the various properties of water.

The language of this item is certainly clear and concise. But what kind of response would be acceptable? Would "water tastes good and gets you wet when you fall in it" be an acceptable answer? Maybe. Only the author of the question knows. Look at the following alternative ways of writing this item. Each one imposes slightly different restrictions on the student's answers, and each one is better than our original item because of those added restrictions.

Describe what happens to water when it is exposed to extreme temperatures.

List the chemical properties of water.

List the nutritional properties of drinking water.

Why does the taste of water vary so greatly from one location to another?

List and briefly describe five ways that water helps to sustain life.

Note that each of these items clearly calls for a different kind of response. Note, too, the variety of ways one can restrict or shape a student's response. Now try your hand at writing essay items by doing the following Your Turn exercise.

YOUR TURN

Writing Essay Items

Write two essay questions. One should be an open-ended question. The second should place restrictions on the response the student is asked to make.

1. Write an open-ended question with few restrictions.
2. Write an essay question that somehow restricts or limits the student's response in one or more of the following ways.
   (a) Limit the amount of time to answer or the number of words that can be used in the answer.
   (b) Limit the topic to certain, specified subtopics.
   (c) Ask the student to focus on one aspect of the topic.
   (d) Restrict the response to only one point of view.

Well-written essay items will help make it easier for the students to respond *and* easier for the teacher to grade. The biggest problem with essay tests is that they are difficult to grade objectively. That problem can be greatly reduced if a model answer is developed and used as a guide when the students' answers are graded. There are two major considerations when writing a model answer.

1. All important content should be included in a model answer.
2. Any important organizational features that would be expected in a comprehensive answer should be specified.

YOUR TURN

Constructing a Model Answer

Write two or three essay questions with various degrees of freedom. Then write a model answer for each question.

First, a model answer should contain any content you hope to find in the students' answers. When comparing a student's answer to the model answer, you should only have to check through the student's answer to see whether or not it includes the items listed as important content in the model answer. Facts, concepts, principles, and acceptable problem solutions are the kinds of things one should list in a model answer. Two examples of model answers follow. The first is for an essay question calling primarily for factual material; the second calls for a specific type of answer but allows the student some freedom in the particular content to be discussed.

Example of a Model Answer for a Factual Essay Question

Question: Describe the steps to take when developing black-and-white film.

Model answer: Student answers should include the following information.

Step 1: In darkened room (red light only), load film onto developing reel, grasp film by edges, check to see that film surfaces are not touching each other.

Step 2: Place reel in developing tank and cover with light-tight lid.

Step 3: Wet down the film, and so forth.

Example of a Model Answer for an Essay Question Allowing Some Freedom of Content

Question: Defend *or* refute the following statement: Civil wars are necessary to the growth of a developing country. Cite reasons for your argument, and use examples from history to help substantiate your claim.

Model answer: All answers, regardless of the position taken, should include (1) a clear statement of the position, (2) at least five logical reasons, (3) at least four examples from history that *clearly* substantiate the reasons given.

Note that in the second example, the student has great freedom to choose what to discuss, but restrictions are placed instead on the *type* of information to be included in the answer. For some essay questions, the order in which topics are included in the answer may be important. Other questions may call for a carefully developed logic, and the specific content is less important. Just remember this basic rule: a model answer should highlight the features that best reflect the learning outcome being measured by the essay question.

Writing Multiple-Choice Questions

Multiple-choice questions are perhaps the most frequently used type of test item. To make it easier to talk about these items, labels have been developed for each part of such an item:

STEM ⟶ Which of the following words is *misspelled?*
(a) Geography
CORRECT ALTERNATIVE ⟶ *(b) Filosophy
(c) History ⟷ DISTRACTORS
(d) Filament

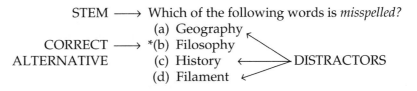

The multiple-choice item is the most versatile of all item types. You can ask questions at almost all levels of understanding with a high degree of reliability. To be both a reliable and a valid measure of a learning outcome, however, a multiple-choice item should meet the following criteria:

1. Present a single problem or question.
2. Measure a learning outcome that can be tested by selecting a right or best answer from among several alternatives.
3. Include alternatives that are terse—most of the item's information occurs in the stem.
4. Include alternatives that are similar in wording, writing style, length, and so forth.
5. Include alternatives that follow logically and grammatically from the stem.
6. Include distractors that are plausible but not correct.

Let's examine a few multiple-choice items to see if they meet the criteria listed. Then you will have an opportunity to evaluate items and try writing some of your own.

Examples of Multiple-Choice Items

Poor item: Alternatives too lengthy, question unclear.

1. Frozen foods
   (a) Can be quick-frozen and then stored at zero degrees and then only for specified periods of time
   (b) Are tastier than any other kind of processed foods
   (c) Should always be washed and blanched before being packed for freezing
   (d) Can be stored at 28° or less if they are properly packaged and sealed

Improved: Question clarified, alternatives shortened.

1. What is most important to a long shelf life for frozen foods?
   (a) 0° temperature
   (b) Air-tight packages
   (c) Blanching foods before freezing
   (d) Selection of food for freezing

Poor item: Alternatives do not follow gramatically from stem.

1. The constituents of air that are essential to plant life are
   (a) Oxygen and nitrogen
   (b) Carbon monoxide

(c) Nitrogen and iodine
(d) Water

Improved: All alternatives are plural, stem shortened.

1. Which of the following pairs are essential to plant life?
   (a) Oxygen and nitrogen
   (b) Carbon oxide and iodine
   (c) Polyethyl and water
   (d) Water and carbon monoxide

Improved: All alternatives are singular.

1. Which of the following is essential to plant life?
   (a) Nitrogen
   (b) Carbon monoxide
   (c) Polyethylene
   (d) Iodine

YOUR TURN

Evaluating and Writing Multiple-Choice Questions

Choose a subject with which you are familiar and write five multiple-choice questions. Write at least two of them at a level of learning higher than just the memorization of facts.

Writing True/False Items

True/false items are often criticized because they are so susceptible to guessing on the student's part. Certain kinds of learning outcomes, however, lend themselves naturally to a true/false format. If the items are carefully written to make them as reliable as possible, it would seem reasonable to include a few true/false items in a test.

The most important rule to remember when writing true/false items is that each item must be clearly true or clearly false. Look at the following examples.

1. Squares have only three sides and two right angles.
2. Liquids always flow in the direction of gravitational pull.
3. Complete sentences include both a subject and predicate.
4. Cities are built on major traffic routes.
5. Our moon reflects the light of the sun.
6. Extroverts are outgoing and always popular.

Note that items 3 and 5 are clearly true and that only item 1 is clearly false. Item 2 is basically true, but "always" is extremely strong language. Might there be some exceptions? And what about item 4? It is a reasonable generalization, to be sure, but not true in every case. Finally, item 6 is partially true (outgoing, yes, but not always popular). Does the part that is false make the whole statement false? The problem with item 6 can often be avoided by remembering a second rule: each true/false statement must present one and only one fact. For example, we could improve item 1 by making two items from it:

(a) Squares have a total of three sides.
(b) Squares have only two right angles.

A final rule to remember when constructing a true/false item is: do not try to trick the students. Don't take a perfectly true statement, for example, and insert a "not" or other qualifying word that would make the statement false.

Good item: The sun is closer to the earth at the equator.

Good item: The sun is farther from the earth at the equator.

Bad item: The sun is not closer to the earth at the equator.

Don't lift a statement out of context, hoping that the student will remember reading it and think it true because it is familiar.

Poor: Nouns modify nouns.

Improved: Although they do not normally do so, in some situations nouns can modify nouns, for example, "baseball bat."

There are many other ways to trick students. You'll know it when you are doing it. Avoid the temptation. Always ask yourself, "Am I measuring an important learning outcome in a straightforward manner?"

Writing Matching Items

Matching items are written as a group of items divided into two lists. The students' task is to match each item from one list with an item from the other list. A well-written set of matching items will illustrate some particular relationship between pairs of items from the two lists. A common use of the matching exercise, for example, is to test the relationship between a term and its definition. Other relationships that might be tested with a matching exercise are:

1. Historical events and dates
2. Novels and their authors
3. Tools and their uses
4. Problems and their solutions
5. Elements and their symbols
6. Causes and their effects
7. Drawings and their interpretations

Relationships like these are relatively easy to test with a matching exercise. Simply make two lists and write a clear set of instructions, telling the student the kind of relationship you are testing (the rationale, or basis, for matching). When writing a matching exercise, make sure that you keep the following points in mind.

Points to Remember When Writing a Matching Exercise

1. An obvious, natural relationship must exist between the items in the two lists.
2. The basis for matching must be made clear to the student.
3. One of the lists should be approximately 50 percent longer than the other list (which makes it difficult to obtain correct matches by the process of elimination).
4. The shorter list should not contain more than seven or eight items.

LEARNING ACTIVITY 3.2

As an optional learning exercise, you may find it helpful to examine a variety of test items, judging them in light of the criteria set down in the last few pages. Ask your instructor to help you locate both standardized and teacher-made tests to examine. For each item, ask yourself what makes the item an effective or ineffective one. Also ask: "What is the writer of this item really trying to measure?" This activity can be done individually or in small groups, but any findings should be shared with others in a general class discussion.

Mastery Test

OBJECTIVE 3 **To write effective test items for assessing achievement**

Write a set of objectives for a unit of instruction. (Choose the subject matter and grade level.) Next, develop a test designed to find out whether students have mastered the objectives. You may wish to put your items on index cards to file for future use.

OBJECTIVE 4

To develop rubrics (including checklists and rating scales) for evaluating student products and performances

LEARNING ACTIVITY 4

There are many times when tests will not give you the information you need. You want to rate a student's musical performance, judge a speech contest, or grade an art project. You are on a committee evaluating textbooks for possible adoption. These and similar situations represent the kind of evaluation problem best solved through the use of checklists or rating scales.

Developing Rubrics

Rubrics provide a scoring system for assessing performance (or products of a performance) and generally take the form of a checklist or a rating scale. We will discuss the development of both of these kinds of rubrics. Rubrics not only provide for a scoring system that allows you to quantify your assessment of a student's performance; they also help you to focus on the critical elements of student performance. This focusing of your attention can reduce errors due to the "halo effect" and other biases.

Checklists

Checklists provide a systematic way of checking whether or not important characteristics are present in someone's performance (or in a product that someone has produced). Note the key consideration: Are some characteristics of this performance or product so important that it is valuable simply to know whether or not they are present? When the answer to that question is yes, a checklist is what you are looking for. The kinds of performances and products that might be evaluated through the use of checklists are:

PERFORMANCES	PRODUCTS
Playing a musical instrument	Drawings and paintings
Singing	Sculptures
Speaking	Maps
Participating in a discussion	Wood products
Leading a discussion	Handicrafts
Conducting an experiment	Outlines
Working through a math problem	
Conducting a library search	
Painting in oils	
Sculpturing	

When developing a checklist for evaluating a performance, your focus will be on behaviors; in developing one for use with products, it will be on observable features or characteristics. Note this difference by comparing the following two checklists. The first has been designed to evaluate a student while he is doing an oil painting (performance). The second has been designed to evaluate an oil painting after a student has completed it (product). How are these lists similar? How are they different?

Example: Evaluating a Student's Oil Painting

PERFORMANCE

______ General layout sketched out first
______ Background wash painted over the large areas
______ Colors mixed on canvas
______ Paints "worked" little, to keep them crisp
______ Brushes and painting knives selected carefully to produce the desired textures

PRODUCT

______ Overall layout pleasing
______ Colors crisp and clean
______ Composition appropriate to subject
______ Sufficient details, but not overdone

The process of developing a checklist is relatively simple. First, list the important behaviors or characteristics. Second, add any common errors to the list. Finally, arrange the list so that it is easy to use.

Listing the important behaviors of a performance is not as easy as listing the important characteristics of a product. That is because when we are good performers, we are often unaware of the things we do that make our performance good. It is especially difficult for a motor-skill performer to verbalize what he or she does when performing. Try to list, for example, the steps you take to balance a bicycle and move it forward. One way to deal with this problem is to watch a good performer and list all the things you observe that person doing. Later, pick out the most important behaviors and include them in your final checklist.

The common errors are most easily listed after you have had an opportunity to watch a beginning performer or to examine a beginner's early products. Note that a checklist is especially useful as a diagnostic tool when it includes common errors. If you anticipate using a checklist only as a final check on performance, there is no need to include common errors.

A well-designed checklist should meet the following criteria:

1. The list should be relatively short.
2. Each item should be clear.
3. Each item should focus on an observable characteristic or behavior.
4. Only important characteristics or behaviors should be included.
5. The items should be arranged so that the total list is easy to use.

Rating Scales

Checklists help us determine the presence or absence of a list of behaviors or characteristics. Rating scales help us determine the quality of a behavior or characteristic. It is helpful to know, for example, that a speaker uses gestures. It is even more helpful to be able to judge the quality of those gestures. A rating scale is used to evaluate that quality of performance. It helps you answer the question: How well does the speaker gesture?

A rating scale is developed by taking a list of behaviors or characteristics (as one might use in a checklist) and constructing a qualitative scale for evaluating each behavior or characteristic.

Example: A Rating Scale for Rating Discussion Leaders*

Directions: Rate the discussion leader on each of the following characteristics by placing an X anywhere along the horizontal line under each item.

1. To what extent does the leader encourage discussion?

Discourages discussion by negative comments	Neither discourages nor encourages discussion	Encourages discussion by positive comments

2. How well does the leader keep the discussion on the right track?

Lets the discussion wander	Only occasionally brings the discussion back on target	Does not let discussion wander from the main topic

3. How frequently does the leader ask controversial questions?

Never asks controversial questions	Occasionally asks controversial questions	Continually asks controversial questions

4. How does the leader respond to inappropriate comments?

Ridicules the one who made the comment	Treats inappropriate comments the same as appropriate ones	Discourages inappropriate comments

*Excerpted from *Evaluation: A Practical Guide for Teachers,* by T. D. TenBrink, pp. 276–277. Copyright © 1974 by McGraw-Hill Book Co. Used with permission.

This rating scale would help an observer focus on specific, observable aspects of each behavior. Each time the scale was used, the same things would be examined. This would help improve the reliability of evaluating a performance and would reduce the errors due to observer bias.

Developing a rating scale involves the same steps used to develop a checklist, plus the step of defining a scale for each characteristic. This added step is sometimes difficult, but it will be easier if you first define the extreme ends of each scale and then describe the midpoints. Defining the extremes is easiest if you can think of some real-life examples. Suppose, for example, that you are developing a rating scale for evaluating the social development of third-graders. Among the many characteristics you feel are important is that of sharing with friends. To define the extreme ends, think first of a child you know who exemplifies this characteristic. This child shares readily with all her friends in an unselfish manner. Imagine this child as she shares with others. See her in your mind. Write down what you see her do; describe her sharing. That description defines the positive end of your scale. To define the extreme negative or low end of the scale, think of a child who is poor at sharing and describe that child's behavior. Now you have the basis for the description at the low end of the scale. By examining these two extremes, you will be able to imagine fairly easily what someone would be like who falls in the middle, and the midpoints of the scale should be easy to define. A completed scale for the characteristic of sharing might look something like:

Sharing with Friends

Complains when a friend has other friends. Won't let others borrow possessions.	Shares occasionally, but is somewhat possessive of friends and possessions.	Encourages others to share friends and possessions.

Note that at this point, we have placed no numbers on the scale. For purposes of scoring, one might number the points along the scale. The lowest point could be assigned 1; the highest, 5. A scale without the numbers is *descriptive;* one with numbers is a *numerical–descriptive* scale. Removing the description and simply using numbers would produce a *numerical* scale. Numerical scales are usually not helpful unless the characteristic can be easily quantified (for example, number of times the child shares toys in one day: 0, 1 or 2, 2–4, 4–6, 6 or more).

Following these suggestions should help you produce some reasonably effective rating scales. There are many techniques for producing scales that are much more sophisticated, however, and these are discussed in some of the works listed in the Additional Resources at the end of this chapter.

Space does not allow a complete treatment of the topic of rating-scale development and use. However, several of the questions teachers ask most often about rating scales follow, along with brief answers. Read these carefully, and ask your instructor for more detailed explanations of any that interest you.

Questions Teachers Often Ask About Rating Scales

Question: What advantage is there to using a rating scale? Isn't it easier to construct a checklist that is effective?

Answer: Whenever you need to know simply whether a characteristic is present or absent, the checklist is a better tool. Checklists simply record quantitative information, however, and are not helpful for judging the quality of a performance or product.

Question: Do I have to have a rating scale in front of me when I evaluate performances? Can't I keep the information that I think is important in my head?

Answer: After you have used a particular rating scale many times, you may be able to evaluate effectively without having the scale in front of you. Even in that situation, however, the scale offers you a convenient way to record the information you have observed. Having an instrument in front of you while you are observing helps you to focus on the important characteristics and greatly reduces observer bias.

Question: How many points should a rating scale have? Is a 5-point scale best? Is a 3-point scale okay?

Answer: Generally speaking, you will get your most reliable results if you use a 5- to 7-point scale. Also, scales with an odd number of points (5 or 7) are usually better than those with an even number of points (4 or 6).

Question: Can students use rating scales to help evaluate each other?

Answer: Definitely. If the scale is well designed and if there are clear instructions for the observer, students can rate each other. Student evaluations can be used quite successfully in the performing arts. Well-designed scales can also be used by students to evaluate their own take-home projects, art projects, and so forth.

Mastery Test

OBJECTIVE 4 **To develop rubrics (including checklists and rating scales) for evaluating student products and performances**

1. Select one of the following (or similar) student products and develop a checklist that lists the most important criteria for evaluating that product.
   (a) Soap sculpture
   (b) Relief map
   (c) Pencil sketch
   (d) Book report
   (e) Model of a village
   (f) Educational game
   (g) Cursive handwriting
   (h) Health poster
2. Use the following format as a guide to develop a rating scale that you might find useful in your own teaching.
   (a) Name the performance or social-personal trait to be evaluated.
   (b) List the major steps to take, or important characteristics to be considered, in the evaluation.
   (c) Select four or five items from the list in item 1 and produce a scale for each item, describing the extremes first and then the midpoints. (You may decide to have more than four or five items in your full scale, but do at least four or five for purposes of this exercise.)

OBJECTIVE 5

To use portfolios to assess ongoing performance and progress

LEARNING ACTIVITY 5

Student Portfolios

A **portfolio** is a carefully selected collection of a student's work designed to provide the opportunity to make very specific kinds of assessments. The two most common types of portfolios used for assessment purposes are "best-work" portfolios and "growth and learning-progress" portfolios.

Best-work portfolios are a collection of a student's best products (e.g., art projects, math papers, writing assignments); they provide a sample of student work over time, across media, and for a variety of problem types. Growth and learning-progress portfolios are used to collect samples of a student's typical work over time. These portfolios allow one to assess such things as the type and quantity of errors as learning progresses, the type of thinking and problem-solving strategies used by students as they learn, and the ability of students to catch and fix their own mistakes as they progress.

For portfolios to be most effective, they should be an integral part of the classroom activities on an ongoing basis throughout the year. To find out some of the things the Kentucky State Educational System did to bring this about, look at the works found in the Additional Resources at the end of this chapter.

Using portfolios as an assessment tool requires at least the following six steps.

1. *Decide on the portfolio's purpose.* The key here is to determine why you want to collect a portfolio of student work. Answering the following questions should help: Which learning objectives could be assessed? What could you and your students learn about the progress being made? Would a portfolio help determine areas of misunderstanding? Do you want to evaluate a sample of a student's best work or are you interested in assessing growth or progress? Do you wish to evaluate process or product? Is a portfolio the best way to obtain the assessment information you need?
2. *Decide who will determine the portfolio's content.* To collect everything a student does is inefficient and makes a portfolio difficult to interpret. A carefully selected sample of work makes a portfolio managable and easier to evaluate. Usually the teacher determines which work samples will be placed in the portfolio, but sometimes you may prefer to have the students choose. A great deal can be learned about students' ability to evaluate their own work if you ask them to select the work to be included. In either case, it is helpful to establish the criteria for determining what should be included.
3. *Establish the criteria for determining what to include in the portfolio.* Which learning objectives are to be evaluated, and what work would best represent progress toward, or accomplishment of, those objectives?

   Do you want a student's best work? Do you want early drafts as well as subsequent revisions, or only the final product? Do you want to see materials related to preliminary work, such as references (perhaps including those identified but not used, as well as those used in the work), note cards, outlines, and so forth? Perhaps an audiotape of interviews conducted in preparation for a report would be useful in determining how a student selects information to report.

4. *Determine how the portfolio will be organized and how the entries will be presented.* How should the entries be labeled? Should there be a "container" for all entries and, if so, how will it be labeled? Would a table of contents be helpful? Besides the student's name and the date of completion, what other information about an entry might be helpful? Would the student's own evaluation of each entry provide useful information? Should the entries be organized chronologically or grouped to represent different learning outcomes or different kinds of problems? If there are several categories of entries, how many entries should be placed in each category? When are entries to be placed in the portfolio? These questions, and others that will be dictated by the type of portfolio being developed, must be addressed *before* students begin the work that will eventually end up in a portfolio.
5. *Determine when and how the portfolio will be evaluated.* Will you be evaluating entries at several points in time as the portfolio takes shape (formative evaluation), or will the evaluation only occur once the entire portfolio is complete (summative evaluation)? Will the teacher or the student evaluate the portfolio, or will the teacher and the student do the evaluation together? Have criteria for evaluating been developed, or has a scoring rubric been designed? Will a single score (or grade) be given, or will a more analytical assessment be made? How much and what kind of feedback will be given to the student? Would written comments be more helpful than a score or grade?
6. *Decide how the evaluations of the portfolio and its contents will be used.* Will the evaluations be used to determine a grade that will be a part of the report card grade? Will the evaluation results be used primarily to assess final achievement, or will they be used to determine progress? Will the findings be used to help students learn from their efforts? Will your teaching strategies change as a result of how effectively and/or efficiently students are learning? What information should be given to the parents that would help them better understand the portfolio and its contents? Will the contents be judged on the basis of established criteria or by comparing a student's work to the work of other students? Will comparisons be made across time, comparing a student's early work with his or her later work? These and similar questions should help you to determine the kind of judgments and decisions that will be made on the basis of the information obtained from portfolio assessment.

Portfolios can be a very powerful tool if they are fully integrated into the total instructional process, not just a "tag-on" at the end of instruction. Read the works about portfolios listed in the Additional Resources at the end of this chapter, and search the Internet for examples of portfolios and discussions of how they can be used to enhance instruction.

Remember, too, that all kinds of materials can be organized into portfolios. Besides the obvious paper-and-pencil entries, one can collect samples of art objects, 3-D models, audiotapes and/or videotapes of performances (music, speeches, interviews), and samples of a student's thinking process (written or recorded). Be creative, but always ask these very important questions: How would samples of students' work help to assess student performance or progress? How would such an assessment help improve my teaching and my students' learning?

Mastery Test

OBJECTIVE 5 **To use portfolios to assess ongoing performance and progress**

1. In your own words, define the term *portfolio.*
2. List three things portfolios can be used to assess concerning student learning.
3. Students should not be allowed to evaluate their own portfolios.
   a. True b. False
4. It is best to wait until a few samples of work have come in before you decide how to organize a portfolio.
   a. True b. False

OBJECTIVE 6

To describe how to use information to evaluate; that is, to grade, to judge student progress, and to judge changes in student attitudes

LEARNING ACTIVITY 6

To evaluate is to judge, to place a value on. When we assign grades, determine that a child is functioning below grade level, evaluate a child's progress, or evaluate a teacher's effectiveness, we are judging. The basic question we will answer in this section of the chapter is: How can one use information that has been obtained (through observation, tests, etc.) to evaluate, to form judgments? Let's take a look at the process of forming **judgments** in general and then examine more carefully several specific kinds of classroom judgments (for example, grading, judging student progress, judging changes in student attitudes, and judging the effectiveness of teaching).

Forming Judgments

The process of forming judgments is well known to all of us because we use it many times each day. We judge the value of a car we want to buy, the quality of a restaurant, the value of a television show, the neatness of our classroom, the warmth of our home, the friendliness of our neighbors, and so forth. Each time we make these judgments, we use the same basic process. We compare information we have about what we are judging to some **referent.** For example, we say that a restaurant is bad because the food is not nearly as good as Mom's. We decide that it's cold in the house because the thermometer reads below 65°. We determine that a car is too expensive because other, similar cars are selling for less, or we may feel that it's too expensive because it's $500 more than we can afford to spend. In each case, we compare information we have to some referent. The following table, which illustrates this process for a variety of judgments, breaks each judgment down into two parts: (1) information used and (2) the referent to which the information is compared.

Common Judgments

Judgment	Information Compared to	Referent
Peter is my best speller.	Peter's spelling test scores	The spelling scores of his classmates
Sally reads above grade level.	Sally's reading achievement score	The average reading score of students at her grade level
This book is the best one I've seen on teaching math.	My perusal of the book	My perusal of other math books
Bobby has an above-average IQ	Bobby's IQ score	The average IQ test score of students Bobby's age
The class is ready to move to the next unit in the math book.	The math achievement scores	The level of math achievement deemed necessary to do the work in the next unit
George is too tall for the Navy.	George's height	Navy's maximum height limit
Elaine has made a great deal of progress in learning to study in her seat.	The number of times Elaine left her seat today	The number of times Elaine left her seat one day last week

Note that different kinds of referents are used in the examples in the table. We frequently compare information we have with some referent or norm (for example, the food in the restaurant compared to food in most other restaurants we have dined in, or the number of problems George got correct compared to the average number answered correctly by the class as a whole). This kind of judgment is based on a *norm-referenced approach.*

Whenever we want to determine whether the persons or things we are judging meet some minimal criterion or standard, we specify that criterion carefully and use it as our basis for comparison. For example, a car is judged to be too expensive when we compare its price to the amount we can afford to spend. The amount we can afford to spend is our criterion, and the kind of judgment we make using such a standard is called a **criterion-referenced judgment.** Criterion-referenced judgments allow us to judge a student's work independently of how well or how poorly the other students have done. It is an important type of judgment when using a mastery learning approach to classroom teaching.

A third type of judgment that is quite useful is called a **self-referenced judgment.** When making this type of judgment, the individual (or thing) being judged serves as his or her own (self) referent. For example, we judge Sam's performance to be very good. Compared to what he was doing yesterday, today's performance was very good. Whenever we are concerned about student progress, we should make self-referenced judgments. Self-referenced judgments should also be used for diagnosing a student's strengths and weaknesses. To answer the question "How are Sarah's math skills compared to her reading skills?" is to make a self-referenced judgment.

Whenever you need to select a few students from among a larger group, you will need to make **norm-referenced judgments.** Comparing a student to a norm group such as other classmates is helpful whenever you need to make comparisons among several individuals to judge their relative merit (for example, who is the best math student). To select one student and not another (as in choosing a class leader) requires you to be able to compare those two students on certain characteristics. That requires norm-referenced judgments. These types of judgments should always be used when you need to compare students.

Criterion-referenced judgments, on the other hand, are most helpful when making decisions about the kind of assignment to give a student or the level of achievement at which to begin a student. In other words, whenever a certain specified standard of performance or achievement is necessary before an action can be taken, criterion-referenced judgments are most useful. When making decisions that rely on information about a student's progress or about his or her relative aptitude in different subjects, self-referenced judgments are in order.

YOUR TURN

Types of Judgments

Answer the following questions to see how well you understand the basic process of forming judgments of different types.

1. What is the heart of the *process* of forming judgments?
   (a) Information
   (b) Comparisons
   (c) People
   (d) Statistics

2. To make a judgment is to place a ________ on.
   (a) mark
   (b) number
   (c) value

For each of the situations in items 3–6, determine the kind of judgment being made. Use the following key: *A*, norm-referenced; *B*, criterion-referenced; *C*, self-referenced.

______ 3. A third-grade teacher discovers that her class scored above the national average on a math achievement test.

______ 4. A high school biology teacher selected his best students to help him set up the experiments for the next day.

______ 5. Misty's teacher was really pleased because of her progress in reading. Her gains since last year are obvious.

______ 6. Four of the students who took the algebra aptitude test failed to get a high enough score, and they were not allowed to take beginning algebra.

Types of Judgments

Grading

Assigning grades has forever been a task teachers dislike. There seems to be no fair way to do it, and any grading system used seems subject to all kinds of interpretation problems. (See articles on grading listed under Additional Resources at the end of this chapter.) The next few paragraphs will not resolve the problems of grading, but they should help you understand better the alternatives available to you.

One of the most common questions teachers get from students concerning grading policy is: Are you going to grade on the curve? Whether grades are fitted to a normal curve or just curved to make a reasonable distribution, the basic idea behind grading on a curve is the same: making norm-referenced judgments, a common form of assigning grades. The class as a whole is used as a norm group, and the class average usually serves as the referent against which all other grades are judged. Usually the average score is assigned a grade of C, and some proportion of scores on either side of that average are also assigned grades of C (the C range usually includes 30 percent to 50 percent of the class). After that, grades are assigned by selecting some cutoff points so that a certain (usually smaller) percentage of students fall into the B and D ranges. Finally, those left fall into the A and F ranges, as their scores deviate above or below C. What do you think are the advantages and disadvantages of this form of grading? List them on a sheet of paper, and then compare your answers later on with the information in the following table. Remember that whenever you grade someone's work by comparing it to someone else's (or to the average of some group), you are using a norm-referenced approach, and all the disadvantages of that type of approach apply.

Another way to assign grades is to establish certain cutoff points for each grade. These cutoff points serve as criteria against which a given student's performance is judged. A common way in which this approach is used is for a teacher to assign points for every assignment and every test. Next, the teacher determines how many total points a student must get to get an A, B, and so forth. Each assignment or test can be graded that way. The total number of points for the marking period can be added together and compared to cutoff totals in the same way to assign report card grades. This could be called criterion-referenced grading. True criterion-referenced evaluation is a bit more complex, however, than what we have just described because the cutoff scores should be determined on the basis of some meaningful external criterion. What do you think are the advantages and disadvantages of this kind of criterion-referenced grading?

Advantages and Disadvantages of Different Types of Grading

Type of Grading	Advantages	Disadvantages
Norm-referenced	1. Allows for comparisons among students. 2. Classes can be compared to other classes. 3. Allows teacher to spot students who are dropping behind the class.	1. If whole class does well, some students still get poor grades. 2. If class as a whole does poorly, a good grade could be misleading. 3. Does not allow individual progress or individual circumstances to be considered. 4. The whole class (or large portions of it) must be evaluated in the same way. 5. Everyone in class (or norm group) must be evaluated with the same instrument under the same conditions.
Criterion-referenced	1. Helps teacher decide if students are ready to move on. 2. Criteria are independent of group performance. 3. Works well in a mastery learning setting. 4. Each individual can be evaluated on different material, depending on his or her level of achievement.	1. It is difficult to develop meaningful criteria (therefore arbitrary cutoff scores are often used). 2. Presents unique problems in computing the reliability of criterion-referenced tests. 3. Makes it difficult to make comparisons among students.
Self-referenced	1. Allows you to check student progress. 2. Makes it possible to compare achievement across different subjects for the same individual.	1. All measures taken on an individual must be taken with similar instruments under similar circumstances. 2. Does not help you to compare an individual with his or her peers.

Teachers often find themselves wanting to give a student a high grade for having made so much improvement. Grading on the basis of improvement is a popular kind of self-referenced grading. Comparing a student to himself or herself is a desirable, humane way to grade; however, this kind of grading has many disadvantages. Can you think of some of them? After writing down your ideas, study the table on page 340.

Using an appropriate referent (norm, criterion, or self) is a first, and important, step toward making sure that grades given are appropriate and meaningful. However, there are a number of other very important factors to consider when assigning grades. Recent concerns over grading practices have brought several of these considerations to the forefront.[2] (See Additional Resources at the end of this chapter for other articles describing various grading practices.)

In the next few paragraphs, several of the common grading practices currently being questioned by parents, educators, and evaluation experts will be discussed. The issues raised here are very important, but solutions to the problems are not always simple. In some cases experts disagree about the best way to handle a given problem. Therefore, this chapter will familiarize you with the problems and indicate which grading practices you should avoid where possible. You should study these problems further on your own, talk further with your instructor about them, or enroll in a test and measurement course that will provide you with some of the measurement and statistics concepts needed to understand the various solutions to these problems.

Inconsistency in the use of grading scales is a problem that plagues virtually every school district in the country and affects education at all levels, kindergarten through graduate school. A student in one class might receive a grade of B for a score of 80 percent, while in another class that 80 percent might merit an A or a C! Grading scales differ from class to class, from school to school, from school district to school district, and may even differ from test to test within the same classroom by the same teacher.

A second, very troubling problem is the practice of averaging grades. Averaging scores can produce inaccurate results because the procedure for obtaining those averages does not consider the difficulty level of the tests or assignments that make up each individual score. This problem can be overcome by converting test scores to standard scores and then averaging the standard scores.

Another problem, not so easily solved, occurs when an extreme score is averaged along with other scores. Suppose, for example, a student has all scores in the A range except one, which he failed (perhaps he was ill, misunderstood a major concept, or studied the wrong material). That one low score could bring his average to a B or a C depending on how many scores were being averaged. Here is a student who probably knows the material as well (and maybe better) than the other students receiving a grade of A. However, because of one test or one assignment, that student receives a much lower grade at report card time.

Assigning zeros for unfinished work or as a disciplinary measure ("You talked out of turn—zero for today!") is another very unfair practice. A zero, when averaged with other grades, is given tremendous weight. A zero, when averaged in with several grades in the A range, could easily drop the average to a D or F range. In such a case, a student whose tested knowledge is at the A level is given a failing, or close to failing, grade because he missed a test or was being disciplined (in most cases for a behavior that had nothing to do with academic ability).

Pop quizzes, testing obscure facts, and other strategies for catching students off guard are other practices that produce grades that reflect something other than academic achievement. Furthermore, these kinds of testing practices usually produce short, unreliable, and invalid measures. Although teachers rarely pay any attention to the reliability or validity of their tests, the impact of measurement error on final grades must be accounted for. A teacher may carefully add up and average a large number of scores, only to end up with an inaccurate grade because of the inaccuracies in the individual scores being averaged. The author has personally analyzed hundreds of teacher-made tests of such low reliability (and, consequently, such high measurement error) that the distribution of grades would have been just as accurate had they been assigned randomly!

Measurement error should be clearly understood by every classroom teacher and every school administrator. Unfortunately, courses teaching these concepts are not always a mandatory part of the teacher preparation curriculum. The tests and measurement and assessment books listed under Additional Resources at the end of the chapter discuss the concept of measurement error. You are encouraged to read those discussions carefully.

One final grading practice that you need to avoid is the practice of averaging every piece of a student's work into the final grade. Students are given assignments so that they can learn new knowledge or gain a new skill. These assignments frequently represent practice exercises. They offer the students an opportunity to try out a skill, to make some errors, and then, with appropriate feedback from the teacher, learn from those errors. Is it really fair to average those grades in with tests given *after* the students have had sufficient time and practice to reach a reasonable level of proficiency?

When the author taught writing skills to junior and senior high school students, he encouraged them to experiment with different sentence structures, different styles of prose, and so forth. Early attempts were often a disaster, but soon students would learn from their mistakes and become very good at using their new skills in subsequent writing assignments. Surely any risk-taking behavior and any exploring of new ideas would have been penalized had those early attempts been graded and the scores averaged in with those of their later, well-written essays.

Assigning grades is more complex than we would like it to be. However, it is important that we do everything we can to make the process fair and the results as meaningful as possible.

Judging Student Progress

Teachers have an ongoing concern about the amount of progress their students are making. If students are making a reasonable amount of progress, the methods, materials, and so forth are probably working. If no progress or too little progress is being made, some changes may need to be made somewhere in the instructional program.

A judgment of student progress is, of course, a self-referenced judgment, and thus all the disadvantages of that type of judgment will hold. It is especially important that progress in achievement be measured the same way each time progress is checked. Suppose that you were trying to check a student's progress in reading. It would be best if you could use the same type of test each time progress was checked (alternate forms of the same standardized tests, observations of oral reading, using the same type of checklist or rating scale, etc.).

The following suggestions should help you assess student progress. Study them carefully, and then discuss with your classmates ways in which these suggestions could be carried out at various grade levels for different subjects.

Suggestions for Assessing Student Progress

1. Determine ahead of time what student characteristics or skills you are going to keep track of (don't suddenly ask, halfway through the semester, "Has any progress been made?").
2. Establish a baseline (achievement level, behavior patterns, etc.) early in the semester.
3. Choose and/or develop instruments (tests, rating scales, etc.) in advance that you can use throughout a student's progress (portfolios are particularly helpful here).
4. Describe the changes you expect will occur as your students progress. This description will help you focus your assessment on appropriate behaviors and achievements.
5. Obtain information often enough so that you can see any progression that might be occurring and so that a single bad sample of information won't throw your evaluation off.

Assessing Changes in Attitude

Most psychologists would define *attitude* as a predisposition to act in a negative or positive way toward some object or person. Note that the attitude is a *predisposition,* which is not observable or measurable; however, it is a predisposition to *act,* and that is observable. This means that to measure attitudes, one must focus on the actions or behaviors of students. Of course, the difficult part is discerning what any given action or pattern of actions means (which attitude is producing the actions).

Usually a teacher becomes concerned about attitude change when he or she discovers that one or more students have a bad attitude. Common among these are negative attitudes toward a given subject, a negative attitude toward the teacher, or feelings of prejudice toward minority students in the class. The important thing to remember when you first become aware of a negative attitude is that there must have been some behaviors that led you to discover that attitude. The student(s) must have said something (speech is an observable behavior), done something, or refused to do something that made you aware of the attitude. Your first step, therefore, is to try to determine what specific behaviors led you to believe that there was an attitude that needed changing.

Once you have determined the behaviors associated with an attitude you think should change, your next step is systematically to obtain information about the frequency of occurrence of those behaviors. These data will serve as the baseline (the referent) against which you will judge any future changes in attitude.

When you are sure that the behaviors you observed are frequent and do indeed represent an inappropriate attitude, you are ready to set down a plan for observing any possible changes in attitude (as they would be reflected in changes in behaviors). There are two important things to consider at this point. First, be certain that you make frequent observations so that you can feel confident that the behavior you are observing is representative, not isolated. Second, look for the behaviors when the student is in the presence of or thinking about the object of his or her inappropriate attitude (for example, look for disruptive behaviors during math if the student dislikes math).

Finally, when the information is obtained, you must judge whether or not the attitude has changed. Remember the disadvantage of making self-referenced judgments. Differences between any two sets of observations may not mean too much. If you find over a period of time (and attitudes usually take considerable time to change) that the undesirable behaviors are decreasing and the desirable ones increasing, an attitude change is probably occurring.

You can use a rating scale to help you summarize the data from your observations. Suppose that you were trying to see if a student's attitude toward math was improving. You might develop a rating scale that would look something like this.

Hates math 1	2	*Tolerates math* 3	4	*Loves math* 5
Complains about math, puts off doing assignments, turns in sloppy math papers		Says, "Don't care about math grade"; does assignment but delays some; never chooses math over other subjects		Says, "I like math"; gets right at assignments; does extra-credit work; chooses math over other subjects

Note that the behaviors characteristic of different attitudes have been placed under the two endpoints and the midpoint of the scale. Each time we observed our student react to math, we could determine which set of behaviors his or her actions were most like and mark an X on the scale accordingly. Several scales each marked in turn over a semester would give us a picture of any progress the student was making.

In summary, the basic steps involved in assessing a student's change in attitude are the following:

1. Determine the behaviors associated with the attitude you think should change.
2. Systematically obtain information about the frequency of occurrence of these behaviors.
3. Decide if the behaviors occur frequently enough and consistently enough to represent an inappropriate attitude.
4. Set down a plan for observing any possible changes in attitude over time.
5. Decide whether the attitude has changed by comparing the information obtained at two or more different times.
6. Record your findings, possibly using a rating scale.

Assessing Instructional Effectiveness

Most teachers have a genuine desire to know whether or not their instruction is effective. They also fear that they, or their principal, will find out that it is not effective. Principals, fellow teachers, students, and parents are all going to judge the quality of instruction. Therefore, it is advantageous for the teacher to have well-documented evidence of his or her teaching effectiveness.

Besides accountability, of course, teachers are concerned about improvement. They are always wanting information to help them upgrade their courses. So let's explore briefly some of the options available to teachers who wish to evaluate their own teaching. The information provided here will help you start thinking about assessing instruction, but it in no way pretends to make you an excellent evaluator. Several books on program evaluation are cited in the Additional Resources at the end of this chapter. Later, you may have an opportunity to enroll in a program-evaluation course. In the meantime, here are a few basic suggestions.

There are two primary considerations in assessing your own instruction. First, you must determine the kind of information you will obtain about the effectiveness of your instruction. Second, you must determine an appropriate referent for judging the effectiveness of your instruction.

There are at least three kinds of information that can be used to determine the effectiveness of your instruction. The first is information about your own behaviors as a teacher. If you feel, for example, that effective instruction occurs when teachers do certain things (for example, provide behavioral objectives for their students, interact a great deal with their students, or ask certain types of questions during instruction), obtaining information about whether or not you do these things is a place to begin in the assessment of your teaching. Many teacher-effectiveness rating scales do focus on such teacher behaviors. Although this kind of information can be helpful to you as you check your own progress as a teacher, it may be misleading about the *effectiveness* of instruction. A teacher's doing certain things doesn't necessarily ensure either effective teaching or improved learning.

A more popular (and slightly better measure) of teaching effectiveness comes from student ratings of teacher effectiveness. There are a number of fairly well-developed instruments that allow students to evaluate their teachers. If you decide to design one of your own, focus on those characteristics of effective teachers that seem to make a difference. Even open-ended questions ("What did you like best about this class?" or "What could be done to make this class more effective?") can sometimes give the teacher useful information.

Of course, the ultimate test of teaching effectiveness is how well the students learn. There are several problems, however, with using learner achievement as a measure of teaching effectiveness. First, students may learn well despite the teacher. Second, it is difficult to know what would have happened had a teacher used a different approach. Even though the students learned well, could they have learned better? Suppose that a class does poorly. Were there extenuating circumstances? Were the textbooks poorly written? Would the students have done that poorly had another teacher taught the lesson? These last questions are not easy to answer, but they do suggest an important solution to the many problems of assessing instructional effectiveness. That solution is to assess the various *components* of the instructional process separately, rather than trying to obtain an overall measure. Suppose, for example, that we were developing a rating scale for students to assess the instruction in a high school English class. Instead of focusing all our questions on the teacher, we would also ask questions about some of the other components of instruction in that classroom. We might ask the students for their opinions about the textbook, workbook, library assignments, small-group discussions, tests, and so forth.

A second major consideration when assessing instruction is the choice of an appropriate referent. You must decide to what you are going to compare your teaching. Will you compare it to that of other teachers (e.g., by comparing your students' standardized achievement scores to the scores of other classes in your school district)? Will you judge your teaching effectiveness by some predetermined criterion (e.g., "At least 80 percent of my students should score at or above grade level on the Iowa Test of Basic Skills")? Will you use a self-referenced approach (e.g., comparing the student ratings from this semester with those of the previous two semesters)? All three types of referents are legitimate. You simply need to decide which would be most useful in improving your teaching. A discussion of this issue with your peers may help to clarify your own thinking.

Alternative Learning Activities

1. Take a poll among your peers, and ask them to list all the things they dislike about the way they have been graded throughout their educational careers. Find out what they think would be the most equitable way to grade. Share these findings with your classmates, and discuss the implications for your own teaching.
2. Ask as many parents as you can what kind of information they would like to have about their children's progress in school. Get them to be as specific as possible.
3. Once you have written effective test questions, you still need to put some of them together in a test format. Ask a teacher you know to tell you some of the important things to consider when putting a test together (e.g., make sure the copy machine produces clear copy).

Mastery Test

OBJECTIVE 6 **To describe how to use information to evaluate; that is, to grade, to judge student progress, and to judge changes in student attitudes**

1. What is the major advantage of grading on a curve?
   (a) Allows comparisons among students
   (b) Produces more accurate judgments
   (c) Allows for differences in individuals

For items 2–5, determine the kind of grading that is involved. Use the following key: *A,* norm-referenced; *B,* criterion-referenced; *C,* self-referenced.

2. A teacher gives George a D because his scores were far below the class average.
3. A high school biology teacher promises an A to anyone scoring above 90 percent on the test.
4. Ms. Kelly tells Jane's parents that she reads well above grade level, as judged by her scores on a standardized test.
5. "I think your language arts grade will soon be up to the same high level as your math grade."
6. What is the biggest problem in judging student progress?
   (a) Deciding when to measure progress
   (b) Getting similar measurements from one time to the next
7. What type of judgment is being made when a teacher evaluates a student's progress?
   (a) Norm-referenced
   (b) Criterion-referenced
   (c) Self-referenced
8. What is being measured or observed in the evaluation of attitude changes?
   (a) Feelings (c) Predispositions
   (b) Ideas (d) Behaviors

OBJECTIVE 7

To describe how to use assessment data to help students learn more effectively

LEARNING ACTIVITY 7

Assessment

Two very important movements in education are having a major impact on how we assess our students and *how we use our assessment results.* The first is the emphasis on state and national standards and the accompanying accountability. The second is the movement toward ever-increasing reliance on authentic assessment techniques. These two movements have made us much more aware of the need to use assessment strategies to help us do a better job of teaching and to help our students do a better job of learning.

Authentic assessment procedures such as portfolios, rubrics, and checklists are especially helpful when trying to determine what students are doing *as they are involved in the learning process.* For example, to find out what students are doing as they learn to write a position paper, one might have them contribute the various "drafts" of the paper to a portfolio (beginning with a list of potential topics from which the final topic was chosen and continuing with an outline, a list of arguments and supportive evidence to be used, a list of resources used, the initial draft, subsequent drafts showing changes made, and ending with the final draft).

Note, too, that many of the local, state, and national standards call for goals that emphasize the process, not just the final product of learning. For example, the mid-continent Research for Education and Learning lists the following as one of its standards for mathematics: "Uses a variety of strategies in the problem solving process."[3]

Historically, classroom evaluation has focused on assessing the products of learning. So we test to see what information has been retained, we check student work for right or wrong answers, and we carefully plan for unit exams and final exams. These final product evaluations can tell us a great deal about how well our students have learned and how successful our teaching has been. However, if we can learn to assess our students *while* they are learning as well as after they have learned, we will be able to adjust our teaching and help the students to make changes in the way they are processing information. We can catch misconceptions earlier, move ahead more quickly when appropriate, and suggest more effective learning strategies to students who are struggling. Observation of students engaged in the learning process becomes an especially helpful tool in this regard. Also, asking students to keep a portfolio of their work, as it develops, can be very revealing. A great deal can be learned, for example, by having students keep each draft of a given writing assignment in a portfolio. The portfolio could contain a list of all the topics they considered writing about, the outline (or outlines) they developed prior to writing, the references they looked up (including those they chose not to use), and their first through their final drafts.

To help students learn more effectively, then, you need to determine what they do (and how they think) as they strive to learn. Often, the strategies of effective learners can be discovered through this process, and those strategies can then be taught to the learners who were less effective.

Mastery Test

OBJECTIVE 7 **To describe how to use assessment data to help students learn more effectively**

1. Why is it important to assess our students while they are learning, not just at the completion of learning?
2. What do you need to find out about students as they learn?

OBJECTIVE 8

To select and use standardized instruments

LEARNING ACTIVITY 8

What Are Standardized Tests?

Standardized tests are helpful when you need highly reliable information to make a wide variety of educational decisions. Although standardized instruments are usually commercially prepared, their most important characteristic is their "standardization." A standardized test has a standard set of procedures that must be followed each time the test is used. There is a fixed set of questions that must be administered according to a carefully specified set of directions, within certain time limitations. Standardized tests have usually been administered to a norm group, and the performance of that group is summarized in a manual so that you can compare the performance of your group to that of the norms. There are three major types of standardized instruments.

1. Aptitude tests
2. Achievement tests
3. Interest, personality, and attitude inventories

Aptitude tests attempt to predict how well someone might do in an area of human endeavor: intelligence tests measure general academic ability, creativity tests measure the ability to be creative, and so forth. Besides these general aptitude measures, there are numerous academic subject aptitude tests that measure ability to learn those subjects (math aptitude, writing aptitude, etc.).

Achievement tests measure how well an individual has achieved in some specific area. There are general achievement tests with subtests covering several different subjects (for example, the Iowa Tests of Basic Skills) and those that measure achievement more in-depth in a given subject (for example, Gates-MacGinitie Reading Tests). Most achievement tests are graded by grade levels, and scores are often reported as grade equivalency scores.

Interest, personality, and attitude inventories are not technically tests because there is usually no single right answer to any given question. These instruments seek to measure typical rather than maximum performance. Inventories that measure interest, study habits, learning style, and attitudes toward academic pursuits are very helpful to school counselors and teachers.

Selecting Standardized Tests

There are four major considerations when selecting a standardized test:

1. Will it give me the information I need?
2. Will the information be reasonably reliable?
3. Is the test easy to administer, score, and interpret?
4. Is the cost within our budget?

Will It Give Me the Information I Need?

To ask this question is to ask if the test is valid for my purpose(s). The **validity** of a test is an estimate of how well it measures what it is supposed to measure. Obviously, if a test is not valid—if it does not provide you with the information you need—then look for another test.

There are many ways to determine the validity of a test. Perhaps the most important of these is **content validity,** which is simply a judgment about how well the items in a test measure what the test has been designed to measure. If you obtain a specimen set of a test you are considering, you can examine the items and compare what they measure with your perception of what you want to measure. If you are examining an achievement test, for example, you could compare the test items to your classroom objectives. By comparing several achievement tests, you could select the one that most closely measures the learning outcomes specified by those objectives.

Predictive validity is an estimate of how well a test predicts scores on some future test or performance. **Concurrent validity** estimates how well a test approximates a score on another test that was designed to measure the same variables. Both tests are given at the same time and their scores are correlated. Predictive validity estimates are generally lower than concurrent validity estimates, so always compare the same kind of validity estimates.

The manuals that accompany a standardized test will usually also provide validity estimates in the form of coefficients of validity. These coefficients will be reported as a number from 0 to 1 (1 being the highest). By comparing tests measuring the same thing, you can get a feel for what size number might represent a reasonable validity coefficient for that type of test. It is important, however, that you compare tests on the same type of validity.

Will the Information Be Reasonably Reliable?

A test is reliable when it measures consistently. **Reliability** is computed several different ways, and the resulting coefficients, like validity coefficients, will be numbers ranging from 0 to 1. Reliability coefficients are generally higher than validity coefficients. Perhaps the most useful reliability estimates are *internal consistency measures*—they estimate how consistently the test measures from item to item. These are usually reported using one or more Kuder Richardson formulas: KR20, KR21. *Test–retest reliability* estimates how consistently a test measures from one time to the next. *Alternate form reliability* is an estimate of how closely two forms of the same test measure the same thing. Always compare tests by comparing similar reliability coefficients.

Is the Test Easy to Administer, Score, and Interpret?

These factors are not as easy to assess when selecting a test, but there are a number of things you should look for. Are the directions for administering the test easy to follow? Are the examples used appropriate, and would they make sense to your students? Are the guidelines for timing clear? Is there an adequate explanation of how to handle student questions? Are the answer sheets easy to use? Is hand scoring a reasonable option? Is machine scoring available, and if so, how much does it cost? What other information (summary statistics, local norms data, response patterns, score interpretation) would be available through the scoring service? Are there adequate charts and/or explanations to help you interpret the data? The answers to these questions can be found by examining specimen sets, or by reading critiques of the test published in journals or in the *Mental Measurements Yearbooks.*

Is the Cost Within Our Budget?

When determining the cost of a test, make certain you consider the cost of each of the following: test booklets, manuals, answer sheets, scoring services, training time (for teachers who will administer the test, if such training seems necessary), report forms (for reporting results to parents), and cost/time involved in interpreting the results.

Sources of Information About Tests

There are valuable sources of information that can help you answer your questions about selecting a standardized test. Read the following descriptions carefully so you will know where to turn for the information you need.

Mental Measurements Yearbooks

There is probably no better single source of information about specific standardized tests than the *Mental Measurements Yearbooks.*[4] Besides basic descriptive information (author, publication date, forms available, types of scores reported, administration time, prices, scoring services available, etc.), these yearbooks provide critical reviews by measurement experts. A bibliography of journal articles that review a given test is also included.

Tests in Print

Tests in Print[5] summarizes information that has appeared in previous *Mental Measurements Yearbooks.* It allows one to make a quick check of pertinent information when narrowing down choices among several tests. A more detailed analysis can be done using the *Mental Measurements Yearbooks.*

Professional Journals

There are numerous journals that contain reviews of tests. To locate those articles not referenced in the *Mental Measurements Yearbooks,* refer to references such as the *Psychological Abstracts* or the *Education Index.*

Specimen Sets

There is no substitute for a careful examination of the tests themselves. Read the administration and technical manual, try taking the test, get a feel for its ease of use, look at the answer sheets, and so forth. You can order specimen sets from most test publishers at a nominal cost, or you can often find them at the testing center or library on a college or university campus.

Using Standardized Tests

Administration

The most important thing to remember when administering a standardized test is that the scores will be difficult, if not impossible, to interpret unless the directions for administering the test are followed exactly. Read those directions carefully ahead of time. For most standardized tests, timing is critical. Be certain that you time the test carefully and that there is a way to hand out and collect the tests so that all students have the same amount of time. For example, ask students to leave their booklets closed until you say open them, and then to close them when you call time and leave them closed on their desk until you pick them up.

Students will have questions during the explanation of the directions and during the test. Handle these questions carefully. Each student must understand the directions, and clarification should be made. If there seems to be ambiguity in the questions themselves, or students don't seem to understand what is being asked, you should help them understand what is being asked of them, but you should do nothing that would give away the answer.

Questions can often be minimized if students are prepared in advance for the test. Respond honestly to their questions about how the test is to be used. Reassure them that standardized tests are designed so that almost no one gets all the answers correct. Tell them to do their best, but not to worry if there are some questions they cannot answer.

Scoring

Most standardized tests are objective and are not too difficult to score manually. A scoring template is usually provided. There are several advantages, however, to using the publisher's scoring service when it is available. The scoring will be accurate. You will often get charts and graphs showing the distribution of the scores for your class. Summary statistics are usually made available, and you can ask for summary data for several classes within your school (or school district). Finally, some services will help you develop local norms.

Mastery Test

OBJECTIVE 8 **To select and use standardized instruments**

1. What is the most important characteristic of standardized tests?
2. Write down, in your own words, the four questions you need to answer when trying to select a standardized test.
3. Which statistical estimate would be important if you were trying to determine if a test measures what it says it does?
   a. Reliability
   b. Validity
   c. Usability
   d. None of the above
4. Which one of the following sources will give you the most information about a specific standardized test?
   a. *Mental Measurements Yearbooks*
   b. *Tests in Print*
5. What is the most important thing to remember about administering a standardized test?
6. Briefly explain how a teacher should handle questions that students ask about a standardized test they are taking.

NOTES

1. For more details, see T. D. TenBrink, *Evaluation: A Practical Guide for Teachers* (New York: McGraw-Hill, 1974).
2. R. L. Canady and P. R. Hotchkiss, "It's a Good Score: It's Just a Bad Grade," *Phi Delta Kappan* (September 1989):68–71.
3. Go to their web site (http://www.mcrel.org) and click on "Standards" for a comprehensive listing of standards in multiple subjects for grades K–12.
4. James C. Impara, *The Fourteenth Mental Measurements Yearbook* (Lincoln: University of Nebraska Press, Buros Institute of Mental Measurements, 2001).
5. Linda L. Murphy, James C. Impara, and Barbara S. Plake, *Tests in Print V* (Lincoln: University of Nebraska Press, Buros Institute of Mental Measurements, 1999).

ADDITIONAL RESOURCES

Reading

Airasian, Peter W. *Classroom Assessment: Concepts and Applications.* New York: McGraw-Hill Higher Education, 2000.

Atkin, Myron J., Paul Black, and Janet Coffey, eds. *Classroom Assessment and the National Science Education Standards: A Guide for Teaching and Learning.* Washington, D.C.: National Academy Press, 2001.

Barton, James, and Angelo Colins, eds. *Portfolio Assessment.* West Plains, N.Y.: Dale Seymore Publications, 1997.

Cohen, Ronald J., and Mark E. Swerdlik. *Psychological Testing and Assessment: An Introduction to Tests and Measurement,* 4th ed. Mountain View, Calif.: Mayfield, 1998.

Evans, E. D., and R. A. Engelbert. "Student Perceptions of School Grading.," *Journal of Research and Development in Education* 21 (Winter 1988):45–54.

Gipps, Caroline V. *Beyond Testing: Towards a Theory of Educational Assessment.* Loomis, Calif.: Palmer, 1994.

Gribbin, A. "Making Exceptions When Grading and the Perils It Poses." *Journalism Educator* 46 (Winter 1992):73–76.

Gronlund, Norman E., Robert L. Linn, and Kevin M. Davis. *Measurement and Assessment in Teaching.* Upper Saddle River, N.J.: Prentice-Hall, 1999.

Kentucky Department of Education. *Portfolios and You.* Frankfort, Ky.: Office of Assessment and Accountability, 1993.

Kentucky Department of Education. *Teacher's Guide: Kentucky Mathematics Portfolio.* Frankfort, Ky.: Office of Assessment and Accountability, 1993.

Koretz, D., et al. "The Vermont Portfolio Assessment Program: Findings and Implications." *Educational Measurement: Issues and Practice,* 13, no. 3 (1994):5–16.

Kuhs, Therese, ed. *Put to the Test: Tools and Techniques for Classroom Assessment.* Westport, Conn.: Heinemann, 2000.

Lyman, H. B. *Test Scores and What They Mean,* 6th ed. New York: Allyn & Bacon, 1997.

McMillan, James H. *Classroom Assessment: Principles and Practice for Effective Instruction,* New York: Allyn & Bacon, 2000.

Mehrens, W. A., and Irvin J. Lehmann. *Measurement and Evaluation in Education and Psychology,* 4th ed. Belmont, Calif.: Wadsworth, 1991.

Nitko, Anthony J. *Educational Assessment of Students,* 3rd ed. Upper Saddle River, N.J., Prentice-Hall, 1996.

Paulson, F. L., P. R. Paulson, and C. A. Meyer. "What Makes a Portfolio a Portfolio?" *Educational Leadership* 49, no. 5 (1991):60–63.

Payne, David Allen. *Applied Educational Assessment.* Belmont, Calif.: Wadsworth, 1997.

Popham, W. James. *Classroom Assessment: What Teachers Need to Know,* 2nd ed. New York: Allyn & Bacon, 1998.

Salvia, John, and James E. Ysseldyke. *Assessment,* 7th ed. Boston: Houghton Mifflin, 1998.

Sunstein, Bonnie S., and Jonathan H. Lovell, eds. *The Portfolio Standard: How Students Can Show Us What They Know and Are Able to Do.* Portsmouth, N.H.: Heinemann, 2000.

Tanner, David Earl. *Assessing Academic Achievement.* New York: Allyn & Bacon, 2000.

Web Sites

Buros Institute of Mental Measurements: http://www.unl.edu/buros
This site provides professional assistance and information to users of commercially published tests.

Buros Institute: Standards for Teacher Competence in Educational Assessment of Students: http://unl.edu/buros/article3.html
This site contains information regarding the approach used to develop standards, the scope of a teacher's professional role and responsibilities for student assessment, and standards for teacher competence in the educational assessment of students.

Central New York Regional Information Center: http://www.cnyric.org
Go to this site and search on "authentic assessment" for interesting articles discussing the value of authentic assessment procedures.

ERIC Digests Index: http://www.ed.gov/databases/ERIC_Digests/Index
This site indexes numerous ERIC Digest articles, including several that discuss assessment and evaluation issues.

The National Center for Research on Evaluation Standards and Student Testing: http://cresst96.cse.ucla.edu
This site contains numerous articles and reports that discuss current assessment and evaluation issues. It also references past conference proceedings of the National Center for Research on Evaluation Standards and Student Testing.

Yahoo!'s Directory of K–12 Lesson Plans: http://dir.yahoo.com/Education/Standards_and_Testing
This site contains a large variety of resources for testing, assessment, measurement, and benchmarking.

Answer Keys

Chapter 2

Answer Keys for Your Turn Exercises

Your Turn: Considering a Real Case

In examining Ted's pre and post maps, make note of changes such as the following:

1. Ted's pre map is limited and reflects his lack of experience in thinking about teaching when he began his teacher preparation program.
2. The two most striking features of Ted's post map are his use of questions and the way his questions emphasize relationships among the various aspects of teacher planning he has identified. His questions show that he has learned to think of teacher planning as a series of decisions. His focus on relationships shows he has learned that these decisions are interrelated, not isolated.
3. Ted's map refers to lessons, but the concepts related to teacher planning that he has identified, and the questions he raises, are equally applicable to long-range planning, for example, unit planning or yearly planning.

In comparing your own map to Ted's and to those of your fellow students, you should consider:

1. What terms have I used that others have omitted, and vice versa?
2. In what ways is the structure of my map similar to or different from the maps of others? For example, how many subconcepts have I included? How have I shown relationships among the terms?

Your Turn: Choosing Key Characteristics

Here is a list of important characteristics of teacher planning. Which of these did you list? Why do you consider the ones you listed more important than the ones you omitted?

1. The four basic types of teacher planning are yearly, unit, weekly, and daily planning.
2. Few experienced teachers begin planning by stating instructional objectives. A basic goal for most teachers is maintaining the interest and involvement of their students, and they begin planning by considering how to accomplish this.
3. One kind of plan is nested within another. Plans made at the beginning of the year affect the daily and weekly plans for the rest of the year.
4. Many teachers say that unit planning is the most important kind of planning they do. Unit plans organize a flow of activities related to a general topic for a period of two weeks to a month.
5. A lesson plan can serve as an organizational tool, and it also provides teachers with a sense of security.
6. Experienced teachers write out complete lesson plans when they are dealing with new content or new curriculum materials. They recommend that student teachers and beginning teachers write out lesson plans.
7. Experienced teachers rely heavily on curriculum guides and textbook materials to determine the content and pace of their lessons.
8. To plan activities that engage students' interest and promote active learning, teachers must draw on a variety of types of resources, including those available through the Internet. Textbooks are not enough.
9. Teachers rarely change their plans drastically in the middle of a lesson, but they do make adjustments based on pupil reactions to the activity.
10. To deal effectively with student diversity, teachers must make adaptations as they implement their plans. Possible adaptations should be considered in advance.
11. Rethinking a lesson after it has been taught is a useful way to improve planning of future lessons.
12. Experienced teachers have established routines for evaluation of instruction, sequencing of lesson activities, and management of classroom interaction. These established procedures free both students and teacher to concentrate on learning and teaching.
13. An effective teacher has a repertoire of alternate strategies, routines, and procedures, all of which serve some important purpose and each of which is especially appropriate in a particular situation.
14. It takes time and a lot of practice to become a successful planner.

Your Turn: Explaining Additional Analogies

There are many ideas you could have mentioned in exploring the analogy, "Teacher planning is like a road map." Here are a few possibilities.

Similarities

1. You use a road map to figure out the best way to reach a certain destination, and teacher planning helps to identify the best way to achieve an instructional goal.
2. A road map shows that there is more than one way to arrive at your destination, and teacher planning helps you to consider alternatives before deciding how to proceed.
3. A road map shows points of interest along the way that you may want to stop and see, and teacher planning can identify special materials that may add interest to a lesson or unit.
4. When you have a routine way to get to a familiar place, you don't use a road map, and when you have a routine procedure that you commonly use in a lesson, you don't need to write it down in your plan.
5. There may be detours along a highway because of road repairs, and road maps don't show these detours. Similarly, there may be interruptions in lessons that are not anticipated in lesson plans.
6. Road maps can show a variety of areas, such as a city, state, or region. Teacher planning can address a variety of time periods, such as a lesson, week, or unit.
7. It is hard to read a road map and drive at the same time, and it is not effective to read your lesson plan while you are in the middle of teaching a lesson.

Differences

1. Road maps are prepared by someone else to be used by a motorist, but teachers prepare their own plans.
2. Road maps are printed in a variety of colors, but teacher plans are written in black and white.
3. A road map is kept in the glove compartment of the car, to be used again and again, but a lesson plan is usually changed or improved before it is used again.

Key Features

1. The road map analogy emphasizes the idea of trying to reach a goal or destination, and this is an important aspect of teacher planning.
2. The road map emphasizes the idea of alternative routes to the same destination, and this is another important aspect of teacher planning.

Answer Key for Mastery Test

A. There are a variety of ways to organize the maxims listed in the mastery test in relation to concepts of importance for instructional planning. The examples provided here do not exhaust the possibilities, but they do provide some suggestions that can be useful for you in evaluating your own categories and explanations.

Maxims Related to the Content Discussed in the Restated "Myths" About Planning

Everybody's Doing It—In a Variety of Ways

Engage a student and the student will learn.
The best discipline strategy is an engaging lesson.
[A basic consideration for most teachers is maintaining the interest and involvement of their pupils.]

A Little Goes a Long Way—Especially at the Beginning

Organization is the key to elation.
[Plans made about classroom organization at the beginning of the year have important effects on plans and activities throughout the year.]

A Plan a Day Keeps Disaster Away—For Novice Teachers

If you fail to plan, you plan to fail.
Overplan—Things can blow big!
Prepare or beware.
[Detailed planning of lessons is an essential activity for novice teachers, who are still developing routines and experimenting to see what procedures work best for them.]

Plans Are Not Made to Be Broken—Just Bent

Be wise—Don't be afraid to improvise.
Plan for the unexpected.
[Effective teachers are flexible enough to note pupil reactions and adjust their plans when necessary.]

One Size Fits All—But Not Very Well

Assume the students' mindset.
Don't underestimate your students.
Not knowing your students is preparing for trouble.
[Classroom diversity compels teachers to make adaptations in their plans to accommodate the instructional needs of different students.]

Time Is of the Essence

Clock watchers end well.
Pace the race.
[Effective teachers use management procedures that save time, so that teacher and students can concentrate on content to be learned.]

Do Look Back—It Helps in Planning Ahead

You can't win 'em all, but you can keep on trying.
[Rethinking lessons recently taught is an effective aid to teachers who want to improve by learning systematically from their own experience.]

You Can Do It Yourself—With a Little Help from Your Friends

Don't be afraid to look outside yourself.
Students can teach, and teachers can learn.
[Teachers rarely rely solely on their own knowledge and inspiration to design classroom instruction.]

Maxims Related to the Basic Parts of a Lesson Plan

Goal/Purpose of Instruction

The more you expect, the more they give.
[Teacher expectations for student performance and learning are explicated in a clear goal statement.]

Content to Be Addressed

Try to be wrong once a week.
[This tongue-in-cheek maxim refers to the fact that novice teachers may not be very familiar with the curriculum being taught and thus need to pay particular attention to careful delineation of content.]

Procedures

Don't do anything for students that they can do for themselves.
Learning can be a team effort.
Put limits on chaos, not creativity.
[Alternative beliefs about appropriate or effective instructional activities are revealed most clearly in the Procedures section of a lesson plan.]

Evaluation

Look for written proof of students' knowledge.
Those who know don't always show.
[While many useful means of evaluation exist, systematic evaluation of student learning is a critical aspect of effective teaching and should be planned for in advance.]

Maxims More Related to Classroom Interaction Than to Prior Planning

A little fun never hurt anyone.
Don't stand still or you'll be a pill.
Kind but firm will help them learn.
Make sure students stay on task.
Never let them see you sweat.
Think before you speak.
Wear a poker face.
[Instructional plans are an important beginning, but teachers need many additional skills to carry out their instructional plans effectively.]

B. Responses will vary according to the lesson plans selected. Here are some things to keep in mind as you evaluate your response. The five essential elements of a complete lesson plan are: (1) stated goal or purpose of instruction, (2) central content to be addressed, (3) list of instructional materials required, (4) set of procedures to be followed, and (5) statement of evaluation process to be used. Additional positive features could be specific aspects of any of the five essential elements, for example, a goal statement with related standard of learning or benchmark, instructional materials with web sites as sources for follow-up investigation, or procedures with alternatives for students with differing abilities.

Chapter 3

Answer Keys for Your Turn Exercises

Your Turn: Recognize Student-Oriented Objectives

1. *S.* A desirable learning outcome.
2. *T.* Students will need to learn proper eye movements, but it is likely that the teacher will have to demonstrate them to the students.
3. *T.* Probably helpful to students, but not an expected student outcome.
4. *S.* A student who can do this has learned well.
5. *T.* How would a teacher do this?
6. *T.* Lecturing is important only if it helps the students reach a desirable learning outcome.
7. *S.* A learning outcome requiring several prerequisite skills.
8. *T.* Of course, maintaining self-discipline may be an important student-oriented objective.
9. *S.* A goal most English teachers hope their students will eventually attain.
10. *S.* A student-oriented objective. The teacher might work through such an evaluation with the students, however, as one activity designed to help them reach this goal.

Your Turn: Clear and Unambiguous Objectives

1. *2*
2. *1*
3. *1*
4. *2*
5. *1*
6. *1*
7. *1*
8. *1*
9. *2*
10. *1*
11. *2*
12. *2*
13. *1*
14. *2*

Your Turn: Specifying General Goals—Parts 1 and 2

Part 1

Here are additional general goals for a high school psychology course. Your goals may not be identical to these, but there should be some similarity between these and the ones you have written. If there is not, have your instructor check your work.

1. Students should be aware of their major personality traits, usual learning strategies, the intrinsic and extrinsic motivating factors that influence their decisions and behavior, and the ways in which they respond under social pressure.
2. Students should have an appreciation for the value of psychological research.
3. Students should have an understanding of the importance of specialists in the area of psychology.
4. Students should have an appreciation for the intricacies of personality development.
5. Students should have developed better study habits based on the principles of learning.
6. Students should have a better understanding of why people act the way they do.
7. Students should have developed attitudes of concern and understanding toward the mentally ill.
8. Students should have developed an attitude toward mental illness that is positive.

Part 2

Here are some additional goals for Unit 1: Psychology as a Science. Many other goals could be written. They need not be written in observable terms, but they should be compatible with the end-of-course goals that have been specified.

Cognitive Goals

1. Students should know the major founders of psychological theory and the important points in their theories.
2. Students should be able to describe those aspects of psychology that make it a science.
3. Students should be able to list the methodological steps in psychological research.
4. Students should be able to define the major concepts and terms found in psychological science and research.

Affective Goals

1. Students should be able to accept differences that exist among the ideas of famous psychologists.
2. Students should enjoy doing simple psychological research.
3. Students should become interested in finding out more about the specific aspects of human behavior that have been studied by psychologists.

Your Turn: Breaking Down a General Goal into Specific, Observable Objectives

Below are three objectives that could have been derived from the goal you were given. Compare your objectives to these. Do your objectives contain the necessary elements to make them understandable and observable? Also, compare your objectives with those written by your classmates.

1. When given a major concept or term used in psychological research, the student should be able to select from among a number of alternatives the one definition or example that best illustrates that concept or term.
2. When asked to write a short paper explaining the methodologies of psychological research, the student should be able to use correctly ten out of fifteen major concepts that were presented in class lecture.
3. When given a description of psychological research problems, the student should be able to select from among a number of alternatives the principle(s) that would be most appropriate to the solution of the problem.

Answer Keys for Mastery Tests

Mastery Test, Objective 1

1. a
2. a
3. a
4. a
5. b
6. a
7. b
8. b
9. b
10. a
11. c
12. a
13. a
14. c
15. b

Mastery Test, Objective 2

1. Specify the general goals.
   Break down the general goals into more specific, observable objectives.
   Check objectives for clarity and appropriateness.

2. True. When broken down into more specific objectives, the end-of-course goals should be observable; however, the general goals are just a step along the way toward the development of usable, observable objectives.

3. (a) Given a description of a learning task, students should be able to describe the process utilized by the learner to accomplish that task.
   Describe the major variables affecting the learning process—tell what makes a learning task easier and what makes it more difficult.
   (b) Given several possible "motivators" and a description of a particular human behavior, students should be able to select the "motivator(s)" that would most likely stimulate the behavior.
   To list the major motivators of human behavior.
   (c) To list at least six benefits of having children from many different backgrounds and cultures in the class and to be able to explain how having children from different backgrounds and cultures makes the class more interesting.

4. (a) A description of subject-matter content.
   (b) An observable, expected response to that content.

5. (a) The conditions under which the student response is expected to occur.
   (b) Level of performance expected, or level of performance that would be acceptable, as evidence that the objective was met satisfactorily.

Mastery Test, Objective 3

1. (a) Focus your planning
   (b) Plan for effective instructional events
   (c) Plan valid evaluation procedure
2. b
3. a
4. Because different kinds of learning require different kinds of thinking and/or different learning conditions
5. c

Mastery Test, Objective 4

1. (a) As handouts prior to instruction
   (b) To prepare students for instruction
   (c) As a guide throughout instruction
2. b
3. (a) Learning outcome
   (b) Learner activities
   (c) Teacher activities
   (d) Assessment activities
4. d

Chapter 4

Answer Keys for Mastery Tests

Mastery Test, Objective 1

1. *General definition:* Should include the idea that a planned beginning is something a teacher does or says to relate the experiences of students to the objectives of the lesson.

   Any three of the following four purposes could be listed: (1) to focus student attention on the lesson, (2) to establish expectations for what is to be learned, (3) to motivate students to become involved in the lesson, and (4) to relate students' prior knowledge to the new material to be learned.
2. You may use any of the situations described in the examples or include situations of your own.

Mastery Test, Objective 2

Of course, responses to any of the five situations will not be the same. If you have carefully read each of the situations, however, each suggests a general direction that you might follow.

Situation 1. A planned beginning to determine how well the students understood the filmstrip or how they could apply what they learned to some new activity seems appropriate here.

Situation 2. A planned beginning to orient students or focus their attention on the significance of pollution and its effect on the environment would be helpful in this case.

Situation 3. In this instance student attention needs to be focused on the search skills they have already acquired in other areas, for example, a table of contents, dictionary, or encyclopedia.

Situation 4. The planned beginning in this situation should incorporate some kind of evaluation activity so that students are actively engaged in using previously learned information and the teacher has an opportunity to see how much students have learned.

Situation 5. This planned beginning should be transitional so that students have an opportunity to integrate previously learned material with new techniques.

Mastery Test, Objective 3

1. *General definition:* Should include the idea that planned discussion permits open interaction between student and student as well as student and teacher. It is student centered and requires all par-

ticipants to adhere to guidelines for acceptable discussion behavior.

2. Any three of the following five purposes could be listed: (1) Students acquire new knowledge and reflect on ideas different from their own. (2) Students learn to express clearly their own ideas. (3) Students learn to evaluate their own thinking and the thinking of others. (4) Students learn to reflect on ideas different from their own. (5) Students learn to share personal feelings.
3. You may use any of the examples described in the Learning Activity or include examples of your own.

Mastery Test, Objective 4

1. Compare your observations with those of other students and prepare a written or oral report on the results of your discussion.

Mastery Test, Objective 5

Of course, responses to this question will not be the same. Your answer should include, however, each of the steps included in the guidelines provided on page 90.

Mastery Test, Objective 6

1. *General definition:* Should include the idea that a planned ending is something a teacher says or does to bring a presentation to an appropriate close.

   Purposes
   1. To draw attention to the end of a lesson
   2. To help organize student learning
   3. To consolidate or reinforce major points to be learned
2. (a) *T.* Whereas the planned beginning initiates instruction, the planned ending terminates it.
   (b) *F.* Clocks tell time, but only teachers can close a lesson.
   (c) *T.* Appropriate use of the planned ending enables students to evaluate their own understanding of a lesson.
   (d) *T.* The planned ending signals the natural conclusion of a presentation sequence.
   (e) *T.* One purpose of the planned ending is to recapitulate the important points in a lesson presentation.
   (f) *F.* An effective planned ending does not occur naturally but requires conscious control by the teacher.
   (g) *T.* An effective planned ending helps provide a coherence to learning through review.
   (h) *T.* Since the planned ending is part of an ordered sequence of instructional events, it requires careful timing.
   (i) *F.* The planned ending terminates a lesson, whereas the planned beginning initiates it.
   (j) *T.* The planned ending helps students organize and retain learning through review.
3. You may use any of the situations described in the examples or include situations of your own.

Mastery Test, Objective 7

Of course, responses to any of the five situations will not be the same. If you have carefully read each of the situations, however, each suggests a general direction you might follow.

Situation 1. A planned ending that reviewed the sequence demonstrated in the presentation would seem most appropriate in this lesson.

Situation 2. A planned ending that would give students an opportunity to practice what they have observed seems appropriate in this instance.

Situation 3. A review of the points, ideas, or concepts developed in the discussion would seem to be the most appropriate planned ending at this point in the lesson.

Situation 4. As in the previous situation, a planned ending that reviews what has gone on and relates to the organizing principle introduced at the beginning of class seems most appropriate.

Situation 5. A planned ending in which students can apply what they have learned in the lesson to a new situation seems most appropriate in this instance.

Chapter 5

Answer Keys for Your Turn Exercises

Your Turn: Characteristics of Effective Questions

1. *F*
2. *T*
3. *T.* Amazing and true.
4. *T*
5. *F.* Sorry.
6. Purposes for asking questions in class: provoke thoughts, crucial role in learning, intellectually demanding, deepen understanding, convergent or divergent thinking, expand multiple intelligences, learn lower- and higher-order content.

   Inappropriate reason(s) for questioning: habit, maintain authority, it's not lecturing, students work harder, cover the subject, keep students on the edge, it's my "job," it gets students involved, it's what was done to me.

Your Turn: Knowledge

1. *F.* Knowledge, or memory, requires recall, a lower-level activity.
2. *T.* Unfortunately.
3. *F.* Memory, or knowledge, questions are important. Learners must have mastery of a wide variety of information. Other levels of thought are not possible without such a base.
4. *T.*
5. *T.*
6. *K.*
7. –. Unless the student has just learned this material and is remembering it, this is *not* a knowledge-level question. It calls for analysis, a higher-level thought process.
8. *K.*
9. –. Calls for higher-order thinking.
10. *K.*
11. –. Calls for a more creative thought process than recall or recognition.
12. –. Unless students have been told what will happen if a recession continues, they must use a thought process at a higher level than memory to answer this question.

Your Turn: Comprehension

1. *F.* Although the student would use original phrasing, only previously provided information could be used.
2. *T.*
3. *T.* That's one reason why comprehension questions are important.
4. *F.* A comprehension question asks students to reorganize information and to phrase it in their own words.
5. *K.* Calls for recall of a fact.
6. *C.* Calls for a comparison.
7. *C.* Asks the student to translate from one medium to another.
8. *K.* Asks for the recall of a fact.
9. *C.* Asks the students to describe something in their own words.
10. *C.* Again, placing information in one's own words is the key.

Your Turn: Application

1. *C.* Interpret in your own words.
2. *Ap.* Learner must apply the skills to solve a problem.
3. *K.* Recall of a name is needed.
4. *Ap.* Must apply information about profit and loss to determine if there will be a profit or loss.
5. *Ap.* To classify the plants, the definitions of the categories must be applied to each case.
6. *C.* Calls for a comparison.
7. *Ap.* To solve the problem, the rules of the definition must be applied.
8. *C.* Rephrasing implies that you use "your own words."
9. *K.* Recalling previous information.
10. *Ap.* To choose the correct answer, the rules of the definition must be applied.

Your Turn: Analysis

1. True.
2. (d) Making evaluations belongs at another level of the *Taxonomy.*
3. True. "Why" questions usually require the analysis of data to locate evidence or to determine causes, reasons, or motives.
4. False. Rephrasing information is required when a student answers a comprehension question.
5. True.
6. *An.* The student must analyze Hamlet's actions to identify a motivation.
7. *K.* Only memory is required.
8. *C.* Rephrasing of a previous discussion.
9. *An.* Evidence to support a statement is sought.
10. *Ap.* Applying a definition to Hamlet to determine an answer.

Your Turn: Synthesis

1. *K.*
2. *K, C,* or *Ap.* Depending on the student response, it could be at any of these levels. Pure repetition would be the knowledge level. Rephrasing the description of the location would place the answer at the comprehension level. Going to a map to point it out would place the response on the application level.
3. *Ap.* Calls for the student to demonstrate or apply the information.
4. *S.* Calls for problem solving, with more than one answer possible.
5. *An.* Calls for evidence to support decision.
6. *S.* Calls for a prediction.
7. *S.* Original communication required.
8. *K.* Memorization of author's comments.
9. *C.* Rephrasing and description needed.
10. *Ap.* The student needs to apply rules to solve a problem.

11. (c). Synthesis is a higher-order activity that calls for much more than memorizing.

12. True.

Your Turn: Evaluation

1. *K.* Recall required.
2. *C.* Description in one's own words needed.
3. *S.* Original communication.
4. *E.* Calls for judgment.
5. *Ap.* Calls for classifying the characteristics of one style with regard to another.
6. *An.* Calls for considering evidence and making a generalization.
7. *E.* Calls for a judgment.

Your Turn: Constructing Questions on the Six Levels of Bloom's *Taxonomy*

Here are some questions on the six levels of the *Taxonomy* that you might have asked about the paragraphs. They are *not* the only questions that could have been asked but are simply meant to provide examples.

1. *Knowledge-level questions*
   1. What action did the three students in Des Moines, Iowa, take that caused their suspension?
   2. What was the ruling of the Supreme Court on their case?
   3. What part of the Constitution did the Supreme Court refer to as a basis for its decision?
2. *Comprehension-level questions*
   1. What is the main idea in this paragraph?
   2. In your own words, explain why the Supreme Court declared the suspensions illegal.
3. *Application-level questions*
   1. Considering the ruling in the Des Moines case, what would the legal ruling be on a student who, despite a ban by school authorities, wore a yellow cloth star sewn on her jacket as a protest against the United Nations policy toward Israel?
   2. Considering the Supreme Court ruling in the Des Moines case, what do you think the legal ruling would be on a group of students who blockaded the entrance to a classroom as a protest against race discrimination?
4. *Analysis-level questions*
   1. Why did the Supreme Court support the rights of students to express their political and social beliefs during school hours?
   2. What evidence, other than the specific case described in this paragraph, can you cite to support the conclusion that young people are now gaining long-denied rights?
5. *Synthesis-level questions*
   1. Develop a short story that portrays a young person seeking to attain a legal right denied to those under twenty-one.
   2. If children gained the full legal rights enjoyed by adults in America, what implications would it have for family life?
6. *Evaluation-level questions*
   1. What is your opinion on the issue of minors enjoying the full legal rights of adults?
   2. If you had been a judge on the court in the case of the Des Moines students who protested the Vietnam War with black armbands despite a school ban, how would you have ruled?

Your Turn: Questioning Strategies

Note the key points that are included in this section. They should serve as the framework of your analysis.

1. Motives for extending wait time: increase the number of students responding; increase the participation rate of students who typically do not take part in class interaction; increase the length, accuracy, creativity, and quality of student answers; provide the opportunity for adequate consideration of higher order questions.
2. Reason(s) for criticism before remediation: it's okay for a student to know an answer is incorrect, especially when it is followed by accurate teacher assistance; criticism need not be sarcastic, threatening, or personal but can encourage students to tune in for remediation; it is a message that they can improve, that you hold high expectations of them, and that they are worth correction rather than neutral acceptance.
3. Using multiple intelligences to promote student-initiated questions: students whose talents and interests are in art or music, for example, are more likely to have their curiosities awakened when the teacher works in these nontraditional intellectual areas; variety in class will also develop and nurture nascent interests in some students, opening up the possibility of still more student-initiated questions; finally, the teacher's openness to new areas and intelligences will contribute to a supportive climate for inquiry and questions.
4. Wait-time summary (here is just one example of a possible, and all-too-common, wait-time summary that students might write): A teacher asked at the end of a lecture, just before we were excused, if anyone had any questions. We had already stacked our books, there was zero wait time, and we all dashed out the door. Sure, there were certainly questions, but no one is going to ask at that point. It was a setup for a quick exit, not thinking.
5. Acceptance as feedback: teachers don't know how often they use acceptance feedback; it doesn't en-

courage achievement; it's easy and requires little thought; it is inoffensive. Acceptance *can* be valuable when opening up questions and encouraging opinions or dialogue.

6. *S.* We hope your work becomes even better through the reciprocal review. If you and your partner agree, that's a good start.
7. *S.* Limerick. Here goes (hopefully, you'll do better):
   There once was a teacher who pondered
   'bout questions and answers that wandered,
   yet when a scaffold was built
   the form came without guilt,
   and the students were ever much fonder!
8. *K/C.* (Often a tough line to draw.)
9. *C.*
10. *Ap.* or *An.* Depending on the difficulty of the passage.
11. *An.*
12. *S.* We *did* the poem. You can't expect us to guess what your question might be. Now it's really . . . Your Turn!

Your Turn: Responding to Diversity

Here's one example to get you started.

Room .25
The teacher is drawn to the active learners. The stereotypic behaviors (by gender and ethnicity) are reinforced. The teacher needs to use an instructional strategy to get everyone participating. One idea is to give every student two "response tickets." They must use them up by the end of class. Some students will have to push themselves to turn in even one ticket. Others will have to filter and select the right answer for the right time. This procedure will remind everyone to "share airtime."

These selected points are to guide you as you rewrite the scenarios.

Room 911
Lack of wait time, especially for students with limited English; low expectations for Hispanic females; teacher avoids embarrassing students by avoiding them altogether, which also suggests low expectations.

Room 411
Factual questions work well for some learners, but many others feel it is boring or the teacher is *dumbing down* to them. The teacher, in search of success, gets stuck at the lowest learning levels. The students too often get stuck there as well.

Room 007
An interesting aspect of this scenario is that this is a generally skillful teacher in an effective class climate. Yet even here, a few quieter students, with a different cultural background, can become invisible.

Room OK
Ho-hum. The minimal interest in student answers suggests that the questions and the content were neither interesting nor challenging. The exceptional praise given the African-American student may be an indicator of low expectations or unconscious bias.

Room 5050
The paragraph that follows the scene uncovers the research disparities, from males getting more questions to females getting less wait time. So, what would you do differently?

Answer Keys for Mastery Tests

Mastery Test, Objective 1

Faculty Presentation
Effective Questioning and Examples

A. What we know about questioning.
   1. Highlight the research on questioning.
      Key points: too many questions, no wait time, too many lower-order questions, most questions come from the teacher.
   2. Identify the traps that trick students.
      Key points: control overhelping, put-downs, manipulation, discrediting, "showering."

B. Seven questioning habits that improve teacher effectiveness *plus* examples.
   1. Asking fewer questions.
      Example:
      (This is where all those unnecessary questions are not being asked.)
   2. Asking better questions.
      Example: How could we create class rules we will respect?
   3. Questioning for depth.
      Example: Consider how are our class rules are like those in your barrio. Design a set that will work in both places.
   4. Questioning for breadth.
      Example: Create a skit, poster, or poem that incorporates our class rules.
   5. Using wait time.
      Example: Yes, that's right, and what other points might you add? (5-4-3-2-1 . . . seconds of silence)
   6. Selecting students.
      Example: I will wait until at least half of the class have their hands up.
   7. Giving useful feedback.
      Example: Your class rules skit was totally entertaining because you showed what might happen on a day without rules. We now see their benefit!

Mastery Test, Objective 2

1. *C*
2. *E*
3. *K*
4. *C*
5. *Ap*
6. *S*
7. *E*
8. *S*
9. *An*
10. *K*
11. *E*
12. *An*
13. *Ap*

Mastery Test, Objective 3

To pass this Mastery Test, you must have constructed twelve questions relating to the given reading selection. There should be two questions on each level of the *Taxonomy;* at least nine of the twelve questions you develop should be well constructed and should accurately reflect the appropriate taxonomic level.

Obviously there is a wide variety of questions that could be constructed on the given paragraphs. Below are three sample questions for each of the six levels of the *Taxonomy.*

1. *Knowledge questions*
   1. What are two somewhat contradictory images that man holds of death?
   2. Who alone, among all things that live, realizes the eventual coming of death?
   3. Who was the author who said, "We fear to be we know not what, we know not where"?
2. *Comprehension questions*
   1. In your own words, what did Dryden mean by his sentence "We fear to be we know not what, we know not where"?
   2. People often hold different images of death. Compare two different conceptions of death that people hold.
   3. What is the main idea of the second paragraph?
3. *Application questions*
   1. Considering our previous study of metaphor and simile, which of these two literary devices applies to the statement in the first paragraph: "Death may be an unwelcome, terrifying enemy, a skeleton with an evil grin who clutches an ugly scythe in his bony hand"?
   2. You have previously been given a list of terms and definitions that characterize various psychological states. Which of these terms best applies to people's tendency to push the reality of death and dying out of their minds?
   3. Give an example of a character from one of the novels we have read this semester who clearly exhibits this tendency to deny the reality of death.
4. *Analysis questions*
   1. Why do you think people push the reality of death and dying out of their minds?
   2. The author suggests that people are unable to face the notion of death. What evidence can you find to support this contention?
   3. Considering the information you have in these paragraphs, how do you think the author feels people should react to death?
5. *Synthesis questions*
   1. Write a poem or short story in which the main character must face death or another's impending death.
   2. What do you predict life would be like if there were no death?
   3. What ideas can you propose to help people become more accepting of their own mortality?
6. *Evaluation questions*
   1. Do you think it would be better for people to ignore death, as many do now, or to be more aware and accepting of death in their daily living patterns?
   2. What do you judge to be the finest literary or artistic expression that has the inevitability of death as its central theme?
   3. In your opinion, is it a good idea for children to read books about death?

Mastery Test, Objective 4

To pass this Mastery Test, you must have designed a scenario that incorporated four effective questioning strategies and labeled them correctly. Since there are many possibilities, here is a sample excerpt.

Scenario

Teacher: Let's do a brief review of lungs for life information so that you're ready for the test next week. What are some of the issues we have studied about the lungs? Take some time to jot down at least four ideas on your organizer sheet. (*Time passes, students write.*) Who has at least six ideas? Okay, wow, almost everybody. Sarita?

Sarita: Smoking is bad for your lungs. (Four seconds pass.)

Sarita: I know this because I have seen photographs of the lungs of smokers. They are terrible to see, black and diseased.

Teacher: Do you remember what we call that disease?

Sarita: Emphysema. I remember from the video.

Teacher: Absolutely correct on the name. Now, you all read a brief description and watched the video about emphysema. (Who has a question about this disease and how it affects the lungs that will help us to review? *SIQ*) Take some time to think. (Five seconds pass. *WT*)

Mastery Test, Objective 5

To complete this Mastery Test, you needed to begin by reviewing the scenario that you developed for Mastery Test, Objective 4. Then, the task was to intersect some of the information on student diversity with questioning strategies. Each strategy would have an example of how your questioning would model knowledge, high expectations, and sensitivity to groups and individuals. As in other cases, your answer is very individualized, so only a portion of a response is included below.

Classroom description: An urban elementary school with predominantly African-American students. I am the music specialist (African-American female) who visits once every other week. Most of the students love listening to and singing "their" songs, but many are tentative when I introduce music theory and notation. Today I am having them make the connection between rest notes (pauses), rhythm, and syncopation.

One African-American male (Jerod) is very musical but doesn't like talking in class. He'll rap and step with friends all the time, but he takes his academic detachment behaviors into music class. He doesn't like participating and really doesn't like being complimented by teachers. Toward the end of the lesson I had the students marking out measures with very complicated rest notes. They were doing this with counting and movement combined and had to demonstrate for four measures.

Specific praise: Jerod took his beat sequence to the front of the room, counted and moved perfectly, and demonstrated the correct rest notes and time signature. My specific praise? "Jerod, way to go! You got it all and you got it right. Somebody help me here. Given all the parts of today's lesson, what was something he did that was really right? There could be at least four or five separate parts that were correct. Who's got one?" The praise will be specific and positive, and it will reinforce the learning objectives. Hopefully, Jerod will be more accepting of the feedback because it comes from his peers.

Chapter 6

Answer Keys for Your Turn Exercises

Your Turn: Developing a Definition of Differentiation

1. Be sure to include how the situation struck you mentally (e.g., were you confused because you were uncertain of what the content was good for—why you needed to learn it, uncomfortable because the language of the classroom wasn't your primary language and explanations went too fast for you to absorb, restless because you kept hearing explanations of things you already knew how to do, frustrated because you finished tasks early and weren't allowed to work on other things that were interesting to you, or resentful of homework because you had to do what you had already mastered?) and affectively (e.g., did you feel rejected by the group because you dressed differently than others in the room, believe the teacher didn't approve of you for some reason, feel torn because many of your peers disapproved of your interest in school?).

2. Be specific about what the adult might have done to modify the learning experience or learning environment to make it work better for you. For example, did he or she
   - make opportunities for students to ask questions individually,
   - have students work in pairs to summarize ideas and clarify uncertain areas,
   - use hands-on examples or models of student work to illustrate ideas,
   - allow students who are still learning English to write in their primary language and then translate their work into English,
   - give students tasks that demonstrate how the ideas and skills are used,
   - give homework alternatives when students already know how to do the basic assignment,
   - find time to build a relationship with each student,
   - help students see one another's strengths?

3. Your definition might include references to differentiation as
   - being actively planned by the teacher (vs. impromptu),
   - based on a teacher's assessment of a student's learning needs,
   - a teacher's attempt to make sure learning works for each child in the classroom,
   - flexible use of time, materials, human resources, and space to help students learn better,
   - providing varied activities, products, ways of learning and support systems for students with varied needs,
   - student-centered instruction,
   - involving multiple ways of teaching and multiple ways of learning.

If you left some of these elements out, why do they seem less significant to you than the ones you included? What else did you include that you feel must be a part of a good definition, and why do you feel strongly about those elements?

Another way of analyzing your definition is to see whether it contains references to what changes in a differentiated classroom (vs. a non-differentiated one), how those things change, and why they change.

4. Think about ways in which your view may be changing in regard to the varied needs of students, the teacher's role in addressing those needs, the role of curriculum and instruction in the classroom, and/or the role of the learning environment in helping each learner succeed.

Your Turn: Developing a Rationale for Differentiation

1. Lists generated by teachers who are asked why they and their colleagues do or do not modify or differentiate instruction often include the following items.

   Why
   Students learn more
   Behavior is better
   Students like school better
   Students develop their strengths
   Fewer students feel frustrated
   Fewer students feel bored
   Students understand and remember better
   The classroom is livelier
   The teacher feels more creative
   Students learn at different rates

   Why Not
   It takes time to plan
   Parents might not understand
   Not enough materials
   Not enough planning time
   Rooms are too small
   Too much material to cover
   It wouldn't be fair
   Don't know how
   Colleagues would resent me
   Room would be noisy
   The students can't work independently

2. Think about ways in which your lists (and the lists of colleagues) are similar to or dissimilar from these lists. Why do you think similarities exist? Dissimilarities? One common pattern in lists such as these is that the majority of reasons for differentiating instruction focus on student needs and benefits, whereas the majority of reasons for not differentiating instruction focus on teacher needs and concerns. What do you make of that pattern? Does it mean teachers put students in second place? Or might it mean something different (e.g., teachers must be comfortable with the ways they teach before they can serve students well)? What implications do you see in your list for yourself as a beginning teacher?

3. Think about what you wrote or said as it relates both to your needs as a developing professional and your students' needs for challenge and success. For example, you may have said you want to help students maintain motivation to learn and will therefore have to discover what motivates different learners. In that case, what will you need to do to understand what motivates your students and to become comfortable using the information you gather?

Your Turn: Examining Classroom Connections in Responsive Teaching

1. In thinking about a graphic representation of how Mrs. Rex links "who we teach," "what we teach," "where we teach," and "how we teach," there are two key considerations. First, her thinking about her students shapes everything else she thinks about. Second, each of the four elements forms a "feedback loop" for all of the other elements. For example, thinking about what the classroom needs to be like (*where* she teaches) so that all students find challenge and success shapes *how* Mrs. Rex teaches at a given point in time. Likewise, thinking about *how* she needs to teach an idea or skill so that each student grows as a result of the lesson helps Mrs. Rex reflect on *what* is truly essential and compelling in her content.

2. In this graphic, it is likely that the four elements either remain distinct from one another and disconnected, or they connect in some way that does not place the student at the apex of thinking. For example, "what we teach" may be at the apex of thinking, and the graphic might suggest the importance of everyone (*who* we teach) covering the same material in the same way (*how* we teach), in an environment that maintains tight control (*where* we teach) to allow for the coverage.

   The important thing in analyzing your graphics for questions 1 and 2 is to be aware of how teacher thinking shifts when planning begins with a focus on student growth and success compared to when that is not central in the teacher's thinking.

3. This answer will vary depending on the beliefs you select. If, for example, you believe that students of a particular age or grade should learn the same content in the same way and over the same time period, that will affect who you teach because you will not feel a need to address their particular learning differences; it will affect where you teach because it will enable you to be comfortable with a more teacher-centered classroom; it will affect what you teach because it will give you permission to use the same materials and goals for everyone without variance; and, it will affect how you teach because you will feel comfortable with the same instructional approaches for all learners at a given time. On the other hand, if you believe strongly that students must feel safe and secure in classrooms in order to progress effectively as learners, that will influence who you teach because you will be looking for what each student needs in order to feel

safe and secure; it will influence where you teach because you will continually look at students' responses to the learning environment and will make adaptations based on what you see; it will influence what you teach because you will see in the content ways to make connections with varied student interest and affect; and, it will have an impact on how you teach because you will be seeking instructional strategies and approaches that maximize success for each learner.

4. Grading in most classrooms assumes that a fundamental role of grades is to "separate the sheep from the goats," or to compare everyone to a norm. In a differentiated classroom, an assumption is that individual growth must be at least one important aspect of grading. Does your response to the question about grading recognize connections between Mrs. Rex's beliefs about students and her likely beliefs about grading? Does your response recognize connections between Mrs. Rex's beliefs about learning environment and her beliefs about grading? Does your response recognize that grades in Mrs. Rex's classroom probably wouldn't continually punish someone for having learning difficulties or reward someone who happens to be more able just for coming to school as they are?

   In thinking about your own beliefs about teaching and grading, did you look for matches between your beliefs about each of the four elements—who you teach, where you teach, what you teach, and how you teach—and your beliefs about grading?

Your Turn: Planning to Differentiate Instruction Based on Learner Need

1. A pre-assessment should ask students to explain and/or demonstrate the knowledge, understandings, and skills that are central to whatever you are pre-assessing. In other words, you have a match between your pre-assessment and a textbook chapter if your pre-assessment contains questions about the most important knowledge, understandings, and skills in the chapter.

2. First, check to make sure your original activity clearly addresses the learning goals you specified for the lesson. In other words, is it highly likely that by completing the task, a learner would accomplish the learning goals?

   When you complete a version of the original learning task for a student who is struggling with the content, be sure you (a) provide support necessary for the student to learn from the task and complete it successfully, (b) develop the task at a level of complexity that seems appropriate for the student, (c) continue to address the essential learning goals in the task. Among the ways you can make a task more accessible for a struggling learner are making what the student needs very familiar to the student, making the task more structured, reducing the number of steps required, using resources that are simpler to read, or modeling what the student needs to do. For example, if your lesson contained a graphic organizer, you might complete a portion of the organizer on the graphic the student receives. That helps illustrate for the student the kind of information called for. If a student needs to do research, you might provide a template to guide collecting and analyzing information. That additional structure may be more helpful to the student than open-ended direction to gather information and figure out what it means.

   When you complete a version of the original learning task for a student who is advanced with the content, be sure you (a) provide a catalyst for extending the student's thought about ideas central to the task and/or application of skills through the task, and (b) continue to address the essential learning goals in the task. Among the ways you can make a task more appropriately challenging for an advanced learner are making the ideas and/or applications more complex or abstract, making the task more open-ended, making the application or format less familiar, developing a task that requires more stages of thinking for successful completion, asking students to work toward criteria that are more expert-like, and providing resources that are more advanced.

3. You might want to reflect on how the teacher extended your interest in the subject or topic as well as how he or she changed your image of yourself as a person and/or a learner. Was there any sort of signal from the teacher to let you know the teacher was aware of your talents? Did it require any extra thought or effort on the teacher's part to extend or develop an interest in you? Did you ever see any evidence that the teacher did similar things for other students? Why do you think the teacher did what he or she did to develop or extend your interests?

4. To what degree did your interviewee talk about how he or she felt in school vs. what he/she learned there? In what ways was that person's impression of teachers, homework, students, life goals, friendships, grades, and classroom routines similar to or different from yours? At this point in your development as teacher, in what ways do you think you would have been an effective or less than effective teacher for your interviewee? Think about why that might be the case.

5. There are many strategies you could add to the figures in the chapter. Here are just a few.

   Readiness: When the Teacher Presents

   Having students choral read key passages of print and important directions is a means of supporting struggling students.

   Asking students to listen and respond to your presentation in the role of a person who might have a different viewpoint on the topic (e.g., listening to a story you are reading as though the student were a character in the story, or listening to a lecture on the Westward Movement as though the student were a Native American) can extend the thinking of advanced learners about a topic.

Readiness: When the Student is Worker

Asking students to work in formats that are quite familiar to support students who are having difficulty with the content of a task, and to work in formats that are quite unfamiliar for students who are advanced with the content (e.g., writing a story is far more familiar to most students than is writing a letter to the editor).

Requiring students to consult with peers who can push their thinking forward as they complete assigned tasks or products can enable everyone to get useful ideas about how to improve their work.

Interest: When the Teacher Presents

Reading selections from famous people who talk about their passions and interests—for example, in a middle school history class, read some of Maya Angelou's thoughts about civil rights; in an art class, read some of John Lennon's thoughts about connections between art and music; in a science class, read Murray Gel-man's thoughts about literature or Lewis Thomas's thoughts about music. There are always people noted in one area whose interests link to other areas, and they provide wonderful bridges between the interests of students and a particular subject.

Making analogies as you present. How is working this math problem like building with blocks? How is the evolution of the U.S. Constitution like working in a darkroom? After students begin to see what you're doing, ask them to make analogies between things they are interested in and ideas you are teaching.

Interest: When the Student is Worker

Having students develop products which compare experts' ways of working and contributions in the field you are teaching and experts' ways of working and contributions they make in fields of particular interest to them.

Providing time for students to generate their own questions about topics they are studying both as a unit begins and as it progresses. Adjust student tasks to address as many of the questions as possible. Also help students cultivate the habit of looking for unanswered questions at the end of a study to help them understand and engage in the on-going quest for knowledge.

Learning Profile: When the Teacher Presents

Asking students to suggest to you ways they have learned best in past settings, and incorporating those into your modes of presentation.

Helping students develop an awareness of your intentional use of varied presentation styles and having them analyze which approaches are working best for them.

Learning Profile: When the Student is Worker

Having students approach tasks or products in varied ways, keeping a record of how they have worked, analyzing results of the various approaches over time, and generating conclusions about their work and study preferences.

Challenging students to examine a topic, complete a task, or develop a product in more than one mode. Then have them think about what happened when they learned through two lenses rather than one, as well as which route was most instructive for them.

Your Turn: Examining the Principles of Effective Differentiation

1. In figures 1–3, most of the strategies would require planning in advance of a lesson. Some, of course, require more planning than others. Among strategies that could be applied "on the spot" with relatively little pre-planning (reactive differentiation) might be
   - using concrete illustrations of complex or abstract ideas,
   - stopping often during presentations to prompt student reflection and questions,
   - asking questions of escalating difficulty in class discussions,
   - coaching for success, and
   - using wait time.

   Even these strategies, however, take a certain amount of thought and planning to be effective—especially in the early stages of teaching when nearly all routines require careful thought. For example, it is not nearly as easy as it seems to ask in a coherent sequence a series of questions that begins with fundamental understandings and becomes more and more complex. Be sure to analyze your own additions to the figures to determine whether they would require pre-planning.

2. There are also multiple ways to see the key principles of differentiation related to the elements of who, where, what, and how we teach. Here are a few ways to think about those connections with three of the principles.
   (a) Effective differentiation is more likely to be proactive rather than reactive.
      Who we teach: Careful attention to student differences draws to the teacher's attention the fact that on-the-spot differentiation is not likely to be robust enough to address learning gaps, provide meaningful challenge, attend to language needs, address a range of interests, and so on.

Where we teach: The teacher is likely to have to plan consistently for flexible and effective use of space and to help students build a positive learning community.

What we teach: It takes careful examination of standards, text materials, and a teacher's own knowledge of a subject to determine what constitutes the essential knowledge, understanding, and skill necessary for each learner to progress in the subject.

How we teach: The teacher will have to carefully plan tasks that are both differentiated and ensure that each student has the opportunity and support to develop key knowledge, understanding, and skill.

(b) The teacher continually assesses student understanding and adjusts instructional plans on what the assessment reveals.

Who we teach: If I value a student, I will use many different resources to find out what that students knows, what he or she is interested in, and what makes learning most effective for that student.

Where we teach: Everyone in the classroom will have to be respectful of student similarities and differences, understand why the teacher takes time to address particular learning needs, and contribute to the routines of a differentiated classroom.

What we teach: Ongoing assessment helps the teacher develop logical sequences of teaching, know when to re-teach or extend teaching related to learning goals, and how to make content more interesting to learners.

How we teach: Using tasks and products at differing levels of readiness or focused on differing interests allows more students to learn more effectively and with greater intrinsic motivation.

(c) An effectively differentiated classroom focuses on growth.

Who we teach: Students cannot generally control the readiness levels and background experiences they bring to class. The teacher is most likely to play a role in maximizing student potential by expecting growth of each learner, supporting each learner in growth, and acknowledging growth when it happens.

Where we teach: The teacher cannot make the classroom a safe learning place if it seems punitive when errors are made or when a student cannot reach a norm on a prescriptive timetable. The teacher cannot make it a challenging place if he or she rewards students for "excellence" which is not earned.

What we teach: As a teacher comes to understand what he or she teaches, there is a sequence of ideas and skills through which the teacher needs to guide students in order to assess and support growth.

How we teach: The teacher will need to teach in a variety of ways and help students learn in a variety of ways to support the maximum growth of each individual.

Your Turn: Thinking about Your Own Response to Academic Diversity

1. The actions you state here will need to stem from your particular beliefs. Here are some examples of how that might look.

   Belief: My students will learn at different rates.
   Action: I will have some time in class where students who need to can continue to work on a task and students who finish have important work to move on to.

   Belief: Making errors in a classroom is part of the learning process and students need to feel safe as they learn.
   Action: On very important assignments, I will make sure students get feedback on how to improve their work before the assignments are turned in.

   Belief: Students learn better when the subject matter interests them.
   Action: I will look for ways to raise student curiosity and to show them how the subject is at work in their own lives.

2. There are many things a teacher could do to help Tia, Carlos, and Sam have a more productive school experience. Here are a few thoughts about each of the students.

   Tia: She is more advanced in this subject than many members of the class, and the pace and sophistication level of the content are frustrating to her because she sits and waits for others to learn far more often than she has a chance to grow herself. In addition, the learning environment is not one where she feels free to express questions and ideas because they make her appear not to "fit in" with her peers.

   Suggestions
   - Provide materials or activities focused on the same learning goals, but requiring a more advanced level of thought and understanding.
   - Develop with Tia an on-going product assignment that relates to the learning goals and on which she can work when she has mastered the key information and skills in the unit.
   - Provide Tia with complex journal prompts on the topic so she can extend her thinking about the topic as she responds in her journal.
   - Make time in class to work with all students (including those who are advanced) in small groups that allow the teacher to push students beyond their current comfort levels with ideas and skills.
   - Make sure Tia often works with peers who are also advanced so they can bounce ideas off of one another at an advanced level.

Carlos: This student is clearly overwhelmed by the amount of content, level of content, and pace in the class. This might be the case because he has a learning disability. It could be the case because he is a second language learner. He may just be missing background knowledge and experiences other students have that enable them to "play the school game" better. He might have an undiagnosed learning problem. Whatever the case, he feels swamped by the class and is discouraged by the repeated sense that he can't keep up.

Suggestions

- Pre-assess student knowledge and skill as a unit begins and plan to use small, teacher-led groups to help students master knowledge and skills needed to close gaps in their thinking.
- Use graphic organizers, including lists of key vocabulary, when students have to take notes in class.
- Help students learn how to determine what key points are in a lecture and what is illustrative or less important.
- Make sure the teacher completes the organizer on the board or overhead projector as students take notes.
- Use "summary groups" after presentations so students can compare what they heard in a presentation to what peers heard. Then follow up with student questions.
- Be sure students get a chance to use skills and knowledge with which they are comfortable as a vehicle for working toward things that are harder for them.
- If a student does not speak English well, help that student build a support system for translating, reteaching, checking ideas, getting feedback on work, developing a study group, and so on.
- If a student does not speak English well, help peers understand the immense task of learning a new language and a new subject at the same time. Enlist their help in figuring out ways to support the student and to celebrate his or her growth.

Sam: For whatever reason, Sam cannot sit still very well. Maybe he is hyperactive. Maybe he's just a wiggler, or someone who learns best when he's moving rather than sitting and listening. He also seems to need a reason for what he's learning—perhaps to see how the information looks when it's used. He seems to need a classroom that is more tolerant of movement and perhaps more practical than informational in nature.

Suggestions

- Allow students to move around in the classroom as long as they do so without disturbing others.
- Help Sam understand his need to move and help him learn to move around when he's studying and reading in order to boost concentration.
- Shift from one activity to another, or from teacher-talk to student-work often.
- Use brief peer discussion groups often to ensure on-going engagement of students and to give everyone a chance to participate actively.
- Consistently include illustrations of the content at work in people's lives.
- Call on Sam to make practical applications of what he's learning, and/or give him class and home tasks that call for practical application.

3. These responses will vary greatly depending on what your own goals for early responsive teaching are. It's likely that almost any steps toward responsive teaching would be helpful in some way to Tia, Carlos, and Sam. Check to see if it's the case that each of your goals would, in fact, be of help to all three of the students, compared to a classroom in which a teacher does not have those goals.

Answer Key for Mastery Test

Use the following information to help you think about your answers to the first two parts of the Mastery Test. There are many ways you could adapt lesson plans and classroom instruction to make the class a good fit for Tia, Carlos, and Sam. The information provides *samples* of learning needs of the three students and possible teacher responses. Answers to the third part of the Mastery Test will be highly individual.

Tia

Student Needs

Work at a fast pace
Greater level of challenge
Meaningful tasks when assignments are completed
Opportunity to answer her own questions
Chance to work with like-readiness peers
Time with the teacher
A sense that excellence stems from effort and growth
Self-efficacy as a learner
A classroom in which individual differences are valued and in which growth is required, supported, and acknowledged

Sample Teacher Responses to the Needs

Provide advanced books and other resources on the topic
Develop tiered tasks with more complex directions, steps, and requirements
Use interest centers, specializations on subtopics, and/or independent studies to allow pursuit of student questions and interests
Use flexible grouping that includes similar-readiness groups
Ensure that you meet with advanced students to coach for continuing growth

Encourage students to develop some of their own criteria for success in tasks and products
Provide rubrics with very advanced indicators of success
Ensure that individual growth is an important factor in feedback and grading
Talk with students about the need for valuing one another's ideas, and model acceptance in your work with students
Call on gifted education resource teachers for suggestions

Carlos

Student Needs

Support with writing
Support with note taking
Support with understanding and following directions
Guidance in seeing the "big picture" of ideas in a topic or unit
Structure and feedback while working in order to promote success
A chance for extra teaching on a topic or skill
A sense that excellence stems from effort and growth
Self-efficacy as a learner
A classroom in which individual differences are valued and in which growth is required, supported, and acknowledged

Sample Teacher Responses to the Needs

Use some task options that call for demonstration of understanding with minimal writing
Use guided note taking in which you model effective note taking on the board or overhead projector
Provide note-taking templates or guides
Ensure small-group peer debriefing about ideas in a lecture or presentation as it proceeds
Use concept maps or similar organizers to help students see how ideas and information connect and make sense
Put directions on a tape recorder
Use reteaching sessions or mini-workshops to reach students who need additional instruction
Use flexible grouping, including opportunities to work in mixed-readiness groups in which all students have an important contribution to make to the group
Use high-interest products or assessments that call on students to use what they have learned in a meaningful way
Provide rubrics with clear guidelines for success
Provide your own and peer feedback as tasks and products evolve
Encourage students to develop some of their own criteria for success in tasks and products
Ensure that individual growth is an important factor in feedback and grading
Talk with students about the need for valuing one another's ideas, and model acceptance in your work with students
Call on special education resource teachers or reading specialists for suggestions

Sam

Student Needs

Opportunity to be an active learner
Hands-on learning
Frequent breaks in intense work
Understanding of the relevance of particular knowledge and work
Practical tasks
Understanding of his own learning style
A sense that excellence stems from effort and growth
Self-efficacy as a learner
A classroom in which individual differences are valued and in which growth is required, supported, and acknowledged

Sample Teacher Responses to the Needs

Provide many hands-on learning opportunities
Use multiple resources and flexible groups to provide variety
Use tasks and options that connect knowledge and skills with people's lives, work, and interests
Use interest centers, interest groups, and high-interest tasks
Use problem-based tasks, products, and assessments
Encourage multiple modes of expressing learning
Use concept maps or similar organizers to help students see how ideas and information connect and make sense
Help students identify, understand, and respond to their own learning styles
Provide rubrics with clear guidelines for success
Ensure your own and peer feedback as tasks and products evolve
Encourage students to develop some of their own criteria for success in tasks and products
Ensure that individual growth is an important factor in feedback and grading
Talk with students about the need for valuing one another's approaches to learning, and model acceptance in your work with students
Call on special education resource teachers or gifted education resource teachers for suggestions

Chapter 7

Answer Keys for Mastery Tests

Mastery Test, Objective 2

Answers for these activities will vary. The following questions are provided to help you focus on important issues.

You should be able to answer the following general questions for every case:

Is instruction organized around meaningful problems?
What kind of scaffolds are being used to support students' problem solving?
What is the role of feedback, reflection, and revision?
Is there evidence of a learning community?

As stated in the introduction, technology can make it quicker or easier to teach the same things in different ways, or it can make it possible to adopt new and better ways of teaching. In this activity, we have created pairs of contrasting cases that describe the same technology being used in two different ways. Each pair of cases highlights issues about specific topics.

You should also be able to answer these specific questions for each pair of cases.

Pair 1: In each case, what is the purpose of the test the students are taking? Who will see the results? How might the results of the test be used by the school system? The teacher? Students? Parents? What is the relationship of the information being tested to what is being taught? Does the use of technology change the assessment in any way?

Pair 2: How likely are students to see the usefulness of what they are learning in each of these cases? What opportunities exist for assessing students' understanding? What are some of the advantages and disadvantages of computer labs over computers in the classroom?

Pair 3: What is the role of students' exploration in each case? What are the advantages and disadvantages of simulations? Of hands-on activities? What difficulties in classroom management might arise in the situations illustrated by these scenarios?

Mastery Test, Objective 3

Answers for this activity will vary depending on the program that is selected for review. The following example can serve as a model. In addition, it provides information on another interesting program.

Program: *Voyage of the* Mimi
Publisher: Sunburst Communication, Pleasantville, NY
Sources for review: Sunburst catalogue: 1-800-321-7511; Sunburst web site: http://www.sunburstonline.com:80/mimi.html

The *Voyage of the Mimi* program provides an interdisciplinary approach to middle school education. It is composed of software, video, and print materials.

Bringing Problems into the Classroom
The cornerstone of the program is a series of thirteen short videos that tell the story of a scientific expedition to study whales. These videos are used to create a context in which students can learn about whales, navigation, map reading, and many other related topics.

Resources and Scaffolds
Support for students is provided via simulation software that allows students to study whales and their environments. These simulations feature the use of probes that measure temperature, pressure, and sound and input this information into the computer. Map-reading software that emphasizes the calculation of distance, rate, and time is also available. The publisher's *Mimi* web site gives a list of Internet resources that link students and teachers studying Mimi to one another and also to information resources on topics such as whales. Lesson plans are available from the publisher and from web sites of participating teachers. Student workbooks are also available.

Feedback, Revision, Reflection
Feedback for students is provided by simulation software. The publisher also provides a collection of checklists organized by episode and expedition and coded by subject area. These checklists can be used as performance indicators that help the teacher target curriculum goals. There are no explicit tools for revision and reflection. The teacher would have to create instructional activities that would accomplish these goals.

Communication and Community
Opportunities for building community can be found through group problem-solving activities. Given the large number of students using the curriculum, there are many possibilities for interaction among classrooms via the Internet. Many good examples of how a community functions are available in the videos themselves by studying the team that makes up the crew of the *Mimi*.

There are no explicit presentation or communication tools in *Mimi*. Teachers would need to develop these. However, the web site does link teachers and classes using *Mimi*. They could develop a plan for cross-class communication and presentation.

Mastery Test, Objective 4

Answers will vary based on the grade level and the subject area. Key items to look for in the reports include:

1. The teaching philosophy of the instructional group.
2. Technology goals of the school and district and how they fit into the teaching philosophy of the group.
3. Suggestions about particular types of software that might be used by the teachers that are consistent with the philosophy and goals outlined in points 1 and 2. For example, a report indicating that the instructional philosophy of the group and goals of the school/district are heavily oriented toward problem-

solving activities but then suggesting that the software purchased be heavily drill-and-practice would not be consistent.

Mastery Test, Entire Chapter

The format and style of the instructional unit should be consistent with those of other units that the student has undertaken for the course. There will be some variation depending on grade level and subject area, but the unit should include the four major points listed in the assignment: (1) broad theme of the unit, (2) specific learning goals and purposes of the lesson, (3) how and what technology will be used, and (4) how learning with understanding is supported by the technology.

Given the emphasis of the chapter, it would be expected that students would take a position about the use of technology that is consistent with the "learning with understanding" stance. This would include (1) goals that reflect problem solving and inquiry, (2) use of technology as a tool to assist in reaching those goals, and (3) assessments that put students into problem-solving situations where deeper understanding of material is needed rather than surface memorization.

The following is a sample response:

A middle school science teacher wants to focus her science instruction on concepts of biological interdependence. She decides to use a challenge known as "The Mystery of Stones River," which she has found on the Challenge Zone of the Learning Cooperative web site. In this unit, the students will engage in scientific inquiry designed to determine the cause of death of a large number of fish in the river. The students can formulate hypotheses and request help from the Challenge Zone to find the cause. The challenge includes a number of subchallenges that scaffold the hypothesis-testing and evidence-gathering process. The Resources section of the Challenge Zone provides pointers to web sites that are extremely useful for exploring challenges.

The students begin with the subchallenge to explain why people might be interested in sampling for macroinvertebrates as they attempt to solve the mystery of the fish kill. A second subchallenge asks students to submit reports on similar types of problems that may have occurred in their local area. In both subchallenges, the students work in groups to research answers to these questions. By accessing the Resources section of the Challenge Zone, the students can connect to relevant web sites and obtain suggestions for books, articles, videos, CD-ROMs, software, and other materials that can enhance their learning experience. For example, they might use a CD-ROM that includes a video anchor showing students beginning to monitor the Stones River and *Macroinvertebrate Sampling* software that is appropriate for subsequent parts of the challenge. This software will allow each student to take a sample and calculate a water quality index for the Stones River. The teacher also has a copy of the University of Michigan's *Model-It* software that she will have the students use to simulate various conditions in the river.

In preparation for submitting published responses to the Challenge Zone, each student will construct a written response to each subchallenge. In this activity, names are removed from papers, and students then review a subset of the responses with the goal of choosing the one that seems to provide the best reasons and explanations for the conclusions. Eventually, students as a group will either choose one of the submitted responses or write a new response that will represent the class as a whole. In this scenario, students know that a subset of submissions to the Challenge Zone will be randomly chosen to be published each week. This opportunity to have their work on public display is highly motivating, and students will make an extra effort to work together to create a high-quality response.

Following the submission of the first set of responses, the students receive a new set of subchallenges related to the Mystery of Stones River. The next subchallenge is to look at responses published by others, compare these to their class's responses, and write a summary of what they learned from the comparison. The students will analyze the responses posted by others and use this as feedback for their own thinking. In looking at the responses of older students, they might note that the older students were careful to differentiate among macroinvertebrates that are tolerant, somewhat tolerant, and intolerant of pollution. The middle school students hadn't noticed that this was even an issue. These opportunities for comparison prompt them to do more research on the topic of macroinvertebrates and summarize it for the Challenge Zone. The summary indicates that their new learning was prompted by the essays from the older students. These opportunities for feedback and revision help overcome traditional barriers associated with the lack of opportunities for formative assessment and the lack of opportunities to extend the walls of the classroom to become part of a larger learning community.

As a culminating activity for the unit, the teacher takes the students on a trip to a local river, testing the water for pollution and submitting their findings both to the department of water conservation and to the Challenge Zone.

Chapter 8

Answer Keys for Mastery Tests

Mastery Test, Objective 1

The four stages of the analytic-pluralistic classroom management process are (1) specifying desirable classroom conditions, (2) analyzing existing classroom conditions, (3) selecting and utilizing managerial strategies, and (4) assessing managerial effectiveness. If you have any reason to believe that your descriptions of these four stages are inadequate, you may want to refer to the appropriate section or sections of Learning Activity 1. Although it is important that you feel reasonably comfortable with your understanding of these four stages, subsequent learning activities are designed to provide the opportunity for more complete understanding.

Mastery Test, Objective 2

The following answers might have been given for the items in this test. Some of your responses might not agree with those here. Where there is disagreement, you may want to analyze your position. As you do so, you should recognize that some managerial strategies may be representative of more than one approach, depending on your interpretation and preference. Thus, it is altogether possible for you to give a correct response that disagrees with the key. What is most important here is that you feel comfortable with your responses, even if you happen to disagree with the key. You should feel that you are familiar with the information presented in this section of the chapter.

If you correctly identified at least forty-five of the statements, you can be fairly confident that you understand the basic principles of the eight managerial approaches described in this Learning Activity. If you did not do as well as you would have liked, you may wish to review the information presented in Learning Activities 2.1 through 2.8 and/or study any of the Readings appropriate for Objective 2 in the Additional Resources section of this chapter. When you are confident that you are familiar with each of the eight approaches, you are ready to move on to the next learning activity.

1. *AU* 2. *SE* 3. *BM* 4. *IN* 5. *SE* 6. *PM* 7. *SE* 8. *IT* 9. *CB* 10. *AU* 11. *BM* 12. *PM* 13. *SE* 14. *GP* 15. *SE* 16. *IT* 17. *BM* 18. *IN* 19. *AU* 20. *SE* 21. *CB* 22. *GP* 23. *BM* 24. *IN* 25. *SE* 26. *CB* 27. *CB* 28. *BM* 29. *GP* 30. *SE* 31. *IN* 32. *GP* 33. *CB* 34. *IT* 35. *IN* 36. *AU* 37. *CB* 38. GP *39.* IN 40. *SE* 41. *PM* 42. *IN* 43. *BM* 44. *IT* 45. *AU* 46. *CB* 47. *BM* 48. *IN* 49. *AU* 50. *GP*

Chapter 9

Answer Keys for Your Turn Exercises

Your Turn: Balancing Learning Teams

Name	Base/Rank	Team*
Alvin	73/9	C
Andy	75/8	B
Carol	64/11	A
Danielle	80/6	B
Eddy	97/2	B
Edgar	82/5	A
Jack	46/12	B
Mary	92/3	C
Sarah	99/1	A
Stan	78/7	A
Tammy	90/4	C
Travis	69/10	C
*Answers may vary.		

Your Turn: Student Team Learning

Team A
Great Team $\bar{x} = 12.5$

Team B
Good Team $\bar{x} = 7.5$

Team C
Super Team $\bar{x} = 22.5$

Team D
(No recognition) $\bar{x} = 4$

Team E
Great Team $\bar{x} = 16$

$\bar{x}$ = improvement point average

Your Turn: Jigsaw

Answers will vary. The following are examples:

1. Four-corners region of the U.S. Southwest: people, water supplies, topography, weather
2. Plot, characters, setting, historical context
3. Flora, fauna, geology, weather
4. Georgians, Armenians, Ukrainians, Moldavians

Answer Keys for Mastery Tests

Mastery Test, Objective 1

1. *F*
2. *T*
3. *T*
4. *F*
5. *F*
6. *F*
7. *T*
8. *F*

Mastery Test, Objective 2

A. Short answers
   1. (a) Positive interdependence—all for one, one for all
      (b) Accountability at the individual and team levels—team success is predicated on the growth of all members
      (c) Face-to-face promotive interaction—helping each other learn
      (d) Interpersonal and small-group skills—social skills are taught directly and explicitly in the context of the academic task
   2. (a) Slavin; primarily academic, detailed team scoring
      (b) Johnsons; equally social and academic, emphasis on teaching social skills
      (c) Kagan; every lesson has elements, some of which are cooperative, that are assembled into a complex event

B. Scenarios:
   1. *CL*
   2. *Other*
   3. *CL*
   4. *Other*
   5. *Other*

C. True/False
   1. *F.* In the first stage of the lesson, the teacher presents information or arranges the presentation of information.
   2. *F.* Productive learning teams are made up of members who are a microcosm of the diversity in class.
   3. *T*
   4. *F.* Academic progress in cooperative learning activities is measured by individual improvement.
   5. *T*
   6. *F.* Team rewards are usually based on achieving preset standards of progress. For example, teams earn rewards when members improve individual test scores by 1–10 points.

Mastery Test, Objective 3

1. Story Buddies
2. 3 by 3 by 3
3. TPS—it offers more practice opportunities
4. Different strategy—too long a time for demonstration
5. 3 by 3 by 3 or different strategy—too long a time for demonstration
6. Numbered Heads Together
7. Numbered Heads Together
8. TPS
9. 3 by 3 by 3 or TPS

Mastery Test, Objective 4

A. 2, 4, 8, 12

B. Answers will vary. However, only one team should have three white students; only one team should have one female; three teams should have two minority students. Each team should have one of the four highest-scoring and one of the lowest-scoring students. Example: Team A—LaTanya, Melissa, Paul, Victor; Team B—Doris, Frank, George, Sam; Team C—Ann, Nan, Ross, William; Team D—Bud, Charles, Hattie, Joy

C. Five elements: form heterogeneous learning teams, present content, have teams practice, assess individual learning, recognize team accomplishments. The applications will vary.

D. Six elements: form learning teams, form expert teams, develop expertise, share expertise, assess individual achievement, recognize team accomplishments. The applications will vary.

Mastery Test, Objective 5

A. Students' Social Skills
   1. Forming—procedural, use Talking Chips to teach turn-taking; functioning—affective routines, restating, paraphrasing, clarifying, use Gambit Chips; formulating—mastering lesson content, Pairs Check; fermenting—expanding on lesson content, probing, critiquing, challenging.
   2. Different cultural groups in any country will have different norms and expectations. Children do not come to school with shared definitions of good manners.

B. Teacher Types
   1. She should address only individuals or teams during group time.
   2. He should let teams take care of their own process questions.
   3. She should encourage his team to engage him.
   4. Students can and should be talking quietly about their work from time to time; it would deepen their learning.

Mastery Test, Objective 6

1. He should move the desks and let folks know why.
2. He should have a special meeting with Ms. Jones to explain what he is doing and ask for her coopera-

tion. Perhaps he can get her to give him daily feedback on the state of the room when she gets to it or give the class such feedback in the form of stickers she places on the posters of teams that are doing a good job of cleaning up.

3. He should do a quick review of the workshop for the principal and lead teacher. He should ask the principal for specific data collection help. Verbatim data are useful and easier for an observer than for the teacher to get.
4. He should explain the cooperative learning approach to Mr. Zack, with special attention to the continued reliance on individual performance for individual grades.
5. He should gather and share data on the benefits to gifted students and describe other opportunities Alison has during the day to stretch her thinking.
6. He should routinely rotate roles and teach leadership skills directly. All students should know how to exercise leadership, even if some have greater natural skill and inclination than others.

Mastery Test, Objective 7

1. *F.* They have both shown achievement effects.
2. *T*
3. *F.* They work best if they target their efforts broadly.
4. *T*
5. *T*
6. *F.* They have learned many requisite skills in the classroom.
7. *T*

Chapter 10

Answer Keys for Your Turn Exercises

Your Turn: Selecting an Information-Gathering Instrument

1. Observation is the best choice because to find out *how* the pupils form their letters, you must watch them forming them.
2. Feelings are best discovered by inquiry. This teacher should ask his students how they feel.
3. Achievement is best measured through testing.
4. Whenever you want a measure of maximum performance of a cognitive skill, test.
5. Observing their performance and perhaps analyzing what she hears—that's the answer to this music teacher's evaluation problem.
6. Observation is best, preferably without the students' knowing that they are being watched.

Your Turn: Selecting the Type of Item

1. *Essay:* To explain, the student needs considerable freedom to respond.
2. *Short answer:* No freedom here, just the steps.
3. *Multiple choice:* Selection from among alternatives is being called for.
4. *Essay:* To discuss requires freedom to respond.
5. *Short answer:* This objective calls for just a list, no explanation.
6. *Multiple choice:* This requires choosing among alternatives or *matching,* with types of malfunctions in one column and the possible causes in another.
7. *Multiple choice:* An example of this type of item might be: "The underlined word represents which of the following parts of speech," or you can use *matching,* with words in one column and parts of speech in the other.

Your Turn: Writing Essay Items

1. *An open-ended question:* This question should allow the student a great deal of freedom to respond, but it should be quite clear about what is being asked. You can see from the following samples that open-ended questions can be difficult to grade because each student may choose to restrict his or her own answer in a different way.

Sample Questions

(a) Discuss ways you might reduce your anxiety when preparing to make an extemporaneous speech.
(b) What could you do to reduce the number of germs on medical instruments if you have no sterilization equipment?
(c) Discuss the pros and cons of the draft registration.
(d) Convince me that it is important to understand the history of the English language.

2. *A restricted essay question:* Again, make certain that your question has been clearly written. Check to see that your question limits the answers in a way that will help the student to respond (the student will know how to answer *if* he or she knows the information being asked for).

Sample Questions

(a) List and explain each of the steps we discussed for setting up an experiment.
(b) In no more than ten lines, describe a typical Eskimo village from the early 1900s.
(c) Cite five reasons for having a 55-mph speed limit. Defend one of your reasons with supporting evidence.

Your Turn: Constructing a Model Answer

Check your model answer against the criteria for model answers. Compare your model answers with those of your peers. If you are uncertain about your answers, ask your instructor to check them.

Your Turn: Evaluating and Writing Multiple-Choice Questions

Check your items against the criteria for effective multiple-choice items. In addition, exchange your items with a classmate and evaluate each other's items.

Your Turn: Types of Judgments

1. b
2. c
3. *A*
4. *A*
5. *C*
6. *B*

Answer Keys for Mastery Tests

Mastery Test, Objective 1

1. Evaluation is the process of obtaining information and forming judgments to be used in decision making.
2. (a) *Preparing for assessment.* In this stage, you need to determine the judgments and decisions you anticipate making (for example, when to begin Unit 2, what assignments to give, where to place Johnny). Next, you must decide what information you will need to make those judgments and decisions (for example, how quickly the students are moving through Unit 1, what the students' interests are, how well Johnny reads). Finally, you will decide when and how to obtain the information needed (for example, weekly, through quizzes; first week of class, using an interest inventory; second week of class, using a standardized test of reading and observing students during oral reading).
   (b) *Obtaining needed information.* Involves asking students (inquiry), observing students (watching students setting up an experiment), or testing students (giving a multiple-choice test of history facts).
   (c) *Forming judgments.* In this stage, you compare the information with some referent and make a value judgment. Grades reflecting achievement and predictions about how well a student might be expected to do are both common examples of classroom judgments.
   (d) *Using judgments in decisions and preparing reports.* Deciding what action to take (for example, move Johnny to a slower reading group) and reporting the evaluation results that led to that decision compose the major tasks of the final stage of assessment. Note that the emphasis is on the *use* of judgments.

Mastery Test, Objective 2

1. d
2. a
3. c
4. b
5. a
6. d

Mastery Test, Objective 3

Evaluate your test against these criteria:

1. The test clearly measures the objectives.
2. The items are clear and concise (unambiguous).
3. The type of items used represents the most direct way to measure the objectives.
4. The readability of the items is appropriate for the grade level you selected.
5. Any necessary instructions to the students are clearly stated.

Mastery Test, Objective 4

1. *Developing checklists:* Your checklist should be clear, concise, and easy to use. If possible, try using it. Ask someone who is an expert at the performance to check your list to see if you have included only the important behaviors.
2. *Constructing rating scales:* Check your scale against the criteria for an effective rating scale. Share your scale with classmates, and ask them if they feel that they would be able to use it successfully.

Mastery Test, Objective 5

1. Carefully selected collection of students' work.
2. Type and quantity of errors, type of thinking or problem-solving strategies, ability of students to catch and fix their own mistakes.
3. b
4. b

Mastery Test, Objective 6

1. a
2. *A*
3. *B*
4. *A*
5. *C*
6. b

7. c
8. d

Mastery Test, Objectve 7

1. The student's answer should include at least: to adjust our teaching as needed, to catch misconceptions early, to determine more effective learning strategies.
2. What they do and how they think during the learning process.

Mastery Test, Objective 8

1. Validity. If a test does not measure what you need measured, it is not valid for your use. It is of no use to you, even if it is extremely reliable.
2. a. Will it give me the information I need?
   b. Will the information be reasonably reliable?
   c. Is the test easy to administer, score, and interpret?
   d. Is the cost within our budget?
3. b
4. a
5. To follow exactly the instructions for administering the test.
6. The teacher should try to clarify and help students understand what is being asked of them but should do nothing that would give away the answer.

INTASC Model Standards for Beginning Teacher Licensing and Development

Principle #1: The teacher understands the central concepts, tools of inquiry, and structures of the discipline(s) he or she teaches and can create learning experiences that make these aspects of subject matter meaningful for students.

Knowledge
The teacher understands major concepts, assumptions, debates, processes of inquiry, and ways of knowing that are central to the discipline(s) s/he teaches.

The teacher understands how students' conceptual frameworks and their misconceptions for an area of knowledge can influence their learning.

The teacher can relate his/her disciplinary knowledge to other subject areas.

Dispositions
The teacher realizes that subject matter knowledge is not a fixed body of facts but is complex and ever-evolving. S/he seeks to keep abreast of new ideas and understandings in the field.

The teacher appreciates multiple perspectives and conveys to learners how knowledge is developed from the vantage point of the knower.

The teacher has enthusiasm for the discipline(s) s/he teaches and sees connections to everyday life.

The teacher is committed to continuous learning and engages in professional discourse about subject matter knowledge and children's learning of the discipline.

Performances
The teacher effectively uses multiple representations and explanations of disciplinary concepts that capture key ideas and link them to students' prior understandings.

The teacher can represent and use differing viewpoints, theories, "ways of knowing" and methods of inquiry in his/her teaching of subject matter concepts.

The teacher can evaluate teaching resources and curriculum materials for their comprehensiveness, accuracy, and usefulness for representing particular ideas and concepts.

The teacher engages students in generating knowledge and testing hypotheses according to the methods of inquiry and standards of evidence used in the discipline.

The teacher develops and uses curricula that encourage students to see, question, and interpret ideas from diverse perspectives.

The teacher can create interdisciplinary learning experiences that allow students to integrate knowledge, skills, and methods of inquiry from several subject areas.

Principle #2: The teacher understands how children learn and develop, and can provide learning opportunities that support their intellectual, social and personal development.

Knowledge
The teacher understands how learning occurs—how students construct knowledge, acquire skills, and develop habits of mind—and knows how to use instructional strategies that promote student learning.

The teacher understands that students' physical, social, emotional, moral and cognitive development influence learning and knows how to address these factors when making instructional decisions.

The teacher is aware of expected developmental progressions and ranges of individual variation within each domain (physical, social, emotional, moral and cognitive), can identify levels of readiness in learning, and understands how development in any one domain may affect performance in others.

Dispositions
The teacher appreciates individual variation within each area of development, shows respect for the diverse talents of all learners, and is committed to help them develop self-confidence and competence.

The teacher is disposed to use students' strengths as a basis for growth, and their errors as an opportunity for learning.

Performances
The teacher assesses individual and group performance in order to design instruction that meets learners' current needs in each domain (cognitive, social, emotional, moral, and physical) and that leads to the next level of development.

The teacher stimulates student reflection on prior knowledge and links new ideas to already familiar ideas, making connections to students' experiences, providing opportunities for active engagement, manipulation, and testing of ideas and materials, and encouraging students to assume responsibility for shaping their learning tasks.

The teacher accesses students' thinking and experiences as a basis for instructional activities by, for example, encouraging discussion, listening and responding to group interaction, and eliciting samples of student thinking orally and in writing.

Principle #3: The teacher understands how students differ in their approaches to learning and creates instructional opportunities that are adapted to diverse learners.

Knowledge

The teacher understands and can identify differences in approaches to learning and performance, including different learning styles, multiple intelligences, and performance modes, and can design instruction that helps use students' strengths as the basis for growth.

The teacher knows about areas of exceptionality in learning—including learning disabilities, visual and perceptual difficulties, and special physical or mental challenges.

The teacher knows about the process of second language acquisition and about strategies to support the learning of students whose first language is not English.

The teacher understands how students' learning is influenced by individual experiences, talents, and prior learning, as well as language, culture, family and community values.

The teacher has a well-grounded framework for understanding cultural and community diversity and knows how to learn about and incorporate students' experiences, cultures, and community resources into instruction.

Dispositions

The teacher believes that all children can learn at high levels and persists in helping all children achieve success.

The teacher appreciates and values human diversity, shows respect for students' varied talents and perspectives, and is committed to the pursuit of "individually configured excellence."

The teacher respects students as individuals with differing personal and family backgrounds and various skills, talents, and interests.

The teacher is sensitive to community and cultural norms.

The teacher makes students feel valued for their potential as people, and helps them learn to value each other.

Performances

The teacher identifies and designs instruction appropriate to students' stages of development, learning styles, strengths, and needs.

The teacher uses teaching approaches that are sensitive to the multiple experiences of learners and that address different learning and performance modes.

The teacher makes appropriate provisions (in terms of time and circumstances for work, tasks assigned, communication and response modes) for individual students who have particular learning differences or needs.

The teacher can identify when and how to access appropriate services or resources to meet exceptional learning needs.

The teacher seeks to understand students' families, cultures, and communities, and uses this information as a basis for connecting instruction to students' experiences (e.g. drawing explicit connections between subject matter and community matters, making assignments that can be related to students' experiences and cultures).

The teacher brings multiple perspectives to the discussion of subject matter, including attention to students' personal, family, and community experiences and cultural norms.

The teacher creates a learning community in which individual differences are respected.

Principle #4: The teacher understands and uses a variety of instructional strategies to encourage students' development of critical thinking, problem solving, and performance skills.

Knowledge

The teacher understands the cognitive processes associated with various kinds of learning (e.g. critical and creative thinking, problem structuring and problem solving, invention, memorization and recall) and how these processes can be stimulated.

The teacher understands principles and techniques, along with advantages and limitations, associated with various instructional strategies (e.g. cooperative learning, direct instruction, discovery learning, whole group discussion, independent study, interdisciplinary instruction).

The teacher knows how to enhance learning through the use of a wide variety of materials as well as human and technological resources (e.g. computers, audio-visual technologies, videotapes and discs, local experts, primary documents and artifacts, texts, reference books, literature, and other print resources).

Dispositions

The teacher values the development of students' critical thinking, independent problem solving, and performance capabilities.

The teacher values flexibility and reciprocity in the teaching process as necessary for adapting instruction to student responses, ideas, and needs.

Performances

The teacher carefully evaluates how to achieve learning goals, choosing alternative teaching strategies and materials to achieve different instructional purposes and to meet student needs (e.g. developmental stages, prior knowledge, learning styles, and interests).

The teacher uses multiple teaching and learning strategies to engage students in active learning opportunities that promote the development of critical thinking, problem solving, and performance capabilities and that help students assume responsibility for identifying and using learning resources.

The teacher constantly monitors and adjusts strategies in response to learner feedback.

The teacher varies his or her role in the instructional process (e.g. instructor, facilitator, coach, audience) in relation to the content and purposes of instruction and the needs of students.

The teacher develops a variety of clear, accurate presentations and representations of concepts, using alternative explanations to assist students' understanding and presenting diverse perspectives to encourage critical thinking.

Principle #5: The teacher uses an understanding of individual and group motivation and behavior to create a learning environment that encourages positive social interaction, active engagement in learning, and self-motivation.

Knowledge

The teacher can use knowledge about human motivation and behavior drawn from the foundational sciences of psychology, anthropology, and sociology to develop strategies for organizing and supporting individual and group work.

The teacher understands how social groups function and influence people, and how people influence groups.

The teacher knows how to help people work productively and cooperatively with each other in complex social settings.

The teacher understands the principles of effective classroom management and can use a range of strategies to promote positive relationships, cooperation, and purposeful learning in the classroom.

The teacher recognizes factors and situations that are likely to promote or diminish intrinsic motivation, and knows how to help students become self-motivated.

Dispositions

The teacher takes responsibility for establishing a positive climate in the classroom and participates in maintaining such a climate in the school as a whole.

The teacher understands how participation supports commitment, and is committed to the expression and use of democratic values in the classroom.

The teacher values the role of students in promoting each other's learning and recognizes the importance of peer relationships in establishing a climate of learning.

The teacher recognizes the value of intrinsic motivation to students' life-long growth and learning.

The teacher is committed to the continuous development of individual students' abilities and considers how different motivational strategies are likely to encourage this development for each student.

Performances

The teacher creates a smoothly functioning learning community in which students assume responsibility for themselves and one another, participate in decisionmaking, work collaboratively and independently, and engage in purposeful learning activities.

The teacher engages students in individual and cooperative learning activities that help them develop the motivation to achieve, by, for example, relating lessons to students' personal interests, allowing students to have choices in their learning, and leading students to ask questions and pursue problems that are meaningful to them.

The teacher organizes, allocates, and manages the resources of time, space, activities, and attention to provide active and equitable engagement of students in productive tasks.

The teacher maximizes the amount of class time spent in learning by creating expectations and processes for communication and behavior along with a physical setting conducive to classroom goals.

The teacher helps the group to develop shared values and expectations for student interactions, academic discussions, and individual and group responsibility that create a positive classroom climate of openness, mutual respect, support, and inquiry.

The teacher analyzes the classroom environment and makes decisions and adjustments to enhance social relationships, student motivation and engagement, and productive work.

The teacher organizes, prepares students for, and monitors independent and group work that allows for full and varied participation of all individuals.

Principle #6: The teacher uses knowledge of effective verbal, nonverbal, and media communication techniques to foster active inquiry, collaboration, and supportive interaction in the classroom.

Knowledge

The teacher understands communication theory, language development, and the role of language in learning.

The teacher understands how cultural and gender differences can affect communication in the classroom.

The teacher recognizes the importance of nonverbal as well as verbal communication.

The teacher knows about and can use effective verbal, nonverbal, and media communication techniques.

Dispositions

The teacher recognizes the power of language for fostering self-expression, identity development, and learning.

The teacher values many ways in which people seek to communicate and encourages many modes of communication in the classroom.

The teacher is a thoughtful and responsive listener.

The teacher appreciates the cultural dimensions of communication, responds appropriately, and seeks to foster culturally sensitive communication by and among all students in the class.

Performances

The teacher models effective communication strategies in conveying ideas and information and in asking questions (e.g. monitoring the effects of messages, restating ideas and drawing connections, using visual, aural, and kinesthetic cues, being sensitive to nonverbal cues given and received).

The teacher supports and expands learner expression in speaking, writing, and other media.

The teacher knows how to ask questions and stimulate discussion in different ways for particular purposes, for example, probing for learner understanding, helping students articulate their ideas and thinking processes, promoting risk-taking and problem-solving, facilitating factual recall, encouraging convergent and divergent thinking, stimulating curiosity, helping students to question.

The teacher communicates in ways that demonstrate a sensitivity to cultural and gender differences (e.g. appropriate use of eye contact, interpretation of body language and verbal statements, acknowledgment of and responsiveness to different modes of communication and participation).

The teacher knows how to use a variety of media communication tools, including audio-visual aids and computers, to enrich learning opportunities.

Principle #7: The teacher plans instruction based upon knowledge of subject matter, students, the community, and curriculum goals.

Knowledge

The teacher understands learning theory, subject matter, curriculum development, and student development and knows how to use this knowledge in planning instruction to meet curriculum goals.

The teacher knows how to take contextual considerations (instructional materials, individual student interests, needs, and aptitudes, and community resources) into account in planning instruction that creates an effective bridge between curriculum goals and students' experiences.

The teacher knows when and how to adjust plans based on student responses and other contingencies.

Dispositions

The teacher values both long-term and short-term planning.

The teacher believes that plans must always be open to adjustment and revision based on student needs and changing circumstances.

The teacher values planning as a collegial activity.

Performances

As an individual and a member of a team, the teacher selects and creates learning experiences that are appropriate for curriculum goals, relevant to learners, and based upon principles of effective instruction (e.g. that activate students' prior knowledge, anticipate preconceptions, encourage exploration and problem-solving, and build new skills on those previously acquired).

The teacher plans for learning opportunities that recognize and address variation in learning styles and performance modes.

The teacher creates lessons and activities that operate at multiple levels to meet the developmental and individual needs of diverse learners and help each progress.

The teacher creates short-range and long-term plans that are linked to student needs and performance, and adapts the plans to ensure and capitalize on student progress and motivation.

The teacher responds to unanticipated sources of input, evaluates plans in relation to short- and long-range goals, and systematically adjusts plans to meet student needs and enhance learning.

Principle #8: The teacher understands and uses formal and informal assessment strategies to evaluate and ensure the continuous intellectual, social and physical development of the learner.

Knowledge

The teacher understands the characteristics, uses, advantages, and limitations of different types of assessments (e.g. criterion-referenced and norm-referenced instruments, traditional standardized and performance-based tests, observation systems, and assessments of student work) for evaluating how students learn, what they know and are able to do, and what kinds of experiences will support their further growth and development.

The teacher knows how to select, construct, and use assessment strategies and instruments appropriate to the learning outcomes being evaluated and to other diagnostic purposes.

The teacher understands measurement theory and assessment-related issues, such as validity, reliability, bias, and scoring concerns.

Dispositions

The teacher values ongoing assessment as essential to the instructional process and recognizes that many different assessment strategies, accurately and systematically used, are necessary for monitoring and promoting student learning.

The teacher is committed to using assessment to identify student strengths and promote student growth rather than to deny students access to learning opportunities.

Performances

The teacher appropriately uses a variety of formal and informal assessment techniques (e.g. observation, portfolios of student work, teacher-made tests, performance tasks, projects, student self-assessments, peer assessment, and standardized tests) to enhance her or his knowledge of learners, evaluate students' progress and performances, and modify teaching and learning strategies.

The teacher solicits and uses information about students' experiences, learning behavior, needs, and progress from parents, other colleagues, and the students themselves.

The teacher uses assessment strategies to involve learners in self-assessment activities, to help them become aware of their strengths and needs, and to encourage them to set personal goals for learning.

The teacher evaluates the effect of class activities on both individuals and the class as a whole, collecting information through observation of classroom interactions, questioning, and analysis of student work.

The teacher monitors his or her own teaching strategies and behavior in relation to student success, modifying plans and instructional approaches accordingly.

The teacher maintains useful records of student work and performance and can communicate student progress knowledgeably and responsibly, based on appropriate indicators, to students, parents, and other colleagues.

Principle #9: The teacher is a reflective practitioner who continually evaluates the effects of his/her choices and actions on others (students, parents, and other professionals in the learning community) and who actively seeks out opportunities to grow professionally.

Knowledge

The teacher understands methods of inquiry that provide him/her with a variety of self-assessment and problem-solving strategies for reflecting on his/her practice, its influences on students' growth and learning, and the complex interactions between them.

The teacher is aware of major areas of research on teaching and of resources available for professional learning (e.g. professional literature, colleagues, professional associations, professional development activities).

Dispositions

The teacher values critical thinking and self-directed learning as habits of mind.

The teacher is committed to reflection, assessment, and learning as an ongoing process.

The teacher is willing to give and receive help.

The teacher is committed to seeking out, developing, and continually refining practices that address the individual needs of students.

The teacher recognizes his/her professional responsibility for engaging in and supporting appropriate professional practices for self and colleagues.

Performances

The teacher uses classroom observation, information about students, and research as sources for evaluating the outcomes of teaching and learning and as a basis for experimenting with, reflecting on, and revising practice.

The teacher seeks out professional literature, colleagues, and other resources to support his/her own development as a learner and a teacher.

The teacher draws upon professional colleagues within the school and other professional arenas as supports for reflection, problem-solving and new ideas, actively sharing experiences and seeking and giving feedback.

Principle #10: The teacher fosters relationships with school colleagues, parents, and agencies in the larger community to support students' learning and well-being.

Knowledge

The teacher understands schools as organizations within the larger community context and understands the operations of the relevant aspects of the system(s) within which s/he works.

The teacher understands how factors in the students' environment outside of school (e.g. family circumstances, community environments, health and economic conditions) may influence students' life and learning.

The teacher understands and implements laws related to students' rights and teacher responsibilities (e.g. for equal education, appropriate education for handicapped students, confidentiality, privacy, appropriate treatment of students, reporting in situations related to possible child abuse).

Dispositions

The teacher values and appreciates the importance of all aspects of a child's experience.

The teacher is concerned about all aspects of a child's well-being (cognitive, emotional, social, and physical), and is alert to signs of difficulties.

The teacher is willing to consult with other adults regarding the education and well-being of his/her students.

The teacher respects the privacy of students and confidentiality of information.

The teacher is willing to work with other professionals to improve the overall learning environment for students.

Performances

The teacher participates in collegial activities designed to make the entire school a productive learning environment.

The teacher makes links with the learners' other environments on behalf of students, by consulting with parents, counselors, teachers of other classes and activities within the schools, and professionals in other community agencies.

The teacher can identify and use community resources to foster student learning.

The teacher establishes respectful and productive relationships with parents and guardians from diverse home and community situations, and seeks to develop cooperative partnerships in support of student learning and well being.

The teacher talks with and listens to the student, is sensitive and responsive to clues of distress, investigates situations, and seeks outside help as needed and appropriate to remedy problems.

The teacher acts as an advocate for students.

Source: Interstate New Teacher Assessment and Support Consortium (1992). *Model Standards for Beginning Teacher Licensing and Development: A Resource for State Dialogue.* Washington, D.C.: Council of Chief State School Officers.

Glossary

Abstract concepts. Those concepts that can be acquired only indirectly through the senses.

Active listening. Differentiating between the intellectual and emotional content of a message, and making inferences about the feelings experienced by the speaker.

Advance organizers. A means of informing students of the way new information that they are about to learn is organized.

Affective goals. Goals that deal primarily with emotion and feeling.

Analysis questions. Questions that require the student to break down a communication into its constituent parts, such that the relative hierarchy of ideas is made clear and/or the relations between the ideas expressed are made explicit.

Anchor activity. A task or series of tasks to which students automatically move when they complete an assigned task. Anchor activities should be meaningful, worthy of a student's time, and designed to further their knowledge, understanding, skill, and/or interests in important content and learning goals.

Application questions. Questions requiring the student to apply a rule or process to a problem to determine the correct answer.

Assessment. Used interchangeably with *evaluation,* the term *assessment* is being used to expand our thinking to include practical and more authentic evaluation procedures and informal as well as formal evaluation tools.

Attitude. A predisposition to act in a positive or negative way toward persons, ideas, or events.

Attraction. Friendship patterns in the classroom group.

Authentic assessment. Assessment that seeks to assess tasks that most directly measure learning outcomes.

Authentic questions. Questions that are motivational and meaningful because they connect with real-life student curiosity, interests, needs, and experiences.

Base score. A percentage score calculated for each student by averaging scores of three recent tests of equal weight to show the student's relative achievement standing in a class and to serve as the point of comparison with later test scores. Base scores are designed to provide a relatively stable indicator of a student's typical performance in a content area.

Checklist. A list of criteria for evaluating a performance or end product.

Classroom management. The set of teacher behaviors by which the teacher establishes and maintains conditions that facilitate effective and efficient instruction—conditions that promote on-task behavior.

Closure. Actions and statements by the teacher designed to help students organize their thinking around the major points of a presentation or discussion.

Cohesiveness. The collective feeling that the class members have about the classroom group; the sum of the individual members' feelings about the group.

Comprehension questions. Questions requiring the student to select, organize, and mentally arrange the materials pertinent to answering the question.

Concept mapping. A procedure for organizing and graphically displaying ideas relevant to a given topic, so that relationships among the ideas are clarified.

Concurrent validity. An estimate of how well a test approximates a score on another test that was designed to measure the same variables.

Conditioned reinforcers. Reinforcers that are learned.

Constructivist theorist. An educator who believes that learners acquire meaning or knowledge by interacting directly with their environment.

Content validity. A judgment about how well the items in a test measure what the test has been designed to measure.

Convergent thinking. Thinking that occurs when the task, or question, is so structured that several people will arrive at similar conclusions or answers, and the number of possible appropriate conclusions is limited (usually one conclusion).

Cooperative learning. An instructional task design that engages students actively in achieving a lesson objective through their own efforts and the efforts of the members of their small, heterogeneous learning team.

Criterion-referenced judgments. Judgments made by comparing the information you have about an individual with some performance criterion; that is, some description of expected behavior.

Decision. A choice among alternative courses of action.

Desist behaviors. Behaviors the teacher uses in an effort to stop student misbehavior.

Differentiated instruction. Varied approaches to what students need to learn, how they will learn it, and/or how they can express what they have learned intended in order to increase the likelihood that each student will learn as much and as efficiently as possible.

Differentiated questions. Teacher questions that respond to and build on student differences, including skill level, learning styles, and individual interests.

Divergent thinking. Thinking that occurs when the task, or question, is so open that several people will arrive at different conclusions or answers, and the number of possible appropriate conclusions is fairly large.

Domain. A field of study, for example, physics, mathematics.

Effective teacher. One who is able to bring about intended learning outcomes.

Embedded data. Information included in a problem statement that must be consulted in order to solve the problem. This is a design feature of the mathematics problem-solving series *The Adventures of Jasper Woodbury.*

Embedded teaching. Scenes included in a problem statement that provide an idea of how to do something without actually providing answers. This is a design feature of the mathematics problem-solving series *The Adventures of Jasper Woodbury*

Evaluation. The process of obtaining information and using it to form judgments that, in turn, are to be used in decision making.

Evaluation questions. Questions requiring students to use criteria or standards to form judgments about the value of the topic or phenomena being considered.

Exit cards. An assessment strategy that takes a quick measure of student understanding as a lesson is ending. Generally, teachers ask students one or two thought or application questions about what they have been learning. Students write their responses in a short period of time (usually no more than 5 minutes) on an index card, and give the card to the teacher as they leave the classroom or move to another activity. The teacher keeps the cards not for a grade, but to determine students' varying needs for next steps in learning.

Expectations. Those perceptions that the teacher and the students hold regarding their relationships to one another.

Expert group. In the cooperative learning strategy Jigsaw, a small group of students whose task is to learn very well certain parts of a complex lesson, in order to effectively coach the members of the (home) learning team.

Extinction. Withholding of an anticipated reward in an instance where that behavior was previously rewarded; results in the decreased frequency of the previously rewarded behavior.

Feedback. Information about the effects or consequences of actions taken.

Generalization. A broad and potentially useful observation about racial, ethnic, class, and gender groups. Such statements are flexible, responsive to individual differences, and can assist teachers in planning for instruction.

Goals. General statements of purpose.

Group-focus behaviors. Those behaviors teachers use to maintain a focus on the group, rather than on an individual student, during individual recitations.

Group investigations. A cooperative strategy in which students group themselves according to particular interests in subtopics in the unit of study. The teacher helps students learn to develop effective research questions, conduct productive research, plan and assess the quality of their work, and present findings in a useful way.

Heterogeneous learning teams. In cooperative learning, working groups made up of four or five students whose differences in entering achievement levels, gender, and ethnicity reflect the variety in the whole class.

Hypermedia. Computer-based documents containing video, graphics, sound, and text that can be controlled by the user. As students explore one topic, they can jump to related topics quickly and easily.

Improvement scores. In cooperative learning, team scores are calculated by comparing the entering achievement levels (see **base score**) with the test scores of each individual. Differences of a given amount translate into "improvement points" and are added to create a team "improvement score" according to a predetermined formula. Improvement scores are the basis of team rewards.

Individual accountability. In cooperative learning, the design of outcome measures to assure that the achievement of each student is measured independently and that individual achievement provides the basis for earning team rewards.

Inference. A conclusion derived from, and bearing some relation to, assumed premises.

INTASC. An acronym standing for "Interstate New Teachers Assessment and Support Consortium." INTASC, a project of the Council of Chief State School Officers, is developing both general and subject specific teaching standards for beginning teachers.

Inquiry. Obtaining information by asking.

Inquiry-based learning. An approach to teaching and learning in which students deepen their understanding of the underlying principles of a domain by conducting investigations. These investigations typically include asking questions, making predictions, gathering evidence, and constructing explanations.

Instructional event. Any activity or set of activities in which students are engaged (with or without the teacher) for the purpose of learning.

Instructional grouping. Dividing a class of pupils into small subunits for purposes of teaching. Groups can be formed according to achievement learning profiles or interest, depending on instructional purpose.

Instructional objectives. Statements of desired changes in student's thoughts, actions, or feelings that a particular course or educational program should bring about.

Interdisciplinary teaching. Integrating the subject matter from two or more disciplines, such as English and history, often using themes such as inventions, discoveries, or health, as overlays to the study of different subjects.

Interval schedule. A type of intermittent reinforcement in which the teacher reinforces the student after a specified period of time.

Jigsaw. A cooperative learning strategy in which students participate first in expert groups, where they learn about a particular aspect of a subject, and then return to learning teams (each having one or more experts of each kind) where the experts in turn teach teammates, who eventually share the knowledge mastered by each expert group.

Judgment. Estimate of present conditions or prediction of future conditions. Involves comparing information to some referent.

Just-in-time learning. A problem-based approach to teaching and learning in which knowledge is acquired just as it is needed to solve a problem.

Knowledge questions. Questions requiring the student to recognize or recall information.

Leadership. Those behaviors that help the group move toward the accomplishment of its objectives.

Learning Situation. Any classroom activity in which students are actively engaged in learning.

Learning Together. The general term for cooperative learning activities of a certain type, developed and advocated by David and Roger Johnson, with a joint emphasis on academic learning and group process skills.

Measurement error. The error that occurs when any measurement is made. Theoretically, it is the difference between the "true" score and any given obtained score.

Metacognition. An awareness of and control over one's own thinking and problem solving processes, for example, knowing what one knows and what still needs to be learned or discovered.

Microworld. A computer program that presents a model of real-world phenomena that students can control and explore.

Movement management. Those behaviors that the teacher uses to initiate, sustain, or terminate a classroom activity.

Multiple intelligences. Distinct forms of human talent that have biological roots and are valued in one or more cultures, identified by Howard Gardner; among those currently known are linguistic, logical-mathematical, spatial, musical, bodily-kinesthetic, interpersonal, intrapersonal, and naturalistic.

Negative reinforcement. The withholding or withdrawal of punishment; the withholding or withdrawal of a negative consequence.

Norm-referenced judgments. Judgments made by comparing the information you have about an individual with information you have about a group of similar individuals.

Norms. Shared expectations of how group members should think, feel, and behave.

Numbered Heads Together. A gamelike cooperative learning strategy in which four- or five-student teams first make sure all members know the answer to a question and then earn points if their randomly selected teammate can respond correctly.

Observation. The process of looking and listening, noticing the important elements of a performance or a product.

On-task behavior. Student behavior that is appropriate to the task.

Overlapping behaviors. Those behaviors by which the teacher indicates that he or she is attending to more than one issue when there is more than one issue to deal with at a particular time.

Pedagogical content knowledge. The blending of content and pedagogy into an understanding of how particular topics, problems, or issues are organized, represented, and adapted to the diverse interests and abilities of learners and presented for instruction.

Peer teaching. A procedure that provides teachers an opportunity to practice new instructional techniques in a simplified setting by teaching lessons to small groups of their peers (other prospective or experienced teachers).

Personal practical knowledge. The understanding that teachers have of the practical circumstances in which they work, which include the beliefs, insights, and habits that enable them to do their jobs in schools.

Portfolio. A collection of work assembled over time to demonstrate the meeting of a learning standard or the acquisition of a skill. Portfolios can be developed by both students and teachers.

Positive reinforcement. The introduction of a reward; the introduction of a positive consequence.

Predictive validity. An estimate of how well a test predicts scores on some future test or performance.

Primary reinforcers. Reinforcers that are unlearned and necessary to sustain life.

Probing (delving) questions. Questions following a response that require the respondent to provide more support, be clearer or more accurate, or offer greater specificity or originality.

Problem solving. A way to organize and interrelate existing knowledge as well as to acquire new information. It combines knowledge already acquired and adds new elements, such as facts, concepts, and generalizations.

Problem-solving instructional strategies. Framing or structuring subject matter to create a psychological state of doubt.

Professional development. The process of acquiring specialized knowledge and skills, as well as an awareness of the alternative actions that might be appropriate in particular situations.

Punishment. Use of an unpleasant stimulus to eliminate an undesirable behavior.

Questionnaire. A list of written questions that can be read and responded to by the student or other respondent.

Rating scales. Instruments that provide a scale of values describing someone or something being evaluated.

Ratio schedule. A type of intermittent reinforcement in which the teacher reinforces the student after the behavior has occurred a certain number of times.

Referent. That to which you compare the information you have about an individual to form a judgment.

Reflection. The process by which teachers inquire into their teaching and think critically about their work.

Reflective decision maker. A model of the teacher that emphasizes the use of reflection as teachers make planning, implementation, and evaluation decisions.

Reinforcement. The process of using reinforcers; in general, any event that increases the strength of a response. A reward for the purpose of maintaining an already acquired behavior is called *positive reinforcement.* Strengthening a behavior through the removal of an unpleasant stimulus is called *negative reinforcement.*

Reliability. A characteristic of a test that measures its consistency. Several kinds of reliability exist, including *internal consistency* (how consistent the test measures from item to item); *test-retest* (estimates how consistently a test measures from one time to the next); and *alternative form* (estimates how closely two forms of the same test measure the same thing).

Repertoire. A set of alternative routines or procedures, all of which serve some common purpose and each of which serves some additional, unique purpose. A person who has a repertoire of procedures available is recognized as being practiced and skillful in use of these procedures, as well as sensitive in selecting the appropriate procedure to use in any given situation.

Routine. An established pattern of behavior.

Rubric. A set of rules for scoring student products or student performance. Typically takes the form of a checklist or a rating scale.

Scaffolding (scaffolds). Instructional assistance—through questions, explanations, and activities—that bridges the gap between what a student knows and what a student needs to learn.

Self-referenced judgments. Judgments made by comparing information you have about an individual to some other information you have about that same individual.

Set. Actions and statements by the teacher that are designed to relate the experiences of the students to the objectives of the lesson.

Standardized test. A test that has a fixed set of questions that must be administered according to a specified set of directions and within time limitations.

Stereotype. A broad and potentially damaging conception about racial, ethnic, class, and gender groups. Such statements are inflexible, ignore individual differences, and can create an obstacle for effective instruction.

Structural Approach. Kagan's framework for cooperative learning, in which complex lessons are assembled from one or more elements, some of which involve cooperative learning activities that address team building, class building, mastery, thinking skills, information sharing, and communication skills.

Student-centered classroom. A classroom in which planning and instruction keep the needs of students in the forefront. The emphasis is on the student as active worker more than passive absorber and on the student as a full participant in developing an effective classroom. Student-centeredness reflects the belief that learning must happen *in* students, not *to* them.

Student-initiated questions. An often neglected aspect of an effective questioning strategy that emphasizes the importance of students, as well as the teacher, asking productive questions.

Student Team Learning. The general term for cooperative learning activities modeled according to the guidelines established by Robert Slavin and associates at Johns Hopkins University. See also **Student Teams Achievement Divisions.**

Student Teams Achievement Divisions (STAD). A cooperative learning strategy in which teacher presentation is followed by team practice and individual testing, with individual improvement scores contributing to team scores and rewards.

Synthesis questions. Questions requiring the student to put together elements and parts to form a whole. These include producing original communications, making predictions, and solving problems for which a variety of answers are possible.

Taxonomy. A classification system; used here in reference to a classification system of educational objectives or skills.

Teaching skill. A distinct set of identifiable behaviors needed to perform teaching functions.

Team packet. In cooperative learning, an envelope or box or file used to expedite distribution and collection of lesson materials.

Team rewards. In cooperative learning, four- or five-member learning teams win certificates and other forms of public recognition on the basis of individual improvement scores.

Teamwork skills. Group-process skills having particular value in cooperative learning activities; they include forming skills that make routines flow smoothly, functioning skills that build group cohesion and participation, formulating skills that promote solid mastery, and fermenting skills that nurture critical thinking.

Terminal goals. Goals one can expect to reach at the end of a given learning experience.

Test. An instrument that presents a common situation to which all students respond, a common set of instructions, and a common set of rules for scoring the students' responses. Used primarily for determining aptitude and achievement.

Theoretical knowledge. Concepts, facts, and propositions that make up much of the content of the disciplines.

Think–Pair–Share (TPS). A cooperative learning strategy in which preformed pairs of students discuss questions or complete short assignments together in the course of a lesson at the direction of the teacher or on an ad hoc basis.

Tiered lessons. An approach to having all students work with essentially the same key information, ideas, and skills, but at different levels of difficulty or sophistication in order to be a match for each student's particular readiness level.

Time out. The removal of a student from a rewarding situation.

Unit plan. A plan for a sequence of several lessons dealing with the same general topic.

Validity. The extent to which the results of an evaluation procedure serve the particular uses for which they are intended. There are several kinds of validity, including content validity, predictive validity, and concurrent validity.

Wait time. The amount of time the teacher waits after asking a question before calling for the answer.

Withitness behaviors. Behaviors by which the teacher communicates to students that he or she knows what is going on.

Zero-noise signal. In cooperative learning, an action that communicates a need for silence and immediate attention, to permit the teacher to provide additional whole-group directions during a team activity.

Index

Through interactive activities, *Classroom Teaching Skills* helps all teachers apply theory to practice.

YOUR TURN

Visit the web site of a school system in your area to see what they have done in regard to plans for technology. [If you can't easily find a site, visit the Williamson County (Tennessee) home page (www.wcs.edu)]. Why are overall district and/or school technology plans important to individual teachers?

Your Turn practice situations help you apply chapter concepts to real life.

OBSERVATION WORKSHEET

Assessment Activities

Talk to a teacher about how he or she decides what to teach, when to teach, and how to teach. Probe for specific answers. Try to identify the various stages in the assessment process as that teacher explains his or her decision making to you. How could you use the terminology of this chapter to explain what the teacher has done?

Directions: Do not use actual names of schools, teachers, administrators, or students when using this worksheet.

Observer's Name: ______

Date: ______

Grade Level: ______

Subject: ______

Class Size: ______

Background Information: Give a brief general description of the school's social, economic, and ethnic makeup.

______

______

What to Record: Observe the teacher in action. Note how assessment is an integral part of his or her teaching. Use the following format to keep track of the information being gathered, the information-gathering techniques being used, and the judgments being made.

Time	Information Obtained	Assessment & Technique	Judgment(s) Made
9:15–9:45	Students' ability to sound words during reading class	Observation	Most did well. George and Mary had trouble with some words.

Reflections on Your Observation:

1. What variety of assessment techniques did the teacher use?

______

______

______

2. In what ways did the teacher use the results of the assessment? Did he or she adjust instruction or learning activities based on assessment results?

______

______

______

3. If so, in what ways? ______

______

______

4. What questions would you want to ask the teacher regarding his or her use of assessment?

______

______

______

Observation Worksheets assist you in making connections between what you learn in college and what's happening on-site in schools.